Block by Block:

The Challenges of Urban Operations

William G. Robertson
General Editor

Lawrence A. Yates
Managing Editor

U.S. Army Command and General Staff College Press
Fort Leavenworth, Kansas

Published by Books Express Publishing
Copyright © Books Express, 2012
ISBN 978-1-78039-671-2

Books Express publications are available from all good retail and online booksellers. For publishing proposals and direct ordering please contact us at: info@books-express.com

Contents

Preface v
Foreword vii
Attacking the Heart and Guts: Urban Operations Through
the Ages 1
    Lieutenant Colonel Lou DiMarco, U.S. Army
The Battle of Stalingrad 29
    S. J. Lewis
"Knock 'em All Down": The Reduction of Aachen,
October 1944 63
    Christopher R. Gabel
The Battle of Manila 91
    Thomas M. Huber
The Battle for Hue, 1968 123
    James H. Willbanks
The 31 December 1994-8 February 1995 Battle for Grozny 161
    Timothy L. Thomas
The Siege of Beirut 205
    George W. Gawrych
The Siege of Sarajevo, 1992-1995 235
    Curtis S. King
The Takedown of Kabul: An Effective Coup de Main 291
    Lester W. Grau
Operation JUST CAUSE in Panama City, December 1989 325
    Lawrence A. Yates
Todo o Nada: Montoneros Versus the Army: Urban Terrorism in
Argentina 373
    Lieutenant Colonel Alan C. Lowe, U.S. Army
Humanitarian Operations in an Urban Environment: Hurricane
Andrew, August-October 1992 407
    Jerold E. Brown
Urban Warfare: Its History and Its Future 439
    Roger J. Spiller
About the Contributors 451
Appendix A. The Future 455

Preface

It is axiomatic in the military community that operations in an urban environment should be avoided if at all possible, given the costs they exact in time, personnel, casualties, and materiel. Yet, throughout history, cities have continuously been at the center of a variety of military undertakings: sieges, street fighting, coups de main, peacekeeping and peace enforcement, stability operations and support operations, and disaster and humanitarian relief. Moreover, this trend continues through the recent past and up to the present as headlines concerning Beirut, Sarajevo, Mogadishu, Grozny, Kabul, and Baghdad indicate.

Given my choice in such matters, I would echo the words of an old song sung by Johnny Cash, among others. The chanted chorus implores, "Don't take your guns to town, son. Leave your guns at home, Bill." Unfortunately, soldiers are not always given that option as a valid course of action. Recognizing that armies cannot always bypass cities, the U.S. military since the mid-1990s has experienced a resurgence of interest in urban operations. As one indication of this renewed attention, the Commander, U.S. Army Training and Doctrine Command (TRADOC), tasked the Combat Studies Institute (CSI), Fort Leavenworth, Kansas, to research and write several in-depth case studies that would provide historical perspectives on the subject. The case studies were to be used for professional development and coursework in all TRADOC schools.

To determine the exact scope of this assignment and the kinds of operations that should be included, I, as CSI's director, met with Dr. Roger J. Spiller, the George C. Marshall Professor of Military History at USACGSC; Dr. William G. Robertson, the U.S. Army Combined Arms Center historian; and Dr. Lawrence A. Yates, CSI's research coordinator. During the meeting, the group reached consensus on the case studies to be examined and determined that the authors of each would come from officer and civilian scholars at Fort Leavenworth. I placed Dr. Robertson in charge of the project as its general editor, with Dr. Yates working closely as managing editor.

The resulting anthology begins with a general overview of urban operations from ancient times to the midpoint of the twentieth century. It then details ten specific case studies of U.S., German, and Japanese operations in cities during World War II and ends with more recent Russian attempts to subdue Chechen fighters in Grozny and the Serbian siege of Sarajevo. Operations range across the spectrum from combat to humanitarian and disaster relief. Each chapter contains a narrative account of a designated operation, identifying and analyzing the lessons that remain relevant today. Before inclusion in this CGSC Press publication, the final draft of each chapter appeared on CSI's website at <http://cgsc.leavenworth.army.mil/CSI/research/MOUT/urbanoperationsintro.asp>. The chapters will remain on CSI's publications website for those who cannot readily access the printed book.

In his foreword, retired General Donn A. Starry, U.S. Army, reflects on the relevance of urban operations today. Dr. Spiller ably reinforces this position in an in-depth conclusion that pulls together the themes of the various chapters while introducing additional issues. It is hoped that today's military professional, as well as interested parties within the general public, will find these studies stimulating and informative. For a more conceptual look at cities and how they affect and are affected by military operations, see Dr. Spiller's *Sharp Corners*, which CSI published in 2001 and can also be found on the CSI publications website.

LAWYN C. EDWARDS
Colonel, Aviation
Director, Combat Studies Institute

Foreword

History instructs that for a variety of reasons, cities have always been targets for attack by adversaries. From the earliest of times, attackers came bearing weapons ranging from knives, arrows, and spears, while in modern times, they have brought weaponry the Industrial Revolution made available: cannon, rocket artillery, and ultimately bombs and rockets delivered from aerial platforms and even thermonuclear warheads, not to mention the potential for chemical and biological payloads. In turn, cities have responded to most of these threats. Early on, for example, they thickened city walls and erected other barriers to entry. But attackers seeking to subdue the cities simply countered with new and better weapons. So the game of measures and countermeasures—the adult, and much more deadly, version of the familiar children's game of rock, scissors, paper—has continued apace for centuries.

A post-1945 visitor to the Allied zones of occupation in Western Europe who had not been on the scene to view firsthand the events of the long war just ended would have immediately noticed several striking features of the landscape. Above all, many, if not most, of the large cities lay in ruin. By one count there were seventy-two such places, virtually all famous, old, large, important. Those cities not destroyed were severely damaged. The Allies had pounded them with strategic and tactical aerial bombing, reduced them to rubble by artillery and sometimes by ground action, consumed them with fire (Hamburg and Dresden), or finally, moving to the Pacific theater in the case of Hiroshima and Nagasaki, atomized them.

Several of these western cities had been bombed flat on the premise that if the city were "rubbled," the resultant demoralization of the working population would adversely affect factory output in that city. Virtually nowhere, however, did such attacks have the predicted effects. The true cost in aircrews and aircraft lost to demonstrate that this operational concept was a seriously flawed hypothesis from the outset was high indeed. Operationally, many cities became targets for destruction purely for political reasons. Remember Berlin. As Antony Beevor dramatically recounts in *The Fall of Berlin 1945*, Joseph Stalin had to have the city for revenge, and for revenge, his armies pillaged, plundered, and raped their way through Berlin's alleys, streets, and undergrounds. Winston Churchill saw Berlin as a political target, necessary for postwar diplomatic clout. General Dwight D. Eisenhower demurred on military grounds because he believed taking Berlin was no longer considered an important objective and thought instead that defeating German armies in the field was the primary goal. Because Churchill linked military concerns to a larger political framework, it is likely that Carl von Clausewitz would have sided with Churchill's position. Because Eisenhower's position focused more on strictly military considerations and less on political factors, Henri de Jomini probably would have agreed with Eisenhower. It is doubtful a civilized person would have sided with Stalin.

Our postwar visitor, in looking around, would see other cities, some quite large, that had seen little if any obvious combat damage. Further, while some smaller towns and villages showed evidence of combat, many, if not most, appeared relatively untouched. But even in urban areas where the visitor encountered extensive damage, it would soon become apparent that many essential functions of the city were still operating, albeit with difficulty. Water and electricity were available; food could be had; populations had gone underground, surviving and living in cellars; and people got to the work place or what was left of it. Not to oversimplify the trauma but simply to state facts, things went on somehow. Postwar Mannheim, for example, leveled in a strategic/operational bombing campaign predicted to demoralize the population and deprive the industrial base of workers, featured a postwar population of cellar dwellers who, while uncomfortable, were living, eating, sleeping, and still working.

Returning to Western Europe ten years later, the visitor would be struck by the extent to which these cities had recovered from their war damage. Marshall Plan dollars and an inherently industrious population had worked wonders. Twenty years later, evidence of war damage was largely limited to remains of buildings left standing as monuments in remembrance of the war: the tower of Berlin's ancient Kaiser Wilhelm Kirche along the Kurfurstendam, for example. New, vibrant cities had emerged from the ruins of the old, a process not entirely unlike that found throughout ancient history when a new city was simply placed on top of another that had been destroyed. The visitor would have observed that cities are not inanimate assemblages of buildings and facilities, but instead, they are more like living things, conceived and born by some means for some reason. They grow and they mature. Some thrive; some become ill and recover. Some die and are forgotten, and some are destroyed and rebuilt. Not only are cities themselves living systems but also they are composed of supporting interstitial systems: water, food, power, communications, transportation, manufacturing, economic, commercial, entertainment, and many others.

Interestingly, those infrastructure systems have seldom been the primary targets of military attack. It is difficult to find a historical example of an attack on a city planned as an operation against a living system, an attack against interstitial and interrelated systems in the organic infrastructure. In looking for insight into such an approach, Dr. James Grier Miller's theory of living systems is indispensable. Its hypothesis is that cells, organisms, organs, animals, humans, organizations—indeed cities—all display common functional characteristics. Understanding the framework of functional systems then provides a parametric baseline for tactical operations against villages and towns and for operational- or strategic-level attacks against large cities. This is in contrast to the little, mock villages created at many U.S. military installations as training sites for urban operations. These are in no way adequate for teaching military operators and planners about attacking large, "living" cities. Nor are they adequate for developing alternatives to bypassing or mounting a conventional military operation against an urban area.

Considering alternatives, operationally as well as tactically, there are families of nonlethal weapons that, when properly employed, can obviate the need for attack using "hard," or kinetic, means. Experiments with enhanced flux nuclear, enhanced blast, and thermobaric devices are currently under way. "Soft" power, as opposed to "hard" power, both discussed by Joseph S. Nye, Jr. in *The Paradox of American Power,* suggests useful nonkinetic alternate strategies.[2] This concept is not especially new as demonstrated by Julius Caesar's *The Civil War*, an account of the great commander's campaigns in Spain during the Roman Civil War.[3] In it, he demonstrates dramatically how it is possible to prevail over determined enemies without laying waste to their cities.

In situations where attacking forces cannot avoid kinetic means, the lessons of the past should not be applied to the future without modification. For example, there is some evidence that transitioning from tactical to operational to strategic levels of war, especially in urban conflict, is confused by transit zones that are more fractal than linear. Operational boundaries may appear quite linear, especially intellectually; so, indeed, might strategic divisions. At the tactical level, however, Benoit Mandelbrot's fractal calculus is far more illuminating a tool than is the essentially linear calculus traditional to virtually all battle (tactical) games and simulations. All is well in one city block, but all hell rages two blocks over. The first floor is cleared here, but why are the miserable illegitimates dropping cocktails on us from two floors above and firing rocket-propelled grenades at us from the cellars below? If the village is afire above ground and the people are gone, why are we taking fire from out of the ground? "By golly, we just may have to destroy this town to save it!" in the words of one Vietnam-era warrior.

In short, there is a need for the U.S. military to explore new ways of conceptualizing urban operations. But that exploration must be grounded, in part, in the empirical data contained in the historical record. Our judgments about the future must be informed by our experiences of the past. And that is what the variety of historical case studies in this book offer: a solid factual and analytical basis on which to conceptualize future urban operations. These studies should not wed today's analysts to traditional ideas and concepts but should serve rather as a "reality check" when those analysts discuss new approaches to the age-old problem of conducting operations on urban terrain and attempt to answer such questions as: How might we expect to have to fight future battles, if any, in cities? Against whom and under what conditions might we expect to fight? What capabilities are resident in the forces and equipment of the threat(s) we might expect to encounter? What does technology offer in terms of countering a threat or providing a margin of capability over an anticipated threat?

Having answered all those interrogatives crisply and with precision, some additional thoughts might be: What capabilities are required in terms of combat equipment—weapons, vehicles, aircraft, and functional systems? What force structures and organizations might be best suited to the operational environment we anticipate? How should soldiers, marines, sailors, and airmen be trained to fight in city environments? What tactics, techniques, and procedures are essential knowledge at tactical and operational levels of war? How are units to be trained for the new environment? How are noncommissioned officers to be educated and trained to perform their essential duties at small-unit levels? How do we educate and train officers who are to lead the forces to plan and train for operations at tactical, operational, and strategic levels of war?

With these questions in mind, the following collection of works will assist military professionals and thoughtful scholars alike in better understanding the complexities of urban combat, an area whose importance grows more urgent for study with each passing day.

General Donn A. Starry
U.S. Army, Retired

Notes

1. James Grier Miller, *Living Systems* (Boulder, CO: University Press of Colorado, May 1995) and Miller, *Measurement and Interpretation in Accounting: A Living Systems Theory Approach* (Westport CT: Quorum Books, 25 October 1989).
2. *The Paradox of American Power: Why the World's Only Superpower Can't Go It Alone* (NY: Oxford University Press, 2002).
3. Julius Caesar, *The Civil War* (Harmondsworth: Penguin, 1976).

Attacking the Heart and Guts:
Urban Operations Through the Ages

Lieutenant Colonel Lou DiMarco, U.S. Army

Cities predate the modern nation-state by several millennia and have long been the focus of culture, politics, economics, religion, and all other aspects of endeavor that represent civilization. Because of their importance, cities have been the dominant focus of military operations for most of human history, and a fundamental purpose of armies has been defending or attacking cities. Attacking defended cities has been one of the most difficult and potentially costly military operations. This was reflected in the ancient Chinese text, *The Art of War*, which recognized the challenges of seizing cities and admonished its readers that the lowest realization of warfare was to attack a fortified city.[1] This maxim has been passed to many modern armies that continue to want to avoid large-scale urban operations. Unfortunately, although strategists have advised against it and armies and generals have preferred not to, the nature of war has required armies to attack and defend cities, and victory has required that they do it well.

The importance of capturing cities has always been evident. In China, it became the dominant requirement of warfare around the second century A.D. (approximately six hundred years after Sun Tzu).[2] In Europe, cities became a primary focus of warfare in the Middle Ages. Almost from their conception, cities raised walls for their own defense, and the walled city remained a significant challenge to armies into the twentieth century. Walls also provided a police and customs barrier, regulating who entered the city and permitting the taxation of goods passing through the gates.[3] The inhabitants of cities realized that through fortifications and a modest number of soldiers they could protect themselves from hostile armies at an economic cost. For most of history, the walled city had the advantage over attacking armies. Gunpowder changed this situation drastically. In the fifteenth century, artillery was developed that was capable of moving with armies and breaching the walls of fortified cities.[4] City dwellers responded with more sophisticated fortifications that included lower, thicker walls and defensive cannon. This initiated a period of increasingly sophisticated siege and fortress warfare that extended into the opening years of the twentieth century. The objective of fortress warfare was control not only of the city and surrounding territory but also of its citizens and its political, cultural, and economic assets. In this respect, siege warfare is the direct predecessor of modern urban warfare, distinguishable primarily in its tactical and technological methods. The objectives of siege warfare, many of its principles, and even many of its tactical considerations remain valid today.

The thought, resources, and effort exerted to defend and capture cities throughout history reflect their importance. That importance is also demonstrated in the manner in which the changing military challenges posed by cities has caused adjustments in the operational art and tactics of urban warfare. A study of warfighting and cities reveals several themes that have characterized urban warfare throughout the ages. This chapter will address some of these themes that warrant consideration in the context of modern urban operations.

Cities have been pivotal within larger operations in two ways. First, they have been important as the object of battle. A study of battles reveals that in many of the most important battles in history, urban areas were central to why the battle was fought, although not always central to how it was fought. Often a battle was fought for control of the city but not fought at the city itself due to terrain, tactics, technology, or other considerations. The Napoleonic battle of Borodino is a case in point. The goal of Napoleon's 1812 campaign was the defeat of Russia. The French army's objective was Moscow. To defend Moscow and defeat the French, the Russians under General Prince Mikhail Kutuzov met the French army near the village of Borodino on 7 September 1812, 75 miles west of Moscow. The Russians picked the most advantageous ground for the defense of Moscow, and given their estimate of the situation, the relative size of both armies, and contemporary tactics and technology, they chose a location that was not the city itself. The French victory at Borodino came at great cost but forced a Russian retreat and the evacuation of Moscow. As a result of this victory, Napoleon entered the city unopposed a week after the battle, on 14 September 1812.[5] This example demonstrates that although the tactical battle may not be fought within the confines of the urban area, the urban area may remain central to the purpose, scope, and execution of the battle and the larger operation.

Another way that cities have influenced major operations is as the geographic location of battle. This is the classic urban battle in and around a city, with forces directly engaged on the urban terrain for domination of the urban area. In this battle, the defender has the advantage of using the complex terrain of the city and its fortifications to provide cover and concealment for his forces. As for the attacker, one option is to assault the city directly from the march. In medieval and early modern times, however, attacking armies did not typically have sufficient mobility to achieve the surprise necessary to make such a tactic reasonable. Most often, the attacker chose to conduct a siege, an option that allowed him to take his time, make extensive preparations, and culminate his operations with a decisive assault on the city. This deliberate operation is the focus of most discussions of premodern urban combat, and within this battle lay most of the major challenges of urban operations.

An examination of urban operations occurring before World War II reveals a number of consistent themes. Subsequent chapters will demonstrate that many of these themes and principles continued to be validated during World War II and after. One of the most important of these themes concerns the reasons armies are compelled to engage in urban combat. Another recurring theme is the significant resources required to conduct urban operations successfully. Additionally, history demonstrates that specialized equipment, personnel, training, and tactics are needed to succeed in urban operations. The unique effects of the complex urban terrain and the presence of the civil population are also issues that continually reoccur in urban battle. These themes of purpose, resources, specialization, and terrain and population factors, although certainly important in all types of operations, are unusually significant in urban operations and have been throughout the history of warfare.

A classic operational question that challenged and teased army commanders was which circumstances properly compelled or warranted the conduct of urban operations. Commanders understood the difficulties and challenges posed by an attack on a city. On the other hand, they also understood the compelling reasons for taking cities. Writing over two millennia ago, Sun Tzu addressed this pivotal decision directly by explaining why a city was not an inviting target:

> As for fortified cities that are not assaulted: We estimate that our strength is sufficient to seize it. If we seize it, it will not be of any advantage to the fore; if we gain it we will not be able to protect it at the rear. If our strength equals theirs, the city certainly will not be taken. If, when we gain the advantages of a forward (position) the city will then surrender by itself, while if we do not gain such advantages (the city) will not cause harm to the rear in such cases, even though the city can be assaulted, do not assault it.[6]

Unfortunately, cities often had to be captured. Sixteenth-century French commander Marshal de Tavannes commented that "great empires and powers must be attacked in their hearts and guts."[7] The heart and guts of most nations was their capital and other important cities. Cities were often the center of leadership, economics, and culture, and thus could represent a strategic center of gravity. Additionally, they often were the location of an essential operational consideration such as geographic position, the enemy force, or an important logistics base. Finally, from a defensive point of view, cities offered important asymmetric advantages in terms of cover and concealment that could offset the advantages of attacking forces.

One of the most important reasons for attacking a city was to capture the enemy's political, economic, or cultural center, thereby destroying his morale, his ability to sustain a war, and his capability to govern. In other words, the city was attacked because it was the enemy's center of gravity. This resulted in numerous battles for capital cities such as Rome and Paris. In ancient times, the Persian Empire's efforts to subdue the independent Greek city-states centered on the most important city-state and its capital, Athens. The Persians mounted three separate unsuccessful campaigns between the years 492 and 479 B.C. aimed at capturing the Greek cultural and economic center.[8] The Greeks succeeded in defending Athens in a series of brilliant battles fought not in the city but on its land and sea approaches. The victory gained in these battles was central to the Greeks' successful resistance to a Persian invasion. In 1453, the successful siege and capture of the Byzantine capital of Constantinople by Islamic forces not only spelled the end of the Byzantine Empire but also ended forever Christian efforts to dominate the Middle East. Thus, the successful attack or defense of a key city could decide the outcome of the campaign, the war, or the fate of an empire.

Attacking the urban political center of an opponent was often decisive but not always. The capture of Mexico City by U.S. forces in 1847 did not compel the surrender of Mexico. Napoleon's successful capture of Moscow in 1812 did not compel the capitulation of Russia, as described by historian David Chandler:

> Every day that passed was allowing the advantage of the strategic situation to move more decidedly in the Tsar's favor. Kutusov appreciated this and did all in his power to protract Napoleon's stay in Moscow, deliberately playing on his opponent's desire for peace....Not only was time playing into the hands of the Russians by

bringing "General Winter" ever closer, but it was also permitting the size of their forces to be rapidly augmented.[9]

Napoleon's focus on capturing the enemy capital and not on destroying the enemy's field army contributed directly to the failure of his Russian campaign and his disastrous retreat. Attacking an urban area as a means to defeat a nation required careful evaluation of the military situation, geopolitical factors, culture, and economics before executing operations. An incomplete understanding of the role and importance of the urban area to the opponent could lead to an extensive expenditure of time and resources with little operational or strategic gain.

An equally compelling reason to attack urban areas was military operational necessity. Commanders sometimes attacked an urban area to destroy an enemy force located there or because of the strategic location of the urban area. Often the urban area contained a capability that was necessary for future operations. When defending, a commander often located his forces in an urban area because of his inferior capability and the increase in combat power provided by the inherent defensive qualities of the urban terrain. These reasons compelled commanders to engage in urban operations to affect the military situation directly.

Strategic geographic position was an important reason for deciding to attack or defend a city. Wellington's bloody siege of Badajoz in 1812 was necessary to secure the primary invasion route into Spain.[10] Grant's decision in the American Civil War to capture Vicksburg was primarily motivated by that city's strategic location on the Mississippi River. When Vicksburg surrendered on 4 July 1863, the Union gained unchallenged control of the river and divided the Confederacy geographically. This success greatly inhibited support and communications between the eastern and western Confederate states and was a devastating blow to the South's morale and prestige.[11]

Often urban operations were required to acquire a capability for future operations. This capability may have been the need for an advance base, logistics facilities, or a harbor. In June and July of 1758 during the Seven Years' War, a 14,000-man English army under General Jeffery Amherst captured the French fortress city of Louisbourg on Cape Breton Island.[12] This city was important as a North Atlantic base for the fleet and facilitated the blockade of French Canada. The loss of the city enabled British land and sea operations and greatly inhibited the operations of the French fleet in North America.

When defending, an army that was outnumbered often took advantage of the inherent defensive qualities of urban areas to compensate for its lack of numbers and to offset other advantages of an enemy. In 1683, an outnumbered Christian force of approximately 20,000 under the command of the Holy Roman Empire took shelter in and defended Vienna rather than meet the Ottoman army of 75,000 in open battle. The fortifications of the city permitted the outnumbered and less mobile European army to avoid defeat for two months until a relief force of 20,000 arrived to lift the siege and drive off the Turks.[13]

As the examples of Mexico City and Moscow indicate, urban operations did not always result in the desired outcome, even when tactical success was achieved and the city occupied. And, as the Turks found out at Vienna, offensive operations against cities often were not successful despite a significant commitment of resources. Thus, it behooved a commander to consider carefully whether urban operations were absolutely essential to the major operation or campaign he was conducting.

Occasionally, the commander could discover viable alternatives to the conduct of a deliberate urban operation. Oftentimes, the mere threat to a capital or key city was enough to compel its surrender. In the Franco-Prussian War, the French surrendered after the Prussians had laid siege to Paris but before an actual assault was mounted. Other times, the attacker could attempt a demonstration or ruse, or conduct a turning movement to entice the garrison of a city to fight in the open. A final technique that armies attempted whenever possible was to use surprise to capture a city before a defense could be organized. Attacking from an unexpected direction or by an unexpected means could achieve this.

British General James Wolfe used several techniques to achieve success and capture the French Canadian city of Quebec without attacking it by the most obvious means. First, he achieved surprise and attacked from an unexpected direction by moving his army stealthily up-river from the city, conducting a night amphibious landing, and scaling the supposedly inaccessible Heights of Abraham. By the morning of 13 September 1759, he had positioned his army in a double rank on the Plains of Abraham west of the city astride Quebec's supply lines. The brilliant and unexpected maneuver unnerved the French commander, Marquis de Montcalm, who decided to attack the British in the open without waiting for reinforcements. In the ensuing battle, British firepower routed the attacking French, destroyed French military capability and morale, and resulted in the city's capitulation on 18 September.[14] In 1702, the Austrians also used surprise and an unexpected approach to capture the northern Italian city of Cremona by infiltrating elite troops into the defense by way of an aqueduct.[15] In 1597, the Spanish captured the city of Amiens in northern France using a ruse. A small group of Spaniards disguised as peasants approached the city gateway, at which point they pretended that their cart had broken a wheel. In the confusion that followed, they rushed and captured the gate.[16] These techniques entailed risk taking and required boldness, imagination, and unique circumstances to be successful.

Bypassing the urban area was a viable technique; however, it had disadvantages. It required that the attacker tolerate the urban garrison in his rear and that he maintain sufficient forces to contain the threat of forays by the city garrison. Another effect of bypassing large important cities was that it often extended the political viability of the opposition and the duration of the campaign, thus jeopardizing the achievement of quick and decisive victory. The mounted Mongol armies that invaded the Chin Empire in northern China in 1211 were not very adept at the nuances of siege warfare and were forced to bypass important large, fortified population centers. The inability of the mounted Mongols to conduct effective sieges was a major factor in the Chin's ability to resist and sustain their Empire for over two decades after the initial Mongol onslaught. Though rarely defeated in open battle, the vaunted Mongol cavalry did not fully conquer the Chin until 1234, after being aided in their efforts by Chinese generals and armies who provided experience in siege warfare.[17]

Another aspect of urban operations that has remained relatively consistent through the ages is the immense resources required for success. Urban operations, particularly from the attacker's perspective, required investments significantly greater than combat operations in open terrain. These investments included time, manpower, special equipment, supplies, and the will and morale of the attacking troops.

Urban operations could take a significant amount of time to execute. Often, the defender relied on the urban fortifications not to defeat but merely to delay the enemy until changed circumstances created conditions for success. The attacker frequently relied on time to starve the garrison into submission. Both sides made calculations that time would work in their favor. Sun Tzu recognized that patience in urban warfare was a virtue and impatience could lead to disaster: "If the general cannot overcome his impatience but instead launches an assault wherein his men swarm over the walls like ants, he will kill one-third of his officers and troops, and the city will still not be taken."[18]

During the siege of the Mediterranean port of Acre by Crusaders in the twelfth century, the goal of the Muslim defenders was to prevent the

Crusaders from taking the city before the arrival of the reinforcing army of Saladin. The Muslims did not realize that what they hoped would be a quick relief would end up as a two-year defense. The Crusaders were hampered by a lack of siege equipment and the fact that the town walls had been reinforced and the town provisioned just before their arrival in August 1189. Saladin arrived to relieve the garrison in mid-September but was unable to break through the ring of Crusaders. Saladin then organized his forces into defensive positions, and the Crusaders were themselves besieged and faced with enemies on two fronts. This circumstance marked the beginning of a series of battles and skirmishes that lasted for twenty-three months. Finally, in July 1191, the Crusaders were reinforced with sufficient naval components to blockade successfully the seaward approach to the city. With the defense totally isolated, famine and disease finally took their toll and the garrison surrendered.[19]

Other external factors that may have intervened in support of a defense over time include the loss of will of the attacking force, logistic constraints on the attacking force, and, in many cases, the impact of disease and illness on the attacking force. Weather was another factor upon which defenders relied to change conditions in their favor. Typically, the defender in a city was much more protected from the elements than the attacker. Thus, some defenders sought to frustrate the attack until adverse weather sapped the strength and morale of the attacker. Before the nineteenth century, most armies considered winter siege operations virtually impossible.

Another resource that the attacker required in urban operations was numerical superiority. Napoleon estimated that the attacker of a fortified city must outnumber the defender by four to one.[20] At Vienna, the Ottomans outnumbered Imperial forces at a ratio of almost four to one. At Vicksburg, Union forces numbered approximately 80,000 while the Confederates numbered approximately 47,000.[21] Here the ratio between forces typically varied between two and three to one. Nevertheless, sufficient Union forces were present to dissuade the Confederates from seeking battle in the open and to prevent the Southern forces from breaking the siege.

Numerical superiority was necessary not only for the combat power to conduct the assault on the city, but also to ensure that the attacker could sustain other tasks associated with the operation. At Badajoz, the British were forced to raise their first siege attempt in 1811 because they had insufficient troop strength to conduct the siege and meet the threat posed by a French field army commanded by Soult.[22] In this case and others, attackers required sufficient force to conduct the siege while discouraging relieving forces. Other factors, such as personnel losses to illness and engineering manpower requirements, also had to be calculated into the attacker's resource requirements. Because of these additional considerations, armies attacking cities needed greater numerical superiority than those opposing the same enemy in open battle.

Urban operations have traditionally required more logistic support than conventional operations. As the length of time of the operation stretched out, the attacker had to ensure that he had sufficient food to last the siege. Initially consolidated into a prepared position, the defender usually had the better supply situation to start. The medieval military strategist de Balsac advised defenders to move all food supplies from the surrounding country into fortified positions, thus denying the wealth of the land to the enemy.[23] An efficient logistics system capable of feeding and supplying tens of thousands of troops far from the home country as they attempted a siege lasting weeks or months was a daunting task for medieval and early modern armies. The magnitude of this task did not get appreciably smaller in more modern times, but more professional and robust logistics systems, combined with better planning and other capabilities such as improved transportation, made sustained siege operations possible even in winter.

Munitions were used in prodigious amounts in the conduct of urban siege operations, and the supply of artillery munitions in particular was a major concern. In the modest English siege of Louisbourg in 1758, the final twelve-hour cannonade by the English expended over 1,000 projectiles.[24] The requirements in terms of artillery support were always very significant. In 1799, the Austrians used 138 field pieces of various types against the city of Turin in northern Italy. In two days, they fired 200 rounds from each cannon and 150 rounds from each mortar. This bombardment compelled the city to surrender without an assault.[25] Beginning in late medieval times, massive artillery support backed by abundant munitions was always vital to success, but it did not always guarantee success. A total of 43,000 rounds of artillery ammunition was expended by a powerful French and Spanish army in an unsuccessful bid to capture the northern Italian fortress of Cuneo in 1744.[26]

A final resource that proved essential for successful urban operations was the morale and will of soldiers and leaders. Urban operations, whether attacking or defending, were physically exhausting and mentally stressful—even more so than regular operations. This was largely a function of the extended duration of the operation, often primitive living conditions, the challenges of overcoming man-made obstacles and fortifications, and the intensity of combat once joined. Urban operations thus required soldiers who were mentally and physically tough, skilled, and motivated to succeed. Frequently, highly motivated soldiers could achieve success even under adverse conditions that would have caused less motivated armies to quit the siege. It was equally important that leaders also be mentally tough. Casualties were likely to be high, and an operation required significant time and patience. The successful storming of the Russian city of Port Arthur in May of 1904 after a four-month siege can largely be attributed to the morale and courage of the Japanese infantryman. Ellis Ashmead-Bartlet, an English reporter who witnessed the siege, stated:

> ...the most striking fact about the siege was the sustained heroism displayed by the Japanese soldiers a heroism never excelled, and seldom equaled in the history of warfare. Every nation has at some time possessed troops capable of performing gallant actions, but I question if any nation has ever produced men who could repeat such feats of bravery as were witnessed before Port Arthur for a continuous period of six months.[27]

Leaders of successful urban operations had to have a clear vision of the operation and the patience to apply tactics, techniques, and procedures systematically to achieve success. At the height of formal siege warfare in the eighteenth century, sieges were expected to last at least thirty days, but often, in fact, lasted much longer. The lengthy siege of Acre discussed previously was successfully sustained and concluded by the Crusaders largely due to the inspiring leadership of the English King Richard, who arrived in time to bolster Christian morale, which was eroding due to the length of the operation. Absent his personal leadership, the battle may have ended differently.

Another important characteristic of urban warfare was the necessity of military forces to deal with the complexities of the urban environment. Those complexities fell into two broad categories: physical and human. The physical complexities of the urban terrain primarily related to the density of man-made structures. Throughout the history of urban operations, the most challenging of the physical structures were man-made fortresses and defensive works that, until the twentieth century, were integral to most important urban areas. The human aspect of urban warfare was represented by the city population. Civilians have always been present on the urban battlefield, and both defending and attacking commanders had to plan for dealing with the urban population.

City fortresses dominated urban warfare in medieval and early modern history. This physical challenge to the employment of military power was primarily found in the defensive walls that surrounded the city. Commanders needed a certain competence and expertise in specific tactics and techniques used to defend or attack a fortified city. The nuances of this type of warfare were such that commanders employed a variety of experts—including artillerists, miners, and engineers—to give advice, supervise, and conduct operations.[28]

The civil structures in the urban area were also important and were often part of the reason the city was being attacked. Historically, commanders have had to be concerned about the vulnerability of civil structures to fire. At Louisbourg, the inability of the garrison to cope with continuous outbreaks of fire was an important consideration in the capitulation of the French command.[29] In that battle, the British were interested in the city's location and its harbor and thus were less than discriminate in attacking civil structures by bombardment.

The human dimension of urban combat was also a factor that commanders had to address in urban operations. On the defense, the question of taking care of the friendly or allied urban population was extremely important. In the defended city, the urban population had to be fed. The morale and disposition of the population could decisively affect the defense. In Londonderry in 1689, the Protestant loyalist civil population of 30,000 was determined to resist a Catholic Irish Jacobite army commanded by King James, even though the city's garrison only numbered 7,000 to the Irish 12,000. Despite the desire of the governor to surrender and the decimation of the population by disease and starvation, the people refused to allow the garrison to surrender the city. The intervention of the population permitted the city to resist for 105 days until the Royal Navy broke the siege. Over half the small garrison perished in the defense, and it is estimated that as many as 15,000 noncombatants perished.[30]

Armies attacking into urban areas also had to deal with the population once they penetrated the city after a successful attack. Ancient and relatively unsophisticated armies often dealt with the civil population by massacre or slavery. The Mongols were often not interested in administering a captured city and frequently put a population to the sword. Ancient historical accounts put the death toll in the Mongol sack of the eastern Persian city Harat at between 1.7 and 2.4 million people.[31] As armies and civilizations became more sophisticated, the advantages of taxes, resources, and commerce inherent in the urban population became apparent. Additionally, as religious influences grew, moral considerations also influenced behavior. Mitigating damage to the urban population was not an easy task because of the density of the population and its proximity to the military operation. It was often made more difficult because the population was frequently openly hostile to the attacking force. The attitude of the attackers also posed problems for the commander. The transition of the attacking army from intense offensive operations to occupation and military administration was psychologically difficult for even well-disciplined troops. The transition could be impossible for troops who were not well trained, were motivated by a hatred of the enemy, had sustained significant casualties, and had been through the stress of a long and difficult siege.

The case of Magdeburg during the 30 Years War is an example of how the stress and ferocity of urban combat could cause commanders to lose control of their troops and perpetuate atrocities. In March 1631, a Catholic Imperial Army under Johan Tzerclaes Count Tilly laid siege to the Protestant city and its more than 30,000 civilian inhabitants. After two months, Tilly's troops were starving and a relieving Swedish army was on the march. The Imperials made one last desperate attempt to capture the city on 20 May. After a furious two-hour assault, Tilly's men took the city. Three days of pillage and slaughter followed the battle. The city itself was burned to the ground and most of the garrison and civil population slaughtered. Estimates of civilian casualties range between 20,000 and 40,000.[32]

Even the legendary discipline of elite British Guard and Rifle brigade regiments could break down under the strain of siege operations culminating in a vicious assault on a fortified city. At Badajoz, the conclusion of the successful assault on the French garrison precipitated 72 hours of uncontrolled rape, drinking, looting, and murder. What was very unusual about Badajoz was that most of the atrocities were perpetuated on the Spanish civilian population who were allied with the British. British officers who attempted to intervene and establish control were ignored, assaulted, and even shot at by their own troops. Ironically, the French soldiers of the garrison that surrendered were largely protected as prisoners of the British during the chaos.[33]

A hostile civilian population could continue to present a challenge even after successful military operations to capture a city were complete. The case of French Louisbourg is an example of one drastic means of controlling a hostile civilian population. After the city's surrender, the French population was put on ships and deported back across the Atlantic to France. In total, more than 8,000 men, women, and children were removed from North America to ensure that the British garrison was not troubled by a hostile civilian population.[34]

Armies often had to deal with urban populations in noncombat situations. Armies were deployed into urban areas under conditions other than combat to maintain order, deal with insurgencies, or support civil authorities coping with natural disasters. Under authoritarian regimes, the use of force or threat of force to control the civil population was so common it was almost unworthy of historical comment. This circumstance began to change with the Age of Enlightenment during the eighteenth century. In more democratic countries, and as international interest increased, the use of force against a domestic or foreign civil population became a much more sensitive issue. Thus by the late nineteenth and early twentieth century, the successful use of military force by modern armies in noncombat situations in cities, though still common, required a fuller understanding of the issues, restraint, and deft execution on the part of the military.

Even in the United States, the Army was employed regularly to deal with disturbances and emergencies in large cities. During the American Civil War, the Union Army—including cadets from West Point—was used to help quell draft riots in New York City. From the end of the Civil War to the end of the nineteenth century, the U.S. Army was called out to deal with civil unrest over three hundred times. The largest deployments were in 1877 when troops were dispatched to augment police forces in Baltimore, Chicago, and St. Louis, and in 1894 when troops from Fort Sheridan were used to restore order in Chicago.[35]

Armies were also used to assist in other kinds of urban emergencies. The American Army's role in providing emergency assistance during the great San Francisco earthquake and fire of 1906 is particularly notable. The earthquake and fire took over 3,000 lives and caused extensive property damage. At one point, four square miles of the city were on fire. Despite this chaos, disorder was not a major problem. General Frederick Funston commanded Army troops who were deployed within hours from the nearby Presidio. He described the effect the troops had:

> San Francisco had its class of people, no doubt, who would have taken advantage of any opportunity to plunder the banks and rich jewelry and other stores of the city, but the presence of the square jawed silent men with magazine rifles, fixed bayonets, and with belts full of cartridges restrained them. There was no necessity for the regular

troops to shoot anybody and there is no well authenticated case of a single person having been killed by regular troops.[36]

A typical example of the use of military force in an urban area is the U.S. Army's last deployment of a large number of troops into an urban area before World War II. On 28 July 1932, President Hoover ordered federal troops to remove the "Bonus Marchers," who were protesting for the payment of World War I veterans' bonuses, from the District of Columbia, using force if necessary. Federal troops, consisting of about 200 mounted cavalry led by Major George S. Patton, 600 infantry and six tanks, drove the veterans from the district and burned their shanty village. Tear gas, bayonets, and sabers were used to move the protesters out.[37] By the next day, the mission was complete and troops returned to their garrisons. No shots were fired and the Army's role in the incident largely reflected General Funston's experience in San Francisco: disciplined Army troops well deployed in an urban area can restore order with a minimum or no use of force.

Fighting for cities caused armies to develop unique weapons, tactics, and equipment to ensure success. Most of this equipment was required by the attacking army, although some could be used in both the defense and offense. In addition, armies also created specialist soldiers who had unique capabilities, training, and expertise necessary for successful urban warfare.

The invention of artillery was one of the most important weapon advances in military history and was a direct response to urban fortification. Artillery was initially designed specifically to deal with the walls of medieval castles and walled cities. It was so effective that it quickly caused the demise of the castle and resulted in drastic changes in the design of fortified cities. Large numbers of artillery were used to attack cities. However, artillery was not normally used against the city itself. The primary purpose of artillery was to create a breach in the surrounding wall. Secondarily, artillery was used to suppress enemy fire, including enemy artillery, during the approach and the assault. Artillery was not commonly used against the population or structures of a city unless a commander specifically decided to compel the city's surrender by the tactic of bombardment.

Before the existence of artillery, defenders behind walls were attacked using mechanical weapons. The three most famous are the catapult, ballista, and the trebuchet. The earliest recorded use of the catapult was in Greece in 398-97 B.C.[38] This weapon did not typically have the kinetic power to defeat well-constructed walls but was somewhat effective at suppressing the enemy manning the walls.[39]

In addition to artillery, other specialized capabilities were developed for the assault on cities. One of the most important munitions was the hand grenade, which was used by both the offense and the defense. Special "grenadier" troops were initially organized to handle this dangerous weapon. Hand grenades became an essential element in siege warfare, as demonstrated by the Spanish who used over 36,000 grenades against the French during the siege of the French city of Valenciennes in 1656. Baron von Wetzel, Austrian governor of the northern Italian city of Brescello, called them "the best means of defense in the event of a siege."[40] They were used by both attackers and defenders during the close quarters fighting just before and during the initial stages of the assault.

Another unique munition was the petard. The petard consisted of an explosive case used to aim and blast a penetrating timber through small fortification doors and gates.[41] It was usually carried forward with the infantry in the assault. The petard permitted infantry to breach obstacles in closed spaces within the city and its fortifications where artillery was not practical.

Armies also developed specialized tactics to seize cities. Before cannon were available to breach walls, armies had to scale them. This was known as attack by escalade, and it could be accomplished only with great difficulty using scaling ladders or siege towers. Once wall-breaching cannon became generally available, an escalading attack was a tactic only used in rare situations where surprise was possible.

Consistent and long-term suppression of enemy defensive fire was a key factor in successful attacks on cities. Suppressive fires covered the approach of assaulting forces, the employment of siege towers, and the process of building trenches. Suppression was accomplished by firing over the heads of the friendly forces approaching the city. Before gunpowder, archers and catapults were key suppression systems. Once cannon were invented, artillery became the key suppression system.

Another tactic important to city fighting was mining and countermining. Attackers mined at a point beginning out of enemy artillery range and ending under the city wall. At the appropriate time, explosives were placed in the mine, detonated, and the wall collapsed. The assault would then follow over the breached wall. Defenders responded to mining with countermines designed to locate the enemy shaft. Countermines caused one or more of the following: the enemy gave up the mine, the mine collapsed, or the force of the mine explosion was dissipated.

Bombardment was another tactical option available to the attacker. This relatively simple tactic required the attacker to surround the city and isolate it from support. When this was accomplished, the attacker used siege lines to bring his artillery into position, and then he proceeded to bombard the city indiscriminately. This tactic attacked the morale and will of the defender. It was sometimes effective when the attacker had the time to wait for the bombardment to slowly erode the morale of the garrison and the population. Bombardment had the advantage of avoiding the casualties of an infantry assault, but it was not an effective technique against a resolute enemy or when time was short. It also was likely to destroy valuable facilities, material, and property inside the city and cause civilian casualties.

The most important, common, complex and successful tactic was the formal siege. The post-medieval, or modern, version of this age-old operation began to be developed late in sixteenth-century Europe and was codified in formal and informal customs and laws of war by the early seventeenth century. It began with a formal demand for and rejection of surrender. This was followed by an official opening of the attack signified by breaking ground on the first trench or by firing the first cannon shot. Its execution was scientific and systematic and thoroughly documented in the writings of the professional military engineers of the period. This tactic made extensive use of very careful reconnaissance and planning, required a lot of time, synchronized a variety of component phases, and made use of unique techniques and specialists. Parallel and zigzag trenches were dug as approaches to the city. These engineering efforts were done in full observation and under the constant fire of the defenders. The trench systems included protected battery positions for friendly artillery. Once friendly artillery was in place, it attempted to blast a breach in the city wall, whereupon infantry stormed from the advance trenches and assaulted the breach. The infantry gained access into the city by climbing the rubble of the collapsed wall. Typically, if the siege was not interrupted by a relieving force, the formal siege ended with a negotiation and agreement on terms once the defender was convinced of its success and before the culmination of the assault on the city.[42]

Walls were the primary means of city protection, but cities also used other obstacles to prevent the attacker from gaining access to the walls. Defensive forces equipped themselves with caltrops, wire, and sharpened stakes pounded into the ground as means to impede the advance of the attacker. These were primarily effective against cavalry and wheeled transportation. Attackers often used bundles of branches, or fascines, to fill ditches and cover wet ground to facilitate the forward movement of men and equipment. Another important piece of equipment was the gabion, a large wicker basket filled with dirt. They were used by the thousands by both attackers and defenders to provide cover and rapidly prepare defensive positions. Sandbags were also invented as a tool of urban sieges and they were used in a similar manner as gabions.[43] To gain access to the walls of the city, attackers often had to cross large ditches, which they accomplished by carrying large bags of hay to throw into the ditches to provide soft landings for troops jumping into them en route to the walls.

Walls are almost as old as cities themselves, and almost as old as walls are the implements used to overcome them. Specialized breaching equipment, such as rams, siege towers, and oversize ladders, offered the primary means of gaining access to cities before gunpowder. Even a small fortress wall required at least a thirty-foot scaling ladder. Most of the basic tools of escalade were invented several millennia before gunpowder. Early rams have been identified in ancient Egypt around 1900 B.C., and the earliest scaling ladder also was found in Egypt around 2400 B.C. Evidence indicates the use of siege towers at least as early as 727 B.C.[44]

Siege towers were an important element of a successful siege before the advent of artillery. These towers were elaborate affairs, and their construction and use required careful engineering support, aid from supporting troops, and very careful synchronization and coordination by the attacking forces. An example of the effective use of siege towers in the assault was the Crusaders' capture of Jerusalem in July 1099 during the first crusade. The Crusaders arrived at the city in June and took six weeks to gather wood and build several siege towers. These towers were over forty feet tall, wheeled, enclosed on three sides by hides (which were sufficient to deflect arrows), and included a built-in bridge and catapult. The Crusaders took three days and nights to fill the defensive ditches on the wall approaches. Finally, the tower was moved forward and approached the wall:

> Resistance was spirited, and the towers were racked by the stones, tar, pitch, and other burning stuffs flung against them. Sacks of cotton and hay, carpets and timber beams had been hung over the walls to absorb the Frankish bombardment. At about midday, while Godfrey's men strove to drive off the Moslem on the walls, the crusaders cut down

two of the beams and pushed them out from the siege tower across to the wall top where they formed a foundation for the bridge when it was lowered. Then they set fire to the sacking. Smoke billowed up and forced the defenders to virtually abandon a section of the wall. The bridge came down and Godfrey and his men rushed across; ladders were hastily erected to give extra support.[45]

This example of the execution of a tower assault demonstrates how engineering efforts to move the tower were coordinated with supporting catapult fires and how smoke was used both to conceal the assault and to drive defenders from the assault point. The complexity and sophistication of this operation demonstrates not only the importance of special equipment, but also the special skills and leadership necessary to employ the equipment properly.

As the defenses of cities became more complicated, it became absolutely essential that armies be manned with specialists in the methods of their defense and attack. The development of grenadiers to handle dangerous explosives has already been mentioned, but first and foremost among the specialists were the engineers. Engineers were not present in medieval armies but made their appearance as sieges became more formal and artillery and fortress design vied for superiority. Engineers began as guilds of civilian specialists, then became quasi-military members, but were only accepted into full status as soldiers in the nineteenth century. Nevertheless, armies, particularly in the attack, relied on their expertise. They advised the commander on which aspect of the fortress to attack and determined the exact breach point. Engineers shared a very hazardous duty as they were constantly in the fore supervising and observing the enemy. An observer of the Seven Years' War commented: "In a single siege an engineer officer must risk his life more frequently, and expose himself to more danger than do many other officers in the entire course of a long war."[46] During the ten-week successful allied siege of French-occupied Lille during the War of Spanish Succession in 1708, all seventy allied engineering officers were killed.[47]

Engineers supervised two types of specialty troops necessary for urban operations: sappers and miners. The engineers generally had exclusive control of the use of miners but had to share with the artillery the direction of sappers. Often this unclear chain of command caused delays in the execution of siege operations. Sapping, the digging of trenches under almost constant fire, was extremely dangerous work. The French engineer Vauban instituted a system of cash rewards based on progress and danger. With these incentives, Vauban's sappers could complete 480 feet of trench every twenty-four hours.[48]

Mining remained an essential element as long as cities were defended by prepared positions and fortresses. Mining could take one of two forms. A deep mine was started well outside the fortification and mined to its foundation. At that point, barrels of explosives were positioned against the foundation and exploded. The result, if done properly, was the exploding of the wall and a huge crater, which became the center of the following infantry assault. The other type of mining was called "attaching the miner." This technique was a direct mine into the base of the fortress wall. The miners quickly burrowed directly into the base of the wall as the enemy above was suppressed by fire. The miners then branched left or right within the wall. At that point, explosives were placed and ignited, bringing down a section of wall.[49] The infantry assault then mounted the wall over the rubble resulting from the explosion. Mining was often used when artillery proved ineffective.

Engineers, sappers, and miners were absolutely critical to successful siege operations. There were never enough of them, and their absence or lack of numbers often caused delays. The failure of Wellington's first siege of Badajoz in 1811 is attributed in part to a chronic shortage of engineers.[50] Mistakes by, or the absence of, engineers could cause significant friendly casualties. Thus, the importance of cities to warfare was recognized in the effort and cost undertaken by armies to develop and train specialized troops to meet the particular needs of successful operations against cities.

Beginning at the end of the seventeenth century, many cities began to change their design, and the fortress city became less common. This process did not occur all at once; by the beginning of the twentieth century, the fortress city was recognized as obsolete and had essentially disappeared. This was a function of several factors. For several hundred years after the Middle Ages, city populations were relatively stable, but urban populations began to increase rapidly in the late eighteenth century.[51] The walled cities began to experience significant crowding and suburbs of the city began to expand beyond the city walls, making the effectiveness of the walls questionable.[52] Additionally, during the eighteenth century, cities in the interior of stable nation-states were not deemed sufficiently threatened to maintain their fortification. Countries such as France intentionally allowed specific city fortifications to erode.[53] Finally, by the time of the Franco-Prussian war in 1870, modern rifled artillery was able to reduce most city fortifications from a range of nearly two miles.[54]

At the same time artillery technology was improving, advances in small arms technology also occurred. Rifled repeating arms made small groups of infantry much more lethal. Small arms technology radically changed infantry tactics. In an urban area, these developments had the effect of turning individual buildings manned by small groups of soldiers into miniature fortresses. Groups of buildings became mutually supporting defensive networks. These man-made defensive networks were much less homogenous than the city wall and hence a much more difficult artillery target. Additionally, the lethality of infantry meant that the integrity of the urban defense was not broken by a break of the walls. Defenders now had the capability of defending effectively throughout the depth of the urban environment—a technique impossible when infantry tactics relied on massed close-knit formations to achieve effective firepower.

One of the early indicators of this phenomenon was the unexpectedly stout defense of the small Chateau de Hougoumont during the climactic Battle of Waterloo in 1815. The allied defense of this position demonstrated the emerging defensive potential of small groups of stone buildings resolutely defended with small arms.[55] By the end of the nineteenth century, the press of urban population growth, the effectiveness of rifled artillery, and the firepower of breech-loading rifles and machine guns led to the obsolescence of the protective city wall and to the capability to defend within individual city buildings and blocks of buildings.

The tactical challenge of the fortified building moved the urban battle from the city wall to the city streets. Thus, the tactics of modern urban warfare, as practiced since the beginning of World War II, differ in many respects from ancient, medieval, and early modern urban tactics. Yet, much about attacking and defending cities remains consistent in principle. Two of the most important consistencies are why armies attack cities, and the fact that the capture and defense of cities remain decisive. Indeed, due to recent urbanization and population trends, it may be argued that the ability to capture and control large urban areas is more important in modern times than in any other time in history.

Other consistencies include the large investment in resources required to properly conduct urban operations. Modern urban operations, like their predecessors, require excessive troops, time, and supplies to be successful. Soldiers and leaders committed to urban combat continue to require inordinately high morale, steadfast will, and patience to endure the stress and grueling physical conditions of the urban environment.

Modern urban operations also require a unique understanding of the physical and human aspects of the urban center. Commanders and their staffs must understand the intricate infrastructure of the modern city, just as the general commanding a besieging army had to understand the design of a fortress city. In addition, even more so than historical commanders whose societies were less sensitive and media aware than modern Western culture, modern commanders must have a thorough understanding of, and a plan to deal with, the urban population. Modern soldiers are subject to many of the same stresses of urban combat, and commanders must be aware of the need for firm discipline regarding interactions with the civil population.

The tactical techniques of urban combat may have changed significantly, but many of the principles remain constant. Modern tactical urban combat still devolves into suppression, breaching, and assaulting fortified positions. Ironically, many cities retain elements of classic fortifications, and these can still affect modern military operations. Twentieth-century urban operations in Metz, Manila, and Hue City all faced the challenges posed by ancient fortress designs that proved to be significant obstacles to modern weapons and tactics. In this regard, twenty-first century armies will be well advised to appreciate the value of direct-fire artillery against stone, concrete, and steel structures.

Although the siege tower is long obsolete, modern forces executing urban operations require special weapons and equipment designed to be optimized in the urban environment. Specialized tactics and troops also continue to have a role against enemies in the urban environment. Modern commanders can benefit from employing specialized troops to act as advisers and to execute specific unique missions in the urban environment. The modern equivalent of grenadiers, sappers, and miners may be civil affairs specialists, snipers, and special operating forces.

Twenty-first century cities are much larger than cities were just a hundred years ago. Cities are not as homogeneous as they once were. Modern-day buildings within cities are generally much more resilient than those of previous ages. In effect, rather than being a single fortified entity, modern cities have the potential of being developed by a defender into dozens or hundreds of individual mutually supporting miniature fortresses. Many of the traditional techniques of fortress assault may be adaptable to this circumstance. The escalade of the twenty-first century may use helicopters instead of scaling ladders, but the principles remain the same.

Cities of the twenty-first century are as challenging to military operations as they have ever been, if not more so. And, as history has demonstrated, armies will continue to have no choice but to execute operations against and within cities. These operations will include the full spectrum of mission types from intense offensive and defensive combat to less lethal but equally vital stability or support operations. Success in these operations will be, as always, a function of understanding the principles illustrated in the past and applying that knowledge to the conditions, technology, organization, and tactics of the present.

Notes

1. Sun Tzu, *The Art of War*, Ralph D. Sawyer, trans. (Boulder, CO: Westview Press, 1994), 177.
2. Ibid., 55.
3. Mark Girouard, *Cities and People: A Social and Architectural History* (New Haven, CT: Yale University Press, 1985), 61.
4. John Keegan, *A History of Warfare* (New York: Random House, 1993), 321.
5. David G. Chandler, *The Campaigns of Napoleon: The Mind and Method of History's Greatest Soldier* (New York: MacMillian Publishing Co., 1966), 808.
6. Sun Tzu, 245.
7. Christopher Duffy, *Siege Warfare: The Fortress in the Early Modern World, 1494 1660* (London: Routledge and Kegan Paul, 1979), 45.
8. Elmer C. May and Gerald Stadler, *Ancient and Medieval Warfare* (West Point, NY: Department of History, U.S. Military Academy, 1973), 11-17.
9. Chandler, 815.
10. Ian Fletcher, *Badajoz, 1812, Wellington's Bloodiest Siege* (Oxford, UK: Osprey Publishing Limited, 2001), 10.
11. James R. Arnold, *Grant Wins the War: Decision at Vicksburg* (NY: John Wiley & Sons Inc., 1997), 298-309.
12. Fred Anderson, *Crucible of War* (NY: Random House, 2000), 250-54.
13. William Seymour, *Great Sieges of History* (London: Brassey's, 1991), 87-100.
14. Anderson, 355-65.
15. For simplicity and clarity, the description of locations of cities in this chapter, except when obvious, will be in modern national and geographic terms rather than in terms of the referenced battle. For example, Cremona is located in the modern northern Italian province of Lombardy, which at the time of the city's conquest by Austria in 1702 was under Spanish rule.
16. Christopher Duffy, Fire and Stone, *The Science of Fortress Warfare, 1660 1860* (London: Greenhill Books, 1996), 116-17.
17. David Morgan, *The Mongols* (Oxford, UK: Basil Blackwell, 1986), 65-73.
18. Sun Tzu, 177.
19. Seymour, 12-27.
20. Ibid., xvii.
21. Arnold, 301-308.
22. Fletcher, 11.

23. *Feeding Mars: Logistics in Western Warfare From the Middle Ages to the Present*, John A. Lynn, ed. (Boulder, CO: Westview Press, 1993), 35.
24. Anderson, 254.
25. Duffy, *Fire and Stone*, 125.
26. Ibid., 130-31.
27. Ellis Ashmead-Bartlett, *Port Arthur: The Siege and Capitulation* (London, UK: William Blackwood and Sons, 1906), 478.
28. Duffy, *Fire and Stone*, 134-35.
29. Anderson, 253.
30. Seymour, 101-20.
31. Morgan, 74.
32. David Palmer, Albert Britt, Gerald Stadler, and Jerome O'Connell, *The Dawn of Modern Warfare* (West Point, NY: Department of History, U.S. Military Academy, 1973), 79.
33. Fletcher, 80-81.
34. Anderson, 255.
35. Russell F. Weigley, *History of the United States Army* (NY: Macmillan Publishing Co. Inc., 1967), 281.
36. Frederick Funston, "How the Army Worked to Save San Francisco," Cosmopolitan Magazine (July 1906) at <http://www.sfmuseum.org/1906/cosmo.html>, 5 March 1996.
37. Robert N. Webb, *The Bonus March on Washington, D.C., May June 1932* (NY: Franklin Watts Inc., 1969), 55-60.
38. Keegan, 150.
39. E. Viollet-Le-Duc, *Annals of a Fortress: Twenty Two Centuries of Siege Warfare* (Barton-under-Needwood, UK: Wren's Park Publishing, 2000), 130.
40. Duffy, *Fire and Stone*, 168.
41. Ibid., 118.
42. Duffy, *Siege Warfare*, 249-50.
43. Duffy, *Fire and Stone*, 134.
44. Keegan, 150.
45. Christopher Gravett, *Medieval Siege Warfare* (Oxford, UK: Osprey Publishing, 1990), 56.
46. Jakob Mauvillion quoted in Christopher Duffy, *The Military Experience in the Age of Reason* (Atheneum, NY: The MacMillan Publishing Company, 1988), 290.
47. David Chandler, *The Art of Warfare in the Age of Marlborough* (NY: Hippocrene Books Inc., 1976), 221.
48. Ibid., 255.
49. Duffy, *Fire and Stone*, 170-75.
50. Fletcher, 19-20.

51. Robert E. Dickinson, *The West European City: A Geographical Interpretation* (London: Routledge & Kegan Paul Ltd., 1951), 461-63.
52. Girouard, 212-13.
53. Dickinson, 418.
54. Ibid., 354.
55. Chandler, *The Campaigns of Napoleon*, 1072.

Bibliography

Anderson, Fred. *Crucible of War*. NY: Random House, 2000. An authoritative history of the Seven Years' War. This work contains excellent discussions of the strategic importance and the battles to secure Louisbourg and Quebec.

Arnold, James R. *Grant Wins the War: Decision at Vicksburg*. NY: John Wiley & Sons Inc., 1997. Arnold's effort is an outstanding discussion of this decisive battle with an emphasis on the tactics and technology of siege warfare.

Ashmead-Bartlett, Ellis. *Port Arthur: The Siege and Capitulation*. London: William Blackwood and Sons, 1906. Ashmead's work is a firsthand perspective of this important battle from the perspective of an English journalist with the Japanese.

Chandler, David. *The Campaigns of Napoleon: The Mind and Method of History's Greatest Soldier*. NY: MacMillian Publishing Co., 1966. This work is the definitive one-volume account of Napoleon's campaigns; an excellent reference to the context of major urban operations during this period.

. *The Art of Warfare in the Age of Marlborough*. NY: Hippocrene Books, Inc., 1976. This effort is an excellent overview of the nature of warfare during the early eighteenth century.

Dickinson, Robert E. *The West European City: A Geographical Interpretation*. London: Routledge & Kegan Paul Ltd., 1951. This volume is a superb analysis of virtually all aspects of urban design and development in Europe. This work places particular emphasis on the development of urban city plans.

Duffy, Christopher. *Siege Warfare: The Fortress in the Early Modern World, 1494 1660*. London: Routledge and Kegan Paul, 1979. This work is the most complete account of fortress warfare in the early modern period.

. *The Military Experience in the Age of Reason*. Atheneum, NY: The MacMillan Publishing Company, 1988. This book is an excellent discussion of the nature of warfare in the mid- to late-eighteenth century and the role of fortifications and engineers.

. *Fire and Stone, The Science of Fortress Warfare, 1660 1860*. London: Greenhill Books, 1996. This work is the authoritative follow-on to Duffy's earlier work and completes the history of fortress warfare.

Fletcher, Ian. *Badajoz, 1812, Wellington's Bloodiest Siege*. Oxford, UK: Osprey Publishing Ltd., 2001. This work is an excellent short, but detailed, account of Wellington's successful effort to seize the key Spanish city of Badajoz.

Girouard, Mark. *Cities and People: A Social and Architectural History*. New Haven, CT: Yale University Press, 1985. This volume is a profusely illustrated history of urban development and culture that helps put urban fortifications and warfare into the context of urban history.

Gravett, Christopher. *Medieval Siege Warfare*. Oxford, UK: Osprey Publishing, 1990. This work is a concise description of medieval siege warfare with an emphasis on siege weapons.

Keegan, John. *A History of Warfare*. NY: Random House, 1993. This work is an excellent one-volume overview of the history of warfare. It is valuable for placing urban warfare within the context of military history and tracing its ancient origins.

Lynn, John A. Editor. *Feeding Mars: Logistics in Western Warfare From the Middle Ages to the Present*. Boulder, CO: Westview Press, 1993. This work is an excellent discussion of the importance of urban areas to logistics and of the impact of logistics on siege warfare.

May, Elmer C. and Gerald Stadler. *Ancient and Medieval Warfare*. West Point, NY: Department of History, U.S. Military Academy, 1973. This work is an excellent concise reference to ancient and medieval warfare.

Morgan, David. *The Mongols*. Oxford, UK: Basil Blackwell, 1986. This work is an excellent history of the Mongols and includes a well-researched description of the Mongol invasion of China and the challenge of Chinese cities.

Palmer, David and Albert Britt, Gerald Stadler, and Jerome O'Connell. *The Dawn of Modern Warfare*. West Point, NY: Department of History, U.S. Military Academy, 1973. This work is an excellent concise reference to early modern warfare.

Seymour, William. *Great Sieges of History*. London: Brassey's, 1991. This book is an excellent reference to some of the most important sieges in history.

Sun Tzu. *Art of War*. Translated by Ralph D. Sawyer. Boulder, CO: Westview Press, 1994. This volume is a complete accounting of the writings of the important ancient Chinese military thinker and is valuable in accessing the thoughts of ancient strategists regarding urban operations.

Viollet-Le-Duc, E. *Annals of a Fortress: Twenty two Centuries of Siege Warfare*. Barton-under-Needwood, UK: Wren's Park Publishing, 2000. This book is a fascinating reprint of the work of a well-regarded nineteenth-century French military engineer. He uses the history of a fictitious French fortress to describe and analyze the development of fortress design and siege tactics.

Webb, Robert N. *The Bonus March on Washington, D.C., May June 1932*. NY: Franklin Watts Inc., 1969. This book is the most complete account of the confrontation between the U.S. government and the Bonus Marchers.

Weigley, Russell F. *History of the United States Army*. NY: Macmillan Publishing Co. Inc., 1967. This book is the most authoritative one-volume history of the U.S. Army.

The Battle of Stalingrad

S.J. Lewis

There is no escaping the fact that in World War II Stalingrad was a decisive campaign from which Germany never recovered. It was one of three "hammer blows" delivered against the Axis in November 1942. The first two were in North Africa: the British victory at El Alamein and the Anglo-American invasion of Casablanca, Oran, and Algiers. The third blow was the Soviet Operation *URANUS*, which would lead to the destruction of the German 6th Army. Stalingrad also represents one of the high points in the art of campaigning, clearly a decisive battle of annihilation with profound strategic implications. Consequently, the campaign has been analyzed extensively at the operational level.

Despite the importance of Stalingrad at the strategic and operational levels, it is at the tactical level that Stalingrad serves as a lens not only to magnify patterns of past warfare but also to provide a possible glimpse into how warfare will be fought in the future. These profound changes are a continuation of long-term trends stemming from both the French Revolution and the industrialization of Western society and warfare. Conventional warfare in Stalingrad required ever-greater numbers of troops that, in turn, produced very high casualties. The increased number of troops required more ammunition, particularly for certain weapon systems. The logistics systems consequently had more supplies to deliver. There were also more casualties to be evacuated. Air forces were especially important, not only in supporting tactical actions but also in interdicting lines of communication (LOC). But perhaps the most significant development at Stalingrad was the tendency for urban operations to impinge increasingly on the operational and strategic levels of warfare.[1]

The city that came to be known as Stalingrad was originally a fortress on Russia's southern flank, resting on the west bank of a bend of the Volga River about 934 kilometers (km) southeast of Moscow. Over time it grew as a trading center, despite the constant threat posed by the Cossacks, and the Russian state formally established the city of Tsaritsyn in 1589. It continued to grow in importance as a trading center on the Volga so that by 1897, the city had a population of 55,914, a harbor, several schools, and eight banks. In 1925, after the Communist Revolution, Tsaritsyn became Stalingrad when Joseph Stalin assumed power. In 1961, it was renamed once again to the name it still has, Volgograd. At the start of World War II the city's population was

600,000, but by July 1941, refugees had swollen that sum to about 900,000.²

The massive German invasion of the Soviet Union that began in June 1941 and accomplished tremendous territorial gains stalled in the harsh winter of 1941-42. In December, Adolf Hitler relieved the commander in chief of the German army and assumed those duties himself. Despite the *Wehrmacht's* failure to complete its conquest, Hitler had never abandoned the idea of conducting an offensive into southern Russia to seize the oil fields in the Caucasus mountains. Hitler consequently issued Directive No. 41 on 5 April 1942. Code-named Operation *BLUE*, it directed that the remaining Soviet military units west of the Don River be eliminated and Russia's vital economic areas be seized. It was an overly complex operation consisting of several phases that were based on wishful thinking, inadequate intelligence, and a presumably passive enemy. Both the Russian and German armies, however, were recovering from the previous year's fighting that had inflicted huge casualties on both sides, making any future outcome uncertain.³

Operation *BLUE*

Before the start of Operation *BLUE*, the Red Army launched a major offensive near Kharkov on 12 May. Army Group South, commanded by Field Marshal Fedor von Bock, countered with a double envelopment that trapped some 240,000 Soviet troops in the Izyum pocket. Throughout summer 1942, Army Group South conducted the preselected phases of the operation, even though the Soviets on 19 June captured documents compromising the plans. Hitler became more and more confident as the German armies advanced across the broad steppes. Von Bock began to worry, however, noticing that Russian units were withdrawing. The German army largely depended on railroads for supply. It could operate comfortably up to the Dnieper River. Any advance farther into southern Russia, however, had to be improvised and would be subject to interruptions. The farther they advanced into southern Russia, the more problematic their supply would become.

In early July, the Germans reorganized, with Field Marshal Wilhelm List's Army Group A fielding the 1st Panzer, 11th, and 17th armies. Hitler replaced von Bock with Maximilian von Weichs and redesignated Army Group South as Army Group B. It consisted of the 2d Hungarian, 4th Panzer, 2d, and 6th armies. Hitler's interference in army operations also increased. He issued Directive No. 45 on 23 July, which sent Army Group A south to the Caucasus region, leaving the 6th

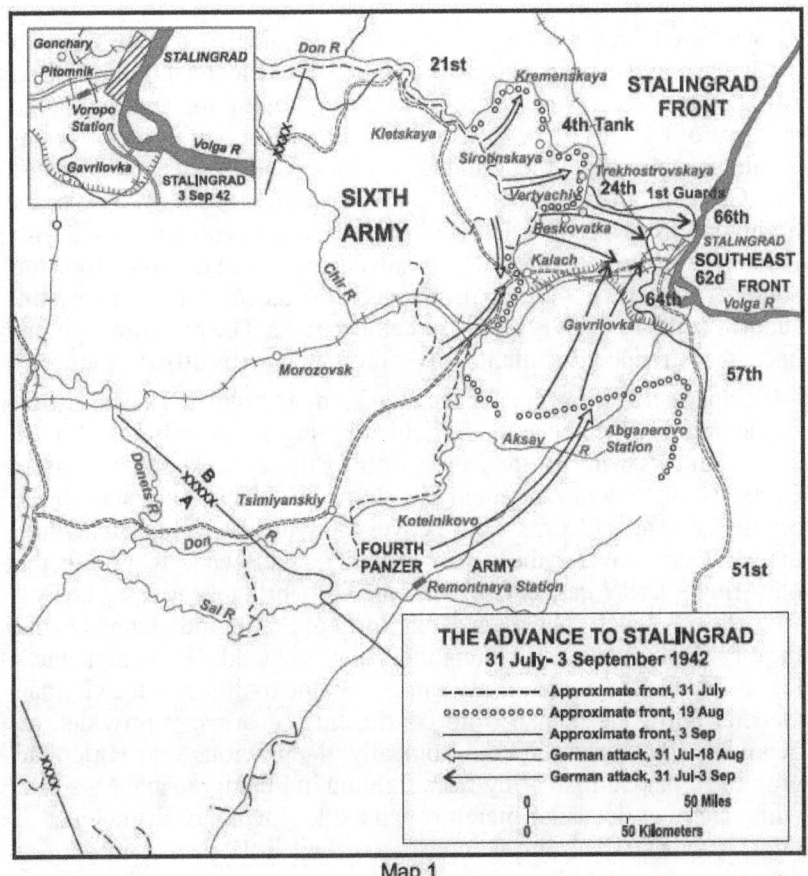

Map 1

Army unsupported to advance on to Stalingrad (see Map 1). It also allowed the Soviets to withdraw most of their troops from the Don bend.[4]

With his early tactical success in the south, Hitler concluded that he was triumphant. He dispatched the 11th Army, the only reserve in southern Russia, north to Leningrad. As the remaining German forces in the area began to fan out, enormous logistics problems ensued. The steppes did not have the infrastructure to support a west European-type army; conspicuously absent were reliable double-tracked railroads and bridges leading to Stalingrad from the west. All the German motorized forces periodically ran out of fuel. The chief of staff of the 4th Panzer Army, whose divisions were to fan out into the Caucasus, described the logistics situation as catastrophic.[5]

Stalingrad had not originally been a major factor in German planning, and the 4th Panzer Army could have reached it much earlier. But Hitler became increasingly fascinated with the city with his issuance of Directive No. 45, a decision that still mystifies historians. It would now constitute the foundation for his conquest of the Caucasus. The German 6th Army under General Friedrich Paulus was to seize Stalingrad from the west. Hitler changed his mind and directed the 4th Panzer Army to assist Paulus by advancing on Stalingrad from the south. It moved forward against tough resistance, only reaching the suburbs south of the city on 10 September 1942. The previous fighting had already reduced its infantry divisions' strength by 40 to 50 percent.[6]

Paulus issued his order for the attack on 19 August. The 6th Army headquarters expected both difficult fighting in the city and Soviet counterattacks with armor from north of the city. The XIV Panzer Corps would conduct the main thrust toward the northern suburbs of Stalingrad. The LI Corps would cover the Panzers' right flank, while the VIII Corps covered the left or northern flank. Even farther north, the 6th Army's XXIV Panzer Corps maintained a bridgehead over the Don River near Kalatch. The main effort north of Stalingrad planned to cut the city's main LOC north along the Volga, although German planners knew this would not cut off all supplies. In the tradition of the German General Staff, the plan had no contingent scenarios; it provided no details on fighting in the city. Ironically, the previous year Hitler had prohibited the German army from fighting in Leningrad and Moscow, while German doctrinal literature tended to downplay the subject of urban combat. Thus, the German army had little if any training or experience in city fighting.[7]

On 21 August, the 6th Army seized a bridgehead over the Don River at Wertjatschij, and two days later the XIV Panzer Corps began its 96.5-km dash eastward. Breaking through scattered opposition, the 16th Panzer Division broke into Rynok the evening of Sunday, 23 August, looking down on the broad Volga north of Stalingrad. It seized Rynok from Red Army antiaircraft units, all-female units that had been deploying north and east of Stalingrad during August. Throughout the remaining hours of the day, troops of the 16th Panzer Division observed as the *Luftwaffe* began bombing Stalingrad.

Luftflotte IV, tasked with supporting the advance into southern Russia, fielded half the air assets on the Eastern Front. It, too, was drawn to Stalingrad—its VIII Air Corps supported the army with an average of 1,000 sorties a day. Throughout 23 August, Colonel General Wolfram von Richthofen's *Luftflotte IV* pounded the city, burning down the wooden houses in the southwest corner. The large petroleum facility burned for days. The walls of the white four- and five-story apartment buildings remained standing, but the bombs burned the interiors, collapsing the floors. The waterworks and communications center were also knocked out. The aerial bombardment during the week killed an estimated 40,000 Russians while the many Soviet antiaircraft units only managed to bring down three aircraft, a consequence of insufficient training and very limited ammunition. Although the *Luftwaffe* created considerable destruction, Anthony Beevor observed, "Richthofen's massive bombing raids had not only failed to destroy the enemy's will, their very force of destruction had turned the city into a perfect killing ground for the Russians to use against them."[8]

Von Richthofen's forces were able to maintain air superiority until late October, by which time combat and mechanical failures had considerably weakened them. Simultaneously, the Russian air force began to receive considerably more and better aircraft, while their antiaircraft forces continued to improve. Most authors, including official historians, maintain that both air forces limited themselves largely to ground support of the army, reconnaissance, and short-range bombing. As historian R.J. Spiller observed, however, we will probably never know the specific sortie patterns of *Luftflotte IV* and the Red air force.[9]

The XIV Panzer Corps remained in its exposed position for several weeks since the 6th Army's infantry divisions were strung out for some 322 km behind it. While the German infantry divisions marched forward, the Red Army repeatedly counterattacked the XIV Panzer Corps. The German infantry divisions reached the heights above Stalingrad on 10 September 1942. From there, they observed the 56-km-long complex of houses, apartment dwellings, and factories pinned against the 1,000-meter-wide Volga by the unending brown steppes. At many points, the city was only 2 km wide. Also visible were several of the Volga's islands and tributaries.

An observer with an eye for tactics would have noticed how the steppes are cut up by innumerable steep-sloped gullies that, in Russian, are called *balka*. The Tsaritsa gully was the major *balka*, which separated the southern third of Stalingrad from the northern two-thirds of the city (see Map 2). At the mouth of the *balka* was the old town center where the czar's officials and businessmen maintained their two-story houses. South of the Tsaritsa was a residential sector. Its train station was near the grain silos across from the large island in the Volga. North of the Tsaritsa was the city center that had its own train station,

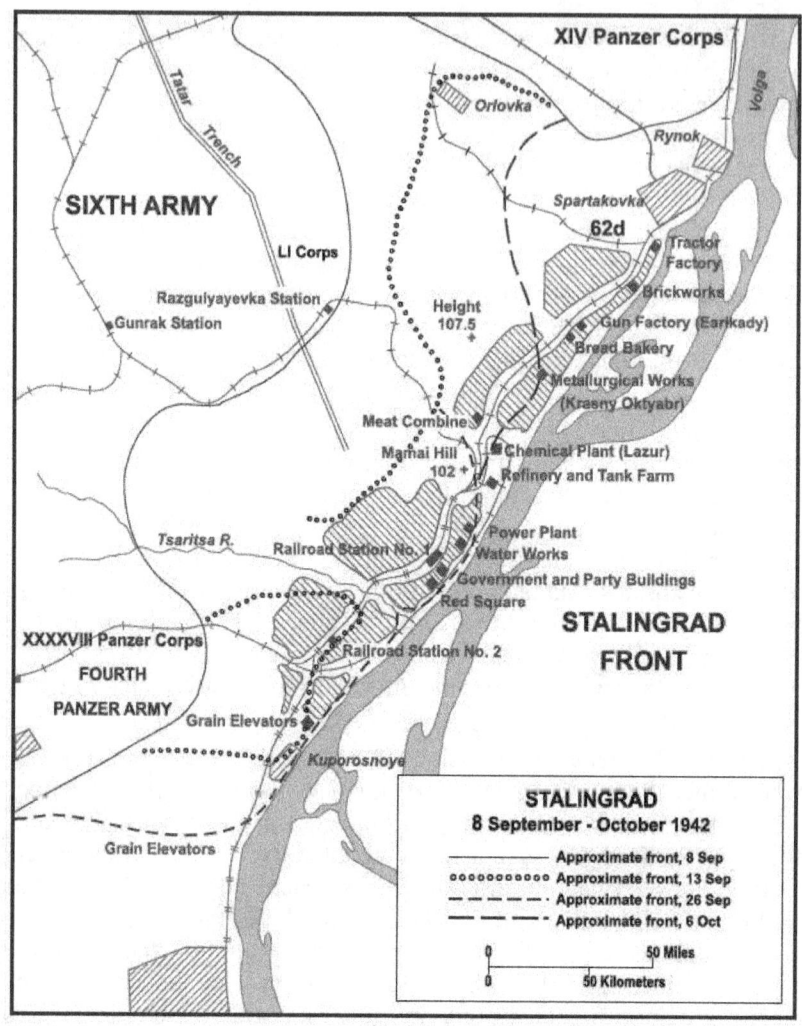

Map 2

several plazas, post office, and waterworks. This area housed the local Communist Party (CP) headquarters. To the north was the large petroleum complex along the Volga. West of the oil complex was Stalingrad's dominant feature, the Mamayev Kurgan (on German maps, *Height* 102), on the northern edge of the residential sector that overlooks the Volga River. To the west of Mamayev Kurgan was the airport. The northern sector was the industrial region. Running south to north were the Lasur Chemical Factory (which from the air resembled half a tennis racket), the Red October Metallurgical Factory, Bread Factory No. 2, the Red Barricade Armaments Factory, and, at the extreme north, a tractor factory.

Despite seeing their city pulverized and the continuing combat operations, 300,000 to 350,000 civilians were still in Stalingrad. Most of them lived in holes, cellars, and homemade bunkers. Since even the German army was incapable of its own logistics support, many civilians faced eventual starvation. Most of those remaining were women, children, and old men. German authorities knew the civilians required evacuation but were unable to carry out the movement. By mid-October, some 25,000 had fled the rubble, walking toward Kalatch. Some of the outskirts of the city still stood, mostly grimy houses occupied by workers. Other than several major streets, most of the roads were unpaved. Russian artillery units that deployed en masse east of the river could hit streets running east and west. Streets running north and south were under Russian small-arms fire.[10]

Besides the enormous military problem of taking Stalingrad, Paulus also had to safeguard his northern flank along the Don River. He never solved this task because the Soviets held a number of bridgeheads from which they launched numerous offensives. Three Soviet armies launched the first offensive on 24 August. Although they suffered great casualties, they succeeded in slowing down the German divisions' arrival in Stalingrad.[11]

Three weeks into the German summer offensive, Stalin remained convinced that the main attack would be against Moscow. He responded clumsily in fits and starts, first splitting Stalingrad between two Front headquarters. In mid-July, however, he corrected this error and created the Stalingrad Front under General A.I. Yeremenko, consisting of the 28th, 51st, 57th, 62d, and 64th armies. The Russians also deployed the North Caucasus, South, Southwest, and Bryansk Fronts in southern Russia. Most men of military age in Stalingrad had already been drafted, but local CP officials mobilized an additional 200,000 men and women to serve in "Worker's Columns" while unneeded workers were placed in militia battalions. Stalin ordered that Stalingrad would not be given up and dispatched the dreaded secret police (NKVD) to enforce discipline. The latter soon controlled all the boats on the Volga and allowed no one out of the city. On 2 August, *Luftwaffe* General von Richthofen noted that Stalingrad seemed to act like a magnet, drawing Russian forces from all directions.

The last major headquarters left in Stalingrad was General Vasili I. Chuikov's 62d Army. While the German 6th Army methodically attacked Stalingrad, Chuikov ferried over the Volga the equivalent of nine rifle divisions and two tank brigades. As the struggle wore on and he gained greater strength, he increasingly resorted to aggressive counterattacks with anywhere from 200 to 800 men, sometimes with tank support. This hyperactive form of defense forced the Germans to shift repeatedly from offense to defense and made the battle of attrition ever more costly.[12]

Stalin's advisers tried unsuccessfully to stop him from launching several major counteroffensives from bridgeheads north of Stalingrad. Three reserve armies filled with untrained conscripts began an attack on 5 September but were checked with substantial losses. The Soviet Union had already suffered millions of losses, including most of its prewar military. The Germans also occupied most of its industrial and manpower centers.[13] Despite this, the Soviets still possessed numerical superiority in men and weapon systems. A German intelligence report of 20 September 1942 estimated the Soviets had 4.2 million soldiers, 3 million of those deployed at the Front. Factories continued to produce enormous numbers of tanks and airplanes, and a new military elite had begun to emerge from the earlier disasters of the war: hard men who understood the Germans' weaknesses and were not afraid of the Germans or of taking casualties. Related to this development was the reemergence of the Soviet General Staff, which had arduously compiled lessons learned from which their recipe for victory evolved. An action symptomatic of this emergence of a new Soviet military elite occurred on 9 October 1942, when the Red Army gave commanders relative autonomy, reducing the old coresponsibility of the political commissar. In late 1942, however, the Soviet military was still recovering from its serious wounds.[14]

As the 6th Army deployed and attacked Stalingrad in September, a crisis occurred in the German High Command. Hitler had become increasingly nervous over what he perceived to be the slow advance into the Caucasus. On 10 September, he fired Field Marshal List and personally assumed command of Army Group A. The mood was tense at Hitler's headquarters at Vinitsa in the Ukraine, aggravated by the hot, humid weather. Hitler had never liked the chief of the General Staff, so General Franz Halder's relief was perhaps unavoidable under the circumstances. Halder managed to last until 24 September, when Hitler replaced him with a relatively junior officer, General Kurt Zeitzler. When the latter arrived to assume his new job, he lectured the General Staff that the only problem Germany faced was its lack of faith in the *Fuehrer*. So, while the fighting for Stalingrad raged, Hitler consolidated his power at the expense of the military professional class.[15]

Soon after the arrival of his infantry divisions on 10 September, Paulus launched a concerted attack on the city. It progressed rapidly through the suburbs but slowed in the inner city. The Germans seized Mamayev Kurgan on 13 September, but it changed hands repeatedly throughout the following months. For both sides, casualties climbed precipitously. The Soviets threw in the 13th Guard Division, which sacrificed many of its 10,000 men in grinding down the German advance. This was the first of four German attacks in Stalingrad. It faltered on 19 and 20 September as a result of massive casualties and dwindling ammunition. This pattern recurred in the three subsequent attacks. The first, from 22 September to 6 October, reached the Volga at the mouth of the Tsaritsa. The attack from 14 October to early November from the north reduced the Soviet hold in Stalingrad to two small bridgeheads. The final futile assault from 11 to 17 November was against the two small bridgeheads.[16]

On 23 September, a German General Staff officer visited the 295th and 71st Infantry Divisions in the center of the town. He noted that the Soviet troops remained as physically close to the Germans as possible to reduce the effectiveness of the Germans' firepower. The Soviet troops were ever alert and whenever they thought they spotted a German weakness, they immediately counterattacked. They were particularly tough now that there was little room left to retreat. The German officer observed that after the heavy artillery bombardment, troops quickly emerged from their cellar holes ready to fire. Despite German countermeasures, the Soviets continued to move supplies across the Volga at night.

The two German divisions the staff officer visited were old, battle-tested formations that had been considerably weakened by infantry casualties. He observed that their combat power was dropping daily and that the average strength of an infantry company was ten to fifteen men. Losses were particularly high for the officers and noncommissioned officers (NCOs). Although replacements had arrived, they were insufficient in number and lacked experience, training, and soldierly bearing. When an officer fell, the men drifted back to their starting point. To get them moving forward again, a higher-ranking officer had to lead them. The soldiers particularly depended on the division *Sturmgeschutze*, heavily armored tracked vehicles whose 7.5-centimeter (cm) guns were designed to take out point targets for the infantry. The small bands of infantry did not want to attack without a *Sturmgeschutz* and viewed it as a failure in leadership if one was not provided to them. This German officer concluded that attacking through the ruins had exhausted the infantry and that they were too tired and dulled. With so few troops, there was no rest because every soldier had to be deployed. There were no reserves.

It was especially hard to get necessary supplies forward to the combat infantry troops. Their diet suffered considerably. The surviving troops expressed bitterness toward the *Luftwaffe's* perceived luxury. They had also become resentful toward the special food bonuses the armored units received. The officers maintained that it was pointless to offer the infantry propaganda since none of the promises could be kept. Out in the steppes of southern Russia, all supplies had to be brought from Germany. Besides food, the infantry's major requirement was 8-cm mortar shells, one of the few ways to get to the enemy's holes in cellars and gully cliffs.[17]

Senior officers noted that they had gotten into a battle of attrition with the Russians, and although their casualties were very high, those inflicted on the Russians were much greater. As soon as the city was captured, however, the divisions would have to be rested and reorganized. They also stated that it was critical to secure sufficient fodder and straw for the horses.[18]

In the last week of September, Paulus launched his second attack on Stalingrad. He exchanged divisions with his northern flank and used the new units to renew the offensive. It pushed the Soviets back into the northern sector of Stalingrad, but casualties and ammunition expenditures were so high that Paulus called off the offensive. The German 6th Army did not begin its third offensive until 14 October. Paulus sent four divisions supported by armor to assist in taking the northern factory complexes. This created a crisis for the defenders, when on the second day, the Germans captured the tractor factory and reached the Volga. Despite the heavy rain, snow, and the consequential mud, the attack made remarkable progress, capturing the ruins of several blocks of houses, the Red October Factory, and some other burned-out hulks. But at the end of the month, the attacks fizzled out from the high casualties and insufficient ammunition. Chuikov's garrison had been reduced to two small pockets, and the block ice in the Volga had created a logistics nightmare, but the Germans were spent. Paulus launched the fourth and final attack on 11 November, based on the arrival of five engineer battalions. The attack advanced very slowly against tough resistance. It, too, expired after several days, and on the 19th, the Soviets launched the counteroffensive that would surround and destroy the German 6th Army.[19]

As autumn wore on, *Fremde Heere Ost's* prediction began to become a reality as more and more Soviet units appeared in southern Russia. The Germans used all-source intelligence, but much of their success at the operational and tactical levels resulted from their ability to intercept Soviet radio traffic. They could pick up newly deployed units; however, the Germans did not know the scope of the deployment or where or when the Soviets would attack. Hitler thought the attack would be against Rostov. *Fremde Heere Ost* still believed the major attack would be against Army Group Center, even though more and more units appeared in the south. Finally, they detected a new Soviet Southwest Front headquarters and, on 12 November, concluded that an attack in the near future against the Romanian Third Army could cut the railroad to Stalingrad. If that happened, it would threaten the German forces farther east, forcing them to withdraw from Stalingrad.[20]

To summarize developments, Hitler had sent the strongest force available toward an objective that would not necessarily win the war. That force could not be logistically supported and advanced into an ever-expanding space against an opponent that was gaining, not losing, strength. He had sent his most powerful army into Stalingrad where it basically destroyed its combat power in costly attacks that played into the enemy's hands. And finally, although intelligence indicated the probability of a major Soviet counteroffensive, the German military leadership resorted to conducting merely cosmetic measures.[21]

Stalin had dispatched two of the *Stavka's* most capable representatives, Generals A.M. Vasilevskiy and G.K. Zhukov, to oversee operations in southern Russia. On 4 October, they conducted a conference that began the planning process for what would be Operation *URANUS*, the counteroffensive against the German 6th Army. Lieutenant General N.F. Vatutin activated the Southwest Front headquarters that fielded five armies along the Don northwest of Kletskaya. The Don Front kept three armies in the central sector. The Stalingrad Front deployed some five armies in the southern sector. Approximately 1 million men and 900 tanks were to conduct a classic double envelopment of the German 6th Army by breaking through the hapless 3d and 4th Romanian armies.[22]

Luftflotte IV had been weakened considerably by the intensive months of combat. By October, the Russian air force wrested air superiority from the Germans as both more and newer equipment arrived. In addition, as the Germans captured more and more of Stalingrad, the Soviet air force could more easily bomb the city. The *Stavka* also dispatched General A.A. Novikov to help coordinate air operations for *URANUS* (see Map 3). He became such a valued team member that when he stated that the air forces were not yet prepared, Zhukov delayed the opening of the offensive.[23]

Timing was critical for the counteroffensive. Zhukov and Vasilevskiy waited for the German 6th Army to expend its combat power in Stalingrad. They also waited for the Anglo-Saxon offensives to succeed in North Africa. By waiting until 19 November, they allowed the ground to freeze, giving their armor greater mobility. The Soviets' artillery preparation was short but powerful, lasting only 90 minutes, after which the offensive launched at 0850. The Romanian defense broke rather easily, allowing Soviet armor to begin the exploitation about 1400. Both Romanian armies collapsed, and there were no Axis reserves to stem the tide. The Soviet forces continued their advance nearly unopposed and on 22 November met at Kalach, encircling Paulus's 6th Army. Some Soviet forces wheeled in against Stalingrad, while others expanded the advance westward to limit any Axis relief efforts.[24]

As has been oft recounted, the German military was unable to orchestrate a breakthrough, and the *Luftwaffe* was never able to even

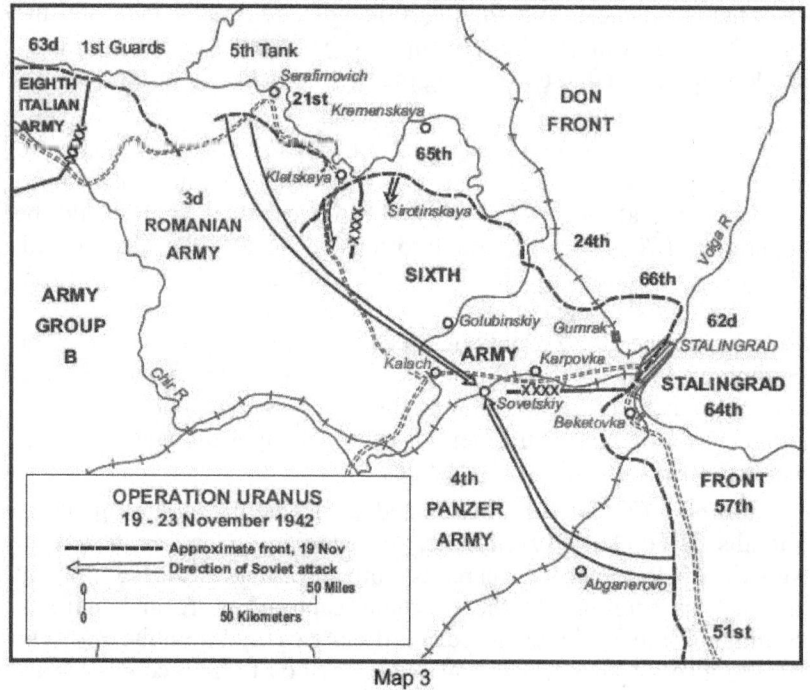

Map 3

approach Hermann Goering's promise to sustain the garrison. At Hitler's headquarters, General Walther Warlimont observed, "On 18 December the Italian Eighth Army collapsed, a decisive factor in the fate of Stalingrad; less than a month later, on 15 January, the Hungarian Second Army disintegrated and on the same day the German ring around Leningrad was broken."[25] Paulus and his army were doomed.

The remnants of the 6th Army deployed into positions resembling an egg 40 km wide and 50 km long, surrounded by the Don Front's seven armies. Despite the Axis and Soviet propaganda, the position could hardly be viewed as a fortress since few if any fortifications were in the open steppes west of Stalingrad. Only a small portion of the German defense was in the remains of Stalingrad. Despite the profound weakness of the 6th Army units, the Soviets achieved little success when, in early December, the Don Front attacked the weakest sector of the line in the west and south. As Earl Ziemke and Magda Bauer observed, this probably occurred because the Soviet units had also been weakened by nearly six months of unbroken combat. German signals intelligence also contributed by intercepting Soviet radio messages and alerting threatened sectors in time to stave off disasters. The 6th Army could ill afford such Pyrrhic victories because its limited strength was wasting away.

The final Soviet offensive began on 10 January after a particularly heavy artillery barrage that cut most of the German communication wires and cables. The ground attack opened large holes in the German line that could not be closed. Although the Germans had an auxiliary airbase at Gumrak, the only serviceable one was Pitomnik, through which casualties, specialists, and vital items departed the trap in exchange for a woefully inadequate flow of food, medicine, petroleum products, and ammunition. Soviet units overran Pitomnik on 12 January, ending resupply in the pocket, after which the defenders' position was hopeless. Paulus noted that artillery ammunition would run out on 13 January. Hitler still prohibited a surrender, however, so the slaughter continued. Final resistance ended on 2 February 1943. The 6th Army ceased to exist.[26]

Tactical Considerations

Evaluating Stalingrad has proved to be difficult, both for participants and for historians. The experience was simply too big. Many participants had never seen a large city destroyed, so the intensity and duration of violence were overwhelming. Soviet and German propagandists assisted in making a large, confusing phenomenon even more difficult to understand. One should not be surprised, therefore, when subsequent accounts focus on exaggeration and the uniqueness of the fighting. Stalingrad has had a remarkable ability to distort perceptions for a long time. It is perhaps too easy to become fixated on exotic ways to kill a human being, whether with knives, blunt objects, or telescopic rifles. Outside of a few new weapon systems, the nature of the fighting and destruction remained identical to that of Flanders and the Somme in World War I. Veterans of those battles, however, were rare at Stalingrad.[27]

At Stalingrad, military operations absorbed more and more troop units. This probably resulted from the infinitely greater compartmentalization that limited not only vision but also the range of direct-fire weapons. As a result, more combatants were required to fill or watch those compartments. For the more important compartments, heavy or specialized weapons were required. Combat in urban areas also magnified the dimension of vertical warfare. The massive destruction of Stalingrad limited vertical combat considerably, although any remaining "high ground" remained critical for observation. Some soldiers described the conflict as "the war of rats" because so much of it concentrated on controlling holes and cellars. It was no accident that the German army sent specially trained engineer battalions to Stalingrad. Their job was to blow up buildings with explosives. Those rapidly advancing attacks limited the amount of vertical warfare. Paulus used this method to create "channels" throughout the city. But this required even more combatants to guard the long flanks of the channel and to reduce pockets of resistance that had survived the demolitions. All those additional troops required more ammunition.

The Soviets and the Germans expended an extraordinary amount of ammunition. Between 10 January and 2 February 1943, the Don Front fired some 24 million rifle and machine gun rounds; 911,000 artillery shells, up to 152-millimeter; and 990,000 mortar shells.[28] In September 1942, the 6th Army expended 23,035,863 rifle and machine gun rounds, 575,828 antitank shells, 116,932 infantry cannon shells, and 752,747 mortar shells. It deployed 14,932 mines and its soldiers expended 178,066 hand grenades.[29] Partisans writing for one side or the other use such figures to assert that the enemy was cowardly or incompetent for such profligate expenditures.[30] Despite the strain on these mass armies and the lack of training in many units, such high monthly ammunition expenditures for both sides would suggest that other factors were involved.

Those larger numbers of troops fighting on urban terrain and firing greater amounts of munitions produced very high casualties. There remains a lack of clarity regarding Soviet losses, but General Chuikov observed that the divisions had already been considerably weakened before they reached Stalingrad. He noted that by 14 September one armored brigade had only one tank left, and two other brigades without any tanks had to be sent across the Volga to refit. One division had two infantry brigades that were full, but the composite regiment of another division only fielded 100 infantrymen. Chuikov stated that another division had a total of 1,500 men—"the motorized infantry brigade had 666 men, including no more than 200 infantrymen; the Guards Division of Colonel Dubyanski on the left flank had no more than 250 infantrymen."[31]

Later, Chuikov went on to explain the effect of the high casualties on his units: "It means that our soldiers (even small units) crawled out from under German tanks, more often than not wounded, to another position, where they were received, incorporated into another unit, provided with equipment, usually ammunition, and then they went back into battle."[32] Early in the battle some 10,000 men of the 13th Guards Rifle Division crossed the Volga but without their heavy weapons. Chuikov threw them into a counterattack against the brick mill and the main train station. The division lost 30 percent of its men in the first 24 hours. By the time the battle ended, only 320 of the original soldiers were left.[33]

Records of the 6th Army did survive and indicate that the intensity of combat was high, both before reaching Stalingrad and later during the city fighting. It crossed the Don River on 21 August 1942. From then until 16 October, it recorded the following losses:

	Officers	NCOs and Men
Killed	239	7,456
Wounded	821	30,360
Missing	8	1,127

During this period, 6th Army recorded capturing 57,800 prisoners of war (POWs) and capturing or destroying 1,950 tanks, 805 guns, and 1,969 aircraft. From 13 September to 16 October 1942, during which much of the city fighting took place, it suffered the following losses:

	Officers	NCOs and Men
Killed	69	2,438
Wounded	271	10,107
Missing	3	298

Paulus's army not only fought in the city but also held a defensive front north of the city. On this northern front, the 6th Army captured 5,625 POWs and captured or destroyed 616 tanks and 87 guns. In the city itself, Paulus's army captured 17,917 POWs while capturing or destroying 233 tanks and 302 guns.[34]

The 71st Infantry and 24th Panzer Divisions

As a rule, Red Army infantry divisions during the war had about 10,000 men, most of whom carried rifles. The dynamics of city fighting wore these units down even further, according to General Chuikov. What city fighting did to the German 71st Infantry Division on 19 September 1942 is shown in Table 1. As can be seen, the regimental support troops suffered proportionately fewer losses than the combat infantry.[35] Table 2 shows 24th Panzer Division casualties after it had been withdrawn from the fighting in Stalingrad.[36]

These statistics should be used with care because they also cover July and August, before Stalingrad. Because the 24th was one of the few panzer divisions in the city, the numbers could represent a statistical aberration. Nevertheless, since it probably was the only division whose records survived, it requires some examination. Since artillery fire was the most destructive agent in both world wars, the figure of roughly 50-percent casualties from artillery is probably typical for conventional urban operations in high-intensity combat. Probably, 11-percent casualties from infantry weapons is too low to be typical. The question remaining is what would have been typical? Just as surprising is the 38-percent loss to enemy air activity. Although this seems very high, the two regiments of armored infantry, one battalion of motorcycle troops, and the antitank battalion all averaged between 9.4-percent and 12-percent casualties from air attacks.

There is also consistency in the losses of the armor regiment and mechanized artillery regiment. It would appear, however, that these losses were incurred during the Battle of Stalingrad rather than before. On 28 September, General Paulus visited the 24th Panzer Division at

Table 1.

191st Infantry Regiment		194th Infantry Regiment		211th Infantry Regiment	
1. Company	25 men	1. Company	12 men	1. Company	24 men
2. Company	17 men	2. Company	22 men	2. Company	*)
3. Company	20 men	3. Company	14 men	3. Company	*)
4. Company	32 men	4. Company	23 men	4. Company	28 men
Staff I. Battalion	7 men	Staff I. Battalion	20 men	Staff I. Battalion	*)
5. Company	10 men	5. Company	7 men	5. Company	27 men
6. Company	13 men	6. Company	13 men	6. Company	22 men
7. Company	12 men	7. Company	10 men	7. Company	*)
8. Company	40 men	8. Company	23 men	8. Company	43 men
Staff II. Bn	17 men	Staff II. Bn	6 men	Btl Staff II.	31 men
9. Company	7 men	9. Company	8 men	9. Company	*)
10. Company	13 men	10. Company	9 men	10. Company	44 men
11. Company	19 men	11. Company	13 men	11. Company	*)
12. Company	35 men	12. Company	27 men	12. Company	38 men
Staff III. Bn	7 men	Staff III. Bn	20 men	Staff III. Bn	17 men
13. Company	53 men	13. Comp.	50 men	13. Company	61 men
14. Company	50 men	14. Comp.	40 men	14. Company	57 men
Regt Staff		Regt Staff		Regt Staff	
Recon Platoon		Recon Platoon		Recon Platoon	
Signal Platoon		Signal Platoon		Signal Platoon	
Eng Platoon	72 men	Eng Platoon	94 men	Eng Platoon	80 men

Bn   battalion
Eng   engineer
Regt   regiment
Recon   reconnaissance

1315, and the operations officer briefed him on the division's considerable losses in armored infantry and tanks. These debilitating losses had occurred in the last several days.[37] If these losses are not a statistical aberration, this should serve as a warning for even a temporary loss of air superiority. These losses also suggest the inadequacy of the *Luftwaffe* and the German air defense.

Despite the presence of the 9th *Luftwaffe* Antiaircraft Division, Russian air strikes inflicted considerable damage in the German rear areas. On the same day that Paulus visited the 24th Panzer Division, the 6th Army observed that destroying artillery ammunition depots by day and night raids had become unacceptable. It attributed these losses

Table 2.

Troop Units	Infantry Weapons	Artillery/Mines	Burns	Aircraft Attacks
24th Panzer Div Staff	6.3	73.8	3.0	19.9
24th Panzer Regt	10.5	63.1	3.0	23.4
24th Arm Inf Bde		31.1		65.9
21st Arm Inf Regt	27.2	63.1	0.3	9.4
26th Arm Inf Regt	30.4	57.2	0.8	11.6
4th Motorcycle Bn	25.5	64.1	0.7	9.7
89th Arm Arty Regt	4.4	70.5		25.1
IV Bn " "	16.7	42.9		40.4
86th Arm Signal Bn	1.2	65.3		33.5
40th Antitank Bn	10.1	77.9		12.0
40th Arm Eng Bn	19.3	42.1	0.4	38.2
40th Supply Bn	14.4	21.8		63.8
Med Company (mot) 1/	12.5	35.7		51.8
Med Company (mot) 2/		58.3		41.7
40th Bakery Company				100.0
40th Butcher Company				100.0
Attached Units	13.1	77.5	0.9	8.5
Distribution of Casualties	11.3	49.8	0.4	38.5

Arm   armored
Arty   artillery
Bn   battalion
Div   division
Inf   infantry
Eng   engineer
Med   medical
Regt   regiment

to dispersing the antiaircraft artillery. It consequently ordered two battalions to return from the Don River bridgeheads.[38]

Just as the 24th Panzer Division's records provide a unique perspective of casualties at Stalingrad, its after-action report constitutes one of the few documents that recounts actual combat experience in the city. Documents are not immune from error, and those who create such reports frequently have their own agendas; nevertheless, the division after-action report provides a rare glimpse into both the strengths and weaknesses of a division fighting in Stalingrad. Consequently, what follows is a summary of that report. The division's after-action report concluded that panzer divisions were created to use their tanks decisively, en masse in open land, not for combat in cities. City fighting threw away armor's advantages of maneuver and mass. Furthermore, tanks were not designed for urban combat, and the rubble frequently limited the effectiveness of their main guns and hull machine guns. Those tanks remained vulnerable to Soviet tank and antitank weapons, so they could not be deployed singly but in groups of ten.[39]

Similarly, the armored infantry had never fought in a large city and had to rethink many of its methods. All German infantry loved the *Sturmgeschutz* because they could take cover behind the heavily armored vehicle as it advanced and fired. It was a serious mistake, however, for the infantry to use tanks in the same manner as the *Sturmgeschutz* because the Mark III and IV tanks were too vulnerable to enemy fire. Instead, the report urged that the armored infantry advance with several tanks behind them, providing fire support.

Although tanks and armored infantry had been working together in combat since 1939, they hardly ever had seen each other on the battlefield. Putting tanks and armored infantry in a small compartment consequently required a different, more intimate level of cooperation. The combined arms team in the compartment required a small number of tanks, armored infantry, and engineers. Rubble, narrow streets, and bomb craters restricted the number of tanks that could operate effectively in such a compartment. The document urged all participating commanders to examine the terrain beforehand, noting obstacles, cover, and the enemy situation. An attack plan had to come from this orientation, reaching an understanding of who would do what. It maintained that the only way to obtain true cooperation was by representing all the participating units. The tank commander had to enter the fight knowing how limited his vision would be and how dependent the tanks would be on the other branches.[40]

Mines were the greatest danger for tanks. The German after-action report recommended that when a tank hit a mine, all tanks in the compartment halt and engineers move forward to clear paths. Infantry had to deploy forward to thwart Russian infantry and to protect recovery teams, for it was critical to retrieve damaged vehicles as soon as possible. It was also necessary to withdraw the tanks before sunset for logistics support because the support vehicles were not armored. A panzer division possessed less infantry and artillery than an infantry division, which made it more difficult to replace infantry losses and punish the enemy with artillery fire.

A large number of knocked-out tanks were strewn about Stalingrad in pods, indicating paths that were once traversable. In late September, the VIII Corps counted sixty-two T-34 hulks in its sector, all manufactured in 1942. The XIV Panzer Corps counted forty-eight hulks of various types but could not approach most of them because of enemy fire. The Russians had retrieved several knocked-out tanks but also found it too dangerous to enter no man's land. Russian POWs stated that most of the tanks had been manufactured at Stalingrad's tractor factory.[41] The XIV Panzer Corps reported that on 30 September it had destroyed 24 Russian and 100 non-Russian tanks. The latter consisted of eight American M3 Lee tanks, forty-seven American M3 Stuarts, and twenty-four British Valentines. They were particularly interested in them, noting that they had not been assembled in Russia and contained instructional materials in English. The Russian tanks consisted of two T-34s, three T-60s, and nineteen T-70s, which apparently came from Gorki.[42]

In the attack, commanders had to make thorough preparations, particularly in synchronizing fire support. It was better for all commanders to meet and, using an aerial photograph, quickly work out who would do what rather than relying on detailed written orders. Before the attack, it was counterproductive to withdraw to protect oneself from the artillery barrage and airstrikes. The Germans discovered that when they did that, the Russians moved forward onto vacated ground. To gain surprise, it was better to attack early in the morning without preparatory fires and then call in adjusted fire as required. In urban operations, it was preferable to halt and regroup upon attaining limited objectives because that was the best way to coordinate the various arms and weapon systems. Informing subordinates of what the daily objective was helped in this process. On occasion, it was necessary to task-organize an armored assault group consisting of tanks, half-tracks, and other units as required. Nevertheless, the purpose of this was still to maximize the infantry combat power and provide one unified command. One constant was the engineers' active participation. To exploit success, reserves had to be kept close by at the ready and yet placed under some cover.[43]

Severely restricted fields of fire and limited observation made defense in Stalingrad very difficult. It proved advisable to use a main line of resistance and to keep reserves at the ready. Heavy mortars used as batteries were very helpful, and the heavy and light infantry cannons were particularly valuable in the defense. Nightly harassment fire by artillery and heavy infantry weapons had to be coordinated in a division fire plan. These fires had the best results between dusk and about 2230 when the enemy carried out most of its logistics activities. It was important to continue to rapidly shift from the offense to the defense. This meant rapidly digging in, organizing a defense in depth, creating new reserves, deploying heavy weapons, planning defensive fires, and if possible, laying mines quickly and contacting units on the flanks.[44]

The 24th Panzer Division reported that it was happy with the coordination of operations with the *Luftwaffe*, which it viewed as vital to its success. *Stuka* dive-bombers were able to drop bombs 100 meters in front of their own lines. German soldiers reported, however, that they really needed to know when the last bomb had been dropped. The *Luftwaffe* liaison officer was in an armored vehicle close enough to see the strikes. German efforts in 1942 to link *Luftwaffe* formations with advancing armored units continued to fail. The situation was too fluid, and too often bombs struck German positions. To the 24th Panzer Division, it seemed much more efficient for the *Luftwaffe* to operate deep against the enemy's LOC. Finally, the ground troops wanted to be better informed of what targets the *Luftwaffe* was going after so they could deploy sufficient light and signals equipment to protect themselves.

It would appear at first glance that fighting in Stalingrad required revising the infantry squad into an assault squad. It required standard light machine guns and riflemen, and also needed sharpshooters, automatic weapons, various kinds of grenades, and explosive charges. Those squads required support from one or more *Sturmgeschutz*, several half-tracks armed with 2-cm antiaircraft or 3.7-cm antitank guns. An engineer squad also had to be available to remove mines and tank obstacles. In addition, the after-action report recommended that a flamethrower squad be available. The heavy infantry weapons required sufficient ammunition. Rifle grenades proved very helpful. To counter enemy snipers or marksmen, the trench mirror was indispensable. And finally, the assault squads required enough radios for efficient communication.[45]

Massive destruction severely restricted movement through the city. Avoiding streets reduced casualties. Since all resistance "nests" had to be reduced, it was preferable to organize the advance in depth. It was important not to become imprisoned by linear conceptions of combat because units had to maneuver backward, forward, or sideways to cover a flank. In Stalingrad, a good deal of effort was expended reducing resistance "nests" (mainly cellars). Particularly dangerous areas were street corners and flat open spaces. These areas without cover demanded smoke screens to facilitate crossing.[46]

A glimpse at the German 71st Infantry Division demonstrates the difficulties of such combat. On 24 September, it advanced against heavy resistance toward the theater and command post buildings.

Soldiers had to fight through the remains of each house. POWs said that traditional concepts such as squads and platoons had generally lost their meaning. The Russian soldiers were led by proven officers and commissars and were still receiving active assistance from civilians. Neither side took many prisoners. Russian casualties were high. The 71st divisional artillery engaged Russian craft on the Volga and managed to silence two enemy batteries, destroying a large ammunition depot on the east bank of the river.[47]

The 24th Panzer Division was satisfied with its artillery regiment but complained that it had limited supplies, particularly ammunition. In the attack, division artillery was not that helpful. To limit friendly fire casualties, only one gun was allowed to provide fire support for an assault squad. At the division, the major problem was the inability to observe. At Stalingrad, the key artillery units were observation battalions that were army troops usually at the disposal of a corps headquarters. They set up their specialized equipment at the few quality observation spots. For example, on 28 September as the LI Corps advanced against the Red October and Red Barricade factories, its observation battalions identified twenty-two enemy batteries and engaged fourteen with counterbattery fire.[48]

It was still possible to coordinate fires; however, the armored artillery regiment's armored observation vehicles proved ideal in supplementing the work of the observation battalions. It was simply too dangerous for the infantry divisions' observation sections to attempt to do this. Sometimes it was necessary to call in fire from the entire regiment. This was so effective that POWs commented on the barrages. In urban combat, the armored artillery reconnaissance assets only had radios. They were, however, in Stalingrad long enough to supplement their signals with wire. For instance, the light/flash unit had to be on the tallest surviving structure in the sector. Hence, it was much more efficient to run wire up to its "nest."

The Red Army experience in Stalingrad proved quite similar, with artillery observers perched in the few available aeries.[49] The panzer division did not have the means to be decisive in counterbattery fire. Its 10-cm cannon had insufficient range and never seemed to have enough ammunition. On occasion, one or two division guns were sent to assist the armored infantry with direct fire. This proved successful, but the guns were particularly difficult to move in the rubble.[50]

The division cooperated with the *Luftwaffe* through radio until its last week in the city when the regimental air support radio unit moved forward to join the tracked observation vehicles. This cooperation sped up prioritization and efficiency of air and fire support. It cut out one level of communication within the *Luftwaffe* and provided many more eyes with which to evaluate the air strikes' effectiveness. In addition, when a target was taken out, this method allowed aircraft to switch rapidly to new targets.

As has already been mentioned, the 24th Panzer Division maintained that it was wasteful to use an armored division in city fighting. Specifically, the tank regimental headquarters had little to do because the largest tank formation deployed was a battalion. The after-action report stipulated that only in rare situations should elements of an armored division be sent to assist another division. Infantry had to be specially trained to cooperate efficiently with tanks. Deploying tanks without infantry was only successful when the enemy was demoralized and lacked antitank weaponry. Local limited tank thrusts were rewarded with success. On the defense, tanks were to be kept as local reserves and used for counterattacks. The major threats were close-range antitank weapons and sharpshooters. The after-action report concluded that before being returned to 4th Panzer Army, the division lost an exceptionally large number of tanks. Many of those losses were unnecessary, the result of having to work with infantry units whose leaders had no idea of tanks' strengths and weaknesses.[51]

Engineers were vital to the combined arms team, but the division commander had serious decisions to make. The engineers maintained the LOC, but when they were also needed for combat engineer missions, the commander had to choose how to allocate them. The 24th Panzer Division recommended deployment by company or platoon. For urban combat they had to be fully equipped with light and heavy infantry weapons and antitank weapons. One of the major problems for German engineers at Stalingrad was their inability to detect rapidly and remove Russian wooden mines.

The Germans had several types of tracked antitank guns. They were very useful in Stalingrad where rubble and partially knocked-down walls provided them with cover up to their hulls. Deployed hull defilade behind infantry, they proved highly effective. Deploying them in the front line, however, made these open-top vehicles too vulnerable to enemy artillery, hand grenades, and sharpshooters. In the defense, they had to be kept even farther back because of enemy observers. Ammunition resupply was difficult for the vehicles. By 1942, it was clear that the version with the 5-cm gun was obsolete.[52]

Regarding individual weapons and systems, the 5-cm antitank vehicle gained notice not only for its insufficient firepower but also for its lack of maneuverability. In autumn 1942, German army divisions still did not have telescopic rifles. The 24th Panzer Division concluded that there were numerous instances when marksmen with telescopic sights could have suppressed resistance nests and prevented casualties. The 8-cm mortar proved effective, as did the 7.5-cm infantry cannon. The 15-cm infantry cannon, however, was too difficult to maneuver in the rubble and proved difficult to resupply.

The report concluded with several recommendations. It urged that the armored and armored artillery regiments receive 2-cm antiaircraft guns. The armored infantry needed a company of tracked heavy infantry cannons. Each panzer battalion required one or two platoons of fully motorized engineers. It also recommended further use of Russian volunteers in armored infantry units. Finally, armored personnel carriers were required to evacuate the wounded completely out of the combat area rather than just to the closest aid station.[53]

These immediate "fixes" indicate the lethality of Russian air operations, insufficient armored infantry firepower in taking out point targets, and insufficient combat infantry and engineers. Since this was one of the most powerful, best-equipped German divisions, one wonders about both the German and Russian infantry units that had much less maneuverability and striking power. This helps explain the phenomenally high casualties of the 13th Guard Rifle Division that was deployed to Stalingrad without its heavy weapons.

Following the visit of a general staff officer to southern Russia on 28 August, the German General Staff's senior medical officer warned Army Group B's doctors that in the hot summer months the soldiers should have an improved diet. What was required was a lower fat diet. Soldiers complained of bread that arrived with mold. Sixth Army could do little to alleviate these problems. The plague of flies lasted until the first freeze. The main problem was that Stalingrad was simply too distant to logistically support. After the 6th Army was encircled, its combat troops were supposed to receive a diet of 200 grams of bread per day. Staff and rear area personnel were to receive only 100 grams.[54]

When 6th Army soldiers rapidly began to die in December without detectable symptoms, Berlin flew a pathologist into the pocket. He found that 6th Army soldiers had the medical problems of old men: changes in bone marrow and internal organs and loss of fatty tissue. The actual cause of death was shrinking of the heart. The right ventricle, however, was enlarged. The pathologist concluded that this resulted from exhaustion, exposure, and undernourishment. Ziemke and Bauer suggest that this phenomenon was probably related to the unique circumstances of being encircled by enemy forces.⁵⁵ It remains possible that not all this damage resulted from the period after the encirclement. The cumulative stress and malnutrition of the previous months' combat may have contributed to this condition.

There is one additional factor that must be mentioned, although it is rather nebulous and remains nearly impossible to quantify. Nevertheless, perhaps Stalingrad's most important revelation was how city fighting impinged on the strategic level of warfare. Regardless of the lack of wisdom behind advancing into southern Russia in 1942, Stalingrad played only a peripheral role in that offensive. Throughout the course of the campaign, however, possession of the city dominated Hitler's thinking. On four occasions, General Paulus reported that city fighting was eroding his army's combat power, but the city had already become a matter of prestige. Hitler made one of his rare public appearances on 30 September at the *Sportpalast* in Berlin. He displayed irritation at the world press's fixation with the Dieppe Raid while ignoring his advance to the Caucasus and Volga. He stated twice that Stalingrad would fall and concluded, "You can be certain no one will get us away from there."⁵⁶ Several days later at one of his military briefings he confessed that Stalingrad was no longer of decisive operational importance but, rather, vital for public opinion around the world and to bolster the morale of Germany's allies. Somehow, a city of relatively minor significance had become a crucial factor in national decision making. Whether this was an isolated miscalculation of a dictator without formal military training or a general tendency in the course of Western warfare gives pause for serious reflection.⁵⁷

We shall never know with certainty the losses caused by the Stalingrad campaign. Approximately 250,000 Axis troops were lost, along with 1,000 tanks and 1,800 guns. Most of the Axis troops were German, but there were 50,000 Austrians killed along with smaller numbers of Romanians, Croatians, and Italians. We also know that there were approximately 50,000 Russian volunteers (*Hilfswillige*) with the German 6th Army, none of whom probably survived the struggle. Of the Axis losses, 150,000 were killed or wounded by January 1943. No one knows the Russian losses, which are estimated at being from four to eight times those of the Axis, and no one knows how many of those losses were civilians.⁵⁸

Notes

The author would like to thank the following, who greatly helped with their time, knowledge, and consideration: Colonel L.C. Edwards, S.B. Gray, Dr. Tim Mulligan, N.E. Sopolsky, and Dr. R.J. Spiller.

1. Roger J. Spiller, *Sharp Corners: Urban Operations at Century's End* (Fort Leavenworth, KS: Combat Studies Institute, 2001), 50-55; Walther Warlimont, *Inside Hitler's Headquarters, 1939 45*, trans. by R.H. Barry (NY: Frederick Praeger, 1966), 267-86; and Timothy W. Ryback, "Stalingrad: Letters From the Dead," *New Yorker* (1 February 1993), 58-71.

2. Spiller, 50-55; Ryback, 58-71; Records of the German Foreign Ministry, file "Russland (Abwehr) Vertreter des Auswaertigen Amts beim Oberbefehlshaber des Heeres," Der Vertreter des Auswaertigen Amts bei einem AOK, Nr. 657g. A.H.Qu. den 10. Oktober 1942, Stalingrad, signed V. Schubert (hereafter V. Schubert, Stalingrad).

3. John Erickson, *The Road to Stalingrad: Stalin's War With Germany*, Vol. I (NY: Harper & Row, 1975), 298-342; *Hitler's War Directives 1939 1945*, H.R. Trevor-Roper, ed. (London: Sidgwick and Jackson, 1965), 116-21; Hans Doerr, *Der Feldzug nach Stalingrad* (Darmstadt, GE: E.S. Mittler & Sohn, GmbH, 1955), 120-24; and Earl F. Ziemke and Magda E. Bauer, *Moscow to Stalingrad: Decision in the East* (Washington, DC: Center of Military History, 1987), 287-324.

4. Erickson, 343-93; *Hitler's War Directives*, Directive No. 45, 23 July 1942, 129-31; Manfred Kehrig, *Stalingrad Analyse und Dokumentation einer Schlacht* (Stuttgart, GE: Deutsche Verlags-Anstalt, 1974), 69-86; and Rolf-Dieter Mueller, "Das Scheitern der wirtschaftliche 'Blitzkriegtrategie,'" in *Das Deutsche Reich und der Zweite Weltkrieg*, Vol. IV, edited by the *Militaergeschichtlichen Forschungsamt* (Stuttgart, GE: Deutsche Verlags-Anstalt, 1983), 936-71. See also H. Dv. g. 90, *Versorgung des Feldheeres, OKH/GenStdH/Gen.Qu.*, 1938, and H. Dv. g. 11a/2 *Erfahrungen aus dem Ostfeldzug fuer Versorgungsfuehrung 1943, OKH/GenStdH/GenQu* 2 Nr. I/17591/42.

5. See previous note. See also Pz AOK 4 file 28183/17 *Chef Notizen zum KTB Nr. 5* (Teil III), entry for 8 September 1942.

6. KTB/OKH/GenStdH/Organisations Abt., 1 August-31 December 1942, Microcopy T-78/roll 417/frames 6386529-531; Spiller, 50-55; Doerr, 30-52; and Ziemke, *Stalingrad to Berlin: The German Defeat in the East* (NY: Fromm Int'l, January 1986), 17-19.

7. *AOK 6 Ia Az.Nr.* 3044/42 g.K. A.H.Qu. den 19. August 1942, *Armeebefehl fuer den Angriff auf Stalingrad*, reprinted in Doerr, 127-29; see also 40-45; and *Battle for Stalingrad The 1943 Soviet General Staff Study*,

Louis Rotundo, ed. (Washington, DC: Pergamon-Brassey's International Defense Publishers, Inc., 1989), 26-30, 41-68. The pertinent German Army manual for city or trench warfare was *Geheim Merkblatt, Angriff gegen eine staendige Front (StoBtrupps)*.

8. Spiller, 50-55; Anthony Beevor, *Stalingrad* (NY: Viking Press, 1998), 119; and Ziemke, 37-42.

9. Vasili I. Chuikov, *The Battle of Stalingrad*, trans. by Harold Silver (NY: Ballantine Books, 1964), 50-72; *Battle for Stalingrad: The 1943 Soviet General Staff Study*, 229-57; Klaus Maier, "*Total Krieg und Operativer Luftkrieg*," in *Das Deutsche Reich und der Zweite Weltkrieg*, Vol. 2, edited by *Militaergeschichtliches Forschungsamt* (Stuttgart, GE: Deutsche Verlags-Anstalt, 1979, 43-69; Kenneth R. Whiting, "Soviet Air Power in World War II," *Air Power and Warfare*, Proceedings of the 8th Military History Symposium, U.S. Air Force Academy, 18-20 October 1978, Alfred F. Hurley and Robert C. Ehrhart, eds. (Washington, DC: Office of Air Force History, 1977), 98-127; Cajus Bekker, *The Luftwaffe War Diaries*, trans. by F. Ziegler (London: Macdonald, 1964); and Spiller, 50-55.

10. V. Schubert, Stalingrad; V. Schubert's Nr. 667, Inf 2081 Mg. *A.H.Qu., dem 26. Oktober, Inh.: Stimmung der Bevoelkerung; Der Vertreter des Auswaertigen Amts bei einem Panzer AOK*. Nr. 126, OU *den 13. Oktober 1942, Geheim, Betr.: Fahrt nach Stalingrad*, signed Muehlen; *AOK 6, Fuehrungsabteilung KTB Bericht ueber eine Fahrt nach Stalingrad*, Menzel, Major *i.G. V.O./OKH b. AOK 6* of 25.9.42; and Spiller, 50-60.

11. Ziemke, 37-41.

12. The NKVD eventually relented and allowed some women and children across the Volga. See Chuikov, 50-168; Beevor, 92-144; and Ziemke, 37-43.

13. Doerr, 55-61, and Ziemke, 41-42.

14. Erickson, 343-93, and Ziemke, 23-36.

15. One of his senior advisers attempted to defend List, which precipitated one of Hitler's most violent outbursts against the officer corps. The dictator announced that he would no longer eat his meals with the officers and directed that stenographers be brought in from Berlin to take down all conversations. Warlimont, 241-60, and Beevor, 123. Warlimont maintained that Halder's departure was precipitated by the latter's argument with Hitler on 24 August. See also Kurt Zeitzer, "Stalingrad," *The Fatal Decisions: Six Decisive Battles of the Second World War From the Viewpoint of the Vanquished*, William Richardon and Seymour Freidin, eds., trans. by Constantine Fitzgibbon, (London: Michael Joseph, 1956), 115-65. The new chief of the General Staff somehow forgot to mention his opening speech but did note that the atmosphere was clouded by mistrust and suspicion.

16. Chuikov, 86-116; Beevor, 129-45.

17. On 18 September, the 6th Army reported there were severe shortages of 10-cm cannon, 8-cm mortar, 5-cm, and 7.5-cm (antitank) shells. AOK 6 *Abt Ia, Tagesmeldung, A.H.Qu. den 18.9.42* in folder AOK 6 *Fuehrungsabteilung Anlagenband zum KTB Nr. 13, Russland*. General Chuikov claims that he ordered his troops to maintain such close physical proximity, which is probably true. Where the idea originated remains open to question, Chuikov, 80.

18. Records of the German 6th Army, *V.O./OKH.b. AOK 6, A.J.Wue., 25.9.42, Bericht ueber eine Fahrt nach Stalingrad*, signed Menzel.

19. Chuikov, 116-94; Ziemke, 44-46; and Ziemke and Bauer, 382-470.

20. Ziemke, 48-49. *Fremde Heere Ost* was the German Army intelligence organization that monitored the Soviet Union.

21. Ibid.

22. Ibid., 50-52.

23. Whiting; Maier; and Bekker, 278-94.

24. Ziemke, 52-55.

25. Warlimont, 285; and Ziemke, 55-65.

26. *Stalingrad Memories and Reassessments*, Joachim Wieder and Heinrich Graf von Einsiedel, eds., trans. by Helmut Bogler (London: Arms & Armour Press, 1998), 67.

27. Records of the German Foreign Office, *Der Vertreter des Auswaertigen Amts beim Pz. AOK 4* (number four crossed out), A.H.Qu., den 6. Oktober 1942, *Betr.: Stimmung der russischen Truppe unter der psychologischen Wirkung des Stalin Befehls*, in folder *Russland (Abwehr)*.

28. Ziemke, 79-80.

29. *KTB A.O.K. 6 Ia, 17. Oktober 1942*, file 30155/33, reproduced on microcopy T-312, roll 1458, frames 961-63.

30. See, for example, Chuikov, 39-41 and 80-93; and Beevor, 127-29, 141-57.

31. Chuikov, 92-93, and *Soviet Casualties and Combat Losses in the Twentieth Century*, Colonel General G.F. Krivosheev, ed. (London: Greenhill Books, 1997), 123-25.

32. Chuikov, 107.

33. Ibid., 131-36; and Zhukov, 373.

34. *KTB A.O.K. 6 Ia, 17. Oktober 1942*, file 30155/33, reproduced on microcopy T-312, roll 1458, frames 961-63.

35. *V.O./OKH b. AOK 6, Bericht ueber eine Fahrt nach Stalingrad, A.H. Wu. 25.9.42* signed Menzel. Excluded from these totals are support troops, lightly wounded soldiers, and soldiers on leave or on detail.

36. Records of the 24th Panzer Division, *Anlage 5 z. 24.Pz. Div. Ia/Op. Nr. 365/42 geh.* of 10.11.42, *Taetigkeitsbericht der Sanitaets Dienst vom 28.6. bis 31.10.1942*.

37. *AOK 6 KTB, Frontfahrt des Oberbefehlshabers am 28.9.1942* in folder *Ia/Ic Anlagenband z KTB 13, Russland*.

38. Ibid.

39. Records of the 24th Panzer Division, *Anlage 2 zu 24. Pz. Div.Ia Nr. 347/42 geh. V.5.11.1942, Richtlinien fuer Zusammenarbeit zwischen Panzer und Grenadieren*.

40. *Richtlinien fuer Zusammenarbeit zwischen Panzer und Grenadieren*.

41. *AOK 6 KTB, V.O./OKH bei AOK 6, A.H.Qu. den 27.9.42 an OKH/Op.Abt. Bezug: Fernspruch vom 19.9.betr. abgeschossene, fabrikneue Feindpanzer* in folder *Ia/Ia Anlagenband z KTB Nr.13, Russland*.

42. *AOK 6 KTB, XIV. Pz.K. 1.10.42 Oblt. Schaefer Hansen, 22.45(Uhr)* in folder *Ia/Ic Anlagenband z KTB Nr. 13, Russland*; and *Richtlinien fuer Zusammenarbeit zwischen Panzer und Grenadieren*.

43. *Richtlinien fuer Zusammenarbeit zwischen Panzer und Grenadieren*.

44. Ibid.

45. Ibid.

46. Ibid.

47. *AOK 6 Ia Lagemeldung, 24.9.42* (LI Corps) in folder *Ia/Ic/AO Anlagenband z KTB Nr. 13, Russland*.

48. When Zhukov briefed Stalin on 12 September on the specific difficulties of fighting in Stalingrad, he mentioned that the Germans held several key elevations. This allowed them to mass and shift artillery fire. See Zhukov, 380-82. *AOK 6 Ia Zwischenmeldung Datum 28.9.42, LI.A.K. meldet 16.45 Uhr* in folder *Ia/Ic Anlagenband z. KTB Nr. 13, Russland*.

49. See Beevor, 148-49.

50. See also *AOK 6 Abt Ia, Tagesmeldung A.H.Qu. den 18.9.42 and AOK 6 Ia Zwischenmeldung, A.H.Qu den 20.9.42* both in folder *Ia/Ic Anlagenband z KTB Nr. 13, Russland. Richtlinien fuer Zusammenarbeit zwischen Panzer und Grenadieren*.

51. Ibid. On 4 October, the 24th Panzer Division was able to deploy thirty-eight tanks: two command tanks, nine short-barreled Mark IIIs, seventeen long-barreled Mark IIIs, and five short-barreled and five long-barreled Mark IV tanks. See *AOK 6 Ia Morgenmeldung Datum 4.10.42, 4.50 Uhr* in folder *Ia/Ic Anlagenband z KTB Nr. 13, Russland*.

52. *Richtlinien fuer Zusammenarbeit zwischen Panzer und Grenadieren*.

53. Ibid.

54. AOK 6 KTB, *Der Heeresintendant im OKH GenSt.dH./GenQu. Az 809 z(I.3) Nr. I/35/800/42 H.Qu.OKH den 23.8.1942 An Armeeintendant* 6 in folder *Ia/Ic/AO Anlagenband z KTB Nr. 13, Russland*; and *Stalingrad Memories and Reassessments*, 51.

55. Ziemke, 69.

56. Ian Kershaw, *Hitler: 1936 1945 Nemesis* (NY: W.W. Norton & Co., November 2000), 534-57;"*Der Fuehrer sprach zum deutschen Volk," Ost Front*, 1 October 1942, *Folge 413 (Ausgabe A)* in *AOK 6 KTB*, folder *Ia/Ic Anlagenband z KTB 13, Russland*; and Ziemke, 44.

57. *Stalingrad Memories and Reassessments*, 22; and *Hitler's Lagebesprechungen*, Helmut Heiber, ed. (Stuttgart, GE: Deutsche Verlag-Anstalt 1962).

58. The Red Army captured some 91,000 Axis troops at Stalingrad. Of that total, fewer than 6,000 ever returned home. *Soviet Casualties and Combat Losses*, 124; Beevor, 439-40; and Ryback.

Bibliography

Unpublished Sources

Documents

Records of the German General Staff

Records of the German Foreign Office

Records of the German Army

Armies

Divisions

Published Sources

Books

Bekker, Cajus. *The Luftwaffe War Diaries*. Trans. by F. Ziegler. London: Macdonald, 1964.

Beevor, Anthony. *Stalingrad*. NY: Viking Press, 1998. A popular account by a journalist.

Chuikov, Vasili I. *The Battle of Stalingrad*. Trans. by Harold Silver. NY: Ballantine Books, 1964. The invaluable memoirs of the Red Army commander in Stalingrad.

Doerr, Hans. *Der Feldzug nach Stalingrad*. Darmstadt: E.S. Mittler & Sohn, 1955. An account of the German advance to Stalingrad by a General Staff officer in southern Russia. Based on interviews and document collections.

Erickson, John. *The Road to Stalingrad: Stalin's War Against Germany*. Vol. I. NY: Harper & Row, 1975. An indispensable source.

_____. *The Soviet High Command 1918 1941*. London: Macmillan, 1962. An invaluable book on the subject.

Funke, Manfred. Editor. *Hitler, Deutschland und die Maechte*. Duesseldorf: Droste Verlag, 1977.

Kehrig, Manfred. *Stalingrad Analyse und Dokumentation einer Schlacht*. Stuttgart: Deutsche Verlags-Anstalt, 1974.

Kershaw, Ian. *Hitler: 1936 1945 Nemesis*. NY: W.W. Norton & Company, 2000. An intriguing chronicle of Hitler's daily activity.

Krivosheev, G.F. editor. *Soviet Casualties and Combat Losses in the Twentieth Century*. (London: Greenhill Books, 1997).

Lewis, S.J. *Forgotten Legions: German Army Infantry Policy, 1918-1941*. NY: Praeger, 1985.

Militaergeschichtliches Forschungsamt. Editors. *Das Deutsche Reich und der Zweite Weltkrieg*. 4 Vols. Stuttgart: Deutsche Verlags-Anstalt, 1983.

Mueller-Hillebrand, Burkhardt. *Das Heer, 1933 1945*. Three volumes. Frankfurt am Main: E.S. Mittler & Sohn, 1969. The foremost study on German army organization, based on document collections and written by the former head of the German General Staff organization branch.

Paret, Peter. Editor. *Makers of Modern Strategy*. Princeton, New Jersey, 1986.

Richardson, William and Seymour Freidin. Editors. *The Fatal Decisions: Six Decisive Battles of the Second World War From the Viewpoint of the Vanquished*. Trans. by Constantine Fitzgibbon. London: Michael Joseph, 1956.

Rotundo, Louis. Editor. *Battle for Stalingrad: The 1943 Soviet General Staff Study*. Washington, DC: Pergamon-Brassey's International Defense Publishers, 1989.

Schmundt, Rudolf. *Taetigkeitsbericht des Chef des Heerespersonalamts General der Infanterie Rudolf Schmundt 1.10.1942 29.10.1944*. Edited by Dermot Bradley and Richard Schulze-Kossens. Osnabrueck: Biblio Verlag, 1994.

Spiller, Roger. *Sharp Corners: Urban Operations at Century's End*. Fort Leavenworth, Kansas: Combat Studies Institute, 2001.

Trevor-Roper, H.R. Editor. *Hitler's War Directives, 1939 1945*. London: Sidgwick and Jackson, 1965.

Voronov, N.N. *Na sluzhbe voennoi*. Moscow: Voevizdat, 1963. A troubled manuscript by yet another Stavka representative to the Stalingrad area. Voronov was an artillery officer.

Warlimont, Walther. *Inside Hitler's Headquarters, 1939 45*. Trans. by R.H. Barry. NY: Frederick A. Praeger, 1966.

Wieder, Joachim and Heinrich Graf von. Einsiedel. *Stalingrad: Memories and Reassessments*. Trans. by Helmut Bogler. London: Arms & Armour Press, 1998. An interesting but overwrought memoir.

Ziemke, Earl F. and Magda E. Bauer. *Moscow to Stalingrad, Decision in the East*. Washington DC: Center of Military History, 1987.

———, *Stalingrad to Berlin: The German Defeat in the East.* Washington DC: Center of Military History, 1987.

Zhukov, Georgii K. *The Memoirs of Marshal Zhukov.* NY: A Seymour Lawrence Book Delacorte Press, 1973. The most authoritative memoir from the Soviet side. It provides a unique glimpse into senior decision making, although Zhukov was not in command at Stalingrad.

Articles

Brosat, Martin. "Deutschland-Ungarn-Rumaenien." *Hitler, Deutschland und die Maechte.* Edited by Manfred Funke. Duesseldorf: Droste Verlag, 1977.

Hillgruber, Andreas. "*Der Einbau der verbuendeten Armeen in die deutsche Ostfront 1941 1944.*" *Wehrwissenschaftliche Rundschau.* Vol. X. 1960.

Isserson, G. "*Razvitiye teorii sovetskogo operativnogo iskusstva v 30 ye gody.*" *Voyenno istoricheskiy zhurnal.* January 1965.

Maier, Klaus. "*Totaler Krieg und Operativer Luftkrieg.*" *Das Deutsche Reich und der Zweite Weltkrieg.* Edited by *Militaergeschichtliches Forschungsamt.* Stuttgart: Deutsche Verlags Anstalt, 1979.

Mueller, Rolf-Dieter. "*Das Scheitern des wirtschaftliche 'Blitzkriegstrategie,*'" in *Das Deutsche Reich und der Zweite Weltkrieg,* edited by the *Militaergeschichtliches Forschungsamt.* Stuttgart: Deutsche Verlags-Anstalt, 1983.

Rice, Condoleezza. "The Making of Soviet Stategy." *Makers of Modern Strategy.* Edited by Peter Paret. Princeton, NJ: Princeton University Press. 1986.

Ryback, Timothy W. "Stalingrad: Letters From the Dead." *New Yorker.* (1 February 1993).

Whiting, Kenneth R. "Soviet Air Power in World War II." *Air Power and Warfare Proceedings of the 8th Military History Symposium, USAF Academy 18 20 October* 1978. Edited by Alfred F. Hurley and Robert C. Ehrhart. Washington DC: Office of Air Force History, 1977.

Zeitzler, Kurt. "Stalingrad," in *The Fatal Decisions: Six Decisive Battles of the Second World War From the Viewpoint of the Vanquished.* Edited by William Richardson and Seymour Freidin. Trans. by Constantine Fitzgibbon. London: Michael Joseph, 1956.

"Knock 'em All Down": The Reduction of Aachen, October 1944

Christopher R. Gabel

The city of Aachen is located in western Germany, just a few miles from the borders of Belgium and the Netherlands. It lies astride one of the two historic axes of advance between France and Germany. In World War II, it was the first major German city to come under direct attack by Allied ground forces. Aachen was not, however, a significant factor in Allied plans for the defeat of Nazi Germany. It was only by chance that American ground troops found themselves involved in urban operations in this ancient city.

The campaign that led to the assault on Aachen began on 6 June 1944 with Operation OVERLORD, the Allied invasion of Normandy. The mission of the multinational force under General Dwight D. Eisenhower's command was to "undertake operations aimed at the heart of Germany and the destruction of her armed forces."[1]

Initial progress toward this goal was slow, owing to frantic German efforts to contain, if not eliminate, the Allied foothold in France. After a prolonged battle of attrition in Normandy, on 25 July the Allies launched Operation COBRA, a deliberate assault designed to break out of the lodgment area. The Germans, who committed everything to a cordon defense, lacked the means of preventing the breakout from becoming a pursuit. During the month of August, the forces under Eisenhower's command liberated most of northwestern France, Belgium, and Luxembourg. Eisenhower's plan for this phase of the campaign envisaged a twin thrust, with the British 21st Army Group on the left, and the American 12th Army Group on the right. The American army group, commanded by Lieutenant General Omar Bradley, planned to cross from France into Germany by way of the "Metz Corridor," in the province of Lorraine. The British army group, under Field Marshal Bernard L. Montgomery, constituted the main effort. Plans drawn up before the invasion called for this force to advance from Liege to Cologne by way of the "Aachen Corridor." It would then cross the Rhine River and assault the vital Ruhr industrial region, the capture of which would effectively destroy Germany's ability to continue the war. The Aachen axis not only constituted the most direct route between Normandy and the Ruhr, but also carried the benefits of proximity to air bases in England and to ports along the English

Channel. Had the Allies adhered to this plan, Aachen would have lain in the path of British, not American, troops.

The circumstances of war often play havoc with plans, and the Allied campaign against Germany was no exception. The rapidity of the Allied pursuit across France prevented the creation of a systematic logistics support base, thus making it essential that the Allies capture quickly the channel ports along the coast of France and Belgium. Another unforeseen demand was the urgent requirement to capture bases along the same coast from which the Germans were launching unmanned flying bombs, known to the Allies as the V-1, against England. Accordingly, once Allied forces crossed the Seine River, Eisenhower shifted 12th Army Group's zone of advance northward, along the channel coast. To maintain contact between the British and American forces, Eisenhower split the 12th Army Group so that the First U.S. Army passed north of the Ardennes, where it covered the right flank of the British. Third Army proceeded alone into Lorraine. This decision placed Aachen in the zone of Lieutenant General Courtney H. Hodges' First Army (see Map 1).

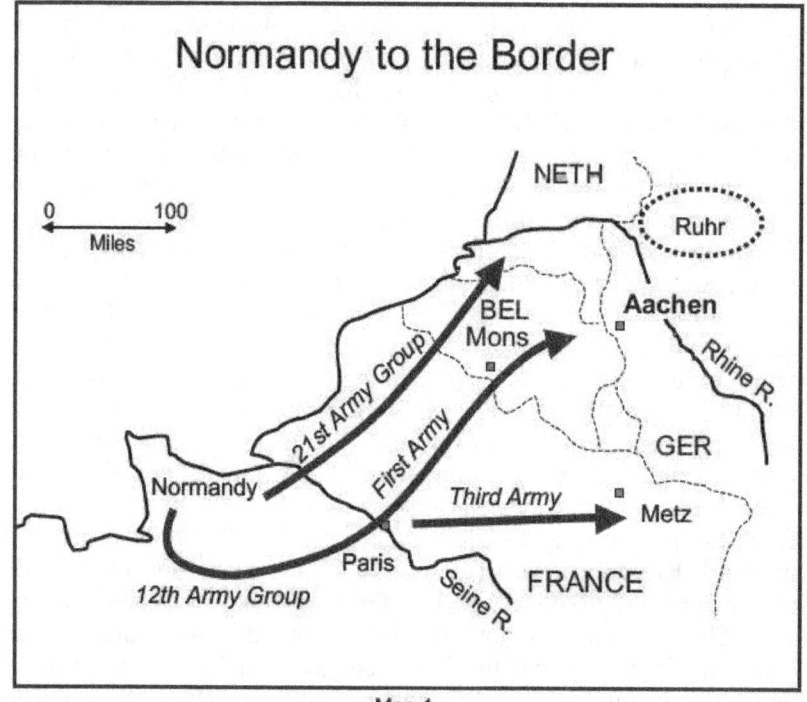

Map 1

One further development during the pursuit dictated which American elements would find themselves fighting in Aachen. First Army advanced northeastward from the Seine with three corps—XIX Corps on the left, V Corps in the center, and VII Corps on the right. The VII Corps, commanded by Major General J. Lawton Collins, was in advance of the two corps to its left. As the pursuit unfolded, a large body of German troops accumulated in front of XIX and V Corps. These troops were remnants of the German Seventh and Fifteenth Armies that were streaming toward Germany in disarray. On 1 September, Hodges ordered Collins to wheel his corps ninety degrees to the left in an attempt to trap the German elements being bulldozed along by his other corps. Accordingly, VII Corps drove north to the vicinity of Mons, Belgium, and on 3 September set up blocking positions to intercept the fleeing enemy. Over the course of the next several days, elements of twenty German divisions ran unaware into the trap. The "Mons Pocket" netted a total of approximately 25,000 German prisoners.[2] In executing its pivot to the north, VII Corps pinched out V Corps to its left, and thus became the center corps in First Army's line. When the eastward advance resumed, VII Corps found itself on the road to Aachen.

Collins' VII Corps crossed the border into Germany on 12 September. Aachen, which lay just ten miles away, was virtually undefended. However, the city was not even an objective at this time. Assuming that the German army was beaten and that the pursuit across France and Belgium would continue into Germany, First Army expected to drive past Aachen and proceed to the Rhine, forty miles beyond. Indeed, pursuit was about all that First Army was capable of at this juncture. It entered Germany 233 days ahead of the planned schedule for logistics support.[3] Equipment and supplies were nearing exhaustion. In VII Corps, the 3d Armored Division was down to one-third of its normal allotment of approximately 230 medium tanks.[4] Supplies for the Army had to be hauled by truck from Normandy, a procedure that had largely ceased to be cost effective. (The trucks hauling supplies for 12th Army Group consumed as much gasoline as either one of the two field armies.) Within First Army, XIX Corps ran out of gas on 9 September and fell behind in the advance to the border. On the day that VII Corps crossed into Germany, First Army had to rely upon captured rations to feed the troops. With priority placed upon the delivery of gasoline needed to continue the pursuit, First Army would find it necessary to ration ammunition until mid-October. The logistics crisis moderated somewhat on 18 September when rail service was advanced to Liege, Belgium, but it would be months before the supply situation was fully resolved.[5]

Moreover, First Army was badly overextended. It reached the German border on a front of eighty miles, of which the VII Corps front was twenty miles. Doctrine for that era prescribed a front of five to ten miles for a force the size of VII Corps.[6] First Army had no reserves. Such extended frontages had been advantageous during the pursuit, but the Allies were about to learn that the pursuit was over. The ever-dangerous German army was in the process of reconstituting after its defeat in France. Determined to defend their homeland, the Germans would enjoy the advantage of a fortified line, the *Westwall*, known to the Allies as the Siegfried Line.

The *Westwall* was a band of some 3,000 mutually supporting pillboxes, bunkers, and observation posts covering the entire western border of Germany.[7] Construction had begun on the *Westwall* in 1936, when German forces occupied the Rhineland in defiance of the Versailles Treaty that had ended World War I. The building effort commenced in earnest in 1938 during the "Munich Crisis." Since the German conquest of France in 1940, the wall had lain unoccupied and was in rather dilapidated condition. Still, the *Westwall* would prove to be a significant combat multiplier for the defenders.

The Germans never supposed that the *Westwall* could stop an invader cold. Its purpose was to slow down an attacker until mobile counterattack forces could arrive. In a sense, this is what Adolf Hitler intended in 1944. He ordered that the Allies be held at the *Westwall* until forces could be amassed for a major counteroffensive through the Ardennes. This counteroffensive, known to Americans as the Battle of the Bulge, eventually took place in December.

Aachen was, for all practical purposes, a part of the *Westwall*. The city nestled within two belts of bunkers and obstacles, one to the west of the city and the other to the east. The Aachen sector was, in fact, one of the most heavily fortified portions of the *Westwall*. Aachen itself, however, was unfortified. It had little to commend it as a battleground from either the German or the American perspective. As a defensive position, Aachen was flawed by the fact that it lay in a depression with higher ground on all sides. From the American point of view, Aachen offered little as an objective. The existing road net made it perfectly feasible to bypass the urban area altogether. Although Aachen was home to some industry and coal mining, it was not vital to the German war effort. Moreover, heavy Allied air raids had already damaged or destroyed half of its buildings. Its prewar population of 165,000 had dropped to fewer than 20,000 by September 1944. A mandatory evacuation of civilians, ordered by Hitler himself, removed most of the remainder. In light of what eventually occurred, it seems ironic that on the day VII Corps entered Germany, the Americans intended to bypass Aachen, and the German commander within Aachen intended, apparently, to yield the city without a fight.[8]

Adolf Hitler had other ideas. He had no intention of yielding a German city to the enemy, particularly a city with Aachen's symbolic significance. Aachen's history extended back to Roman times, when it was known as "Aquisgranum." The Roman name derived from the hot mineral springs located there, which the Romans converted into baths. The supposed medicinal qualities of Aachen's baths continued to attract visitors into the twentieth century. More to the point, Aachen was the capital city of Charlemagne's European empire in the early Middle Ages and was the coronation site for the Holy Roman Empire from 813 to 1531. Hitler, who styled his regime the Third Reich (or empire), considered the Holy Roman Empire founded by Charlemagne to be the First Reich. It would not do to lose Charlemagne's city to an invader.

As a battleground, the city of Aachen in 1944 contained three different types of urban terrain (see Map 2). The core of the city was a relic of the Middle Ages, with crooked streets and close-packed buildings. Masonry construction predominated here. To the north, on higher ground, were the mineral springs and the resort hotels built around them. Here the streets were wider and straighter, and much of the area consisted of wooded parks around the resorts. Surrounding both the downtown and resort areas was an industrial belt consisting of factories, coal mines, and residential areas. The American soldiers who eventually found themselves fighting in Aachen would at least have the benefit of excellent maps (obtained in France) and, thanks to Allied air superiority, access to aerial photographs.[9] Although a complex battlefield, Aachen would not be a mysterious one.

The battle of Aachen began on 12 September with neither side intending to fight for the city itself. On that date, VII Corps began a penetration of the *Westwall* south of the city in hopes that it would quickly break through into the Cologne plain beyond. By 15 September elements of the 1st Infantry Division and 3d Armored Division had achieved penetrations, but progress was slow and casualties heavy (see Map 3). Even when manned by second-rate troops, the fortifications of the *Westwall* represented a formidable obstacle. Bad weather further hampered the American drive. Rain-soaked ground limited off-road mobility, and cloudy skies afforded the Germans an opportunity to reinforce the Aachen sector without interference from Allied air power.

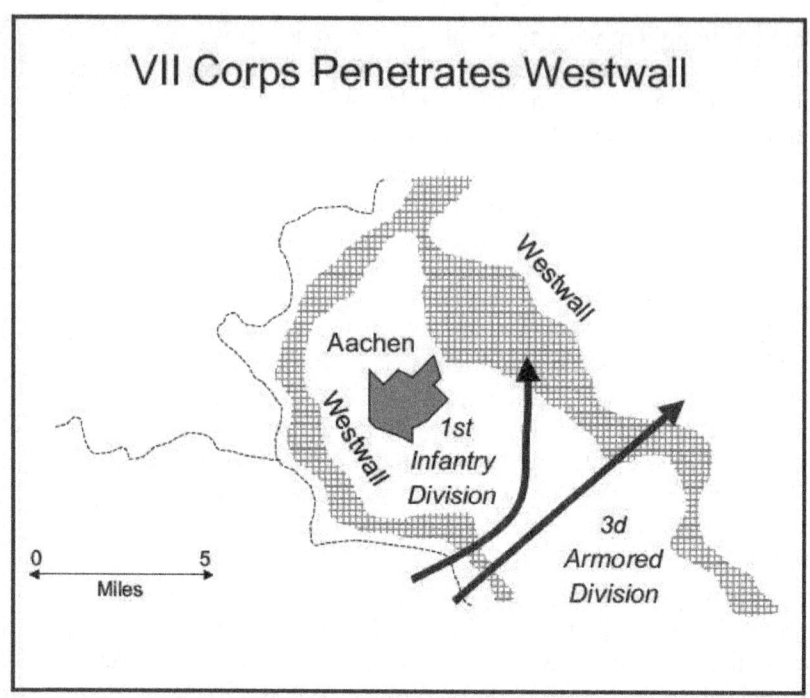

Map 2

American intelligence officers noted the arrival of the first German reinforcements on 14 September.[10] By 17 September, the Germans had strength enough to begin mounting counterattacks.

With progress effectively stalled by German resistance, bad weather, and logistics scarcity, the American high command recognized that the pursuit was over. On 22 September, First Army went on the defensive. By 24 September, the Rhine had ceased to be an immediate objective. Instead, First Army decided it would be necessary to reduce Aachen, which by now constituted a dangerous salient on the left flank of VII Corps' penetration of the *Westwall*.

When First Army resumed offensive operations a week later, the first order of business was to encircle Aachen. On 2 October, XIX Corps launched a deliberate assault against the *Westwall* north of the city. Twenty-six artillery battalions and 432 tactical aircraft bombarded German positions, following which the 30th Infantry Division attacked eastward, forcing a crossing of the Wurm River and entering the *Westwall*. Neither the air nor the artillery preparations had much impact upon the *Westwall* fortifications, so the infantry, organized into small

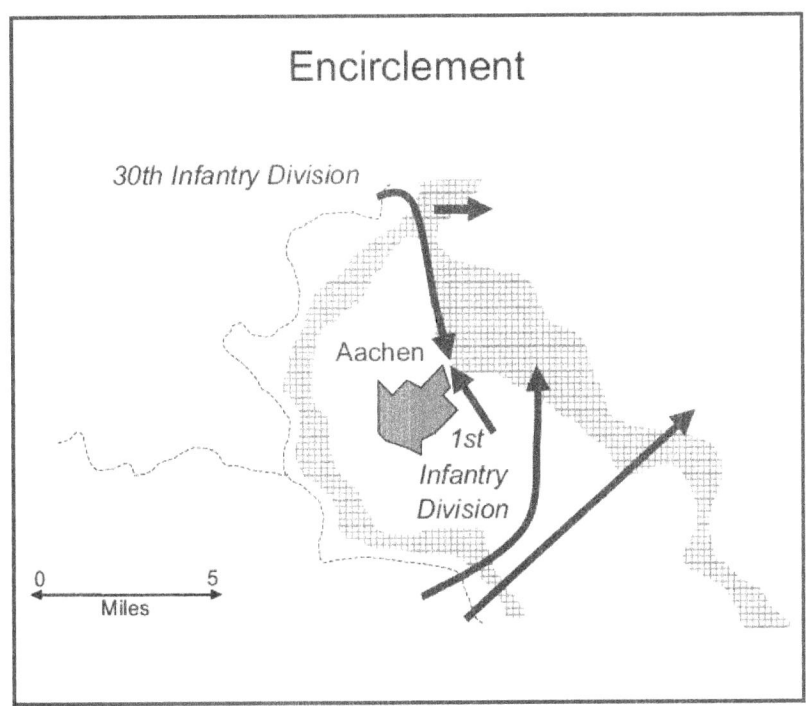

Map 3

teams, proceeded to reduce the pillboxes one by one with grenades, pole charges, and flamethrowers. The 2d Armored Division began crossing into the slowly expanding bridgehead on 3 October. By 6 October, the 30th Infantry Division had penetrated the *Westwall* and turned south, with the 2d Armored Division facing east to protect the infantry's left flank. The German reaction to this incursion was vigorous but uncoordinated. Violent, piecemeal counterattacks began on 4 October. Among the German troops committed to stopping the 30th Infantry Division was a depleted grenadier regiment withdrawn from the garrison in Aachen (see Map 4).[11]

On 7 October, First Army ordered the 1st Infantry Division to attack north toward the 30th, forming the southern jaw of the encirclement. The 18th Infantry Regiment, which drew the assignment, attacked laterally along the *Westwall* through suburban and industrial terrain. The regiment formed special pillbox assault teams built around flamethrowers, Bangalore torpedoes, and demolition charges. Reinforcing the regiment were a battery of self-propelled 155mm guns, a company of self-propelled tank destroyers, and a company of M4

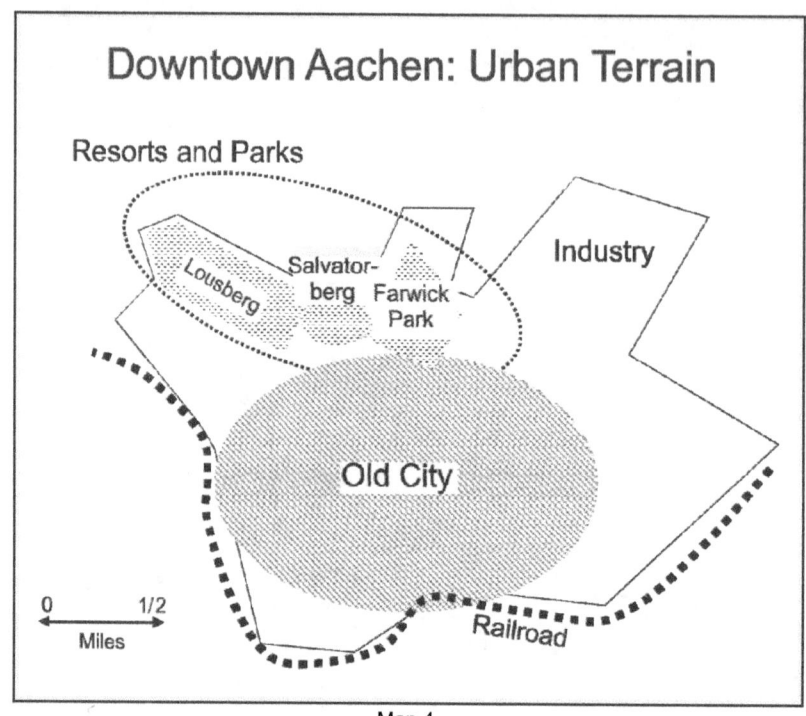

Map 4

"Sherman" tanks. An air liaison officer accompanied each battalion. Eleven artillery battalions and a company of 4.2-inch mortars provided supporting fires. The 18th Infantry's mission was to advance 2.5 miles, capturing three hills that lay consecutively along its route. The first of these, Verlautenheide, fell to the Americans in a predawn attack on 8 October that followed closely upon a heavy artillery bombardment. On the afternoon of the same day, the 18th Infantry took the second elevation, called Crucifix Hill, once again by hitting the German defenders just as the artillery prep lifted. For its attack on the third and final hill, the 18th Infantry changed its tactics. On the night of 9 October, two companies infiltrated among the German pillboxes and occupied the crest of Ravel's Hill without firing a shot. After clearing the bypassed enemy positions, the 18th dug in and awaited the advance of the 30th Infantry Division from the north.[12]

With the Americans perched precariously on Ravel's Hill, the gap between 1st Infantry Division in the south and 30th Infantry Division in the north was just over a mile wide. However, German reinforcements continued to arrive. General Friedrich J. Koechling's LXXXI Corps, defending the Aachen sector, began to receive elements of the I SS Panzer Corps consisting of the depleted 3d Panzer Grenadier and 116th Panzer Divisions. Koechling's mission was to eliminate the American penetrations of the *Westwall*. However, the pressure of events forced him to commit the arriving elements piecemeal rather than massing them for a general counteroffensive. Consequently, both the 30th and 1st Infantry Divisions were able to hold their ground in the face of repeated counterattacks and artillery bombardments, but only with massive artillery and air support. It would take the 30th Infantry Division another week to close the gap.

At this juncture, First Army decided to proceed with the reduction of Aachen itself, even though the encirclement was incomplete. First Army arrived at this decision not so much from a desire to own Aachen, but from a need to shorten the American lines and free up the forces containing Aachen so they could be used to counter the German forces arriving from the east. In essence, the reduction of Aachen was a secondary effort. First Army's main effort was the encirclement battle east of the city. This being the case, the only forces immediately available for the capture of Aachen were two battalions of the 1st Infantry Division.

Fortunately for the Americans, the defense of downtown Aachen was also a secondary priority for the Germans, who were more concerned with eliminating the penetrations of the *Westwall* north and south of town. The garrison of Aachen proper consisted primarily of the 246th Volksgrenadier Division, minus four of its seven infantry battalions. Volksgrenadier divisions, which first appeared in the German order of battle in the autumn of 1944, were hastily constituted formations composed largely of survivors from other divisions wrecked in battle. These divisions lacked a full complement of artillery, but were abundantly provided with automatic weapons as compensation. The commander of the 246th Volksgrenadier was Colonel Gerhard Wilck. Also under Wilck's command were elements of two "fortress battalions" (static-defense forces composed of second-rate troops), some *Luftwaffe* (air force) ground troops, and 125 city policemen. To support his infantry, Wilck had five Panzer IV medium tanks armed with high-velocity 75mm guns, and 32 artillery pieces ranging in caliber from 75mm to 150mm.[13] Perhaps the most dangerous weapons in Wilck's arsenal were *panzerfausts*, hand-held recoilless antitank weapons that delivered a hollow-charge warhead capable of penetrating eight inches of armor. The main drawback of the *panzerfaust* was its short range—30 to

80 meters—but in the close confines of urban fighting it could be deadly.[14]

Wilck assumed command in Aachen on 12 October, one day before the American assault on the city began. He established his headquarters in the luxurious Hotel Quellenhof, located in the resort district on the north side of town. Wilck's position was not an enviable one. Hitler himself had ordered a "last stand" in Aachen, and Wilck was aware that soldiers who failed to do their duty could expect their families to face retribution from the German secret police. Yet, his force numbered only some 5,000 troops of uneven quality, exclusive of reinforcements that would become available during the fight.[15]

Although he did not know it, Wilck's force outnumbered by a ratio of three or four to one the Americans who would launch the attack on Aachen. Moreover, the two battalions of the 1st Infantry Division given the task of reducing Aachen had no experience in urban operations. At best, they had received word-of-mouth accounts of urban fighting conducted by other units, and that news was far from reassuring.

Published doctrine would have been little help to the Americans.[16] The closest that the relevant field manuals came to urban operations doctrine was a few pages on fighting in towns and villages. There were no references to major cities. Moreover, those manuals made it clear that reducing a town by "frontal attack" was the least preferable means of coping with such objectives. They recommended enveloping the town or avoiding it altogether.

On the other hand, published doctrine presented a fairly accurate picture of the type of defense one could expect to encounter in a builtup area. The manuals predicted that the enemy would defend in depth throughout the town, and that buildings and especially cellars would be fortified into strongpoints capable of all-round defense. Perhaps the most helpful piece of advice found in the manuals was to warn that streets would be swept by fire, and that the best way for infantry to advance would be to pass from building to building by piercing holes in the walls.

As for the actual tactics to be employed, the manuals advocated methodical, firepower-intensive procedures. Operations would of necessity be decentralized, due to the lack of observation. Units should advance in a series of bounds, reducing strongpoints one by one with artillery bombardments followed closely by infantry assaults. Frequent halts along phase lines (main streets) would be necessary to restore contact among adjacent units. As for tanks, doctrine suggested rather unhelpfully that "opportunities will present themselves frequently where the support of tanks in such situations becomes desirable."[17]

One might argue that the Army's published doctrine was sound in general principle, but clearly the American troops assaulting Aachen would have to work out the details for themselves. One factor working in the Americans' favor was that the force given the mission was among the most experienced units in the U.S. Army. The 1st Infantry Division's 26th Infantry Regiment, commanded by Colonel John F.R. Seitz, had been in action since the invasion of North Africa in November 1942. Two of the regiment's three battalions were available for the reduction of Aachen—the 2d, commanded by Lieutenant Colonel Derrill M. Daniel, and the 3d, under Lieutenant Colonel John T. Corley. Expecting that the German defenses in Aachen would be oriented to the south, where American forces had been in position for a month, the commander of the 1st Infantry Division, Major General Clarence R. Huebner, directed the two assault battalions to swing around to the east and attack the city along an east-west axis. The 1106th Engineer Combat Group, consisting of two battalions, received the mission of holding the perimeter on the southern side of Aachen while the attack crossed its front.

Colonel Seitz assigned to the 2/26 the mission of clearing the heart of downtown Aachen. On its right, the 3/26 was designated the main effort, its objectives being the hills on the north side of the city, Salvatorberg and Lousberg. Both battalions received orders to remove all civilians encountered. The Americans intended that no Germans, civilian or military, would remain unaccounted for behind U.S. forces as they advanced through the city.

From 8 to 12 October, the two assault battalions worked their way up to jump-off positions east and southeast of Aachen, taking the opportunity to practice tactics and techniques of urban fighting as they advanced. By nightfall of 12 October, the 2/26 on the left had drawn up to the foot of the railroad embankment of the Aachen-Cologne railway. To its right, the 3/26 occupied its line of departure in the industrial area just east of Aachen proper (see Map 5).

Meanwhile, on 10 October Major General Huebner delivered an ultimatum to the garrison of Aachen giving the Germans twenty-four hours to surrender. When the ultimatum expired unanswered on 11 October, the Americans began a two-day preparatory bombardment of the city. Twelve battalions of VII Corps and 1st Infantry Division artillery poured 4,800 rounds into the city on 11 October, to which four air groups of the IX Tactical Air Command, totaling some 300

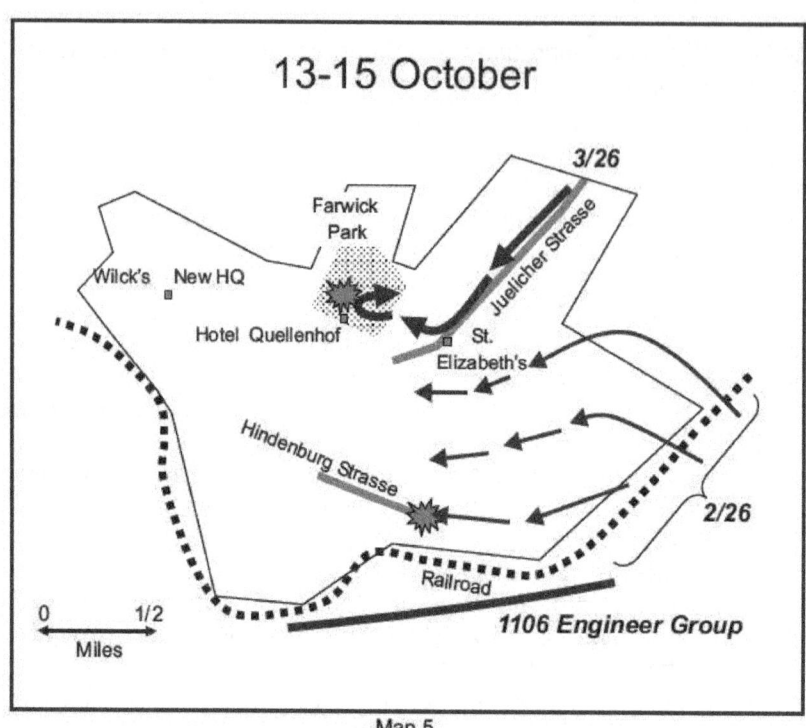

Map 5

fighter-bombers, added 62 tons of bombs. Another 5,000 shells and 99 tons of bombs hammered the city on 12 October.[18] It is not likely that this display of firepower had much impact on the German defenders, who had long since established themselves in basements, bunkers, air raid shelters, and other protected positions.

The 1106th Engineer Group, overlooking Aachen from its positions on the high ground south of the city, made its own unique contribution to the preparatory fires. The engineers loaded streetcars with captured explosives, to which they attached time fuses, and then set them rolling downhill into the city center. The 1106 dispatched three of these weapons, which the engineers dubbed "V-13s." The first V-13 exploded prematurely, and the second derailed on the wreckage of the first. After a patrol succeeded in clearing the tracks, the third V-13 rolled into the heart of Aachen and exploded, without discernible impact on the German defenses.[19]

In analyzing the reduction of Aachen itself, it is important to recognize that the two American battalions involved faced different challenges and fought different battles. For analytical purposes, it is best to treat the two battalions separately.

The 2/26, given the mission of clearing the densest part of the old city, conducted a methodical, specialized urban operation. Fortunately, Lieutenant Colonel Daniel, the battalion commander, wrote a detailed account after the war of the methods employed.[20] His preparations began with a reconfiguration of his battalion that integrated the combat arms at the small-unit level. Each rifle company became a task force. In addition to the company's three organic rifle platoons and weapons platoon (light machine guns and 60mm mortars), Daniel added three tanks or tank destroyers, which the company then assigned down to the rifle platoons. The tanks, M4 Shermans, weighed approximately 35 tons and mounted general purpose 75mm main guns capable of firing armor-piercing, high-explosive, and white phosphorus rounds. The tank destroyers were M10s, based upon the M4 tank, that mounted high-velocity 75mm guns highly valued for their ability to penetrate walls and fortifications. It should be noted that the M4 and M10, both of which were about twenty feet long and nine feet wide, were small enough to maneuver even in the close confines of an urban environment.[21] Daniel further augmented each of the rifle companies with two 57mm antitank guns, drawn from the regimental antitank company, two bazooka teams, one flamethrower, and two heavy machine guns (water-cooled .30 caliber weapons capable of sustained fire).[22]

Each of the 2/26's companies was assigned a zone of advance, within which each platoon, with its accompanying tank or tank destroyer, was assigned a specific street to clear. Using the detailed maps at his disposal, Daniel set up a "measles system" in which all intersections and prominent buildings were numbered to speed up communication and ensure coordination among the battalion's elements. Daniel further ordered that constant, positive liaison be maintained between adjacent units at all times. As units advanced, Daniel mandated stops at designated checkpoints for the reestablishment of contact along the line. Offensive operations halted at nightfall along designated phase lines (major streets) to avoid the confusion and loss of observation inherent in night combat.[23]

Logistics posed a special set of problems for the 2/26. Anticipating high expenditures of ammunition, Daniel improvised a mobile battalion ammunition dump that could keep pace with the advancing companies.[24] To facilitate medical evacuation in the rubble-filled streets, Daniel obtained some M29 cargo carriers, known as "Weasels."[25]

These versatile little vehicles were fully tracked and measured only 10.5 feet long and 5.5 feet wide but could carry a payload of 1,200 pounds.[26]

On 13 October the reduction of Aachen began, with the two battalions moving out in simultaneous but separate attacks. The first obstacle that confronted the 2/26 was a railroad embankment, fifteen to thirty feet high, that ran from southwest to northeast along the battalion front. Three artillery battalions delivered a 23-minute preparatory fire on the far side of the embankment, followed by a "grenade barrage," in which every man of the two lead companies tossed grenades over the obstacle.[27] At 0930 the troops clambered over the embankment, only to find that the area behind was undefended. The embankment remained, however, a formidable obstacle to the tanks and other vehicles. Two tanks, though, succeeded in traversing the embankment when it was discovered that vehicles could drive straight through a railroad station built into the embankment, once a few walls had been knocked down.[28] After clearing the embankment, the two assault companies pivoted left so that they faced west. The 2/26's third company filled in behind, ready to take its place in the line.

On 14 October, the 2/26 began its methodical advance through Aachen, though with one eye over its shoulder. Due to the intensity of German counterattacks against the forces still attempting to complete the encirclement, the 26th was warned to be ready to suspend its advance and go over to the defense. Despite this distraction, Daniel put all three of his companies on line and moved into the city.

With a front of some 2,000 yards (two to four times the frontage prescribed by doctrine) and no reserve, the 2/26 relied upon patience, thoroughness, and firepower to maintain its advance. The battalion's catchphrase for this operation was "Knock 'em all down." There was no attempt to avoid collateral damage; in fact, the troops displayed a degree of enthusiasm in wrecking a German city. More pragmatically, Daniel reasoned that German soldiers could not be expected to fight effectively with buildings falling down around their ears.[29] Stated generally, Daniel's procedure was to use all available firepower to pin down the defenders and chase them into cellars, where the infantry closed with and eliminated them with bayonet and grenade.

"Knock 'em all down" started with artillery fire. Heavy artillery struck German lines of communication to isolate the battle area. Medium artillery and mortars fired across the front itself. Artillerymen used delayed fuses to ensure that rounds penetrated buildings before exploding. Division and corps artillery was arrayed south of the city, which allowed artillery to fire parallel to the front of troops fighting in the city. With the danger of short rounds falling on American troops thus minimized, artillerymen were able to adjust fires within yards of the infantry lines. However, since the encirclement battle still raged, the forces fighting in Aachen could not count upon artillery support all the time.[30]

Tanks and tank destroyers assigned to the platoons were, on the other hand, an ever-present source of mobile firepower. The American troops, acutely aware of the dangers posed by German *panzerfausts* in close-quarters fighting, developed combined arms tactics in which infantry protected the armor from *panzerfausts* while the armor engaged strongpoints that impeded the infantry. Platoons generally kept their armor one street back from the street being cleared. The tank or tank destroyer would nose cautiously around the corner and pour fire into a specific building. Then, the infantry would assault the building, whereupon the armor would shift fire to the next in line. Once the block had been systematically cleared, all available weapons would fire into every possible *panzerfaust* firing position while the armor dashed forward into the street just cleared.[31]

As for the infantry, the rifle platoons stayed out of the streets as much as possible. Heavy machine guns maintained steady fire up the streets along the axis of advance, thus impeding German lateral movements, while the American infantry moved from building to building by blowing holes through adjoining walls with bazookas and demolition charges. The preferred mode of clearing a building was to fight from the top down, with grenades being the weapon of choice.[32]

The 2/26 eliminated every German position as it was encountered, intentionally bypassing none. Every sewer manhole was blocked off to prevent the reoccupation of positions behind American lines. In accordance with orders from higher headquarters, all civilians encountered were evacuated from the city.

As fighting progressed on 14 October, the 2/26 received augmentation from VII Corps in the form of a self-propelled 155mm gun. (The 3/26 was likewise reinforced on this date.) This weapon fired a 95-pound armor-piercing projectile at a muzzle velocity of 2,800 feet per second—sufficient kinetic energy to penetrate an entire block of buildings. Daniel was strictly enjoined to take good care of this asset.[33]

At day's end, the 2/26 reached its designated phase line, but a gap remained between its right flank and the left of the 3/26 to the north. Daniel blamed the 3/26 for anchoring its left on the wrong landmark.

Fortunately, the Germans did not exploit this gap, though the 2/26 did lose one of its 57mm antitank guns to fire from this open flank.

The 2/26 continued its methodical advance on 15 October. It achieved a linkup with the 3/26, thus securing its right flank. Company G, on the left wing, encountered a massive three-story fortified structure that proved to be a gigantic above-ground air raid shelter. One burst of fire from the company's flamethrower induced the surrender of 200 soldiers and 1,000 civilians sheltering behind the structure's fifteen-foot walls.[34]

At dusk, the Germans launched a counterattack in company strength, with tank support, along Hindenburg Strasse. It took the 2/26 two hours to contain the attack and restore the line. This action cost the Americans one tank destroyer, one antitank gun, and a heavy machine gun. The Germans lost one tank and about a platoon's worth of infantry.[35] This would prove to be the largest single action that the 2/26 would fight during the reduction of the city.

On the next morning, 16 October, the 1st and 30th Infantry Divisions finally linked up east of Aachen, thus completing the encirclement of the city. The Germans responded with heavy counterattacks, prompting the 1st Infantry Division to suspend offensive operations within the city as a precautionary measure. The 2/26 took advantage of the pause to secure its position. On the battalion's left flank, the 1106th Engineer Group pivoted its right wing forward from its position south of the city to conform to the 2/26. The battalion also decided to take measures against a supposed pillbox spotted at the far end of Hindenburg Strasse. Daniel brought up his attached 155mm self-propelled gun for the purpose. To protect it, he ordered tank destroyers to fire into the intervening cross streets. To protect the tank destroyers, infantry secured the buildings within *panzerfaust* range of the armor. Once in place, the 155 utterly demolished the "pillbox," which later proved to be a camouflaged tank.[36]

The 2/26 continued its methodical advance on 17 and 18 October (see Map 6). The 1106th Engineer Group continued to displace forward to cover the battalion's flank. As it advanced, the 2/26's front widened. The 1st Infantry Division attached Company C (1/26 Infantry) to Daniel's command, where it assumed responsibility for a zone on the right flank.[37]

During this period, the 2/26 found itself taking fire from the rear, despite all its precautions to assure that no Germans were bypassed. After a careful search, the Americans discovered that the fire was coming from a church steeple that had been reinforced with concrete, making it a fortified observation post. This position proved to be impervious to both small arms and 75mm tank destroyer fire, whereupon Daniel again called upon his 155mm artillery piece. One shot from the 155 brought the entire structure crashing to the ground.[38] This use of a 155mm gun as an anti-sniper weapon is perhaps the epitome of "Knock 'em all down."

The 2/26's front continued to widen as it entered the western portion of the city on 19 October. Another battalion, the 2/110 (28th Infantry Division), was made available "for defensive missions only."[39] This force, which had been battered in earlier fighting, occupied a gap that emerged between the 2/26 and the 1106th Engineers. That same day, operating in conjunction with the 3/26 to its right, elements of the 2/26 occupied the lower slopes of Salvatorberg.

On 20 October, the battalion's right wing became embroiled in a difficult battle for the Technical School. (Unknown to the Americans, the German headquarters in Aachen was just a few blocks away in the 3/26 zone.) Conversely, resistance faded on the left as the battalion neared the western edge of the city. The Technical School fell on 21 October, yielding several hundred prisoners. This was the last organized resistance encountered by the 2/26. The battalion crossed a railway embankment at the western edge of the city with a repeat of the grenade barrage with which it had entered Aachen. It was securing the ground beyond when word arrived that the German commander, Colonel Wilck, had surrendered to the 3/26.[40]

Whereas the actions of the 2/26 in Aachen were largely in the nature of a clearing operation against poorly organized defenders, the 3/26 experienced something more like a pitched battle. Its battlefield environment was also different. Unlike the dense urban terrain that confronted the 2/26, the 3/26 first encountered an industrial area, and then advanced through the parks and resorts that covered the hills on the north side of town. Control of those hills, which overlooked the city center, was key to the possession of Aachen, a fact that both sides recognized. Colonel Wilck placed the best of his defenders in the path of the 3/26.

The 3/26 launched its attack on 13 October through factories and apartment houses on the northeast side of Aachen (see Map 5). Although its front was considerably narrower than that of the 2/26, the 3/26 advanced with both flanks open. After progressing steadily along Juelicher Strasse for several hours, the battalion was halted by 20mm cannon fire that drove the infantry out of the street, exposing two tanks to *panzerfaust* fire. One tank was destroyed, and the other damaged and abandoned by its crew. Some infantrymen later succeeded in retrieving the damaged tank.[41]

On 14 October, the 3/26 concentrated two of its three companies in the reduction of a German strongpoint in St. Elizabeth's Church. By the end of the day, elements of the battalion advanced to the edge of Farwick Park, only a few blocks from Wilck's headquarters in the Hotel Quellenhof. In response, Wilck moved his headquarters to an air raid bunker 1,200 yards west of the hotel. That evening, Wilck received the only reinforcements that would come his way during the battle. SS Battalion Rink, a task force of infantry and eight assault guns, reached Wilck's position after fighting its way past the U.S. 30th Infantry Division. Although this force was rather badly depleted, as an SS unit it was manned with the best, most fanatical personnel that Germany had to offer. Wilck assigned this battalion the task of stopping the 3/26.[42]

The next day started out well for the 3/26. The battalion achieved a linkup with the 2/26 on its left, securing one flank. The attack against Farwick Park made steady progress, with the help of some 4.2-inch mortars provided by division headquarters. Advancing across once-luxurious lawns and gardens, the 3/26 reached the vicinity of the Hotel Quellenhof, Wilck's old headquarters, when SS Battalion Rink counterattacked in force. The counterattack drove the Americans back out of Farwick Park in disarray. Not until 1700 did the 3/26 stop the German attack and stabilize its lines.[43]

Following this setback, the 3/26 went on the defensive for two days. The American forces outside the city completed their encirclement on 16 October, in the face of heavy German counterattacks. The 3/26 used the pause to lick its wounds and await reinforcements from VII Corps. On the German side, Wilck knew that the 4,392 effectives at his disposal on 16 October were not likely to be reinforced.[44]

The 3/26 resumed offensive operations on 18 October (see Map 6). A patrol sent out beyond the right flank made contact with the 30th Infantry Division, thus affording a degree of security in that direction.[45] The battalion renewed its attack on Farwick Park, regained the ground lost on 15 October, and assaulted the Hotel Quellenhof. After bitter fighting through the once-luxurious rooms of the hotel, the Americans forced their opponents into the basement and subdued them with grenades and machine gun fire poured point-blank through the windows. The 3/26 controlled Farwick Park by day's end.[46] The ground gained on 18 October placed the 3/26 in position to attack Salvatorberg and Lousberg, the key terrain in the battle for Aachen. What is more, the

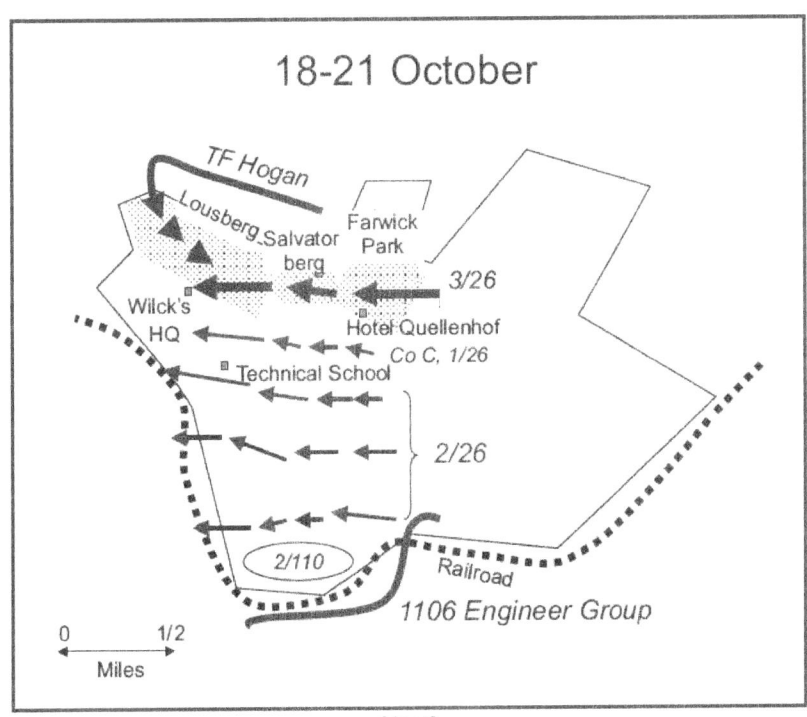

Map 6

battle for Hotel Quellenhof seems to have broken the back of SS Battalion Rink and, thus, of the German defense in general.

For the final assault, VII Corps reinforced the 3/26 with Task Force Hogan, consisting of one armored infantry battalion and one tank battalion (minus a medium tank company) from the 3d Armored Division.[47] The attack, coordinated by 1st Infantry Division headquarters, jumped off at 0730 on 19 October. Task Force Hogan, advancing on the right, passed behind Lousberg and attacked from the northwest while the 3/26 attacked from the east. Both advances progressed steadily against weakening resistance. The 3/26 seized Salvatorberg and moved onto the slopes of Lousberg proper. Task Force Hogan's advance cut the last possible escape routes for the Germans in Aachen and, at 1202, established contact with the 3/26 on Lousberg.[48]

With defeat staring him in the face, Wilck sent out an order to his command calling for a fight to the last man and bullet. How many German troops received this directive is not known, but resistance clearly was crumbling. On 20 October, as Task Force Hogan and the

3/26 cleared the last German troops from Lousberg, the issue was no longer in doubt.

The end came on 21 October, when elements of the 3/26 closed in on an air raid bunker south of Lousberg, unaware that it was Wilck's headquarters. Lieutenant Colonel Corley, the battalion commander, dispatched his attached 155mm self-propelled gun to reduce the position. Before the gun could open fire, Wilck sent out a white flag in the hands of some American prisoners who were being held in the bunker. He broadcast a last radio message proclaiming his loyalty to Hitler and to Germany and then turned himself over to the 3/26. The surrender of the Aachen garrison took effect at 1205.[49]

With the German communications system broken down, Wilck had no means of communicating the surrender to most of his troops. The Americans found it necessary to drive one of Wilck's staff officers around town in an armored car to collect the German troops still holding out.[50] The two battalions of the 26th Infantry, the 1106th Engineers, and Task Force Hogan accounted for 1,600 German prisoners after Wilck's surrender, bringing the total haul of prisoners collected during the reduction to 3,473.[51]

At 1615, the 26th Infantry reported, "Mission out here complete as of now and are through with TF 'Hogan.'"[52] The regiment patrolled Aachen for two more days, then was relieved by a field artillery battalion. Aachen was secured but, for the 26th Infantry, the war was far from over. The next day it took up a position in the front lines facing east into Germany.

The military garrison of Aachen was not the only group of Germans with whom the victors had to contend. Some 7,000 civilians still inhabited the city when the reduction began, and all of these had to be evacuated and processed. Two agencies were responsible for handling the civilians. The Counter Intelligence Corps screened the evacuees, looking for any spies, would-be saboteurs, and high-ranking officials. Suspected spies were to be turned over to the First Army Military Commission for trial. German military deserters were sent to the Provost Marshal for processing as prisoners of war. The task of the Counter Intelligence Corps was greatly simplified by the Nazi regime's obsession with documentation—every German carried identity papers. After the screening process, military government personnel registered the evacuees and provided them with food and shelter.[53]

Of the 7,000 civilians in Aachen, approximately 6,000 were removed in the course of the fighting. At first, the evacuees were simply taken to an open field for screening by the Counter Intelligence Corps before being removed to displaced persons camps behind Allied lines. As the reduction of Aachen picked up pace and the number of evacuees swelled, military government took over some German army barracks at Brand, four miles from Aachen. Here the evacuees could be kept under shelter (and behind fences) while the screening and registration took place.[54]

Overall, the Americans responsible for handling the civilian evacuees from Aachen found them to be passive, and even cooperative. The hard-core Nazis had left town during the evacuation that preceded the battle. Those who remained seemed to be quite content to let the U.S. Army take care of them. After a decade of increasingly brutal Nazi rule, not to mention the horrors that war had brought upon them, the evacuees from Aachen found American military rule to be relatively benign. The happiest group of evacuees was undoubtedly the Polish and Russian forced laborers liberated by the Americans.[55]

Within captured Aachen itself, teams from the Counter Intelligence Corps searched specific buildings for military information, but found little. Other teams secured communications centers and collected all radio transmitters to prevent any stay-behind spies from communicating with the outside. One report stated specifically that "no pigeons were found." This was in response to rumors that German spies behind Allied lines were using homing pigeons to communicate with their homeland. Counter Intelligence personnel in Aachen also screened some 1,000 civilians who had avoided evacuation during the battle.[56]

It would appear that the Germans made no preparations for subversion against occupying forces in anticipation of the American capture of Aachen. The Counter Intelligence Corps reported that there were no confirmed cases of sabotage, no booby traps, and no resistance cells to be found within the city.[57] For all its prowess at the tactical and operational levels of war, Nazi Germany proved to be singularly inept at covert operations such as espionage, counterespionage, and subversion. At no point in the Allied conquest of Germany did a coherent popular resistance movement menace the occupying forces, Adolf Hitler's rhetoric notwithstanding.

Urban operations may well represent the coming face of battle in an increasingly urbanized world. Today there is a tendency to regard urban operations as a distinct, rather esoteric form of warfare demanding specialized military capabilities. As the foregoing account should make clear, the reduction of Aachen posed challenges that invoked a certain degree of innovation and adaptation. Most notable were the creation of small, combined arms teams and the measures undertaken to cope with civilians. What should not be overlooked, however, is the degree to which the battle of Aachen resembled conventional combat, even though it was fought in urban terrain.

First, it should be noted that Aachen was a linear battle, most particularly in the sector of the 2/26. The battalion took great pains to assure that all Germans were either in front of its line or on their way to detention centers. It was remarkably successful in keeping the battle linear. Even in the zone of the 3/26, where the situation was more fluid, linearity prevailed.

Second, the tactics employed within Aachen embodied the standard fire-and-maneuver concepts that were common to open-field battle of the day. The tactical intent, which the Americans routinely accomplished, was to pound the enemy into helplessness with firepower, so that when the infantry attacked, it encountered an enemy who was ready to surrender. Much the same could be said for Army combined arms doctrine in general, as practiced in World War II.

Third, it should be noted that both the attackers and defenders in Aachen were conventional, "heavy" forces. The American forces were able to shift from conventional to urban operations in a matter of days. They possessed no equipment specially designed for urban operations, nor did they have much in the way of formal doctrine to guide their efforts. Although none of the American units involved had ever reduced a city before, they did possess experience in fighting among the close confines of the Normandy hedgerows. Not surprisingly, the task organization and tactics employed in Aachen somewhat resemble those used with success in Normandy.

The battle for Aachen challenges conventional wisdom in another respect. Urban operations are commonly regarded as bloody, time-consuming operations in which the defender can exact many times his own number in enemy casualties. In Aachen, however, the defenders outnumbered the attackers, and yet managed to hold out for only nine days because of the American offensive methods and the incoherent nature of the German defense. The two battalions of the 26th Infantry (plus attachments) that bore the brunt of the fighting in Aachen lost 75 killed, 414 wounded, and 9 missing in securing a city defended by over 5,000 enemy troops.[58] For the U.S. Army, the true bloodbath of the 1944 campaign was not an urban operation, but rather the battle of the Huertgen Forest.

The Germans, on the other hand, lost virtually all of the troops committed to Aachen. Over half of the total surrendered, despite Hitler's admonition that they were to fight to the last man. A small number probably succeeded in exfiltrating, but the rest were killed or wounded. The German cause did not gain much from the sacrifice of these troops.

In two respects, however, the battle for Aachen bears out conventional wisdom. First, although Aachen itself was unfortified, war made it a fortress. Stone walls erected for any purpose can be a significant combat multiplier for a defender. Moreover, when the Americans reduced the city to rubble with artillery and air bombardment, they rendered buildings unfit for civilian use but did not destroy them as fighting positions. Urban rubble is as much of a problem for an attacker as intact buildings would be.

Second, Aachen showed that civilians add an inescapable dimension to urban operations. Despite two mandatory evacuations (one by the German government before the battle, and one by the Americans during it), an estimated 1,000 civilians were still in the city when Wilck surrendered the German garrison. Although this number represents only a small fraction of the city's prewar population, it was large enough to require the attention of the victors. Future planners can never assume away the presence of civilians during urban operations.

In the context of the U.S. Army's 1944 campaign in Europe, urban operations were not a major problem. Partly by chance and partly by planning, Americans avoided combat in truly large cities such as Paris and Berlin. When they did have to fight in builtup areas, U.S. troops adapted and pushed on. Given the intensity of the war, "Knock 'em all down" served admirably as a technique. The reduction of Aachen, a sideshow for the U.S. First Army as it drove into Germany, was just another day's work for an experienced, competent military force.

Notes

1. Gordon A. Harrison, *Cross Channel Attack,* U.S. Army in World War II (Washington, DC: Office of the Chief of Military History, 1950), 457.

2. Elbridge Colby, *The First Army in Europe*, 91st Congress, 1st Session, Senate Document No. 91-25 (Washington, DC: U.S. Government Printing Office [GPO], 1969), 92-95.

3. Charles B. MacDonald, *The Siegfried Line Campaign,* U.S. Army in World War II (Washington, DC: U.S. Army Center of Military History, 1963), 4.

4. Ibid., 68.

5. Colby, 97-108.

6. Field Manual (FM) 100-5, *Field Service Regulations, Operations* (Washington, DC: GPO, 1944), 11. This manual calls for a battalion in a "main attack" to occupy a frontage of 500 to 1,000 yards. Extrapolating this figure yields a frontage of approximately 5 to 10 miles for a corps.

7. See MacDonald, 30-35 for information on the *Westwall* and its component fortifications.

8. Ibid., 71.

9. Ibid., 26-27.

10. H.R. Knickerbocker et al., *Danger Forward: The Story of the First Division in World War II* (Washington, DC: Society of the First Division, 1947), 256.

11. MacDonald, 261-73.

12. Ibid., 285-88.

13. MacDonald, 81. See also 1st U.S. Infantry Division, "Report of Breaching the Siegfried Line and the Capture of Aachen, 7 November 1944," Combined Arms Research Library (CARL) manuscript collection, Fort Leavenworth, KS (hereafter referred to as CARL).

14. Alex Buchner, *The German Infantry Handbook, 1939 1945* (West Chester, PA: Schiffer Publishing, 1991), 149-51. The *panzerfaust* was comparable in performance and employment to the rocket-propelled grenade of modern times.

15. MacDonald, 307-308.

16. In addition to FM 100-5 (1944), the following FMs were consulted: FM 100-5, *Tentative Field Service Regulations, Operations* (Washington, DC: GPO, 1939) 218-22; FM 7-5, *Infantry Field Manual: Organization and Tactics of Infantry, The Rifle Battalion* (Washington, DC: GPO, 1940), 99.

17. FM 100-5 (1944), 248.

18. Colby, 107, and MacDonald, 309-310.

19. Ibid., 310n.

20. Derrill M. Daniel, "The Capture of Aachen," CARL manuscript collection.

21. *The American Arsenal* (Mechanicsburg, PA: Stackpole, 1996), 29, 51.

22. Daniel, 7-9, and MacDonald, 310.

23. Daniel, 6, and MacDonald, 310-11.

24. Daniel, 5-6.

25. MacDonald, 311.

26. *The American Arsenal*, 72-73.

27. 1st Infantry Division, "G-3 Report of Operations, 1 October to 31 October 1944," 5 November 1944, CARL manuscript collection.

28. Daniel, 8-10.

29. Ibid., 5.

30. Daniel, 11, and MacDonald, 310.

31. Daniel, 6-7, and MacDonald, 310.

32. Daniel, 11, and MacDonald, 310-11.

33. *The American Arsenal,* 159.

34. Daniel, 12-13.

35. Ibid., 13.

36. Ibid., 14-15.

37. Ibid., 15.

38. Ibid., 15-16.

39. 1st Infantry Division, "G-3 Report," 114 and 118-19, and 1st Infantry Division, "Report of Breaching the Siegfried Line," 11.

40. Daniel, 16.

41. MacDonald, 311-12.

42. Ibid., 312.

43. Ibid., 312-13.

44. Ibid., 313-14.

45. 1st Infantry Division, "G-3 Report," 117.

46. MacDonald, 315.

47. 1st Infantry Division, "G-3 Report," 118-19.

48. Ibid., and 1st Infantry Division, "Report of Breaching the Siegfried Line," 11.

49. MacDonald, 316.

50. 1st Infantry Division, "G-3 Report," 124.

51. MacDonald, 316-17, and 1st Infantry Division, "G-3 Report," 124.

52. 1st Infantry Division, "G-3 Report," 124.

53. 1st CIC Detachment, "CIC Operations in Aachen and Vicinity September, October, and November," 1.

54. Ibid.

55. Ibid., 3-4.

56. Ibid., 2-3.
57. Ibid., 2.
58. MacDonald, 318.

Annotated Bibliography

The basic source for study of the Aachen battle is *The Siegfried Line Campaign* by Charles B. MacDonald (Washington, DC: U.S. Army Center of Military History, 1963). This work is a volume in the Army's official history series, *United States Army in World War II*. MacDonald, a combat veteran of the war, encompasses Aachen, the Huertgen Forest, and Operation MARKET GARDEN in this thoroughly researched, well-written book. He devotes ten pages to the urban operation within the city of Aachen itself.

Of particular value is an unpublished manuscript titled "The Capture of Aachen, A Lecture Presented by Lieutenant Colonel Derrill M. Daniel." This 19-page typescript document contains details on task organization, control measures, and tactics employed by the 2/26 Infantry in Aachen. A copy is available in the Combined Arms Research Library (CARL), Fort Leavenworth, Kansas. Other documents available from this library include reports of the 1st Infantry Division G3 section, a 1st Infantry Division after-action report, and a compilation of documents from the Counter Intelligence Corps. CARL also possesses a valuable collection of field manuals from the World War II period.

Three readily available secondary works are of interest to the student of the Aachen operation. *Danger Forward: The Story of the First Division in World War II* (Washington, DC: Society of the First Division, 1947) includes ten pages on the operations in and around Aachen. Charles Whiting has produced a mass-market account titled *Bloody Aachen* (NY: Military Heritage Press, 1988 [1976]). This book relies in part on MacDonald's official volume, cited above. Irving Werstein's *The Battle of Aachen* (NY: Thomas Y. Crowell, 1962) is an anecdotal account upon which serious researchers will not wish to rely.

Among the most useful reference works is George Forty's *U.S. Army Handbook 1939 1945* (NY: Scribner, 1980). This handy volume contains a wealth of information on Army organization, weapons, and equipment. The *German Infantry Handbook, 1939 1945* (West Chester, PA: Schiffer, 1991) by Alex Buchner, provides comparable information on German forces. *The American Arsenal* (Mechanicsburg, PA: Stackpole, 1996), a reprint of an official Ordnance Department publication, provides authoritative information on American weapons and equipment.

Two government publications offer information on Army doctrine in World War II. *Seek, Strike, and Destroy: U.S. Army Tank Destroyer Doctrine in World War II* (Fort Leavenworth, KS: U.S. Army Command and General Staff College [USACGSC], 1985) by Christopher R. Gabel discusses the integration of tank destroyers into small-unit combined arms teams. Michael D. Doubler's monograph, *Busting the Bocage: American Combined Arms Operations in France, 6 June 31 July 1944* (Fort Leavenworth, KS: USACGSC), explores the organizational and tactical innovations used in

Normandy, which bore some resemblance to those employed in later urban operations.

The Battle of Manila

Thomas M. Huber

The Battle of Manila, 3 February 1945 to 3 March 1945, was the only struggle by the United States to capture a defended major city in the Pacific War. Manila was one of few major battles waged by the United States on urban terrain in World War II. It is arguably one of the most recent major urban battles conducted by U.S. forces. The case of Manila offers many lessons large and small that may be instructive for planning future urban operations. Basically, Manila was an instance of modern combined arms warfare practiced in restrictive urban terrain in the presence of large numbers of civilian inhabitants. Manila provides many lessons relevant both to the combined arms aspect of the struggle and to the civilian affairs aspect of the struggle.

The road to Manila was a long one. After the Japanese navy's attack on Pearl Harbor in December 1941, the United States mobilized for an extended struggle. U.S. forces in the Philippines had resisted Japanese invasion doggedly but unsuccessfully from December 1941 to May 1942. Late in 1942, however, U.S. forces under General Douglas MacArthur's Southwest Pacific Area theater command fought their way back through the Solomons and New Guinea. Beginning in November 1943, forces under Admiral Chester Nimitz's Pacific Ocean Areas theater command seized Tarawa, the Marshalls, and the Marianas. By October 1944, MacArthur was prepared once again to contest the Philippines and landed major forces at Leyte Gulf. Leyte was secured after hard fighting so that by January 1945, MacArthur was ready to land forces on the shores of Luzon (the main island in the northern Philippines) and drive toward the Philippine capital city itself, Manila.

The city of Manila in 1945 was one of urban contrasts. In some highly traditional sections, the teeming population still lived in nipa-thatched huts. In other sections, citizens lived in modern air-conditioned apartments. The city covered an area of approximately 14.5 square miles, extending 5.5 miles north to south and 4 miles east to west, from the eastern edge of Manila Bay. The metropolitan population in 1944 was 1,100,000.[1]

Manila was bisected by the Pasig River, which flowed roughly east to west, and was interlaced with many smaller streams called "esteros." Six bridges spanned the Pasig in January 1945, all of which the Japanese severed during the battle for the capital. North of the Pasig, along the bay, was the North Port area, and north of that was the Tondo district, a populous working class residential district. Just inland from the port area was a business district that housed retail stores, manufacturing plants, movie houses, and restaurants. East of that lay older middle- and upper-class residential areas.

South of the Pasig along the bay were more modern port facilities, and just inland from that was Intramuros, the old Spanish walled city. Intramuros was an arrowhead-bastioned sixteenth-century fort with walls 40 feet thick at the base. The north wall faced the Pasig, and the other walls were fronted by park land formed by filling in the fortress's moat. East and south of Intramuros were major government buildings, hospitals, and schools. These were constructed of reinforced concrete and many were built to be earthquake proof. Large apartment buildings also of reinforced concrete could be found in this area. Eastward from the civic buildings and parks surrounding Intramuros were prosperous modern residential districts, more recently built than the prosperous eastward suburbs north of the Pasig. In February 1945, American forces found themselves fighting their way through all these areas and conducting their final siege operations against the old walled city of Intramuros.

By the time U.S. forces reached Manila on 3 February 1945, much of the city was already fortified by the Japanese defenders, especially south of the Pasig. The overall commander of the Japanese army forces in the Philippines was General Tomoyuki Yamashita. Yamashita's command was subdivided into several "groups," with the Shimbu Group under Lieutenant General Shizuo Yokoyama responsible for Manila. Yamashita wished to pull all his forces into a mountainous stronghold in northern Luzon, so he ordered Yokoyama to conduct an orderly evacuation from Manila and not defend it. This order included Japanese naval forces in the Manila area, which were under Yokoyama's command. However, Vice Admiral Denshichi Okochi, commander of the Southwestern Area Fleet based in the Philippines, who reported to Combined Fleet, not to Yamashita's 14th Area Army, had ordered naval personnel to defend naval facilities in Manila regardless of Yamashita's withdrawal strategy. So as Americans approached Manila in January 1945, Japanese army troops moved out of the city while Japanese naval troops moved in. Okochi organized the Manila Naval Defense Force (MNDF) and placed in command Rear Admiral Sanji Iwabuchi, already the commander of the 31st Naval Special Base Force in the Manila area. Okochi himself relocated to Baguio,

Yamashita's headquarters, early in January, but ordered Iwabuchi to hold Manila and Nichols Field south of the city as long as possible, and then to destroy all Japanese naval facilities and supplies in the Manila Area.[2]

What this meant was that Iwabuchi in Manila was ordered by General Yamashita, his legal superior, to withdraw, but ordered by Vice Admiral Okochi, his superior by way of loyalty and training, to stand firm. It eventually became clear that Iwabuchi intended to resist Japanese army expectations, and instead to fulfill his naval missions at all costs. Yamashita and Yokoyama evidently wished throughout that Iwabuchi would leave Manila and not fight there. Yokoyama's and Iwabuchi's staffs held a series of probably tense conferences from 8 to 13 January, in which the latter made clear that they intended to defend Japanese naval facilities in Manila. Yokoyama felt he had little choice but to accept this; however, at the end of January, he issued still somewhat equivocal orders to Iwabuchi that authorized defense of the city. Yokoyama, in accord with standard Japanese practice, placed Japanese army forces still in Manila under Iwabuchi's command. These army elements were gathered under Colonel Katsuzo Noguchi as the Noguchi Detachment and would later be given responsibility to defend north of the Pasig.[3]

Nonetheless, even as late as mid-February, when U.S. forces had already invested Manila, Yokoyama was still trying to get Iwabuchi to leave the city. On 13 February, Yokoyama ordered Iwabuchi to move to Fort McKinley (southeast of Manila) and then to break out of the American ring as Shimbu Group forces broke in with coordinated attacks on 17-18 February. Iwabuchi did not move to Fort McKinley at this time, however, and instead radioed to the Shimbu Group that leaving the city was now impossible. Still, the several thousand Japanese troops already in Fort McKinley did managed to evacuate eastward to join the Shimbu Group in the mountains during the Shimbu Group's otherwise largely ineffectual attacks toward Manila on 17-18 February.[4]

To Yokoyama at Shimbu Group headquarters, Iwabuchi radioed his response to the order to evacuate to Fort McKinley: "In view of the general situation, I consider it very important to hold the strategic positions within the city. . . . Escape is believed impossible. Will you please understand this situation?" Meanwhile to Okochi, commander of Southwest Area Fleet, he radioed, "I am overwhelmed with shame for the many casualties among my subordinates and for being unable to discharge my duty because of my incompetence. . . . Now, with what strength remains, we will daringly engage the enemy. 'Banzai to the Emperor!' We are determined to fight to the last man." Iwabuchi reported legally to one commander, but morally to another.[5]

The gap in understanding between the Japanese army and navy at Manila may strike some readers as unusual. The basis for this gap lay not only in the particular circumstances at Manila, but also in the traditions of the respective services. The prewar Japanese army and navy were well known for their insularity. Each strove to operate independently of the other as much as possible. They were engaged in bitter budgetary struggles at each other's expense and tended not to share intelligence. The Japanese army operated its own maritime shipping system—to include its own cargo submarines at the end of the war—so as not to depend on the navy. The prewar Japanese army and navy constituted a good case study of the high cost of failing to achieve effective interservice cooperation.

The Japanese navy fought in Manila without the help of the Japanese army and in defiance of the Japanese army joint commander's direct orders to evacuate. Fighting alone had enormous consequences. The MNDF would operate with no armor, little artillery, and with what was probably a limited supply of close-combat weapons. Moreover, the MNDF had no prior organization or training for urban warfare. Iwabuchi's force consisted of the 31st Naval Special Base Force as its core, to which were added ship and aviation crews stationed in the Manila area, Korean and Formosan construction troops, and some civilian employees of the naval base.[6] The MNDF were naval staff of every description. Few had had training for ground warfare of any kind, let alone urban warfare. One of the lessons of Manila was that it is possible to defend a city for a time without prior doctrine, organization, training, or equipment for urban warfare.

The MNDF defended Manila using found equipment. Their most abundant weapon was the 20mm machine cannon, intended primarily for aviation and anti-aviation use. They deployed 990 of these guns, evidently dismantled from naval aircraft. They used 600 machine guns of 7.7mm and other calibers, and sixty 120mm dual-purpose naval guns. They had a few field pieces, including ten 100mm and 105mm guns and howitzers. The MNDF appear not to have had flamethrowers or submachine guns. Apparently not all had rifles, and some of those who did carried a variety of American weapons captured in 1942. Some defenders carried spears made of bayonets fixed to poles. Grenades seem to have been generally available, though MNDF defenders sometimes used Molotov cocktails, suggesting local shortages.

Artillery shells and depth charges buried fuse up became mines. In some cases, they dropped aerial bombs from upper floors of buildings.[7]

All of the Japanese naval defenders' equipment was improvised. They had almost no equipment for ground warfare already supplied to them or routinely included in their organizational requirements. They were aided first by the proximity of naval and air bases and second, by the city itself, which served as a kind of great warehouse for much of what they needed: American rifles stored in the city since 1942, barbed wire, gasoline, and the like. Cities by their nature provide not only restrictive terrain for the defense, but also abundant materiel for the defense.

Iwabuchi's command evidently consisted of about 17,000 troops. Some 4,500 of these were deployed north of the Pasig in the Noguchi Detachment. Iwabuchi directly commanded about 5,000 troops south of the Pasig. In that Iwabuchi had expected major U.S. attacks to come from the south, approximately 5,000 more were stationed south of the city in defense of Fort McKinley and Nichols Field. A few thousand more Japanese naval troops were deployed in partially sunken ships in the bay or east of the city toward the Shimbu Group.[8]

Deployment and creation of fighting positions was all done hastily, because it had only been in December 1944 that the Japanese navy decided to defend Manila in the wake of the Japanese army's departure.[9] This meant not only that the Japanese defenders had no training, doctrine or equipment of siege warfare, but also that they had little time to fortify their positions. Consequently, they could fortify existing structures but not dig deeply into the earth, which would have allowed them to shelter more of their force from American firepower. Nonetheless, when U.S. forces encountered Japanese lines north of the Pasig on 3 February 1945, their impression was that they faced a well-prepared and formidable adversary.

In January 1945, U.S. commanders were also engaged in an animated debate over whether and when to capture Manila. MacArthur, commander of the Southwest Pacific Area, believed it was essential to seize the city as soon as possible. Manila provided port and aviation facilities needed for the coming invasion of Japan, and also had major political significance as the Philippine capital. Nonetheless, Lieutenant General Walter Krueger, commander of the U.S. 6th Army, apparently believed that Manila was not a genuine center of gravity and planned to bypass it. Krueger, whose force landed on the beaches of Lingayen Gulf on 27 January 1945, also favored delaying any attack on Manila until he could build up his assets and consolidate his position on the Lingayen coast. He was concerned, with some justification, that if he immediately advanced 100 miles to Manila, his lines of communication would be exposed to counterattacks from Yamashita's Kembu and Shobu Groups.[10] MacArthur, however, favored entering Manila as soon as possible. He hoped that the Japanese would abandon the city and declare it open, as he himself had done in 1942. In fact, Yamashita's 14th Area Army's policy was to do exactly this; at the end of January, MacArthur's intelligence told him, accurately, that the Japanese army was evacuating Manila.[11]

The principal U.S. units involved in the Battle of Manila, the 37th Infantry Division and the 1st Cavalry Division, had not fought in cities before, but they apparently had to some extent been trained for city fighting and followed established doctrine for urban warfare (see the figure). Their methods differed from doctrine on only two points: air strikes were not allowed within the city, and artillery fires in the early phases of the battle were prohibited except against observed pinpoint targets known to be enemy positions. Both the 37th Infantry Division

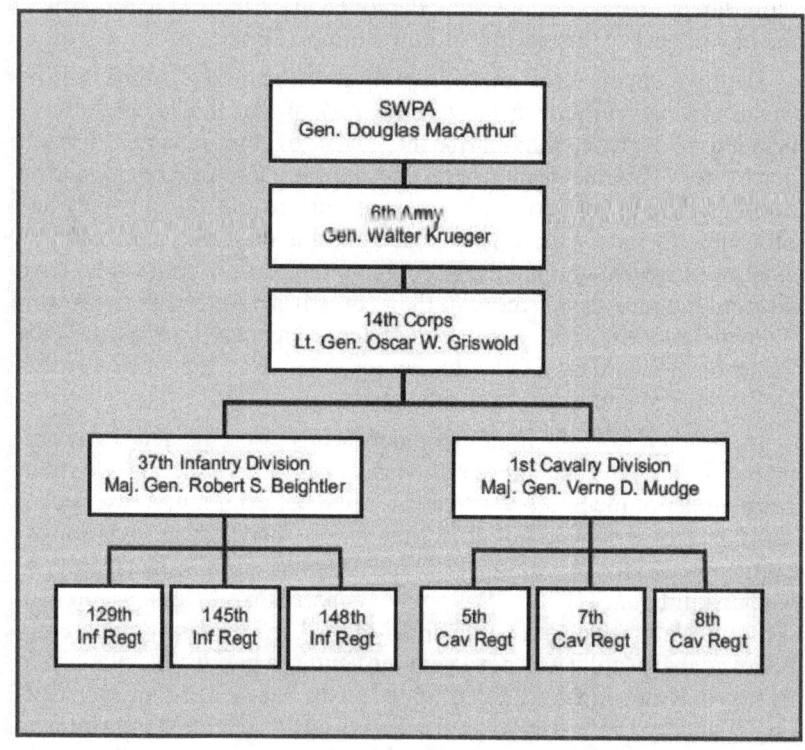

and the 1st Cavalry Division had had abundant recent experience in jungle warfare and were trained, organized, and equipped for fighting in restrictive terrain. While jungle fighting and urban fighting differ in many respects, tactically both fights have an important similarity in that both take place in restrictive terrain. Although by happenstance more than planning, these units were fairly well prepared for the kind of tactical fighting they would face in Manila.[12]

MacArthur set the Manila operation in motion personally on the night of 31 January by visiting 1st Cavalry Division headquarters, then still in the vicinity of the Lingayen beachhead. The division set out for Manila at one minute after midnight on 1 February, without 24-hour reconnaissance or flank protection. It employed "flying columns," battalion-size forces entirely on wheels to expedite the advance, covered the 100 miles to Manila in 66 hours, and entered the outskirts of the city on 3 February. MacArthur visited the other major unit that would assault Manila, the 37th Infantry Division, on 1 February and set it in motion toward the city. It reached the Manila area on 4 February.[13]

MacArthur ordered the 1st Cavalry to seize three objectives: Santo Tomás University, where U.S. and Allied internees were held by the Japanese; Malacanan Palace, the presidential residence; and the Legislative Building. The division's flying columns moved easily to capture the first two of these, but heavy Japanese resistance kept it from reaching the Legislative Building that lay south of the Pasig River.[14]

On 3 February, the 8th Cavalry Regiment entered and liberated Santo Tomás at 2330. The guards, mostly Formosans, offered little resistance. Some 3,500 jubilant internees were freed, but 275 Americans were still held hostage in the education building by 63 Japanese troops. On 5 February, these 63 were escorted through American lines in exchange for release of the hostages. Suddenly, the 1st Cavalry Division was responsible for feeding and otherwise accommodating the 3,500 freed internees. This task was complicated by the fact that Japanese forces had cut the division's lines of communication by blowing up the Novaliches bridge. By 5 February, the 1st Cavalry was very low on food for both itself and the internees. The division was surrounded, as historians of the plodding 37th Infantry Division point out. The 37th Infantry Division had to "rescue" the 1st Cavalry Division on 5 February by breaking through Japanese positions and reestablishing 1st Cavalry's supply. A convoy with food and ammunition reached the division on the evening of 5 February. The division's lines of communication continued to be insecure, however. Japanese forces killed twelve 1st Cavalry drivers during these weeks.[15]

Administering a city requires not only looking out for the needs of the individual inhabitants, but also safeguarding city functions such as water and power. Lieutenant General Krueger was therefore eager to preserve the water and power supplies of Manila as U.S. forces entered the city. Manila's steam power generating plant was on Provisor Island, on the south side of the Pasig, and elements of the 37th Infantry Division would not reach it until 9 February. Manila's water system lay northeast of the city, and securing and protecting it was one of the first missions assigned to the 1st Cavalry Division. The main features of the system were the Novaliches Dam, the Balara Water Filters, the San Juan Reservoir, and the pipelines that carried water among these and to Manila. From 5 to 8 February, the 7th Cavalry Regiment captured all of these facilities intact, despite some being wired for demolitions. They spent the rest of the battle for the city guarding these installations.[16]

The 37th Infantry Division moved into Manila shortly after the 1st Cavalry Division, on an axis of advance just west of 1st Cavalry Division's. On 4 February, the 37th Infantry Division moved through the working class Tondo residential district adjacent to the bay and, on its left flank, reached the Old Bilibid Prison where it discovered 1,330 U.S. and Allied prisoners of war and civilian internees left under their own recognizance by retreating Japanese. The division left them there for the time being because the area outside was not yet secure. On 5 February, however, fires in the city threatened Bilibid, so the 37th Infantry Division had to evacuate the 1,330 internees hastily and care for them elsewhere. All available troops and transportation assets were devoted to this emergency move, which was complicated by the fact that many internees were unable to walk. Divisional troops were heavily engaged in this work, and the internees were moved to the Ang-Tibay Shoe Factory north of the city—the 37th Infantry Division's command post. The division provided cots and food for the internees and dug latrines. The next day, the fires subsided and the internees were moved back to Bilibid, where their needs could finally be provided for more thoroughly.[17]

In the vicinity of Bilibid Prison and southward toward the Pasig, the 37th Infantry Division and the 1st Cavalry Division began encountering major Japanese resistance (see Map 1). As the 1st Cavalry Division moved southward on the multilane Quezon Boulevard, it encountered a defended barricade just south of Bilibid Prison. The Japanese had driven steel rails into the roadbed, wired a line of trucks together, laid mines in front, and covered the whole roadblock with fire from four machine gun positions. The barricade of trucks was unusual in Manila, but

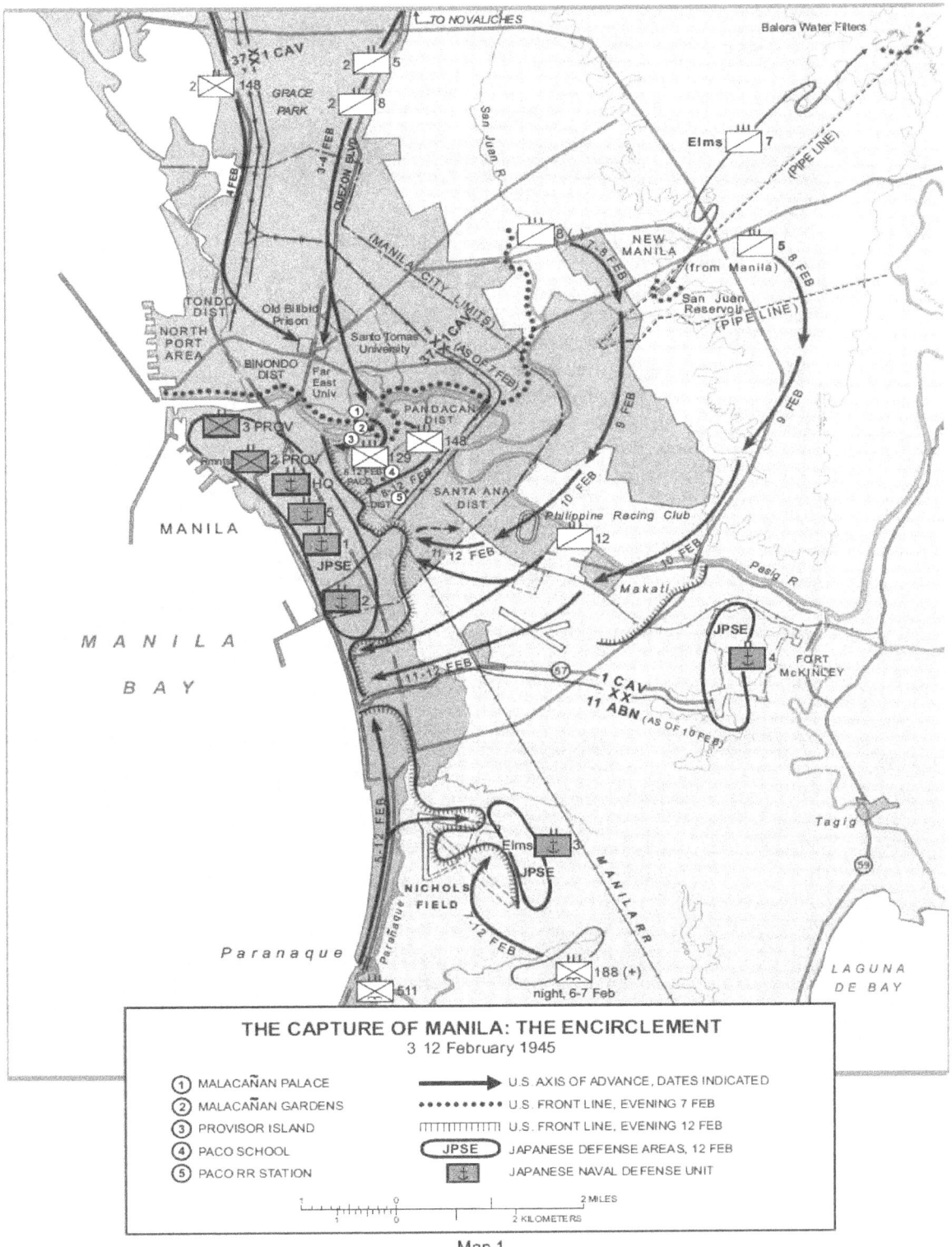

the minefield covered by obstacles and machine guns would be a common feature of the Japanese defenses both north of the Pasig and elsewhere.[18]

The 148th Infantry Regiment had to cross the Estero de la Reina bridge to approach the Pasig but was stymied by mines and five 500-pound bombs on the bridge, by blazing fires in buildings to its right and front, by exploding demolitions and gasoline drums, and by machine gun fires trained on intersections and streets. Most of the American units approaching the Pasig probably faced similar challenges. Another feature of the early fighting north of the Pasig was that the Japanese Noguchi Detachment on 5 February set fire to major buildings near the river in order to halt the U.S. advance; the Japanese also exploded demolitions in major buildings and in military facilities. Until these fires could be brought under control on 6 February, U.S. personnel were forced back from the river, and the U.S. advance was delayed. The 37th Infantry Division also on 5 February faced interactions with civilians that it would see more of, such as when ". . . swarms of the native population . . . crowded the streets cheering the American troops, forcing gifts upon them, and . . . engaged in unrestrained looting." Both the jubilation and the looting obstructed military operations, and the 37th Infantry Division would see more of both.[19]

By 7 February, U.S. forces were in control of Manila north of the Pasig. Surviving Noguchi Detachment troops had withdrawn south across the river and destroyed all of the bridges. On 5 February, Lieutenant General Oscar W. Griswold, commander of 14th Corps, extended the 37th Infantry Division's area of control eastward into what had been the 1st Cavalry Division's zone and also gave 1st Cavalry responsibility farther to the east. This change made possible the next phase of operations in which the 37th Infantry Division would fight its way across the Pasig in the downtown area while the 1st Cavalry Division swept wide around the city, east, south and west again to the bay, thus isolating the Japanese defenders from any source of resupply or relief.[20]

Many cities contain harbors or lie on rivers so that urban warfare frequently requires some amphibious warfare assets. On 7 February, the 37th Infantry Division began the difficult work of crossing the Pasig. The 148th Infantry Regiment crossed first at 1515. Troops had the benefit of an amphibious tractor battalion and thirty engineer assault boats. They were covered by artillery fire and smoke and departed from four different concealed launch points. The first wave crossed without incident, but the second was raked by machine gun and automatic cannon fire from Japanese positions lying to the west on the south bank of the Pasig. These fires shattered some of the plywood boats and oars. Troops paddled on as best they could with oar handles and rifle butts. The landing area was the Malacanan Gardens, the only point on the south bank without a seawall that would obstruct amphibious tractors and disembarkment. Troops found few Japanese in the disembarkment area and established a bridgehead with little difficulty. On 8 February, the 37th Infantry Division built a pontoon bridge across the Pasig to support the bridgehead. The bridge had two tracks, one for personnel and one for vehicles. No sooner was the bridge built, however, than hundreds of Philippine civilians began pouring across it from south to north, trying to escape the fighting.[21]

The 37th Infantry Division completed its crossing of the Pasig on 8 February and began deploying south and west out of its bridgehead.[22] The hardest fighting the 37th Infantry Division would face in Manila was in this district south of the river, between the crossing of the Pasig on 7 February and the assault on Intramuros on 23 February. Japanese defenders had established a series of strongpoints in major buildings in this area and contested them fiercely. On 8 February, the 129th Infantry Regiment moved westward along the Pasig shore and on 9 February crossed the Estero de Tonque by boat to assault Provisor Island where Manila's steam electrical generation plant was located. The Japanese defenders placed sandbagged machine gun emplacements in buildings and at entrances and were able to blanket the whole island with machine gun positions to the west, southwest, and south. The 129th Infantry Regiment approached the island in engineer assault boats, then conducted a cat and mouse struggle with Japanese for control of the buildings, fighting with machine guns and rifles among the structures and heavy machinery. The 129th was able to secure the island on 10 February, but lost twenty-five troops killed in the process. The vital electrical generation equipment, which Krueger in 6th Army's plans had hoped to capture intact, was hopelessly damaged by both Japanese defenders and American fires.[23]

While the 129th Infantry Regiment swept west out of the Malacanan bridgehead in a close arc, the 148th Infantry Regiment swept southeast in a broad arc, then back westward. The two regiments moved in line through the Pandacan district to the southeast with relatively little resistance, but then found themselves in a pitched battle in the Paco district for control of the Paco Railroad Station, Paco School, and Concordia College. On 9 February, both 129th Infantry Regiment and 148th Infantry Regiment advanced only 300 yards.[24]

Given the new intensity of the fighting in the 37th Infantry Division's sector, the division requested and received a lifting of the restrictions previously imposed on artillery fires. To that point, fires had been restricted to observed enemy positions but had failed to force an enemy withdrawal. Thereafter, fires would be allowed "in front of ... advancing lines without regard to pinpointed targets." In other words, fires could blanket enemy positions U.S. troops were assaulting. "Literal destruction of a building in advance of the area of friendly troops became essential," as the *37th Infantry Division Report After Action* put it.[25]

The Japanese defensive positions U.S. troops encountered in the Paco district were well developed, as they would be for the rest of the battle. Japanese observers were present in almost every building. At street intersections, machine gun pillboxes were dug into buildings and sandbagged so as to cover the intersection and its approaches. Artillery and antiaircraft weapons were placed in doorways or in upper story windows. Most streets and borders of streets were mined, using artillery shells and depth charges buried with their fuses protruding an inch or so above the surface. The streets were a fireswept zone forcing Americans to move between streets and within buildings. Americans entered and searched each building and house, top to bottom, and neutralized whatever enemy they found.[26]

Besides controlling the urban terrain with fires, the Japanese in the Paco district and points west had fortified particular sturdy public buildings as urban strongpoints. In some cases, these buildings were mutually supporting. The first of the urban strongpoints the 37th Infantry Division encountered was the Paco Railroad Station. The Japanese had machine gun posts all around the station, and foxholes with riflemen surrounded each machine gun post. Inside at each corner were sandbag forts with 20mm guns. One large concrete pillbox in the building housed a 37mm gun. About 300 Japanese troops held Paco station. The Japanese placed observers in the Paco church steeple, and the station could not be approached until the Paco School and other neighboring positions had been cleared.[27]

Americans inched forward to within 50 yards of the Paco station building, set up a bazooka or Browning Automatic Rifle (BAR), and pounded the building as riflemen rushed forward covered by fire. The station was finally seized at 0845 on 10 February after 10 assaults. Between the Provisor fighting and the Paco station fighting on 9 and 10 February, the 37th Infantry Division suffered 45 killed in action (KIA) and 307 wounded in action (WIA).[28]

American troops would have much more such fighting ahead. Once the 129th Infantry Regiment and the 148th Infantry Regiment had secured Provisor Island and the Paco Railroad Station respectively, both swept westward toward Intramuros and the bay. The 129th Infantry Regiment collided with the Japanese strongpoint at the New Police Station, and the 148th Infantry Regiment collided with the strongpoint of the Philippine General Hospital (see Map 2). The 129th Infantry Regiment began its assaults on the New Police Station on 12 February. The strongpoint consisted of the police station itself, the shoe factory, the Manila Club, Santa Teresita College and San Pablo Church. By nightfall, the 129th Infantry Regiment had consolidated its lines on Marques de Camillas Street fronting the strongpoint. Maintaining lines—keeping units that advanced faster than others from leaving hazardous gaps in the line—offered many challenges in the highly compartmented urban environment.

The bitter fighting at the New Police Station went on for eight days, until 20 February. On 17 February, the relatively fresh 145th Infantry Regiment replaced the battle-worn 129th Infantry Regiment. The first tanks arrived on 14 February to assist the Americans. Tanks were not present earlier in this part of the city because they could not cross the Pasig. Once committed, they were used for direct-fire bombardment on the New Police Station and in later operations.

The American method was to bombard the resisting structure with tanks and 105mm guns and howitzers, then to conduct an assault. Sometimes the Japanese defenders counterattacked, driving the Americans out, in which case the whole process was repeated. The Japanese had trenches and foxholes outside the buildings and numerous sandbagged machine gun positions inside. U.S. artillery reduced the exterior walls to rubble, but infantry still had to go into the buildings and clear them room by room and floor by floor. The preferred American method was to fight from the roof down, but the troops were unable to do this at the New Police Station, probably because no structures were near enough to give roof access. Thus, they had to work from the ground up. Japanese defenders cut holes in the floors and dropped grenades through them. They also destroyed the stairways to prevent access to upper stories. Nevertheless, the 145th Infantry Regiment managed to secure the New Police Station strongpoint by 20 February.[29]

From 20 to 22 February, the 145th Infantry Regiment repeated this exercise a block to the east at the city hall and general post office. At the city hall, the regiment employed the usual method of having artillery pound the exterior walls and then assaulting into the structure that remained. As at the New Police Station, the process of bombardment and assault had to be repeated several times. Americans in the assault made generous use of "submachine guns, bazookas, flame throwers, demolitions, and hand grenades." At one point when Japanese resisters in a first floor room refused to surrender, the Americans blew holes in the ceiling, put flamethrowers through them, and annihilated all of the defenders. Americans sometimes had to fight their way into prepared positions in the darkened basements of these buildings. By the evening of 22 February, the 145th Infantry Regiment had fought its way through the worst of the strongpoints to the walls of Intramuros.[30]

Meanwhile, the 148th Infantry Regiment was fighting its way through the Philippine General Hospital and the University of the Philippines, operating parallel to and just south of the 129th Infantry Regiment and its follow-on 145th Infantry Regiment (see Map 2). The tactical battle here was similar to that elsewhere but complicated by the fact that there were still civilian patients in the hospital. When the 148th Infantry Regiment discovered this on the afternoon of 16 February, it tried to limit its artillery fires to Japanese positions in the foundations of the hospital buildings. During the day of 17 February, the 148th escorted 2,000 patients out of the hospital, and 5,000 more that night.[31]

On the morning of 19 February, the 5th Cavalry Regiment, having been assigned to the 37th Infantry Division from the 1st Cavalry Division, relieved the battle-worn 148th Infantry Regiment. The 5th Cavalry Regiment continued attacks in this sector on the University of the Philippines strongpoint. The Japanese here not only had established the usual defenses of sandbagged machine gun nests, but also had cut firing slits through the foundations just above the ground and put machine gun nests on the flat roof. After assaults on Rizal Hall, the 75 Japanese survivors of the original complement of 250 committed suicide on the night of 23 February. The next morning, the 5th Cavalry Regiment made the final assaults into University Hall, so concluding the strongpoint fighting for the 148th Infantry Regiment and the follow-on 5th Cavalry Regiment. For these units, as for the northerly 129th and follow-on 145th Infantry Regiments, the hardest strongpoint fighting was now over, and U.S. forces had secured Manila south of Intramuros.[32]

While the battle of the strongpoints raged, 7 to 24 February, the 1st Cavalry Division was sweeping wide east, south, and west, around the city to Manila Bay (see Maps 1 and 2). When the 37th Infantry Division crossed the Pasig at Malacanan Gardens, the 129th Infantry Regiment pivoted sharply west, campaigning toward the east wall of Intramuros.

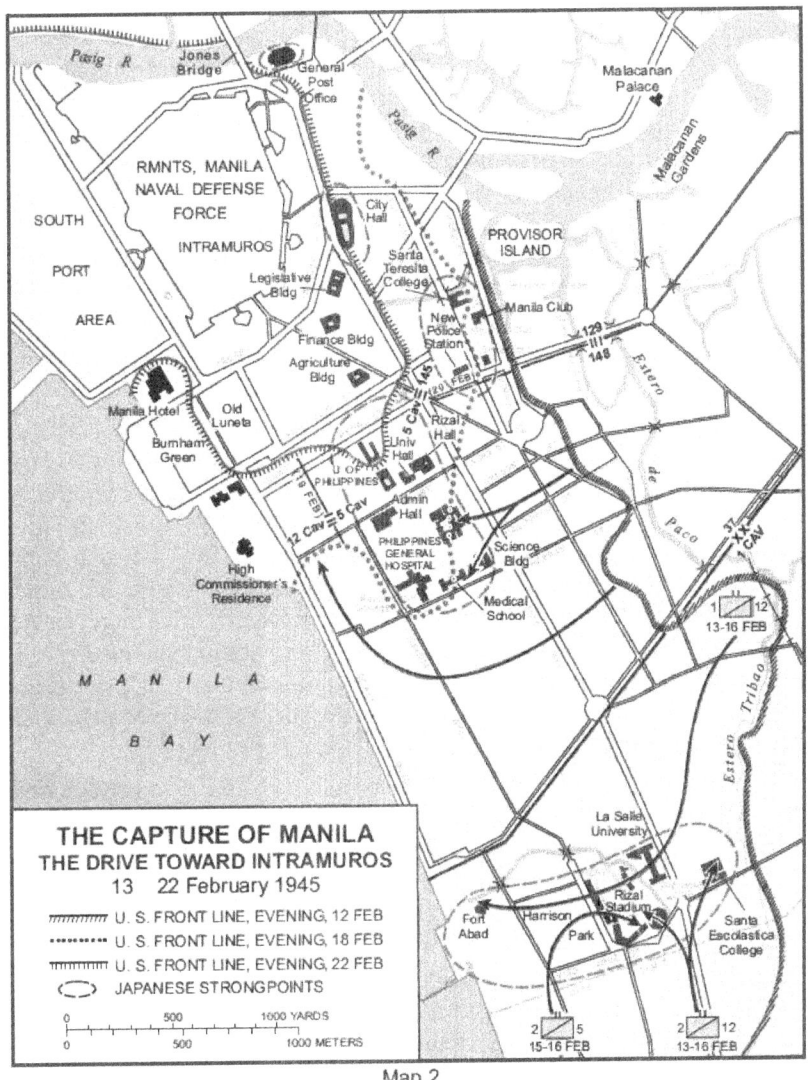

Map 2

The 148th Infantry Regiment swung more broadly south, west, and north, bringing it up against the south wall of Intramuros. The 1st Cavalry Division swung on an axis parallel to these, but flung farther out, around the whole city. Thus, the 1st Cavalry Division implemented a standard element of siege doctrine: isolate the defenders.

On 8 February, as the 37th Infantry Division was crossing the Pasig at Malacanan Gardens, the 5th and 8th Cavalry Regiments began a sweep around the east and south sides of Manila (see Map 1). The 8th Cavalry Regiment swung close and the 5th Cavalry Regiment swung wide. The 8th Cavalry Regiment crossed the Pasig at the Philippine Racing Club against little opposition; the 5th Cavalry Regiment crossed at the suburb of Makati against intermittent machine gun fire. On 10 February, the 5th Cavalry Regiment secured the Makati electrical power substation, following Krueger's policy of sparing as much city infrastructure as possible. By 12 February, both the 12th Cavalry Regiment, relieving the 8th Cavalry Regiment, and the 5th Cavalry Regiment had reached the waterfront, completing the encirclement of the city. They both had contact with the 37th Infantry Division on their right.[33]

Once they reached the waterfront, the 12th Cavalry Regiment and the 5th Cavalry Regiment immediately turned northward, to move up the shore and join their forces to those of the 37th Infantry Division as it closed in on Intramuros (see Map 2). Moving abreast, the two regiments encountered a developed Japanese strongpoint in the Harrison Park area, which contained Rizal Stadium, La Salle University, and other structures. The 1st Cavalry Division fought pitched battles there, as the 37th Infantry Division had at the Paco Railroad Station and elsewhere. Japanese defenders had constructed heavy bunkers all over the baseball diamond at Rizal Stadium, which the 1st Cavalry finally overcame with the use of flamethrowers, demolitions, and three tanks.[34]

On 16 February, the 1st Cavalry Brigade (5th and 12th Regiments) passed from the 1st Cavalry Division's operational control to that of the 37th Infantry Division for the assault on the central city. At this point, the 5th Cavalry Regiment relieved the 148th Infantry Regiment, and the 12th Cavalry Regiment continued advancing northward and on 20-22 February cleared the High Commissioner's Residence, Burnham Green, and the Manila Hotel. There was a hard fight, floor by floor, for the Manila Hotel, and MacArthur himself appeared on the scene, since he had resided in a penthouse apartment of the Manila Hotel during his former stay in the Philippines.[35]

By 23 February, the 37th Infantry Division had fought its way to the eastern wall of the Japanese stronghold of Intramuros and was prepared to assault it. Intermittent bombardment of the fortress began on 17 February. There was then a focused bombardment from 0730 to 0830 on 23 February, the day of the assault. This preparation employed an abundance of 105mm and 155mm howitzers, 75mm tank guns, 4.2-inch mortars, a few 8-inch howitzers, and other pieces; in other words, it was almost all of the 37th Infantry Division's artillery assets. The 8-inch howitzers proved most effective against the thick walls of Intramuros. Thirty machine guns were used for the artillery preparations, of which 26 were trained on Japanese machine gun positions and four were reserved for targets of opportunity before and during the assault. Overall, 7,487 high-explosive shells were dropped on Intramuros.[36]

At 0830, a red smoke signal was fired to mark the end of the artillery preparation and the beginning of the assault. Ten minutes later, a second bombardment began placing a smokescreen east to west across the central section of Intramuros to obscure the north-lying assaults from Japanese gunners in the south-lying Legislative, Finance and Agriculture Buildings (see Map 3). The 129th Infantry Regiment assaulted southward across the Pasig in engineer boats at 0830, the first troops disembarking at 0836. Simultaneously the 145th Infantry Regiment assaulted the east wall. Japanese fires within Intramuros evidently were less intense than in earlier encounters because the heavy bombardment had destroyed or disorganized them. Both the 129th Infantry and the 145th Infantry Regiments therefore moved easily through the breached walls and then through the streets of Intramuros. The 145th Infantry Regiment's progress was soon blocked, however, by the flow of 2,000 refugees, women and children, from Del Monico

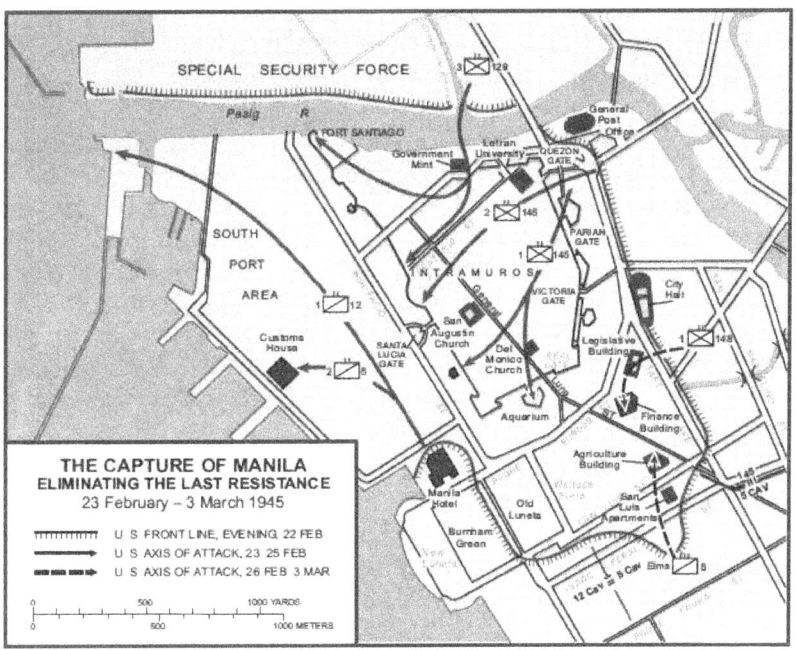

Map 3

Church on General Luna Street where the Japanese had been holding them. Many would be evacuated from the west gate of Intramuros by a truck convoy of the 37th Quartermaster Company. Male civilians had evidently been separated by the Japanese, detained in the Intramuros' old citadel, Fort Santiago, and executed there en masse. By nightfall of 23 February, the 129th and 145th Infantry Regiments held nearly all of Intramuros and would secure the rest the next day.[37]

The hardest fighting in Intramuros was the 129th's effort to capture Fort Santiago in the northwest corner of the old walls. They fought room to room, and then through subterranean dungeons and tunnels, using flamethrowers, phosphorus grenades, demolitions, and bazookas. In some cases, they poured gasoline or oil through holes in the floor then ignited it to flush out the die-in-place defenders. The regiment did not secure the last of the fort's tunnels until 1200 on 25 February.[38]

During the fighting in Intramuros, some Japanese troops attempted to exfiltrate wearing U.S. uniforms and carrying M1 rifles. Others showed a white flag in the belfry of Del Monico Church only to follow up with rifle fire. None of this helped them. Only twenty-five Japanese surrendered in the Intramuros fighting, all of them Formosans of the Imperial Japanese Labor Force. At dawn on 26 February, seeing that the Intramuros stronghold had fallen, Rear Admiral Iwabuchi and his staff committed suicide at their headquarters in the Agriculture Building.[39]

Despite the loss of Intramuros, the Japanese still held three strong positions, the Legislative, Finance and Agriculture Buildings, which lay just southeast of the old fortress. Since Iwabuchi had expected U.S. attacks to come from the south, he had fortified these buildings more thoroughly than the more northerly strongpoints. It is probably also for this reason that Iwabuchi had put his headquarters in the Agriculture Building. The Legislative, Finance, and Agriculture Buildings were of reinforced concrete. Window-sited machine guns covered exterior approaches. Sandbags and barricades blocked all ground-level doors and windows. Interiors were also fortified as in other strongpoints.

The U.S. artillery preparation on the buildings began on 25 February. However, the 1st Cavalry Division, then deployed along the bay shore west of Intramuros, reported shells falling on its positions. These were 37th Infantry Division rounds that had overshot the government buildings to fall on the 1st Cavalry Division. Major General Robert S. Beightler, commander of the 37th Infantry Division, immediately ordered a cease-fire at 1050 to resolve this problem by shifting troops out of the fire zone. Fires resumed at 1245.[40]

On 26 February, the 148th Infantry Regiment assaulted the Legislative Building and secured it by 28 February. The regiment's troops were harassed by Japanese firing up through holes in the floor and had to withdraw after their first assault to allow more shelling of the still vigorously resisting defenders. On 26 February, the 5th Cavalry Regiment assaulted the Agriculture Building after an artillery preparation, but troops had to withdraw because of withering Japanese covering fire from the nearby San Luis Terrace Apartments. The 5th Cavalry Regiment had to spend 27 February clearing out the apartments. On 28 February, the regiment returned to the Agriculture Building with a three-hour artillery preparation. Point-blank 155mm howitzer fires alternated with point-blank tank and tank-destroyer fires, with all of these fires aimed no higher than the first floor of the Agriculture Building so as to avoid endangering friendly troops. Much of the Agriculture Building thus pancaked on its own first floor, and the 5th Cavalry Regiment assaulted into what was left. A flamethrower tank reduced a pillbox on the southeast corner, and other tanks swarmed around the building to provide point-blank 75mm fire. The 5th Cavalry Regiment otherwise used flamethrowers, bazookas, and small arms.

On 1 March, the 5th Cavalry Regiment made a surrender appeal to Japanese survivors. When there was no response, the regiment employed demolitions and burning gasoline and oil against remaining defenders. An artillery preparation was applied against the sole remaining Japanese position, the Finance Building, on 28 February and 1 March. A surrender appeal this time garnered twenty-five Japanese responses. After more artillery preparation on 2 March, the 148th Infantry Regiment assaulted the building. They cleared the last of the Japanese defenders from the elevator shaft on top of the building on the morning of 3 March.[41]

On the afternoon of 3 March Lieutenant General Oscar W. Griswold, commander of 14th Corps, reported to General Krueger of 6th Army that all resistance had ceased. The struggle to capture Manila was over.[42] The struggle to administer the battle-torn city, however, was just beginning. U.S. military assets on the scene would play a major part in reviving and running Manila for several weeks after the battle. The task of administering the city was complicated by the enormous toll the battle had taken. U.S. casualties in the battle were 1,010 KIA and 5,565 WIA, for a total of 6,575. Japanese counted dead were 16,665. In addition, there were an estimated 100,000 civilian casualties, of varying degrees of seriousness and of diverse causes; most were probably generated by Japanese executions and atrocities toward

Philippine civilians, by friendly fire from American artillery, and by mishap or exposure associated with dislocation. Much of Manila itself was in ruins. The water system within the city needed extensive repairs. Sewage and garbage collection systems were not functioning. The electrical system was out. Most streets were ruined and public transportation no longer existed. The major government buildings, the Philippine General Hospital, and the University of the Philippines were destroyed, along with many residential districts. The port installations were severely damaged. Besides all this, numerous homeless civilians were milling about seeking food, shelter, and medical care.[43]

U.S. forces in Manila were immediately enlisted for occupation duty. After the battle, the 37th Infantry Division bivouacked near Grace Park, in the northern suburbs. On 5 March, the division was removed from 14th Corps, placed directly under 6th Army, and given the mission of providing security for the city. Troops from the division were distributed to Filipino police stations, and so they had to deal with collaborators brought in by civilians until the Counterintelligence Corps could investigate. Looting was a major problem for the division's security troops. Large-scale looting was conducted during the battle by organized bands of Filipinos who moved just behind the American advance. The looters placed a point man in the American front lines to identify where the spoils were richest, allowing those behind to carry off the goods without delay. American security troops did not try to reverse the looting done during the battle. They stopped further looting when the battle was over, however, by mounting guard and patrol duty throughout the city, 24 hours a day.[44]

Security forces faced the problem of the city being strewn with numerous mines, unexploded shells, and booby traps. Areas where fighting had been heaviest were roped off from the public by military police until the 37th Infantry Division's engineer companies could clear them. On 8 March, the track was blown off a U.S. bulldozer on Dewey Boulevard. There were occasional casualties from mines throughout March. The 117th Engineer Battalion piled fifty tons of cleared mines and shells in Burnham Green Park, where on 16 March these exploded from causes unknown. There were no casualties. The 117th Engineers were also busy repairing warehouses, plumbing and electrical facilities, and building an airstrip and Red Cross recreation center.[45]

Troops of the 37th Infantry Division carried weapons in Manila until 17 March. Since the end of the fighting on 3 March, things had been done on a more relaxed basis. New movies were brought to the units every other night. Seats for the troops were placed in open air, and the block of seats then roped off because of the crowds of civilians who also came and watched. Most of the units began holding dances weekly, attended by Filipinos and expatriate women. The Division Special Service Band sometimes played for these events, although the 2d Battalion, 129th Infantry Regiment had its own orchestra. Troops had fresh food every day, and there were no epidemics. Unit staffs also caught up on paperwork, replenished supplies, and began training the hundreds of arriving replacements. This respite was short-lived, however. 37th Infantry Division marched out of Manila on 29 March to begin its next campaign.[46]

The Japanese defense of Manila had failed. Nevertheless, there are some remarkable features of the Japanese effort. On the one hand, Japanese operations show the shortcomings of trying to fight without training, doctrine, or equipment, and without significant joint support. On the other hand, the Japanese showed how much could be done in defense of a city with nothing to work with but resolute personnel and the resources of a great metropolis.

Japanese tactics were simple but effective. Troops fought in small units that tenaciously defended particular assigned positions. They conducted a static defense with almost no maneuver or coordinated action between positions. On the streets north of the Pasig, they set up minefields and obstacles covered by interlocking machine gun fires. The mines were often made of artillery shells, depth charges, or aerial bombs, and the machine guns were often dismounted naval aviation machine guns. In strongpoints south of the Pasig, the Japanese set up positions in sturdy reinforced-concrete buildings and sometimes put foxholes outside. Typically they swept the approaches with automatic fires sighted through windows or loopholes. They put sandbagged machine gun nests throughout these buildings, sometimes fortified cellars and roofs, and sometimes fired through holes cut in walls, ceilings and floors. In most cases, they chose neither to surrender nor retreat, but instead died in place.

U.S. infantry who faced these positions perceived them as formidable. Nonetheless, it is remarkable what these positions lacked. They had little artillery, no armor, no air support, and few suppressive fire weapons for the close fight. They had almost no field radios allowing communication between units, and almost no trenches or tunnels connecting units. They had almost no underground positions except cellars in buildings. There were limited numbers of Japanese to man these positions: Iwabuchi had only 5,000 troops in the central

Manila force. There was also limited time to prepare: the Japanese army had decided to leave Manila in December 1944.

The Japanese had few artillery pieces compared to the Americans, most of them converted naval guns. They fired isolated rounds randomly or against preregistered junctions or bridges. Apparently, they had no forward observers with radios to direct fires and perhaps also had comparatively limited ammunition. The Japanese appeared to be short on close-range suppressive fire weapons also. There is no report of their using flamethrowers or submachine guns. They had grenades, but sometimes used Molotov cocktails, suggesting local shortages. Most but not all had rifles. Some of the rifles were U.S. makes captured in 1942. In place of rifles, some carried jury-rigged spears made of bayonets on poles. In other words, the Japanese were woefully lacking in both heavy weapons and light weapons. All they really had in abundance were machine guns and automatic cannon. They were fighting the Battle of Manila with naval aviation equipment, not ground warfare equipment.[47]

The Japanese naval defenders in Manila had military discipline and dedication. But they had no doctrine, no training, no armor, no air, little artillery, no communication between positions, no maneuver, no coordination, and no reinforcements. Nonetheless, they held the Americans at bay for four weeks. They showed what could be done by defenders who had nothing to work with but their own resoluteness, urban terrain, and the abundant resources of a great city. The Battle of Manila shows that urban warfare significantly favors the defender.

Although the Japanese navy conducted a remarkable ad hoc defense in Manila, U.S. forces ground their way steadily through the Japanese positions. American tactics were decisively more effective. What were the Americans doing that allowed them to advance? U.S. forces in Manila were practicing modern combined arms warfare against a static defense. They were trained ground forces with abundant troops, equipment, and service assets. They were experienced in fighting in restrictive jungle terrain. To their credit, they used all the assets available to them, except for some capabilities of airpower.

Corps and division staffs made sure that regiments and battalions were operationally and tactically coordinated. Tanks were used to the maximum for direct fires and suppressive fires from the time they became available to 37th Infantry Division on 14 February, and by 1st Cavalry Division throughout. Airpower, however, was never used to bomb or strafe Japanese positions in the city of Manila, as MacArthur repeatedly denied requests from subordinate units for air bombardment. This was a major departure from U.S. combined arms doctrine, justified by MacArthur's desire to spare Philippine civilians in the city. Airpower was used in other ways, however. Cub planes were used continuously for artillery spotting. The 1st Cavalry Division used airpower, indeed joint airpower, for close air support and scouting in the division's sweep around the outer edge of the city. Marine Air Groups 24 and 32, flying from an airstrip near Lingayen Gulf, kept nine shipborne dive-bombers over the 1st Cavalry Division's leading elements, and P-40s from the 5th Air Force flew reconnaissance missions to 1st Cavalry's left and front. Moreover, U.S. airpower closed the skies completely to Japanese aircraft.[48]

The restrictions on air bombardment within the city may have mattered little, however, because the enemy was contained within a confined space easily within artillery range. U.S. forces had abundant artillery assets and could get effects similar to those of air bombardment by employing massed artillery. Initially, artillery fires were also limited by MacArthur to "observed fire on known targets." These restrictions were abandoned on 10 February because of mounting U.S. casualties. This was shortly after the 37th Infantry Division had crossed the Pasig and encountered developed Japanese strongpoints. Permission was obtained for "area artillery fire in front of advancing lines."[49]

The American method, once area artillery fires and tanks became available, was to pulverize the building they faced and then to assault into the remains. They used bazookas and flamethrowers against machine gun nests. They used abundant light suppressive fire weapons, grenades, and mortars, as well as small arms. Sometimes U.S. assaults failed because of withering fire or counterattacks, in which case troops would pull back and repeat the process. Tanks and tank destroyers were used in a direct-fire role for the artillery preparation. Their use beyond that was limited by mines, rubble, and the heavy concrete walls of the buildings themselves. Tanks could not follow infantry into the cellars and onto the roofs. Americans in Manila evidently learned to use their assets as they went along and used them to full advantage. Casualties suffered by the 37th Infantry Division when artillery restrictions were first lifted from 10-12 February averaged twenty-six KIA per day. By 21-23 February, when the division was fighting at city hall and assaulting Intramuros, casualties were down to six KIA per day on average.[50]

The Americans at Manila learned fast. They used artillery and tanks to the fullest to achieve their objectives with minimal loss of friendly troops' lives. The falling friendly casualty rates suggest that American troops between 3 February and 23 February had refined all manner of urban warfare methods, at all operational levels, that allowed them to advance more efficiently at the end than at the beginning. American troops had superior assets from the start; by the end, they knew how to use them. Americans won at Manila because they applied a full range of combined arms methods against a static defense. They got better at it as they went along.

The Battle of Manila offers many lessons and insights that may be applicable to future instances of urban warfare. Some of these insights are tactical in nature. They show how to cope with the enemy force. Others are civil in nature. They show how to cope with the civilian population and with objectives relating to the civilian population. Many of the tactical lessons of Manila we have already explored in examining the methods of Japanese and U.S. forces. Some of these lessons are applicable to combined arms warfare in general, not exclusively to urban warfare. Some of the tactical features of Manila, however, are peculiar to cities and likely to recur in operations in other cities.

The tactical battle of Manila, like many other urban conflicts, was a tale of fire and water. On 5 February, the 37th Infantry Division was stymied by raging fires that it had no way to fight or bring under control. The possibility of fire is endemic to urban environments. Manila showed that firefighting may be a feature of urban warfare for ground forces. The Manila fighting also demonstrated that urban warfare may have an amphibious war aspect. Both the 37th Infantry Division and the 1st Cavalry Division repeatedly had to cross rivers and esteros in assault boats and on pontoon bridges, often under fire. Though little came of it, the Japanese defenders attempted an amphibious envelopment of American lines on 7 February, using barges on Manila Bay. The final Manila operation for Americans was the search on 6-7 March by elements of the 129th Infantry Regiment, deployed on landing craft, of 32 ships sunk in the harbor where Japanese continued to resist.[51] The amphibious element is not unique to Manila. Almost all great cities are situated on a river or harbor or both. Urban fighting usually requires some projection over water.

Several artillery issues at Manila are characteristic of urban warfare. To avoid counterbattery fire, Japanese defenders put 75mm guns on trucks and moved them after firing. A shell passing through a target was a concern in Manila; shelling a building could jeopardize friendly troops on the other side. This is a case where some urban operations would necessitate more coordination than other forms of ground warfare. Some other artillery issues are more difficult to resolve. When is it justified to use massive area artillery bombardment, or air bombardment, when civilians may be present? It is a question that probably must be answered case by case. Commanders may be prudent to think through this question before they are in an operational situation. Study of the Manila battle may help them to do that.

Manila offered some tactical lessons for armor. Urban warfare is often siege warfare. Driving tanks around the city will not bring victory in itself, but it may achieve the first stage of victory, which is to isolate the enemy. Within Manila, tanks were useful for direct artillery fire and to suppress pillboxes in the open. Tanks could not get into the buildings, however, just as tanks cannot get into caves. Tanks accompanied infantry to the wall. Once through the wall, infantry were on their own. Tank movement was inhibited in Manila. Tanks did not reach the 37th Infantry Division until 14 February because they could not cross the light pontoon bridges over the Pasig. Japanese defenders had mined approach routes, so mine-clearing operations delayed tank movement every time lines moved forward. Electromagnetic mine detectors did not work because of all the metal already present in debris on the street.[52] Sometimes rubble thrown down by the giant artillery bombardments obstructed the tanks. Tanks were useful in Manila, but not as decisive as they would be in maneuver battles over open ground.

Infantry did the hardest work at Manila. Artillery reduced the walls, and armor accompanied them to the walls. The greatest challenge, however, lay inside the walls. Indoor fighting in Manila resembled World War I trench warfare in that it was heavily reliant on light suppressive fire weapons, flamethrowers, bazookas, mortars, and grenades. As in World War I, force fatigue was a potential problem, a problem that U.S. commanders astutely minimized by replacing fighting regiments with fresh regiments after about 14 days of heavy engagement.[53]

While Manila offers many tactical lessons pertinent to the military dimension of urban warfare, it also offers many lessons in the other dimension of urban warfare—the civic dimension. In this dimension, problems were not always as amenable to technical solutions as they had been in the military dimension.

What were Manila's lessons for civil affairs? Operators faced two categories of problems, one being to preserve or revive the functions of the city as a whole, and the other being to provide for the multitude of citizens as individuals. The Sixth Army was keen to keep the major collective services in the city—water and electricity—from being destroyed. The 1st Cavalry Division succeeded in preserving most of the water system, which lay outside the city, but the electrical steam power generator at Provisor Island within the city was destroyed, in spite of Sixth Army's good intentions. Moreover, the city's refuse collection stopped, the sewage system was damaged, public transportation ceased to function, and roads and bridges were destroyed throughout the central city. Local government barely had existed in Manila during the early weeks of the battle but was revived soon after MacArthur reestablished the Commonwealth Government on 28 February. Local authorities, although they existed after 28 February, were heavily assisted by the 37th Infantry Division until the latter's departure on 29 March. The division also performed major service after the battle by keeping order, clearing mines, and helping repair facilities. The lesson of Manila as regards collective municipal functions—government, water, electricity, and the like—is to do as the 1st Cavalry Division and the 37th Infantry Division did: safeguard them as much as possible and, failing that, restore them as soon as possible.

The multitude of civilians also provided many challenges for U.S. forces in Manila. Civilians in pursuit of various purposes sometimes obstructed military activity for the 37th Infantry and the 1st Cavalry Divisions. One of these cases was the celebration by jubilant crowds at the beginning of the battle. This public celebration impaired force movement, though it may also have helped troop morale. On several occasions during the battle, civilians fled against or across the U.S. axis of advance, obstructing movement or fire. The presence of civilians made U.S. authorities unwilling to use air bombardment and reluctant to use area artillery fire. Americans believed Japanese were establishing positions in facilities such as hospitals and churches where civilians were present, knowing U.S. artillery would not fire on them there.[54] In one case, at Santo Tomás, civilians were held hostage by Japanese troops in exchange for safe passage of lines.

Besides hampering military operations, civilians often made positive demands on U.S. service support activities that could not be ignored. At Bilibid Prison, the 37th Infantry Division was suddenly forced to evacuate, then house some 1,300 internees in the way of an advancing fire. Civilians injured in the battle, some of whom were victims of Japanese atrocities, came to U.S. medical aid stations for help.[55] Finally, individual civilians immediately after the battle depended on military personnel to maintain order and protect them from looting and other transgressions.

The lesson here for operators in an urban warfare environment is that they must be prepared to exercise patience in their operations given that in urban terrain, more than any other terrain, there are likely to be numerous nonbelligerents present. The lesson for planners in an urban warfare environment is to make sure that friendly forces have a superabundance of food and medical supplies, and of service assets, medical transportation, engineering, and so on. During and especially after the battle, they may have to devote these to that part of the mission objective that is to reestablish the fabric of civic life. The Manila battle is rich in lessons for urban warfare in its civil dimension as well as in its military dimension.

Notes

1. For this and following information on Manila, see Robert R. Smith, *Triumph in the Philippines, The War in the Pacific, United States Army in World War II* (Washington, DC: Center of Military History, 1993 [1963]), 237-40, and Stanley A. Frankel, *The 37th Infantry Division in World War II* (Washington, DC: Infantry Journal Press, 1948), 243-47.
2. Smith, 241-42, appendix D and appendix E.
3. Ibid., 242-44.
4. *Reports of General MacArthur, 2v.*, Gordon W. Prange, ed., Volume II, Part II (Washington, DC: Center of Military History, 1944 [1966]), (hereafter *MacArthur Reports II*), 498; Smith, 271-73; Richard Connaughton, John Pimlott, and Duncan Anderson, *The Battle for Manila* (Novato, CA: Presidio Press, 1995), 142.
5. Ibid., 141-42.
6. Ibid., 143, 187; and U.S. Army, 37th Infantry Division, *Report After Action on Operations of the 37th Infantry Division, M 1 Operations* (Headquarters, 37th Infantry Division, 1945) (hereafter 37th Infantry Division), 47. For organization of Japanese forces in Manila area see Smith, appendix D.
7. Smith, 308; Connaughton, 189-91; and 37th Infantry Division, 51.
8. Smith, 244-45.
9. Ibid., 241-42, and Connaughton, 186-87.
10. Ibid., 83, 180-81.
11. Smith, 249; Connaughton, 83, 179-81; and *Reports of General MacArthur, 2v.*, Gordon W. Prange, ed., Volume I (Washington, DC: Center of Military History, 1994 [1966]), (hereafter *MacArthur Reports I*), 276.
12. Smith, 249-50. For U.S. urban warfare doctrine of the day, see U.S. War Department, Field Manual 31-50, *Attack on a Fortified Position and Combat in Towns* (Washington, DC: 31 January 1944).
13. Connaughton, 83-84; Smith 217-18; Frankel, 242; and Bertram C. Wright, *The 1st Cavalry Division in World War II* (Tokyo: Toppan Printing Co., 1947), 128-29.
14. Wright, 129.
15. Smith, 251-52; Wright, 132-33; and Frankel, 255.
16. Smith, 250-51, 256, and Wright, 133.
17. Smith, 253-54; 37th Infantry Division, 41, 43; and Frankel, 254, 259.
18. Smith, 253.
19. Frankel, 252, 254-57; Smith, 255; and 37th Infantry Division, 41.
20. 37th Infantry Division, 43, and Smith, 254.
21. Connaughton, 109; 37th Infantry Division, 45; Smith, 259-60; and Frankel, 272.

22. 37th Infantry Division, 47.
23. Smith, 260-63; 37th Infantry Division, 49, 51; and Frankel, 275-76.
24. 37th Infantry Division, 49.
25. Ibid., 51.
26. Ibid.
27. Frankel, 273-75, and 37th Infantry Division, 49.
28. Frankel, 273, 275, and 37th Infantry Division, 49, 52.
29. Above account of New Police Station strongpoint drawn from Frankel, 276-80, and Smith, 280-83.
30. Above account of city hall and general post office strongpoints drawn from Smith, 284-85, and Frankel, 280.
31. Smith, 285-87.
32. Ibid., 287-90.
33. Wright, 134, 136; Smith, 264-65, 269; and Connaughton, 84-85.
34. Smith, 277-78.
35. Smith, 279-80, and Connaughton, 180.
36. *The 129th Infantry in World War II*, Regimental Staff ed. (Washington, DC: Infantry Journal Press, 1947) (hereafter *129th Infantry*), 107; Smith, 294, 296; and 37th Infantry Division, 77, 79.
37. Smith, 297-300; 37th Infantry Division, 79, 81; and Frankel, 291.
38. *129th Infantry*, 108; Smith, 298; and 37th Infantry Division, 83.
39. 37th Infantry Division, 81; Connaughton, 170-71; and Frankel, 292-93.
40. Smith, 303; Connaughton, 188; Frankel, 293-94; and 37th Infantry Division, 86.
41. Smith, 303-306; Frankel, 294-95; and 37th Infantry Division, 86.
42. Smith, 306.
43. Ibid., 307; Frankel, 295-96; General Walter Krueger, *From Down Under to Nippon, The Story of Sixth Army in World War II* (Washington, DC: Combat Forces Press, 1953), 251; Wright, 136; and *129th Infantry*, 97.
44. Frankel, 297-98; 37th Infantry Division, 88; and *129th Infantry*, 109.
45. Frankel, 299.
46. Ibid., 299-303, and *129th Infantry*, 110.
47. 37th Infantry, 43; Smith, 308; and Connaughton, 190-91.
48. On coordinating advance and consolidating lines, see Frankel, 276. On tanks, see 37th Infantry Division, 59. On airpower, see Smith 235, 249-50, 264, 294.
49. Ibid., 249-50, 263-64, 296, and 37th Infantry Division, 51.
50. 37th Infantry Division, 53, 55, 75, 77, 81.
51. Frankel, 261, and *129th Infantry*, 109.
52. 37th Infantry Division, 59.
53. Ibid., 65, 67.

54. Connaughton, 123; 37th Infantry Division, 53; and Frankel, 278.
55. Frankel, 277. For atrocities, see Connaughton, 113-25.

Bibliography

The 129th Infantry in World War II. Regimental Staff, ed. Washington, DC: Infantry Journal Press, 1947. History of the 129th Infantry Regiment in the Pacific in World War II, prepared by the regimental staff. Describes operational events as seen at the regimental level. Useful appendixes.

Connaughton, Richard, John Pimlott, and Duncan Anderson. *The Battle for Manila.* Novato, CA: Presidio Press, 1995. Excellent single-volume treatment of the Manila battle. Synthesizes earlier literature and provides interesting insights of its own.

Frankel, Stanley A. *The 37th Infantry Division in World War II.* Washington, DC: Infantry Journal Press, 1948. A history of the 37th Infantry Division's service in the Pacific written apparently on behalf of the 37th Division's Veterans Association. Describes operational events and is especially good for details relating to divisional morale and unusual challenges the division faced. Useful appendixes.

Krueger, General Walter. *From Down Under to Nippon, The Story of Sixth Army in World War II.* Washington, DC: Combat Forces Press, 1953. Memoir of the commander of Sixth Army in the Pacific. Describes succinctly Sixth Army's Pacific operations.

Reports of General MacArthur, 2v. Gordon W. Prange, ed. Washington, DC: Center of Military History, 1994 [1966]. Authoritative account of the Pacific war compiled by MacArthur's staff in Japan shortly after World War II. Volume I addresses U.S. operations in the Pacific, and Volume II addresses Japanese operations in the Pacific.

Smith, Robert R. *Triumph in the Philippines, The War in the Pacific, United States Army in World War II.* Washington, DC: Center of Military History, 1993 [1963]. Official U.S. Army history of the Philippine campaign of 1944-1945. Contains detailed coverage of combat events, maps, casualty figures, and the like for U.S. ground forces.

U.S. Army. 37th Infantry Division. *Report After Action on Operations of the 37th Infantry Division, M 1 Operations.* Headquarters, 37th Infantry Division, 1945. The day-by-day after-action report of the 37th Infantry Division. Describes daily deployments and results for the division. Thoughtful commentary is provided at many points by division staff officers.

U.S. War Department. Field Manual 31-50. *Attack on a Fortified Position and Combat in Towns.* Washington, DC, 31 January 1944. Field manual describing U.S. Army doctrine for urban warfare during World War II.

Wright, Bertram C. *The 1st Cavalry Division in World War II*. Tokyo: Toppan Printing Company, 1947. History of the Pacific campaigns of the 1st Cavalry Division compiled by the division historian. Colloquial in tone. Contains numerous photos and useful appendixes.

The Battle for Hue, 1968

James H. Willbanks

On 8 March 1965, elements of the U.S. 9th Marine Expeditionary Force came ashore in Vietnam at Da Nang, ostensibly to provide security for the U.S. air base there. A month later, President Lyndon Johnson authorized the use of U.S. ground troops for offensive combat operations in Vietnam. These events marked a significant change in U.S. involvement in the ongoing war between the South Vietnamese government and its Communist foes. Heretofore, U.S. forces had been supporting the South Vietnamese with advisers and air support, but with the arrival of the Marines, a massive U.S. buildup ensued that resulted in 184,300 American troops in Vietnam by the end of 1965. This number would rapidly increase until over 319,000 troops were in country by the end of 1967.[1]

Eventually, U.S. ground troops were deployed in all four corps tactical zones and actively conducted combat operations against the southern-based Viet Cong (VC) and their counterparts from North Vietnam, the People's Army of Vietnam (PAVN—also known as the North Vietnamese Army or NVA). The first major battle between U.S. forces and PAVN troops occurred in November 1965 in the Ia Drang Valley. Over the next two years, U.S. forces conducted many large-scale search-and-destroy operations such as MASHER/WHITE WING, ATTLEBORO, CEDAR FALLS, and JUNCTION CITY. These operations were designed to find and destroy the enemy forces in a war of attrition. By the end of 1967, however, the war in Vietnam had degenerated into a bloody stalemate. U.S. and South Vietnamese operations had inflicted high casualties and disrupted Communist operations, but the North Vietnamese continued to infiltrate troops into South Vietnam. Nevertheless, General William Westmoreland, commander of U.S. forces in Vietnam, was very optimistic that progress was being made; on 21 November 1967, he appeared before the National Press Club in Washington and asserted, "We have reached an important point when the end begins to come into view. I am absolutely certain that, whereas in 1965 the enemy was winning, today he is certainly losing. The enemy's hopes are bankrupt."[2] Events in 1968 would prove him wrong.

The plan for the 1968 Tet Offensive was born in the summer of 1967. Frustrated with the stalemate on the battlefield and concerned with the aggressive American tactics during the previous year, Communist leaders in Hanoi (the North Vietnamese capital) decided to launch a general offensive to strike a decisive blow against the South Vietnamese and their U.S. allies. This campaign was designed to break the stalemate and achieve three objectives: provoke a general uprising among the people in the south, shatter the South Vietnamese armed forces, and convince the Americans that the war was unwinnable. The offensive would target the previously untouched South Vietnamese urban centers. The Communists prepared for the coming offensive by a massive buildup of troops and equipment in the south. At the same time, they launched a series of diversionary attacks against remote outposts designed to lure U.S. forces into the countryside away from the population areas. In the fall of 1967, the plan went into effect with Communist attacks in the areas south of the Demilitarized Zone (DMZ) separating North and South Vietnam along South Vietnam's western border in the Central Highlands. The main effort of this preliminary phase of the offensive began on 21 January 1968 at Khe Sanh in northwestern South Vietnam, where two PAVN divisions lay siege to the Marine base there. Believing that the Communists were trying to achieve another Dien Bien Phu, President Johnson declared that Khe Sanh would be held at all costs.[3]

With all eyes on Khe Sanh, the Communists launched the main offensive itself in the early morning hours of 31 January 1968, when 84,000 North Vietnamese and VC troops, taking advantage of the Tet (lunar New Year) cease-fire then in effect, mounted simultaneous assaults on thirty-six of forty-four provincial capitals, five of the six autonomous cities, including Saigon and Hue, sixty-four of 242 district capitals, and fifty hamlets. Many of the South Vietnamese troops were on holiday leave, so the Communist forces initially enjoyed widespread success. Within days, however, all of the attacks in the smaller towns and hamlets were turned back. Heavy fighting continued for a while longer in Kontum and Ban Me Thuot in the Central Highlands, in Can Tho and Ben Tre in the Mekong Delta, and in Saigon itself.

The longest and bloodiest battle of the Tet Offensive occurred in Hue, the most venerated city in Vietnam. Located astride Highway 1 ten kilometers west of the coast and a hundred kilometers south of the DMZ, Hue was the capital of Thua Thien Province and South Vietnam's third largest city, with a wartime population of 140,000 (see Map 1). It was the old imperial capital and served as the cultural and intellectual center of Vietnam. It had been treated almost as an open city by the VC and North Vietnamese and thus had remained remarkably free of war. Although there had been sporadic mortar and rocket attacks in the area, Hue itself had been relatively peaceful and secure prior to Tet in

Map 1

1968. Nevertheless, the city was on one of the principal land supply routes for the allied troops occupying positions along the DMZ to the north, and it also served as a major unloading point for waterborne supplies that were brought inland via the river from Da Nang on the coast.

Hue was really two cities divided by the Song Huong, or River of Perfume, which flowed through the city from the southwest to the northeast on its way to the South China Sea ten kilometers to the east. One-third of the city's population lived north of the river within the walls of the Old City, or Citadel, a picturesque place of gardens, pagodas, moats, and intricate stone buildings. Just outside the walls of the Citadel to the east was the densely populated district of Gia Hoi (see Map 2).

The Citadel

The Citadel was an imposing fortress, begun in 1802 by Emperor Gia Long with the aid of the French and modeled on Peking's Forbidden City. Once the residence of the Annamese emperors who had ruled the central portion of present-day Vietnam, the Citadel covered three square miles and really included three concentric cities and a labyrinth of readily defensible positions. The Citadel was protected by an outer wall 30 feet high and up to 90 feet thick, which formed a square about 3,000 yards on each side. Three sides were straight, while the fourth was rounded slightly to follow the curve of the river. The three walls not bordering the river were encircled by a zigzag moat that was 90 feet wide at many points and up to 12 feet deep. Many areas of the wall were honeycombed with bunkers and tunnels that had been constructed by the Japanese when they occupied the city in World War II.

The Citadel included block after block of row houses, parks, villas, shops, various buildings, and an airstrip. Within the Citadel was another enclave: the Imperial Palace compound, where the emperors had held court until 1883 when the French returned to take control of Vietnam. Located at the south end of the Citadel, the palace was essentially a square with 20-foot-high walls that measured 700 meters per side. The Citadel and the Imperial Palace were a "camera-toting tourist's dream," but they would prove to be "a rifle-toting infantryman's nightmare."[4]

South of the river and linked to the Citadel by the six-span Nguyen Hoang Bridge, over which Route 1 passed, lay the modern part of the city. This was about half the size of the Citadel and included about two-thirds of the city's population. The southern half of Hue contained the hospital, the provincial prison, the Catholic cathedral and many of the

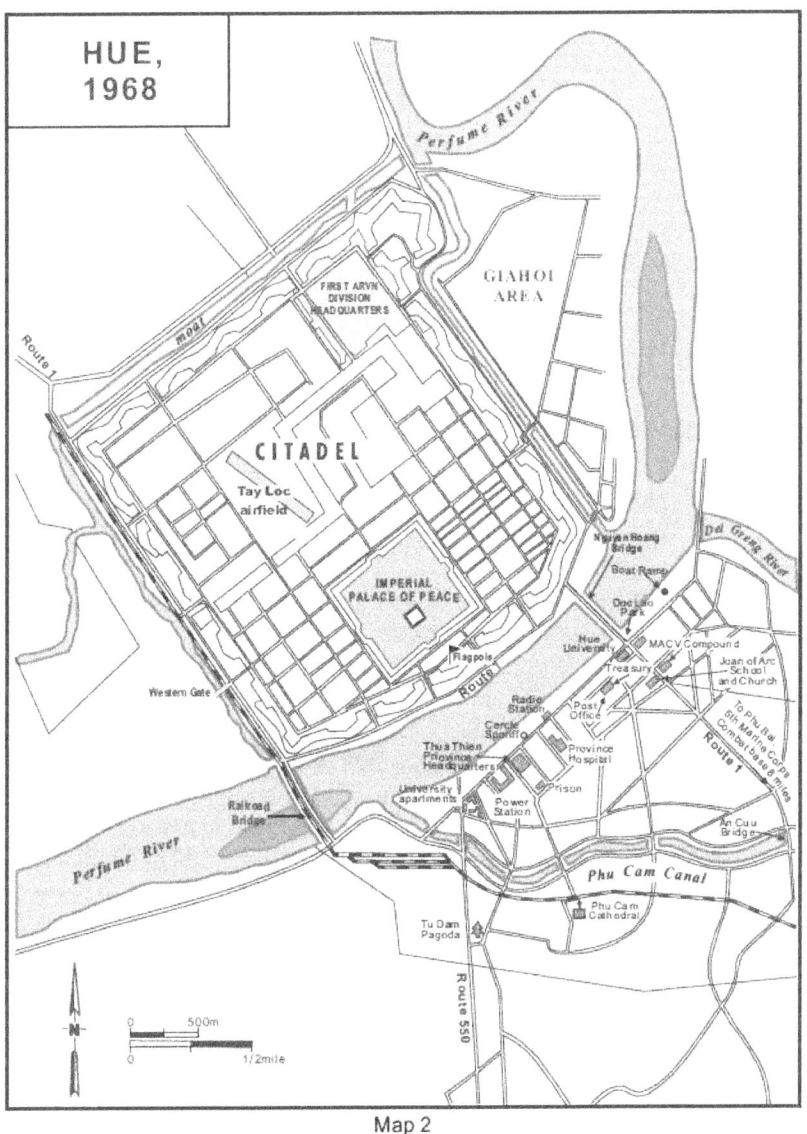

Map 2

city's modern structures, to include government administrative buildings, the U.S. Consulate, Hue University, the city's high school, and the newer residential districts.

The 1st Infantry Division Army of the Republic of Vietnam (ARVN) was headquartered in Hue, but most of its troops were spread out along

Highway 1, from Hue north toward the DMZ. The division headquarters was located at the northwest corner of the Citadel in a fortified compound protected by 6- to 8-foot-high walls, topped by barbed wire. The closest South Vietnamese unit was the 3d ARVN Regiment, with three battalions, that was located 5 miles northwest of Hue. A fourth ARVN battalion was operating some miles southwest of the city. The only combat element in the city was the division's Hac Bao Company, known as the "Black Panthers," an elite all-volunteer unit that served as the division reconnaissance and rapid reaction force. Security within the city itself was primarily the responsibility of the National Police.

The only U.S. military presence in Hue when the battle began was the MACV (Military Assistance Command, Vietnam) compound, which housed 200 U.S. Army, U.S. Marine Corps, and Australian officers and men who served as advisers to the 1st ARVN Division. They maintained a lightly fortified compound on the eastern edge of the modern part of the city south of the river about a block and a half south of the Nguyen Hoang Bridge.

The nearest U.S. combat base was at Phu Bai, 8 miles south along Route 1. Phu Bai was a major Marine Corps command post and support facility that was the home of Task Force X-Ray, which had been established as a forward headquarters of the 1st Marine Division. The task force, commanded by Brigadier General Foster C. "Frosty" LaHue, assistant commander of the 1st Marine Division, was made up of two Marine regimental headquarters and three battalions—the 5th Regiment with two battalions and the 1st Regiment with one battalion. Most of these troops, including LaHue, had only recently arrived in the Phu Bai area, having been displaced from Da Nang, and they were still getting acquainted with the area of operations when the Communists launched their attack on Hue.

In addition to the U.S. Marines, there were also U.S. Army units in the area. Two brigades of the 1st Cavalry Division were scattered over a wide area from Phu Bai in the south to landing zone (LZ) Jane just south of Quang Tri in the north. The 1st Brigade of the 101st Airborne Division had recently been attached to the 1st Cavalry and had just arrived at Camp Evans (located north along Highway 1 between Hue and Quang Tri), coming north from its previous area of operations.

Opposing the allied forces in the Hue region were 8,000 Communist troops, a total of ten battalions. These were highly trained North Vietnamese regular army units that had come south either across the DMZ or more likely, down the Ho Chi Minh Trail. They were armed with AK-47 assault rifles, RPD machineguns, and B-40 rocket-propelled grenade launchers. In addition, the PAVN had 107-millimeter (mm), 122mm, and 140mm free-flight rockets; 82mm and 120mm mortars; recoilless rifles; and heavy machine guns. The North Vietnamese units were joined by six VC main force battalions, including the 12th and Hue City Sapper Battalions.[5] A typical main-force VC infantry battalion consisted of 300 to 600 veteran, skilled fighters. The VC soldiers were armed similar to the PAVN except that they did not have some of the heavier weapons.[6] During the course of the battle for Hue, the total Communist force in and around the city would grow to twenty battalions when three additional infantry regiments were dispatched to the Hue area from the Khe Sanh battlefield.

Before the Tet Offensive began, the Communists had prepared extensive plans for the attack on Hue, which would be directed by General Tran Van Quang, commander of the B4 (Tri Thien-Hue) Front. The plan called for a division-size assault on the city, while other forces cut off access to the city to preclude allied reinforcements. Quang and his senior commanders believed that once the city's population realized the superiority of the Communist troops, the people would immediately rise up to join forces with the VC and PAVN against the Americans and the South Vietnamese, driving them out of Hue. Possessing very detailed information on civil and military installations within the city, the Communist planners had divided Hue into four tactical areas and prepared a list of 196 targets within the city. They planned to use more than 5,000 soldiers to take the city in one swift blow.

Communist documents captured during and after the Tet Offensive indicate that enemy troops received intensive training in the technique of city street fighting before the offensive began.[7] Extremely adept at fighting in the jungles and rice paddies, the PAVN and VC troops required additional training to prepare for the special requirements of fighting in urban areas. This training, focusing on both individual and unit tasks, included offensive tactics, techniques, and procedures to assist in taking the city and defensive measures to help the Communists hold the city once they had seized it.

While the assault troops trained for the battle to come, VC intelligence officers prepared a list of "cruel tyrants and reactionary elements" to be rounded up during the early hours of the attack.[8] This list included most South Vietnamese officials, military officers, politicians, American civilians, and other foreigners. After capture, these individuals were to be evacuated to the jungle outside the city, where they would be punished for their crimes against the Vietnamese people.

The enemy had carefully selected the time for the attack. Because of the Tet holiday, the ARVN defenders would be at reduced strength. In addition, bad weather that traditionally accompanied the northeast monsoon season would hamper aerial resupply operations and impede close air support, which would otherwise have given the allied forces in Hue a considerable advantage.

The city's defense against the impending attack hinged in large part on the leadership of Brigadier General Ngo Quang Truong, commander of the 1st ARVN Division, regarded by many U.S. advisers as one of the best senior commanders in the South Vietnamese armed forces.[9] A 1954 graduate of the Dalat Military Academy, he had won his position through ability and combat leadership and not because of political influence or bribery, as was the case with many of his ARVN peers.

On the morning of 30 January, the beginning of the Tet holiday, Truong received reports of enemy attacks on Da Nang, Nha Trang, and other South Vietnamese installations during the previous night. Sensing that something was up, he gathered his division staff at the headquarters compound and put them and his remaining troops on full alert. Unfortunately, over half of his division was on holiday leave and out of the city. Believing that the Communists would not attack the "open" city directly, Truong positioned the forces left on duty around the city to defend outside the urban area. Therefore, when the Communist attack came, the only regular ARVN troops in the city were from the Hac Bao "Black Panther" reconnaissance company that was guarding the airstrip at the northeastern corner of the Citadel.

Unknown to Truong as he prepared for whatever was to come, there was a clear indication that there would be a direct attack on his city. On the same day that the South Vietnamese commander put his staff on alert, a U.S. Army radio intercept unit at Phu Bai overheard Communist orders calling for an imminent assault on Hue. Following standard procedure, the intercept unit forwarded the message through normal channels. Making its way through several command layers, the intercept and associated intelligence analysis did not make it to the Hue defenders until the city was already under attack.[10]

Even as the intelligence report made its way slowly through channels, the Viet Cong had already infiltrated the city. Wearing civilian garb, Communist troops had mingled with the throngs of people who had come to Hue for the Tet holiday. They had easily transported their weapons and ammunition into the city in wagons, truck beds, and other hiding places. In the early morning hours of 31 January, these soldiers took up initial positions within the city and prepared to link up with the PAVN and VC assault troops. At 0340, the Communists launched a rocket and mortar barrage from the mountains to the west on both old and new sectors of the city. Following this barrage, the assault troops began their attack. The VC infiltrators had donned their uniforms, met their comrades at the gates, and led them in the attack on key installations in the city.

The PAVN 6th Regiment, with two battalions of infantry and the 12th VC Sapper Battalion, launched the main attack from the southwest and moved quickly across the Perfume River into the Citadel toward the ARVN 1st Division headquarters in the northeastern corner. The 800th and 802d Battalions of the 6th Regiment rapidly overran most of the Citadel, but Truong and his staff held the attackers off at the 1st ARVN Division compound, while the Hac Bao Company managed to hold its position at the eastern end of the airfield. On several occasions, the 802d Battalion came close to penetrating the division compound, so Truong ordered the Black Panthers to withdraw from the airfield to the compound to help thicken his defenses there. By daylight on 31 January, the PAVN 6th Regiment held the entire Citadel, including the Imperial Palace. The only exception was the 1st Division compound that remained in South Vietnamese hands; the PAVN 802d Battalion had breached the ARVN defenses on several occasions during the night, but each time they were hurled back by the Black Panthers.

The story was not much better for the Americans south of the river in the new city. It could have been worse, but the North Vietnamese made a tactical error when they launched their initial attack on the MACV compound. Rather than attack immediately on the heels of the rocket and mortar barrage, they waited for approximately 5 minutes. This gave the defenders an opportunity to mount a quick defense. The PAVN 804th Battalion twice assaulted the compound, but the attackers were repelled each time by quickly assembled defenders armed with individual weapons. One U.S. soldier manned an exposed machine gun position atop a 20-foot wooden tower; his fire stopped the first rush of North Vietnamese sappers who tried to advance to the compound walls to set satchel charges, but he was killed by a B-40 rocket. The PAVN troops then stormed the compound gates where they were met by a group of Marines manning a bunker. The Marines held off the attackers for a brief period, but eventually the PAVN took out the defenders with several B-40 rockets. This delay, however, slowed the North Vietnamese attack and gave the Americans and their Australian comrades additional time to organize their defenses. After an intense firefight, the Communists failed to take the compound, so they tried to reduce it with mortars and automatic weapons fire from overlooking buildings. The defenders went to ground and waited for reinforcements.

While the battle raged around the MACV compound, two VC battalions took over the Thua Thien Province headquarters, police station, and other government buildings south of the river. At the same time, the PAVN 810th Battalion occupied blocking positions on the southern edge of the city to prevent reinforcement from that direction. By dawn, the North Vietnamese 4th Regiment controlled all of Hue south of the river except the MACV compound.

Thus, in very short order, the Communists had seized control of virtually all of Hue. When the sun came up on the morning of 31 January, nearly everyone in the city could see the gold-starred, blue and red National Liberation Front flag flying high over the Citadel. While the PAVN and VC assault troops roamed the streets freely and consolidated their gains, political officers began a reign of terror by rounding up the South Vietnamese and foreigners on the special lists. VC officers marched through the Citadel, reading out the names on the lists through loudspeakers and telling them to report to a local school. Those who did not report were hunted down.[11] The detainees were never seen alive again; their fate was not apparent until after the U.S. and South Vietnamese forces recaptured the Citadel and nearly 3,000 civilians were found massacred and buried in mass graves.

As the battle erupted at Hue, other Communist forces had struck in cities and towns from the DMZ to the Ca Mau Peninsula in the south. Allied forces had their hands full all over the country, and it would prove difficult to assemble sufficient uncommitted combat power to oust the Communists from Hue. Additionally, U.S. and South Vietnamese forces had been moved to the west to support the action in and around Khe Sanh, thus reducing the number of troops available in the entire northern region. This situation would have a major impact on the conduct of operations to retake Hue from the Communists.

Brigadier General Truong, who only had a tenuous hold on his own headquarters compound, ordered his 3d Regiment, reinforced with two airborne battalions and an armored cavalry troop, to fight its way into the Citadel from positions northwest of the city. En route these forces encountered intense small-arms and automatic weapons fire as they neared the Citadel. They fought their way through the resistance and reached Truong's headquarters late in the afternoon.

As Truong tried to consolidate his forces, another call for reinforcements went out from the surrounded MACV compound. This plea for assistance was almost lost in all the confusion caused by the simultaneous attacks going on all over I Corps. Lieutenant General Hoang Xuan Lam, commander of the South Vietnamese forces in I Corps, and Lieutenant General Robert Cushman III, Marine Amphibious Force (MAF) commander, were not sure what exactly was happening inside the city. The enemy strength and the scope of the Communist attack was less than clear during the early hours of the battle, but the allied commanders realized that reinforcements would be needed to eject the Communists from Hue. Accordingly, Cushman ordered TF X-Ray to send reinforcements into Hue to relieve the besieged MACV compound.

While both ARVN and U.S. commanders tried to assess the situation and made preparations to move reinforcements to Hue, the North Vietnamese quickly established additional blocking positions to prevent those reinforcements from reaching the beleaguered defenders. The PAVN 806th Battalion blocked Highway 1 northwest of Hue while the PAVN 804th and K4B Battalions took up positions in southern Hue. At the same time, the 810th Battalion dug in along Highway 1 south of Hue.

Responding to III MAF orders, Brigadier General LaHue, commander of TF X-Ray, dispatched Company A, 1st Battalion, 1st Marines (A/1/1), to move up Route 1 from Phu Bai by truck to relieve the surrounded U.S. advisers. The initial report of the attack on Truoung's headquarters and the MACV compound had not caused any great alarm at LaHue's headquarters. The TF commander, having received no reliable intelligence to the contrary, believed that only a small enemy force had penetrated Hue as part of a local diversionary attack; little did he know that almost a full enemy division had seized the city. He therefore sent only one company to deal with the situation. LaHue later wrote that "initial deployment of force was made with limited information."[12]

Not knowing exactly what to expect when they reached the city, the Marines from A/1/1 headed north as ordered, joining up with four M48 tanks from the 3d Tank Battalion en route. The convoy ran into sniper fire and had to stop several times to clear buildings along the route of march. When the convoy crossed the bridge that spanned the Phu Cam Canal into the southern part of the city, the Marines were immediately caught in a withering crossfire from enemy automatic weapons and B-40 rockets that seemed to come from every direction. They advanced slowly against intense enemy resistance, but became pinned down between the river and the canal, just short of the MACV compound they had been sent to relieve. The company commander, Captain Gordon D. Batcheller, was wounded during this fight, as were a number of his Marines.

With his Company A pinned down, Lieutenant Colonel Marcus J. Gravel, the battalion commander of 1/1 Marines, organized a hasty reaction force: himself; his operations officer; some others from his battalion command group; and Company G, 2d Battalion, 5th Marines (G/2/5), a unit from another battalion that had just arrived in Phu Bai earlier that day. Gravel had never met Captain Charles L. Meadows, the Company G commander, until that day, and he later said that the only planning he had time to accomplish was to issue the order: "Get on the trucks, men."[13]

With little information other than that its fellow Marines were pinned down, the relief force moved up the highway, reinforced with two self-propelled, twin 40mm guns. The force met little resistance along the way and linked up with A/1/1st Marines, now being led by a wounded gunnery sergeant. With the aid of the four tanks and the 40mm self-propelled guns, the combined force fought its way to the MACV compound, breaking through to the beleaguered defenders at about 1515. The cost, however, was high: ten Marines were killed and thirty were wounded.

Having linked up with the defenders of the MACV compound, Lieutenant Colonel Gravel received new orders from LaHue, directing him to cross the Perfume River with his battalion and break through to the ARVN 1st Division headquarters in the Citadel. Gravel protested that

Co H, 2d Bn, 5th Marine troops take cover in heavy fighting in Hue City.

his "battalion" consisted of only two companies, one of which was in pretty bad shape, and that part of his force would have to be left behind to assist with the defense of the MACV compound. Nevertheless, LaHue, who still had not realized the full extent of the enemy situation in Hue, radioed back that Gravel was to "go anyway."[14] Sending Gravel's battered force to contend with the much stronger PAVN and VC north of the river would ultimately result in failure.

Leaving Company A behind to help with the defense of the MACV compound, Gravel took Company G, reinforced with three of the original M48 tanks and several others from the ARVN 7th Armored Cavalry Squadron, and moved out to comply with LaHue's orders. Leaving the tanks on the southern bank to support by fire, Gravel and his Marines attempted to cross the Nguyen Hoang bridge leading into the Citadel. As the infantry started across the bridge, they were met with a hail of fire from a machine gun position at the north end of the bridge. Ten Marines went down. Lance Corporal Lester A. Tully, who later received the Silver Star for his action, rushed forward and took out the machine gun nest with a grenade. Two platoons followed Tully, made it over the bridge, and turned left, paralleling the river along the Citadel's southeast wall. They immediately came under heavy fire from AK-47 rifles, heavy automatic weapons, B-40 rockets, and recoilless rifles from the walls of the Citadel.

As mortar shells and rockets exploded around them, the Marines tried to push forward but were soon pinned down by the increasing volume of enemy fire. Gravel determined that his force was greatly outnumbered and decided to withdraw. However, even that proved very difficult. According to Gravel, the enemy was well dug-in and "firing from virtually every building in Hue city" north of the river.[15] Gravel called for vehicle support to assist in evacuating his wounded, but none was available. Eventually, the Marines commandeered some abandoned Vietnamese civilian vehicles and used them as makeshift ambulances. After 2 hours of intense fighting, the company was able to pull back to the bridge. By 2000, the 1st Battalion had established a defensive position near the MACV compound along a stretch of riverbank that included a park (which they rapidly transformed into a helicopter LZ). The attempt by the Marines to force their way across the bridge had been costly. Among the casualties was Major Walter D. Murphy, the S3 Operations Officer of the 1st Battalion, who later died from his wounds. Captain Meadows, commander of Company G, lost one-third of his unit killed or wounded "going across that one bridge and then getting back across the bridge."[16]

At Phu Bai, despite detailed reports from Gravel, LaHue, and his intelligence officers still did not have a good appreciation of what was happening in Hue. As LaHue later explained, "Early intelligence did not reveal the quantity of enemy involved that we subsequently found were committed to Hue."[17] The intelligence picture in Saigon was just as confused; General Westmoreland, commander of U.S. MACV, cabled General Earle Wheeler, Chairman of the Joint Chiefs of Staff, that the "enemy has approximately three companies in the Hue Citadel and Marines have sent a battalion into the area to clear them out."[18] This repeated gross underestimation of enemy strength in Hue resulted in insufficient forces being allocated for retaking the city.

With Brigadier General Truong and the 1st ARVN Division fully occupied in the Citadel north of the river, Lieutenant General Lam and Lieutenant General Cushman discussed how to divide responsibility for the effort to retake Hue. They eventually agreed that ARVN forces would be responsible for clearing Communist forces from the Citadel and the rest of Hue north of the river, while TF X-Ray would assume responsibility for the southern part of the city. This situation resulted in what would be, in effect, two separate and distinct battles that would rage in Hue, one south of the river and one north of the river.

In retaking Hue, Lam and Cushman were confronted with a unique problem. The ancient capital was sacred to the Vietnamese people, particularly so to the Buddhists. The destruction of the city would result in political repercussions that neither the United States nor the government of South Vietnam could afford. Cushman later recalled, "I wasn't about to open up on the old palace and all the historical buildings there."[19] As a result, limitations were imposed on the use of artillery and close air support to minimize collateral damage. Eventually these restrictions were lifted when it was realized that both artillery and close air support would be necessary to dislodge the enemy from the city. However, the initial rules of engagement played a key role in the difficulties incurred in the early days of the battle.

Having divided up the city, Cushman—with Westmoreland's concurrence—began to make arrangements to send reinforcements into the Hue area in an attempt to seal off the enemy inside the city from outside support. On 2 February, the U.S. Army 1st Cavalry Division's 3d Brigade entered the battle with the mission of blocking the enemy approaches into the city from the north and west. The brigade airlifted the 2d Battalion, 12th Cavalry (2/12 Cav), into an LZ about 10 kilometers northwest of Hue on Highway 1. By 4 February, the cavalry troopers had moved cross country from the LZ and established a blocking position on a hill overlooking a valley about 6 kilometers west of Hue. This position provided excellent observation of the main enemy routes into and out of Hue.

During the same period, the 5th Battalion, 7th Cavalry (5/7 Cav), conducted search-and-clear operations along enemy routes west of Hue. On 7 February, they made contact with an entrenched North Vietnamese force and tried for the next 24 hours to expel the Communists. However, the enemy forces held their position and stymied the cavalry advance with heavy volumes of automatic weapons and mortar fire. On 9 February, Headquarters, 3d Brigade, 1st Cavalry Division, ordered 5/7 Cav to fix the PAVN in place and directed 2/12 Cav to attack northward from its position. The latter ran into heavy resistance near the village of Thong Bon Ti but continued to fight its way toward 5/7 Cav's position. For the next ten days, the two cavalry battalions fought with the entrenched Communists who held their positions against repeated assaults. Despite the inability of the cavalry troops to expel the North Vietnamese, this action at least partially blocked the enemy's movement and inhibited its participation in the battle raging in Hue.

For almost three weeks, the U.S. cavalry units tried to hold off the reinforcement of Hue by North Vietnamese troops from the PAVN 24th, 29th, and 99th Regiments. The Americans were reinforced on 19 February when the 2d Battalion, 501st Infantry (2/501st) was attached to the 3d Brigade, 1st Cavalry Division, from the U.S. Army's 101st Airborne Division. The battalion was subsequently ordered to seal access to the city from the south. The 1st Battalion, 7th Cavalry (1/7 Cav), deployed south to the Hue area also on that day after being relieved from its base defense mission at Camp Evans. While these U.S. Army units saw plenty of heavy action in these outlying areas and contributed greatly to the eventual allied victory at Hue, the fighting inside the city was to remain largely in the hands of South Vietnamese troops and U.S. Marines.

As allied reinforcements began their movement to the area, the ARVN and Marines began making preparations for counterattacks in their assigned areas. Making their task more difficult was the weather, which took a turn for the worse on 2 February when the temperature fell into the 50s (F) and the low clouds opened up with a cold drenching rain.

As the rain fell, Lieutenant Colonel Gravel's "bobtailed" 1st Battalion, 1st Marines, was ordered to attack to seize the Thua Thien Province headquarters building and prison, six blocks west of the

MACV compound. At 0700, Gravel launched a two-company assault supported by tanks to take his assigned objectives, but the Marines immediately ran into trouble. An M79 gunner from Company G recalled: "We didn't get a block away [from the MACV compound] when we started getting sniper fire. We got a tank...went a block, turned right and received 57mm recoilless which put out our tank"; the attack was "stopped cold," and the battalion fell back to its original position near the MACV compound.[20]

By this time, Brigadier General LaHue had finally realized that he and his intelligence officers had vastly underrated the strength of the Communists south of the river. Accordingly, he called in Colonel Stanley S. Hughes, the new commander of the 1st Marine Regiment, and gave him overall tactical control of U.S. forces in the southern part of the city. Assuming control of the battle, Hughes promised Gravel reinforcements and gave him the general mission to conduct "sweep and clear operations . . . to destroy enemy forces, protect U.S. Nationals and restore that [southern] portion of the city to U.S. control."[21] In response, Gravel ordered Company F, 2d Battalion, 5th Marines (F/2/5), which had been placed under his operational control when it arrived the previous day, to relieve a MACV communications facility near the VC-surrounded U.S. Consulate. The Marines launched their attack, fighting most of the afternoon, but failed to reach the U.S. Army signal troops, losing three Marines killed and thirteen wounded in the process. At that point, Gravel's troops established night defensive positions; during the night, Gravel made plans to renew the attack the next morning.

The next day, the Marines made some headway and brought in further reinforcements. The 1st Battalion finally relieved the MACV radio facility in the late morning hours, and after an intense 3-hour fight, reached the Hue University campus. During the night, the Communist sappers had dropped the railroad bridge across the Perfume River west of the city, but they left untouched the bridge across the Phu Cam Canal. At 1100, Company H, 2d Battalion, 5th Marines (H/2/5), commanded by Captain Ronald G. Christmas, crossed the bridge over the canal in a convoy, accompanied by Army trucks equipped with quad .50-caliber machine guns and two ONTOS, which were tracked vehicles armed with six 106mm recoilless rifles. As the convoy neared the MACV compound, it came under intense enemy heavy machine gun and rocket fire. The Marines responded rapidly, and in the ensuing confusion, the convoy exchanged fire with another Marine unit already in the city. As one Marine in the convoy remembered, "our guys happened to be out on the right side of the road and of course nobody knew that. First thing you know everybody began shooting at our own men . . . out of pure fright and frenzy."[22] Luckily, neither of the Marine units took any casualties. Company H joined Gravel where the 1st Battalion had established a position near the MACV compound. The PAVN and VC gunners continued to pour machine gun and rocket fire into the position, and by day's end, the Marines at that location had sustained two dead and thirty-four wounded.

On the afternoon of 2 February, Colonel Hughes decided to move his command group into Hue where he could more directly control the battle. Accompanying Hughes in the convoy that departed for the city was Lieutenant Colonel Ernest C. Cheatham, commander of 2d Battalion, 5th Marines, who had been sitting frustrated in Phu Bai while three of his units—companies F, G, and H—fought in Hue under Gravel's control. Hughes quickly established his command post in the MACV compound. The forces at his disposal included Cheatham's three companies from 2/5 Marines and Gravel's depleted battalion consisting of Company A, 1/1 Marines, and a provisional company consisting of one platoon of Company B, 1/1, and several dozen cooks and clerks who had been sent to the front lines to fight.[23]

Hughes wasted no time in taking control of the situation. He directed Gravel to anchor the left flank with his one-and-a-half-company battalion to keep the main supply route open. Then he ordered Cheatham and his three companies to assume responsibility for the attack south from the university toward the provincial headquarters, telling him to "attack through the city and clean the NVA out." When Cheatham hesitated, waiting for additional guidance, the regimental commander who, like everyone else going into Hue, had only the sketchiest information, gruffly stated, "if you're looking for any more, you aren't going to get it. Move out!"[24]

Cheatham devised a plan that called for his battalion to move west along the river from the MACV compound. He would attack with companies F and H in the lead and Company G in reserve. Although the plan was simple, execution proved extremely difficult. From the MACV compound to the confluence of the Perfume River and the Phu Cam Canal was almost 11 blocks, each of which the enemy had transformed into a fortress that would have to be cleared building by building, room by room.

The Marines began their attack toward the treasury building and post office, but they made very slow progress, not having yet devised workable tactics to deal with the demands of the urban terrain. As the

Marines, supported by tanks, tried to advance, the Communists hit them with a withering array of mortar, rocket, machine gun, and small-arms fire from prepared positions in the buildings. According to Cheatham, his Marines tried to take the treasury and postal buildings five or six different times. He later recalled, "You'd assault and back you'd come, drag your wounded and then muster it [the energy and courage] up again and try it again."[25]

The Marines just did not have enough men to deal with the enemy entrenched in the buildings. The frontage for a company was about one block; with two companies forward, this left an exposed left flank, subject to enemy automatic weapons and rocket fire. By the evening of 3 February, the Marines had made little progress and were taking increasing casualties as they fought back and forth over the same ground.

The following morning, Colonel Hughes met with his two battalion commanders. Hughes ordered Cheatham to continue the attack. He told Gravel to continue to secure Cheatham's left flank with his battalion, which now had only one company left after the previous day's casualties. As Gravel ordered his Marines into position to screen Cheatham's attack, they first had to secure the Joan of Arc school and church. They immediately ran into heavy enemy fire and were forced to fight house to house. Eventually, they secured the school but continued to take effective fire from PAVN and VC gunners in the church. Reluctantly, Gravel gave the order to fire on the church, and the Marines pounded the building with mortars and 106mm recoilless rifle

Co L, 3d Bn, 5th Marine troops use walls and houses to cover their advance in street fighting in the Citadel.

fire, eventually killing or driving off the enemy. In the ruins of the church, the Marines found two European priests, one French and one Belgian, who were livid that the Marines had fired on the church. Gravel was sorry for the destruction but felt that he had had no choice in the matter.[26]

With Gravel's Marines moving into position to screen his left flank to the Phu Cam Canal, Cheatham launched his attack at 0700 on 4 February. It took 24 hours of bitter fighting just to reach the treasury building. Attacking the rear of the building after blasting holes through adjacent courtyard walls with 106mm recoilless rifle fire, the Marines finally took the facility but only after it had been plastered with 90mm tank rounds, 106mm recoilless rifles, 81mm mortars, and CS gas, a riot-control agent.

In the rapidly deteriorating weather, the Marines found themselves in a room-by-room, building-by-building struggle to clear an 11-by-9-block area just south of the river. This effort rapidly turned into a nightmare. Fighting in such close quarters against an entrenched enemy was decidedly different from what the Marines had been trained to do. Accustomed to fighting in the sparsely populated countryside of I Corps, nothing in their training had prepared them for the type of warfare this urban setting demanded.[27] Captain Christmas later remembered his apprehension as his unit prepared to enter the battle for Hue: "I could feel a knot developing in my stomach. Not so much from fear—though a helluva lot of fear was there—but because we were new to this type of situation. We were accustomed to jungles and open rice fields, and now we would be fighting in a city like it was Europe during World War II. One of the beautiful things about the Marines is that they adapt quickly, but we were going to take a number of casualties learning some basic lessons in this experience."[28]

It was savage work—house-to-house fighting through city streets—of a type largely unseen by Americans since World War II. Ground gained in the fighting was to be measured in inches, and each city block cost dearly: every alley, street corner, window, and garden had to be paid for in blood. Correspondents who moved forward with the Marines reported the fighting as the most intense they had ever seen in South Vietnam.

The combat was relentless. Small groups of Marines moved doggedly from house to house, assaulting enemy positions with whatever supporting fire was available, blowing holes in walls with rocket launchers or recoilless rifles, then sending fire teams and squads into the breach. Each structure had to be cleared room by room using M16 rifles and grenades. Taking advantage of Hue's numerous courtyards and walled estates, the PAVN and VC ambushed the Marines every step of the way. Having had no training in urban fighting, the Marines had to work out the tactics and techniques on the spot.

One of the practical problems that the Marines encountered early was the lack of sufficiently detailed maps. Originally their only references were standard 1:50,000-scale tactical maps that showed little of the city detail. One company commander later remarked, "You have to raid the local Texaco station to get your street map. That's really what you need."[29] Eventually, Cheatham and Gravel secured the necessary maps and numbered the government and municipal buildings and prominent city features. This permitted them to coordinate their efforts more closely.

Making the problem even more difficult was the initial prohibition on using artillery and close air support. The Marines had a vast arsenal of heavy weapons at their disposal: 105mm, 155mm, and 8-inch howitzers; helicopter gunships; close air support from fighter-bombers; and naval gunfire from destroyers and cruisers with 5-inch, 6-inch, and 8-inch guns standing just offshore. However, because of the initial rules of engagement that sought to limit damage to the city, these resources were not available to the Marines at the beginning of the battle.

Even after Lieutenant General Lam lifted the ban on the use of fire support south of the river on 3 February, the Marines could not depend on air support or artillery because of the close quarters and the low-lying cloud cover. Lieutenant Colonel Gravel later explained part of the difficulty: "Artillery in an area like that is not terribly effective because you can't observe it well enough. You lose the rounds in the buildings in the street . . . and you have a difficult time with perspective."[30] Additionally, the poor weather, which also greatly limited close air support, had a negative impact on the utility of artillery because with low clouds and fog obscuring the flashes, the rounds had to be adjusted by sound.

The Marines had other firepower at their disposal. They used tanks to support their advance but found they were unwieldy in close quarters and drew antitank fire nearly every time they advanced. The Marines were much more enthusiastic about the ONTOS, with its six 106mm recoilless rifles that were used very effectively in the direct-fire mode to suppress enemy positions and to blow holes in the buildings so the Marines could advance.[31] Despite their preference for the 106mm recoilless rifle, the Marines used every weapon at their disposal to dislodge the PAVN and VC troops.

Progress was slow, methodical, and costly. On 5 February, Captain Christmas' H/2/5 Marines took the Thua Thien province capitol building in a particularly bloody battle. Using two tanks and 106mm recoilless rifles mounted on mechanical mules (a flat-bedded, self-propelled carrier about the size of a jeep), the Marines advanced against intense automatic weapons fire, rockets, and mortars. Responding with their own mortars and CS gas, the Marines finally overwhelmed the defenders in mid-afternoon.

The province headquarters had assumed a symbolic importance to both sides. A National Liberation Front flag had flown from the flagpole in front of the headquarters since the initial Communist takeover of the city. As a CBS television crew filmed the event, the Marines tore down the enemy ensign and raised the Stars and Stripes. This was a politically sensitive situation; the Marines should have turned over the provincial headquarters building to the ARVN and continued the fight, but Christmas told his gunnery sergeant, "We've been looking at that damn North Vietnamese flag all day, and now we're going to take it down."[32] To Lieutenant Colonel Cheatham, this proved to be the turning point of the battle for Hue. He later said, "When we took the province headquarters, we broke their back. That was a rough one."[33]

The provincial headquarters had served as the command post of the PAVN 4th Regiment. With its loss, the integrity of the North Vietnamese defenses south of the river began to falter. However, the fighting was far from over. Despite the rapid adaptation of the Marines to street fighting, it was not until 11 February that the 2d Battalion, 5th Marines, reached the confluence of the river and the canal. Two days later, the Marines crossed into the western suburbs of Hue, aiming to link up with troopers of the 1st Cavalry and 101st Airborne Division who were moving in toward the city. By 14 February, most of the city south of the river was in American hands, but mopping-up operations would take another 12 days as rockets and mortar rounds continued to fall and isolated snipers harassed Marine patrols. Control of that sector of the city was returned to the South Vietnamese government. It had been very costly for the Marines who sustained 38 dead and 320 wounded. It had been even more costly for the Communists; the bodies of over 1,000 VC and PAVN soldiers were strewn about the city south of the river.[34]

While the Marines fought for the southern part of the city, the battle north of the river continued to rage. Despite the efforts of the U.S. units trying to seal off Hue from outside reinforcement, Communist troops and supplies made it into the city from the west and north, and even on boats coming down the river. On 1 February, the 2d ARVN Airborne Battalion and the 7th ARVN Cavalry had recaptured the Tay Loc airfield inside the Citadel but only after suffering heavy casualties (including the death of the cavalry squadron commander) and losing twelve armored personnel carriers. Later that day, U.S. Marine helicopters brought part of the 4th Battalion, 2d ARVN Regiment, from Dong Ha into the Citadel. Once on the ground, the ARVN attempted to advance but were not able to make much headway in rooting out the North Vietnamese. By 4 February, the ARVN advance north of the river had effectively stalled among the houses, alleys, and narrow streets adjacent to the Citadel wall to the northwest and southwest, leaving the Communists still in possession of the Imperial Palace and most of the surrounding area.

On the night of 6-7 February, the PAVN counterattacked and forced the ARVN troops to pull back to the Tay Loc airfield. At the same time, the North Vietnamese rushed additional reinforcements into the city. Brigadier General Truong responded by redeploying his forces, ordering the 3d ARVN Regiment to move into the Citadel to take up positions around the division headquarters compound. By the evening of 7 February, Truong's forces inside the Citadel included four airborne battalions, the Black Panther company, two armored cavalry squadrons, the 3d ARVN Regiment, the 4th Battalion from the 2d ARVN Regiment, and a company from the 1st ARVN Regiment.

Despite the ARVN buildup inside the Citadel, Truong's troops still failed to make any headway against the dug-in North Vietnamese who had burrowed deeply into the walls and tightly packed buildings. All the time, the PAVN and the VC seemed to be getting stronger as reinforcements made it into the city. With his troops stalled, an embarrassed and frustrated Truong was forced into appealing to III MAF for help. On 10 February, Lieutenant General Cushman sent a message to Brigadier General LaHue directing him to move a Marine battalion to the Citadel. LaHue ordered Major Robert Thompson's 1st Battalion, 5th Marines, to prepare for movement to Hue. On 11 February, helicopters lifted two platoons of Company B into the ARVN headquarters complex (the third platoon from the unit was forced to turn back when its pilot was wounded by ground fire).

Twenty-four hours later, Company A, with five tanks attached, plus the missing platoon from Company B, made the journey by landing craft across the river from the MACV compound along the moat to the east of the Citadel and through a breach in the northeast wall. The next day Company C joined the rest of the battalion. Once inside the Citadel, the Marines were ordered to relieve the 1st Vietnamese Airborne TF in the southeastern section. At the same time, two battalions of Vietnamese Marines moved into the southwest corner of the Citadel with orders to sweep west. This buildup of allied forces inside the Citadel put intense pressure on the Communist forces, but they stood their ground and redoubled efforts to hold their positions.

The following day, after conferring with South Vietnamese President Nguyen Van Thieu, Lieutenant General Lam authorized allied forces to use whatever weapons were necessary to dislodge the enemy from the Citadel. Only the Imperial Palace remained off limits for artillery and close air support.

The mission of the 1/5 Marines was to advance down the east wall of the Citadel toward the river with the Imperial Palace on their right. At 0815 on 13 February, Company A moved out under a bone-chilling rain, following the wall toward a distinctive archway tower. As they neared the tower, North Vietnamese troops opened up on the men with automatic weapons and rockets from concealed positions that they had dug into the base of the tower. The thick masonry of the construction protected the enemy defenders from all the fire being brought to bear on them. Within minutes, several Marines lay dying, and thirty more were wounded, including Captain John J. Bowe, Jr., the company commander. These troops, fresh from operations in Phu Loc, just north of the Hai Van Pass, were unfamiliar with both the situation and city fighting; finding themselves "surrounded by houses, gardens, stores, buildings two and three stories high, and paved roads littered with abandoned vehicles, the riflemen felt out of their element."[35]

Under heavy enemy fire, the Marine advance stalled; in the first assault on the south wall, the Marines lost fifteen killed and forty wounded. Major Thompson pulled Company A back and replaced it with Company C, flanked by Company B. Once again, the Marines were raked by heavy small-arms, machine gun, and rocket fire that seemed to come from every direction, but they managed to inch forward, using airstrikes, naval gunfire, and artillery support. The fighting proved even more savage than the battle for the south bank. That night, Thompson requested artillery fire to help soften up the area for the next day's attack. At 0800 on 14 February, Thompson renewed the attack, but his Marines made little headway against the entrenched North Vietnamese and VC. It was not until the next day when Captain Myron C. Harrington's Company D, 1st Battalion, 5th Marines (D/1/5), was inserted into the battle by boat that the wall tower was finally taken but only after six more Marines were killed and more than fifty wounded. That night, the PAVN retook the tower for a brief period, but Harrington personally led the counterattack to take it back.

On the morning of 16 February, Major Thompson's Marines continued their push southeast along the Citadel wall. From that point until 22 February, the battle seesawed back and forth while much of the Citadel was pounded to rubble by close air support, artillery, and heavy weapons fire. The bitter hand-to-hand fighting went on relentlessly. The Marines were operating in a defender's paradise—row after row of single story, thick-walled, masonry houses jammed close together up against a solid wall riddled with spider holes and other enemy fighting positions. The Marines discovered that the North Vietnamese units in the Citadel employed "better city-fighting tactics, improved the already formidable defenses, dug trenches, built roadblocks and conducted counterattacks to regain redoubts which were important to . . . [their] defensive scheme."[36] The young Marines charged into the buildings, throwing grenades before them, clearing one room at a time. It was a battle fought meter by meter; each enemy strongpoint had to be reduced with close-quarter fighting. No sooner had one position been taken than the North Vietnamese opened up from another.

M48 tanks and ONTOS were available, but these tracked vehicles found it extremely difficult to maneuver in the narrow streets and tight alleys of the Citadel. At first, the 90mm tank guns were ineffective against the concrete and stone houses; the shells often ricocheted off the thick walls back toward the Marines. The Marine tankers then switched to concrete-piercing fused shells that "resulted in excellent penetration and walls were breached with two to four rounds."[37] From that point on, the tanks proved invaluable in assisting the infantry assault. One Marine rifleman later stated: "If it had not been for the tanks, we could not have pushed through that section of the city. They [the North Vietnamese] seemed to have bunkers everywhere."[38]

As a result of the intense fighting, Hue was being reduced to rubble, block by block. By the end of the battle, estimates tallied 10,000 houses either totally destroyed or damaged, roughly 40 percent of the city.[39] Many of the dead and wounded were trapped in the rubble of homes and courtyards. Enemy troops killed by the Marines and South Vietnamese troops lay where they had fallen. One of the MACV advisers later wrote: "The bodies, bloated and vermin infested, attracted rats and stray dogs. So, because of public health concerns, details were formed to bury the bodies as quickly as possible."[40] For those who fought in

Hue, the stench and horrors of the corpses and the rats would never be forgotten.

By 17 February, 1/5th Marines had suffered 47 killed and 240 wounded in just five days of fighting. Constantly under fire for the whole time, the Leathernecks, numb with fatigue, kept up the fight despite having slept only in three- to four-hour snatches during the battle and most not even stopping to eat. The fighting was so intense that the medics and doctors had a very difficult time keeping up with the casualties. Because of the mounting casualties, Marine replacements were brought in during the battle, but many of them were killed or wounded before their squad leaders could even learn their names. Some replacements arrived in Hue directly upon their completion of infantry training at Camp Pendleton, California. The rapid rate of attrition was evident from the fact that there were Marines who died in battle while still wearing their stateside fatigues and boots.[41]

On 18 February, with what was left of his battalion completely exhausted and nearly out of ammunition, Major Thompson chose to rest his troops in preparation for a renewal of the attack. They needed time to clean their weapons, stock up on ammunition, tend the walking wounded, and gird themselves for the next round of bitter fighting. The following morning, Thompson and his Marines again attacked toward the Imperial Palace. They inched forward, paying dearly for every bit of ground taken. After another 24 hours of bitter fighting, they secured the wall on 19 February but had virtually spent themselves in doing so.

As the U.S. Marines had fought their way slowly toward the Imperial Palace, the Vietnamese Marine TF entered the battle. At 0900 on the 14th, the South Vietnamese launched their attack from an area south of the 1st ARVN Division headquarters compound to the west. They were to make a left turning movement to take the southwest sector of the Citadel but did not get that far because they immediately ran into heavy resistance from strong enemy forces as they engaged in intense house-to-house fighting. During the next two days, the South Vietnamese advanced fewer than 400 meters. To the north of the Vietnamese Marines, the 3d ARVN Infantry Regiment in the northwest sector of the Citadel was having problems of its own and making little progress. On the 14th, enemy forces broke out of their salient west of the Tay Loc airfield and cut off the 1st Battalion, 3d ARVN Regiment in the western corner of the Citadel. It would take two days for the ARVN to break the encirclement and then only after bitter fighting.

The enemy was also having his own problems. On the night of 14 February, a U.S. Marine forward observer with ARVN troops inside the

Citadel, monitoring enemy radio frequencies, learned that the PAVN was planning a battalion-size attack by reinforcements through the west gate of the Citadel. The forward observer called in Marine 155mm howitzers and all available naval gunfire on preplanned targets around the west gate and the moat bridge leading to it. The forward observer reported that he had heard "screaming on the radio," monitoring the PAVN net.[42] Later, it was confirmed by additional radio intercepts that the artillery and naval gunfire had caught the North Vietnamese battalion coming across the moat bridge, killing a high-ranking North Vietnamese officer and a large number of the fresh troops.

Shortly after this incident, U.S. intelligence determined that the PAVN and VC were staging out of a base camp 18 kilometers west of the city and that reinforcements from that area were entering the Citadel using the west gate. Additionally, intelligence identified a new enemy battalion west of the city and a new regimental headquarters with at least one battalion 2 kilometers north of the city. Acting on this information, elements of the U.S. 1st Cavalry Division were ordered to launch coordinated assaults on the city from their blocking positions to the west. On 21 February, the 1st Cavalry troopers attacked and were able to move up to seal off the western wall of the fortress, thus depriving the North Vietnamese of incoming supplies and reinforcements and precipitating a rapid deterioration of the enemy's strength inside the Citadel. The North Vietnamese were now fighting a rear guard action, but they still fought for every inch of ground and continued to throw replacements into the fight.

As elements of the 1st Cav advanced toward Hue from the west and action continued in the Citadel, fire support coordination became a major concern. On 21 February, Brigadier General Oscar E. Davis, one of the two assistant division commanders for the 1st Cav, flew into the Citadel to take overall control of the situation and to serve as the area's fire support coordinator. He collocated his headquarters with Brigadier General Truong in the 1st ARVN Division headquarters compound.

For the final assault on the Imperial Palace itself, a fresh unit, Captain John D. Niotis' Company L, 1st Battalion, 5th Marines, was brought in. By 22 February, the Communists held only the southwestern corner of the Citadel. Niotis led his Marines along the wall to breach the outer perimeter of the palace. Once inside, they were faced with devastating fire from the entrenched Communists. Niotis ordered his Marines to pull back so plans could be made for another attack.

While the Marines prepared for the next assault on the Imperial City, it was decided that it was politically expedient to have the South Vietnamese liberate the palace.[43] On the night of 23-24 February, the 2d Battalion, 3d ARVN Regiment, launched a surprise attack westward along the wall in the southeastern section of the Citadel. The North Vietnamese were caught off guard by the attack but quickly recovered. A savage battle ensued, but the South Vietnamese pressed the attack. The Communists, deprived of their supply centers to the west by the linkup between the 1st Cavalry and 2/5th Marines, fell back. Included in the ground gained by the South Vietnamese attack was the plot upon which stood the Citadel flagpole. At dawn on the 24th, the South Vietnamese flag replaced the VC banner that had flown from the Citadel flagpole for twenty-five days. Later that day, the ARVN 1st Division reached the outer walls of the Citadel where it linked up with elements of the 1st Cavalry Division. The last Communist positions were quickly overrun by the allied forces or were abandoned by VC and North Vietnamese troops who fled westward to sanctuaries in Laos.

On 2 March 1968, the battle for Hue was officially declared over. It had been a bitter ordeal. The relief of Hue was the longest sustained infantry battle the war had seen to that point. The losses had been high. In the twenty-six days of combat, the ARVN had lost 384 killed and more than 1,800 wounded, plus 30 missing in action. The U.S. Marines suffered 147 dead and 857 wounded. The U.S. Army suffered 74 dead and 507 wounded. The allies claimed over 5,000 Communists killed in the city and an estimated 3,000 killed in the fighting in the surrounding area.

Although the U.S. command had tried to limit damage to the city by relying on extremely accurate 8-inch howitzers and naval gunfire, the house-to-house fighting took its toll, and much of the once beautiful city lay in rubble. In the twenty-five days of fighting to retake Hue, 40 percent of the city was destroyed, and 116,000 civilians were made homeless (out of a pre-Tet population of 140,000).[44] Aside from this battle damage, the civilian population suffered terrible losses from the Communist attackers: some 5,800 were reported killed or missing. After the battle was over, South Vietnamese authorities discovered that VC death squads had systematically eliminated South Vietnamese government leaders and employees. Nearly 3,000 corpses were found in mass graves—most shot, bludgeoned to death, or buried alive, almost all with their hands tied behind their backs.[45] The victims included soldiers, civil servants, merchants, clergymen, schoolteachers, intellectuals, and foreigners. It was estimated that the VC and PAVN murdered many of the other missing South Vietnamese during the battle or as Communist forces withdrew from the Citadel.

The fighting had been intense and bloody, but in the end, the allies had ejected the Communists and recaptured the city. The battle of Hue is a textbook study of the difficulties involved in combat in an urban area. A number of factors that played a key role in the conduct of the battle are worthy of particular note; they include intelligence, command and control, training, rules of engagement, medical support, and population control.

Intelligence, or the lack thereof, had a major impact on the course of the battle for Hue. The intelligence system completely failed to anticipate that an attack on the city was imminent. Even when there were attack indicators, they were not provided to the commanders on the ground who could have best used the warning. Once the attack was launched, the intelligence systems failed to provide an adequate appreciation for enemy strength and intentions in Hue. This greatly inhibited the effectiveness of the allied response, especially in the early days of the battle when both the ARVN and the Marines were unclear as to how many enemy units were in the city. This resulted in a piecemeal approach that saw units thrown into battle against vastly superior numbers.

Command and control was also a crucial factor. The division of labor between the ARVN and U.S. Marine and Army forces resulted in a lack of coordination and unity of effort that inhibited the attempt to retake the city. This can be seen even before the battle began. When a radio intercept indicated that an attack on Hue was pending, it was the convoluted command channels that led to a sluggish response and the failure of the Hue defenders to be alerted in time.[46] Until Brigadier General Davis was placed in overall charge on 21 February, the various allied forces had acted in isolation of each other. The Marines took their orders from TF X-Ray; the ARVN obeyed the commands of Brigadier General Truong; and the U.S. Army troops to the west, largely ignorant of what the Marines and ARVN forces were doing inside the city, operated on their own. The result was three separate battles that raged simultaneously with no overall commander coordinating allied efforts. By the time that Davis was given overall control, the battle was effectively over. As one Marine later remarked, Davis "didn't have anything to coordinate, but he had the name."[47]

The lack of an overall hands-on commander meant that there was no general battle plan for retaking Hue, no one to set priorities, no one to deconflict the requests for artillery and close air support, and no one person to accept the responsibility if things went wrong. Also, there was no overall system to ensure an equitable distribution of logistics resupply. The U.S. Marines and Army scrambled to take care of their own while the ARVN got next to nothing. It was a command arrangement that almost guaranteed difficulty in achieving any meaningful unity of effort.

The command and control situation caused problems in other areas as well. With no single commander orchestrating the battle, it was difficult to coordinate the isolation of the city from outside reinforcement as the Marines and South Vietnamese tried to clear the city. This permitted the North Vietnamese and VC to rush replacements in to replace the troops they lost during the intense fighting. Thus, they were able to replenish their ranks even as the fighting intensified and after they began to take increasing numbers of casualties. When the elements of the 1st Cavalry Division effectively sealed the city from the northwest on 21 February, it had a decisive impact on the battle inside the city. Perhaps this could have been achieved earlier had there been a single commander to better synchronize the efforts of the units outside the city with those fighting inside the city.

The command and control situation also had the potential for increased fratricide because of the lack of coordination between the battles north of the river and those south of the river. The piecemeal insertion of forces also contributed to the potential of fratricide, as can be seen in the incident on 3 February when forces being rushed to the battle exchanged fire with forces already in the city.

Training played a key role in the conduct of the battle for Hue, particularly on the part of the Marines from TF X-Ray. The struggle for the city was made even more difficult by the fact that the allies were unprepared for the type of fighting required during combat in a builtup area such as Hue. The Marines who played such a crucial role in retaking the city were accustomed to fighting an enemy in jungle or open terrain away from populated areas of any significance. They had no training for urban warfare and essentially had to develop their own tactics, techniques, and procedures as they went along. The first three days of the battle had been a bloody learning process as the Marines went through what was, in effect, on-the-job training in house-to-house fighting.

The tactics the Marines had used so effectively in previous operations in I Corps had little application inside the city. The Marines therefore had to devise ways to defeat an entrenched enemy who used the myriad of buildings, walls, and towers so effectively.[48] Different techniques were tried. One of the best used an eight-man team. Four riflemen covered the exits while two men rushed the building with grenades and two other riflemen provided covering fire. The team would rotate the responsibilities among the eight men and move on to the next building. Lieutenant Colonel Cheatham, commander of 2/5 Marines, later described the tactics used: "We hope to kill them inside or flush them out the back for the four men watching the exits. Then, taking the next building, two other men rush the front. It sounds simple but the timing has to be just as good as a football play."[49]

The Marines learned quickly that more heavy weapons were needed. Tactics of fire and maneuver would not work in street fighting without the threat of heavy weapons. Objectives often could be reached only by going through buildings. Tanks, 106mm recoilless rifles, and 3.5-inch rocket launchers proved essential in the house-to-house fighting. The rocket launchers, called "bazookas" in World War II, were easily the more portable and, according to some Marines, the most effective.[50] The 106mm recoilless rifles were also extremely effective. The gun could be employed singularly, either mounted on jeeps or mules or carted around by hand (even though it weighed over 400 pounds dismounted), or it could be used in a unit of six on the ONTOS tracked vehicles. The Marines used these weapons to create holes in compound walls and the sides of buildings through which they would rush. They were also extremely useful for providing suppressive fire and as countersniper weapons.

Tear gas was used as an effective weapon to chase enemy troops from their bunkers and spider holes. The Marines had tried using smoke grenades on the treasury building south of the river, but what little smoke they produced was quickly dispersed by the breeze coming off the river. One Marine officer suggested using an E8 tear gas launcher that he had seen stacked against the wall of an ARVN compound adjacent to the MACV compound. The launcher, about 2 feet high, could hurl as many as sixty-four 35mm tear gas projectiles up to 250 meters in four 5-second bursts of sixteen each. Unlike the grenades, the E8 could flood an entire area so that the gas would permeate every room and bunker. The Marines used the CS dispenser very successfully throughout the remainder of the battle, and one company commander credited this approach with limiting his casualties during the fighting.[51]

In the early days of the battle when the Marines were trying to work out ways to deal with the entrenched enemy in the city, they had to do it largely without the artillery and close air support they were so accustomed to using. The rules of engagement the allied senior commanders initially agreed upon limited the use of artillery and close air support to minimize the damage to the historic and symbolic city. This made it extremely difficult, particularly during the early days of the battle, for the Marines to dig the North Vietnamese out of their prepared positions inside the city. These restrictions, which the Marines generally obeyed, were later abandoned when the allies argued successfully that adhering to that standing order was causing unacceptable casualties. Nicholas Warr, who had served as a platoon leader in Company C, 1/5 Marines, during the battle for Hue, later wrote, "These damnable rules of engagement . . . prevented American fighting men from using the only tactical assets that gave us an advantage during firefights—that of our vastly superior firepower represented by air strikes, artillery, and naval gunfire—these orders continued to remain in force and hinder, wound and kill 1/5 Marines until the fourth day of fighting inside the Citadel of Hue."[52]

Because of the initial restrictions on artillery and air strikes and the fact that most of the available artillery from Phu Bai was directed at interdicting enemy escape routes to the rear and not on the city itself, the Marines had to use their own mortars for close-in fire support, using them as a "hammer" on top of the buildings. Lieutenant Colonel Cheatham later observed, "If you put enough [mortar] rounds on the top of a building, pretty soon the roof falls in."[53] The mortars also proved useful against enemy soldiers fleeing from buildings being assaulted by the Marines. By preregistering on both the objective building and the street to that building's rear, the Marines were able to inflict heavy casualties by shifting fire from the objective to the rear street as they pushed the enemy soldiers out of the building.[54]

The intensity of the bitter fighting resulted in a tremendous amount of casualties. Because the bad weather inhibited medical evacuation by helicopter, it soon became apparent that there was a need for forward medical facilities. The 1st Marine Regiment established the regimental aid station at the MACV compound with eight doctors in attendance. This facility provided emergency care and coordinated all medical evacuation. Each of the forward battalions had its own aid station. Cheatham, commander of 2/5 Marines, later lauded this highly responsive medical support, declaring that it was "a throwback to World War II. [I] had my doctor . . . one block behind the frontline treating the people right there."[55] The Marines used trucks, mechanical mules, and any available transportation to carry the wounded back to the aid stations. From there, U.S. Marine and Army helicopters were used for further evacuation, often flying with a 100-foot ceiling. In the battle for Hue, if a Marine reached an aid station alive, his chances of survival were close to 99 percent.[56]

Due to the heavy fighting in the city, population control quickly became a problem. In urban warfare, the people are often caught in the middle between the two opposing forces. Hue was no exception. The initial attack provided the first trickle of civilians seeking refuge in the relative safety of the MACV compound. The trickle would become a flood over the next weeks, creating a logistics and security nightmare for the U.S. and South Vietnamese forces in Hue as the refugee problem reached staggering proportions. Every turn in the fighting flushed out hundreds of Vietnamese civilians of every age. Whole families were able to survive the shelling and street warfare by taking refuge in small bunkers they had constructed in their homes. Out of the rubble came old men, women, and children, waving pieces of white cloth attached to sticks. Something had to be done about this growing flood of refugees and displaced persons as the battle continued to rage.

A U.S. Army major from the MACV advisory team was placed in charge of coordinating the effort to manage the refugee situation. Temporary housing was found at a complex near the MACV compound and at Hue University where the number of refugees swelled to 22,000. Another 40,000 displaced persons were in the Citadel area across the river. Most of the refugees were innocent civilians, but some were enemy soldiers or sympathizers, and many were ARVN troops trapped at home on leave for the Tet holidays. All of these ARVN soldiers who were fit for duty were put to use helping the Marines and MACV advisers with the refugees.

In addition to dealing with shelter for the refugees, U.S. and South Vietnamese officials had to restore city services, including water and power; eliminate heath hazards, including burying the dead; and secure food. With the assistance of the local Catholic hierarchy and American resources and personnel, the South Vietnamese government officials tried to restore order and normalcy in the city. By the end of February, a full-time refugee administrator was in place, and the local government slowly began to function once more.

The battle of Hue remains worthy of study when considering the complexities and requirements for urban operations. It was a bloody affair that resulted in a severe casualty toll, largely because of the aforementioned reasons, not the least of which were intelligence failures and lack of centralized command and control. It was only through both the American and South Vietnamese Marines' and soldiers' valor that they prevailed against a determined enemy under combat conditions in an urban environment that far exceeded anything that any of the allies had previously experienced. However, the victory at Hue proved irrelevant in the long run. Despite the overwhelming tactical victory the allies achieved in the city and on the other battlefields throughout South Vietnam, the Tet Offensive proved to be a strategic defeat for the United States. U.S. public opinion, affected in large part by the media coverage of the early days of the offensive, began to shift away from support for the war.[57] On 31 March 1968, the full impact of the Tet Offensive was demonstrated when President Lyndon B. Johnson halted all bombing of North Vietnam above the 20th parallel and gave notice that he would not seek reelection to a second term in the White House. Thus, the Communists won a great strategic victory. However, in doing so, they lost an estimated 30,000 fighters, and the VC would never recover. Nevertheless, the Tet Offensive resulted in a sea change in U.S. policy in Vietnam, and the United States soon began its long disengagement from the war.

Despite the outcome of the war, the battle of Hue remains a classic study in urban warfare that clearly demonstrates not only the rigors and demands of fighting in a builtup area but also the valor and fortitude demanded of the soldiers who are to fight in such situations. The U.S. Marines and South Vietnamese soldiers retook the city from the Communists and paid for the effort in blood; many of the lessons they learned the hard way are just as valid for urban fighting today as they were in 1968.

Notes

1. U.S. military troop strength reached its peak of 543,300 in April 1969.
2. Spencer Tucker, *Vietnam* (London: UCL Press, 1999), 136.
3. The Viet Minh defeated the French forces in a decisive battle at Dien Bien Phu on 7 May 1954 after a two-month siege. The French subsequently withdrew from Vietnam.
4. Edward F. Murphy, *Semper Fi Vietnam: From Da Nang to the DMZ, Marine Corps Campaigns, 1965 1975* (Novato, CA: Presidio Press, 1997), 189.
5. The Viet Cong, or as it was more properly known, the People's Liberation Armed Forces (PLAF), included regular forces, called main force VC, full-time guerrillas, and a part-time self-defense militia. The main-force VC battalions were organized, trained, and equipped similarly to the PAVN battalions.
6. Pham Van Son. *Tet—1968* (Salisbury, NC: 1980), 458.
7. Ibid., 459.
8. Don Oberdorfer, *Tet!* (New York: Avon, 1972), 225.
9. George W. Smith, *The Siege at Hue* (New York: Ballentine Books, 2000), 17, and Keith W. Nolan, *Battle for Hue* (Novato, CA: Presidio Press, 1983), 3.
10. James J. Wirtz, *The Tet Offensive: Intelligence Failure in War* (Ithaca, NY: Cornell University Press, 1991), 98.
11 Pham, 272-76.
12. Jack Shulimson, Leonard A. Blasiol, Charles R. Smith, and David A. Dawson, *U.S. Marines in Vietnam: The Defining Year 1968* (Washington, DC: Headquarters, U.S. Marine Corps, 1997), 171.
13. Ibid., 172.
14. Ibid., 173.
15. Ibid., 174.
16. Ibid.
17. Ibid.
18. Westmoreland message to Wheeler, dated 31 Jan 68, Westmoreland Messages, Westmoreland Papers, Center of Military History, quoted in Shulimson et al., 174.
19. Quoted in Shulimson et al., 176.
20. Shulimson et al., 176.
21. 1st Marines (Rein), 1st Marine Division (Rein) Combat Operations After-Action Report (Operation HUE CITY), dated 20 Mar 1968, 11 (hereafter 1st Marines AAR).
22. Ibid., 13, and Marine quoted in Shulimson et al., 176.

23. Murphy, 198-99.
24. Quoted in Shulimson et al., 179-80.
25. Ibid.
26. Ibid., 182.
27. 1st Marines AAR, 79.
28. Quoted in Stanley Karnow, *Vietnam, A History* (New York: Penguin Books, 1997), 545.
29. Quoted in Shulimson et al., 185.
30. Ibid., 186.
31. Ibid.
32. Quoted in Murphy, 206; Nolan, 77-79.
33. Smith, 161.
34. Shulimson, 191.
35. Murphy, 209.
36. Quoted in Shulimson et al., 201.
37. 1st Marines AAR, 80.
38. Quoted in Shulimson et al., 202.
39. Nolan, 183.
40. Smith, 162.
41. Murphy, 213.
42. Shulimson et al., 204-205.
43. Ibid., 211, and Nolan, 172.
44. Shulimson et al., 219.
45. Ibid., 214.
46. Wirtz, 98.
47. Quoted in Shulimson et al., 223.
48. 1st Marines AAR, 79.
49. Quoted in Smith, 141-42.
50. 1st Marines AAR, 81.
51. Capt. G. R. Christmas, "A Company Commander Reflects on Operations Hue City," in *The Marines in Vietnam 1954 1973, An Anthology and Annotated Bibliography*, Edwin H. Simmons et al., eds. (Washington, DC: Headquarters, U.S. Marine Corps, 1974), 162.
52. Nicholas Warr, *Phase Line Green: the Battle for Hue, 1968* (Annapolis, MD: Naval Institute Press, 1997), 124.
53. Quoted in Shulimson et al., 188.
54. Christmas, 161-62.
55. Shulimson et al., 219.
56. Ibid.
57. There are indications that public opinion had already begun to shift by the end of 1967, but the Tet Offensive certainly accelerated this shift.

Annotated Bibliography

Arnold, James R. *Tet Offensive 1968: Turning Point in Vietnam.* London: Osprey, 1990. One of the Osprey Military Campaign Series that contains extremely good maps, diagrams, and photographs.

1st Cavalry Division, 14th Military History Detachment, Combat After-Action Report—Op Hue, Period 2-26 February 1968, dated 16 August 1968.

1st Marine Division, 1st Marine Division Commander's AAR, Tet Offensive, 29 January-14 February 1968, dated 25 May 1968.

1st Marine Division, TF X-Ray AAR, Operation Hue City, with enclosures, dated 14 Apr 68.

1st Marines (Rein), 1st Marine Division (Rein) Combat Operations After-Action Report (Operation HUE CITY), dated 20 Mar 1968.

Ford, Ronnie E. *Tet 1968: Understanding the Surprise.* London: Frank Cass, 1995. Addresses the intelligence breakdown that contributed to the surprise and impact of the Tet Offensive.

Hammel, Eric M. *Fire in the Streets: the Battle of Hue, Tet 1968.* Chicago: Contemporary Books, 1991. A very thorough hour-by-hour, day-by-day account of the battle that also addresses the strain that the surprise attack put on the South Vietnamese-U.S. alliance.

Karnow, Stanley. *Vietnam: A History.* 2d revised and updated ed. New York: Penguin Books, 1997. One of the most comprehensive overall accounts of the entire American experience in the Vietnam war that provides a useful context for the events that unfolded in Hue in 1968.

Krohn, Charles A. *The Lost Battalion: Controversy and Casualties in the Battle of Hue.* Westport, CT: Praeger Publishers, 1993. A first-hand account from the battalion intelligence officer of 1/12 Cavalry of operations by the 1st Cavalry Division against the PAVN forces on the outskirts of Hue in February 1968.

Murphy, Edward F. *Semper Fi: From Da Nang to the DMZ, Marine Corps Campaigns, 1965 1975.* Novato, CA: Presidio Press, 1997. Addresses U.S. Marine Corps operations in I Corps tactical zone during the Vietnam war.

Nolan, Keith William. *Battle for Hue: Tet, 1968.* Novato, CA: Presidio Press, 1983. A detailed account of not only U.S. Marine operations in Hue but also the actions of the South Vietnamese soldiers and Marines who participated in the fight to retake the city.

Oberdorfer, Don. *Tet!* New York: Doubleday, 1971. The classic work on the 1968 Tet Offensive; includes a particularly good description of the roundup and massacre of civilians by the Viet Cong at Hue.

Pearson, Willard. *The War in the Northern Provinces, 1966 1968*. Washington, DC: Department of the Army, 1975. An official history of U.S. Army operations in the I Corps tactical zone, including the action around Hue in 1968.

Pham Van Son. *Tet—1968*. Salisbury, NC: Documentary Publications, 1980. A study written by the Military History Division, Joint General Staff, Republic of Vietnam Armed Forces. It provides the South Vietnamese perspective of the fighting during the Tet Offensive, including the action at Hue.

Shulimson, Jack; Leonard A. Blasiol; Charles R. Smith; and David A. Dawson. *U.S. Marines in Vietnam: The Defining Year 1968*. Washington, DC: Headquarters, U.S. Marine Corps, 1997. An official Marine Corps history that addresses operations in 1968, focusing on the fighting at Khe Sanh and Hue; impeccably documented with detailed maps.

Simmons, Edwin H. et al. *The Marines in Vietnam 1954 1973, An Anthology and Annotated Bibliography*. Washington, DC: Headquarters, U.S. Marine Corps, 1974. A compendium of articles and first-hand accounts of Marine Corps operations during the Vietnam war.

Smith, George W. *The Siege at Hue*. New York: Ballentine Books, 2000. A first-hand account of the fighting in Hue by a former MACV adviser with the 1st ARVN Division in 1968.

Tucker, Spencer. *Vietnam*. London: UCL Press, 1999. A detailed overview of the numerous wars of Vietnam concentrating on the period of U.S. involvement. It is particularly useful in putting the action at Hue in the larger context of North Vietnamese strategy and tactics.

Warr, Nicholas. *Phase Line Green: The Battle for Hue, 1968*. Annapolis, MD: Naval Institute Press, 1997. A first-hand account by a platoon commander in Company C, 1/5 Marines.

Wirtz, James J. *The Tet Offensive: Intelligence Failure in War*. Ithaca, NY: Cornell University Press, 1991. Focuses on the failure of allied intelligence to anticipate the timing and scope of the enemy offensive; draws heavily on Viet Cong and declassified U.S. sources.

The 31 December 1994-8 February 1995 Battle for Grozny

Timothy L. Thomas

The Chechen Republic of the Russian Federation is located in the federation's southwestern corner near the Caspian Sea. It covers approximately 6,500 square miles, measuring nearly 100 miles by 70 miles at its widest points. Several terrain features dominate the republic. In the north, there is a plain that runs nearly 35 to 40 miles until it empties into the center of Chechnya (where Grozny is located). The foothills begin south of Grozny and run close to 20 miles until they merge into the Caucasus Mountains in the south. Elevations in Chechnya range from 200 feet in the northern plains to 12,000 feet in the mountains. The republic has one major river, the Terek, which runs west to east across the plains in the north of Chechnya (see Map 1).

From late December 1994 until 8 February 1995, Russia's armed forces fought against its own citizens in the city of Grozny, Chechnya, the capital of the republic.[1] The roots of the conflict are historical. The entire region was part of Imperial Russia and the Soviet Union. Russian expansion into the region began in the late eighteenth century as Russia sought allies among the Christian population and suppressed local revolts that had tribal and religious content. In the Soviet period, the region briefly enjoyed independence from Moscow but was reconquered by the early 1920s. Some national groups in the region, the Chechens being one of them, sided with German invaders during World War II and were treated as traitor-nations when areas were reconquered by the Soviets. Joseph Stalin deported the population of Chechnya to Kazakhstan and other areas in 1944 for Chechen disloyalty. It was not until 1957 that the Chechens returned on the order of then General Secretary Nikita Khruschev. Regardless of this act, a simmering hatred of Russians remains just below the level of consciousness for many Chechens. A local saying supporting this attitude is that "a shot is fired in the Caucasus, but the echo lasts for 100 years."[2]

The term "Grozny" means terrible or formidable. Russian General Alexy Yermolov founded Grozny on 10 June 1818. It served as a fortress or outpost for Russian forces operating in the Caucasus against the Chechens. When Yermolov assumed command of the Caucasus in 1816, he quickly appreciated the difficulty of defending the 700-mile Caucasian perimeter against raiders and established Grozny to help

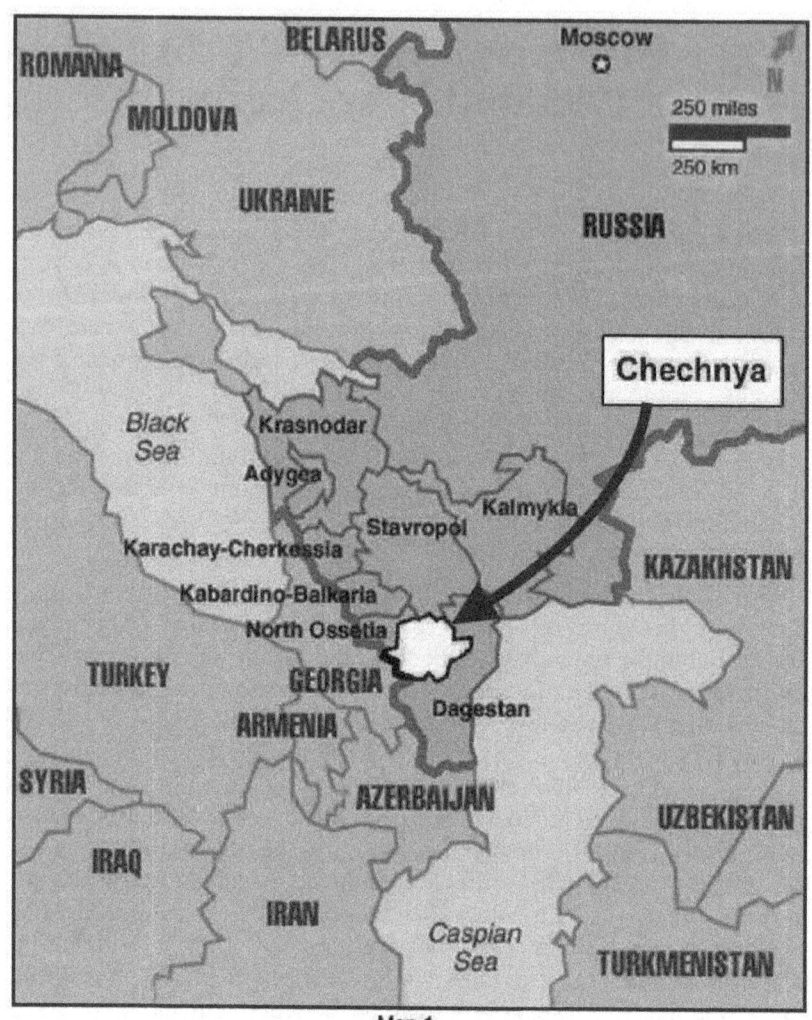

Map 1

protect it. In 1994, it was a city of approximately 490,000 inhabitants. It had a mixture of Chechens and Russians, along with a few other nationalities, and covered nearly 90 square miles if the suburbs are included. The city runs predominantly from the northwest to the southeast. It is cut into four sectors by two features: the Sunzha River running from the northeast to the southwest and a railroad line running from the southwest to the center of the city and then departing the city due east. A refinery complex is located in the southwestern portion of the city, and there are two airports, one to the northwest and one due east of the city. The city has a mixture of buildings ranging from 10- to 15-story structures to those with only one story. These buildings are made of concrete for the most part. Approximately 123 roads lead in and out of Grozny.

Russian authorities became concerned with activities in Chechnya in 1991, in particular with the intentions of Chechen President Dzhokhar Dudayev. He publicly sought to create a "single trans-Caucasian republic stretching to include parts of Russia and Ukraine as well as all of the Caucasian and trans-Caucasian region."[3] This was of immense concern to Russia, since critical oil and natural gas pipelines run through the region, as well as trade routes to the Middle East. In fact, the Caucasus is a key geostrategic door for Russia to the Middle East.

The 1994-95 fight for Grozny was precipitated by a strange, even bizarre sequence of events. Boris Yeltsin, president of the Russian Republic and serving under the Soviet Union's General Secretary Mikhail Gorbachev, stated in 1991 that the republics should "chew off all the sovereignty they can swallow." The Russian Republic's president soon came to wish he had never uttered that phrase. Chechnya, a component part of the Russian Republic, took Yeltsin at his word. A small, localized revolution began on 21 August 1991 in Chechnya, two days after the August coup in the former Soviet Union. Chechnya declared its independence from Russia on 6 September 1991, citing Yeltsin's proclamation concerning sovereignty. The Amalgamated Congress of the Chechen People invited former Soviet Air Force General Dzhokhar Dudayev, living in Estonia, to be president. Later, he was popularly elected in Chechnya and stated he wanted to free Chechnya from Russian rule. Many Russians in the current regime considered the elections illegal and therefore characterized Dudayev's presidency as illegitimate.[4] Russia's Fifth Congress of People's Deputies not only decreed the elections illegal but also declared Dudayev's regime unconstitutional.[5]

In early September, the Yeltsin administration had transferred power in Chechnya to a provisional supreme council under the command of a professor named Hussein Akmadov. Dudayev, whose power had been growing, decided to take a risk, and he used national guard forces to dissolve the council and occupied its building in the spring of 1993. Russia sent a delegation to negotiate with the Chechen president, but it was too weak to engender military support from Yeltsin to remove Dudayev. In June, Dudayev's presidential guard clashed with protestors of the parliament's dissolution and killed nearly fifty people. In addition, Russia protested the ongoing violations of the Russian

Constitution in Chechnya, the sharp increase in criminal activity in the region, the seizure of hostages by Chechens, and the increased number of deaths among the civilian population. All of these issues increased tension between President Yeltsin and Chechen President Dudayev.[6]

By the latter half of 1993, a group in opposition to Dudayev emerged in Chechnya, primarily in the northern part of the republic. This group initiated a small-scale guerrilla war. In spring 1994 the opposition called upon Russia to support it and help restore constitutional order. Russia's security services eventually supported the opposition covertly during an unsuccessful attack on Grozny in November 1994.[7] Russian complicity was exposed but not before Russian Defense Minister Pavel Grachev had publicly declared that no Russian soldiers were involved. Humiliated by the loss to the Dudayevites during this so-called Black Operation, Yeltsin ordered an immediate intervention into Chechnya. It began on 11 December 1994. Article 88 of the Russian Constitution and a decree from Yeltsin on 30 November served as the legal basis for the Russian action. The tasks of the Russian forces were to stabilize the situation, disarm armed bands, and reestablish law and order.

The situation itself was unique for Russia's armed forces. The command designation, a combined force operation of troops from the Ministry of Internal Affairs (MVD) and the Ministry of Defense (MOD), had not been tried before under such circumstances and on such a scale with such short notice. In addition, before the intervention, there was no serious thought given to the current condition and relative strength of Russia's forces. A special command was created in the North Caucasus Military Region to direct the operation's joint grouping.[8] The operational plan was designed:

> With the goal of disarming illegal armed bands and confiscating weapons and armaments from the population and reestablishing constitutional law and order on the territory of the Chechen Republic, the formations and units of the armed forces, together with other military forces of the Russian Federation, are to implement a special operation in four stages.[9]

Stages one and two were movement plans from outside of Chechnya into the republic. Stage three of the operation focused on objectives:

> Formations and units advance from the north and south to capture the Presidential Palace, government buildings, television and radio facilities, and other important structures in Grozny. Then, together with Special Forces subunits of the Internal Affairs Ministry and FSB, continue to confiscate weaponry and materiel.[10]

Finally, stage four was the stabilization of the conflict after capturing key objectives in Grozny.

The Russians believed that Dudayev's men totaled some 10,000 in the city and that they were armed with up to 80 D-30 122-millimeter (mm) howitzers, 25 tanks, and 35 BTRs and BMPs.[11] A few multiple-rocket launchers were also among the Chechens' equipment, as seen on local television reports. The Chechen account of its force size is different. Ilias Akhmadov, a fighter during the first battle for Grozny and now the republic's foreign minister, stated that only 450 Chechen fighters were "permanent," while the others were locals or those who came from neighboring villages. The republic's vice president at the time, Yanderbaiyev, believed the number was closer to 4,500 to 6,000. The actual size of the Chechen force thus remains in doubt.

According to the Russian description of their own forces, they had nearly 24,000 men, 19,000 from the armed forces and 4,700 from the MVD Internal Forces. For equipment, the Russians had 34 battalions (five motorized rifle, two tank, seven airborne, and twenty MVD battalions), which yielded 80 tanks, 208 BMPs, and 182 artillery pieces and mortars. Some 90 helicopters supplemented this effort. Thus, the Russians clearly had an advantage in men and equipment. Some of the Russian forces were real professionals such as the airborne units. Other Russian units, however, not only had never seen combat but also had not been involved in an exercise of this magnitude. Chechen forces were equally diversified. Some Chechens had fought in Abkhazia and were tried veterans. Others were fighting for the first time, although Chechen Ilias Akmadov noted that it took only a few days to turn most Chechens into competent fighters.

Three Russian force groupings were created to move troops into Chechnya from three directions: Mozdok, Vladikavkaz, and Kizliar (see Map 2). The operational plan was for the force groupings to advance on Grozny from six directions (additional directions were variants of the three main movement routes) and to blockade the city by forming two concentric rings. The outer ring, the MVD's responsibility, was to coincide with Chechnya's administrative border, and the inner ring, the MOD's responsibility, was to coincide with Grozny's outer city limits. By the end of December, everything was more or less ready for the Russians to advance on Grozny. Reconnaissance was conducted, vehicles and positions camouflaged, and engineers cleared lanes for passage. Defense Minister Grachev's forces believed that the Chechen command had created three defensive rings to defend Grozny. There was an inner circle with a radius of 1 to 1.5 kilometers (km)

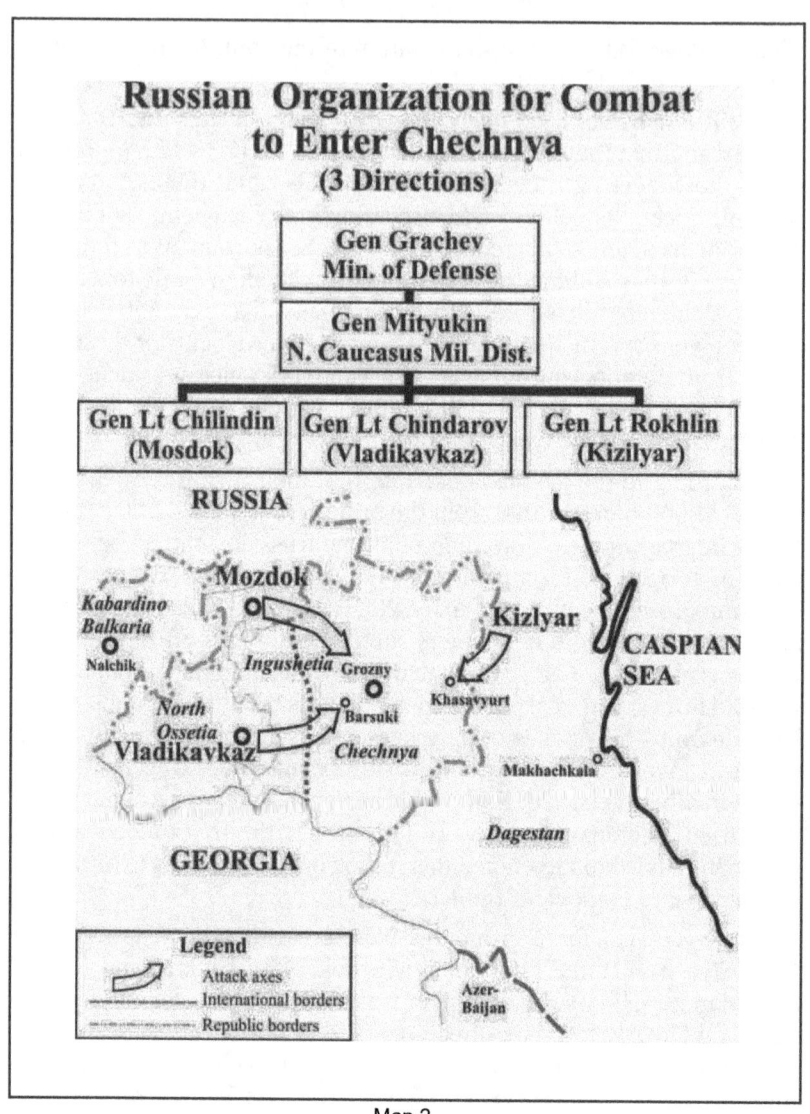

Map 2

around the presidential palace, a middle circle to a distance of up to 1 km from the inner borderline in the northwestern part of the city and up to 5 km in its southwestern and southeastern parts, and an outer circle that passed mainly through the city outskirts. The outer and middle defense rings were based on strongpoints, while the inner line consisted of prepared positions for direct artillery and tank fire. Lower and upper floors of buildings were prepared for the use of firearms and antitank weapons.[12]

The Mozdok grouping under the command of General Lieutenant V.M. Chilindin, moving from the northwest, was composed of the 131st Independent Motorized Rifle Brigade (MRB), the 106th Paratroop Division, and the 56th Independent Paratroop Brigade. Before moving into the city, the units of the northern group were situated in the following way. On the left flank was the 81st Motorized Rifle Regiment (MRR), the 131st MRB was in the center, and on the right was the 276th MRR, according to an interview with force commander General Major Konstantin Pulikovsky (it is assumed these regiments were part of the 106th Paratroop Division). Forces had to cross the small Neftyanka River on the way into Grozny. The western Vladikavkaz axis under the command of General Lieutenant Chindarov contained the 693d MRB of the 19th Motorized Rifle Division, a regiment from the 76th Paratrooper Division, and a paratrooper battalion from the 21st Independent Paratrooper Brigade. The east grouping from Kizlyar under the command of General Lieutenant Lev Roklin contained the 20th Motorized Rifle Division. Commanders, however, were unprepared to move quickly enough, and as the groupings advanced through Chechnya on their way to the city, only the forces from Mozdok and Kizlyar kept to their initial schedules. Other groups only reached initial positions by 20 or 21 December, and as a result, the blockade of the city was never completed. The south remained open to escaping refugees and to Chechen resupply routes, which the Russians did not foresee.[13]

On 26 December 1994, Russia's National Security Council authorized the final move on Grozny. The majority of Dudayev's forces and armaments were thought to be in the city, while armed attacks on Russian forces continued in the outlying areas. As one general noted about the plan of attack:

> The operational plan called for the separation of Grozny into areas or zones, with the railroad tracks and the Sunzha River serving as boundaries in the east west and north south directions, respectively. Storm detachments were to attack from several directions at once: from the north, west and east. Upon entering the city they were to coordinate with Special Forces of the MVD and the Federal Security Service and capture the Presidential Palace.[14]

Four columns advanced on Grozny (see Map 3). From the east, General Lieutenant Nikolay Staskov, deputy commander of airborne

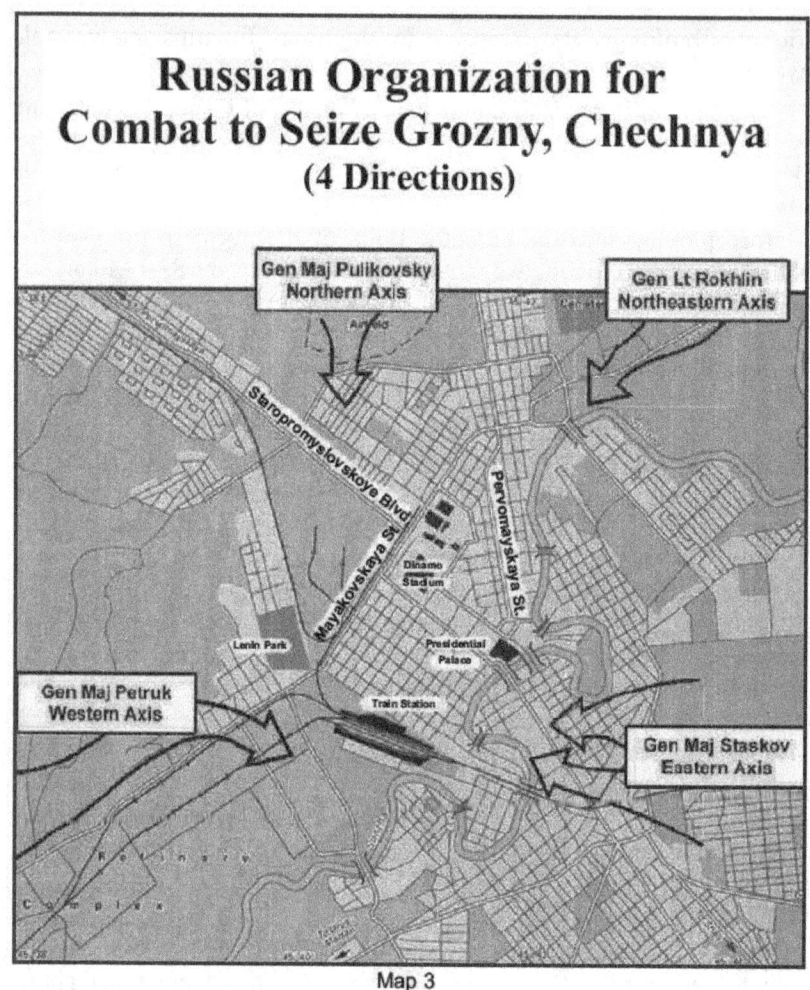

Map 3

forces for peacekeeping activity, commanded storm detachments of the 129th MRR and a parachute battalion from the 98th Airborne Division. They were to capture the bridges across the river and link up with the Northern and Western Force Group to block the central part of the city. From the west were two storm detachments of the 19th Motorized Rifle Division from Vladikovkaz under the command of General Major V. Petruk (overall commander of the western direction) and a regiment of the 76th Airborne Division from Pskov under the command of General Ivan Babichev (who was later designated the commander of western forces when Petruk was relieved). These forces were to attack along a zone bordered on the right by the railroad tracks and on the left by Popovicha Street. Their objectives were to capture the train station and then blockade the presidential palace from the south. In the north, General Major K. Pulikovsky commanded the 131st MRB, the 276th MRR, and the 81st MRR that were to isolate the Chechen formation from the city proper. General Lieutenant Lev Rokhlin commanded the final direction (he also commanded the move from Kizlyar toward Chechnay), the northeast, and he had under his command the 255th MRR. Their job was to block off the northern part of the city and the presidential palace from the north.

On 31 December, when the forces were told to move on the city, the western column commanded by General Petruk still had not arrived at his unit's assembly area outside Grozny. This caused the movement on the city to be disjointed and uncoordinated. According to Pulikovsky, the operation was unfolding so rapidly that the command almost did not have time to name it.

Russian Minister of Defense Pavel Grachev, who planned the attack and hoped to celebrate his birthday on the 31st with the rout of the Chechens, estimated that in 5 to 6 days the town would be fully cleansed of bandit formations.[15] The 81st MRR in the north moved into the city and became ensnared in an ambush on Pervomayskaya Street at about 1500 on 31 December. There was not enough infantry present, according to Pulikovsky, to sniff out the ambush, and the Chechens fired on the tanks in the column repeatedly from the upper windows of multistoried buildings. Pulikovsky, who thought the army would arrive to face little resistance and the Chechens would run, hide in the hills, or at least hide their weapons, later admitted that this initial resistance caught him by surprise. It was hard to imagine the Chechens doing anything while the Russians were in the town.

The 131st Maikop Brigade had moved at 0600 to the bridge over the Sunzha on 31 December and then into the city. Leaflets were distributed stating Chechen combatants should take their magazines out of their weapons, put their weapons over their left shoulder, and slowly advance toward Russian troops. The Chechens laughed at these instructions. In fact, a real but extremely small army was facing the Russians, one with former Soviet officers who understood the basics of Russian city tactics and operating procedures. The 131st entered Grozny unopposed. It was to have taken up a blocking position on the western side of the city but, sensing no opposition, reported back to Pulikovsky that it was ready to move on to its next objective. Apparently unaware of the situation of the 81st MRR, Pulikovsky authorized the 131st Maikovskiy Brigade to proceed to the train station near the city's center, also around 1500 on 31 December. Perhaps there was no opposition because Dudayev had only a few hundred fighters at the time and had focused most of his attention on the 81st MRR, the initial unit in contact. Colonel Savin led his forces into the city as if participating in a parade, according to Russian reports. He went along Staropromyslovskoye Boulevard to Mayakovskaya Street and then to the train station in the city center. All units were to link up there, and Savin got there first.

Savin reported that nothing was happening and that troops were lined up at the ticket counter arranging their rides home. Later in the day, however, Savin's communications chief reported that he had heard the phrase "welcome to hell" through his headset. Savin did not know if this was some type of joke or a warning. Suddenly, without warning, some Chechen fighters appeared behind the train station, and all hell broke loose. The Russians did not understand initially what had happened. Since the situation appeared so calm, they had gone into the train station, hardly securing their vehicles or even bothering to post guards. In the meantime, Chechen mobile units had fallen back on the city center and had surrounded them at the train station. They methodically began to destroy the Soviet BMPs with rocket-propelled grenade (RPG) fire. Not in their wildest dreams could the Russians imagine how unpredictable and vulnerable their situation had become.

According to one participant, everything happened very fast, as if a nuclear war had started with no one around. In addition to the shooting, the Chechens attempted to demoralize the Russians, using communications intercepts to relay threats. For the Russians, of course, there was no thought of surrender. But after a few hours, Russian ammunition began to run low (they had not planned on extensive battles in the city), and they began to lose scores of soldiers to the Chechen onslaught. The 74th Brigade was to have advanced at nearly the same time as the 131st, which would have offered some reinforcements, but they stopped to celebrate New Year's Eve. The 503d Regiment was supposed to be sent into Grozny to support the movement as well, but it refused to move, citing lack of preparation. The commander of the 503d said he had fulfilled his order already and saw no reason to put everyone at risk that way at night in a city. The 131st then attempted a breakout from the train station and lost 60 more men, including Colonel Savin. The Chechens also took severe losses in the fighting. Estimates later were that the Russians had 300 soldiers in the train station to fight against 1,000 Chechens, figures that the Chechens contest.

Clearly, the Chechen plan of defense perceived by Grachev (the three concentric rings) did not appear to be the case in reality as the Chechens were apparently organized quite differently. Otherwise, the Russian force could not have proceeded to the city center with such ease. According to Chechen Ilias Akmadov, the Russians were not "lured" into the city center but "driven" there because there were no concentric rings or forces available for such resistance. The Chechens, in fact, noted that no such plan existed. Instead, the "situation did the organizing." One fighter noted that the attack on 31 December came as a surprise to him, a statement supported by the fact that no barricades or fighters met the Russian force moving into the city that day. The Chechens lacked enough numerical strength to organize even one echelon of defense around the city.

However, the company or group commanders had a great deal of autonomy. Mobile groups of ten to twelve people operated relatively independently, each group consisting of one grenade launcher, two snipers, and the rest with automatic weapons. There simply were no well-defined lines of defense. The groups were always on the move. The greatest weakness was their inability to coordinate Chechen regular forces with local militias, although intimate knowledge of the city helped overcome this weakness. At times, seventy people made their way through dead space while Russians were only 30 to 40 meters away. This was especially true at night when the Russian soldiers lost the desire to move around, according to a Chechen fighter.[16] The Chechens had little if any urban combat training, a fact that makes one marvel at their success. Akmadov noted that everything was so condensed and quick that it only took a few days to turn a raw recruit into the Chechen concept of "a professional."

According to interviews conducted after the fighting ended, the Chechens also had a fixed method of conducting ambushes. The ambush was based on using 25-man groups composed of three mobile squads of two heavy machine gunners, two RPG gunners, one sniper, and three riflemen. Three of these 25-man groups (supported by an 82mm mortar crew with two tubes) would conduct an ambush as a 75-man unit. Three of the eight-man squads would serve as a "killer team" and set up in three positions along the ambush route. They would occupy the lower level of buildings in the ambush zone to prevent being wounded by incoming artillery. The remaining fifty men would occupy blocking positions to ensure the entrapped Russians could not escape and to prevent reinforcements from entering the ambush area.[17] To counter this tactic, the Russians would conduct extensive artillery fire on a proposed route of advance, attempting to reduce buildings along the route to rubble. This method proved effective, although on occasion, the rubble served as excellent ambush positions for the Chechen fighters.

In fairness to the Russians, however, it must be noted that the Russian force was poorly trained. As General Boris Gromov, commander of the Soviet Union's 40th Army in Afghanistan, noted about Russia's armed forces:

> The troops taking part in the combat operations had not been prepared for this either morally or physically or professionally. The armed forces are not distinguished today by a high degree of training or personnel and they lack a sufficient quantity of equipment that is in good working order and combat ready, communication and control facilities, technical and rear support, and so forth. All this condemned the military campaign in Chechnya in advance to big casualties on both sides.[18]

State Duma deputy Viktor Sheynis' eyewitness information about the 31 December operation was available in newspapers on 2 January. He indicated that the initial attack on New Year's Eve was a total disaster for Russia. According to an interview with a participant of the operation, the 131st MRB and the 81st MRR took the brunt of the losses. In one column alone, 102 of 120 armored personnel carriers and 20 of 26 tanks were destroyed by Chechen antitank fire; all six "Tunguska" surface-to-air missile systems were destroyed. Seventy-four servicemen, including a corps operations officer, were captured.[19] The commander of a division surface-to-air missile platoon, Lieutenant Colonel Aleksandr Labzenko, added that:

> ... they were not trained to fight in cities and an enormous amount of armored equipment, thoughtlessly left in narrow streets without any cover, was not protected by the infantry ... there is a lack of even basic cooperation between different subunits and their commanders and subordinates.[20]

In short, the Chechens nearly brought the Russian force to its knees from 1-3 January. One Russian close to the fighting reported that "many officers in Chechnya have confessed to me in mid-January 1995 that at the beginning of that month the Russian Army was on the verge of refusing to obey the ridiculous orders of its commanders and the government."[21] Later in the year, the head of Yeltsin's personal security force, Alexander Korzhakov, allegedly noted that "Grachev dragged Yeltsin into the Chechen mess, and a man of integrity [in Grachev's shoes] would have shot himself."[22]

According to retrospective reports, there were three principal reasons for the initial disaster. First, the Russian army worked under severe restrictions, some self-imposed and some imposed by nature. One officer noted that the rules of engagement did not allow for the Russians to open fire first, resulting in the deaths or wounding of many soldiers.[23] Military support was most severely affected, however, by some commanders refusing to participate in the coordinated attack on Grozny (in particular, the commanders of axes west and east who did not enter the city despite their radio reports that they had). Most likely this was not due to cowardice on the part of the officers in charge of the western and eastern columns but, rather, to confusion and a lack of administrative and air support available after entering the city's outskirts, leaving their forces vulnerable. This left the 131st MRB and 81st MRR without support and at the mercy of the Chechens. In addition, nature worked against the Russian force. Not only was it winter but also bad weather limited air support on 1 and 2 January.

Second, the Russian army was unprepared and untrained for immediate combat, let alone combat in cities. To fight under such circumstances was simply absurd and doomed to failure. Anne Garrels of National Public Radio was in the basement of the presidential palace on 3 January and interviewed Russian prisoners of war (POWs).[24] Some of the young recruits told her that they did not know with whom they were riding as they entered the city because they had been thrown together as a crew only a day or so before; that they did not understand who was fighting whom; that some of the soldiers thought they were going into Grozny for police or law enforcement duty and not to fight; and that some of the soldiers had neither a weapon, ammunition, a map, nor a mission. Some, in fact, were sleeping in the back of their BMP or BTR as it entered the city. In addition, there was little training to coordinate units' and subunits' actions. This was particularly true for missions involving the armed forces and the MVD troops.

Third, the Russian leadership did not do a good job of preparing the "theater" for warfare. The High Command neither sealed off the republic's borders nor took the time required to rehearse properly for the potential scenarios that Dudayev had prepared for them. One general, choosing anonymity, noted that after liberating several city districts, Russian forces realized that Dudayev had created numerous firing points, communications nets, and underground command points that made the job much more difficult. In this respect, the main military intelligence (GRU) and federal counterintelligence service (FSK) did poor jobs of providing information on the armed formations that the Russian force faced, compounding the fate of the untrained soldiers.[25]

Still unexplained in the initial plan is the Russian commanders' apparent disregard of the lessons learned from the "Black Operation" the anti-Dudayev opposition forces conducted in November 1994. For example, Major Valeriy Ivanov, speaking to State Duma deputies about the failed 26 November attack, noted that he was told "special forces would be at work there [in Grozny] and helicopters would provide fire support from the air. Infantry would be attached to the tanks." None of this support appeared. Lieutenant Dmitriy Volfovich supported Ivanov, noting that the tankers could not respond with machine gun fire because "the machine guns were not loaded." And a plan to paint tank hatches white to allow helicopter pilots to identify friend from foe backfired when no helicopter support appeared, and Dudayev's force fired on "white caps" against a gray background.[26] Chechen forces fought according to their own plans, which Defense Minister Grachev, for one, viewed as inhumane. For example, he noted that Chechen forces conducted attacks under cover of civilian "human shields" and fought from positions in hospitals, schools, and apartment blocks.[27]

The shocking defeat of 1-3 January changed the course of the remainder of the fight for the city. In fact, the battle of Grozny can be divided into three separate parts. Part one is the 31 December-3 January fight described to this point. Part two refers to actions taken between 4-17 January when the Russians recovered and captured President Dudayev's palace and the northern portion of the city while Chechen resistance evacuated the presidential palace and took up defensive positions on the other side of the Sunzha River. Part three focuses on the fighting from 17 January to 8 February when Russian forces managed to rid Grozny of the major Chechen fighting elements on the southern side of the Sunzha (see Map 4).

Despite the shock and heavy losses suffered in the attack of 1-3 January, the worst appeared over by 4-5 January due to an apparent Chechen retreat. Moscow's official mood once again appeared to be one of optimism. First came reports of Chechens moving out of Grozny and aircraft strikes on their remaining tanks and other combat vehicles (or those the Chechens captured in the first four days of the fight).[28] Chechen convoys moving in a southerly and southeastern direction were passing through outlying villages along two routes—either through the villages of Shali, Serzhen-Yurt, and Benoy-Vedeno or the villages of Shali, Kirov-Yurt, and Makhkety—while the center of Grozny remained under Chechen control.[29] Enemy groups were also re-

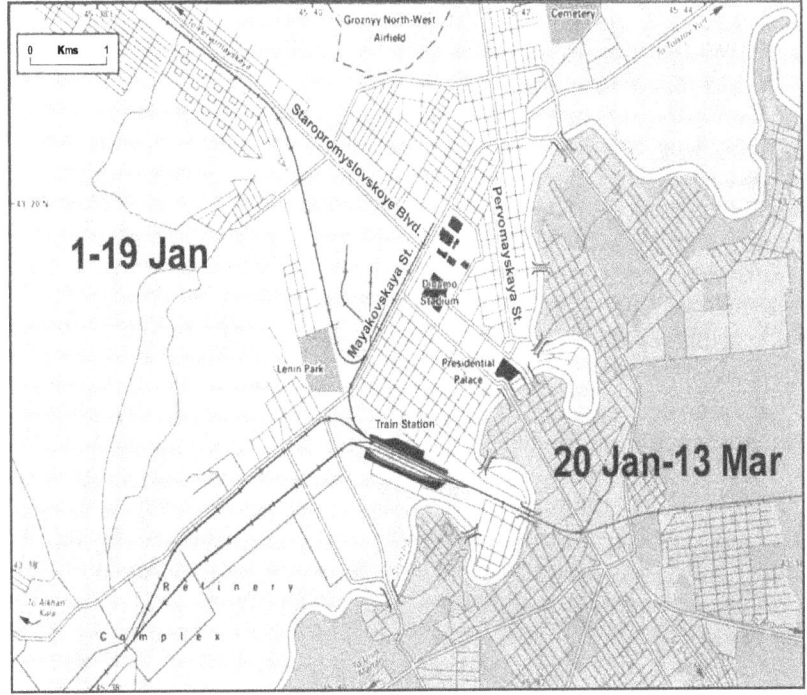

Map 4

portedly moving in a northeasterly direction away from Grozny but were repulsed from entering Dagestan by OMON (special purpose militia detachments), border troops, and Internal Forces, as well as fire support from the air, according to official sources.[30] Russian Vice Premier Yegorov noted that Grozny should be taken on 5 January without any further fighting and the legitimate government established simultaneously.[31] This information was contradicted by live reporting from the area by Russian journalists who reported that Dudayev subunits controlled the streets and had many Russian units surrounded.[32] Thus, when viewed in hindsight, reports that the worst appeared over indicate that Russian officials tried to cover up their shortcomings while the independent media thwarted this attempt at official deception.

It was clear to those on the ground that the battle would indeed proceed according to a different scenario. On the 6th, the Interfax news agency reported that special units of the Russian MOD destroyed a Chechen commando group using weapons "with elements of artificial intelligence." These elements included using aerial reconnaissance and satellite data as well as laser- and television (TV)-guided air-to-surface missiles. According to the source, this would not be the last use of weapons designed for other "theaters of operation."[33]

By 7 January, Orthodox Christmas, it was evident that the Russian military was in a dogfight, and no amount of optimistic press reports would change the story. Ostankino TV noted that the fighting was the most fierce since 31 December-1 January, reporting on the 7th that the entire town was ablaze, along with the refinery and other outlying industrial companies.[34] Clearly, the war was not getting any easier for the Russian forces. Ham radio operators in Chechnya transmitted information on Russian troops that allowed the Chechens to pinpoint Russian locations.[35]

Russian reconnaissance units searched for Russian POWs, while federal troops continued to fight well-armed mobile groups of Chechens. The Chechens used civil defense as well as underground sewage and water tunnels both to flank and to get into the rear of military units. Chechen tactics added to the advancing Russians' psychological stress. They booby-trapped tanker trucks, mined roads, and held civilians hostage.[36] In addition, Russian artillery shells were reportedly falling in the city of Grozny at a rate of 15 to 20 per minute (the latter report from a Duma representative).[37]

One Chechen commander reported having 85 to 125 men defending a district of Grozny that extended 1 km. He added that he had only two RPG-7s at the time and that he doubted if Chechen Chief of Staff Aslan Maskhadov had more than 400 men total. His unit's tactic:

> was to fire at the enemy everywhere without being seen anywhere. The Russians did not know where and who the enemy was. We shot, destroyed, withdrew, went home to sleep, returned to start military actions again. No organization or planning. We were independent hunters.[38]

At the same time, journalists were striking back at Russian military leaders for the latter's criticism of the reporting from Grozny. Members of the news media pointed out that it was nearly impossible to report from military bases because they could not go anywhere and their cameras and film were confiscated, whereas the Dudayevites helped reporters. This resulted in "one-sided" reporting from the Dudayev perspective according to some journalists who asked who was to blame for portraying events under such conditions, the journalists or the Russian military commanders who refused the journalists access to Russian soldiers?[39] Even the Russian command later indicated it had made a serious mistake in this area. Counterintelligence head Sergei

Stepashin noted that "we began the operation in Chechnya without having prepared public opinion for it at all... I would include the simply absurd ban on journalists working among our troops . . . while journalists were his [Dudayev's] invited guests."[40]

Regrouping took place on 8 and 9 January after the ferocious fighting of the 7th. Russian Internal Forces busily tried to restore the Chechen police force, a necessity to return Grozny to self-rule. They appealed to anyone among the local populace who wished to work to restore law and order.[41] Russian military commanders talked to militants in buildings through megaphones, urging them to lay down their arms. As these efforts were under way, indications were that young Chechen volunteers aged 16 to 18 arrived to reinforce their republic's armed formations as well as "a regiment of kamikazes" wearing black headbands.[42] Chechens also were sent to the Russian side to misinform the federal armed forces about Chechen plans, and a network of informers advised on all movements of internal and defense forces as the latter proceeded through North Ossetia, Ingushetia, and Dagestan.[43] Another report indicated that in early January a group of sixty fighters, half of them women, swore on the Koran an oath of allegiance to sovereign Chechnya and its president, vowing to go to Moscow to commit subversive and terrorist actions.[44] There also was a report that up to a hundred Russians had surrendered in Grozny on 7 and 8 January, some of them special forces troops. In a few instances, some soldiers were drunk. Reporting ended on the stark note that in recent days, in the freezing basements where the civilians were huddled, babies were being born.[45] This indicates the extent of the varied missions and problems confronting soldiers in urban environments and the difficulty in uncovering the truth.

On 9 January, the Russian government declared a cease-fire. It would begin at 0800 on 10 January and last for 48 hours, according to the official announcement. Just two hours after the cease-fire started on the 10th, Russian artillery shells began raining down on the Chechen presidential palace.[46] The head of the Chechen General Staff, Aslan Maskhadov, declared the 48-hour cease-fire a Moscow "trick." It is not known if Russia's forces simply disobeyed the order on purpose or if the continuation of firing was due to Chechen actions and the Russian forces were merely acting in self-defense:

> The Russians reported on the 10th of January that the Chechens were breaking the cease fire of the 9th (which the Chechens reported was already broken by the Russians), and so federal troops were merely responding according to the principle of "adequate response."[47]

This tactic of double-crossing one another after an agreement was to be repeated many times in the coming months.

By 10 January, the Russian force had managed to make two corridors into the city for supplying the army and evacuating wounded servicemen to hospitals, but talks with authorities to remove the bodies of Russian soldiers lying on Grozny's streets were fruitless.[48] However, the Chechens did allow a Russian POW and representatives of the Russian Orthodox Church in Grozny to do the negotiating with the Russian side (with General Babichev, the new commander of Russian forces entering Grozny from the west). Moscow radio reported that the Chechens had gathered the bodies of Russians lying near the presidential palace and piled them in one place, with sentries firing short volleys to drive hungry dogs away from the bodies.[49]

Also on 10 January, a report indicated that federal forces attacked in the direction of the presidential palace but were beaten back. If the attack occurred, it was not a serious one, and only rarely were mortars heard. Russian troops remained about 400 meters to the north and 1.5 km to the west of the city center.[50] Radio Ekho Moskvy was, as usual, much more negative in its reporting (Radio Ekho Moskvy talked with Chechens and did not rely on strictly official Russian reports), noting that two Chechen negotiators carrying white flags were killed, Chechen villages were bombed, and Russian units appeared to be preparing for a new assault on 12 January, when the cease-fire officially ended.[51] The contradictions in these two reports indicate just how much ITAR-TASS's official reporting and the nongovernmental reporting from agencies such as Ekho Moskvy differed.

During the cease-fire that finally took place later on the 10th, Russian Prime Minister Victor Chernomyrdin offered an interesting concession worthy of note. He proposed to villagers in Chechnya that if they ensured that armed formations did not open fire from or within populated areas, he would guarantee that the federal troops would not conduct combat operations there.[52]

On the combat front, Dudayev's militants continued to resist in scattered regions of the city, especially in the Katayama, Baranovka, and Oktyabrskiy districts, and they continued to disguise themselves as local inhabitants or even Russian soldiers. Internal forces focused on guarding administrative borders of the Chechen republic and on conducting operations to locate local gangs to disarm and/or liquidate them. Federal forces continued the search for POWs.[53] On 11 January, a Russian TV documentary depicted the fighting in Chechnya for the first time from a Russian perspective. Titled "Hell" and produced by

Aleksandr Nevzorov, who previously held anti-Yeltsin views, the documentary clearly was a progovernment production designed to bolster army morale and to show the country the difficulties the average soldier in Chechnya faced. For the first time, the character of the conflict was given a new understanding, as the Chechen force's strength and their atrocities were depicted. Nevzorov, speaking with commander Lev Rokhlin, noted that the Chechens could only be considered an army and not merely bandit formations. Rokhlin agreed and added, "it is a mercenary army."[54]

In another report, more difficult to believe but supported by later interviews with Chechen fighters, Radio Ekho Moscow tape recorded interviews with Russian soldiers and reported that special troops stood behind the soldiers when they went into battle and threatened to shoot them if they retreated or tried to give up; the soldiers also reported that they had an order to kill women, old people, and children.[55] This statement was reminiscent of the actions of the old People's Commissariat for Internal Affairs (NKVD) to prevent Russian and Soviet desertions in past hostilities.

At 0800 on 12 January, the cease-fire officially ended. During the cease-fire, an additional 100 vehicles arrived to reinforce Russian positions. Federal forces regrouped, rotated troops, and prepared for the next assault. The Russians apparently could not wait for 0800 to arrive. At 0700, Russian forces pounded the city center incessantly with artillery (shells landed every ten seconds for over three hours), and at 0930, forty Grad rockets slammed into the main city square. Russian snipers also gained some ground.[56] Fighting was intense, and the Russian assault continued during 13-14 January, with most of the combat activity centered at the buildings of the presidential palace, the Council of Ministers, Chechen Internal Affairs, and security ministries and at the railway station.[57] Simultaneously, MVD forces blockaded the main departure routes out of Grozny as well as Chechnya's administrative borders. An indicator of how intense the fighting had become was that doctors no longer put on their white smocks because Chechen snipers were using them for targets. Earlier, Chechen militants downed three ambulance helicopters displaying red crosses, according to Moscow reports.[58]

It was not until 15 January that the whole town was sealed off, including its southern sector.[59] This was the first time the armed forces had succeeded in accomplishing this, a fact many viewed as a prerequisite to entering the town in the first place. Chechen forces immediately tried to deploy additional troops in the south to prevent the encirclement from becoming permanent.⁶⁰ The 15th also witnessed continued attacks by Russian shock units and assault detachments to dislodge Dudayev's fighters from a number of buildings and continued attempts by paratroopers, motorized infantry units, and marines to get inside the presidential palace, an effort that would take another four days. Female snipers were rumored to be fighting for the Chechens, and during the assault, Interfax news agency reported that a female sniper from Belarus had been killed.⁶¹ However, when asked his opinion, Russian 8th Army Corps commander Lev Rokhlin noted that the militants' resistance had slackened, and the only reason the Russians had not taken the presidential palace was to keep the casualty rate low since Russian POWs reportedly were still in the basement. Rokhlin noted the militants were short of ammunition, supplies, and food, and on orders from the Chechen leadership, the militants were now possibly being issued drugs.⁶²

On 19 January, the Mayak Radio Network reported that the Russian Federation flag was flying over the presidential palace in Grozny. While many assumed that the fighting was over, combat continued for a month or so. The battle to date had only included the northern and central parts of Grozny. South of the Sunzha, the Chechens still controlled much of the city. Therefore, raising the flag was mostly a symbolic act. It did, however, confirm Russian control over President Dudayev's center of power and symbol of resistance.

ITAR-TASS reported on 19 January that Dudayev had lost control over his forces, Chechen communications had become unreliable, and foreign mercenaries were now in the second echelon. Dudayev's militants reportedly killed those who ran away.⁶³ Dudayev moved to the southeastern district of the town (to the opposite side of the Sunzha River) and replaced his bodyguard with Lithuanian mercenaries.⁶⁴ Another report had Dudayev taking refuge in the bomb shelter of City Hospital No. 5 along with a 150- to 200-man guard force while a new headquarters was being prepared for him in the mountain regions of Chechnya.⁶⁵

Meanwhile, battles continued to rage in the southern sections of Grozny. Russian reinforcements continued to be rushed in from as far away as the Pacific Fleet. It was not until 21 January that group West and group North (now containing elements of group East and the remnants of the main assault force from the north) met in the center of Grozny. The Chechens moved to the southeast section of the city and established a bridgehead on the other side of the Sunzha River. A few days later, the Russian army began a month-long final assault on those positions.[66]

Also on 21 January, Russian reporting indicated that the situation in the center of Grozny had somewhat eased.[67] Russian Federal Counterintelligence Service director Sergey Stepashin noted that about 3,500 Chechen militants still remained in Grozny, however. Vladimir Polozhentsev of Ostankino TV reported that military and political leaders of the Chechen Republic were preparing provocations in the region, aiming to exacerbate ethnic tensions and destabilize the situation in the North Caucasus in general.[68] On 22 January, news agencies reported that elements of the Chechen population were beginning to insist that Dudayev's men occupying villages surrounding Grozny leave and take their weapons with them, to include mobile missile launchers.[69] In Grozny, however, militants continued to lay mines along their routes of retreat, to recruit new fighters, to bring in reserves, and to set up command posts to the south of the Sunzha River. Fifty new mercenaries with blue berets and the inscription "Ukraine" had also appeared.[70]

On 24 January, ITAR-TASS reported that army troops and internal forces were preparing to form "commandant zones." They also formed a garrison procurator's office. Militant actions now were only occurring at night and appeared to lack synergy. However, some Chechen units were bribing people to provoke aggressive actions, and some representatives of the Chechen clergy still were reported to be calling on local residents for terrorist acts against Russian servicemen.[71] Russian forces continued artillery bombardment of the outlying districts of Grozny. Russian Defense Minister Grachev felt the scattered resistance was insignificant and believed that there were no population centers in Chechnya where bandit formations could mount serious opposition to federal forces.[72] This assessment would be proven tragically wrong.

The normally antigovernment radio station, Ekho Moskvy, noted that federal forces had basically completed their tasks and that the MVD would have the city under its total control by the end of January. Then only the MVD and troops from the North Caucasus Military District would be left in Chechnya.[73] On 26 January, Radio Rossii reported that Security Council Secretary Oleg Lobov disclosed that, until a general election was held, an interim administrative body would be set up to rule Chechnya.[74] Also on 26 January, ITAR-TASS offered a final situation report. Clearly, the essence of the report was that the internal forces now were in charge. While federal troops continued to combat militants on the Sunzha River left bank, internal forces:

> ... blocked the main routes of movement of Chechen militants, sealed off the areas of dislocation of armed formations, and blocked the administrative border of the Chechen republic in order to prevent an inflow of bands, mercenaries, weapons, and military hardware, as well as protected communications, roads and bridges, and inspected transport vehicles.[75]

Finally, on 26 January, control of the fighting on the Russian side was transferred to the MVD in the person of General Anatoliy Kulikov, commander of the internal forces of the Ministry of Internal Affairs (some 290,000 soldiers at the time). All Russian armed forces in Chechnya were now under his control. He still had much work to do to capture the city.

Reporting from 31 January indicated that Russian troops were blocking streets, engaging in street fighting, and repulsing armed groups' attacks. Thus, the indication was that the Chechens would not leave the city quickly or easily. In addition, Russian troops reported directing intensified shelling on Minutka Square, a key transport and communication intersection a few km southeast of the presidential palace. A large number of Chechen forces were reportedly concentrating there. Mobile groups as large as thirty to forty men were in the area.[76]

On 2 February, Kulikov noted that the army and internal forces were continuing to succeed in pushing the Chechens out of Grozny, underscoring that the larger part of the city was under Russian control. Part of Oktyabrskiy District, another key road intersection in the south of the city near Minutka Square, remained under Dudayev's control. Russian forces used the Shmel flamethrower to destroy strongpoints and snipers, and began to demonstrate more confidence in their operation.[77] Troops continued disarming Chechen formations in Grozny and organized police work in the Leninskiy district of Grozny. The Chechens, however, maintained that they retained control of the right bank of the Sunzha and that they continued to smash Russian special subunits. On 3 February, the Russian bridgehead was expanded to Leningrad Street where it crossed Yakutskiy Street. As a result, Kulikov noted that a "turning point" was now in sight, and on 5 February, Minister of Defense Grachev stated that control was established over Minutka Square and over the southern approaches to the city.[78]

The Chechens, however, still held out and decided not to give up the city without a fight. On 6 February, Kulikov noted that some of his forces in the city were under multiple rocket launcher and heavy artillery attacks from the few items of this sort in the Chechen inventory (obtained before the war illegally or acquired during the fight for

Grozny). Countering these threats required the operational subordination of Defense Ministry tanks and helicopters to the internal forces, equipment not standard issue to the MVD. The Chechens reported that they still held most of the Oktyabrskiy District and the suburb of Chernorechye in the southern and southwestern parts of Grozny, while Russian reporting countered these claims. In addition, snipers and small formations of Chechens infiltrated the city in some regions and continued to battle the Russian blockade in other areas. On 8 February, the city was reported to be 80 percent under the control of General Kulikov's internal forces, but Chechen mobile assault groups still remained. At night, the Chechens continued to rule the streets, and it was then that most of the Russian casualties occurred. Supposedly, the Chechen main command had evacuated the city and moved to other, smaller cities, leaving only a reconnaissance and harassment force in place.[79] This tactic of "successive cities" was a recurrent theme throughout the war.

A significant development very much related to the battlefield activities under way was the announcement on 8 February that a Bureau for Current Information and a Mobile Information Center were being established under the federal executive authorities' Territorial Administration in the Chechen Republic. Yevgeniy Ivanov was appointed chief of the Press Service Mobile Information Center. Representatives of the public relations center of all the security services were also included in the work of the center.[80] This would finally allow the Russian press service to control some of the reporting from Chechnya and would allow all of the services to sing from a common sheet of music. To date, Russia had completely lost the "information war" because it had allowed the Chechens (who even gave reporters access to operational material) to control the reporting.

The battle for Grozny continued until 23 February. On 16 February, a cease-fire was declared to exchange prisoners and the wounded. Combat resumed on the 20th, and the Russians seized the heights above the area of Novye Promysly. This was important in that Dudayev's TV broadcasting center was located there on Hill 373. The Chechens tried to retake the hill three days later but failed and instead fled to other cities or into the mountains. By 23 February, Dudayev's remaining detachments were surrounded in the areas of Novye Promysly, Aldy, and Chernorech'e.

Chechen Chief of Staff Aslan Maskhadov commented on the final withdrawal of his forces from Grozny. He expressed pride at his men's accomplishments over the past month and termed the current situation not a retreat but a planned withdrawal. He added that his Chechen force did not possess Russia's superiority in artillery, tanks, and planes but that if one of his men had ten RPGs, then he expected eight tanks to be destroyed. One Chechen fighter added the following:

> I never thought that I would see this happen. There will be much blood paid for this. The Russians have made a bad, bad mistake. But we did manage to hold out here for 37 days Berlin lasted only two weeks in 1945. This war will continue, only now it will be one without front lines.[81]

When a shot is fired in the Caucasus, the echo lasts 100 years.

Thus, at the end of February, after nearly 40 days of sustained battle, the fight for Grozny was over. The Chechens moved on to other cities, a habit they followed throughout the course of the war, which ended in August 1996. Perhaps the Chechens' initial success in Grozny was the motivation for this tactic. They found out in the first few weeks of January 1995 that, even when badly outmanned and outequipped, the city offered them unique advantages—familiarity with the terrain, the element of surprise, and the use of nonlinear and asymmetric tactics, among others. The Chechens gained confidence in their ability to withstand even the most ferocious Russian armed offensive. They did so despite having no air support at all. The Russians, for their part, did not consider the battle for Grozny a victory as much as they did a successful operation. They suffered incredible losses in the first week of fighting and then drew on the experience of their artillery forces and storm detachments to collect themselves and conduct block-by-block fighting until they eventually drove the Chechens out of the city. Simultaneously, the Russian forces began the process of turning the local population against them. Unfortunately, the Russians maintained an air of arrogance after this success that eventually led to their defeat and expulsion from the republic in the August 1996 battle for Grozny.

The January 1995 battle for Grozny offered lessons learned from a variety of perspectives. What follows are four different looks at the fighting. First, there is the reporting of Russian military correspondents—beginning with Igor Korotchenko—who were in the city during the fight. Second, there are named and unnamed Russian military specialists who wrote for journals and magazines, trying to explain what happened in January 1995. Third, there are some professional analyses by Russian leaders of the operation, such as Minister of Defense Grachev and the leader of the main assault and later head of the North

Caucasus Military District, General Kvashnin. Finally, there are testimonies from Chechens who fought the Russians.

News correspondent Korotchenko, a civilian who had studied the ongoing fighting in Chechnya closely over the months of December and January, stated that it was critical to increase dramatically the use of special troops and especially electronic warfare units in the combat zone. He advocated creating a total information vacuum by putting remotely controlled portable jammers near guerilla bases and by suppressing satellite communications channels Dudayev used. He also believed it was vital to force tactics on the Chechens that put them at a disadvantage such as night operations. He also recommended not sending composite units to Chechnya with servicemen selected from several units and thrown together for a particular mission. Such a selection process results in losses two to three times higher than usual, according to Korotchenko.[82]

Another reporter, Anatol Lieven, offered telling observations about the fight for Grozny that could apply to any armed force. For example, the effectiveness of even the best technologies for urban warfare will depend on how confused and afraid the man using them is. Furthermore, the capacity of social tradition to mobilize fighters and impose a discipline on them goes beyond the "surface discipline" (imposed by basic training) of a modern army. Finally, failure can result from the limitations of firepower when fighting a dispersed infantry opponent behind good cover.[83]

Other lessons Russia's military learned based on information analysis also seeped into the papers. FSK director Sergey Stepashin noted that the enemy's potential was underestimated, Russia's strength was overestimated, Dudayev's Moscow connections were not identified, and Dudayev's informers with connections in high places continued to operate in place during the war.[84] Now we understand, Stepashin added, that special services must have special subdivisions to resolve the struggle against bandit groups and particularly dangerous criminals who head criminal structures.[85] Another commentator noted that the Russian army had to fulfill its task while an "information war" was conducted behind its back with its own country's propaganda machine firing the shots![86] The truth of the matter was that the Russian military refused to allow cameramen or journalists to interview their soldiers. Dudayev, on the other hand, understood full well the implications of the press and had it dancing to his tune. He showed the press what he wanted it to see, put his own spin on events through interviews, and along with his propaganda chief Udugov, literally won the information war without opposition.

The second lesson learned was that opinions of Russian military professionals writing for journals and newspapers had influence. One lengthy critique of the operation, supposedly written by an unidentified but highly placed military officer writing for *Novaya Yezhednevnaya Gazeta*, noted shortcomings in so many areas that it appeared that the Russian armed forces must nearly be incompetent (which was not the case).[87] The officer listed troop preparation shortcomings such as poor morale and physical preparations. He noted a lack of training for a march or offensive combat, weak knowledge of materiel and armaments, weak fighting and weapon skills, poorly trained drivers, and a lack of confidence in using armaments. He added that the force lacked an overall knowledge of the rules of engagement against targets of opportunity and moving targets, first aid and administering antishock drugs, ambush preparations and means of movement, and target designation with smoke. Finally, he stated that there was poor use of smoke screens and sniper groups to neutralize enemy gun crews; poor preparation of assault groups to destroy enemy fire positions, pillboxes, and emplacements; and poor training in using flamethrowers and grenade launchers. In addition, personnel did not carry identification tags according to this officer, making their identification in case of death difficult.[88]

In April 1995, an article about the fight for Grozny appeared in the Russian military journal, *Armeyskiy Sbornik* (*Army Journal*). One of the first to address lessons learned in a professional journal, the article, titled "Sweeping Built Up Areas," did more than hint at some of the problems Russian commanders encountered. It noted the importance of unexpectedly, quickly, and completely sealing off areas to the enemy and the requirement to establish two rings of encirclement, the first 2 to 3 km from the main objective and the second on the outskirts of the city. Another problem was inability of tanks, BMPs, and other vehicles to cover the advance of ground troops and the lack of even "amateur" improvements to fighting vehicles and firing positions (such as putting screens on armor made from fine mesh metal netting or filling cartridge and shell boxes with crushed rock, broken brick, or gravel to reduce the effect of rounds fired at the vehicle).[89] The article also revealed that on many occasions one Russian unit fired on another due to Chechen chicanery. For example, during the assault on Grozny:

> Mortars mounted on Kamaz trucks fired one salvo and immediately moved to another area. They have learned to skillfully disorient fire

spotters [forward observers], often creating a friendly fire situation. Thus, on the eve of the taking of the palace, a Russian Grad multiple rocket launcher fired on its own reconnaissance forces. Troops subjected each other to a half hour of fire on approaches to Grozny, while motorized riflemen tested the strength of airborne personnel while moving up to the train station.[90]

According to Russian guidelines, the Russian force was undermanned for the operation. For combat in cities, the ratio of offensive and defensive forces must be 4:1 or 5:1 in favor of the attacker.[91] This was not the case in Grozny. It was apparent that 50,000 to 60,000 men were needed to storm Grozny. In 1941 when Kalinin was liberated, a ratio of 4:1 was needed. On 3 January 1995, only 5,000 Russian soldiers were in the city. In addition, the element of surprise was lost, and Dudayev reinforced his men with replacements from the south. This general situation sometimes is forgotten during the interpretation of lessons learned after the fight ended, but it greatly affected the course and outcome of the battle.

Russian officers interviewed in Moscow after the fight noted that elements of the Russian force appeared unprepared in both training and planning to fight in builtup areas. There were few local guides to move Russian forces through the city. As a result, Russian forces ended up in gardens and dead-end streets. A major problem both the MVD and the army encountered was identifying Chechen guerilla forces that would walk around the city, sometimes wearing Red Cross armbands, and then fire at Russian personnel from windows or dark alleyways. To distinguish fighters from peaceful city dwellers, the army and MVD began looking at men's shoulders for evidence of bruising from firing weapons and at forearms for burned hair or flesh from extracting hot cartridges. They closely examined clothing and smelled for gunpowder residue.[92] Further, to identify a Chechen artilleryman, Russian soldiers looked for glossy spots left by artillery and mortar rounds on the bends and cuffs of sleeves. Pockets that carried cartridges, if turned inside out, showed a shiny, silvery, leaden hue. A grenade launcher operator or mortar man was recognized from fibers and crumpled pieces of gun cotton on clothing.[93]

According to many Russian officers, Chechen use of the antitank, or RPG launcher, was the most effective city weapon. It could be used in the direct- or indirect-fire (that is, set up like a mortar) mode and was effective against people, vehicles, or helicopters as an area or point weapon. Russian forces used flamethrowers to drive snipers from their nests and clear buildings for their initial entry. Two other initial Russian mistakes were that the Russians did not always properly employ infantrymen to support armor attacks (they followed behind armor instead of feeling out Chechen ambush sites), and they did not hold an area once it had been cleared.[94]

The third lesson learned was that some high-ranking Russian defense officials offered a more optimistic picture of what had transpired. Defense Minister Pavel Grachev and General Staff Chief Anatoliy Kvashnin, in interviews on 1 and 2 March 1995, presented their urban combat lessons learned. Their comments indicated they understood clearly the problems their forces encountered and that their forces now had to implement solutions. To Grachev, the main reasons for the initial failure to fulfill tasks were the lack of experience in fighting in cities, some commanders' lack of resolve, and the inadequate morale and psychological preparation of personnel.[95] Different rules, different laws, and a different pace applied since forces were fighting within Russia. The armed forces and MVD units lacked coordination. This forced some units to slow down or stop on some routes. The General Staff had to coordinate training and planning with other ministries in peacetime and in wartime, and to review relationships with the mass media and public organizations to keep patriotism high during a conflict.[96] Grachev underscored that Grozny demanded tactical changes in the way Russian forces would conduct city fights, especially in terms of manning assault units, improving sniper activities, carrying out intelligence operations, and explanatory work among the population. Colonel General Kvashnin noted that this was a real war, one that politicians began and they had to end. The army is merely a means of waging a large or small war and is unfamiliar with the techniques of waging a war on Russian territory.[97]

Finally, Chechen lessons learned were worthwhile to study for their insights on fighting a force that both greatly outnumbers them and is theoretically more organized for urban warfare. The Chechens fought in a nontraditional way, with rapid mobile units instead of fixed defenses. One key lesson was the importance of the sniper and the RPG gunner, or a combination of the two. For example, snipers were employed to draw fire from a Russian force, and then a Chechen ambush position overlooking the sniper's activities would open fire on the Russian column fighting the sniper. Additionally, forces could operate successfully in an independent mode. Both regular and volunteer forces under President Dudayev learned to work in a specific area or to respond to calls for assistance. While command was less centralized than in the Russian force, Motorola radios made coordination possible.

Chief of Staff Maskhadov directed his forces to fight in small groups, although this limited their ability to engage in extended combat. When the Chechens were able to force Russian soldiers from a building:

> They left at most five of their fighters in the building. After some time, the Russians would counterattack and concentrate at least a company against the building . . . but having taken back the building they invariably found only a few bodies of Chechen fighters. Also whenever the Russian soldiers took up defensive positions, they customarily positioned several people in every building, thus diluting their forces.[98]

It was also reported that the Chechens would fire a "fuga" into a window before attacking. A fuga was an RPG-7 round with two 400-gram pieces of trotyl explosives attached with adhesive tape. The Chechens also attached napalm to antitank grenades that could help damage the turret of the target.[99]

The most detailed Chechen lessons learned came from interviews with Chechen fighters some three or four years after the fighting ended. In one interview, titled "Chechen Commander: Urban Warfare in Chechnya," a Chechen commander listed some recommendations for conducting urban operations against both regular and irregular forces based on his experience.[100] First, study the people. One must understand the enemy in detail, not only from a military and political sense but also from a cultural sense. Chechen forces suffered only minimal psychological trauma due to their warrior ethic, their heritage of resisting Russian control, and their sense of survival. Chechens also used noncombatants to exercise psychological deception on the urban battlefield. They declared some villages and suburbs as "pro-Russian" or noncommitted when, in fact, these same areas were centers for strategic planning, command and control, and logistics purposes. This was a well-conducted information operation against the Russians.

Second, know the territory. Key terrain in a city is at the micro level. Do not rely on streets, signs, and most buildings as reference points. Use prominent buildings and monuments instead, as they usually remain intact. It was better to conduct reconnaissance by day and attack at night, which the Russians did not like to do. When forty Ukrainian volunteers signed up to support the Chechens, they were required to conduct detailed reconnaissance with Chechens before entering combat.

Third, study the opposition's weapons and equipment, and how this equipment might be employed in an urban environment. The

Chechens' "national weapon" was the RPG. Destroying armor was a great psychological defeat for the Russians and a great morale booster for the Chechens. The most effective weapon system employed against pure infantry was the sniper, a casualty producer, psychological weapon, and impediment to rapid movement. Nothing could slow down a force as much as a sniper. Chechens feared the Russian mortars more than any other weapon in the city but learned to employ their own with great skill as well. The Chechen force began the battle for Grozny with individual protective equipment but soon discarded it because it impaired mobility in the urban environment. The Motorola hand-held radio was the primary communications device. There was one radio for every six combatants, but it would have been preferable to have one per combatant. Little encryption was used, only the Chechen language. At the national equivalent of a headquarters, access was available to Inmarsat.[101]

The Chechen force also was very successful in redirecting Russian artillery and fighter fire to rain down on Russian forces. Chechen hunter-killer units would sneak between two Russian positions in the city, especially at night, and fire in one direction and then the other before moving out of the area. Thinking they were under attack, the Russian units would fire at each other, sometimes for hours. Many such episodes of fratricide were reported among the Russian ranks. The Chechens were also very interested in capturing or obtaining any Shmel thermobaric weapon system available. The Shmel is a 93mm Russian flamethrower that is 920mm long and weighs 12 kilograms. It has a maximum range of 1,000 meters, a sighting maximum of 600 meters, and a minimum range of 20 meters. The Shmel strongly resembles the U.S. Army's light antitank weapon (LAW) of the 1970s. The Russian force, to explain extensive damage to buildings in Grozny, stated that the Chechens had captured a boxcar full of Shmel weapons and were now using them indiscriminately. The Shmel was important because both sides realized a "heavy blast" direct-fire weapon system was a must for urban warfare. They also could be used against vehicles and fortified positions as a breaching device.

Finally, the Chechen force, by necessity, went into battle as light as possible. Mobility was the key to success against the slower and heavier Russian force, in the opinion of the Chechen commander. Organizationally, the Chechen force had seven-man subgroups (armor hunter-killer teams, a number slightly different than the six-man groups reported earlier) that contained three riflemen/automatic riflemen/ammunition bearers, two RPG gunners, one sniper, and one medic/corpsman. Three of these subgroups made up most of a 25-man group or platoon, and three of these platoons formed 75-man groups. The Chechen force exploited Russian disorientation by moving behind and parallel to the Russian force once it entered the city. Snipers set up in hide positions that supported their respective platoons. The Chechen commander, according to the person who interviewed him, described the ambushes/assaults as follows:

> Each 75 man ambush group set up in buildings along one street block, and only on one side of the street never on both sides of a street because of the cross fires a two sided ambush would create. Only the lower levels of multi story buildings were occupied to avoid casualties. One 25 man platoon comprised the 'killer team' and set up in three positions along the target avenue. They had the responsibility for destroying whatever column entered their site. The other two 25 man platoons set up in the buildings at the assumed entry points to the ambush site. They had responsibility for sealing off the ambush entry from escape by or reinforcement of the ambushed forces. The killer platoon established a command point (platoon HQ) with the center squad. As the intended target column entered the site, the squad occupying the building nearest the entry point would contact the other two squads occupying the center and far building positions. Primary means of communications was by Motorola radio. Once the lead vehicle into the site reached the far squad position, the far squad would contact the other two squads. The commander at the central squad would initiate or signal to initiate the ambush. Minefields were employed to reinforce ambushes by taking out reinforcing armor and to relieve pressure on the killer platoons in case the ambush bogged down.[102]

U.S. Marine Corps Intelligence Activity analyst Arthur Speyer, speaking about the battle for Grozny to an audience at RAND, noted several Chechen weaknesses from a U.S. perspective. First, the Chechens' greatest weakness was their inability to conduct an extensive engagement. The small size of the Chechen units, coupled with their limited ammunition supplies, caused them to avoid large-scale battles. The Russians discovered that drawing the Chechens into a long engagement would allow the Russian force the time to surround the position and use overwhelming fire support. Control was another problem for Chief of Staff Aslan Maskhadov. He stated that many of the independent groups decided for themselves when, where, and how long they would remain in combat. On more than one occasion, Maskhadov noted that local militia forces would simply pick up and go home when they got bored, tired, or cold. Troops were required to withstand long periods of intense combat with limited resupply and rest.

The lessons of the fight for Gronzy are many and quite sobering for anyone who contemplates using troops in an urban environment. While some of the lessons learned by Russian and Chechen combatants are peculiar to that region, others have wider applicability. No army wants to engage in urban combat, but increasing urbanization and the danger of strikes from high-precision weapons may well force the fight into the city where the defender has the advantage. The Chechen decision to continue to fight from "successive cities" is indicative of their reliance on this tactic.

Most Russian analysts viewed the Grozny operation as a success but one that fell far short of a victory. Many pointed directly to the high command as being guilty of sending troops into battle before they were prepared and for implementing a less than complete plan. One analyst called the top brass the "Children of August 1991," a reference to those who came to power after the failed coup in 1991 against then General Secretary Mikhail Gorbachev. Their dramatic upward climb came after they disobeyed their superiors, such as Defense Minister Pavel Grachev's decision to support Boris Yeltsin and not his superior at the time, Soviet Defense Minister Dmitri Yazov, the first such case in the army's history.[103] Colonel General Boris Gromov, the last commander of the 40th Army to leave Afghanistan, was relieved of his duties by one of the Children of August. Gromov had hesitated in putting his support behind the fight in Chechnya. He noted that Russian specialists did not take into account the historical, national, religious, geographical, and meteorological factors, all of which should have affected the planning and time of year for such an intervention. Most unfortunate of all, the battle for Grozny was only two months of what would become a 21-month war.

One Russian officer noted that Russian military and political leaders required a deeper understanding of when and how to use force. As a result, it was recommended that political leaders participate in short courses at the General Staff Academy. This idea is not new. For the past five or so years, Harvard University has been conducting classes for selected members of the Russian leadership. Each class received instruction in the basic principles of the use of force from a U.S. perspective. Obviously the planners of the battle for Grozny ignored this military-political guidance. The Russian armed forces lacked criteria for the development of rules of engagement. Advanced instruction in combat in cities was lacking in the curriculum of the academies, even if at the expense of large-scale wars (for example, the tactics of assault detachments and shock groups need updating to include modern equipment and techniques). Further, the Russian government did not understand how low the military had sunk in terms of readiness in the past five years. Lip service to military reform by politicians had not worked, and the military leadership needed to throw off its pompous attitude.

Preparation for urban combat begins in peacetime and requires the development of an extensive set of conditions under which the fight will be attempted. A vast template of courses of action, options, constraints, limitations, force mixes, enemy compositions, legal factors, and city characteristics must be studied and digested before decisions are made. Two of the most important conclusions drawn from Grozny are that there is no standard urban combat operation and reinforcing failure to attain success does not necessarily result in culmination. First, each operation is unique to the opponent, the city, specific operational and tactical issues, and geopolitical considerations, among other factors. This is a difficult, crucial task for any army but especially for one moving from a forward-deployed to an expeditionary state as the United States is attempting. The requirements to sufficiently sustain or support urban combat become enormous. Second, the Chechens were eventually evicted from Grozny after 37 days of fighting. This initial Russian success in Grozny did not last. In August 1996, the Chechen force recaptured the city, and the Russians were never able to culminate their effort and left Chechnya later that month. However, the Chechens were only to lose Grozny again to the Russians in January 2000 in the second Chechen-Russian conflict. As more information becomes available, a look at the latter battles for Grozny would also be educational and informative for the military professional.

Notes

1. Varied sources, speaking from their own national perspective, are used in the writing of this chapter. It is impossible to check the reliability of each account because the authors cannot be reached personally. Thus, the reader should keep in mind that each account of an incident depended to a great degree on one's perspective (Russian military, Chechen fighter, Russian journalist). This chapter includes all perspectives in retelling this battle and avoids terms such as freedom fighter or rebel when describing the Chechens.

2. Luisa Meireles, Interview with Ramazan Abdulatipov, *Expresso* (4 February 1993), 20 as reported in Foreign Broadcast Information Service (FBIS)-SOV-95-025, 7 February 1995, 13.

3. Anatoliy Sergeevich Kulikov, "The First Battle of Grozny," Appendix B of RAND report, *Capital Preservation: Preparing for Urban Operations in the Twenty First Century*, 13-58, based on Kulikov's remarks at a March 2000 conference in Santa Monica, California.

4. "Chechnya," *Moscow News*, 16-22 December 1994, No. 50, 1, 2.

5. Valeriy Vyzhutovich, "Chechnya Will Spurn Kremlin's Representatives," *Izvestiya*, 20 December 1994, 2, as reported in FBIS-SOV-94-244, 19.

6. Kulikov.

7. "Chechnya."

8. Ibid.

9. Ibid.

10. Ibid.

11. Ibid.

12. A. Kvashnin, "Troops Acquired Combat Maturity in Grave Ordeals; From Speech Delivered by Colonel General A. Kvashin at 28 February Assembly of Armed Forces Leading Personnel," *Krasnaya Zvezda*, 2 March 1995, 3, as translated and published in FBIS-SOV-95-044, 7 March 1995, 23.

13. Kulikov, 29-31.

14. Ibid., 34.

15. Moscow Mayak Radio, 1 January 1995, as reported in FBIS-SOV-95-001, 3 January 1995, 24.

16. Dodge Billingsley, "Interview with Ilias Akhmadov," *The Harriman Review* (Winter 1999-2000), 38-42.

17. Based on an interview with Arthur Speyer who interviewed several Chechen fighters after the first battle for Grozny.

18. Aleksandr Zhilin, Interview with Colonel General Boris Gromov, *Moskovskiy Novosti* (8-15 January 1995), 1, 5.

19. Viktor Litovkin, "Shooting the 131st Maykop Brigade," *Izvestiya* (11 January 1995), 4, as reported in FBIS-SOV-95-008, 12 January 1995, 37.

Litovkin included in his report actual interviews with participants from the battle. In another report, a high-ranking Russian officer said losses were not as great as this. He said 210 of the 450 men originally listed as missing were discovered in hospitals or other units. Only 26 were registered as killed. See Interfax, 17 January 1995, as reported in FBIS-SOV-95-011, 18 January 1995, 27. A report appeared in *Red Star* on 11 January that said the losses the 81st Guards MRR sustained in Grozny on 1 January were greatly exaggerated. To date, only sixteen soldiers and six officers died in combat, according to the article. However, the report also noted that no data was available on 463 servicemen listed as missing. The report indicated many soldiers were scattered all over Grozny and were slowly returning to the unit. How many may have been in the pile of bodies near the presidential palace was not mentioned. See Aleksandr Bugay and Oleg Bedula, "About the 81st MRR: Reliable Information With No Sensations," *Krasnaya Zvezda* (11 January 1995), 1, as reported in FBIS-SOV-95-007, 11 January 1995, 31. As it turned out, this was a Russian attempt to cover up its massive losses in the first few days of January 1995.

20. Ibid., Litovkin.

21. Pavel Felgenhauer, "The Chechen Campaign," from a talk given at a conference in Monterey, California, 7 November 1995, 14.

22. Natalia Gevorkyan, *Moskovskoiyi Novostii* (17-24 December 1995), 6, as printed in *The Current Digest*, Vol. XLVII, No. 50 (1995), 17, 18.

23. ITAR-TASS, 19 January 1995, as reported in FBIS-SOV-95-013, 20 January 1995, 22.

24. From the author's discussion with Ms. Garrels in Moscow, March 1995.

25. Interfax, 19 January 1995, as reported in FBIS-SOV-95-013, 20 January 1995, 23.

26. Konstantin Merezhko, "Caucasian Prisoners, or Pawns are in the Hands of Amateurs," *Sluzhba* (20 December 1994), 1, as reported in Japan Registry Service (JPRS)-UMA-95-003, 31 January 1995, 11.

27. "Pavel Grachev: Russian Unity Defended," *Rossiyskaya Gazeta* (2 March 1995), 2, as reported in FBIS-SOV-95-042, 3 March 1995, 21.

28. Moscow Russian TV, 4 January 1995, as reported in FBIS-SOV-95-003, 5 January 1995, 12.

29. Moscow Mayak Radio, 4 January 1995, as reported in FBIS-SOV-95-004, 6 January 1995, 15.

30. ITAR-TASS, 5 January 1995, as reported in FBIS-SOV-95-004, 6 January 1995, 8.

31. ITAR-TASS, 4 January 1995, as reported in FBIS-SOV-95-002, 4 January 1995, 24.

32. Moscow Mayak Radio, 5 January 1995, as reported in FBIS-SOV-95-004, 6 January 1995, 17.
33. Interfax, 6 January 1995, as reported in FBIS-SOV-95-005, 9 January 1995, 23, 24.
34. Ostankino TV, 7 January 1995, as reported in FBIS-SOV-95-005, 9 January 1995, 27.
35. ITAR-TASS, 9 January 1995, as reported in FBIS-SOV-95-006, 10 January 1995, 4.
36. ITAR-TASS, 7 January 1995, as reported in FBIS-SOV-95-005, 9 January 1995, 25.
37. Moscow TV, 7 January 1995, as reported in FBIS-SOV-95-005, 9 January 1995, 24.
38. Marine Corps interview with Grozny unit commander.
39. Nikita Vaynonen, "Television Camera Does Not Shoot, But It is Unmerciful," *Rossiyskiye Vesti* (10 January 1995), 1, as reported in FBIS-SOV-95-006, 10 January 1995, 8. For other reports on the military "victimizing" journalists, see Oleg Panfilov, "The Next Target—Journalists," *Izvestiya* (6 January 1995), 3, as reported in FBIS-SOV-95-005, 9 January 1995, 35, and Interfax, 10 January 1995, as reported in FBIS-SOV-95-007, 11 January 1995, 24.
40. Vladimir Georgiyev, "The Chechen People Are for a Peaceful Life," *Rossiyskiye Vesti* (24 January 1995), 1, 2, as reported in FBIS-SOV-95-015, 24 January 1995, 23.
41. Moscow TV, 8 January 1995, as reported in FBIS-SOV-95-005, 9 January 1995, 11.
42. ITAR-TASS, 8 January 1995, as reported in FBIS-SOV-95-005, 9 January 1995, 29.
43. Ibid.
44. Interfax, 8 January 1995, as reported in FBIS-SOV-95-005, 9 January 1995, 30.
45. Moscow Mayak Radio, 8 January 1995, as reported in FBIS-SOV-95-005, 9 January 1995, 31.
46. Paris AFP, 10 January 1995, as reported in FBIS-SOV-95-006, 10 January 1995, 14.
47. ITAR-TASS, 10 January 1995, as reported in FBIS-SOV-95-007, 11 January 1995, 35.
48. Moscow RIA, 9 January 1995, as reported in FBIS-SOV-95-008-A, 12 January 1995, 11.
49. Moscow Radiostantsiya Ekho Moskvy, 8 January 1995, as reported in FBIS-SOV-95-005, 9 January 1995, 28.
50. Interfax, 10 January 1995, as reported in FBIS-SOV-95-007, 11 January 1995, 34.

51. Radiostantsiya Ekho Moskvy, 10 January 1995, as reported in FBIS-SOV-95-007, 11 January 1995, 35.

52. Moscow RIA, 10 January 1995, as reported in FBIS-SOV-95-008-A, 12 January 1995, 5.

53. ITAR-TASS, 11 January 1995, as reported in FBIS-SOV-95-007, 11 January 1995, 30.

54. Moscow Ostankino TV, 11 January 1995, as reported in FBIS-SOV-95-009, 13 January 1995, 32.

55. Radiostantsiya Ekho Moskvy, 12 January 1995, as reported in FBIS-SOV-95-009, 13 January 1995, 38.

56. Paola Messana and Catherine Triomphe, Paris AFP, 13 January 1995, as reported in FBIS-SOV-95-009, 13 January 1995, 14.

57. Moscow 2x2, 14 January 1995, as reported in FBIS-SOV-95-010, 17 January 1995, 31.

58. ITAR-TASS, 16 January 1995, as reported in FBIS-SOV-95-010, 17 January 1995, 37.

59. Moscow Radiostantsiya Ekho Moskvy, 15 January 1995, as reported in FBIS-SOV-95-010, 17 January 1995, 31.

60. ITAR-TASS, 14 January 1995, as reported in FBIS-SOV-95-010, 17 January 1995, 33.

61. Interfax, 16 January 1995, as reported in FBIS-SOV-95-010, 17 January 1995, 32. For a more complete account of shock units and assault detachments, see Mr. Les Grau, "Russian Urban Tactics: Lessons From the Battle for Grozny," National Defense University Strategic Forum, Number 38, July 1995.

62. Interfax, 17 January 1995, as reported in FBIS-SOV-95-010, 17 January 1995, 43.

63. ITAR-TASS, 19 January 1995, as reported in FBIS-SOV-95-013, 20 January 1995, 19.

64. Interfax, 19 January 1995, as reported in FBIS-SOV-95-013, 20 January 1995, 19.

65. Mayak Radio, 19 January 1995, as reported in FBIS-SOV-95-013, 20 January 1995, 19. Apparently, contracts were also being concluded with those Chechens of this district who wanted to participate in opposing the Russians.

66. Felgenhauer, 17.

67. ITAR-TASS, 21 January 1995, as reported in FBIS-SOV-95-014, 23 January 1995, 24.

68. Moscow Ostankino TV, 21 January 1995, as reported in FBIS-SOV-95-014, 23 January 1995, 26.

69. Interfax, 22 January 1995, as reported in FBIS-SOV-95-014, 23 January 1995, 28.

70. ITAR-TASS, 22 January 1995, as reported in FBIS-SOV-95-014, 23 January 1995, 28.

71. ITAR-TASS, 24 January 1995, as reported in FBIS-SOV-95-016, 25 January 1995, 26.

72. Ibid.

73. Radiostantsiya Ekho Moskvy, 23 January 1995, as reported in FBIS-SOV-95-015, 24 January 1995, 30.

74. Radio Rossii, 26 January 1995, as reported in FBIS-SOV-95-017, 26 January 1995, 12.

75. ITAR-TASS, 26 January 1995, as reported in FBIS-SOV-95-018, 27 January 1995, 41.

76. ITAR-TASS, 31 January 1995, as reported in FBIS-SOV-95-021, 1 February 1995, 15.

77. Pavel Felgenhauer, "The Russian Army Will Be in Chechnya for a Long Time..." *Segodnya*, 25 January 1995, 1, as reported in FBIS-SOV-95-022, 2 February 1995, 12.

78. ITAR-TASS, 1318 GMT, 3 February 1995, as reported in FBIS-SOV-95-024, 6 February 1995, 21; and Interfax, 1416 GMT, 6 February 1995, as reported in FBIS-SOV-95-025, 7 February 1995, 23.

79. Anatoliy Yurkin, ITAR-TASS, 1529 GMT, 7 February 1995, as reported in FBIS-SOV-95-027, 9 February 1995, 25.

80. "Objectively and Promptly," *Rossiyskaya Gazeta* (8 February 1995), 2, as reported in FBIS-SOV-95-028, 10 February 1995, 25.

81. Anthony Loyd, "Fleeing Chechens Pledge 'War With No Front Lines,'" *The Times*, 8 February 1995, 11.

82. Igor Korotchenko, "The Operation in Chechnya: Success or Defeat of the Russian Army," *Nezavisimoye Voyennoye Obozreniye*, supplement to *Nezavisimaya Gazeta* (February 1995), 1, 2, as reported in JPRS-UMA-95-008, 28 February 1995, 1-3.

83. Anatol Lieven, "The World Turned Upside Down," *Armed Forces Journal* (August 1998), 40-43. Lieven's article is worth the time to look up and read.

84. Ibid., and Vyzhutovich interview with Stepashin, as reported in FBIS-SOV-95-043, 6 March 1995, 35.

85. Gregoriyev, 23.

86. Sergey Pavlenko, "The Chechen Drama: Why is its Essence Often Better Understood by the Ordinary Soldier Than by Many Politicians?" *Krasnaya Zvezda* (7 February 1995), 1, as reported in FBIS-SOV-95-027, 9 February 1995, 29.

87. Yelena Afanasyeva and Dmitriy Muratov, "Minister Grachev's Statement That He Would Take Grozny With a Single Regiment Had a Deleterious Effect on the Consciousness of Commanders," *Novaya*

Yezhednevnaya Gazeta (28 January 1995), 1-2, as reported in JPRS-UMA-95-007, 21 February 1995, 6-9.

88. Afanasyeva, 7, 8.
89. Colonel Oleg Namsarayev, "Sweeping Built Up Areas," *Armeyskiy Sbornik* (April 1995), 35-37, as reported in FBIS-UMA-95-139s, 20 July 1995, 20, 21.
90. Namsarayev, 21.
91. Igor Sibirtsev, on press conference of Lieutenant General Mayorov, "On the Northern Front of Grozny," *Vecherniy Novosibirsk* (30 January 1995), 4, as reported in JPRS-UMA-95-005, 7 February 1995, 6.
92. From a conversation with an MVD officer, Moscow, June 1995.
93. Namsarayev, 22.
94. From the author's discussions with Russian officers who fought in Grozny.
95. Ibid., and Kvashnin, 25.
96. Pavel Grachev, *Krasnaya Zvezda* (2 March 1995), 2.
97. Ibid., and Kvashnin, 27.
98. Stasys Knezys and Romanas Sedlickas, *The War in Chechnya* (College Station, TX: Texas A&M University Press, 1999), 108.
99. Ibid.
100. "Chechen Commander: On Urban Warfare in Chechnya," working draft received from the Marine Corps, 1999.
101. Ibid.
102. Ibid. Other significant Chechen lessons learned and related by the Chechen commander were: The tracer round is useless in urban areas due to serious negative tradeoffs. Operations security is especially important in the urban fight. Chechen commanders were so concerned about secrecy that they did not brief their men about the objective of an operation until they were already on the way to their objective. Chechen commanders did not move by "flanking maneuvers" but instead by "chess-like maneuvers" to hit the Russians where they least expected it. "Hugging" techniques were also used (setting up positions within 50 to 250 meters from Russian positions to render Russian artillery and rocket fire ineffective). As a rule, the Chechens did not place mines or booby traps inside buildings. The possibility of "friendly" casualties was not worth any possible benefit gained.
103. Feliks Babitskiy, "Dismissals for Generals, That May Be the Outcome of the Chechen Crisis," *Rossiyskiye Vesti* (21 January 1995), 1, as reported in FBIS-SOV-95-013, 20 January 1995, 19.

Bibliography

English-Language Sources

Gall, Carlotta and Thomas de Waal. *Chechnya: Calamity in the Caucasus*. New York and London: New York University Press, 1998.

Glenn, Russell W. *Capital Preservation: Preparing for Urban Operations in the Twenty First Century*. Arroyo Center: RAND, 2001.

Knezys, Stasys and Romanas Sedlickas. *The War in Chechnya*. College Station, TX: Texas A&M University Press, 1999.

Lieven, Anatol. *Chechnya: Tombstone of Russian Power*. New Haven and London: Yale University Press, 1999.

Nivat, Anne. *Chienne De Guerre*. Public Affairs 2001.

Oliker, Olga. *Russia's Chechen Wars: 1994 2000*. Arroyo Center: RAND, 2001.

Smith, Sebastian. *Allah's Mountains: The Battle for Chechnya*. NY: St. Martin's Press, 1998.

Russian Sources

Kulikov, Anatoliy and Sergei Lembik. *Chechenskiy Uzel (Chechen Knot)*. Moscow: House of Pedagogiki, 2000.

Troshev, Gennadiy. *Moya Voina (My War)*. Moscow: Vagrius, 2001.

Articles

Afanasyeva, Yelena and Dmitriy Muratov. "Minister Grachev's Statement That He Would Take Grozny With a Single Regiment Had a Deleterious Effect on the Consciousness of Commanders." *Novaya Yezhednevnaya Gazeta*, 28 January 1995. Reported in JPRS-UMA-95-007, 21 February 1995.

Babitskiy, Feliks. "Dismissals for Generals, That May Be the Outcome of the Chechen Crisis." *Rossiyskiye Vesti*, 21 January 1995. Reported in FBIS-SOV-95-013, 20 January 1995.

Billingsley, Dodge. "Interview With Ilias Akhmadov." *The Harriman Review*. Winter 1999-2000.

Bugay, Aleksandr and Oleg Bedula. "About the 81st MRR: Reliable Information With No Sensations." *Krasnaya Zvezda,* 11 January 1995. Reported in FBIS-SOV-95-007, 11 January 1995.

"Chechen Commander: on Urban Warfare in Chechnya." Working draft received from the Marine Corps, 1999.

"Chechnya." *Moscow News*, 16-22 December 1994, No. 50.

Felgenhauer, Pavel. "The Russian Army Will Be in Chechnya for a Long Time." *Segodnya*, 25 January 1995. Reported in FBIS-SOV-95-022, 2 February 1995.

"The Chechen Campaign." A talk given at a conference in Monterey, California, 7 November 1995.

Gevorkyan, Natalia. *Moskovskoiyi Novostii*, 17-24 December 1995. Printed in *The Current Digest,* Vol. XLVII, No. 50 (1995).

Grachev, Pavel. *Krasnaya Zvezda*, 2 March 1995.

Interfax, 6 January 1995. Reported in FBIS-SOV-95-005, 9 January 1995.

10 January 1995. Reported in FBIS-SOV-95-007, 11 January 1995.

16 January 1995. Reported in FBIS-SOV-95-010, 17 January 1995.

17 January 1995. Reported in FBIS-SOV-95-010, 17 January 1995.

19 January 1995. Reported in FBIS-SOV-95-013, 20 January 1995.

22 January 1995. Reported in FBIS-SOV-95-014, 23 January 1995.

1416 GMT, 6 February 1995. Reported in FBIS-SOV-95-025, 7 February 1995.

ITAR-TASS, 4 January 1995. Reported in FBIS-SOV-95-002, 4 January 1995.

5 January 1995. Reported in FBIS-SOV-95-004, 6 January 1995.

7 January 1995. Reported in FBIS-SOV-95-005, 9 January 1995.

8 January 1995. Reported in FBIS-SOV-95-005, 9 January 1995.

9 January 1995. Reported in FBIS-SOV-95-006, 10 January 1995.

10 January 1995. Reported in FBIS-SOV-95-007, 11 January 1995.

11 January 1995. Reported in FBIS-SOV-95-007, 11 January 1995.

14 January 1995. Reported in FBIS-SOV-95-010, 17 January 1995.

16 January 1995. Reported in FBIS-SOV-95-010, 17 January 1995.

19 January 1995. Reported in FBIS-SOV-95-013, 20 January 1995.

>21 January 1995. Reported in FBIS-SOV-95-014, 23 January 1995.

>22 January 1995. Reported in FBIS-SOV-95-014, 23 January 1995.

>24 January 1995. Reported in FBIS-SOV-95-016, 25 January 1995.

>26 January 1995. Reported in FBIS-SOV-95-018, 27 January 1995.

>31 January 1995. Reported in FBIS-SOV-95-021, 1 February 1995.

>1318 GMT, 3 February 1995. Reported in FBIS-SOV-95-024, 6 February 1995.

Lieven, Anatol. "The World Turned Upside Down." *Armed Forces Journal*, August 1998. Lieven's article is worth the time to look up and read.

Litovkin, Viktor. "Shooting the 131st Maykop Brigade."*Izvestiya*, 11 January 1995. Reported in FBIS-SOV-95-008, 12 January 1995.

Loyd, Anthony. "Fleeing Chechens Pledge 'War With No Front Lines.'" *The Times*, 8 February 1995.

Marine Corps interview with Grozny unit commander.

Mayak Radio, 1 January 1995. Reported in FBIS-SOV-95-001, 3 January 1995.

>19 January 1995. Reported in FBIS-SOV-95-013, 20 January 1995.

Merezhko, Konstantin. "Caucasian Prisoners, or Pawns are in the Hands of Amateurs." *Sluzhba*, 20 December 1994. Reported in JPRS-UMA-95-003, 31 January 1995.

Messana, Paola and Catherine Triomphe. *Paris AFP*, 13 January 1995. Reported in FBIS-SOV-95-009, 13 January 1995.

Moscow 2x2, 14 January 1995. Reported in FBIS-SOV-95-010, 17 January 1995.

Moscow Mayak, 4 January 1995. Reported in FBIS-SOV-95-004, 6 January 1995.

>5 January 1995. Reported in FBIS-SOV-95-004, 6 January 1995.

>8 January 1995. Reported in FBIS-SOV-95-005, 9 January 1995.

Moscow Ostankino TV, 11 January 1995. Reported in FBIS-SOV-95-009, 13 January 1995.

>21 January 1995. Reported in FBIS-SOV-95-014, 23 January 1995.

Moscow Radiostantsiya Ekho Moskvy, 8 January 1995. Reported in FBIS-SOV-95-005, 9 January 1995.

15 January 1995. Reported in FBIS-SOV-95-010, 17 January 1995.

Moscow RIA, 9 January 1995. Reported in FBIS-SOV-95-008-A, 12 January 1995.

10 January 1995. Reported in FBIS-SOV-95-008-A, 12 January 1995.

Moscow Russian TV, 4 January 1995. Reported in FBIS-SOV-95-003, 5 January 1995.

Moscow TV, 7 January 1995. Reported in FBIS-SOV-95-005, 9 January 1995.

8 January 1995. Reported in FBIS-SOV-95-005, 9 January 1995.

Namsarayev, Oleg. "Sweeping Built Up Areas." *Armeyskiy Sbornik*, April 1995. Reported in FBIS-UMA-95-139s, 20 July 1995.

"Objectively and Promptly." *Rossiyskaya Gazeta*, 8 February 1995. Reported in FBIS-SOV-95-028, 10 February 1995.

Ostankino TV, 7 January 1995. Reported in FBIS-SOV-95-005, 9 January 1995.

Panfilov, Oleg. "The Next Target Journalists." *Izvestiya*, 6 January 1995. Reported in FBIS-SOV-95-005, 9 January 1995.

Paris AFP, 10 January 1995. Reported in FBIS-SOV-95-006, 10 January 1995.

"Pavel Grachev: Russian Unity Defended," *Rossiyskaya Gazeta*, 2 March 1995. Reported in FBIS-SOV-95-042, 3 March 1995.

Pavlenko, Sergey. "The Chechen Drama: Why is its Essence Often Better Understood by the Ordinary Soldier Than by Many Politicians?" *Krasnaya Zvezda*, 7 February 1995. Reported in FBIS-SOV-95-027, 9 February 1995.

Radio Rossii, 26 January 1995. Reported in FBIS-SOV-95-017, 26 January 1995.

Radiostantsiya Ekho Moskvy, 10 January 1995. Reported in FBIS-SOV-95-007, 11 January 1995.

12 January 1995. Reported in FBIS-SOV-95-009, 13 January 1995.

23 January 1995. Reported in FBIS-SOV-95-015, 24 January 1995.

Vyzhutovich, Valeriy. "Chechnya Will Spurn Kremlin's Representatives." *Izvestiya*, 20 December 1994. Reported in FBIS-SOV-94-244.

Vaynonen, Nikita. "Television Camera Does Not Shoot, But it is Unmerciful." *Rossiyskiye Vesti*, 10 January 1995. Reported in FBIS-SOV-95-006, 10 January 1995.

Yurkin, Anatoliy. ITAR-TASS, 1529 GMT, 7 February 1995. Reported in FBIS-SOV-95-027, 9 February 1995.

Zhilin, Aleksandr. Interview with Colonel General Boris Gromov. *Moskovskiy Novosti*, 8-15 January 1995.

Interviews

Garrels, Anne. Reported for National Public Radio from Grozny in January 1995. She was interviewed by the author in Moscow, March 1995.

Speyer, Arthur. Interviewed several Chechen fighters after the first battle for Grozny. Interviewed by the author in March 2000 at the RAND conference.

The Siege of Beirut

George W. Gawrych

But was it a siege when most civilians could come and go between artillery rounds?

Robert Fisk, reporter[1]

The siege of Beirut turned into the single most intensely televised and reported war in living memory. Journalists were able to operate on both sides of the encounter and thus produce vast quantities of uniquely synoptic material every day.

Avner Yaniv[2]

In invading Lebanon on 6 June 1982, Israel sought to deal a major blow to the Palestinian Liberation Organization (PLO), an umbrella organization that included all Palestinian resistance groups opposed to the Israeli state. The 1982 campaign into Lebanon drew the Israel Defense Forces (IDF) into an unanticipated siege of Beirut. Despite detailed coverage by the international media of the human suffering in the city, the Israeli coalition government persevered in maintaining pressure on the Lebanese capital for seventy days without resorting to a full-scale ground assault. The siege turned into a saga of Israeli bombardment from the air, land, and sea, with limited ground attacks into the city. In the end, Israel forced the PLO to evacuate its political leadership and fighters from Beirut to other Arab countries. The Israeli success resulted from a combination of Israeli military and economic pressures and American diplomacy.

Background

By 1982, Israeli Prime Minister Menachem Begin, Defense Minister Ariel Sharon, and Chief of the General Staff Lieutenant General Raful Eitan were all determined to remove the PLO threat from Lebanon. In the 1970s, the PLO had established its headquarters in west Beirut and had turned most of southern Lebanon into a mini Palestinian state, popularly known as Fatahland. Israel viewed Fatahland as a serious threat, in that Palestinian resistance groups used it as a base for launching artillery shells and guerrilla operations into Israel's northern region of Galilee.

PLO strength derived, in large measure, from Lebanon's weakness. In 1975, the Lebanese civil war broke out, fragmenting the country into numerous fiefdoms headed by heads of various Lebanese confessional groups. The central government had no power in the face of warlords with their own militias. In 1976, Syria, given its own political and territorial ambitions in Lebanon, had taken advantage of the internecine strife to occupy large parts of the country, including the important Bekaa Valley (see Map 1). An election for a new president was scheduled for August 1982, and under the terms of a decades-old agreement, the holder of that office had to be a Maronite Christian. Christians constituted 40 percent of Lebanon's three million people; Muslims and Druse formed 60 percent. Much of the political power resided in the Maronite and, to a lesser extent, the Sunni Muslim communities.

In response to the emerging Palestinian threat, Israel had slowly and clandestinely developed close ties with the Phalangists, the most powerful political party and military organization in the Maronite community. Pierre Gemayel, the patriarch of the Gemayel family, headed the Phalange Party but left control of the militia to his son Bashir. The Phalange Party opposed the PLO's presence in Lebanon, and Phalange militiamen had fought Palestinian guerrillas on numerous occasions. Consequently, Israel and the Phalange found a common interest in wanting the destruction of Fatahland and Syria's withdrawal from the country.

Bashir Gemayel was a rising political figure in Lebanon. A charismatic and ruthless individual, he was slowly positioning himself to be elected as Lebanon's new Maronite president. Begin and Sharon came to view the Phalange as an instrument for furthering Israel's security interests on its northern border. During the first half of 1982, both men held a number of secret meetings with Bashir in the hope of forging an Israeli-Lebanese Christian alliance against the PLO and the Syrian presence in Lebanon. Apparently, throughout his discussions with Israeli officials, Bashir welcomed Israel's support but avoided committing to military cooperation.[3]

In the meantime, Begin and Sharon also sought a pretext for launching a major invasion against the Palestinian threat in southern Lebanon. An assassination attempt against the Israeli ambassador in London, Shlomo Argov, on 3 June 1982 provided them with the opportunity they were looking for. In a shrewd calculation, Begin limited Israel's immediate response to air strikes, and on 4 June, Israeli planes bombed PLO targets in Beirut and southern Lebanon. In particular, the Israeli air force pulverized the PLO's munitions depot in

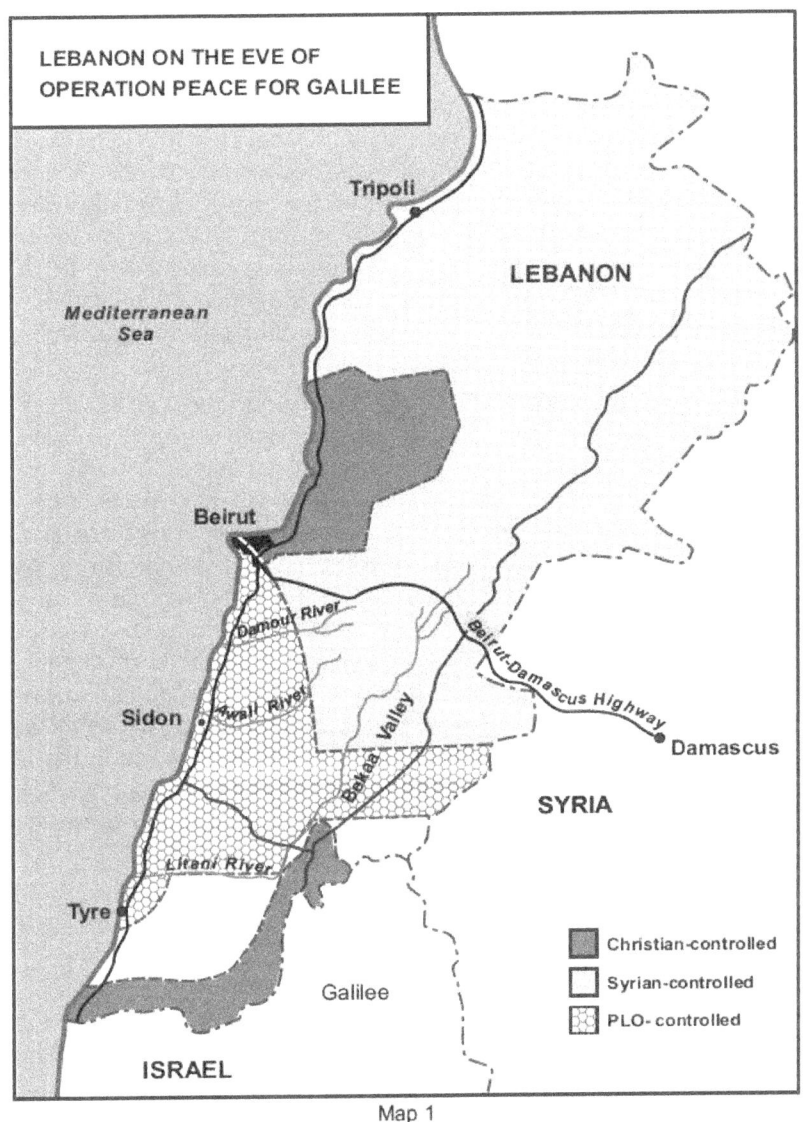

Map 1

Beirut's sports stadium. Now, Begin and Sharon fully expected the PLO to retaliate by shelling Israel's northern settlements. When the Palestinians did in fact fire back with artillery rounds, they fell right into the Israeli trap. Late on 5 June, the Israeli cabinet used the Palestinian retaliation as the sought-after pretext for approving a land campaign into Lebanon.

The Israeli cabinet named the operation *PEACE FOR GALILEE*. A secondary objective was to sign a peace treaty with Lebanon. The main objective was to "place all the civilian population of Galilee beyond the range of the terrorist fire from Lebanon by attacking [the Palestinian guerrillas], their bases, and their headquarters."[4] At the cabinet meeting, Sharon assured his fellow ministers that the campaign plan limited ground operations to 40 kilometers (km), thus leaving Beirut outside of the area of operations.[5] In his directive to the armed forces, however, the defense minister ordered the IDF to be prepared to execute a junction with Lebanese Christian militia near Beirut within 96 hours of the operation's commencement.[6]

Suspicious of Sharon's sincerity and concerned about possible Syrian intervention, the cabinet decided to monitor the campaign closely, thus leaving any military escalation subject to its approval. Begin told the ministers that "the cabinet will meet daily and make decisions according to the evolving situation."[7] Such political supervision of tactical events would prove unprecedented in modern Israeli history. As Sharon noted, "For the first time in all of Israel's war experience, cabinet meetings were held every day and sometimes twice a day. For the first time the government set specific goals for the army on an ongoing basis."[8] To address the cabinet's daily scrutiny, Sharon appointed a brigadier general as permanent liaison to the cabinet, and all the ministers received a special defense ministry phone number that they could dial at any time for "updates or clarification."[9] Daily cabinet supervision of the campaign would directly affect the conduct of the siege of Beirut.

In this war, unlike any other in the Arab-Israeli conflict, "Israel's advantage was absolute in every category."[10] The IDF committed 75,000 troops; 1,250 tanks (including the highly prized Israeli-made Merkava); and 1,500 armored personnel carriers organized into four independent divisions, an amphibious brigade, a two-division corps, and a reserve division. The Lebanese army of 23,000 regulars was a nonplayer, remaining neutral throughout the campaign. The main forces facing the Israelis were 30,000 Syrian troops and 20,000 Palestinian fighters. The Syrians, deployed mainly in the Bekaa Valley and along the Beirut to Damascus highway, sported some 600 tanks (the older Soviet-made T-54s and T-62s) and 300 artillery pieces and antitank guns. For their part, the Palestinians counted 100 T-34 tanks, 100 artillery tubes, and 60 rocket launchers mounted on trucks.[11] The IDF thus possessed a clear numerical superiority in troops and weapons for an initial advance of only 40 km, anticipated to take two days to reach the Awali River and the southern tip of the Bekaa Valley. Few Syrian troops were located in this area. Therefore, the PLO presented the main military obstacle in southern Lebanon.

On 6 June at 1100, the IDF launched Operation *PEACE FOR GALILEE*. Despite a marked superiority in troops and weaponry, the Israeli army fell behind its timetable as friction and Palestinian resistance proved more formidable forces than expected. Advance units had expected to go 40 km within 48 hours but failed to do so. Moreover, this goal of 40 km itself quickly emerged as a matter of controversy. In a letter on 6 June to U.S. President Ronald Reagan, the Israeli prime minister indicated that the military operation would be limited to 40 km. Two days later, on 8 June, Begin went public and informed the Israeli parliament of this territorial limitation. The announcement surprised the IDF. No one had heard of such a restriction. Major General Amir Drori, the commander of the invading troops, later stated that he first learned of the 40-km limit from the media.[12] Another Israeli general put it differently: "The prevailing understanding among the senior officer cadre of the IDF [was a] prompt penetration into the depth of Lebanese territory all the way to Beirut."[13] Sharon had failed to inform the IDF of any territorial limitation.

In the five days that followed Begin's announcement of 8 June, Sharon did everything he could to gain approval for tactical moves that inched the IDF to an encirclement of Beirut. The resultant piecemeal movements aggravated the question in the IDF concerning the final objectives of the campaign. Meanwhile, confusion started to grow in both the cabinet and the public when military operations began to exceed the publicly stated 40-km limit. Finally, on 13 June, fully one week after the commencement of the war, Israeli units linked up with the Phalange forces at the presidential palace in Baabda. Beirut lay in full view in the valley below.

The City

In 1982, Beirut was but a shell of its former splendor. By the 1960s, the city had gained the deserved reputation as the Paris of the Middle East. Palm trees and outdoor cafes lined the main thoroughfares. *Suqs* (marketplaces and shopping centers) attracted wealthy tourists from the Middle East and Europe. Sun worshippers could bask on its lovely beaches under the shadow of luxurious hotels while skiers came down the slopes on the mountains overlooking the city. In addition to offering the fine pleasures of life, Beirut served as a financial, educational, and cultural center for the Arab world. Rue de Banques was rumored to possess half the Arab wealth. American University and St. Joseph University were both prestigious institutions of higher learning, attracting students from the Arab elites in the entire Middle East. The press was relatively free, and many Arabs could print their ideas in the publishing houses of the city.

Unfortunately, the Lebanese Civil War, begun in 1975, dramatically changed the city's quality of life. War brought much destruction and left a divided capital, one part primarily Christian, the other primarily Muslim. The Maronite Christian family of the Gemayels controlled east Beirut, collecting taxes and providing many basic services. Lebanese Muslims and the PLO dominated west Beirut. The Green Line—a narrow patch of trees, bushes, and earthen works stretching for some 10 miles—separated the two parts, in effect, acting as a moat. Three crossing sites along the Green Line connected west and east Beirut. West Beirut showed evidence of the civil war more than its Christian counterpart. Entire streets lacked any intact buildings; many families lived in war-damaged structures.

In 1982, Beirut and its suburbs sported a population of over 1,000,000 (see Map 2). West Beirut was the newer section of the city, containing some 600,000 residents and 25,000 buildings squeezed into an area of 10 square miles. The port area still contained elegant beachfront hotels. American University and most Western embassies, including that of the United States, were located here as well. South of the port area stood Corniche Mazraa with its business district. Here, high-rise buildings served as offices, apartments, or hotels. Built mainly in the post-1950s, these buildings used glass extensively. Hamra Street served as the commercial heart of the Muslim sector.

Adjacent to Corniche Mazraa was the Fakhani district where the PLO had established its headquarters. A few buildings rose to fourteen stories, but the construction was generally of lower quality than that in Corniche Mazraa. Fakhani contained a sports stadium that the PLO had converted into a major ammunition depot and a recruiting and training center. Fakhani, as well as the Sabra and Shatilla camps to its south, contained many Palestinian refugees who lived in one-story buildings with no foundation and only one or two rooms. Streets were very often too narrow for large military vehicles. Finally, the southernmost area contained the large refugee camp of Burj al-Barajinah, the Shiite slums, and Beirut International Airport. Here, the terrain was flat and sandy.

The PLO had turned west Beirut into a Palestinian capital in exile, therefore a strategic center of gravity for the IDF's targeting. In anticipation of an Israeli invasion or a major flareup in the Lebanese Civil

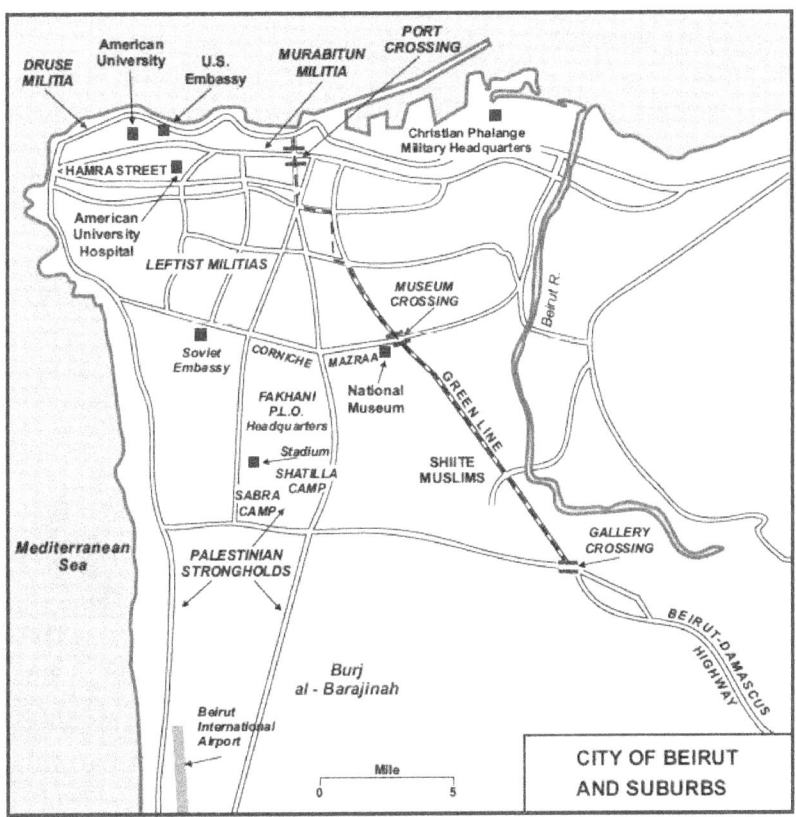

Map 2

War, the PLO headquarters had constructed three levels underground. West Beirut had also become home to many Palestinian bourgeoisie, some of whom had obtained Lebanese citizenship. Most of the city's 200,000 Palestinians, however, were poor and concentrated in the three major Palestinian refugee camps mentioned above. Essentially, west Beirut was divided into two parts, a Lebanese sector in the north and a Shiite and Palestinian part in the south.

Geography gave the Israeli invader two advantages. Mountains in the east, southeast, and south, some rising to over 6,000 feet, overlooked Beirut and provided excellent observation and artillery positions. Moreover, the Palestinians were concentrated in the southern area where the terrain was more open. The IDF could thus concentrate its bombing on Fakhani and the three refugee camps without placing most of the Lebanese inhabitants at great risk, at least in theory.

Opposing Forces

The siege of Beirut involved at least ten separate armed forces, each fighting for its own interest. Figures vary considerably as to the size of the various militia groups, for in siege warfare, civilians often function as combatants. At the beginning of the war, the PLO had some 3,000 full-time fighters in west Beirut. This force increased as Palestinians fled southern Lebanon in the face of advancing Israeli forces. By 13 June, there were over 16,000 Arab fighters in the city. These included 12,000 Palestinian forces, 2,000 Lebanese militiamen, and 2,300 Syrian troops. Syria controlled several thousand of the Palestinian forces. Together, the fighting groups in west Beirut formed a "plethora of competing organizations," devoid of unity of command.[14] Each group fought its own battle with a minimum of coordination with other groups.

The PLO was an umbrella organization for a number of different Palestinian groups. Yasser Arafat was the chairman of the PLO Executive Committee as well as the commander in chief of all PLO military forces. He also directly controlled Fatah, the largest group. In addition to Fatah, whose strength inside the city had grown to 8,000 fighters, at least four other Palestinian organizations were in west Beirut: the Popular Front for the Liberation of Palestine, the Democratic Front for the Liberation of Palestine, the Popular Front for the Liberation of Palestine-General Command, and *al-Saiqa*, controlled by Damascus. The Palestinian fighters concentrated on protecting the PLO headquarters and the three refugee camps of Sabra, Shatilla, and Burj al-Barajinah. The PLO relied on some forty T-34 tanks, a few dozen DM-2 scout cars, fifty to seventy obsolete antiair guns, and twenty BM-21 Katyusha multiple rocket launchers. Lebanese Muslims divided into two main groups, the leftist Sunni Murabitun and the Shiite Amal. Each Lebanese militia had fewer than 1,000 fighters in the city. The Murabitun defended the port area and National Museum crossing, while Amal concentrated its forces on protecting the Shiite slum areas in the south. A small Druse contingent guarded the port area.[15]

To exert its interest in the city, Syria had stationed its 85th Mechanized Infantry Brigade in west Beirut as well. Comprising some 2,300 men, the brigade possessed thirty to forty T-54/55 tanks, armored personnel carriers, D-30 122-millimeter (mm) howitzers, 82mm mortars, Katyushas, 130mm field artillery, and 57mm antiair guns. The Syrians deployed in the southern parts of west Beirut, an area relatively open and hence good defensive terrain for Syrian tanks. They also guarded the area around the Soviet embassy. The Syrian brigade, however, had suffered heavy damage south of the airport fighting Israeli units advancing from the coastal road toward the Beirut to Damascus highway.[16]

By the time of Operation *PEACE FOR GALILEE*, the PLO had prepared underground bunkers and tunnels in anticipation of an Israeli invasion. It had stockpiled arms, fuel, food, and medicine. In 1981, the Palestinians had also begun constructing a number of secret emergency command posts.[17] These prewar preparations paid dividends for the besieged fighters. As noted by a Western reporter in Beirut during the siege, "the PLO suffered no serious shortages. Their generators could be heard roaring away during the night."[18] Civilians suffered from want but the fighters not as much.

East Beirut fell under the control of the Gemayel family. Bashir Gemayel commanded a militia force of 8,000 fighters called the Lebanese Forces (LF). Between 1975 and 1982, the IDF had trained some 250 LF officers and 1,000 noncommissioned officers in Israel. The LF was a paramilitary force, organized on paper into companies and battalions but employed more at the platoon and squad levels. Essentially a light force sporting M16s and AK47s, Bashir's militiamen possessed a small number of T-54/55 tanks, Katyushas, and artillery pieces.[19] During the Israeli siege, the LF provided indirect support: blocking northern and northeastern approaches to west Beirut, manning checkpoints along the Green Line, and offering intelligence to the Israelis. Despite this assistance, Bashir proved a poor ally for Israel because he refused Israel's demand to commit his forces to capture west Beirut.

The siege of west Beirut thus fell squarely on the shoulders of the IDF. All three services—army, air force, and navy—participated in the attempt to pound the Palestinian defenders into submission. Israeli ground forces stood between 35,000 to 50,000 with 400 tanks and over 100 heavy artillery pieces, including 105mm, 155mm, and 175mm cannons.[20] The navy committed most of its small fleet to a blockade and provided naval gunfire as needed. The air force conducted thousands of combat sorties. The IDF clearly possessed a marked numerical advantage in men and equipment for the siege of Beirut.

Israeli Doctrine

In undertaking its siege, "the IDF was in uncharted waters, both doctrinally and in terms of what they had planned for before the invasion."[21]

Certainly, the army had had some experience in urban warfare in previous wars. But, in 1982, the Israeli Army faced a seemingly formidable challenge: an Arab capital with a million inhabitants. The IDF's previous urban battles paled before the siege of Beirut.

At the operational level, IDF doctrine for urban warfare stressed that "cities should be encircled before anything else."[22] At the tactical level, the IDF had refined its tactical doctrine and stepped up its training program for urban warfare, based in large measure on the battle for Suez City in the 1973 war. Israeli urban operations (UO) doctrine called for armor to lead or to support infantry. The army favored using tanks in urban warfare because the tank afforded both firepower and protection, and the IDF placed a premium on minimizing casualties in war. Unfortunately for Israel, the emphasis on armor in the IDF force structure left the army with a shortage of qualified infantry for a major urban operation. Regular infantry received adequate preparation, but reservists generally gained limited training for UO in their refresher courses. As a result, reserve infantry troops suffered greater casualties in the war. Training exercises before operations helped alleviate some deficiencies.

Doctrine emphasized using combined arms in city fighting. Tank units were trained to task organize with other combat arms for battle. Thus, Israeli UO doctrine stressed flexibility in force design. Generally, when employed in an attack, tanks fought under infantry command. The infantry commander was expected to be in the lead tank where he could focus on navigation while the crew fought the battle. Artillery observers accompanied troops to help provide timely fire support. Doctrine writers encouraged using loudspeakers whenever appropriate to convince civilians to leave the targeted area. Moreover, patrols were encouraged to find civilians willing to provide information and help guide troops through the maze of streets to their objectives.[23]

A Missed Opportunity?

The linkup between Israeli and Phalange forces on 13 June signified the encirclement of west Beirut. That same day, Sharon met with Bashir Gemayel, expecting that the Lebanese warlord would seize west Beirut with his own forces, supported by the IDF. What transpired should have been no surprise to Sharon. Bashir again backed away from such military cooperation with Israel. He was maneuvering to be elected as Lebanon's next president in the August election. Although the Israelis had helped him a great deal, Gemayel stressed that he needed time to build bridges to the United States and mend fences with the various Muslim groups.[24] Clearly, the Lebanese warlord wanted to avoid the appearance of doing Israel's dirty work of clearing the Palestinians out of Beirut. Such an image would seriously damage his credibility with the Lebanese people, and he was determined to be president of all Lebanon.

Apparently at this juncture in the war, the IDF missed a golden opportunity to capture west Beirut in quick order. A Western reporter inside Beirut at the time observed how "the sheer speed and depth of the mass Israeli invasion stunned both the Palestinians and the Syrians."[25] In interviews conducted after the war, a number of Palestinians depicted the Arab forces in the city as "demoralized, dispirited, and panic-stricken as a result of the crushing defeat they had suffered in the previous week."[26] In fact, "The key [for the IDF] lay in the ability of its troops in the field to win a rapid, indisputable, and psychologically overwhelming triumph."[27] On 12 June, Arafat had already expressed a desire for a cease-fire between Israel and the PLO in the hope of gaining valuable time.

Political considerations, not military possibilities, weighed heavily on Begin and Sharon in assessing their next move. Both men wanted to remove the PLO from Lebanon, which meant destroying its center of gravity in Beirut. They had hoped that Gemayel would take the lead in securing west Beirut, but that had proved to be wishful thinking. Occupying west Beirut would represent a major military escalation in the war. Such a move definitely required cabinet approval, and most of the ministers opposed such an attack, expressing concern over Israeli casualties and the strategic ramifications of escalating the conflict with an assault on an Arab capital.[28] Moreover, Sharon and Begin were fully aware of the public's abiding concern about casualties. Urban fighting would certainly have increased Israeli losses. Israel had already suffered 214 killed, 1,176 wounded, and 23 missing in action.[29] Finally, Begin had informed the Israeli parliament publicly and President Reagan privately that Israel was limiting its operation to 40 km. Beirut clearly lay outside this geographical limit.

Rather than seek cabinet approval for a forced entry, Sharon decided to strengthen his position around west Beirut. He admitted in his memoirs to being "intent on achieving the strongest position we could" in this phase of the war.[30] The immediate military objective became pushing the Syrians out of positions in the surrounding hills and along the Damascus to Beirut highway. The IDF spent the next thirteen days fighting in the hills east of Beirut. By 26 June, the IDF controlled 22 km of the strategic highway. While maintaining its hold around west Beirut, the IDF periodically shelled the Lebanese capital, mainly with artillery.

In response to Sharon's encirclement of Beirut, the Israeli cabinet changed the objectives of Operation *PEACE FOR GALILEE*. Instead of placing Galilee's civilian population out of artillery range, Israel now demanded that all Palestinian fighters and Syrian troops depart from Beirut. The Lebanese army would enter west Beirut to accept arms from the PLO fighters who, in turn, would leave without their weapons. In contrast to its demands on the PLO in Beirut, Israel offered a different arrangement to the Syrians. The Syrian brigade could depart the city, fully armed and with assurances of safe passage. Damascus declined this offer. Clearly, at this point in the war, military operations were driving policy. Sharon's decision to secure the hills surrounding Beirut altered the strategic and tactical situation significantly. The cabinet now found itself widening the war's objectives in response to Sharon's military escalation.

Arafat rejected Israel's demand to leave the city with his organization and decided to bide his time. Meanwhile, Arab forces in west Beirut took advantage of the Israeli delay in assaulting the city by frantically fortifying their own positions. "They mined the southern approaches to the city, booby-trapped junctions, placed explosives in buildings so that they could be blown up to collapse on advancing forces, dug trenches, and fortified bunkers."[31] Eventually, a system of strongpoints and barricades guarded all possible avenues of entry into the city.

While strengthening defenses around the city, Arafat and other Palestinian leaders began making extravagant claims: "We are ready for this battle, which will be . . . the Stalingrad of the Arabs."[32] Increasing numbers of defenders took heart. Brigadier General Abu al-Walid, the PLO chief of military operations, reversed his earlier pessimistic assessment. On 13 June, the retired colonel from the Jordanian army saw the Palestinian situation militarily hopeless. By the end of the month, however, he could boast of defensible positions ringing west Beirut. More important, perhaps, the passage of time indicated to many Palestinian fighters that Israel lacked the will for heavy casualties associated with urban warfare.[33]

In addition to strengthening Palestinian resolve, the Israeli delay in attacking west Beirut offered Arafat an opportunity for an honorable end to the siege. The PLO leader concluded that Israel had little stomach for city fighting. Attrition and time together might work to the

Palestinians' advantage. Israel could tire of a long siege with its concomitant high casualties. Moreover, the international media would certainly expose the suffering of civilians, especially of children, women, and the elderly. Arafat expected to appeal to Western conscience in this regard: "In being beleaguered in Beirut, I am imposing a moral siege on all capitals."[34] Arafat seemed to hope that the PLO might end up maintaining a political presence in Beirut, with or without a small militia force.

Strategic Context

After securing control around Beirut, Sharon was ready at the beginning of July to tackle the city directly. The cabinet, however, remained opposed to a major ground assault on west Beirut. Cabinet members expressed concern over the international repercussions from such an escalation and over the anticipated loss of Israeli soldiers from urban combat. Sharon would thus have to rely on general bombardments and limited ground operations designed to pressure the PLO into agreeing to depart Beirut.

The Israeli domestic front remained generally supportive of the Begin government during the siege. However, public approval for the war did drop from 93.3 percent at the onset of Operation *PEACE FOR GALILEE* to 66 percent within the first month.[35] Although a significant drop, domestic support remained sufficiently strong throughout the length of the siege, despite sporadic antiwar rallies in the streets of Israeli cities. Countermarches took place as well. In fact, most of Israel stood behind the government in the war.

Polls showed both Begin and Sharon gaining in popularity during this period. Begin saw his approval rating rise from 47.7 percent at the beginning of June to 57.6 in July; Sharon witnessed an increase from 48.9 to 59.6 percent. And the main opposition party backed the government in the war. Both Shimon Peres and Yitzak Rabin, the heads of the Labor Party, offered only mild criticism, and neither called for an end to the siege of Beirut.[36] Israeli politicians and the public were thus willing to accept Arab civilian casualties in the fight against the PLO, an organization perceived as a threat to the Jewish state. Consequently, the IDF had the time it needed to force the PLO's withdrawal from west Beirut.

On the diplomatic front, the United States remained essentially a steady ally of Israel during the siege. Some friction existed between the two countries, however. Washington sought a quick end to the invasion and generally pushed to reduce the level of violence, especially during the siege of Beirut. Although at times critical of Israel for inflicting suffering on civilians, the Reagan administration avoided any direct confrontation with Israel over Lebanon. In the end, Washington used its diplomatic offices to help negotiate the PLO's withdrawal from west Beirut. Israel could thus claim a military victory over the PLO.

Desirous of a speedy end to the war, the Reagan administration relied on Ambassador Philip C. Habib as its special envoy to seek a diplomatic solution. Habib, a Lebanese-American career diplomat, faced numerous problems. During negotiations, Arafat played for time, hoping to avert a political disaster. Moreover, because the United States refused to recognize the PLO, Habib had to negotiate with Arafat through intermediaries, primarily Sunni Prime Minister Shafik al-Wazzan and Saeb Salem, a former holder of the office. Complicating matters, both Wazzan and Salem lived in west Beirut and declined to leave their part of the city. Consequently, Habib had to deal with both men mainly by phone. The wheels of diplomacy moved very slowly in this strategic environment.

Since Israel's establishment in 1948, Palestinians have generally come to view Arab states as wanting in their support of the Palestinian plight, especially during crises. It was no different in 1982. Conservative states led by Saudi Arabia preferred quiet diplomacy and avoided directly challenging U.S. support for Israel. Arafat had strained relations with Hafiz al-Asad, the Syrian president. Asad wanted to control the PLO, and Arafat stood in his way. Egypt offered general support to the Palestinians but refused to sever diplomatic relations with Israel.[37] Habib, for his part, experienced difficulty gaining the Arab states' quick and full cooperation to accept the PLO fighters from Beirut. No Arab state was eager to offer to accept all the Palestinian fighters, especially before Arafat agreed to depart the city.

Finally, the Palestinians were essentially strangers in Lebanon, and the PLO had overstayed its welcome in the country. Many Lebanese initially welcomed the Israeli invasion in the hope that the Israelis might dismantle the Palestinian ministate in the country. In a similar vein, Lebanese Muslims in Beirut wanted to keep their city from becoming an Arab Stalingrad. The PLO had to show some sensitivity toward the Lebanese people's suffering. In this light, on 2 July, Arafat promised the Muslim Lebanese leadership of west Beirut that the PLO would do everything to spare the city death and destruction.[38] It took six weeks to fulfill that pledge. Meanwhile, the IDF slowly laid waste to west Beirut.

Battle for Beirut

At the beginning of July, the IDF shifted its main focus to Beirut and away from the hills surrounding it.[39] Before any major military move, Israel first warned the PLO and the civilian population of an impending attack on the city. The Begin government also softened its earlier position and announced that the Palestinian fighters could leave with their light weapons. At dusk on 1 July, Israeli aircraft suddenly swooped down on the city in mock bombing runs, making loud noise and lighting the sky with flares. Meanwhile, Israel's Arabic-speaking radio encouraged civilians to flee the city before the military attacks. The next day the IDF command confidently announced its readiness for an assault on the city.

On 3 July, the IDF tightened its economic blockade. A force of some 200 tanks moved from east Beirut and quickly secured the Green Line separating the Christian and Muslim parts of Beirut. Now Israeli soldiers and LF militiamen at checkpoints stopped all but essential personnel (doctors or policemen, for example) from entering west Beirut. The IDF also shut off all fuel, food, and water into the city. This situation lasted until 7 July, when the Reagan administration convinced the Begin government to rescind its order for a brief period.

While Sharon ordered artillery to pound Palestinian sections of west Beirut, the Israeli air force limited its operations to fake bombing raids and dropping flares and leaflets. Meanwhile, on the ground, a column of armor and infantry advanced toward the Burj el-Barajinah refugee camp in the southern part of the city. After a heavy firefight, this force managed to gain only a shallow penetration but deep enough to signal Israel's firm resolve to defeat the PLO. On 8 July, the Israeli high command stressed the army's willingness to conduct the siege through the winter if necessary.

The next two weeks saw the PLO and IDF conduct artillery duels. These were mostly one-way exchanges, as the Palestinians had to husband their ammunition wisely if they wanted to prolong the siege as long as possible. On a number of occasions, the Palestinians directed their fire into east Beirut to disrupt the otherwise tranquil life there. Israel maintained a steady military pressure on west Beirut. One Israeli officer underscored the need for a regular bombardment: "If a city is supposed to be under siege and nothing happens, they will start doing their laundry and making coffee."[40] Artillery shelling took place almost daily.

Then, on 21 July, the IDF escalated its bombing campaign. According to Israel, the Palestinians launched several raids into Israeli positions killing five IDF soldiers. Israel used the Palestinian action to justify a major attack on west Beirut. For the first time since 25 June, the air force launched a major strike. Residents in Beirut experienced ninety minutes of intense shelling by the air force, artillery, and tanks.[41] From 22 to 30 July, Israel increased its air strikes, artillery shelling, and naval gunfire.

At the end of July, Sharon decided to complement the bombardment of west Beirut with ground attacks designed to tighten the noose around the PLO headquarters and the Palestinian camps.[42] He seemed determined to force a military resolution to the PLO's withdrawal from the Lebanese capital rather than to see a diplomatic one under American auspices. The new strategy began on 31 July with a prolonged bombardment of the city. Then, on 1 August at 0300, a task force of Israeli infantry, paratroopers, and tanks launched an attack in the south and captured Beirut International Airport by the end of the day. During daylight hours, the IDF pounded west Beirut for fourteen straight hours with air, naval, and artillery bombardment. As ground troops consolidated their gains, the IDF continued a bombardment of west Beirut for two more days.

Then, on 4 August, Sharon launched the war's largest ground operation against the city. Beirut residents now experienced twenty straight hours of shelling as the IDF conducted a general bombing attack that day. Israeli gunboats blasted the entire shoreline from the hotel district in the north to Ouzai in the south. Planes and artillery struck other areas of west Beirut. Especially hard hit were the refugee camps and the Fakhani district. No place, however, appeared safe, as every civilian seemed to have been in close proximity to an exploding shell.

The attack of 4 August inflicted significant damage on west Beirut. Shells had hit many of the city's most important landmarks and institutions. Among the damaged buildings were the American University Hospital, the prime minister's building, the Central Bank, the Ministry of Information, the offices of *Newsweek* and *United Press International*, and the two luxury hotels housing foreign journalists. Residential areas also experienced damage. To increase suffering on the civilian population, the IDF maintained a blockade of water, electricity, and fuel, so much so that American University Hospital appealed on the radio for diesel fuel to help doctors and staff treat the many wounded. Unable to inflict serious damage on the IDF, the Arab defenders fired rockets and artillery into Christian east Beirut, leaving many streets temporarily deserted. Sections of the business district appeared as a ghost town for a brief period.

Sharon launched a ground operation in conjunction with the bombing campaign (see Map 3). On the eastern front, Israeli forces crossed into west Beirut at the three checkpoints on the Green Line. The main effort appeared to take place at the Museum Crossing in the direction of the PLO headquarters in Fakhani. Here, engineers and bulldozers led the way for tanks, infantry, and paratroopers, clearing barricades and other barriers set up on the streets. The fighting proved quite difficult, often house to house, but the IDF managed to capture the National Museum and the Hippodrome. Heavy Palestinian resistance prevented the Israelis from severing the Fakhani district from northern sections of west Beirut.

Meanwhile, on the southern front, the IDF launched attacks in two areas. One thrust headed north along the coast and captured a number of PLO strongpoints in Ouzai. The Israelis managed to advance a km or so before Palestinian fighters stopped their advance. A second attack fanned out from Beirut International Airport and headed northeast, managing to drive a wedge between Palestinian positions in Ouzai and the Burj al-Barajinah camp. By this time, however, most of the 80,000 or so residents of Burj al-Barajinah had fled to Fakhani district or the Sabra and Shatilla camps, leaving a sparsely populated slum area. Both Israeli attacks made limited progress. Arab defenders relied mainly on rocket-propelled grenades (RPGs), machine guns, and 130mm artillery guns to stop the Israelis.

By the end of 4 August, the Israeli army had established positions closer to the three refugee camps and the PLO headquarters. But that day would prove the costliest twenty-four hours of the siege for the IDF. Israel suffered nineteen killed and sixty-four wounded. On the diplomatic front, the ground assault temporarily stalled Habib's negotiations and, therefore, drew sharp criticism from Washington because Israel escalated the battle at a time when negotiations were seemingly bringing some progress. Socially, the attack on 4 August caused more civilians to abandon the city, upwards of 6,000 per day for the next week according to some accounts.

Time was clearly running out for the PLO at the beginning of August. The IDF had begun to demonstrate its willingness to use ground forces to squeeze and defeat the Palestinians. Moreover, Israel's bombardment was becoming more widespread, threatening to level Lebanese sections of west Beirut. Diplomatically, the PLO was

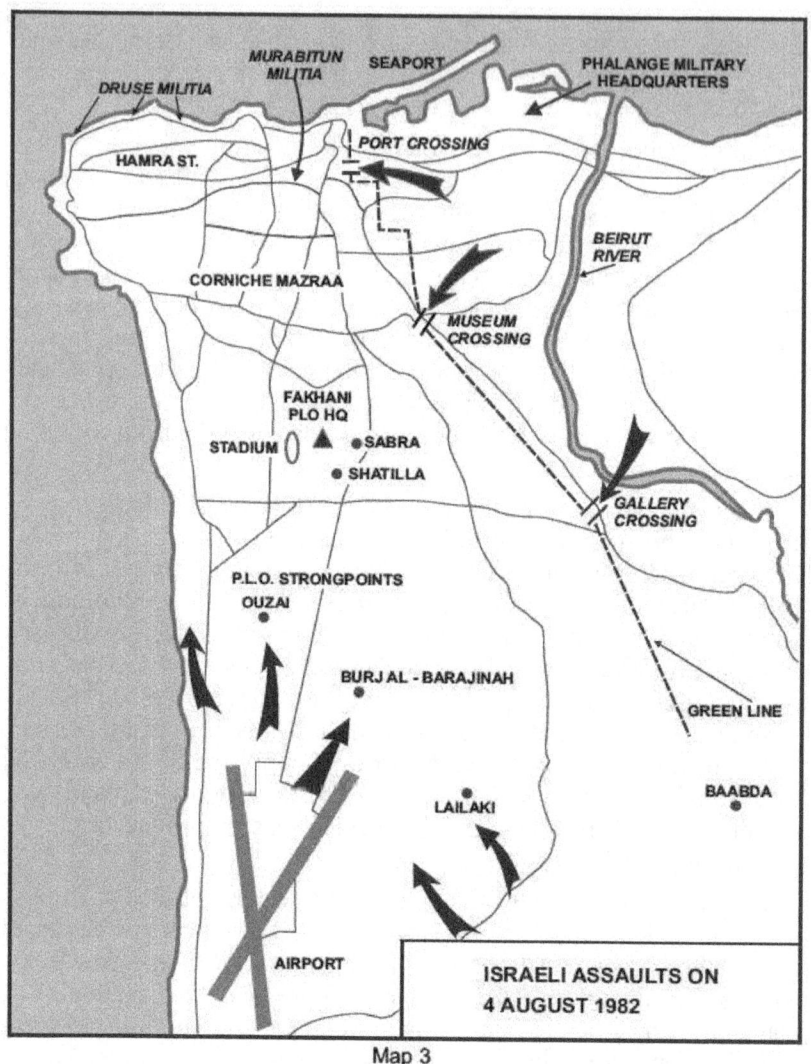

Map 3

essentially isolated, under pressure from Washington and with largely ineffective support from the Arab world. Virtually every PLO leader realized that there remained little if any hope for better terms.[43] So on 6 August, Arafat agreed to evacuate, albeit with minor reservations. Israel received the document on 9 August. On 11 August, the Israeli cabinet offered its approval in principle but expressed its own concerns over a number of details. A military surprise awaited the politicians and the diplomats.

On 12 August, despite diplomatic progress under American sponsorship, Sharon ordered, without cabinet approval, the IDF to launch its most massive bombardment of the city. The aerial assault lasted from 0600 to 1700, a day that became known as "Black Thursday." Targeting focused on the refugee camps and the area around PLO headquarters. At the end of the day, losses stood at 128 killed and 400 wounded, mainly civilians. Sharon apparently had wanted military pressure to convince Arafat to accept the American-sponsored evacuation plan. In this way, Israel could claim its military had clearly defeated the PLO.

When challenged by the cabinet to explain his independent action, Sharon tried to justify the attack by claiming that PLO artillery fire had killed two and wounded seventy-seven Israeli soldiers the day before. Unconvinced by this explanation, the cabinet stripped Sharon of all authority to order military operations. Any air force or ground attacks now required the prime minister's approval in the event the cabinet was unable to meet.[44]

The American administration was also upset with Sharon. Washington felt his action had undermined the diplomatic effort, and Reagan, affected by new images on television and in the newspapers of innocent women and children being killed or wounded, personally called Begin to express outrage and demand an end to the shelling and bombing. That night, 12-13 August, Arafat did drop his last demands and agreed to evacuate Beirut. By this time, Habib had lined up seven Arab states to receive the Palestinian fighters. For the next five days, diplomats labored feverishly to work out the final details for the PLO's departure.

Finally, on 19 August, Israel offered its consent to the evacuation plan. The PLO would withdraw under the protection of a Multi-National Force (MNF) comprising 800 U.S. Marines, 800 French troops, and 400 Italian troops. An advance contingent of 350 French troops arrived on 21 August. That day, the first 395 Palestinian fighters boarded ships and departed Beirut. On 30 August, with much fanfare, Arafat sailed off on a ship destined for Greece. The Palestinian exodus ended on 3 September. Counts of the number of evacuees vary slightly, from 14,614 to 14,656.[45] These fighters left Beirut with guns blazing in the air in defiance.

Lebanese sources placed the official toll of dead in Beirut at 6,776. This figure included those victims of the 4 June bombing, two days before Operation *PEACE FOR GALILEE* actually commenced. Lebanese police claimed that civilians accounted for 84 percent of the fatalities. This figure squares with the estimate of 80 percent often cited by international doctors who had served in Beirut during the siege. Of the 1,100 combatants among the killed, Palestinians accounted for 45.6 percent; Lebanese, 37.2 percent; Syrians, 10.1 percent; and other nationalities, 7.1 percent.[46] The IDF lost 88 killed and 750 wounded in the battle for Beirut. Total IDF losses up to this point in the war stood at 344 soldiers killed and over 2,000 wounded. Beirut thus accounted for 23 percent of Israelis killed and 32 percent of the wounded for Operation *PEACE FOR GALILEE*.[47]

Although the siege had officially ended on 21 August, the story of violence in west Beirut had not. Bashir Gemayel was elected president on 23 August, only to be assassinated on 14 September. The IDF used his assassination as an excuse to enter west Beirut and destroy elements of the Palestinian infrastructure in the city. Sharon also permitted units of Bashir's militia to move into the refugee camps of Sabra and Shatilla, where Phalange fighters, clearly intent on revenge for the loss of their leader, massacred innocent civilians from 16-18 September. Political repercussions were felt in Washington and Tel Aviv. Reagan, having guaranteed the safety of Palestinian civilians, now ordered the Marines back into west Beirut to provide security. The Israeli public demanded an investigation of the events. The massacres at Sabra and Shatilla proved a tragic ending to the siege. As noted by a retired Israeli general, "These atrocities led to the loss of legitimacy of the entire campaign, to direct intervention by the U.S. and the U.N., and to the beginning of the Israeli withdrawal from Lebanon."[48]

Battle Dynamics

The world watched for over two months as the IDF gradually tightened its grip on Beirut. Israel's main aim in the siege remained constant: the expulsion of Arafat and Palestinian fighters from the city. Sharon expected that the Sunni Lebanese leadership in west Beirut would seek to avoid destruction and would therefore apply pressure on the PLO to leave. To achieve its goal, Israel resorted to diplomacy, an information campaign, military pressure, and economic strangulation. The military effort employed all three services.

The Israeli navy, though small, performed three missions during the siege. First, it imposed a naval blockade on the port of Beirut. A ring of patrol boats, gunboats, and missile boats, supported by submarines, maintained a tight naval blockade. The Reshef class was Israel's premier ship in the blockade. Sporting a crew of forty-five, this fast patrol boat contained six Gabriel missile launchers and two 76mm guns. The

Reshef boats could operate on the sea for long periods. Second, the navy threatened the Arab defenders with an amphibious landing on the beaches. A precedent had been set earlier in the campaign when, on the first evening of the war, naval boats landed forces at the Awali River north of Sidon. To avoid being outflanked from the sea, the Arab defenders deployed fighters to guard the coastline. The IDF never attempted a major sea landing. Third, the navy provided naval gunfire in conjunction with air strikes and artillery barrages. For this, the navy relied largely on the Gabriel missile and the 76mm gun.[49] Directed by radar or optical sighting, the Gabriel missile possessed a maximum range of 38 km and carried a delayed-action fuse on its 150-kilogram warhead.

The Israeli air force also played a major role in the siege of Beirut. Fixed-wing aircraft conducted the air war over Beirut. F-15 Eagles and F-16 Flying Falcons generally provided cover while F-4 Phantoms, A-4 Skyhawks, French-built Mirages, and Israeli-made Kfirs conducted bombing runs. Israeli aircraft dropped smart munitions, cluster bombs, missiles, and rockets. Because Arab air defenses were ineffective except against helicopters, Israeli pilots approached their targets with a 30-degree dive angle and dropped their payloads at 3,000 to 4,000 feet. After an attack, an RF-4 reconnaissance aircraft would generally fly over the target area to take pictures for assessing the damage. The air force avoided using helicopters in combat roles and instead assigned them missions of transporting supplies or carrying wounded.[50]

Israel used cluster, incendiary, and concussion bombs. Cluster bombs maximized the killing of human beings. In this vein, the Israelis employed the American-made GBU58, MK180, M42, and M434E1. After the siege, a thirteen-member American ordnance team spent six weeks helping the Lebanese army de-mine the western and southern parts of Beirut. The Americans counted 1,144 explosive devices—rockets and mines, grenades and booby traps, 256 cluster bombs, 18,500 pounds of explosives, 47,500 rounds of ammunition, and 30 gallons of chemical explosives.[51]

To the media, Israel stressed its employment of precision weapons against military targets, but general bombing also took place. As described firsthand by retired British Major Derek Cooper, "From early July the attacks from sea, land and air got intense, sustained and indiscriminate, often by night as well as in the day time; little warning was given and the creeping barrage of destruction grew as the days went by and the siege and blockade began to bite . . . the shelling and bombing were indiscriminate as building after building was destroyed from sea, land and air."[52]

Several districts were especially hit hard. Fakhani district and the three refugee camps saw the greatest damage. The port area and Corniche Mazraa experienced less damage, but this was all relative. Virtually all the embassies and seventeen of twenty-six hospitals suffered damage. "In a city that was an armed camp, hospitals were not going to escape the contamination of their patients' politics."[53] The siege left the city devastated. As noted by an Israeli historian, "Come August Beirut was in shambles: running out of food and medicines; electricity cut off; and water supplies so short that inhabitants used artesian wells."[54]

Artillery and tanks played an important role in providing ground firepower. The IDF relied on artillery as the main weapon for shelling west Beirut. Ground operations emphasized combined arms. Tanks (mainly M-60s) generally led the attack formation, with 155mm howitzers bringing up the rear, ready to be brought forward.[55] Artillery, especially the 155mm self-propelled howitzer, saw employment in a direct-fire role against buildings or strongpoints. The M163 Vulcan 20mm antiaircraft gun with its high-elevation capability, mounted on an M-113 armored personnel carrier (APC), proved extremely useful against upper-level floors in tall buildings. M-113 APCs transported troops and supplies, but the IDF understood their vulnerability to RPGs and used them sparingly as a result. Engineers played an important role in clearing road obstacles and mines. The D-9 bulldozer was the vehicle of choice.[56]

Israeli infantry sported American small arms as well as the domestically produced Galil assault rifle. The Galil borrowed heavily from the Soviet AK47 assault rifle. The Israeli rifle had a thirty-five-round magazine and a fifty-round magazine for the machine gun version. This weapon proved very effective at close range. To fight on foot in Beirut, Israeli soldiers received additional equipment: hand radios, hand grenades, RPG launchers, light antitank weapons, and illumination rounds for mortars. Flak jackets helped reduce casualties, but still some 55 percent of Israeli casualties resulted from small-arms fire, many in the head or neck. Snipers proved most troublesome. Rules of engagement allowed for the application of heavy ordnance on buildings hiding Palestinians firing on Israeli troops.

PLO forces relied heavily on the AK47. They also quickly grasped the effectiveness of RPGs in urban warfare and distributed them widely. Small mobile teams of three to six fighters formed around a single RPG; they manned the outer circle of defense against Israeli ground attacks. RPGs were most effective against M-113s, less so against tanks. Palestinians also employed Katyusha truck-mounted, multiple rocket launchers. Because the Israelis had good fields of observation, the Palestinians fired the rockets and then quickly hid the trucks in alleys, garages, and between buildings.[57]

Noncombatant Aspects

To isolate the PLO and the Syrians, Israel encouraged the civilian population to flee the city using leaflets (dropped by planes), loudspeakers, and radio broadcasts. The IDF even sent personalized flyers to the Syrian brigade, naming its commander and providing instructions for its safe passage to Damascus. Israeli soldiers kept checkpoints open for townspeople to leave. Some people returned after the bombing ceased. These Lebanese were afraid to leave their apartments or businesses for too long lest squatters occupy them. Many did not return. By the end of the siege, over 250,000 residents of the original 600,000 had abandoned west Beirut. Journalists especially took advantage of Israel's open-door policy that permitted some traffic back and forth. "In the morning, we could talk with the Palestinian defenders of west Beirut. In the afternoon, we could take tea with the army that worked to destroy them."[58]

The IDF also resorted to economic sanctions, trying to make life difficult for the people. Periodic cuts in fuel, water, and electricity were expected to persuade the people to abandon the city. Inhabitants faced severe water shortages and resorted to artesian wells. International pressures forced resumption of water and electricity for brief periods. Enterprising Christian merchants in east Beirut found ways to smuggle supplies into west Beirut. Telephones, however, were left intact. Despite the hardships, on some days, women took to the beaches to sunbathe in swimsuits. People defiantly struggled to maintain some normalcy in the midst of the siege.

Israel maintained a steady information campaign for international consumption. But it was extremely difficult to put a positive spin on a siege that brought misery and death to children, women, and the elderly. The IDF could not hide this human suffering because reporters moved freely back and forth across the Green Line and could verify either side's claims. Television became an emotive source of daily reporting. On several occasions, for example, the Israelis were shown to practice misinformation. Claiming a desire to minimize civilian casualties, Israeli spokesmen stressed precision bombing methods targeting only the PLO "terrorists" and denied using cluster bombs. Then the truth came out that the IDF was using them. In another case, the IDF blamed Lebanese Christians for cutting off water and electricity to west Beirut until reporters discovered Israelis helping to man the pumping stations. Israeli censors even tried to edit newsreels, so the major networks sent their material to Damascus.[59]

Israeli bombardment of west Beirut produced unforeseen political consequences. Many Lebanese welcomed the Israeli invasion, wanting to see an end to Palestinian autonomy within Lebanon. But most of these individuals turned against the IDF as the war brought significant death and destruction to the country. As early as 7 July, Nabih Berri, the head of the Shiite organization Amal, prophetically stated the future role of his Shiite community. "If the Israelis stay in Lebanon, we'll become the new Palestinians."[60] For the next eighteen years of Israeli occupation, Shiite organization Hizbullah proved Israel's main threat in Lebanon, eventually forcing the IDF to withdraw unilaterally from the country in May 2000.

Dissent against the war did emerge early in Israel, even in the army. During the third week of July, Colonel Eli Geva, a brigade commander, refused an order to fire his artillery into areas of west Beirut. He argued to his superiors that such bombardment would naturally cause numerous civilian casualties. The senior leadership relieved Geva of his command. Eventually, several hundred Israeli officers and soldiers refused to serve in Lebanon, and some formed a peace organization. Of these, 170 faced trials and imprisonment. Such dissent within the military, though limited in numbers, was unprecedented in the annals of the IDF and therefore a shock to the society.[61] Siege warfare did stir the conscience of many Israelis, both civilian and military, but not enough to derail military operations.

The IDF launched Operation *PEACE FOR GALILEE* without cabinet approval for expanding the war to Beirut. This political constraint prevented the IDF from attempting a rapid capture of west Beirut. Determined to defeat the PLO in Beirut, Begin and Sharon adopted a strategy that avoided Israeli casualties as much as possible. Initially, both men had sought an alliance with Bashir Gemayel, hoping that he would assume the principal role in west Beirut's capture. This proved a strategic miscalculation. When the Maronite leader refused to cooperate, Sharon slowly dragged the IDF into a siege based on a strategy of attrition, combining military pressure and economic strangulation. At times, military operations drove policy. On other occasions, policy restrained military operations.

After seventy days of siege, Arafat and the PLO surrendered, owing to a combination of factors. First, the Begin government and the Israeli people possessed the will to stay the course in forcing the PLO's exodus from the city. Second, the IDF enjoyed a marked superiority in numbers and technology that slowly constricted the area the PLO fighters controlled. Israeli ground forces employed combined arms centered on the tank. Third, the PLO had become isolated diplomatically. American diplomacy essentially helped Israel attain its war aim of expelling the PLO from Beirut.

By the end of the first week of August, the PLO faced little, if any, hope of a compromise. Nevertheless, the IDF lacked a political mandate to attempt a decisive military defeat of the PLO with ground forces, and the Reagan administration would not countenance such a dramatic escalation. Taking advantage of international guarantees, Arafat finally abandoned Beirut to fight Israel another day in other places. The city of Beirut had provided enough shelter for the PLO leader to depart defeated but not destroyed.

Notes

1. Robert Fisk, *Pity the Nation: The Abduction of Lebanon* (NY: Atheneum, 1990), 295.

2. Avner Yaniv, *Dilemmas of Security: Politics, Strategy, and Israeli Experience in Lebanon* (NY: Oxford University Press, 1987), 145.

3. Ariel Sharon, *Warrior: An Autobiography of Ariel Sharon* (NY: Touchstone, 1989), 437-44, 450-51; Avraham Tamir, *A Soldier in Search of Peace: An Inside Look at Israel's Strategy* (NY: Harper & Row, 1988), 119-21; and Avi Shlaim, *The Iron Wall: Israel and the Arab World* (NY: Norton, 2000), 398. Tamir, a major general and Sharon's military adviser at the time, attended some of the meetings.

4. Itimar Rabinovich, *The War in Lebanon, 1970 1983* (Ithaca, NY: Cornell University Press, 1984), 121-22; Tamir, 127; and Shlaim, 406.

5. Sharon, 457, and Shlaim, 405.

6. Author, discussions with Israeli officers attending the U.S. Army Command and General Staff College (CGSC), Fort Leavenworth, Kansas, 1999-2001.

7. Rabinovich, 134.

8. Sharon, 463.

9. Ibid., 464.

10. *The Middle East Military Balance, 1983*, Mark Heller, ed. (Tel Aviv: Tel Aviv University, 1983), 12.

11. Dov Tamari, "Military Operations in Urban Environments: The Case of Lebanon, 1982," *Soldiers in Cities: Military Operations on Urban Terrain*, Michael C. Desch, ed. (Carlisle Barracks, PA: Strategic Studies Institute, 2001), 36. For higher figures, see Trevor N. Dupuy and Paul Martell, *Flawed Victory: The Arab Israeli Conflict and the 1982 War in Lebanon* (Fairfax, VA: Hero Books, 1986), 86-91; and Roman Gabriel, *Operation Peace for Galilee: The Israeli PLO War in Lebanon* (NY: Hill and Wang, 1984), 47-54, 81, 233.

12. Israel Shahak, "New Revelations on the 1982 Invasion of Lebanon," *Middle East International* (7 October 1994), 19.

13. Tamari, 39.

14. R.D. McLaurin and Paul A. Jureidini, *Battle of Beirut, 1982* (Aberdeen, MD: U.S. Army Human Engineering Laboratory, 1986), 35.

15. Ibid., 23-24.

16. Ibid., 25, 48, and Gabriel, 141.

17. Rashid Khalidi, *Under Siege: P.L.O. Decision Making During the 1982 War* (NY: Columbia University Press, 1986), 59.

18. Fisk, 289.

19. *Middle East Military Balance, 1983*, 263-65; Gabriel, 129-30; and McLaurin and Jureidini, 20-21.

20. Ibid., 19.

21. Khalidi, 56.

22. Tamari, 37.

23. Discussion is based on McLaurin and Jureidini, 17-20, 29-30; The MOUT Home Page, "Operation Peace for Galilee," at <www.specialoperations.com/mout/pfg.html>; and author, discussions with Israeli officers attending CGSC, Fort Leavenworth, Kansas, 1999-2001.

24. Rabinovich, 139, and Tamir, 132.

25. Fisk, 215.

26. Dupuy and Martell, 152-53. Others have echoed this assessment. See Khalidi, 55, and Anthony H. Cordesman and Abraham R. Wagner, *The Lessons of Modern War, I: The Arab Israeli Conflicts, 1973 1989* (Boulder, CO: Westview Press, 1990), 144, 151.

27. Khalidi, 47.

28. Rabinovich, 139.

29. Cordesman and Wagner, 144.

30. Sharon, 476.

31. Dupuy and Martell, 150.

32. Khalidi, 118.

33. Ibid., 112.

34. Ze'ev Schiff and Ehud Ya'ari, *Israel's War in Lebanon* (NY: Simon and Schuster, 1984), 207.

35. Martin van Creveld, *The Sword and the Olive: A Critical History of the Israeli Defense Force* (NY: Public Affairs, 1998), 298.

36. James F. Clarity, "Antiwar Minority Remains Vocal and Visible and Small," *New York Times*, 8 August 1982, A12, and Yaniv, 127-28.

37. Khalidi, 148-54.

38. Thomas L. Friedman, *From Beirut to Jerusalem* (NY: Anchor Books, 1989), 147, and Khalidi, 115-16.

39. The account draws heavily upon the following sources: *New York Times*, 1 June to 21 August 1982; Gabriel, 139-58; Schiff and Ya'ari, 195-229; Dupuy and Martell, 155-63; Cordesman and Wagner, 146-47; and McLaurin and Jureidini, 43-45.

40. James M. Markham, "Israelis Keep Reminding Beirut That Siege Is On," *New York Times*, 5 July 1982, A4.

41. Gabriel, 146-47.

42. For a flow of the siege in the month of August, see Ibid., 151-54; Dupuy and Martell, 160; Cordesman and Wagner, 147; Khalidi, 96; and Michael Jansen, *The Battle of Beirut: Why Israel Invaded Lebanon* (Boston,

MA: South End Press, 1982), 39-64. Also see the numerous articles in the *New York Times* during the period 1 to 21 August 1982.

43. Khalidi, 174.
44. Schiff and Ya'ari, 225-27; Gabriel, 158; Yaniv, 147; and Shlaim, 413.
45. Dupuy and Martell, 179.
46. "Lebanese Add 1,200 to Beirut Siege Toll," *Washington Post*, 2 December 1982; John Yemma, "New Figures Emerge on the Cost of Lives in Israel's War in Lebanon," *Christian Science Monitor*, 21 December 1982; Franklin P. Lamb, *Reason Not the Need: Eyewitness Chronicles of Israel's War in Lebanon* (Nottingham, UK: Spokesman, 1984), 342.
47. Gabriel, 169.
48. Tamari, 51-52.
49. McLaurin and Jureidini, 62.
50. Ibid., 67.
51. David Zucchino, "In Weary Beirut, the Litter of War Kills, Too," *Philadelphia Inquirer*, 23 January 1983.
52. Lamb, 338.
53. Fisk, 286.
54. Van Creveld, 297.
55. McLaurin and Jureidini, 39.
56. Ibid., 55.
57. Ibid., 33-34, and The MOUT Home Page.
58. Fisk, 300.
59. Ibid., 286-89, and Lamb, 432, 455-56.
60. Khalidi, 88.
61. Van Creveld, 299.

Selected Bibliography

Few English sources provide a detailed treatment of tactical and technological events of the siege. Consequently, this study has given more attention to the strategic dimensions.

Dupuy, Trevor and Paul Martell. *Flawed Victory: The Arab Israeli Conflict and the 1982 War in Lebanon*. Fairfax, VA: Hero Books, 1986. Little on the siege; better on the military events leading to the encirclement.

Fisk, Robert. *Pity the Nation: The Abduction of Lebanon*. NY: Atheneum, 1990. The best account of life inside Beirut by a reporter who witnessed the siege.

Friedman, Thomas L. *From Beirut to Jerusalem*. NY: Anchor Books, 1989. Award-winning book with surprisingly very little on the siege even though the author filed daily reports on the siege for the *New York Times*.

Gabriel, Roman. *Operation Peace for Galilee: The Israeli PLO War in Lebanon*. NY: Hill and Wang, 1984. Offers a succinct but superficial chapter on the siege from the Israeli perspective.

Jansen, Michael. *The Battle of Beirut: Why Israel Invaded Lebanon*. Boston, MA: South End Press, 1982. Good overview of the siege based on quotes taken from various newspapers in the English language.

Khalidi, Rashid. *Under Siege: P.L.O. Decision Making During the 1982 War*. NY: Columbia University Press, 1986. Provides insight into the Palestinian resistance to the Israeli siege. A must read for balance.

McLaurin, R.D. and Paul A. Jureidini. *Battle of Beirut, 1982*. Aberdeen, MD: U.S. Army Human Engineering Laboratory, 1986. Most detailed treatment of tactical, technological, and doctrinal aspects of the siege.

MOUT Home Page. "Operation Peace for Galilee." <www.Specialoperations.com/mout/pfg.html>. A list of lessons learned from the Israeli siege. Complements McLaurin and Jureidini's study.

New York Times, 13 June to 21 August 1982. Excellent daily coverage of the siege. Several good maps depicting Israeli attacks into the city.

Schiff, Ze'ev and Ehud Ya'ari. *Israel's War in Lebanon*. NY: Simon and Schuster, 1984. A scathing treatment of the Israeli invasion. Schiff is a well-respected military journalist in Israel.

Tamir, Avraham. *A Soldier in Search of Peace: An Inside Look at Israel's Strategy*. NY: Harper and Row, 1988. Senior Israeli general who attended several important meetings before and during the war.

Tamari, Dov. "Military Operations in Urban Environments: The Case of Lebanon." *Soldiers in Cities: Military Operations on Urban Terrain*, edited by Michael C. Desch. Carlisle Barracks, PA: Strategic Studies Institute, 2001. Interesting strategic-operational analysis of the siege.

Van Creveld, Martin. *The Sword and the Olive: A Critical History of the Israeli Defense Force*. NY: Public Affairs, 1998. Chapter on Lebanon is best short summary of the entire war and the subsequent Israeli occupation from 1982 to 1998.

Yaniv, Avner. *Dilemmas of Security: Politics, Strategy, and Israeli Experience in Lebanon*. NY: Oxford University Press, 1987. A critical, detailed treatment of the war from the perspective of Israeli politics.

The Siege of Sarajevo, 1992-1995

Curtis S. King

Like all of the studies of this volume, the struggle for Sarajevo from 1992 to 1995 offers a unique perspective on urban operations (UO). Within the wide range of UO, the siege of Sarajevo seems to fall at a mid-intensity level roughly halfway between full-scale house-to-house fighting and noncombat disaster relief. Yet, perhaps more than most other entries in this collection, the three-year clash at Sarajevo represents the largest variety of UO in a single campaign. At various times, the siege included moments of high-intensity street fighting, lengthy siege operations dominated by bombardments and sniper fire, and political posturing. In fact, all factions in the Bosnian war found that operations in Sarajevo could serve more as a tool for propaganda than as a means for military advantage. All the while, UN forces were involved in the struggle, initially in a limited and almost impossible effort to bring humanitarian aid to the city and later in a more active peacekeeping and mediation role.

The complexity of the conditions and conduct of the siege are a cautionary tale and a lesson in the pitfalls of attempts to simplify the bitter war in Bosnia-Herzegovina and the role of Sarajevo in that fight. Still, there are some themes that emerge from the conflict for Sarajevo that provide insight into UO. First, the reluctance of all factions to commit to an intensive house-to-house struggle for the city reinforces the impression that urban fighting demands greater resources, especially manpower and ammunition, than battles on most other terrain. Second, as the factions realized they were unable or unwilling to pay the price for the complete capture of the city, they also discovered that they could still use the battle for the city for political gain. This realization spawned a wide variety of tactical techniques that contributed little to capturing or relieving the capital but was designed to elicit political dividends. Finally, in connection with the potential political advantages to be gained in Sarajevo, many of the combatants came to view the city's civilian population as a chip in the game of Bosnian power politics.

The siege of Sarajevo was part of a vicious war in Bosnia-Herzegovina (for brevity, hereafter referred to as Bosnia) from 1992 to 1995. While historians have debated the supposed "ancient ethnic" origins of this war, the more immediate causes lay in Yugoslavia's collapse after the death of Josip Broz Tito.[1] Since World War II, this former partisan leader had held together the diverse republics of

Map 1

Yugoslavia with a combination of propaganda, incentive, and brute force. Without Tito, nationalistic movements reemerged and drove several of the republics toward independence. This nationalism ultimately led to conflict among the newly independent states of the old Yugoslavia, and it was a key element of the political and military factors that dominated the fighting in Bosnia and the siege at Sarajevo (see Map 1).

The first republic to leave Yugoslavia was Slovenia, which initially declared itself a sovereign state on 27 September 1989. For the next year, there was high tension, but relatively light military conflict, between Slovenia and the federal government of Yugoslavia, which was becoming increasingly dominated by Serbia and its leader, Slobodan Milošević. According to several accounts, Milošević agreed in January 1991 to allow Slovenia its independence primarily because there were so few ethnic Serbs in Slovenia.[2] This decision revealed that Milošević had shifted from his earlier goal of maintaining a united Yugoslavia to a more nationalistic aim of building a "greater Serbia."

Croatia's assertion of independence in June 1991 was far less simple and much bloodier than that of Slovenia. Most Croatians were Catholic, but helping to generate friction with Serbia, the new Croatian Republic also included a significant population of Eastern Orthodox Serbs located primarily in a region known as the Krajina. In addition, parts of Croatia bordered Serbian and Bosnian Serb lands. In spring 1991, Milošević and Croatian President Franjo Tudjman maneuvered militarily and politically as conflict loomed between the two republics. Milošević had the stronger military forces, while Tudjman hoped to portray the Serbs as aggressors to the international community. At the same time, extremist groups on both sides sent forces to the Krajina to stir up passions among the local population.[3] Open warfare broke out in summer 1991, and the brutality of the struggle came to be symbolized by the fight for Vukovar from September to November 1991. After the fall of Vukovar to pro-Serbian forces, Croatia and the Krajina Serbs (backed by the Serb Republic) came to an uneasy truce, and by early 1992, UN soldiers were in Croatia administering a cease-fire between the warring factions.

The Croatian war exhibited several factors that influenced the war that later engulfed Bosnia. First, at the highest political levels, both Milošević and Tudjman were flexible in tactics and goals. They were capable of extreme nationalistic pronouncements, yet willing to sacrifice nationalistic allies for the sake of support from the international community. Second, the fighting in Croatia transformed the Yugoslav People's Army (known by the Serbo-Croatian acronym of JNA) from a multiethnic force fighting for a federal Yugoslavia to a pro-Serb force that supported Milošević's agenda for a greater Serbia.[4] Additionally, one of the JNA's major commanders in Krajina who became familiar with the conditions of urban fighting was Ratko Mladić. He later emerged as the overall Bosnian Serb commander at Sarajevo. Third, the problems UN forces encountered after the cease-fire in Croatia prefigured the difficulties UN forces faced in Bosnia.[5] Their underlying neutral stance and their general lack of substantial military strength meant that they had to perform their mission with great awareness of political conditions and the limits of their own military power.

Finally, pro-Serb forces used tactics in the battle for Vukovar that were similar to those later employed at Sarajevo. The JNA showed its sympathies to the Serbs and used its heavy weapons outside Vukovar to bombard and devastate the city. Serb paramilitaries (soldiers Bosnian Serb leaders raised outside of the official military structure) were more willing to do the urban fighting but found that the cost of fighting from house to house was costly. Although the Serbs had taken the city, the price for Vukovar was high, not only in the manpower and time expended but also in the international support lost in the effort.[6] After Vukovar, the JNA and Serb paramilitary forces tended to rely on heavy weapons to bombard urban areas while remaining reluctant to commit to costly street fighting.

Unlike Slovenia, which did not have a significant ethnic minority, and Croatia, which had a single and relatively concentrated Serb minority, Bosnia consisted of three ethnic groups, none of which commanded an absolute majority of the population. According to the April 1991 census, Bosnia's ethnic mix was 43.6 percent Muslim, 31.3 percent Serb, 17.3 percent Croat, and 5.2 percent Yugoslav (this last category mainly representing people of mixed ethnic backgrounds).[7] This demographic factor meant that no single ethnic group could rule Bosnia with an absolute majority, making it difficult to create a workable unified political structure. It was just as difficult to partition Bosnia along reasonable and simple ethnic lines. These ethnic groups were not divided into clearly defined geographic areas. In the cities, especially Sarajevo, the ethnic groups were often intermingled, and in the countryside, the more ethnically homogenous villages dotted the landscape in a mixed fashion that defied a regional pattern.

These problems had been apparent in Bosnia's first free elections in November 1990. Each of the republic's three ethnic groups formed strongly nationalistic parties that dominated the elections, with the vote dividing almost strictly along ethnic lines (the one party that fostered multiethnic unity gathered few votes). Thus, the Muslims captured the most votes but not a majority, and after some complicated political maneuvering, one of the Muslim leaders, Alija Izetbegović, became Bosnia's president.[8] The three national parties agreed to govern as a coalition, but relations were strained.

The new coalition government in Bosnia watched events in Slovenia and Croatia with a careful eye. Izetbegović initially had hoped that Bosnia could remain in Yugoslavia, along with Slovenia and Croatia, in an autonomous status. However, once both Slovenia and Croatia had declared their independence from Yugoslavia, Bosnia was forced to choose between remaining in a Serb-dominated rump Yugoslavia or declaring its own sovereignty. By spring 1991, Izetbegović had become a proponent of an independent Bosnian state, while the Bosnian Serbs, under the leadership of Radovan Karadić, preferred to remain a part of Yugoslavia. The Bosnian Serb members of Parliament often boycotted legislative sessions, and finally on 14 October 1991, they left Parliament indefinitely.[9]

As nationalist elements gained ascendancy on all sides, the possibility for compromise diminished. The Bosnian Serbs threatened to create their own Bosnian state if Izetbegović pushed toward independence, and they called on the JNA to protect the four self-declared Bosnian Serb autonomous regions within Bosnia. Ironically, Izetbegović also tried to woo the JNA to his side, hoping that the federal army could prevent the Serb paramilitaries' intervention.[10] These efforts collapsed. Subsequently, Izetbegović, perhaps hoping for international recognition and protection, called for a referendum on Bosnian independence that took place on 29 February and 1 March 1992. Karadić and the Bosnian Serb leadership called for a boycott of the referendum. Most Bosnian Serbs did not vote, and the overall turnout was 64 percent. However, the Muslims and Bosnian Croats voted almost unanimously for independence.[11] The day after the vote, at a Bosnian Serb wedding ceremony in Sarajevo, Muslim gunmen killed a member of the wedding party, and tension in the city reached a new high. The factions managed to avoid open fighting in Sarajevo for another month, but by late spring, war seemed inevitable.

In the events leading up to the outbreak of the war, all of the major factions and their leaders staked out their positions, which was to have considerable influence on the siege of Sarajevo. Alija Izetbegović, the Bosnian Muslim leader, wanted a united and independent Bosnia, multiethnic but with Muslims as the largest segment of the population. Radovan Karadić, leader of the Bosnian Serbs, initially pushed for all of Bosnia to remain in a Serb-dominated Yugoslavia, but by 1992, his aim was to partition Bosnia and bring the Serb regions, as a contiguous unit, into Yugoslavia. This goal required physically relocating significant parts of the ethnic populations and "ethnic cleansing." This term came to describe a variety of actions—threats, house burnings, beatings, rape, and executions—designed to force opposition ethnic groups out of a region, thus leaving that area ethnically pure. These actions were not a full-scale policy of genocide but were usually designed to create larger, contiguous regions populated by single ethnic groups. In the Bosnian war, the Bosnian Serbs were the first to employ this tactic, but all factions eventually engaged in ethnic cleansing. Milošević initially supported Karadić because they shared the common goal of a greater Serbia; however, the occasional conflicts between these two leaders grew worse as the war continued. Karad ić tried to keep some measure of independence from Belgrade for the Bosnian Serbs while Milošević distanced himself from the Bosnian Serbs when their ethnic cleansing brought increasing international pressure and economic sanctions.

The final Bosnian faction, the Bosnian Croats, wavered between supporting the Muslim and Serb sides. In the independence referendum and at the opening of the war, the Bosnian Croat leadership supported the concept of a multiethnic Bosnia, but the idea of a partition—with segments of Bosnia being incorporated into newly independent Croatia—was always a possibility. Bosnian Croat leader Mate Boban supported partition, but the Croatian president, Tudjman, had firmer control over his Bosnian counterpart than Milošević had over Karad ić. Tudjman appeared to be the ultimate opportunist, willing to support any policy in Bosnia that benefited Croatia. He wavered between a partition that could add parts of Bosnia to Croatia and keeping a unified Bosnia as a buffer between Croatia and Serbia. The one constant for Tudjman was to support any action that could aid in the recovery of the Krajina.

The role of actors outside Bosnia also had a major influence on the conflict. The most obvious external players were Serbia and Croatia, whose political goals clearly influenced (but did not control) their Bosnian clients' policies. Just as important, the Bosnian Serbs and Bosnian Croats could count on military support from contiguous benefactor states. This support included heavy weapons and money. Additionally, the JNA was clearly a pro-Serb force, and it would be the crucial force that enabled the Bosnian Serbs to lay siege to Sarajevo. The Muslims had no adjacent ally, and Izetbegović hoped that the international community, primarily the UN and NATO, would aid the Muslim side. However, a UN arms embargo on Bosnia actually hurt the Muslims the most because they started the war with no heavy weapons and could not smuggle them in from adjacent allies. Later in the war, Izetbegović's forces would get some support from Muslim nations that managed to get weapons through the embargo.

All of the factions in Bosnia with their varied aims fought for more than three years. During this time, the fighting spread to almost every region of the country, but throughout the conflict, Sarajevo remained a focal point of the struggle and the most visible symbol of the war. During the siege, as it does today, the city of Sarajevo stretches out along both sides of the Miljacka River in a narrow, oblong shape approximately 13 kilometers (km) long from east to west but generally only 3 to

4 km wide as it follows the river (see Map 2). The urban area contained virtually all of the types of terrain and structures that are found in most modern cities. However, the truly dominant characteristic of the city was the ring of mountains surrounding it, placing the city in a bowl visible and vulnerable to anyone who occupied the rim of high ground on the outside edges. Keeping in mind that there was only limited fighting in the streets of Sarajevo itself, it is worth examining key pieces of terrain that influenced the siege both militarily and politically.[12]

Transportation routes into and out of the city, rivers and roads, provided only limited capacity. The Miljacka River, like almost all watercourses in Bosnia, was nonnavigable, and thus Sarajevo had no port facilities. The river roughly divided the Bosnian capital in half. The Miljacka is a tributary of the Bosna River that, along with the eljeznica River, bounded the city on its western border. There were numerous bridges across the Miljacka throughout the city, including the famous "Latin Bridge" where Archduke Franz Ferdinand was assassinated. The Miljacka was only a limited barrier to movement between the northern and southern portions of the city and played only a minor role in the siege.

The city's major roads were a much larger factor in the struggle. As might be expected, Sarajevo was (and is) a nexus of major highways for Bosnia (see Map 3). Two roads led out of the city north toward Tuzla, a major Bosnian Serb stronghold, and Zenica, one location the UN designated as a safe haven. Toward the east, one highway connected the city with Višegrad, and more important Pale, which was the capital of the Bosnian Serb faction within Bosnia (later to be called the *Republika Srpska*, or RS, in its Serbo-Croatian acronym). One major route from the city passed near the airport and continued south to Trnovo, Foča, Dubrovnik, and Split. This was the main path connecting the city with Bosnian Croat strongholds and, to a lesser extent, the Muslim ones in the south. Finally, the main road to the west connected Sarajevo with Mostar, the scene of some of the bitterest fighting of the war when Bosnian Croats and Muslims turned against each other in 1993 and 1994. All factions, as well as the UN, used the roads to attempt to transport supplies and humanitarian aid and to evacuate refugees, children, the sick, and the elderly.

One other road, the infamous "sniper's alley," is also noteworthy. Starting in the west, the road name changed several times until becoming Marshal Tito Boulevard as it entered the old city. This was the main east-west path through the city. It was not a highway, but for much of its route, it was a wide, four-lane street with a median in the

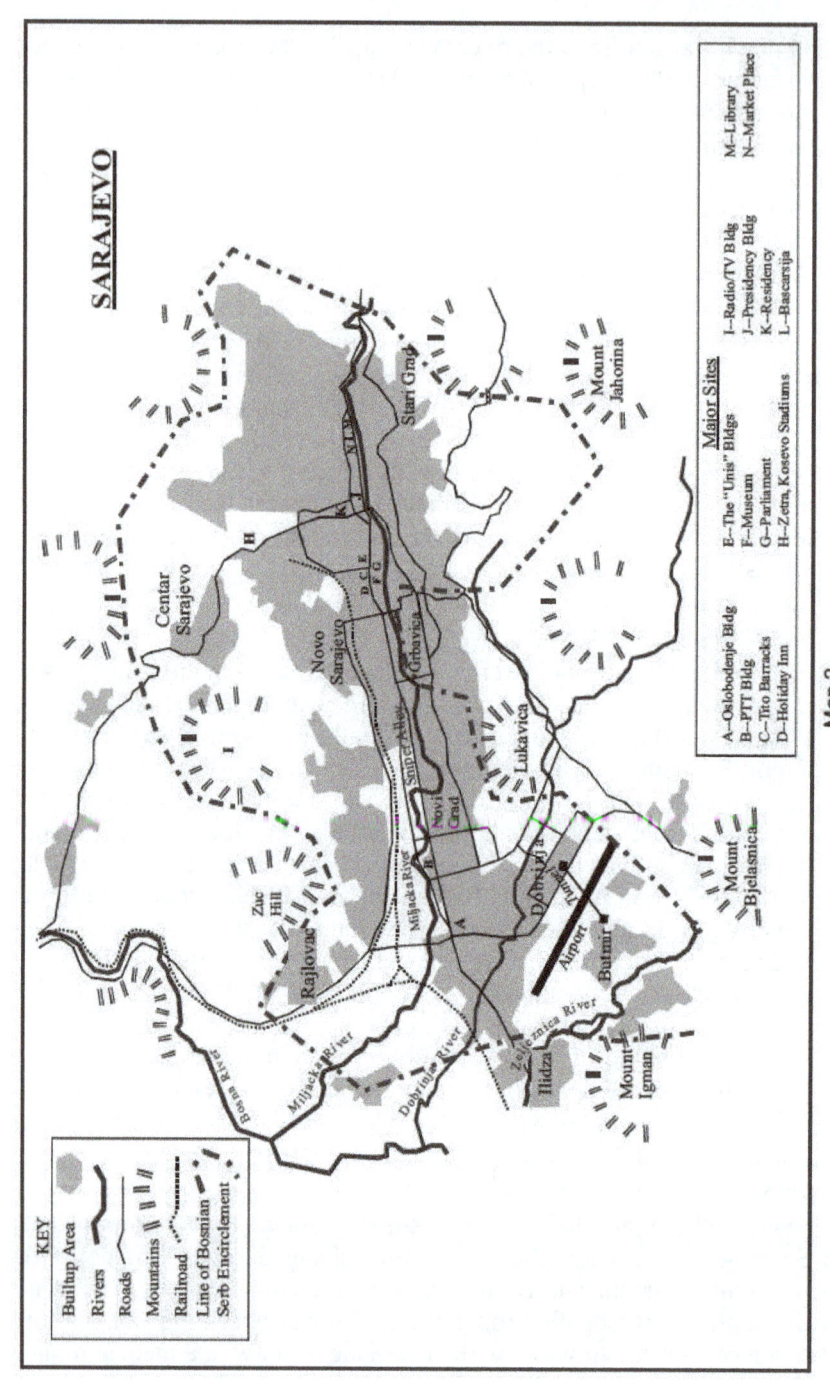

Map 2

Map 3

middle for the city's tram. From its origins on the west side of the city up to the point where it split near the "old city," the street was an open area that was visible from many high buildings and most of the surrounding mountains, thus rendering it vulnerable to sniper fire. The single, ground-level tram down the center of the boulevard was Sarajevo's only internal mass transit system, but as a transportation line, it often did not run during much of the siege and had little effect on the fight for the city. However, the tram cars were sometimes turned on their sides and used as obstacles and barricades.

Looking at the various sectors of the city, one can start with the western area of Sarajevo, best known during the siege for the suburb of Ilid a and the Sarajevo airport. Ilid a is split by the eljeznica River and, at the time of the siege, consisted of modern residential homes and small apartment buildings. Its most famous site is a spa consisting of several hotels that served as a Bosnian Serb headquarters during much of the siege and later was the headquarters for the multinational Implementation Force (IFOR) that replaced the UN Protection Force (UNPROFOR) in 1996. The airport lies slightly east of Ilid a, and like the highways emanating from the capital, its significance at the time was more political than military. Neither side used the airport for combat aircraft or military supply, but it became a symbol of contact with the international community and a major connection for humanitarian aid.

Just north and east of the airport was the sector of the city known as Dobrinja. It consisted largely of three- and four-story apartment complexes. The open area of the airport on the southwest side of Dobrinja gave clear fields of fire from the surrounding mountains, and much of Dobrinja was devastated during the siege. This part of the city also became known for being the eastern end of a tunnel that ran under the airport. The Bosnian (Muslim and Croat) forces built the tunnel to aid in resupplying the city while avoiding the Bosnian Serb guns that dominated the region around the airport. It is also interesting to note that the tunnel was the one example of underground operations in the siege; Sarajevo did not have a subway and had only a small sewer system. Unlike some other urban conflicts, Sarajevo saw virtually no subterranean fighting.

Just north of Dobrinja, but still south of the Miljacka River, was the area of town known as Novi Grad. Most of this sector was made up of housing for the city's industrial laborers, and it included several massive apartment buildings built in the old Communist style of repetitive, high-rise structures. These tall buildings provided perches for snipers from all of the factions. Also in this region was the Oslobodjenje building, the home of Sarajevo's pro-Bosnian (Muslim) press, which was devastated in the siege. Farther east was the Postal, Telephone, and Telegraph (PTT) building, which was the headquarters for UNPROFOR during part of the siege.

Moving farther east in the city past residential apartments and moderately sized buildings on both sides of the Miljacka, the center of the city contained several areas and structures that figured prominently in the struggle. On the north side of the main east-west boulevard (sniper's alley) lay Tito Barracks, a complex of large concrete buildings that housed the old JNA garrison for the city. Close by was the Holiday Inn that gained fame as the favorite location for the international press during the conflict. Slightly farther east were two high-rise buildings called the *Unis*, also known locally as *Mono* and *Uzier*, two famous characters from jokes told by Sarajevo's residents. Although tall, the *Unis* buildings were not a popular site for snipers because they were subjected to heavy mortar and artillery fire throughout the struggle. Across the boulevard from the Holiday Inn—but still north of the Miljacka—were the Parliament Building and National Museum. These buildings received only moderate damage during the fighting; the Muslim defenders held trench lines closer to the river rather than occupying the structures themselves. Just across the Miljacka from the parliament and museum was the district of Grbavica, a residential area of mostly two- and three-story apartments. This district marked the farthest advance of the Bosnian Serbs into the city itself.

Continuing eastward toward the old sector of the city, a road called Alipašina branched north from Marshal Tito Boulevard. This road climbed rapidly upward toward mountains on the north side of the city. About 2 km from the center of the city, the Alipašina passed two stadiums built for the 1984 Olympics: the Koševo outdoor stadium and the Zetra indoor ice rink. Across the Alipašina from the stadiums was a large open hillside that contained a small cemetery before the siege. During the war, many of the dead bodies were stored in Zetra stadium before being buried on the hillside across from the rink. Often, snipers killed mourners during these funeral processions. By 1995, the cemetery was four times its original size.

Returning to the area near the intersection of the Alipašina and Tito Boulevard, there were two significant buildings: the Residency and the Presidency. Neither structure is particularly large or militarily important, but both had political significance. The Residency was Tito's old vacation home in the city, and it later functioned as UNPROFOR headquarters. The Presidency was the office of Bosnian President Izetbegović during the war.

Finally, the eastern sector of the city is a mixture of closely packed residential buildings, stores, and famous historical structures centered on the Muslim old city known as Baščaršija. The old city was interlaced with numerous narrow streets and cobblestone pedestrian paths. On the eastern tip of this sector, a large stone building constructed in the Austro-Hungarian era (1894) as the City Hall later became the city's library. Although not a major factor in the siege, the building suffered heavy artillery fire, which tragically destroyed a substantial number of priceless books. Just west of the library, the most prominent Muslim mosque, Catholic cathedral, and Orthodox church lay within 500 meters of each other—miraculously little damaged during the war—perhaps symbols of the potential for peaceful coexistence. Near these places of worship lay a more tragic symbol, the central market place (the Markale market), a small open area (a square about 200 meters on all sides) filled with wooden stands for produce and other vendors. It had no military importance, but bombings of the market and the resultant civilian deaths had a great impact on the politics of the siege.

The high ground surrounding Sarajevo was the dominant terrain of the struggle. During the siege, almost every road to Sarajevo had to go through a pass dominated by mountains the Bosnian Serbs controlled. The most publicized of these high points was Mount Igman on the southwest outskirts of the city. Two other sectors of elevated terrain stand out. First, on the south side of the city, the Bosnian Serbs held a series of hills starting at Lukavica and continuing east past the location of the bobsled run of the 1984 Olympics. Control of these southern heights gave the Bosnian Serbs their best artillery and sniper shots into the city. Second, although the Bosnian Serbs also controlled much of the high ground on the northern half of the city, the Bosnian Muslims held one hilltop less than 1 km from the Zetra stadium, which was also the location of the Bosnian television broadcasting station. This station continued to broadcast throughout the siege.

As mentioned earlier, the population of Sarajevo was cosmopolitan and relatively tolerant of religious differences. Its ethnic groups extensively intermingled throughout the city. According to the 1991 census, the total population was 428,617. Sarajevo had a relatively small land area for a major urban area and, therefore, was more densely populated than many comparable cities. As in the nation at large, the Muslims made up the largest percentage of the city population at 49.3 percent. The Bosnian Serbs were 27.4 percent of the total. Interestingly, the Yugoslav percentage of the city population (12.1) was greater than the Croat portion (7.3). This factor shows that a sizable segment of Sarajevo's population was the product of mixed ethnic backgrounds. Finally, 3.9 percent of the city was listed as "others," which included a small but growing Jewish population.

Before the siege, the distribution of the ethnic groups throughout Sarajevo was so mixed that almost no sector, except for the old city (Baščaršija), could claim a majority of one faction. The large apartment buildings had people from each group, and the residential areas usually had Muslim, Orthodox, and Catholic homes side by side. However, not long after the siege began, segments of the population shifted. In particular, significant numbers of Bosnian Serbs left their homes to seek safety behind Bosnian Serb lines around the city. Thus, in addition to the old city, a few other sectors of Sarajevo became predominantly Muslim and subject to bombardment.

The opposing forces at Sarajevo were a mix of military, paramilitary, pseudo-military, armed civilian, and even some criminal elements that represented the myriad of factions vying for control of the city. For simplicity, it is useful first to discuss the concept of Total National Defense and then each of the factions' forces in turn: the JNA, Bosnian Serb irregulars, Croat and Bosnian Croat units, and the Muslim-dominated forces initially designated as the Bosnian Defense Force (BDF) and eventually renamed the Army of the Federation of Bosnia and Herzegovina (known by its Serbo-Croatian acronym of AFBiH). After examining the factions, we will examine the other major player in Sarajevo, UNPROFOR. Scrutiny of the leadership, organization, weaponry, doctrine, training, and experience of all of the fighting elements reveals a general lack of UO preparation and a shortage of the resources (and in some cases the will) needed to carry out a sustained city fight.

Before its breakup, Yugoslavia's armed forces were based on a concept called Total National Defense. Not surprisingly, this concept grew out of Yugoslavia's experience in World War II as well as the nature of the country's terrain and Yugoslavia's position as a nonaligned player between the Soviet Union and the United States in the Cold War.[13] Under Total National Defense, the active army (JNA) was not expected to defeat a major power in a conventional war. Instead, the JNA acted more as a training vehicle for conscripts who became members of the Territorial Defense Force (TDF) after completing their two-year term in the JNA. The TDF, fighting as partisans, was expected to carry most of the fight against any invader (much like in World War II).

The forces needed for Total National Defense doctrine had several unique characteristics. Both the JNA and TDF trained in small-unit tactics with an emphasis on partisan warfare. The TDF was locally based and reflected the ethnic composition of its region. The JNA was multiethnic (at least before 1990) and answered to the Yugoslav federal government. The TDF had access to small-arms caches that were distributed throughout the country, with a particular concentration of weapons in the rugged terrain of Bosnia. The JNA had all of the heavy weapons: tanks, armored personnel carriers (APCs), artillery, and mortars. As the Yugoslav wars evolved after 1990, the TDF fragmented into supporting its local regions while the JNA generally became more of a pro-Serbian force.

When fighting broke out in Sarajevo in April 1992, the Yugoslav federation controlled the JNA units in Bosnia. By this time, Slovenia and Croatia had departed Yugoslavia, leaving the federation dominated by Serbia, and thus Milošević had a preeminent influence on the JNA's role. This being said, it is important to emphasize that the JNA, especially at the outset of the war, was not simply an unquestioning tool of Serbian nationalism. It still contained some non-Serbian officers and several moderate Serb officers who hoped to restore Yugoslav unity or at least to mitigate the suffering in Bosnia. Additionally, at the beginning of the Bosnian war, the Bosnian Serb leader, Karad ić, had only limited influence on JNA operations. Finally, not long after the fighting erupted in April 1992, the federal government ordered the JNA to withdraw from Bosnia. However, only limited parts of the JNA withdrew, while many of the JNA soldiers and most of their heavy equipment remained behind and eventually became the basis of the Bosnian Serb Army (later known by its Serbo-Croatian acronym as the VRS).[14]

Just as fighting erupted in Sarajevo, General Ratko Mladić, a veteran commander of JNA forces fighting in Croatia, became the JNA commander in Bosnia. Mladić was a Serb nationalist who did not hesitate to take whatever measures he felt were necessary to eradicate Croat and Muslim opposition in Bosnia. Initially, as a JNA officer, he reported to the Yugoslav government, but he did all he could to support the Bosnian Serbs. Later in 1992, when parts of the JNA departed Bosnia and the rest became the Army of *Republika Srpska* (VRS), Mladić received command of this new force. At that point, he no longer kept up the façade of Yugoslav unity, and he worked directly for Karad ić. Mladić remained the VRS commander for the rest of the war.

The JNA leader in the Sarajevo region was Colonel-General Milutin Kukanjac. While he disliked Izetbegović and the new Muslim-dominated Bosnian government, Kukanjac focused on protecting and preserving his JNA forces and was uninterested in taking the city by storm. He seemed to have a genuine interest in acting as a moderating force, but he nonetheless permitted Bosnian Serbs to occupy dominant positions in the hills around Sarajevo, gave them heavy weapons, and occasionally assisted in bombarding the city. Kukanjac's actions reflected the JNA's mixed role at the beginning of the war.

The fighting in Slovenia and Croatia had prompted a significant reorganization of the JNA in December 1991 that had a major influence on the composition of Kukanjac's forces around Sarajevo. The Yugoslav federation shuffled its old military districts (MDs) and created a new one, the 4th MD, to operate in Bosnia with its headquarters at Sarajevo.[15] The 4th MD was actually redesignated once more before April 1992, when it became the 2d MD. It consisted of four corps and approximately 60,000 men throughout Bosnia. The 4th Corps was positioned at Sarajevo and consisted of 15,000 to 20,000 men. These soldiers reflected a transition in the composition of the JNA in 1991 and early 1992; the JNA lost its multiethnic mix as Muslim and Croat soldiers, and particularly officers, left the federal army or were purged by the dominant Serbian leadership. By the time fighting broke out in Sarajevo, the 4th MD consisted largely of Bosnian Serb, Serb, and Montenegrin soldiers. (Montenegro was the only Yugoslav republic to remain with Serbia in the rump Yugoslavia that remained after 1992).

The JNA forces were the best equipped of any of the factions fighting for Sarajevo, including possessing heavier weapon systems than those of UNPROFOR. While there are rough estimates of the total number and types of JNA equipment throughout former Yugoslavia (about 800 to 900 tanks, 740 APCs, 6,400 mortars, and about 1,300 field guns), it is difficult to estimate the numbers available for the Sarajevo fight. Simple mathematics would indicate that the 2d MD in Bosnia might have had about one-quarter of the JNA totals, while the JNA troops at Sarajevo had only a portion of the 2d MD's total (for example, perhaps 50 tanks, 400 mortars, and 80 field guns). In any case, the JNA at Sarajevo deployed a wide mix of heavy weapon systems that included T-34, T-54/55, and M-84A tanks; wheeled and tracked APCs from both Western and former Soviet stocks; some multiple rocket launchers; an extensive variety of artillery and mortars (from 60-millimeter [mm] up to 155mm); and Gazelle and Mi-8 helicopters. The number and types of JNA equipment may not seem impressive, but this was virtually the only heavy equipment available in the siege for any of the factions.

By April 1992, the JNA was in the process of transforming its role and doctrine based on experiences in Slovenia and Croatia. The federal army was no longer a training ground for multiethnic conscripts to join the TDF. Instead, the JNA became a force of long-term Serb and Montenegrin soldiers whose mission was to support the Serb-dominated federal government in Yugoslavia's internal wars. Despite this change in roles, the JNA transformation was incomplete. It still carried traditions of partisan doctrine and training (small-unit actions, decentralized control), and it lacked the numbers to conduct a large-scale conventional war in Bosnia's rugged terrain. Increasingly, the JNA relied on its heavy weapons to destroy or intimidate its opponents while Bosnian Serb irregulars did the close fighting. The JNA, like all of the factions in Sarajevo, had no special UO training or doctrine. Some of the JNA officers had seen the high cost of the fighting in Vukovar, and they were reluctant to commit their forces in house-to-house fighting in Sarajevo.

The Bosnian Serb irregular forces were initially more aggressive than the JNA and more willing to engage Izetbegović's Bosnian forces in urban combat. However, they lacked the strength necessary to take the city, and after parts of the JNA converted to a Bosnian Serb force, the irregulars adopted the JNA tactics that relied on heavy weapons in order to avoid casualties that might result from a city fight.

To imply that all of the irregulars in support of the Bosnian Serbs at Sarajevo were Bosnian Serbs under Karadić's control is an oversimplification. While most of the irregulars were probably Bosnian Serbs, some were Serbians, Montenegrins, and even Croatian Serbs who were fighting for the overall cause of Serb nationalism.[16] Karadić certainly had more control over most of these units than he had over the JNA, but due to the irregulars' disparate nature, the Bosnian Serb political leader never had complete command of them.

Similarly, the Bosnian Serb irregulars did not have a unified military commander in April 1992. The most infamous of the irregular leaders went by the *nom de guerre* of "Arkan" (his real name was eliko Ranjatović). He commanded a unit known as the Tigers, similar to other irregular units called the White Eagles and Panthers. Although Arkan did not participate significantly in the siege at Sarajevo, the collection of virtually independent battalion-level commanders like him at Sarajevo only loosely reported to Karadić while intermittently working with the JNA.

The irregulars were mostly light infantry, and they began the war in Bosnia with sufficient quantities of small arms and ammunition but limited numbers of heavy weapons. However, they could often count on the support of JNA weaponry, and in fact, they inherited most of the 4th MD's equipment when the JNA ostensibly withdrew from Bosnia. Estimates of Bosnian Serb irregular strength vary between 20,000 and 35,000 throughout all of Bosnia, thus leaving a very rough estimate of 4,000 to 8,000 men immediately available for the fight in Sarajevo. These forces usually operated in battalion-size units or smaller, and it was difficult for the Bosnian Serb leadership to coordinate the irregulars' efforts.

Reflecting their light infantry structure (and aspects of their former partisan training), the Bosnian Serb irregulars relied on small-unit doctrine that emphasized sudden attacks on enemy weak points while avoiding decisive confrontations with enemy strengths. The irregulars did not have a specific UO doctrine, but some of the units deployed near Sarajevo had fought in builtup areas in Croatia and probably knew more about city fighting basics (for example, methods for clearing a building) than the JNA.

Overall, the Bosnian Serb irregulars presented an unusual combination of characteristics. They were more ideologically motivated than most of the JNA soldiers, and they had some city fighting experience; thus they seemed more likely to engage, and succeed, in a house-to-house struggle for Sarajevo. However, their numbers were limited, their units and leadership were divided, and heavy casualties in the urban battles of Croatia had tempered their enthusiasm for city fighting.

Croat and Bosnian Croat forces had less influence on the conflict in Sarajevo than in other parts of Bosnia because the Bosnian Croats tended to focus on terrain that was adjacent to Croatia, particularly Herzegovina. At the start of the Bosnian war, there were two Bosnian Croat armies fighting in Bosnia: the Croatian Defense Forces (HOS) and the armed forces of the Croatian Defense Council (HVO). The HOS started as local paramilitary units, while the HVO clearly had closer ties with the more regular units of the Croatian Army (HV). In August 1992, the HOS merged with the HVO. Their combined forces often wavered between supporting the Muslims and the Bosnian Serbs, depending on the political situation.[17] A group of moderate Bosnian Croats, under Stjepan Kljuić, supported Izetbegović, but a large percentage of Bosnian Croats, particularly those in Herzegovina, sided with the more nationalistic Boban. As the Bosnian Croats shifted their support, they had a significant but not decisive effect on the siege.

Overall, the HVO was under the political control of Boban, and just as Boban clearly relied on the support of Croatian President Tudjman, the HVO often called on the HV for assistance in its campaigns. In addition, the HVO command largely seemed to answer to orders from the HV main staff in Zagreb. The HVO was organized on a territorial basis, with locally recruited soldiers serving close to home. They had some heavy weapons and were generally better armed than the Bosnian (Muslim) forces and less well armed than the Bosnian Serbs. HVO doctrine carried some of the old partisan traditions, and, except in Mostar, the troops proved reluctant to engage in city fighting. The

HVO's overall strength in Bosnia was about 35,000 troops, but few of these troops took part in the siege.

The only HVO force in the Sarajevo region was a regiment of 2,000 men in the suburb of Stup. During the siege, these troops did not directly engage in city fighting or even in shelling Sarajevo. Their main effect was in holding one of the resupply routes into the city. Throughout 1992, the HVO forces in Stup usually allowed Bosnian (Muslim) convoys to proceed to the city. For parts of 1993, the HVO closed this route as part of the bitter Muslim-Croat fighting of that year. However, after the Washington Accord between Muslims and Croats in February 1994, the route was reopened to Bosnian supplies. Some Bosnian Croat soldiers who served in Izetbegović's forces had a more direct role in the fight for Sarajevo, as will be discussed later in this chapter.

The forces that supported Izetbegović's Bosnian government were usually more numerous than their opponents, especially in the Sarajevo region, but they started with little organization and experience and were woefully lacking in equipment and heavy weapons. Before the outbreak of fighting in Bosnia, paramilitary Bosnian Muslim units such as the Green Berets and the Patriotic League of the People had formed in Sarajevo and other Muslim-dominated regions in Bosnia. However, most of the BDF came from former TDF soldiers and local police forces. In any case, the BDF had to start virtually from scratch, taking elements from a variety of sources.[18]

The ad hoc nature of the early BDF makes it difficult to determine its exact structure, strength, equipment, and ethnic composition. On the issue of ethnic composition, writers and observers of the Bosnian war have offered widely varying views of Izetbegović's forces. Some accounts portray the BDF as a true multiethnic force that reflected the Bosnian government's desire to tolerate an inclusive Bosnian unity. Other works argue that only a small number of Bosnian Serbs and Bosnian Croats joined Izetbegović's forces, usually because they were coerced, and that the Bosnian government made a cynical show of multiethnic participation without sharing any real power. There are elements of truth in all of these accounts, but in the end, the Bosnian government, even if only out of necessity, was the only faction that made any effort to incorporate all of Bosnia's ethnic groups. Only a few Bosnian Serbs continued to serve in the BDF, but the Bosnian Croats made up a significant percentage of the BDF units. During the siege, Bosnian Croat units serving in the BDF do not appear to have openly turned on the Muslim forces and engaged them in combat, but in several cases, Bosnian Croat units refused to cooperate with BDF attacks and gave tacit assistance to the Bosnian Serbs.

Whatever the post facto arguments of BDF composition, most accounts agree that Izetbegović's Bosnian government was the least prepared faction at the outbreak of war in April 1992. The Green Berets were available but were small in number. At first, Izetbegović negotiated with the JNA, perhaps naively in an attempt to woo it to the Bosnian side, and thus neglected efforts to build his own force. It was his belated recognition of the need for more substantial Bosnian forces that led to his call to mobilize the Bosnian TDF and police forces on 4 April 1992, which was the immediate cause (or excuse) for the outbreak of the war. Even after these events and the significant fighting that continued for two months, it was not until 26 June that the Bosnian government declared a formal state of war.

Initially, the Bosnian government relied on three types of forces to hold Sarajevo: Muslim paramilitary units, TDF and police forces (containing some multiethnic troops), and Muslim "criminal" elements. This last group, as might be expected, have been the subject of much controversy, with some accounts portraying the Izetbegović government as nothing more than a collection of Muslim thugs. While some members of the Bosnian government (and Izetbegović's family) probably had connections to organized crime, using Muslim gangs seems to have come more out of military necessity than out of profit. In any case, the initial defense of Sarajevo fell to disparate units that were ill equipped, lacked centralized control, and were untrained in UO doctrine. However, perhaps out of desperation, the Bosnian troops showed a willingness to engage in costly street fighting to hold the city. Many of these soldiers also had the advantage of knowing the terrain—as residents of Sarajevo—and thus felt more comfortable in a city fighting for their own neighborhoods.

It was only after the outbreak of fighting that the Bosnian government began to structure its forces and formally create the Bosnian Army (later known as the BDF). The commander in chief of the Bosnian forces was President Izetbegović, and his defense minister was Jerko Doko, a Bosnian Croat. While the political leaders provided overall guidance, details of the fighting were left to the Bosnian main staff in Sarajevo. The chief of staff was Colonel Safir Halilović, a Muslim, and his two deputies were Colonel Stjepan Šiber, a Bosnian Croat, and Jovan Divjak, a Bosnian Serb. Almost all members of the main staff had been former members of the JNA or TDF. Although the main staff divided control of the BDF into seven district staffs with one located in

Sarajevo, the main staff and the Bosnian government stayed in Sarajevo throughout the war, and they exercised what amounted to direct control of the city's defense.

Arms and equipment were a constant problem for the BDF. At the beginning of the conflict, small arms and ammunition were barely adequate at best while heavy equipment (artillery, mortars, tanks, and APCs) was almost nonexistent. This is part of the reason for the Bosnian government's willingness to turn to organized crime in Sarajevo where the local "mafia" provided small arms to the pro-government forces. The UN embargo on arms hurt the Bosnian government more than its enemies because Bosnia began the war with the fewest weapons on the ground, and it did not have an adjacent benefactor nation to supply it arms. Beginning in late 1992, Izetbegović turned to other Muslim nations (especially Arab) to help finance the purchase of arms and ammunition, some of which were smuggled through Croatian ports. Although the BDF was never as well equipped as its adversaries, the Bosnian forces eventually acquired some T-54 (and later, T-62) tanks; APCs; 60mm, 82mm, and 120mm mortars; a hodgepodge of old Yugoslav and former Eastern bloc artillery pieces; the Soviet-designed RPG-7; and German and Yugoslav antitank missiles.

The pro-Bosnian forces did not have UO doctrine or experience at the beginning of the war, although the units fighting within the city had the advantage of fighting on familiar terrain. As the BDF became more structured, it does not seem to have adopted any formal UO doctrine, but the units within the city became more experienced in urban fighting, thus making any Bosnian Serb attempt to take the city more difficult as the war progressed.

UNPROFOR soldiers rarely engaged the factions in direct combat during the siege; however, they engaged in various activities such as escorting convoys and guarding the airport. Their mere presence at key points in the conflict significantly influenced the struggle for the city. UNPROFOR units were in Sarajevo at the onset of hostilities almost by accident, as UN leaders chose the Bosnian capital as the headquarters of the peacekeeping forces deployed in Croatia (for the Krajina conflict) over the objections of UNPROFOR's military leaders who felt that Sarajevo was too far from Croatia. Thus, UNPROFOR troops in Sarajevo were initially only a small headquarters guard force not intended for intervention in Bosnia's conflict.[19]

The UNPROFOR commander in 1992 was Lieutenant General Satish Nambiar, an experienced Indian officer. His deputy was a flamboyant French officer, Major General Philippe Morillon. Both Nambiar and Morillon were focused on the deployment of UNPROFOR in Croatia. They spent most of their time outside of Sarajevo, and they were not heavily involved with UN operations in the city in the early months of the Bosnian war. By default, the UNPROFOR officer most involved in the early fight for Sarajevo was third in the UNPROFOR hierarchy, Brigadier General Lewis MacKenzie, a Canadian officer with considerable experience in peacekeeping operations.

In accordance with their initial mission in Sarajevo as an administrative headquarters, UNPROFOR forces located in the Bosnian capital were small. The staff included officers and support personnel from multiple nations. The only real fighting force in April 1992 was a company-size unit of Swedish guards whose mission was to protect the headquarters. These guards performed their mission admirably, but clearly, UNPROFOR lacked the physical strength to influence events in the city, and MacKenzie had to rely mostly on negotiation, persuasion, and bluff to have some restraining effect on the conflict. The initial small UNPROFOR was located in the PTT building in downtown Sarajevo.

Although UNPROFOR gained some strength as the war progressed, it never had the mission of direct military intervention. This increased strength included troops from several nations who occupied the airport and a French battalion at Mount Igman that endeavored to keep this dominating height neutral. All of the UN contingents that rotated through service in Sarajevo came with their own national equipment. This included sufficient small arms, some APCs, and wheeled vehicles, but no heavy weapons (tanks and artillery). Toward the end of the siege, the main source of military striking power for UNPROFOR became NATO airpower.

Describing the full course of the siege of Sarajevo presents unique challenges. The conflict lasted over 30 months—along with Leningrad, arguably the longest siege of the twentieth century. Events of some importance occurred almost each day, including bombardments and sniper fire, yet neither side made an effort to achieve a decisive victory within the city's urban environment. Perhaps the best way to capture the importance, as well as the feel, of the struggle for Sarajevo is to trace the siege chronologically with a focus on three areas: major attempts to take the city or lift the siege, efforts to cut or open supply lines into Sarajevo, and actions that had significant political effects on the conflict.

Although tensions had been mounting for some time in Bosnia and armed conflict had erupted in Bijelina, Bosanski Brod, and other locations in early April, all of the factions seemed unprepared for the outbreak of fighting in Sarajevo.[20] On 4 April, Izetbegović made preliminary steps toward mobilizing the Bosnian TDF—on paper, still accountable to the Yugoslav government—in support of his Bosnian government. The next day, students and other residents from all of Sarajevo's ethnic groups conducted a peace march along Tito Boulevard that protested the nationalistic policies of each of the factions' political leaders. Snipers from the Holiday Inn fired on the crowd, killing a young medical student from Dubrovnik, Suada Dilberović, the "first casualty" of the siege. Muslim police entered the Holiday Inn and arrested several armed Bosnian Serbs. Also that day, Bosnian Serb paramilitaries attacked the Sarajevo Police Academy.

All sides now scrambled to mobilize forces. On 6 April, the same day that the European Community (EC) formally recognized Bosnia, Izetbegović completed the mobilization of the Bosnian TDF and called on the Sarajevo police to support the Bosnian government. The Sarajevo chief of police, Dragan Vikić (a Muslim), took nominal command of the combined TDF and police forces and issued a decree that attempted to reassure the city's population: "the defenders of Sarajevo will not open fire on members of the Yugoslav People's Army and will not pose a threat to any citizen." However, another account claims that Vikić was far less sanguine and felt that the situation in Sarajevo was "out of control." Bosnian Serb paramilitaries began setting up checkpoints and roadblocks on the roads surrounding the city, and they seized control of the airport. The JNA took little action, largely because its forces were divided and positioned in several locations. At the outbreak of the fighting, a large part of Kukanjac's troops was located at Tito Barracks near the center of the city. Bosnian forces quickly surrounded these soldiers, and Kukanjac devoted much of his effort to getting them out of the city. Another large element of the federal army was located in the barracks at Lukavica, and these soldiers also hesitated to join in the city struggle. The rest of the JNA was split into smaller units and positioned in the mountains surrounding the city. The JNA's divided positions hindered its ability to make a concerted effort in the fighting. [21]

After Izetbegović declared a state of emergency throughout Bosnia on 7 April, the JNA stepped up its air strikes on Sarajevo's suburbs. Still, the JNA ground troops within Sarajevo remained quiet while pro-Muslim forces (TDF, police, and irregulars) set up roadblocks throughout the city. By 8 April, Bosnian roadblocks controlled the routes within the interior of Sarajevo, and Bosnian Serb roadblocks on the perimeter of the city controlled access from the outside. At the same time, Izetbegović called for the formal organization of the BDF, and he declared that any irregular forces in Bosnia not submitting to the control of the Bosnian Ministry of Interior were considered "enemies." In effect, the Bosnian president was condemning the use of Bosnian Serb paramilitaries while trying to avoid completely alienating the JNA "regular" forces.[22]

As the opposing sides settled into their positions for the siege, there were some last-minute attempts at compromise. Kukanjac, perhaps concerned for the safety of his troops at Tito and Lukavica Barracks, declared that paramilitaries were the main cause of the conflict (he did not specify which faction's paramilitaries), that the JNA's main aim was "protecting the town and citizens from clashes and so forth," and that the JNA would not bombard Sarajevo. Although this last claim proved hollow, Kukanjac seems to have genuinely hoped to minimize the conflict. As the JNA preached moderation to an extent, Izetbegović met one of Karadić's key subordinates, Momćilo Krajišnik, in Sarajevo to attempt an eleventh-hour agreement. The discussions came to naught, and Krajišnik left the city. He would not return for almost three years.[23]

For the next several weeks, there was sporadic fighting in and around the city. Mostly this took the form of air and artillery bombardments and sniper fire. None of the factions endeavored to take the city by storm. The Bosnian forces were far too weak and fully engaged in building their army's strength, the JNA forces in the center of the city remained in their barracks, and the Bosnian Serb irregulars devoted their efforts to strengthening the ring around the city. The JNA retained control of the airport and kept it closed for part of the month. All sides put up more and more checkpoints and roadblocks but no clearly discernable front line separated the opposing forces.[24]

The situation changed in early May with two major events: a substantial assault on the city by the Bosnian Serbs and the kidnapping of Bosnian President Izetbegović. The Bosnian Serb attack on 2 May 1992 seems to have been intended to split the city in two, and it coincided with offensives throughout much of the rest of Bosnia. For the assault on Sarajevo, the Bosnian Serbs advanced in two columns of armored vehicles. One column came from the south out of Vraca and the Trebovic mountains. It advanced into the district of Grbavica and attempted to cross the Miljacka River at Skenderija. The other column advanced from the west, near the airport, and appeared to be aiming for the *Oslobodjenje* building. Both columns were supported with mortar and artillery fire.[25] This fire support probably included JNA units surrounding the city, but Kukanjac's troops in the barracks within the city did not join in the attack. Clearly, the Bosnian Serbs and the JNA were reluctant to engage in a dismounted house-to-house fight; they relied on troops mounted in armored vehicles, supported with heavy indirect fire.

The results of the attack were some limited gains against ill-equipped, but desperate, Bosnian resistance. The western column advanced far enough to take the suburbs of Nedarići and Mojmilo and isolate the suburb of Dobrinja near the airport. However, this column stalled quickly once it ran into more serious Bosnian defenders in and around Dobrinja. The eastern column pressed its attack with more determination. It reached the river, took all of Grbavica, and even fired some tank rounds into the Presidency building. Nonetheless, Bosnian TDF, police, and Muslim irregulars—armed with a few crucial antitank weapons—fought from the surrounding buildings and halted the advance. One key shot took out a lead Bosnian Serb vehicle on one of the narrow streets leading to the bridge at Skenderija, thus blocking a large part of the attacking force. Other portions of the Bosnian Serb attackers were reluctant to advance into kill zones, and they would not dismount to clear the defenders from the surrounding buildings. Although the ground attacks had stopped, the heavy shelling continued throughout 2 May and into the next day. One report claimed that the shelling was the worst yet in the war, "setting buildings ablaze and covering streets with debris and shrapnel."[26]

The Bosnian Serb attack revealed several aspects of the fight for Sarajevo. First, whether from doctrine and experience with the costs of taking a city or from a simple lack of ground soldiers, the Bosnian Serbs showed that they were going to rely heavily on armored vehicles and firepower. In fact, they grew more reluctant to commit any forces (armored or otherwise) into the urban area, and for the rest of the siege, they put most of their effort into fighting on the perimeter of Sarajevo to close routes into the city. Second, the Bosnian Serb difficulties confirmed the vulnerability of armored columns without dismounted support in an urban fight. Armored vehicles gave the Bosnian Serbs mobility (but only on the roads), protection against small-arms fire, and additional firepower from mounted machine guns and tank main guns. But they were too vulnerable to hand-held antitank weapons and bombs that could be thrown from adjacent buildings. The armored columns needed to be teamed with dismounted infantry to clear the buildings and with engineers to clear obstacles and mines. Finally, although the Bosnian Serbs ultimately failed in their goal to split the city, they made significant gains in many of their other offensives throughout Bosnia. They came to realize that Sarajevo had a large symbolic value to the Izetbegović government, as well as to the Western media, and that they could use the city as a diversion for their more general goal of partitioning the rest of Bosnia.

The other crucial event of early May, Izetbegović's kidnapping, also helped shape the future fighting in Sarajevo. The Bosnian president was returning from negotiations in Spain on 2 May when, after several delays, his flight landed at the Sarajevo airport. Usually, an UNPROFOR escort would pick up Izetbegović to take him to the Presidency building, but after waiting several hours (and perhaps thinking that the heavy fighting had canceled the flight), the escort had departed. The president had now fallen into the lap of the JNA that controlled the airport. From Tito Barracks, Kukanjac ordered the JNA commander at the airport to detain Izetbegović and move him to Lukavica Barracks. At first, Izetbegović refused to go to Lukavica. In a bizarre sequence of events, while Izetbegović argued with his captors, a phone call from a woman in downtown Sarajevo rang at the airport desk. She was calling to see about canceled flights, but Izetbegović quickly picked up the phone and held the following remarkable conversation:

> Good evening Madam, this is Alija Izetbegović, the President of Bosnia on the phone. There was a brief pause. She was confused. He said, Yes, yes. That's right, Alija Izetbegović, the President of Bosnia. Could you please be so kind, I am here at the airport, sitting in the director's office, and the Army won't let us go. We are kept here. Could you please call the Presidency and tell them that you talked to me, that I am here, at the airport, and if you can't reach the Presidency, please call radio and TV and inform them.[27]

Amazingly, the astonished woman informed both the Presidency (Izetbegović's deputy, Ejup Ganić, eventually got word of the kidnapping) and the local television and radio stations, which broadcast the "detention" to Bosnia and the West. Izetbegović, concerned for the safety of his daughter who was detained with him, later agreed to go to Lukavica, but the unusual phone conversation at the airport and the subsequent publicity certainly gave him some leverage in negotiating his release.

While the Bosnian resident wrestled with his situation, Kukanjac telephoned Belgrade for guidance. The JNA leader was not interested in removing Izetbegović from power, but he asked for and received permission to use his captive as a bargaining chip in getting the JNA troops out of their city barracks. Kukanjac told the press that he wanted a cease-fire and exchange of Izetbegović that would allow the JNA to "pack and peacefully leave the centre of Sarajevo."[28]

The UNPROFOR commander in Sarajevo, MacKenzie, acted as a mediator and helped to arrange the exchange between Kukanjac and Izetbegović. UNPROFOR elements in Sarajevo were still basically headquarters units with minimal security (the main peacekeeping mission remained in Croatia), and MacKenzie wanted to keep the UN intervention to a minimum. After much arguing, the plan was for a column consisting of a few UNPROFOR APCs along with 20 empty JNA vehicles to escort Izetbegović and his daughter from Lukavica to Tito Barracks. The convoy would then pick up Kukanjac and a large segment of the JNA garrison and return to Lukavica (where they could later be moved outside the city). Along the way, a part of the convoy with the UNPROFOR escort would break off and deliver Izetbegović to the Presidency building.

Not unexpectedly, the convoy did not go exactly as planned on 3 May; in his diary, MacKenzie called 3 May "the worst day of my life." The initial leg of the journey to Tito Barracks proceeded relatively well. Once at Kukanjac's headquarters, there were delays and additional demands from Kukanjac (he wanted to evacuate a larger number of men) and confusion between Izetbegović and Ganić over whether the Bosnian government could guarantee the convoy's safety. The convoy finally left Tito, and within about 1 km, it came under fire. The Bosnian forces wanted to disarm the JNA troops in the convoy, but Kukanjac refused. Neither the small UNPROFOR escort nor the road-bound JNA were able to battle the Bosnian forces that controlled the buildings surrounding the convoy. Even with the tension and some casualties, cooler heads prevailed. Izetbegović switched to another vehicle, and MacKenzie dismounted to help diffuse a confrontation farther back in the column. After moving about another km, some of the UNPROFOR vehicles, along with Izetbegović and his daughter, left the column and arrived safely at the Presidency building. The main column was hit once more before reaching Lukavica. Kukanjac managed to keep the convoy moving, and it finally arrived late that night. After its arrival, JNA and Bosnian Serb mortars and artillery unleashed a heavy barrage on the city. Overall, twenty-five were killed and wounded during the exchange, and over ninety JNA soldiers were taken prisoner, most of whom were exchanged by 5 May.[29]

The kidnapping and convoy ambush had a major impact on the combatants. Izetbegović finally abandoned all hope of using the JNA as a moderating force in the conflict and was convinced that he needed to build the Bosnian units (the BDF) into a force capable of defending his government on its own. The old-guard members of the JNA, including Kukanjac, were only too happy to get out of Sarajevo and the rest of the Bosnian conflict. Following the JNA's major reorganization on 8 May, the Serb-dominated government of Yugoslavia removed most of the old Titoist officers. This date also marked the beginning of the JNA's official withdrawal from Bosnia; however, as noted earlier, most Bosnian Serb soldiers of the JNA remained behind, along with much of their heavy equipment. They joined the Bosnian Serb irregulars to form the VRS and came under Mladić's command (and Karadić's control). Those JNA forces that did not remain behind conducted the initial part of their withdrawal from Sarajevo between 19 and 25 May with some harassment at Bosnian checkpoints along the way.[30] After May, the lines separating Bosnian Serb forces surrounding the city and Bosnian forces within Sarajevo were set, with only minor changes, for the rest of the siege.

In addition, the kidnapping and convoy incident illustrated the primacy of political factors in the war. It hardened all of the factions' positions and soured the UNPROFOR leadership's attitude. Even at the tactical level, political considerations came to the fore. The UNPROFOR-JNA convoy of vehicles was completely at the mercy of the Bosnian forces—particularly so in the urban environment where the Bosnians held the buildings that dominated the road. This had nothing to do with an unsure UN mission or supposedly restrictive rules of engagement; UNPROFOR would have needed large numbers of ground troops ready to fight house to house to guarantee the convoy's safety. However, the Bosnian militia did not annihilate the convoy, partly because of political repercussions. In fact, although pundits have criticized Izetbegović, Kukanjac, and MacKenzie over their role in the convoy ambush, all three leaders effectively used persuasion rather than military force to keep a bad situation from getting out of control.

For the next several weeks, sniper fire and bombardments punctuated several cease-fires. On 27 May, artillery shells hit a group of Sarajevo citizens lined up outside of a store. The incident gained notoriety in the West as the "bread queue bombing" and placed the Bosnian Serbs in a negative light.[31] At about the same time, another series of artillery strikes received less publicity, but a recorded radio conversation revealed that the purpose of Mladić's VRS bombardments was clearly psychological and political:

"Mladić: [to Colonel Vukasinovic, artillery chief]: Are you up there?

Vukasinovic: Yes, everything is ready.

Mladić: Which weapons have you got ready?

Vukasinovic: I have those up there, in Kresa.

Mladić: What can you hit?

Vukasinovic: I can fire all the way to the garrison.

Mladić: Do not fire at the garrison. Can you pound Velesici?

Vukasinovic: I can.

Mladić: Are your guns pointed toward the target?

Vukasinovic: They are.

Mladić: And tell me, can you pound Baščaršija [the old Muslim historic area]?

Vukasinovic: I can.

Mladić: What?

Vukasinovic: Yes, no problem.

Mladić: Keep the Presidency and the Assembly building under steady, direct fire and pound slowly in intervals until I give the order to stop."[32]

Mladić was clearly more concerned with destroying historic, cultural, and political targets than he was with striking at the enemy's military forces (the garrison).

At the end of May and early June, negotiations for withdrawing the last JNA elements from Tito Barracks continued while bombardments and sniper fire grew more intense. MacKenzie recorded in his diary that "things are heating up. Very heavy fighting in Sarajevo," and that "all hell has broken loose in Sarajevo. Heaviest shelling yet." A *London Times* account confirmed "the worst night of shelling in almost two months of seige."[33] That same *Times* article also reported a Bosnian Serb attack on the coastal town of Dubrovnik. As was to happen on several occasions, a major Bosnian Serb offensive in some region of Bosnia coincided with actions in Sarajevo, thus dividing the attention of the Western media and the international community. On 5 June, the last remnants of JNA troops at Tito Barracks, perhaps 300 soldiers, departed the city during a brief cease-fire. Shortly thereafter, the

Bosnian Serbs unleashed a particularly heavy bombardment aimed at Tito and nearby locations that appeared to be targeted at destroying JNA equipment left behind by the evacuation.[34]

As the JNA departed the center of the city, it also negotiated with UNPROFOR and the Bosnian presidency to turn over the Sarajevo airport. These negotiations proved tortuous. An initial trilateral agreement on 5 June fostered optimism within UNPROFOR's leadership and among the citizens of Sarajevo.[35] However, both the Bosnian Serbs and the Izetbegović government obstructed the implementation of the agreement, and fighting around the airport continued.[36] Tactically, the JNA troops at the airport were subject to harassing fire from the three- to five-story apartment buildings in the adjacent pro-Bosnian community of Dobrinja. Yet, the JNA could retaliate with heavier weapons such as tanks positioned at the airport as well as artillery and mortars in the hills to the south and west. Neither side needed the airport for military purposes—the factions lacked combat aircraft, and the airport was too vulnerable to ground fire to be a good base for such tactical aircraft. Given this situation, the withdrawing JNA had no desire to hold the airport, but it and the Bosnian Serb forces hoped to extract as much political benefit as possible from the "concession" of turning over the airport to UN control. At the same time, Izetbegović's Bosnian government seemed just as interested in provoking the JNA and Bosnian Serbs into retaliations and bad publicity as in letting UNPROFOR control the airport.

French President François Mitterand's dramatic visit to Sarajevo helped to give UNPROFOR control of the airport. Mitterand's appearance illustrates how much the political machinations of the warring factions dominated their military actions. The JNA, Bosnian Serb irregulars, and pro-Izetbegović forces could have easily stopped the French president's visit; they all could sweep the airport runways with direct and indirect fire. Instead of choosing military options, the fighting factions seemed to focus on the benefits of gaining favor with Mitterand and Western opinion.[37] While the French president's visit was delayed as UNPROFOR frantically tried to negotiate his safe arrival, Mitterand finally arrived in Sarajevo on 28 June. He had originally planned to meet only with Izetbegović, but UN representatives scrambled to ensure that he also saw Karadić. Both leaders gave Mitterand their standard speeches. After listening to their combination of pleas and harangues, the French president departed the next day.

While some accounts portray Mitterand's visit as self-serving, the French president deserves credit for considerable personal courage as well as helping to push the factions into fulfilling the terms of the airport agreement. Soon after his visit, the fighting around the airport was considerably reduced, and UNPROFOR was able to occupy it at the end of the month. Although under UNPROFOR control throughout the rest of the siege, the airport still was bombarded and had to close on several occasions. However, it is significant that the Bosnian Serbs did not attempt to cut completely this line of communication from the West to the city. Again, they may have feared the political repercussions, and perhaps they thought they could better use the city as a diversion with Western journalists and relief efforts focused on Sarajevo.

At the end of June, the Bosnian forces (now officially the BDF) made their first serious effort to break the ring around the city. The main attack was in the suburb of Vraca, but it failed after only modest gains. The BDF lacked heavy weapons (although they made moderate use of mortars for the first time), and the VRS forces, using inherited JNA weapons, had too much firepower to be dislodged.[38] Two other factors may have influenced the battle. First, Vraca is a suburb of small residential buildings that lies on the outskirts of the city. Thus, the terrain—while still containing buildings—was more open than the more constricted area near the city center, thus favoring the larger firepower of the VRS. Second, the BDF command complained that its Croatian units were not supporting their attacks, a complaint voiced even earlier by Deputy Commander Jovan Divjak.

After this attack, Sarajevo settled back into its siege routine for a few months. During this time, the UN approved an expansion of the UNPROFOR mission that finally added Bosnia to the original mandate for peacekeeping in Croatia. The new, combined UN forces were designated UNPROFOR-2 (although, for simplicity, we will continue to refer to it as UNPROFOR). Many of the Canadians, including MacKenzie, rotated out of Sarajevo, and a mixed force of troops from Egypt (Muslim), France (Catholic), and Ukraine (Eastern Orthodox) took over peacekeeping duties in Bosnia and Sarajevo. Lieutenant General Nambier retained overall control of UNPROFOR, and his former deputy, French Major General Morillon, took command of the forces in Bosnia from MacKenzie after a short interlude. Morillon soon moved UNPROFOR headquarters from Sarajevo to the smaller town of Kiseljak. In fact, the new commander of UNPROFOR's Bosnian contingent—though active in many confrontations in Bosnia, particularly Srebrenica—showed little concern with events in Sarajevo and had little influence on the siege. The new UN forces in Bosnia totaled 1,500 troops, with perhaps fewer than 300 in the capital, and while this contingent was larger than the original headquarters in Sarajevo, it was still far too small to attempt to enforce the UN mission through force.[39]

At the end of August, the Bosnian Serbs unleashed some of their heaviest bombardments coinciding with the opening of the London Peace Conference, a new round of peace talks hosted in the British capital. One series of strikes killed eleven and wounded fifty-five. Another barrage left fourteen dead and 126 wounded in downtown Sarajevo. During this heavy fire, the BDF attempted to open a reliable lifeline to the city. It employed an armored train on the rail line through Ilid a, but the Bosnian Serbs repulsed its attack. Also during this time, the Bosnian Serbs targeted the Bosnian National Library with indirect fire and destroyed priceless books and manuscripts representing Bosnian culture.[40]

After the heavy shelling of August, which culminated a flurry of activity that had started in April, the city settled into a tragic routine of bombardments and sniper fire. Often, it was difficult to pinpoint the origins of this fire, and all of the factions used this uncertainty to accuse their opponents of unprovoked aggression. On the Bosnian (pro-Izetbegović) side, the lack of heavy weapons and the disadvantage of occupying positions in the low ground of the city did not allow for using indirect fire. It appears that the pro-Izetbegović forces often shifted their mortar positions within the city, perhaps aided by observation from the radio/television building that was located on the one piece of high ground in Bosnian hands, the hill just northwest of Zetra stadium. Bosnian snipers were also located throughout the city. Not surprisingly, they were almost always in the taller buildings that provided the best fields of fire. This included the Holiday Inn, the *Unis*, the Europa Hotel, and the workers' apartment complex at Alipašino Polje (in Novi Grad). Perhaps the favorite location for Bosnian snipers and even some heavier weapons was the suburb of Dobrinja, a location that gave the Bosnians opportunities to harass the VRS positions on the western side of the airport near Ilid a.

The VRS held dominant high ground on all sides of the city, but their preferred locations for bombardments and sniper fire were on the south side of Sarajevo. The most well-known VRS artillery and mortar position was the former JNA barracks at Lukavica. In fact, this was only one of several locations for VRS indirect fire south of the city—locations that spread from Mount Igman to Lukavica, past Vraca, and farther east to the former Olympic bobsled run in the Stari Grad section of the city. Even today, one can see the Bosnian Serb artillery and mortar positions along this path, marked by cement foundations and buildings without roofs to allow for emplacement of cannons and mortars. These same hills also provided commanding positions for snipers who dominated sniper's alley in the center of Sarajevo. In addition, the VRS position at Grbavica provided an excellent location for snipers in moderately high buildings adjoining the Miljacka River. Positions on Mount Igman and Mount Bjelasnica gave the VRS good fields of fire on the airport and the Muslim stronghold at Dobrinja. Although less popular than the positions south of Sarajevo, the VRS occasionally used firing positions on the Zuc hills northwest of the city.

The regular rhythm of the siege included other repeating, if sporadic, events. Cease-fires would come and go on a frustratingly routine basis. Occasionally, these cease-fires allowed valuable humanitarian aid into the city and medical evacuations out. However, they rarely lasted more than 48 hours. The airport frequently opened and closed due to shelling, and relief aircraft received fire on several occasions. The UN would usually suspend flights for several days at a time when its aircraft received fire. The city's water and power supplies were frequently disrupted, making life even more miserable for its citizens.

In December, Karadić offered a cease-fire for "humanitarian" evacuations from Sarajevo. The Izetbegović government rejected the offer as a ploy to partition Sarajevo, a means of ethnically cleansing the capital by consent. At about the same time, the BDF reinforced its positions near Mount Igman to keep open that vital route to the city.[41] Additionally, the Bosnian government began to bring the varied pro-Bosnian combat units under better control and put the BDF into a regular structure. By the end of 1992, the BDF had formed five infantry corps totaling about 80,000 men, although perhaps only 44,000 of these were fully armed. The 1st (Sarajevo) Corps was deployed in the Sarajevo region with a rough strength of 35,000 men (it is not known how many of these troops were fully armed). The 1st Corps was divided into brigades, but the actual number and designations of these brigades changed repeatedly. It appears that the corps relied on three to four brigades derived from the local Sarajevo region, one brigade recruited from Visoko, and the 1st Tactical Group (about a battalion-size unit) from Kiseljak. Similarly, the VRS furthered the integration of former JNA forces and equipment with the Bosnian Serb irregulars. The VRS designated its units in the Sarajevo region as the 1st (Sarajevo-Romanija) Corps under the command of General Momir Talić. VRS infantry troop strength was only 29,000, but they continued to retain their advantage in weapons over their BDF foes.[42]

The new year began with considerable tension when Bosnian Serb irregulars killed Bosnian Deputy Prime Minister Hakija Turajlić on a road entering Sarajevo. He had been traveling in a convoy with UNPROFOR escorts, but the UN troops were unable (or unwilling depending on accounts) to intervene.[43] Despite this incident and the continued routine of sniper, mortar, and artillery fire, there were no major moves in Sarajevo for the first four months of 1993 as all sides seemed engrossed with the negotiations surrounding the Vance-Owen Peace Plan.

In fact, political events involving the international community took center stage during this period. The Vance-Owen plan, named after UN envoys Cyrus Vance and Lord David Owen, divided Bosnia into a series of provinces (three Muslim, three Serb, two Croat, and one Muslim-Croat) with a weak federal Bosnian government. Sarajevo was to be its own multiethnic province.[44] During the negotiations for the plan, relations between Karad ić and Milošević soured; the Serbian leader feared economic sanctions and urged Karad ić to accept the plan, while the Bosnian Serb chief did not want to cede any of the territory that his forces had gained in the first six months of the war. While the Bosnian Serbs hesitated to accept the agreement, NATO began enforcing the UN-approved "no fly" zone over Bosnia on 12 April (more in response to events in Srebrenica than in Sarajevo). The no fly zone over Bosnia meant that NATO aircraft patrolled Bosnian airspace to ensure that none of the factions flew combat aircraft in the country. It was the first time that the UN turned to NATO to apply military pressure to its peacekeeping effort in Bosnia. Near the end of the month, the Vance-Owen plan was finalized and Karad ić reluctantly signed, but the RS Assembly rejected the plan on 5 May. The next day, the UN approved the concept of safe havens in Bosnia, one of which was Sarajevo. This new designation for the city had little practical effect on the siege.

Events heated up in early July with a VRS offensive south of Sarajevo that captured the town of Trnovo and blocked the route to Gora de. Shortly thereafter, the Bosnian Serbs attacked the northern slopes of Mount Igman, but the BDF clung to a part of the mountain and barely held open that path to the city. Clearly, the Bosnian Serbs, while still avoiding the urban terrain in the city, were renewing their efforts to close the routes surrounding Sarajevo. These efforts intensified throughout July with renewed assaults at Hrasnice (near the airport), a fresh attack on the suburb of Rijlovac, and more efforts on Mount Igman and its neighboring heights of Mount Treskavica and Mount

Bjelasnica.[45] In each case, the attacks were on open, if mountainous, terrain or suburbs with low residential houses, ground more favorable than the center of Sarajevo for the VRS advantage in armored vehicles and heavy firepower. Each attack made limited gains but could not achieve its entire objective.

During the course of the fighting for Igman, the pro-Izetbegović forces finished a tunnel under the Sarajevo airport that, at the time, the Western media and Bosnian Serbs did not notice. This tunnel could only provide limited relief to the supply difficulties of the BDF and Sarajevo's citizens, but these supplies also provided a morale boost to the city's defenders. In January 1993, the Bosnian forces began construction on the tunnel from both ends at the same time: Butmir on the west side of the airport and the Muslim stronghold in Dobrinja on the east. The tunnel was completed on 30 July 1993. It was 800 meters long and 1.5 meters high, and the main mode of transport was a manual pushcart on rail tracks that carried 50 kilograms of supplies at a time. Gas, electric, and telephone lines also ran along the side of the tunnel, a considerable safety risk given that the tunnel often had ankle-deep water on its floor.[46]

On 2 August, Mladić renewed the efforts to take Mount Igman. He threw in the newly arrived 1st Krajina Brigade and took a few more bits of ground against stubborn BDF resistance. The situation was desperate for the BDF, and the Bosnian delegation walked out of the Geneva talks in protest over the VRS attack on Sarajevo, a supposed safe haven. Allegedly, UN officials made a false report that Karadić would order Mladić to pull back from Mount Igman if the Bosnians would return to the Geneva negotiations. By 4 August, three-quarters of Mount Igman was in VRS hands, but the offensive appeared to have run its course. In addition, the increasing international pressure may have deterred Mladić from more assaults. In any case, the VRS commander met with UN observers and agreed to pull back some of his forces and allow UN (French) peacekeepers to take up positions on part of the mountain. A few days later, Mladić kept his word and pulled part of his force back to Mount Bjelasnica. He also rotated the 1st Krajina Brigade out of the Sarajevo region to use in other offensives in Bosnia.[47]

After the Mount Igman struggle, Sarajevo settled back into the routine of the siege for the next several months. However, during this time, relations between the Muslims and Croats reached a low point. These two groups conducted open warfare in several regions of Bosnia, although Sarajevo saw very little. In an attempt to crack down on organized crime in the city, Izetbegović removed some of his military commanders who had ties to the criminals in late October. While the goal of minimizing the criminal element seemed genuine, it also gave Izetbegović a cover for dismantling the few separate HVO units in Sarajevo. After November, the Bosnian government had firm control of the remaining pro-Bosnian Croat units in Sarajevo, which were broken into smaller groups and made to report through the BDF chain of command. Perhaps in response to Izetbegović's actions, a particularly heavy barrage (nine dead, forty wounded) occurred on 9 November, and this barrage appears to have been from HVO-controlled units outside of the city.[48]

The year ended with increasing suffering for the citizens of Sarajevo. A Christmas truce fell apart, and the resulting week's bombardments killed thirty-two people and wounded 200 more. There was virtually no electricity in the city, and water supplies were constantly interrupted. UN attempts to evacuate the elderly made only the barest progress, and most of the elderly remained behind to suffer the winter with little or no heat.[49] Despite these conditions, UN and private humanitarian efforts deserve credit for bringing at least a bare minimum of food and medical supplies. Although there was much malnutrition in Sarajevo, the city's civilians did not experience mass starvation or epidemics.

In early 1994, two Bosnian Serb bombardments forced the international community into further action. On 22 January, shells fell in an area where Bosnian children were playing, killing six and wounding thirty-five. On 5 February, mortar rounds hit the old central (Markale) market, resulting in sixty-eight dead and 197 wounded. Four days later, NATO announced a ten-day ultimatum. Bosnian Serbs had to withdraw their heavy guns 20 km from Sarajevo or face NATO air strikes. Karad ić protested and walked out of the Geneva talks, an act called "the height of brinkmanship" by one observer. As tension mounted and NATO planes went on alert, the new UNPROFOR commander, General Sir Michael Rose, worked to avoid the NATO bombardment. He was helped when Russian troops arrived as part of the rotation of units in UNPROFOR and occupied parts of Grbavica, allowing their fellow orthodox Slavs to withdraw in one area and save face. On 20 February, the NATO deadline passed, but Rose claimed that the Bosnian Serbs had pulled back in twenty-three of forty-two artillery sites. Some reports suggest that Rose exaggerated these claims, but NATO decided that there had been enough progress and did not launch airstrikes. However, NATO did shoot down several Serb warplanes over Bosnia, and on 7 March, all factions agreed to an uneasy cease-fire in Sarajevo.[50] Although occasionally violated, the cease-fire eased living conditions in the city for the next three months. However, the Bosnian Serbs maintained their control of almost all of the surrounding routes, and they kept supplies flowing into the city to a bare minimum.

Two major factors influenced the Bosnian Serb's limited concessions in Sarajevo and the subsequent, albeit temporary, cease-fire. The most obvious factor was the threat of NATO air strikes and the actual downing of Serbian fighter aircraft. However, the VRS also may have loosened the grip on Sarajevo because it was beginning its major offensive on Goraţde. All of the posturing at Sarajevo had succeeded initially in distracting Western media and BDF attention from Goraţde.

In July, the cease-fire broke down when Karadţić rejected a new peace proposal from the "Contact Group" (Russia, the United States, France, Germany, and Britain). By the end of the month, the Bosnian Serbs were tightening their hold on Sarajevo, and sniper fire and bombardments grew in intensity.[51] The Bosnian Serb rejection of the Contact Group proposal brought about the final split between Milošević and Karadţić. The Serb leader, upset that RS intransigence was keeping the international community from lifting sanctions on Serbia, cut off supplies from Serbia to the RS (the UN had imposed economic sanctions in May 1992 and tightened them after the RS rejection of the Vance-Owen plan in May 1993). The siege continued for the next six months at a level only slightly less than that of 1993 while fighting raged in other parts of Bosnia, particularly in Bihać. During this time, the Muslims and Croats reached an agreement that formed a federation of their factions in Bosnia, ended their open warfare, and paved the way for some cooperation in the war against the Bosnian Serbs. Also, Milošević, angered over the Bosnian Serbs rejecting the Contact Group proposal, withdrew much of his support from the Karadţić regime. The war was beginning to turn against the RS.

In March 1995, Karadţić, Mladić, and other RS leadership members developed a plan to bring a favorable end to the war. They decided to increase pressure on Sarajevo and complete its isolation while conducting offensives to wipe out the Muslim enclaves in eastern Bosnia, all of which were UN safe havens. The offensives began throughout Bosnia in April, with the first immediate step in Sarajevo being the Bosnian Serbs forcing the humanitarian airlifts into the city to end. Bosnian Serb shelling also increased, and in May, one bombardment killed eleven people in the suburb of Butmir. Later in the month, the VRS took the bold step of attacking UNPROFOR (French) peacekeepers holding the Vrbanja bridge open on the outskirts of Sarajevo. Acting with direct military action, uncommon for UN forces,

UNPROFOR counterattacked and retook the position, losing two men and killing four Bosnian Serbs.[52]

The next month, BDF forces launched an offensive in an attempt to break the siege of Sarajevo, their largest such attack of the war. However, the Bosnian forces still lacked the heavy weapon systems needed to drive the VRS from the high ground around the city. The Bosnian Serbs repulsed the attacks, and the BDF suffered heavy losses. One account called the renewed struggle the "heaviest fighting since 1993." During this time, UNPROFOR abandoned the weapons-collection sites around Sarajevo, and the Bosnian Serb forces had complete freedom to bombard the city. The renewed fighting in Sarajevo again distracted some of the attention from outside battles, in particular the struggle for Srebrenica.[53]

After the failed BDF offensive, the Bosnian Serbs continued to increase pressure on Sarajevo with heavy artillery, mortar, and sniper fire. This increase was reflected in the growing number of civilian and military casualties in the city. The year had begun with the relatively light losses of one killed and twenty-one wounded in January. By May the numbers had grown to sixty-four dead and 221 wounded, and by July the losses were 152 dead and 547 wounded.[54] This expanded pressure on the city coincided with a major VRS offensive on the last Muslim town deep within RS territory, Gora de. However, if the Bosnian Serb leaders hoped that they could use the Sarajevo siege to divert Muslim-Croat attention from the war in the rest of Bosnia, they miscalculated. The Muslims held Gora de with renewed determination. Bosnian Muslim-Croat forces, now acting with better cooperation as the AFBiH, launched successful offensives, particularly in central Bosnia, that took back significant land that the Bosnian Serbs had captured earlier in the war. The success of the Muslim-Croat offensive was a crucial factor in convincing the Bosnian Serbs to accept a peace agreement in 1995, but it took a more publicized event in Sarajevo to bring the international community to firm action that forced the Bosnian Serbs to accept peace terms.

The signal event that finally ended the siege was a second bombing of the central marketplace on 28 August that killed thirty-eight people. It occurred more than eighteen months after the tragic market bombing that brought the first significant NATO involvement in the war in 1994, and despite some similarities between the two events, essential differences contributed to the end of the siege. Initially, as in 1994, the Bosnian Serbs denied any responsibility for the bombing and accused the Izetbegović government of manufacturing the market bombing to gain sympathy for the Muslim cause. They even dredged up a former JNA "ballistics expert" to accuse the Muslims of firing on the market. Not surprisingly, the Bosnian government accused the Bosnian Serbs of conducting the tragic shelling, and Izetbegović promised retaliation. However, unlike their vacillation in the 1994 bombing, the international community reacted decisively in 1995. UNPROFOR inspectors quickly determined that the Bosnian Serbs had launched the shells that hit the marketplace, and most European nations and the United States did not hesitate to condemn the Bosnian Serbs for the massacre. Even the normally cautious UN Secretary General, Boutros Boutros-Ghali, demanded action.

The market tragedy finally steeled the international community to unleash NATO air strikes and artillery fire. The strikes began on 30 August 1995 and included heavy attacks on Bosnian Serb radar sites; artillery positions; and ammunition dumps around Sarajevo and on Bosnian Serb positions in Tuzla, Gora de, epa, Mostar, and the RS capital in Pale. One report talked of "wave upon wave" of NATO aircraft ranging over the Bosnian capital in the largest operation in NATO's history. The aircraft were joined by the UN's Rapid Reaction Force (RRF): British, French, and Dutch combat units that had been inserted on Mount Igman in 1994 to ensure that the Igman resupply route to the city stayed open. The RRF bombarded Bosnian Serb positions surrounding Sarajevo with 105mm and 155mm artillery fire. The air and artillery attacks were effective; the Bosnian leaders, while expressing the usual complaint about UN hesitations since 1992, expressed their approval of the NATO offensive. Even the Bosnian Serb government admitted that their forces in Sarajevo and elsewhere had suffered "immense" damage.[56]

After two days of bombardment, NATO paused, hoping that the Bosnian Serbs would comply with their demands to withdraw their heavy weapons from around the capital city. The United States made a peace proposal in Geneva that the UN and NATO hoped would draw a reply from the Bosnian Serbs. Mladić and Karad ić sent out feelers that they might accept the peace offer, but they remained defiant with their weapons around Sarajevo. On 4 September, the NATO strikes resumed and continued to take a heavy toll on the Bosnian Serbs, who finally agreed on 9 September to the Geneva proposal that would eventually become the Dayton Accords ending the fighting in Bosnia and Sarajevo.[57] The Bosnian Serbs also began withdrawing their heavy weapons. The long siege was over.

While some city struggles have produced generally straightforward outcomes (for example, Aachen and Stalingrad), Sarajevo's results are more ambiguous. The Bosnian Serbs never took the city, and thus the BDF—in various permutations as pure Muslim, Muslim-Croat, and multiethnic forces—could claim victory for having held the city. On the other hand, the Bosnian Serbs made only limited attempts to take Sarajevo, and they quickly concluded that a less costly siege could achieve their ultimate military and political goals. For a time, the siege accomplished this purpose; the Bosnian Serbs used events in Sarajevo to distract attention from their larger goal of taking other Bosnian territory that could be joined into a unified state and ultimately linked to a Serb-dominated Yugoslavia. However, the Bosnian Serbs overplayed their hand. Their intransigence at Sarajevo, along with atrocities in other regions, eventually aroused the outrage of the international community. In short, the concept of using Sarajevo as a diversion for other operations may have been a sound initial concept, but the Bosnian Serbs failed to adjust when the siege became more of a liability.

At the operational and tactical levels, politics continued to have a huge impact on the siege. For example, the lack of airpower involvement in the fight (until the last month of the siege) was not because of the urban terrain but was related to concerns over political fallout and UN and NATO no fly zones. The airport and ground routes into the city probably could have been closed completely, but instead they opened and closed intermittently based on the potential political gain, particularly with the international community. Bosnian Serb bombardments (and occasionally BDF strikes) were aimed at political or psychological targets rather than at any target that could help take the city. Sniper fire was random and designed to make life miserable for the citizenry, not to support an overall military assault as at Stalingrad. Understanding the dominance of these political factors, it is worth emphasizing several considerations of the urban siege at Sarajevo.

First, the early Bosnian Serb decision not to engage in a street fight for the city was based on experience at Vukovar, the perceived high demand for dismounted infantry in an urban environment, and the high casualties that could result from such a fight. Because the VRS never pressed home an attack, the fight for Sarajevo does not prove the widely held concepts of troop-intensive, high-casualty fights for urban areas. However, Sarajevo does stand as an example of how the perceptions of these concepts permeate modern military thinking and act to discourage an attacking force from an all-out struggle for any city.

Second, despite the paucity of street fighting, some aspects of urban tactics were confirmed. Armored columns, without dismounted support, proved relatively ineffective. Dismounted troops, armed with even the most rudimentary antitank weapons, can occupy buildings that dominate city streets and block armored advances. On the other hand, the lightly armed BDF had difficulty in its own offensives against the Bosnian Serbs' heavy firepower, especially when the urban terrain was not as compact as in the inner city. In addition, neither side had adequate engineer support, which is normally essential to clear blocked streets in a city fight. In the end, all of the factions lacked aspects of the full combined arms team, and all struggled to succeed.

Third, sporadic, if occasionally heavy, shelling and sniper fire might have made life miserable for the city populace, but it did not bring about its surrender. This was particularly true because Sarajevo continued to have some lifelines for resupply. While the Bosnian Serbs clearly had political considerations behind their harassing fires, a true siege designed to bring about the city's capitulation would have had to close off the city completely and use much heavier fires.

Finally, looking at the UNPROFOR role in Sarajevo, it appears that the urban environment made it virtually impossible for peacekeeping (and peace enforcement) forces to use military force to impose their will on the opposing sides. These missions are difficult enough in more open terrain, but the need to control so many buildings and key terrain features in a city would have called for prohibitively high numbers of peacekeepers. This does not mean that peacekeeping cannot be done in a city. In fact, despite some harsh and unfair criticisms, UNPROFOR certainly moderated the conflict and helped with considerable humanitarian aid. Those cases of UNPROFOR success usually resulted from politically savvy negotiations and threats of international condemnation, not from using their own military units. Clearly, peacekeeping forces need to be adequate for inspection, observation, manning some checkpoints, convoy escort, and their own self-defense, but they are not designed to engage the factions in combat and compel them to come to the peace table.

Notes

1. Unfortunately, the conflict in Bosnia was (and is) so politicized that substantial parts of its historiography are little more than biased propaganda sometimes bordering on diatribe. Four of the more respected works on Bosnia and background of the Balkans in general include: Noel Malcolm, *Bosnia: A Short History* (London: MacMillan Publishers Ltd., 1996); Robert D. Kaplan, *Balkan Ghosts: A Journey Through History* (NY: St. Martin's Press, 1993); Rebecca West, *Black Lamb and Grey Falcon* (NY: Viking Press, 1941); and Barbara Jelavich, *History of the Balkans*, 2 volumes (Cambridge: Cambridge University Press, 1983).

Although all four of these works are clearly superior to much of the self-serving material available on Bosnia, they still present widely diverse views on the nature of conflict in Bosnia and the Balkans. In particular, Kaplan and Malcolm represent opposing views on the depth and severity of the ethnic roots of the fighting. Kaplan, a journalist who is well traveled in the Balkans, wrote that deeply engrained ethnic hatreds, particularly between Serbs and Croats, were the base cause of the fighting that erupted as Yugoslavia collapsed. Kaplan recognized that Sarajevo was a sophisticated urban center, but he saw the rest of Bosnia as villages "full of savage hatreds, leavened by poverty and alcoholism," and he claimed that the "fact that the most horrifying violence—during both World War II and the 1990s—occurred in Bosnia was no accident."

Malcolm, who is generally sympathetic to the Muslim cause, takes a dramatically different view of the Bosnian conflict from Kaplan. For Malcolm, one "great piece of misinformation" grasped by Western leaders was that the struggle in Bosnia was "the expression of 'ancient ethnic hatreds' welling up of their own accord." For Malcolm, "the animosities which did exist were not absolute and unchanging. Nor were they inevitable consequences of the mixing together of religious communities." Malcolm believes that while ethnic conflict has existed in Bosnia, it is not the essential root of the war of 1992-1995—a war driven by the self-seeking interests of groups and leaders outside of Bosnia rather than intractable differences within Bosnia's ethnic communities.

2. Laura Silber and Allan Little, *The Death of Yugoslavia* (London: Penguin Books Ltd., 1995 and 1996), 76-78 and 112-14; Christopher Bennett, *Yugoslavia's Bloody Collapse: Causes, Courses, and Consequences* (London: Hurst & Company Ltd., 1995), 13-14 and 143-45; and Malcolm, 214, 215-17, and 223.

3. Silber and Little, 170, and Bennett, 161-65.

4. See Jasminka Udovicki and Ejub Stitkovac, "Bosnia and Hercegovina: The Second War," in *Burn This House: The Making and Unmaking of Yugoslavia*, Jasminka Udovicki and James Ridgeway, eds. (Durham, NC: Duke University Press, 2000), 175 for an account of the deal struck between Tudjman and Milošević for the partitioning of Bosnia. This deal, which both sides later renounced, shows that both the Croatian and Serbian leaders were unsure of their ultimate aims in Bosnia; they wavered between outright annexation and support of separate, but dependent, Bosnian client regimes. See Silber and Little, 171-72 and 175, and Bennett, 166-67, for accounts of the pro-Serb leanings of the JNA.

5. Silber and Little, 187-88, and Bennett, 172.

6. Silber and Little, 177-79, and Bennett, 168. See also Silber and Little, 224, and Malcolm, 226-27, who describe the initial use of Serb paramilitaries under Zeljko Raznjatovic (known by the pseudonym Arkan). Arkan's Tigers gained a reputation for doing the dirty work of ethnic cleansing within Croatian urban areas, while the JNA remained on the cities' outskirts and used their heavy weapons to keep the towns isolated.

7. Bennett, 180. Bosnia's total population in 1991 was 4,354,911. It is also interesting to note that of Bosnia's 109 municipalities, 17 had no majority of one group; of the rest, the majority group rarely had more than 70 percent of the municipality's total population. These numbers bear out the difficulty in trying to draw boundaries based on ethnic composition.

8. Silber and Little, 206-11. Although the vote divided along ethnic lines and the one multiethnic party received little support, the parties that won were not extremist parties. None of them campaigned on separatism, and all agreed to govern as a coalition.

9. Silber and Little, 211-20. Also see Jasminka Udovicki and Ejub Stitkovac, 178-86. Some accounts of Izetbegović's conduct before the opening of the war criticize him for his handling of the European community's recognition of Bosnia and his reversal on the Badinter Commission peace proposal. Even so, even the most negative views recognize that Izetbegović faced a hard decision between independence (and possible war) and remaining in a Serb-dominated Yugoslavia. At the same time, Izetbegović supporters join his critics in recounting his naiveté that led to Bosnia's unpreparedness for war.

10. Malcolm, 227-30, and Silber and Little, 218.

11. Malcolm, 230-31.

12. The description of the terrain in and around Sarajevo comes from my personal observations. I was stationed in Bosnia with the multinational Stabilization Force (SFOR) from November 1999 to April 2000. During that time, I worked as the assistant SFOR historian and lessons learned analyst. I was able to travel through the city and its surrounding countryside to observe the build-

ings and terrain that were key during the war. I must also thank a member of the SFOR Multinational Division Southwest Liaison Team, Corporal N. Marshall, Royal Air Force (RAF), who took me on a battlefield tour of the city. The liaison team put together an information pamphlet of the tour: Corporal Mark Bladen, RAF; Corporal Chris Stone, RAF; and Corporal Gary Woodard, RAF, *Sarajevo Battlefield Tour*, prepared in August 1999.

13. David C. Isby, "War Returns to Europe: Military Aspects of the Conflicts in Yugoslavia,1991-93," *Command Magazine, Military History, Strategy and Analysis* (July-August 1993), 28-35.

14. Silber and Little, 218.

15. Dr. Milan Vego, "The Yugoslav Ground Forces," *Jane's Intelligence Review* (June 1993), 247-53.

16. Edgar O'Ballance, *Civil War in Bosnia, 1992 94* (NY: St. Martin's Press, 1995), 29-30, and Isby, 31. O'Ballance puts the Bosnian Serb irregular strength at only 20,000; Isby estimates the irregular strength at 35,000 (these figures are for all of Bosnia).

17. Dr. Milan Vego, "The Croatian Forces in Bosnia and Herzegovina," *Jane's Intelligence Review* (March 1993), 99-103. See Bennett, 199-200 for a good description of the shifts in Bosnian Croat politics and the roles of Boban and Tudjman during the Bosnian war. Also see Silber and Little, 131-32 and 144-45, and Bennett, 146-47, for a discussion of Milošević and Tudjman's relationship. Most sources agree that these two leaders, while engaged in war over the Croatian Krajina, were willing to make a deal that divided Bosnia between them at the expense of Bosnia's Muslims.

18. Steven L. Burg and Paul S. Shoup, *The War in Bosnia Herzegovina: Ethnic Conflict and International Intervention* (London: M.E. Sharpe, 1999) 128-31; Dr. Milan Vego, "The Army of Bosnia and Herzegovina," *Jane's Intelligence Review* (February 1993), 63-67; Christopher Collinson, "Bosnia This Winter—A Military Analysis," *Jane's Intelligence Review* (December 1993), 547-50; Jovan Divjak, "The First Phase, 1992-1993: Struggle for Survival and Genesis of the Army of Bosnia-Herzegovina," *The War in Croatia and Bosnia Herzegovina, 1991 1995*, Branka Magas and Ivo Zanic, eds. (London: Frank Cass Publishers, 2001), 162-65; and O'Ballance, 29-30. Divjak gives an excellent explanation of the complex interplay of police, territorial forces, and paramilitaries in creating the BDF. He also has a table with detailed information on weapons and strengths, comparing 1992 and 1995. O'Ballance puts the police strength in Bosnia at 40,000 in mid-April with an additional 30,000 "available."

19. General Lewis MacKenzie, *Peacekeeper: The Road to Sarajevo* (Vancouver: Douglas & McIntyre, 1993), 103-107 and 200-202.

20. Tim Judah and Dessa Trevisan, "Serb Assaults Push Bosnia to Edge of War," *London Times* (4 April 1992), 15.

21. O'Ballance, 28, and Silber and Little, 225-27. O'Ballance disagrees with Silber and Little on the initial date of TDF mobilization, but it is probably just a case of differing interpretations of the initial call for increased readiness on 4 April 1992 and placing TDF forces under the presidency's control on 6 April. See Silber and Little, 226-27, for a description of the first casualty of the war. See "Sarajevo Defense Units at 'Full Combat Readiness,'" excerpts from Sarajevo Radio Network Broadcast on 7 April 1992 in *Foreign Broadcast Information Service (FBIS), Daily Reports: East Europe* (hereafter *FBIS EEU*) (8 April 1992), 18, and O'Ballance, 29, for views of Vikic's proclamation and attitude. Finally, see "Federal Army Takes Control of Airport," from Zagreb Radio, Croatia Network Broadcast of 6 April 1992, *FBIS EEU* (6 April 1992), 39, and Silber and Little, 228, for descriptions of the JNA takeover of the airport.

22. O'Ballance, 28-29. For a report on the air strikes, see Tim Judah, "Yugoslav Jets and Snipers Join Battle in Sarajevo," *London Times* (6 April 1992), 14. Also note that the *London Times* places the "state of emergency" on 8 April. See "Sarajevo Leadership Declares Emergency," *London Times* (9 April 1992), 15. However, the declaration was probably issued to pro-Izetbegović forces on 7 April before being given to Western media sources on 8 April.

23. For Kukanjac's comments, see "Army Will Not Bombard Sarajevo," Sarajevo Radio, Sarajevo Network, 7 April 1992, *FBIS EEU* (8 April 1992), 19. For the meeting of Krajisnik and Izetbegović, see Silber and Little, 229.

24. The sporadic fighting in April 1992 is reflected in several FBIS reports. See "Army Denies Shooting; Sarajevo Airport Closed," Sarajevo Radio, Sarajevo Network, 13 April 1992, *FBIS EEU* (13 April 1992), 26; "Muslim Forces Blockade Sarajevo District," Belgrade Radio, Belgrade Network, 11 April 1992, *FBIS EEU* (13 April 1992), 26; "Sarajevo Municipality Blockaded by Serbs," Zagreb Radio, Croatia Network, 20 April 1992, *FBIS EEU* (21 April 1992), 18; "Sarajevo Radio Reports Hits From Mortars," Belgrade TANJUG in English, 21 April 1992, *FBIS EEU* (21 April 1992), 18; "More Fighting Breaks Out in Sarajevo," Sarajevo Radio, Sarajevo Network, 23 April 1992, *FBIS EEU* (24 April 1992), 20. See also Jonathan Landay and Louise Branson, "Beseiged Sarajevo Braced for Onslaught," *Sunday London Times* (26 April 1992), 17.

25. See Silber and Little, 232-34, for a description of the two-column attack. Also there are reports of heavy involvement of Serbian irregulars such as "Arkan troops" and "White Eagles," vice the JNA, in the attack. See "U.S. Ambassador Talks to Izetbegović," Zagreb Radio, Croatia Network, 2 May 1992, *FBIS EEU* (4 May 1992), 29.

26. Louise Branson, "Yugoslav Troops Capture Bosnian Leader," *Sunday London Times* (3 May 1992), 15.

27. Silber and Little, 231 and 235-37 (see 235 for Izetbegović's phone conversation). See also "Detained on Arrival," Belgrade TANJUG, 2 May 1992, *FBIS EEU* (4 May 1992), 29, and Branson.

28. Ibid.; "Release Negotiations Underway," Sarajevo Radio, Sarajevo Network, 2 May 1992, *FBIS EEU* (4 May 1992), 29-30; "Izetbegović Discusses Detention," Sarajevo Radio, Sarajevo Network, 2 May 1992, *FBIS EEU* (4 May 1992), 30-31; and "Presidency's Ganić on Izetbegović's Release," Belgrade TANJUG Domestic Service, 3 May 1992, *FBIS EEU* (4 May 1992), 31.

29. Silber and Little, 237-43; "Izetbegović Released; JNA Convoy Surrounded," Sarajevo Radio, Sarajevo Network, 3 May 1992, *FBIS EEU* (4 May 1992), 31; "Hostage Deal Ends in Bloodshed," *London Times* (4 May 1992), 1; Tim Judah and Dessa Trevisan, "Army Column Attacked After Releasing the Bosnian Leader," *London Times* (4 May 1992), 7; "Central Sarajevo Hit by Heavy Shelling," *London Times* (5 May 1992), 1; Roger Boyes, "Belgrade Guides Campaign to Dismember Bosnia," *London Times* (5 May 1992), 8; Tim Judah and our Foreign Staff, "Sarajevo Spares 156 Yugoslav Soldiers," *London Times* (5 May 1992), 8; and MacKenzie, 164-71.

30. O'Ballance, 41 and 46.

31. Ibid., 44.

32. "Recording of Order to Bomb Sarajevo," Zagreb HTV Television, 29 May 1992, *FBIS EEU* (1 June 1992), 36, and Tim Judah and Dessa Trevisan, "Serbs Defy UN and Bomb Old Dubrovnik," *London Times* (30 May 1992), 1.

33. MacKenzie, 194-95, and Tim Judah and Dessa Trevisan, "Serbs Defy UN and Bomb Old Dubrovnik."

34. MacKenzie, 200-201, and Bill Frost and Dessa Trevisan, "Besieged Troops Leave Sarajevo," *London Times* (6 June 1992), 13.

35. MacKenzie, 198-200. MacKenzie gives most of the credit for the initial agreement to UN negotiator Cedric Thornberry.

36. MacKenzie, 207-40; "Sarajevo Fighting Said Fiercest of the War," Belgrade TANJUG, 8 June 1993, *FBIS EEU* (9 June 1992), 37-38; "Roundup of Battles," Sarajevo Radio, Sarajevo Network, 9 June 1992, *FBIS EEU* (9 June 1992), 39-40; Bill Frost, "Serbs Savor Artillery Power Over Muslims," *London Times* (7 June 1992), 10; Dessa Trevisan, "UN Sarajevo Convoy Comes Under Attack," *London Times* (11 June 1992), 12; "Serb Guns and Snipers Break Bosnian Truce," *London Times* (16 June 1992), 12; John Holland, "Airport Setback for Serbs," *London Times* (19 June 1992), 13; and John Holland et al., "Serbs Move to Take Suburb After Vow to Evacuate Airport," *London Times* (20 June 1992), 12.

37. MacKenzie, 241-64; "Roundup of Battles," Sarajevo Radio, Sarajevo Network, 9 June 1992, *FBIS EEU* (9 June 1992), 39-40; "Heavy Fighting Prevents Withdrawal," Belgrade TANJUG, 27 June 1992,

FBIS EEU (29 June 1992), 38; Louise Branson and Ian Glover-James, "Mitterand Flies to Sarajevo as EC Backs Military Action," *London Times* (21 June 1992), 1; and Tim Judah and Dessa Trevisan, "Mitterand Opens Way for Sarajevo Airlift," *London Times* (29 June 1992), 1.

38. O'Ballance, 57; and "Muslim Forces Reportedly Attack Serb Positions," Belgrade Radio, Belgrade Network, 30 June 1992, *FBIS EEU* (1 July 1992), 26.

39. O'Ballance, 76-77 and 98-103; MacKenzie, 298-323; John Holland et al., "UN Troops Bring Hope to Sarajevo," *London Times* (3 July 1992), 1; and Dessa Trevisan and Tim Judah, "UN Supplies Relieve 71-Day Serb Siege of Sarajevo Suburb," *London Times* (13 July 1992), 8. According to MacKenzie, the temporary French UNPROFOR commander was Colonel Davout d'Auerstadt, and the temporary Egyptian commander was Colonel Abdel Abdelouahab Altahllawi.

40. Robert Seely and Dessa Trevisan, "UN Centre Hit as Shelling of Sarajevo Intensifies," *London Times* (22 August 1992), 7; Roger Boyes and Nicholas Wood, "Bosnian Muslims Launch Attack to Regain Territory," *London Times* (24 August 1992), 1 and 4; Michael Binyon et al., "Talks Blighted by Gunfire and Carrigan Resignation," *London Times* (26 August 1992), 1; Robert Seely, "Relentless Artillery Barrage Takes Toll on Civilian Morale," *London Times* (29 August 1992), 10; Robert Seely and Adam Le Bor, "16 Die as Serbs Shell Sarajevo Marketplace," *London Times* (31 August 1992), 1; "Serbs Deny Responsibility for Sarajevo Attack," Belgrade TANJUG Domestic Service, 30 August 1992, *FBIS EEU* (31 August 1992), 27; "Sarajevo Shelled; Chemical Agents Reportedly Used," Sarajevo Radio, Bosnia-Hercegovina Network, 28 August 1992, *FBIS EEU* (31 August 1992), 28; and O'Ballance, 85.

41. O'Ballance, 118-19, 121-22, 125-26, and 134-35; "UNPROFOR HQ Partially Moved From Sarajevo," Belgrade TANJUG Domestic Service, 26 December 1992, *FBIS EEU* (28 December 1992), 27; "Serb Leaders, Morillon Discuss Sarajevo Situation," Belgrade SRNA, 26 December 1992, *FBIS EEU* (28 December 1992), 27; "Karazdic, Morillon Discuss Evacuations of Civilians," Belgrade Radio, Belgrade Network, 25 December 1992, *FBIS EEU* (28 December 1992), 27; "Serbs Agree to Open Aid Corridor to Sarajevo," Belgrade TANJUG Domestic Service, 25 December 1992, *FBIS EEU* (28 December 1992), 27-28; "Sarajevo Civilians Not Permitted to Leave City," Belgrade TANJUG Domestic Service, 25 December 1992, *FBIS EEU* (28 December 1992), 28; "Muslims Reject Plan to Evacuate Civilians," Belgrade TANJUG, 27 December 1992, *FBIS EEU* (28 December 1992), 28; "Muslim Plan for Sarajevo Aid Corridor Rejected," Belgrade TANJUG, 26 December 1992, *FBIS EEU* (28 December 1992), 28; "Sarajevo Radio Reports Shelling," Sarajevo Radio, Bosnia-Hercegovina

Network, 29 December 1992, *FBIS EEU* (29 December 1992), 38; "Civilians Prevented From Leaving Sarajevo," Zagreb Radio, Croatia Network, 28 December 1992, *FBIS EEU* (29 December 1992), 39.

42. Vego, "The Army of Bosnia and Herzegovina," 63-67; Collinson, 547-50; Jovan Divjak, 162-65. See also "Wargamer" Internet site, copyright 2001, accessed on 5 March 2002 <www.wargamer.com/sp /military/bih/ armija>. As with many Internet sites, it is difficult to verify the information posted on the site, and the orders of battle listed here give an impression of well-structured units that did not really exist in Bosnia on either side. However, the site includes some good information, including the unit designations of the brigades fighting on each side.

43. O'Ballance, 138; "Intense Fighting Reportedly Continues in Sarajevo," Paris AFP, 1 January 1993, *FBIS EEU* (4 January 1993), 58; "TANJUG Reports Muslim Offensive in Sarajevo," Belgrade TANJUG, 2 January 1993, *FBIS EEU* (4 January 1993), 58-59; "Deputy Prime Minister Shot by Serb Troops," Paris AFP, 8 January 1993, *FBIS EEU* (11 January 1993), 31; "Met With Turkish Officer," Ankara TRT Television Network, 8 January 1993, *FBIS EEU* (11 January 1993), 31; "Turajlic Buried in Sarajevo," Paris AFP, 9 January 1993, *FBIS EEU* (4 January 1993), 31-32; "Government Issues Communique," Sarajevo Radio, Bosnia-Hercegovina Network, 9 January 1993, *FBIS EEU* (11 January 1993), 32; "Government Holds UNPROFOR Responsible," Sarajevo Radio, Bosnia-Hercegovina Network, 8 January 1993, *FBIS EEU* (11 January 1993), 32; "Ganić Orders Halt to Talks," Sarajevo Radio, Bosnia-Hercegovina Network, 9 January 1993, *FBIS EEU* (11 January 1993), 33; "Serbs Issue Statement," Belgrade TANJUG Domestic Service, 9 January 1993, *FBIS EEU* (11 January 1993), 33; "Serb Army Blames UNPROFOR," Belgrade TANJUG Domestic Service, 10 January 1993, *FBIS EEU* (11 January 1993), 33-34; "Morillon Reacts to Shooting," Paris France-2 Television Network, 9 January 1993, *FBIS EEU* (11 January 1993), 34-35; and David Rieff, *Slaughterhouse: Bosnia and the Failure of the West* (NY: Simon & Schuster, 1995), 150-51. Rieff is particularly critical of the French commander, Colonel Patrice Sartre, of the UN column escorting Turajlic.

44. Silber and Little, 276-90, and Susan Woodward, *Balkan Tragedy: Chaos and Dissolution After the Cold War* (Washington, DC: The Brookings Institution, 1995), 242-44 and 307-308. David Owen, *Balkan Odyssey* (NY: Harcourt, Brace, & Co., 1995), 94-159, covers the details of the plan; 160-97 cover the ultimate rejection of the plan. These three works offer interesting variations on the Vance-Owen plan. Silber and Little see the plan as an honest, but misguided, attempt at peace—an example of Western efforts that failed to understand the complexity of the Bosnian situation. They also point out the cynical attitudes of the factions (particularly the Serbs) who feigned support of

the plan but never expected it to be implemented. Owen, not surprisingly, views the plan favorably. He is more critical of the American role in the struggle, which he sees as undermining the peace efforts with constant threats of air strikes but an unwillingness to commit ground troops. Woodward is one of the most vociferous critics of Western efforts at peace, but her book has surprisingly little detail on the Vance-Owen plan.

45. O'Ballance, 184-90; "Bosnian Army Prepared to Repel Attacks on Sarajevo," Sarajevo Radio, Bosnia-Hercegovina Network, 14 July 1993, *FBIS EEU* (15 July 1993), 36; "Serbs Respond to Attack on Ilid a," Belgrade Radio, Belgrade Network, 19 July 1993, *FBIS EEU* (20 July 1993), 25; "'Considerable' Serb Losses Reported on Mt. Igman," Sarajevo Radio, Bosnia-Hercegovina Network, 19 July 1993, *FBIS EEU* (20 July 1993), 25-26; "Muslims Continue to Repel Serbs," Sarajevo Radio, Bosnia-Hercegovina Network, 19 July 1993, *FBIS EEU* (20 July 1993), 26; "Muslim Offensive 'Continuing Unabated,'" Belgrade TANJUG, 20 July 1993, *FBIS EEU* (20 July 1993), 26; "'Considerable' Muslim Losses," Belgrade TANJUG Domestic Service, 20 July 1993, *FBIS EEU* (21 July 1993), 29; "Muslim Counteroffensive," Sarajevo Radio, Bosnia-Hercegovina Network, 20 July 1993, *FBIS EEU* (21 July 1993), 29; "Serbs Continue Attacks," Zagreb Radio, Croatia Network, 20 July 1993, *FBIS EEU* (21 July 1993), 29; "Muslims Continue Attack," Belgrade Radio, Belgrade Network, 20 July 1993, *FBIS EEU* (21 July 1993), 30; "'Unusually Intense' Shelling," Paris AFP, 22 July 1993, *FBIS EEU* (22 July 1993), 49; "Muslim Attacks Repelled," Belgrade TANJUG, 22 July 1993, *FBIS EEU* (23 July 1993), 34; "Serb Shelling of Mt. Igman Continues," Sarajevo Radio, Bosnia-Hercegovina Network, 22 July 1993, *FBIS EEU* (23 July 1993), 34; "Mt. Igman Front Reactivated," Sarajevo Radio, Bosnia-Hercegovina Network, 28 July 1993, *FBIS EEU* (29 July 1993), 30.

46. Alix Kroeger, "Sarajevo's Tunnel of Hope," BBC News Online, posted 16 April 2001, accessed 10 February 2002 at <http://news.bbc.co.uk/hi/english/world/europe/newsid 128000/1280328.stm> and the author's visit to the Tunnel Museum and personal conversations with Edis Kolar. Edis and Bajro Kolar (and their father) are owners and proprietors of the museum, which lies on the western end of the tunnel in Butmir. The Bosnian forces selected the Kolar farm as its start point for the western terminus of the line under the airport in January 1993. At the time, both Kolar brothers and the father were serving in the BDF. Edis stated that his family was willing to lend its farm to the cause, but he also admitted some trepidation over the fact that their land would certainly come under heavy fire and be useless as farmland for the duration of the war. On the other hand, his face lit up with unrestrained pride when he described the time that he was given the honor of pushing a

special railcar with a chair that carried Izetbegović safely into the city during one occasion when the airport was closed.

47. O'Ballance, 194-98 and 202; "UNPROFOR Says Serbs Poised to Capture Mt. Igman," Paris AFP, 3 August 1993, *FBIS EEU* (4 August 1993), 36; "Serbs Consolidating Positions," Paris AFP, 4 August 1993, *FBIS EEU* (4 August 1993), 37; "UNPROFOR Arrives on Mt. Bjelasnica," Belgrade TANJUG Domestic Service, 4 August 1993, *FBIS EEU* (4 August 1993), 37; "Serbs Continue Offensive on Mt. Igman Front," Sarajevo Radio, Bosnia-Hercegovina Network, 5 August 1993, *FBIS EEU* (5 August 1993), 25; "Attacks on Igman, Bjelasnica Continue," Sarajevo Radio, Bosnia-Hercegovina Network, 4 August 1993, *FBIS EEU* (5 August 1993), 25-26; "UN Officer, Mladić on 'Fall of Igman,'" Paris AFP, 4 August 1993, *FBIS EEU* (5 August 1993), 26; "Serbs Invite UNPROFOR Observers to Bjelasnica," Belgrade TANJUG Domestic Service, 3 August 1993, *FBIS EEU* (4 August 1993), 28; "Gen Mladić: Army Will Not Take Sarajevo," Belgrade TANJUG, 6 August 1993, *FBIS EEU* (6 August 1993), 39; "Agrees to 'Framework of Withdrawal' From Igman," Paris AFP, 6 August 1993, *FBIS EEU* (6 August 1993), 39; "Karadić: UN to be Allowed on Igman," Belgrade TANJUG, 6 August 1993, *FBIS EEU* (6 August 1993), 40; "Muslims Say Serb Offensive Continuing," Sarajevo Radio, Bosnia-Hercegovina Network, 5 August 1993, *FBIS EEU* (6 August 1993), 40-41; "Serbs Preparing New Strikes on Bjelasnica," Sarajevo Radio, Bosnia-Hercegovina Network, 6 August 1993, *FBIS EEU* (6 August 1993), 41-42; "UNPROFOR Arrives on Peaks," Belgrade TANJUG, 9 August 1993, *FBIS EEU* (10 August 1993), 31; "Military Leaders Sign Cease-Fire Agreement," Belgrade Radio, Belgrade Network, 11 August 1993, *FBIS EEU* (11 August 1993), 33; "Commanders on Agreement," Belgrade TANJUG Domestic Service, 11 August 1993, *FBIS EEU* (11 August 1993), 33; "Sarajevo Radio on Talks," Sarajevo Radio, Bosnia-Hercegovina Network, 10 August 1993, *FBIS EEU* (11 August 1993), 33-34; "UNPROFOR: Serbs 'Not Budging,'" Paris AFP, 10 August 1993, *FBIS EEU* (11 August 1993), 34; "Serbs Repel Muslim Infantry Attack on Mt. Igman," Belgrade TANJUG Domestic Service, 10 August 1993, *FBIS EEU* (11 August 1993), 34; "Mladić's Serbs Continue Offensive," Sarajevo Radio, Bosnia-Hercegovina Network, 10 August 1993, *FBIS EEU* (11 August 1993), 34-35; "UNPROFOR Deployment Reported," Belgrade TANJUG, 10 August 1993, *FBIS EEU* (11 August 1993), 35; "Sarajevo Radio Reports Withdrawal," Sarajevo Radio, Bosnia-Hercegovina Network, 11 August 1993, *FBIS EEU* (12 August 1993), 22; "Serb Army, UNPROFOR Chiefs Visit Mount Igman," Belgrade TANJUG Domestic Service, 13 August 1993, *FBIS EEU* (13 August 1993), 39; "UN Commander on Withdrawal," Belgrade TANJUG, 10 August 1993, *FBIS EEU* (11 August 1993), 39-40; and "Last Serb Unit

Leaves," Zagreb Radio, Croatia Network, 16 August 1993, *FBIS EEU* (17 August 1993), 38.

48. O'Ballance, 222-25; "Presidency Arrests Commanders in Sarajevo," Sarajevo Radio, Bosnia-Hercegovina Network, 26 October 1993, *FBIS EEU* (26 October 1993), 22; "Commanders Held in 'Isolation,'" Sarajevo Radio, Bosnia-Hercegovina Network, 26 October 1993, *FBIS EEU* (26 October 1993), 22; "Rebel Commanders Surrender, Topalovic Killed," Sarajevo Radio, Bosnia-Hercegovina Network, 27 October 1993, *FBIS EEU* (27 October 1993), 23; "TANJUG Reports Clashes," Belgrade TANJUG Domestic Service, 27 October 1993, *FBIS EEU* (27 October 1993), 23; "Delic, Alispahic Discuss Sarajevo Crackdown," Sarajevo Radio, Bosnia-Hercegovina Network, 27 October 1993, *FBIS EEU* (28 October 1993), 33-34; and "Army Disbands Croatian Forces in Sarajevo," Sarajevo Radio, Bosnia-Hercegovina Network, 6 November 1993, *FBIS EEU* (8 November 1993), 25.

49. O'Ballance, 234.

50. Ibid., 237-39; Silber and Little, 309-18; General Sir Michael Rose, *Fighting For Peace, Bosnia 1994* (London: The Harvill Press, 1998), 16-17 and 42-68. Silber and Little are highly critical of Rose, accusing him of deliberately misleading the UN and NATO as to the extent (or lack) of Serbian withdrawals of heavy guns around Sarajevo. Rose's own account emphasizes that air strikes would have placed the ground UNPROFOR troops in danger with little benefit. Even though Rose does seem inclined to give the Bosnian Serbs a bit too much credit for their efforts, he still concludes that the market bomb was from a Bosnian Serb mortar, 43-44.

51. Silber and Little, 335-44.

52. Roger Cohen, *Hearts Grown Brutal: Sagas of Sarajevo* (NY: Random House, 1998), xlvi-xlvii.

53. "Sarajevo Being Strangulated," Sarajevo Radio, Bosnia-Herzegovina Network, 8 May 1995, *FBIS EEU* (8 May 1995), accessed 26 February 2002 (note that in late 1994, the FBIS reports have been placed on the Internet instead of on microfiche at <http://199.221.15.211>; all remaining FBIS notes refer to this website); "1st Corps Reports Intensified Attacks on Sarajevo," Sarajevo Radio, Bosnia-Herzegovina Network, 10 May 1995, *FBIS EEU* (10 May 1995), accessed 26 February 2002; "Heaviest Fighting in Sarajevo Since 1993," Paris AFP, 10 May 1995, *FBIS EEU* (10 May 1995), accessed 26 February 2002; and Cohen, xlvii-xlviii.

54. "Army Reports on Military Situation in Sarajevo," Sarajevo Radio, Bosnia-Herzegovina Network, 3 August 1995, *FBIS EEU* (3 August 1995), accessed 26 February 2002; "Presidency Appoints 1st, 4th Corps Commanders," Sarajevo Radio, Bosnia-Herzegovina Network, 16 August 1995, *FBIS EEU* (16 August 1995), accessed 26 February 2002; "Government Reports on Sarajevo Casualties," Ljubljana OSLOBODJENJE, 17 August 1995,

FBIS EEU (17 August 1995), accessed 26 February 2002; "Muslims Launch 'All-Out' Attack on Serb Sarajevo," Belgrade TANJUG, 22 August 1995, *FBIS EEU* (22 August 1995), accessed 26 February 2002; and Stacy Sullivan, "UN Pounds Serb Guns as Sarajevo is Shelled," *London Times* (23 August 1995), 12. During the increased fighting in August, the Bosnian 1st (Sarajevo) Corps commander, Vahid Karvelic, became the head of the Bosnian General Staff's operations and planning division. He was replaced by Brigadier General Nedzad Ajnadzic, the former 37th Division commander. This appears to have been a normal rotation of duties for both men, not a comment on their performance.

55. Silber and Little, 364-65; "Sarajevo Shelled; 30 Casualties Reported," Sarajevo Radio, Bosnia-Herzegovina Network, 28 August 1995, *FBIS EEU* (28 August 1995), accessed 26 February 2002; "Sarajevo Shelled; 30 Casualties Reported; Serbs Deny Responsibility," Belgrade SRNA, 28 August 1995, *FBIS EEU* (28 August 1995), accessed 26 February 2002; "Sarajevo Shelled; 30 Casualties Reported; UN 'in Contact With' NATO," Paris AFP, 28 August 1995, *FBIS EEU* (28 August 1995), accessed 26 February 2002; "Boutros-Ghali Condemns Massacre, Demands Action," Belgrade TANJUG, 28 August 1995, *FBIS EEU* (28 August 1995), accessed 26 February 2002; "Izetbegović Promises Retaliation for Shelling," Sarajevo Radio, Bosnia-Herzegovina Network, 28 August 1995, *FBIS EEU* (28 August 1995), accessed 26 February 2002; "Bosnian Serbs Reject UN Statement on Sarajevo Mladić Proposes Commission," Belgrade TANJUG Domestic Service, 28 August 1995, *FBIS EEU* (28 August 1995), accessed 26 February 2002; "Motives of 'Muslim Terrorists' in Sarajevo Massacre," Belgrade SRNA, 28 August 1995, *FBIS EEU* (28 August 1995), accessed 26 February 2002; "'Overwhelming' Evidence of Serb Attack; UN Considers Military Response," Paris AFP, 29 August 1995, *FBIS EEU* (29 August 1995), accessed 26 February 2002; "Serbs Resume Artillery, Tank Attacks on Sarajevo," Sarajevo Radio, Bosnia-Herzegovina Network, 29 August 1995, *FBIS EEU* (29 August 1995), accessed 26 February 2002; "Bosnian Serbs Reject UN Statement on Sarajevo," Paris AFP, 29 August 1995, *FBIS EEU* (29 August 1995), accessed 26 February 2002; "'Ballistics Expert' Says Muslims Fired Shell," Belgrade SRNA, 29 August 1995, *FBIS EEU* (29 August 1995), accessed 26 February 2002; Stacy Sullivan, "Shell in Sarajevo Market Kills 33," *London Times* (29 August 1995), 1; and Michael Dynes and Ian Brodie, "Germany Leads the Condemnation of Market Massacre," *London Times* (29 August 1995), 8.

56. Stacy Sullivan, James Bone, and Eve-Ann Prentice, "Nato Bombers Attack Serbs Near Sarajevo," *London Times* (30 August 1995), 1; Eve-Ann Prentice, "West Fears Attack May Derail Balkan Deal," *London Times* (30 August 1995), 7; Stacy Sullivan, Michael Evans, and James Bone, "NATO to

Press on With Attack," *London Times* (31 August 1995), 1; Michael Evans, "NATO Unleashes Full Air Power Against Bosnian Serb Guns," *London Times* (31 August 1995), 3; "Air Strikes Not 'Declaration of War,'" Paris AFP, 30 August 1995, *FBIS EEU* (30 August 1995), accessed 26 February 2002; "UN Action Aimed to Eliminate 'All Threats,'" Paris AFP, 30 August 1995, *FBIS EEU* (30 August 1995), accessed 26 February 2002; "Start of Joint NATO, RRF Action Reported," Sarajevo Radio, Bosnia-Herzegovina Network, 30 August 1995, *FBIS EEU* (30 August 1995), accessed 26 February 2002; "Start of Joint NATO, RRF Action Reported RRF Fires Over 600 Shells," Belgrade TANJUG, 30 August 1995, *FBIS EEU* (30 August 1995), accessed 26 February 2002; "NATO Action 'Far-Reaching,'" Sarajevo Radio, Bosnia-Herzegovina Network, 30 August 1995, *FBIS EEU* (30 August 1995), accessed 26 February 2002; "Air Strikes 'a Success'; Serb Radio 'Damage Immense,'" Banja Luka Srpski Radio Network, 30 August 1995, *FBIS EEU* (30 August 1995), accessed 26 February 2002; "Air Strikes 'a Success' 1st Corps on Raid Damage," Sarajevo Radio, Bosnia-Herzegovina Network, 30 August 1995, *FBIS EEU* (30 August 1995), accessed 26 February 2002; "Air Strikes 'a Success'; Radar Systems, Artillery Hit," Sarajevo Radio, Bosnia-Herzegovina Network, 30 August 1995, *FBIS EEU* (30 August 1995), accessed 26 February 2002; "Air Strikes 'a Success'; Ammunition Dumps in Lukavica Hit," Sarajevo Radio, Bosnia-Herzegovina Network, 30 August 1995, *FBIS EEU* (30 August 1995), accessed 26 February 2002; and "Serb Sources Report on NATO, RRF Strike Damage; Sarajevo Damage Detailed," Pale Srpski Radio-Televizija Studio Sarajevo, 30 August 1995, *FBIS EEU* (30 August 1995), accessed 26 February 2002.

57. Silber and Little, 364-69; Michael Evans, "Military Chiefs Given Free Rein," *London Times* (31 August 1995), 2; Michael Evans, Eve-Ann Prentice, and Susan Bell, "NATO Aircraft Renew Attack on the Serbs," *London Times* (1 September 1995), 1; Michael Evans, "NATO Commander Hails Success of Precision Bombing," *London Times* (1 September 1995), 13; Stacy Sullivan, Sam Kiley, and Michael Evans, "NATO Suspends Raids on Serbs," *London Times* (2 September 1995), 1; Michael Evans and Stacy Sullivan, "Serbs Facing Renewed Air Onslaught," *London Times* (4 September 1995), 1; Michael Evans and Stacy Sullivan, "Mladić Risks New Strikes by Defying NATO Ultimatum," *London Times* (5 September 1995), 1; Sam Kiley and Michael Evans, "NATO Bombers Strike Again as Serbs Keep Shelling," *London Times* (6 September 1995), 1, 9; Peter Capella and Michael Evans, "Bosnia Deal Ends Greater Serbia Dream," *London Times* (9 September 1995), 1; "No Serb Withdrawal of Heavy Weapons," Paris France-2 Television Network, 31 August 1995, *FBIS EEU* (31 August 1995), accessed 26 February 2002; "Izetbegović on NATO Raid, Fate of Sarajevo," Paris LE MONDE, 1 September 1995, *FBIS EEU* (1 September 1995),

accessed 26 February 2002; "Strikes to Continue Until Serbs Comply," Sarajevo Radio, Bosnia-Herzegovina Network, 5 September 1995, *FBIS EEU* (5 September 1995), accessed 26 February 2002; "Strikes 'Rather Successful'; Radar on Jahorina Under Attack," Sarajevo Radio, Bosnia-Herzegovina Network, 5 September 1995, *FBIS EEU* (5 September 1995), accessed 26 February 2002; "NATO Air Strikes Target Serb Communications Pale Telephone Links Cut Off," Paris AFP, 5 September 1995, *FBIS EEU* (5 September 1995), accessed 26 February 2002; "Serbs Fire Artillery at Sarajevo in Retaliation," Sarajevo Radio, Bosnia-Herzegovina Network, 5 September 1995, *FBIS EEU* (5 September 1995), accessed 26 February 2002; and "'War Is Over'; U.S. Soldiers Coming," Sarajevo Radio, Bosnia-Herzegovina Network, 9 September 1995, *FBIS EEU* (9 September 1995), accessed 26 February 2002.

Bibliography

Bennett, Christopher. *Yugoslavia's Bloody Collapse: Causes, Course, and Consequences*. London: Hurst and Co., 1995. Good summary of Yugoslavia's collapse after Tito's death. Focus is on political issues, not as much on the military.

Bladen, Mark, Corporal, Royal Air Force (RAF); Corporal Chris Stone, RAF; and Corporal Gary Woodard, RAF. *Sarajevo Battlefield Tour*. Prepared by the Multinational Division (Southwest) Liaison Team of the Stabilization Force (SFOR) in August 1999. Small unpublished pamphlet of principal wartime sites in Sarajevo from the author's personal collection.

Blank, Stephen J., Editor. *Yugoslavia's Wars: The Problem From Hell*. Carlisle Barracks, PA: U.S. Army War College, 1995. Interesting collection of essays addressing the international community's role in the Balkans, but with little on military actions.

Briquemont, Lieutenant General Francis. *Do Something, General! Chronique de Bosnie Herzegovine 12 julliet 1993 24 janvier 1994*. Brussels: Collection La Noria, Editions Labor, 1997. Memoirs, in French, of the Belgium UNPROFOR commander from July 1993 to January 1994.

Burg, Steven L. and Paul S. Shoup. *The War in Bosnia Herzegovina: Ethnic Conflict and International Intervention*. London: M.E. Sharpe, 1999. Although generally focused on the international aspects of the war, there is a large chapter on the war operations that is very useful.

Cohen, Roger. *Hearts Grown Brutal: Sagas of Sarajevo*. NY: Random House, 1998. Mainly a human account of the suffering through the eyes of several families that are friends of Cohen.

Collinson, Christopher. "Bosnia This Winter—A Military Analysis." *Jane's Intelligence Review*. December 1993. This article, like the others from *Jane's*, is an analysis of military forces in Bosnia by intelligence experts that contains good information on units and equipment.

"Bosnian Army Tactics." *Jane's Intelligence Review*. January 1994.

Donia, Robert J. and John V.A. Fine, Jr. *Bosnia and Hercegovina: A Tradition Betrayed*. London: Hurst and Co., 1994. Excellent work on the history of Bosnia with a final chapter on the war; not much on military operations but good background.

Foreign Broadcast Information Service (FBIS). *Daily Reports: East Europe*. 1992-1995.

Glenny, Misha. *The Fall of Yugoslavia: The Third Balkan War*. Third Revised Edition. NY: Penguin Books, 1996. Detailed volume that focuses on politics and international activity but lacks military detail.

Gow, Dr. James. "Settling Bosnia—The Balance of Forces." *Jane's Intelligence Review*. April 1994.

Hoare, Quintin and Noel Malcolm, Editors. *Books on Bosnia*. London: The Bosnian Institute, 1997. Very useful bibliography with extensive, if sometimes harsh, annotations on each book.

Isby, David C. "War Returns to Europe: Military Aspects of the Conflicts in Yugoslavia, 1991-93." *Command Magazine, Military History, Strategy, and Analysis*. July-August 1993. Article from a wargame magazine that has some good information on unit composition and the Total National Defense concept.

Jelavich, Barbara. *History of the Balkans*. 2 Volumes. Cambridge: Cambridge University Press, 1983. Classic work on the Balkans but concludes before the 1992-1995 war; great for background.

Kaplan, Robert D. *Balkan Ghosts: A Journey Through History*. NY: St. Martin's Press, 1993. A personal account of travels through the Balkans with strong opinions of the politics; not much on military operations.

Little, Allan and Laura Silber. *The Death of Yugoslavia*. London: Penguin Group and BBC Worldwide Ltd., 1996. Excellent work on the entire war heavily based on interviews with and actual television and video transcripts of the participants.

London and Sunday Times. April 1992-December 1995.

MacKenzie, General Lewis. *Peacekeeper: The Road to Sarajevo*. Vancouver: Douglas & McIntyre, 1993. Memoirs of the first UNPROFOR commander in Sarajevo that are disarmingly honest in expressing his frustrations.

Magas, Branka and Ivo Zanic, Editors. *The War in Croatia and Bosnia Herzegovina, 1991 1995*. London: Frank Cass Publishers, 2001. An excellent collection of essays. Divjak's chapter is particularly useful.

Malcolm, Noel. *Bosnia: A Short History*. Revised Edition. London: MacMillan Publishers Ltd., 1996. Superb overview of the nation but too broad to include detail on operations in 1992-1995. Excellent source to use for background.

Morillon, General Philippe. *Croireet oser; chronique de Sarajevo*. Paris: Grasset, 1993. Memoirs of the most flamboyant UNPROFOR commander. Not much information on Sarajevo because his efforts were focused on Srebrenica.

O'Ballance, Edgar. *Civil War in Bosnia, 1992 1994*. NY: St. Martin's Press, 1995. Sometimes flawed account of the war (some details are incorrect), but it goes into the most detail on the military campaigns of any English-language work.

Owen, David. *Balkan Odyssey*. NY: Harcourt, Brace, & Co., 1995. Owen's own account of the peace process; often critical of the United States' role.

Ridgeway, James and Jasminka Udovicki. Editors. *Burn This House: The Making and Unmaking of Yugoslavia*. Durham, NC: Duke University Press, 2000. Covers the human aspects of the war, not much on the military.

Rieff, David. *Slaughterhouse: Bosnia and the Failure of the West*. NY: Simon & Schuster, 1995. Highly critical volume of the West's lack of resolve on Bosnia; lacks in military detail.

Rogel, Carole. *The Breakup of Yugoslavia and the War in Bosnia*. Westport, CT: Greenwood Press, 1998. Good overview of the political aspects of Yugoslavia's breakup but not much on military operations.

Rose, General Sir Michael. *Fighting for Peace, Bosnia 1994*. London: The Harvill Press, 1998. Memoirs of the UNPROFOR commander's time in Bosnia; filled with frank, but perhaps biased, assessments.

Vego, Dr. Milan. "The Army of Bosnia and Herzegovina." *Jane's Intelligence Review*. February 1993.

"The Croatian Forces in Bosnia and Herzegovina." *Jane's Intelligence Review*. March 1993.

"The Yugoslav Ground Forces." *Jane's Intelligence Review*. June 1993.

West, Rebecca. *Black Lamb and Grey Falcon*. NY: Viking Press, 1941. An overview of the entire Balkans; good for background but not much detail on the Bosnia war, 1992-1995.

Woodward, Susan. *Balkan Tragedy: Chaos and Dissolution After the Cold War*. Washington, DC: The Brookings Institution, 1995. A pessimistic view of Balkan affairs with a focus on the international community's errors. Not much on military operations.

The Takedown of Kabul: An Effective Coup de Main[1]

Lester W. Grau

On 27 April 1978, Afghan officers who had trained in the Soviet Union conducted a military coup, bringing Communist power to Afghanistan. Nur M. Taraki, the new Soviet-backed president, announced sweeping programs of distributing land, emancipating women, and destroying Afghanistan's old social structure. Armed resistance immediately challenged the new government. The Army of the Democratic Republic of Afghanistan (DRA) disintegrated as bloody purges swept the officer ranks. In March 1979, the city of Herat rose in revolt. Most of the Afghan 17th Infantry Division mutinied and joined the rebellion. Forces loyal to President Taraki advanced and occupied the city while the Afghan Air Force bombed the city and the 17th Division. More than 5,000 people, including Soviet citizens, died in the fighting.

Soldiers, units, even entire brigades deserted to the resistance, and by the end of 1979, the Afghan army had fallen from about 90,000 to about 40,000 soldiers. Over half the officer corps was purged, executed, or had deserted. In September 1979, Taraki's prime minister, Hafizullah Amin, seized power and secretly executed Taraki. Amin led the Soviets to believe that Taraki was alive long after he had been killed. But Amin's rule proved no better than Taraki's, and the Soviet Union watched this new Communist state spin out of control and out of Moscow's orbit. The Soviet politburo moved to stabilize the situation.

The Soviet Union had significant experience with stability operations in maintaining its socialist empire. Its experience subjugating the Hungarian Revolution of 1956 (where the Soviet forces suffered tremendous losses) led to improved methods and techniques, so that in the 1968 invasion of Czechoslovakia, the Soviet army only lost 96 killed.[2] By that point, the elements of its coup de main model now included the preinvasion insertion of an in-country Soviet military and KGB element and the production of a cover or deception operation to divert attention away from the imminent attack. A General Staff group would tour the country before the invasion, under some pretense, to assess and fine-tune operational plans. When the invasion began, the in-country Soviet military and KGB element would disarm or disable key nodes of the national military forces. Airborne and Spetsnaz forces would spearhead the invasion and seize major airfields, transportation chokepoints, the capital city, key government buildings, and communications facilities.[3] They would also seize or execute key government leaders. Soviet ground forces would cross into the country, seize the major cities and road networks, suppress any local military resistance, and occupy the key population centers. A new government would then be installed, supported by the armed might of the Soviet armed forces and officially recognized by the Soviet government and its satellites.

This invasion model was used successfully in Afghanistan. Beginning in 1978, Soviet military and KGB advisers permeated the structure of the Afghanistan armed forces and security forces down to battalion level. In March 1979, eight Mi-8 helicopters, a transport squadron of AN-12s, a signal center, and a paratroop battalion transferred to Bagram air base in Afghanistan. The aircraft and all the crews were Soviet, yet the aircraft had Afghan markings and the personnel wore Afghan uniforms. The paratroopers, who provided security, wore Afghan flight suits.[4] The squadron conducted extensive reconnaissance of the country. In April 1979, General of the Army Aleksiy A. Yepishev, the head of the Main Political Directorate, led a delegation of several generals in a visit to Afghanistan to assess the situation. Yepishev had made a similar visit to Czechoslovakia before the 1968 invasion.

In August 1979, General of the Army Ivan G. Pavlovski, commander in chief (CINC) of the Soviet Ground Forces, led a group of some 60 officers on an extended reconnaissance tour of Afghanistan that lasted for weeks. In 1968, he also had been involved in the Czech crisis as commander of the invasion force. In November 1979, a Spetsnaz battalion, clad in Afghan uniforms, deployed to Afghanistan and was incorporated into the presidential security forces, guarding the outer perimeter of Amin's residence. This so-called Muslim battalion was made up of Soviet Central Asian soldiers who spoke Pashtu, Dari (a dialect of Farsi), Tadjik, or Uzbek. In December, two thirty-man Spetsnaz groups, code-named "Grom" (Thunder) and "Zenit" (Zenith) deployed to Kabul and began reconnaissance of the thirteen objectives that they would have to take out in the coming assault.[5] More members of Zenith deployed later in the month.

The initial Soviet invasion of Afghanistan was based on the newly reconstituted 40th Army. It consisted of the 5th and 108th Motorized Rifle Divisions, the 103d Airborne Division, the 860th Separate Motorized Rifle Regiment, the 56th Separate Air Assault Brigade, the 345th Separate Parachute Regiment, the 2d Air Defense Brigade, and the 34th Composite Aviation Corps.[6] Airborne elements would fly in and help the in-place Spetsnaz take the capital city of Kabul and the main airfields. Ground elements would seize and occupy the eastern and western corridors (see Map 1).[7] President Amin helped the planning process along greatly by continually requesting Soviet help and Soviet troops to prop up his beleaguered regime. The Soviets were happy to comply, only they were not coming to help Amin. The stage was set to seize the country.

Welcome to Kabul

Kabul is an ancient city that Alexander the Great passed through in 330 B.C. while en route to India.[8] The largest city in Afghanistan, its population was 435,202 in 1969.[9] Three major mountains push through the city in various directions, and the Kabul River cuts the city in half. Like other Central Asian cities, Kabul's center is composed of ancient adobe buildings set in a rabbit warren of narrow streets and narrower passages. This tight, teeming bazaar is divided into separate sections where large groups of specialists live in an Eastern version of the medieval guild. Leather workers, jewelers, brass workers, and carpet merchants all have their own time-honored section of the bazaar for production and sales. Individual artisans and factories also produce items for sale in the town bazaars and for export.

In 1979, government officials normally lived in the "new city" where the ministries, foreign embassies, hotels, restaurants, and cafes are located. The "new city" is generally north and southwest of the center. The "microrayon" is a region northeast of the city that consists of Soviet-style prefabricated buildings that were produced in a Soviet-constructed factory. At the time of the invasion, these multiple-storied concrete buildings pierced the skyline, and new restaurants, stores, supermarkets, and garages catered to the foreign colony and the growing Afghan middle class. The city was electrified, although power was unstable and problematic. Running water was not potable, although the Japanese were constructing a water system for Kabul. Modern plumbing was confined to the new sections of the city.[10] By regional standards, Kabul was a liberal, open city where women in cosmopolitan miniskirts contrasted with those who were completely covered and veiled, and discotheques blared Western and Eastern music into the early hours.

On the eve of the Soviet invasion, it was winter in Afghanistan, and the snow was belt-deep in parts of the capital. Far to the north, at 0700 on 25 December 1979, two Soviet pontoon bridge regiments began

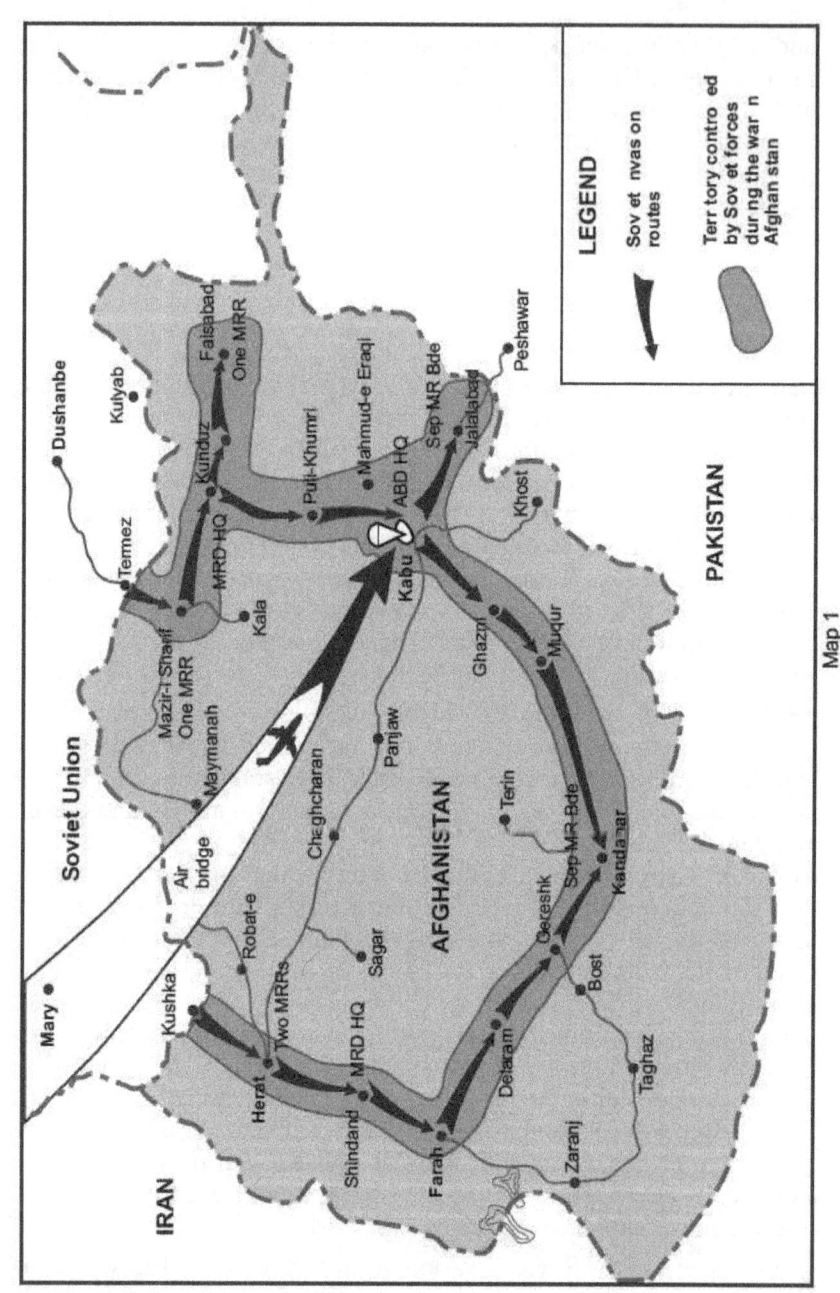

Map 1

guiding their floating bridges into position on the Amu Darya River in the vicinity of Termez, a Soviet city on the Afghan border. Meanwhile, the 40th Army commander, General Lieutenant Yuri Vladimirovich Tukharinov, met with the chief of operations of the DRA General Staff, General Baba Jan, in Kunduz, Afghanistan, to coordinate actions in the deployment area.

By noon, the Soviet forces had received their orders from Soviet Minister of Defense Marshal of the Soviet Union Dmitri Fedorovich Ustinov. These orders directed that the 40th Army and Soviet air force planes would begin crossing the DRA's borders at 1500 (Moscow time) on 25 December. The Soviet forces began their incursion precisely at the established time. The scouts and air assault battalion of Captain L.V. Khabarov were the first to cross. They were tasked with seizing the Salang pass, a crucial chokepoint on the road to Kabul (twelve Soviet scouts would die in an ambush at the pass). The remainder of the 108th Motorized Rifle Division followed the troops across the pontoon bridges.

Simultaneously, Soviet military transport aviation aircraft crossed the border carrying elements of the 103d Airborne Division, commanded by General Major I.F. Ryabchenko, and the 345th Separate Parachute Regiment to airfields in the capital and nearby Bagram. It took a total of 343 flights and 47 hours to transport the paratroopers and their vehicles and gear. The first aircraft touched down at 1615 on 25 December, and the last touched down at 1430 on the 27th. General Colonel I.D. Gaydaenko directed the military air transport operation. The effort did not occur without casualties. At 1933 on the 25th, an IL-76 that Captain V.V. Golovchin piloted crashed into a mountain and burned during its approach landing. All thirty-seven paratroopers and seven crew members were killed.

On the 25th, the chief Soviet advisers to the Afghan military met in Kabul. They were ordered to prevent any Afghan units, which were opposed to the Soviet presence, from approaching Kabul. Those military advisers and technicians who worked with the DRA air defense forces were directed to prevent actions against the paratroopers' air movements by controlling all the air defense systems and their ammunition storage bunkers. The advisers temporarily disabled some air defense systems by removing the sights or by physically locking them. Consequently, the Soviet air armada flew into Afghanistan unopposed.[11]

For the coup de main to succeed, Amin had to be eliminated and Kabul had to be taken quickly, which meant that the inbound airborne and motorized rifle divisions would not be available for the mission.

The primary strike force would be the Spetsnaz forces already in Kabul and Bagram, advance units of the 345th Separate Parachute Regiment, and Soviet military advisers serving in Kabul. The operation plan to seize Kabul provided for the capture of thirteen key points: the Tadzh-Bek palace, President Amin's residence; the Central Committee of the National Democratic Party of Afghanistan (NDPA), the Communist Party building; the Ministry of Defense (GRU); the Ministry of the Interior; the Ministry of Foreign Affairs; the Ministry of Communications; the General Staff; the headquarters of the Central Army Corps; the military counterintelligence (KAM) building; the prison for political prisoners in Pul-e Charki; the radio and television center; the central post office; and the central telegraph office (see Map 2).[12] Simultaneously, the Soviets planned to block units of the DRA armed forces deploying in the Afghan capital.[13]

The objectives were spread throughout the city, but the majority was located north of the Kabul River in the newer section of town. Three of the key objectives (Amin's palace, the General Staff building, and the GRU) were south of Kabul, well into the suburbs. The thirteen groups tasked with taking these objectives were normally composite groups of KGB Spetsnaz, GRU Spetsnaz, paratroopers, advisers, and a few cooperative Afghans. The GRU Spetsnaz, paratroopers, and advisers provided the vehicles for the assaults. The signal for the attack to begin would be an explosion that would destroy "the shaft" that housed the international telephone cables as well as those connecting the country's military units. The shaft was located next to the Central Telephone Exchange. General Drozdov, the ranking KGB representative present in the country, would determine the time of the assault. While the overall planning was centralized, the execution was decentralized. The assault commander for each objective did his own reconnaissance, determined his own routes, and developed his own maneuver plan for rapid execution.

Taking the Tadzh-Bek Palace

The purpose of the Soviet intervention was to replace President Amin with Moscow's candidate. The KGB had orders to kill Amin, and since he lived in the Tadzh-Bek palace, the best place to kill him was in the palace. The palace was situated on a terraced hill on the southern outskirts of the city, and there was no high-speed approach. Rather, a serpentine road wound around the hill to the palace entrance. Amin's personal bodyguard was drawn from his tribe, so most of the bodyguards inside the palace had blood ties with the president. This

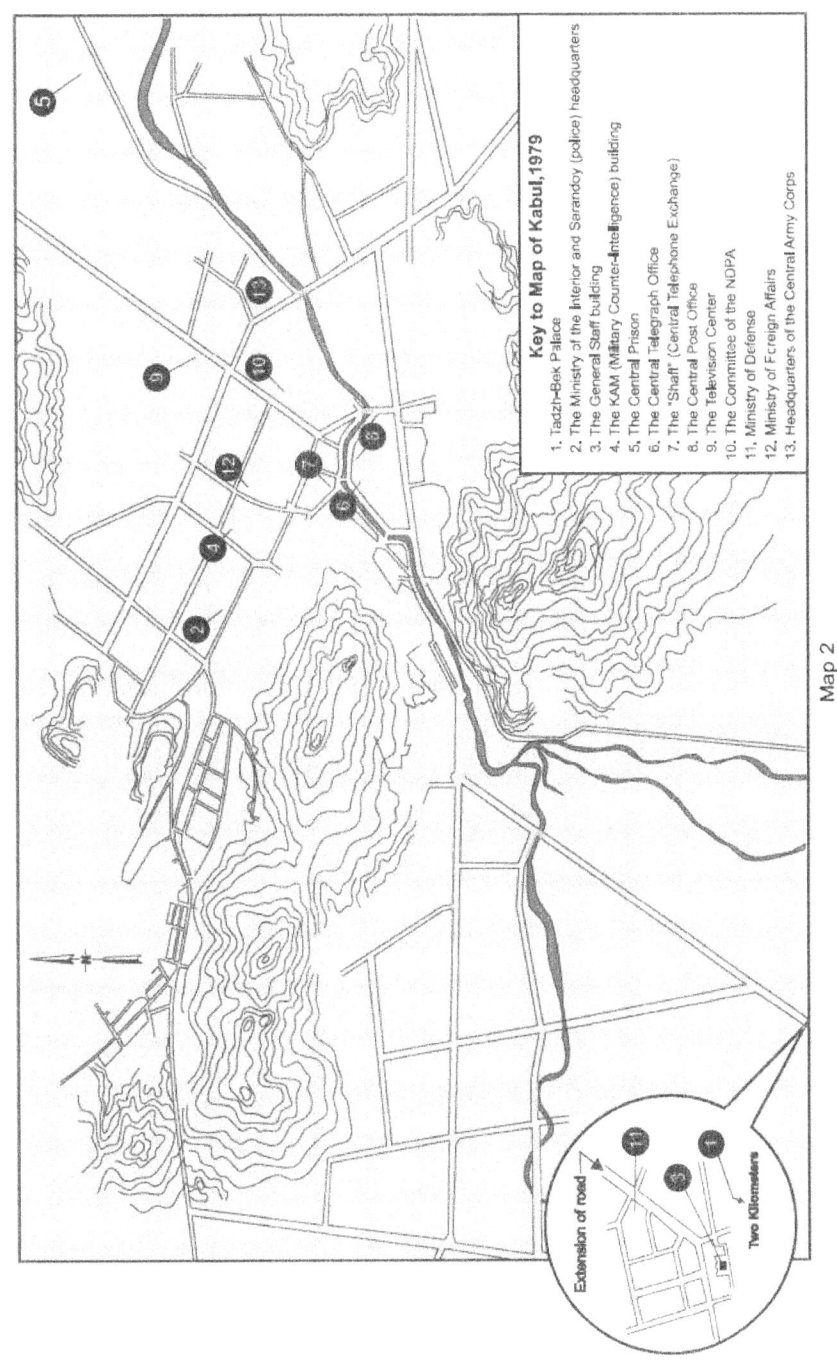

Map 2

company-size group occupied positions inside the palace and immediately on the outside. Soviet military doctors provided Amin's medical care, and Soviet cooks prepared his meals. Soviet military advisers were present within Amin's security brigade, and KGB advisers were present in his bodyguard.

The Soviet Muslim battalion held the eastern side of the external perimeter. The battalion's official designation was the 154th Separate Spetsnaz Detachment. It included 520 officers and soldiers plus equipment. This detachment/battalion was a unique organization that served as a pattern for the eight GRU Spetsnaz battalions that would eventually deploy to Afghanistan. In addition to the command and staff group, the detachment had four companies. The 1st Company was mounted on tracked BMP-1s, and the 2d and 3d companies were mounted on wheeled BTR-60PBs.[14] The 4th Company was a weapons company with an AGS-17 automatic grenade launcher platoon, a "Lynx" RPO flamethrower platoon, and a platoon of sappers. The detachment also included three separate platoons: signal, ZSU 23-4 "Shilka," and an automotive and materiel support platoon.[15] A mobile field dressing station with a doctor-anesthesiologist and a surgeon was also assigned to the battalion.

Every company had a translator—a cadet from the Military Institute of Foreign Languages—assigned for duty. However, there was practically no problem with language training in the detachment since all the Tajiks, about half of the Uzbeks, and some of the Turkmen knew Farsi, one of the principal Afghan languages. Major Kh. Khalbaev commanded the battalion. It was billeted in some uncompleted barracks on mountains overlooking the palace.[16]

Amin's security brigade manned positions within the palace, machine gun positions outside the palace on the palace hill, the traffic control posts on the approach road, and an overwatch position on the nearby mountain. The security brigade also maintained a ring of encircling positions around the palace. The security brigade headquarters caserne was near the overwatch position. Three DRA tanks on the overwatch position could fire on anyone crossing the open ground to attack the palace. A DRA antiaircraft regiment occupied high ground overlooking the palace to protect it from air attack. The regiment's twelve 100-millimeter (mm) antiaircraft guns and sixteen dual-barreled DShK heavy machine guns could also fire on ground targets on the palace approaches. There were a total of some 2,500 DRA personnel protecting the palace. In addition, there were two tank brigades garrisoned near Kabul that could rapidly intervene.[17]

Amin's death had to be coordinated with achieving other important objectives in the city. The first attempt to kill Amin would be by poison. Should that fail, the palace would be taken by assault. The assault force had to cross an expanse of open ground covered by carefully sited fighting positions and tanks in overwatch; it then had to follow a winding, channeled road up to the objective.[18] This was a hazardous route, and consequently, the Soviets considered a helicopter assault using the Mi-8 helicopters of the covert Soviet unit at Bagram airfield to airlift the assault force onto the palace roof. However, the Tadzh-Bek palace's roof was steep and probably icy. If the air assault went in at night, the risk was unacceptable. Further, the antiaircraft regiment would have to be neutralized before the assault at the risk of losing tactical surprise. For these reasons, a ground assault was necessary.[19]

The Soviets decided to assault the palace using a combination of three forces: the Muslim battalion Spetsnaz, which belonged to the GRU, and Spetsnaz groups Thunder and Zenith, which both belonged to the KGB. Thunder was an organized covert group masquerading as professional athletes. Zenith was an ad hoc group composed of Spetsnaz officers who were graduates of the Officer Professional Development Course in Balashikh and members of the Spetsnaz KGB reserve. The vehicles for the assault would come from the Muslim battalion.

The most difficult and important objective in Kabul was the Tadzh-Bek palace, and the Soviets devoted particular attention to its capture. In a preliminary move to minimize resistance, the Muslim battalion arranged a reception for the Afghan security brigade commanders on 25 December. They prepared pilaf, although there were difficulties getting alcoholic drinks. The embassy KGB personnel helped out with a box full of "ambassadorial" vodka and cognac plus various delicacies such as caviar and fish. The reception table was well appointed.[20] Since this was an Islamic country, the vodka and cognac were served out of teapots to preserve the appearance of propriety.[21]

Fifteen Afghan security brigade personnel, led by its commander, Major Dzhandad, and its political deputy, Ruzi, attended the reception. During the reception, the Soviets engaged the Afghans in conversation while they toasted Soviet-Afghan friendship and military cooperation. Sometimes the Soviet soldiers, who were serving as waiters, poured water instead of vodka into the Soviet officers' glasses. The security brigade's political deputy became especially talkative and told Captain Lebedev that President Taraki was suffocated under Amin's orders. This was important information and confirmed Soviet suspicions.

Major Dzhandad immediately ordered the political deputy to leave the room.[22] The Soviets now knew that the Afghans had lied to them about Taraki's death.

Colonel Kozlov, the senior GRU representative in Kabul, planned the assault on the palace (see Map 3). His first concern was the antiaircraft regiment. He determined that the engineer platoon, reinforced with two AGS-17 automatic grenade launchers and their crews, would take on the regiment. The AGS-17s would fire to cut off the antiaircraft personnel from their weapon positions, while the engineers, under AGS-17 covering fire, would move to the guns and machine guns and blow them up. Lieutenant Colonel Shvets, Kozlov's deputy, would command this group.

The dug-in tanks were the next concern. Kozlov's other assistant, Captain Sakhatov, selected personnel to capture them. He chose three tankers, four KGB Spetsnaz, two snipers, and two machine gunners. They would ride on a GAZ-66 truck up to the third battalion position and capture the three tanks.

The Muslim battalion's 2d and 3d companies, along with a company of paratroopers commanded by Senior Lieutenant Vostrotin, would block and contain the DRA 2d and 3d battalions and the combined 1st Battalion and tank battalion in their barracks area. The Soviet 1st Company, commanded by V. Sharipov, would transport KGB Spetsnaz Thunder and Zenith groups to the palace where they, along with two groups from the 1st Company, would conduct the direct assault on the palace.[23]

On the evening the reception was held, KGB General Drozdov held a meeting with KGB Spetsnaz commanders. He assigned everyone's position for seizing the Tadzh-Bek palace. Everyone was ready. The only thing missing was the plan of the palace. The next day, the Soviet advisers to Amin's security brigade, who were members of the KGB 9th Directorate, led some Spetsnaz personnel through the palace. They looked at everything attentively. Subsequently, Drozdov later made a floor-by-floor plan of Tadzh-Bek. However, the Soviet adviser to the Afghan Security Brigade commander, Yuri Kutepov, refused to relay Drozdov's request that the palace guard be weakened because such a request would heighten suspicion.

The commanders of Thunder and Zenith, KGB Majors M. Romanov and Ya. Semenov, conducted a reconnaissance of the external area and examined the firing positions and the nearby locale. Not far from the palace, on the hill where the tanks were in overwatch, was a restaurant/

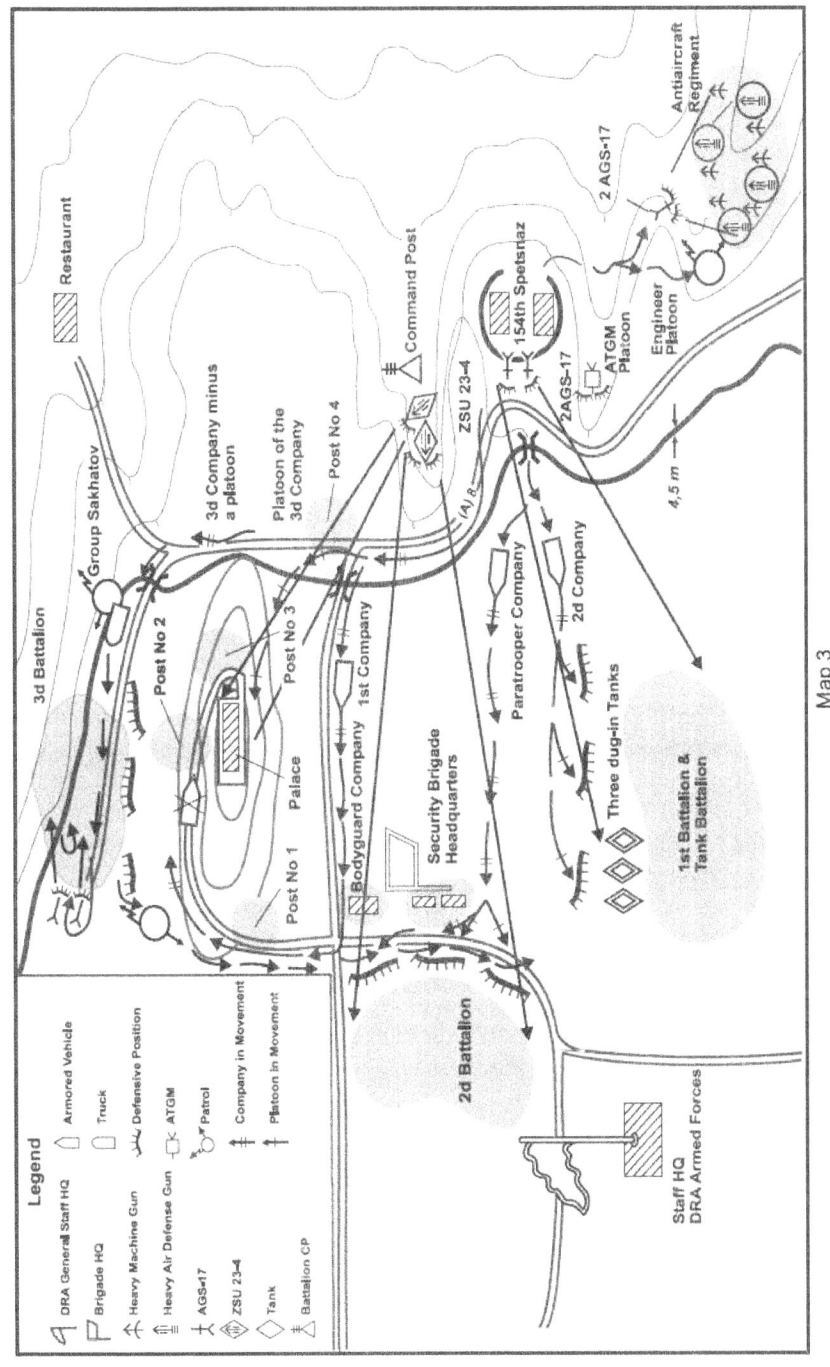

Map 3

casino where high-ranking officers of the Afghan army usually gathered. Under the pretext of finding a place for their officers to gather for a New Year's celebration, the Spetsnaz commanders visited the establishment. From there, the Tadzh-Bek was clearly visible, as were the approaches to the palace and the outposts sited to protect it. The commanders conducted a thorough reconnaissance and then started to drive back to brief their findings. At the second outpost, a suspicious Afghan officer stopped, disarmed, and held them for four hours. Finally, after much tea drinking and conversation, the commanders were released. It was a day before the assault, and the reconnaissance was accomplished. The KGB Spetsnaz knew the approach routes; the guard schedule; the total number of Amin's guards and bodyguards; the location of machine gun nests, armored vehicles, and tanks; the internal arrangement of rooms and corridors in the palace; and the location of radios and telephone equipment.

That night, the Aghan president to be, Babrak Karmal, and some members of his entourage secretly flew into Kabul from the Soviet Union with the 103d Airborne Division. They were whisked to the Soviet embassy and late that night hidden in a truck convoy bound for Bagram airfield. They were kept in the Muslim battalion base camp at the airfield, guarded by KGB Spetsnaz.

The morning of 27 December dawned, and Soviet personnel prepared for the assault. The Spetsnaz commanders made another reconnaissance, and while they were scrutinizing the area through binoculars, they saw Major Dzhandad and a group of his officers studying the Muslim battalion's defenses. Lieutenant Colonel Shvets went over to Dzhandad and invited him for dinner, ostensibly in honor of one of the officer's birthday. The Afghan brigade commander replied that he and his men were conducting training, but they would come by that evening. Then Shvets asked Dzhandad to release his Soviet advisers for the dinner and took them away with him. This act saved many Soviet lives. Reports of the Afghans' reconnaissance was reported to KGB Central, which sent back the message, "Begin the assault at 1500."

At this time, President Amin, not suspecting the imminent coup, was in a state of euphoria. He had achieved his goal of bringing Soviet troops into Afghanistan. On the afternoon of 27 December, he held a magnificent dinner, bringing several members of the Afghan politburo and his ministries, along with their families, into his luxurious palace. It was a formal occasion marking both the anniversary of the founding of the People's Democratic Party of Afghanistan (PDPA) and the return of the Secretary of the Central Committee of the PDPA, Pandsheri, from

Moscow. This return assured Amin that the Soviet leadership was satisfied with his version of Taraki's natural death and the change of leadership in the country. Pandsheri's visit seemed to have strengthened the new regime's relationship with the Soviet Union and confirmed that the Soviets would provide a broad range of military assistance. At the reception, Amin solemnly addressed those present. "The Soviet divisions are already on the way here. Paratroopers have landed in Kabul. All is going well. I am constantly on the telephone communicating with Comrade Gromiko, and we are discussing the best way to inform the world about this Soviet military assistance."[24]

At 1500, KGB General Drozdov transmitted a message from the Soviet embassy changing the time of the assault (H-hour) to 2200. He later changed it again, this time to 2100. Still later on, other changes were made until H-hour finally stood at 1930. Soviet cooks had prepared the dinner, and Amin, his children, and his daughter-in-law, as well as many guests, suddenly fell ill. Some, including Amin, lost consciousness. Amin's wife quickly called the security brigade commander, Major Dzhandad, who called the Central Military Hospital and the Soviet Embassy's medical clinic to summon help. The food and pomegranate juice were immediately sent to the hospital for examination. The cooks were detained, and the guard was reinforced. However, the primary perpetrators disappeared, and eventually the cooks were freed unharmed.

The Soviet surgeons who were stationed in Kabul, along with Afghan Lieutenant Colonel Veloyat Habbi, chief of the Central Military Hospital, and Abdul Kayum Tutakhel, the chief surgeon, arrived at the palace. They were there at the request of the Afghan chief of the Main Political Directorate, M. Ekbabla Waziri, and the chief of the political department of the apparatus of the main armed forces in the DRA, General Major S.P. Tutushkina.

When Colonel Anatoli Vladomirovich Alekseyev, commander of the Soviet surgical group that was supplementing the hospital staff; Colonel Viktor Petrovich Kuznechenkov, a doctor; and other medical personnel approached the interior guard post, they handed in their weapons as usual. However, they were subjected to a search, which had not happened before. Further, they were addressed sharply. At the entrance to the palace, their documents were checked much more carefully than usual. Then they were searched again. They understood why when they entered the lobby and saw people lying down or sitting unnaturally in the lobby, on the stair steps, and in the rooms. Those who had regained consciousness were writhing in pain. The doctors diagnosed the problem at once—widespread poisoning. They started to help the suffering people, but Lieutenant Colonel Veloyat Habibi ran up to them and took them with him to Amin. The head of state was in serious condition. Amin lay in one of the rooms, undressed and looking like a corpse with a slack jaw and rolling eyes. He was in a deep coma. Was he dead? They took his pulse. There was a barely perceptible beat.

Colonels Kuznechenhov and Alekseyev did not consider that they might be interfering with someone's plan and began to save the chief "friend of the USSR." First they closed his jaw and then restored his breathing. They put him in a bathroom, cleaned him up, and began administering liquids to force diuresis. After that, they again transferred him to a bedroom. They gave him injections and more injections, then intravenous (IV) drips. There were IV needles in both his hands. Their work continued until 1800, during which time they managed to save Amin's life. But, feeling that disturbing events were afoot, Alekseyev sent the women out of the palace and insisted that a laboratory analysis be conducted to determine the source of the problem. A long time passed until Amin regained consciousness and, expressing surprise, asked, "Why did this happen in my house? Who did it? Was it an accident or sabotage?"

The incident greatly upset the Afghan security brigade officers. They established additional security posts, including internal posts manned by Afghan military personnel, and put a tank brigade on alert to be ready to provide assistance. But help had no way to arrive. Soviet paratroopers had completely isolated the Afghan military units garrisoned in Kabul. Soviet adviser V.G. Salkin described the events in Kabul:

> In the evening at approximately 1830, Captain Achmed Dzhana, the brigade commander, received the order to move one battalion into the city. At that time, Colonel Viktor Nikolaevich Pyasetskiy, the adviser to the brigade commander, and I were colocated with the brigade commander. The commander ordered that the first tank battalion be brought to full combat alert. Movement orders would follow. Instantly tank engines roared and the first battalion was ready for action. Pyasetskiy looked at his watch from time to time, expecting new orders from the security brigade. At 1900, Colonel Pyasetskiy himself asked Captain Dzhana to contact his higher headquarters. However, he was unable to call since the telephones were not working.
>
> Colonel Pyasetskiy advised the commander to check on the integrity of the telephone wire within the brigade's territory. The signal platoon

> was quickly summoned and the soldiers began to check the connections thoroughly. This lasted about thirty minutes.
>
> Suddenly, a column of four BMDs knocked down the garrison gates and quickly surrounded the brigade headquarters building. A Soviet captain jumped down from the lead vehicle. He entered the building, introduced himself, took Colonel Pyasetskiy aside and conversed with him, then took out a flask of spirits and proposed a drink. The captain addressed the commander of the brigade and stated that the city was restless and that the presence of the tank brigade in the city would be undesirable. After consultation, the brigade commander gave the order to stand down the first battalion.[25]

Shortly before 1900, KGB Colonel Kozlov called General Magomedov, the chief Soviet military adviser, and told him that due to unforeseen circumstances, the time of the assault had changed and it was necessary to start as soon as possible. After some fifteen minutes, the twelve-man assault group led by Captain Sakhatov boarded its truck and started to drive to the hill where the tanks were dug in. Their mission was to seize the tanks and prevent their being used against the assault groups. Further, they were to deceive the defending palace guard, pretending that the members of the Afghan Security Brigade had revolted and were attacking the palace. The Soviets had to create the impression that the first volleys fired came from the security brigade headquarters caserne. The 2d Company of the Muslim battalion lay in wait at its designated position ready to support the movement of Group Sakhatov by fire.[26]

As planned, Sakhatov's group moved out fifteen minutes before the beginning of the assault. As they drove through the Afghan 3d Battalion area, they saw that the battalion was on alert. The battalion commander and deputies were standing in the center of the parade ground while weapons and ammunition were being issued to battalion personnel. Quickly estimating the situation, Sakhatov decided to capture the 3d Infantry Battalion's command group. Moving at top speed, the truck full of Spetsnaz suddenly braked by the Afghan officers, and within a few seconds, the officers were lying on the floor of the truck. The GAZ-66 jumped forward, leaving a cloud of dust behind.

During the first few minutes, the soldiers of the battalion did not understand what had happened, but then they opened fire on the fleeing vehicle. It was too late. The dust cloud hid the vehicle, and the firing was ineffective. Sakhatov drove 200 meters and then, reaching advantageous terrain, stopped the vehicle and unloaded his personnel. The Spetsnaz immediately lay down and opened fire on the pursuing 3d

Battalion soldiers. The leaderless Afghans bunched up, presenting a fine target. The two machine guns and eight assault rifles from Sakhatov's group killed more than 200 personnel. In the meantime, the snipers removed the guards by the tanks. When the vehicle holding Group Sakhatov left the Afghan 3d Battalion's position, Colonel Kozlov heard the firing and quickly gave the commands "Fire" and "Advance" to the officers and soldiers of the Muslim battalion, paratroop company, and KGB Spetsnaz groups. Red rockets flew into the air. Wristwatches showed 1915. Over the radio crackled the code word to begin the assault, "Storm-333."

Senior Lieutenant Vasiliy Praut opened the initial direct fire on the palace using two ZSU Shilka 23-4 self-propelled air defense guns, pouring out a stream of bullets. Two other ZSU-23-4s fired on the 2d Battalion in support of Group Sakhatov. AGS-17 automatic grenade launchers fired on the tank battalion position, preventing the crews from reaching their tanks.

The Soviet 2d and 3d companies and the paratrooper company moved out in their armored vehicles to block the security brigade's battalions. Meanwhile, the 1st Company, together with the KGB Spetsnaz groups, headed toward the palace. Most of Zenith was mounted on four BTRs that were to lead out and drive to the western part of the hill. There, dismounting, they would climb the stairs to the western facing of Tadzh-Bek and then move around to the front of the building to link up with Thunder. Five BMPs from the first company had most of KGB Spetsnaz Group Thunder onboard. They were to drive to the front entrance of the palace and dismount.

Zenith moved out. The BTRs drove past the external outposts and moved onto the single road that snaked up the mountain to the dismount area in front of the palace. The road was well protected, and other approaches were mined. Hardly had the first vehicle passed the first turn when it was hit by heavy machine gun fire. The following BTR was immediately hit and set on fire, causing the personnel inside to evacuate the vehicle. Some were wounded. The vehicle commander was shot in the groin with a bullet entering just below his flak jacket. It was impossible to rescue him, and he bled profusely. The Zenith personnel disembarking from the BTR had to lie down and return fire at the windows of the palace and then begin to climb up the hill using assault ladders.

At this time, subgroup Thunder began to move out. The lead vehicle came under fire, and the driver stopped the vehicle, opened the hatch, jumped out, and ran for cover. The vehicle was under fire from outpost

1, which it had just passed. The BMP's back doors swung open to dismount troops to deal with this outpost. The first two out were translators who were immediately killed. All the BMPs then opened fire on the outpost and subdued it. The lead vehicle's driver reappeared, and the column again moved out and began to climb the serpentine road. The BMPs were firing their onboard machine guns and turret cannon furiously as they snaked around the palace. They ran out of ammunition before they reached the dismount point. Searchlights from the palace picked up the assault groups, and fire sprayed the vehicles. Unable to penetrate the thick palace walls, bullets from the ZSU-23-4s ricocheted wildly against the armored vehicles and among the dismounting troops. As the assault force continued to dismount, heavy defensive fire ripped into it, killing or wounding many soldiers and destroying a BMP. Fortunately for the Soviets, the palace guard was armed with 9mm West German Heckler & Koch MP5 submachine guns that could not penetrate the Soviet flak jackets. Still, the flak jackets did not stop bullets from striking limbs and groins, and the ricocheting 23mm rounds and defenders' heavy machine gun bullets ripped through the flak jackets.

The survivors from Zenith arrived at the front entrance of the palace and, joining the survivors from Thunder, climbed through a window into the building. One group began to clear the ground floor while another charged up the stairs in a hail of fire. V. Grishin of the KGB Spetsnaz recalls:

> There were shots from everywhere. Lenya Gumenniy stood by a box near the stair landing and gave me some ammunition while I reloaded assault rifle magazines. There were other guys there. We began to gather by the entrance door leading to the corridor that opens onto the rooms on the second floor. We had to open the doors and rush the corridor. We got ready and reloaded magazines. Then it became dark. Before we rushed forward, we had to fire our assault rifles or throw grenades, as we learned in training. We kicked open the door. Sergey Aleksandrovich threw a grenade, but the door flew back so hard that it rebounded off the wall and slammed shut. The grenade hit the door and bounced back at us. Lenya and I managed to jump down off the stair landing and lay flat. Everyone else instantly lay down as the grenade exploded.[27]

The group picked itself up and rushed inside and down the corridor. Intense fire filled the building. On both floors, the Spetsnaz began clearing the rooms, throwing a grenade inside and then raking the room with fire. They were worked into a killing frenzy, and their orders were to leave no witnesses.

Amin was upstairs wandering around in shorts and an Adidas tee-shirt. He had IV drips in both arms and was dragging the IV stand with him. His terrified five-year-old son clung to his leg. Amin ordered his aide to notify his Soviet military advisers about the attack on the palace. Amin told him, "The Soviets will help us." But his aide replied, "The Soviets are doing the shooting." These words upset the president, and he picked up an ashtray and threw it at his aide, shouting, "You are lying, it cannot be!" Then Amin, himself, tried to call the chief of the General Staff, but communications were already cut. Amin quietly said, "I suspected it. I was right." He lay down on the counter of a large wooden bar. He was still alive when the first Soviet assault troops cleared the room. When they returned later, someone had killed Amin. His body lay wrapped in a carpet. The assault force cleared the third floor to complete the capture of the palace. The action lasted 45 minutes. They passed the word to KGB General Drozdov. Drozdov immediately contacted KGB Chief Yuri Andropov in Moscow and confirmed that Amin was dead. A main goal had been achieved.[28]

Outside the palace, the Muslim battalion, supported by the captured tanks and the ZSU-23-4 antiaircraft machine guns, smashed and scattered the Afghan Security Brigade. The tanks and ZSU-23-4s were moved in around the palace as the Muslim battalion and assault force formed a perimeter defense on the frozen ground, anticipating an Afghan tank attack that never came.

The Soviets began evacuating their dead and wounded. After the fight, they counted casualties. In the KGB Spetsnaz group, five men, including overall palace assault commander Colonel Grigoriy Boyarinov, were killed during the assault on the palace. Practically all the thirty-six remaining Spetsnaz were wounded, but those who could still hold a weapon continued to fight. Five Spetsnaz were also killed in the Muslim battalion, and thirty-five were wounded. Of these, twenty-three wounded men remained with the formation during the fight. One of the Soviet doctors who treated Amin was also killed.

The Afghans suffered major losses. Although a significant number of the security brigade soldiers surrendered, the fighting continued after the palace was captured. The Muslim battalion fought the remainder of the 3d Battalion for a full day, after which the Afghans fled into the mountains. Most of the Afghan officers and soldiers were captured. The entire antiaircraft regiment surrendered without a fight, and the tank battalion did not offer any resistance. Amin's personal bodyguard had 300 men, of which half were captured and the rest killed, wounded, or missing. His security brigade was shattered and scattered. Total

Afghan prisoners numbered nearly 1,700 men. Amin's five-year-old and eight-year-old sons were killed, and his daughter was wounded.

Blowing Up the Shaft

At 1930, Kabul thundered with strong explosions. A ten-man KGB subgroup from Zenith blew up the so-called shaft communications juncture, disconnecting the Afghan capital from the outside world. Aleksei Polyakov, a Spetsnaz commander recalls:

> I received the order to conduct the sabotage. I conducted another visual reconnaissance of the target and returned to the villa. . . . I gathered my group, briefed the time we would carry out the sabotage, and assigned the mission to blow up the cable communications shaft at 1930.
>
> At 1845, we left on three motor vehicles to carry out the mission of the high command. I left one man behind at the villa and gave him the order that, in case our operation failed, he should close down everything and leave our embassy, and go to the border guards company. Since I did not have enough interpreters for my group, I requested that an interpreter be allocated to my detachment. As developments demonstrated, if my detachment had not had an interpreter, we could not have carried out the operation bloodlessly.
>
> When we arrived at the target area, I was with the subgroup which would provide cover. We were in a UAZ 469 jeep which moved close to a traffic regulators post. The second covering group was in a 'Volga' sedan which parked close to a hotel. Boris Pleshkunov's subgroup had the interpreter, Khayatov, and was seated in a UAZ 450 jeep which moved up to the 'shaft.' It was necessary to distract the communications center guard post while the cover to the 'shaft' was opened. The interpreter trotted up to the guard, explained that there was going to be a communications check, offered him a cigarette, and distracted him with conversation.[29]

The hatch was locked, so the padlock had to be cut with bolt cutters. Then the hatch was opened, and a rucksack loaded with two explosive charges and timers was lowered to the bottom of the water-filled shaft. A tear gas grenade was also tossed down the shaft to complicate repair. The whole thing took a few seconds. The timers were set for 15 minutes. The group got back in their cars, leaving the interpreter to chat with the guards. After several minutes they were back at their villa.[30] At 1930, a strong explosion, the signal for the general assault on Kabul, thundered.

Taking Down the General Staff

The Afghan Army General Staff building was another difficult objective. While preparing for the mission, subgroup Zenith commander KGB Major Valeriy Rozin accompanied Soviet adviser for combat training General A. Vlasov on a visit inside the newly occupied General Staff building. Until recently, the building had been a museum. Rozin was only able to examine part of the building, but subsequently, he visited an architect who was able to draw up a complete floor plan of the entire building, including the guard posts, based on Rozin's reconnaissance. Rozin worked out a detailed plan of operation, assigning tasks to each member and working out coordination.

At 1850 on 27 December, Rozin, two border guards, and fourteen Spetsnaz from subgroup Zenith boarded vehicles and left the Soviet Embassy heading to the General Staff building. Abdul Vakil', an Afghan accomplice, accompanied them. They arrived at the site about 1900. One group of Spetsnaz went up to the first floor in the left wing of the building where the offices of the Afghan chief of staff were located. The rest of the Spetsnaz stayed on the ground floor and in the lobby, waiting for the appointed time.

Rozin noticed that the number of Afghans in the building—at the external guard posts, the posts in the lobby and on both floors, plus the number of civilians and officers present—was considerably more than during his earlier reconnaissance. In the communications center, there were three communications specialists on duty, plus about fifteen Afghan soldiers with assault rifles. The two normal sentries were at the building facings on the left and right side of the entrance, reinforced by seven to ten other Afghan soldiers. Several soldiers were located in ground floor rooms. Apparently some information about the operation may have leaked out—possibly even the planned starting time. The Afghans were watching the Soviets attentively. The "legend" or cover that got the group inside the building was a scheduled meeting between General I.F. Ryabchenko, commander of the 103d Airborne Division, and General M. Yakub, chief of the Afghan General Staff.

About 1900, Ryabchenko, General P.G. Kostenko (the Soviet adviser to the chief of the Afghan General Staff), General A.A. Vlasov, Rozin (who had airborne coveralls over his Spetsnaz uniform and was playing the role of Ryabchenko's deputy for technical units), and A. Pliev (the interpreter) entered the chief of staff's office, depositing their weapons at the reception desk. The Afghans searched them. An officer, L. Lagoiskiy, and Spetsnaz personnel V. Irvanev and I. Vasil'ev accompanied Ryabchenko, who remained in the corridor during the reception. General Yakub affably greeted his visitors and invited them to sit at his table. The meeting began. General Vlasov introduced the division commander to the chief of General Staff of the Armed Forces of the DRA. They began to discuss questions of mutual cooperation. Ryabchenko had not been briefed on the coming action, therefore he behaved normally. As the time for the start of the action neared, Vlasov and Kostenko left Yakub's office under various pretexts.

At the same time, the Spetsnaz dispersed in the lobby and corridors of the ground and first floor of the General Staff building. They covered the majority of the Afghans located there. To distract the Afghans' attention and achieve surprise, the Spetsnaz became acquainted with the Afghans, offered them cigarettes, and talked with them about accompanying the division commander and providing his protection.

At 1930, a strong explosion rocked the city. Yakub also heard the noise but continued to speak. Obviously he had already guessed everything but did not lose his self-control. Then he rushed to the table where a German 9mm MG-5 submachine gun lay. Major Rozin rushed to cut him off. Hand-to-hand combat ensued. Yakub was physically very powerful (he was under six feet tall and weighed over 250 pounds) and was an agile and well-trained individual. He had graduated from the Ryazan Airborne Academy, spoke Russian very well, and was a great friend of the Soviet Union. It would not have gone easily for Rozin, but at that moment, three Soviet soldiers and several Afghans burst into the room. Ryabchenko, not understanding what was happening, remained seated, but Pliev, the interpreter, joined the fight. In the cross-fire that ensued, Yakub was wounded and one of his assistants was killed. The chief of the General Staff quickly disappeared into a break room, where, it turned out, there were some more well-equipped Afghan army soldiers and also a deputy to the Minister of Internal Affairs. Pliev offered the Afghans in the break room the chance to surrender. They began to come out, one at a time, with their hands raised.

At this time, three Spetsnaz disarmed the sentry at the communications center in a short hand-to-hand fight, cut the telephone wires leading out of the building at the stairway, and suppressed the guards' resistance with automatic weapons fire. Then the Spetsnaz smashed the most vulnerable and important communications gear. This paralyzed the command of the divisions and regiments located in Kabul and supported the success of all Soviet actions in the Afghan capital. Two Zenith officers blocked the ground floor entrance of the building's right wing, denying entry to Afghan guards. Two others similarly controlled the entry to the left wing. Simultaneously, they prevented the Afghan soldiers from exiting the rooms. Meanwhile, I. Pestsov and two border guards remained in the lobby and liquidated the guards at the front entrance.

After knocking out the communications center, V. Kudrik, V. Stemilov, and A. Maskov ran upstairs to the first floor to help Yu. Titov and Yu. Klimov with their fight. Hand-to-hand combat and gunfights in the upstairs rooms of the first floor were long and fierce. The Soviets moved into these rooms firing furiously. Part of the Afghan military personnel sheltered on the second floor. The Spetsnaz did not assault the second floor. The Afghans sheltering there could not leave since the warriors of Zenith controlled all the exits.

In the meantime, the chief of the General Staff's guards were tied up and placed under guard. The wounded General Yakub lay down in the break room. When the fight was over, Abdul Vakil' came into the chief of staff's break room. He spoke with the wounded general for a long time in Pashtu and then shot him with a pistol.

As Afghan resistance was suppressed in various parts of the building, the Spetsnaz collected about 100 prisoners in the large hall. Many were in shock, and although they were all disarmed, they still represented a real threat to the handful of Spetsnaz. Major Rozin ordered that all of them be tied up immediately. There was no rope, so they used ripped-out telephone wire.

The fight had lasted more than an hour. When it began to calm down, a company of paratroopers arrived at the General Staff building on BMDs. They began firing at the windows with their machine guns and assault rifles. The Spetsnaz had to lie down on the floor or find shelter to avoid fratricide. Tracer bullets clawed into the walls of the rooms, burning with a red light and creating a unique show. Rozin began to shout to the division commander to stop the firing. General Ryabchenko ordered one of his officers to contact the company commander immediately. Somewhat later, a signalman with an R-105 radio arrived, and the division commander took command. The paratroopers quickly overcame the remaining pockets of resistance and captured the second floor. The Afghans lost twenty men, and more than 100 officers and soldiers were captured. In the assault group, two men were lightly wounded.[31]

We Interrupt This Program to Bring You a Special Announcement

The reconnaissance company of the 345th Separate Parachute Regiment, reinforced by a ZSU-23-4 and nine Spetsnaz from Zenith, was supposed to capture the radio and television center. For this reason, the reconnaissance company moved from Bagram to Kabul on 21 December and deployed not far from the embassy communications center. The company commander, Senior Lieutenant Aleksandr Popov, and the commander of the Zenith group, KGB Major Anatoliy Ryabinin, planned the upcoming mission. The paratroopers would capture the center's outside grounds and destroy the weapons deployed there; the Spetsnaz would fight inside the buildings.

They understood that success in battle could be ensured only by careful preparation; therefore, they prepared for this operation very thoroughly. Major Ryabinin had earlier visited the site twice. Posing as an automatic switching engineer, he found out where the radio and television studios were, where the signals were sent into the ether, where the switching terminals were, and where the primary and backup power systems were.

Initially, Lieutenant Popov drove around the radio and television center with some Spetsnaz from Zenith and determined its general arrangement and the primary approaches to it. Then he changed into civilian clothes and, along with his platoon leaders, conducted a detailed reconnaissance of the approaches to the objectives, the entrances and exits, and the location of the guard posts and weapons. Popov determined the location of the guard posts, military equipment, the caserne, and the distribution of personnel and weapons. Then the platoon leaders calculated the driving time to the objective on various routes. Using these data, they planned the assault.

The plan was to seize the radio and television center and surrounding area using two axes. Two platoons, commanded by Deputy Company Commander Senior Lieutenant S. Loktev would attack from the vicinity of the American Embassy, cut off the tank crews from their tanks, and then either destroy or capture them. The other attack would be on the left axis using the reconnaissance platoon, the command group, and the squad of Zenith Spetsnaz. This main attack would break down the gate, seize the site, and support the capture group. Two variants were also planned. One plan was to conduct the attack mounted on BMDs. The other variant was a surprise night attack on foot without fire preparation.

In the middle of the day on 27 December, the company commander received his combat mission from Colonel A. Kukushkin, the chief of reconnaissance of the airborne forces. Lieutenant Popov relayed the order to his platoon leaders, and they, in turn, gave every paratrooper his specific mission. The BMD drivers and vehicle commanders received particular instructions. An Afghan accomplice, A.M. Vatandzhar, accompanied the Soviet soldiers. The order to begin the operation arrived at 1830. It stipulated that the assault would begin at 1930. They would seize the objective and then defend it. Major Ryabinin was in a BMD with the company commander. The Spetsnaz group from Zenith was in a BTR along with Vatandzhar.

At the appointed time, the combat vehicles began to move, but unexpectedly, the march column was cut in two by a battalion of Soviet paratroopers. The BTR with the Spetsnaz and Vatandzhar lagged behind. A. Popov, recalling that time, stated, "We did not know that there were other paratrooper regiments in Kabul, therefore we were extremely surprised and did not understand where these paratroopers came from." The reconnaissance company arrived at the objective at the designated time. The paratroopers attacked the objective on two axes, knocked down the gate, and shot the sentries. They attacked with RPG-18 hand-held antitank grenade launchers and destroyed three tanks and a BMP. The paratroopers captured another tank and took the crew captive. The rest of the tanks and BMPs—there were eleven tanks and four BMPs on the objective—did not offer any resistance. Not one Afghan tank fired its main gun, although all the weapons were loaded and the crews had been on combat alert since 1700. They were not told whom they were to fight against. They simply fired their machine guns, then drove away from the objective and parked, waiting for something.

In the meantime, the Spetsnaz group rushed into the radio and television buildings and took possession of them. The fight lasted about 40 minutes. After seizing the building, the Spetsnaz searched the Afghan radio and television personnel and moved them under guard to a single room. Vatandzhar provided major assistance to the group. He arranged the surrender of the crews from the tanks that were standing some distance away. He explained the situation to them and guaranteed their safety with the change in regime. All the crews from seven tanks and three BMPs surrendered. The Soviets collected weapons and 106 prisoners. Seven Afghans were killed and twenty-nine wounded. One paratrooper was wounded in the leg.

Vatandzhar then addressed the radio and television center employees and, working with the Afghan experts, set up the transmission of a broadcast to the people by Babrak Karmal declaring the formation of a new government. The paratroopers monitored the transmissions and guarded the buildings. Subsequently, the radio and television center was transferred to representatives of the new government of Afghanistan. Its guard force was changed to a company of the 103d Airborne Division.[32]

Telegraphing the Blow

At 2020, Aleksandr Puntus led a platoon of paratroopers and nine Spetsnaz from Zenith as they drove up to the telegraph building. Finding the gate locked, Puntus and his interpreter got out of their vehicle and began to explain to an Afghan officer who approached them that they had come to reinforce the telegraph guard and asked him to let them in. The officer replied that he had orders not to let anyone near the site. The officer said that approximately an hour earlier there had been a strong explosion near the telegraph building. As a result, there was a large crater, and the building was damaged. Since none of the attempts to persuade the Afghan officer worked, a peaceful entry into the building was impossible.

After reporting the situation, the group was ordered to seize the telegraph building by force. The operation began at 2100 when a BTR knocked the gate down and drove into the courtyard. The group's fire neutralized the guards near the building and patrolling the premises. Then the paratroopers and Spetsnaz rushed into the building and quickly captured all three floors. The operation took 20 minutes and was carried out successfully despite the initial resistance of the thirty-two Afghan soldiers at the site.

The Afghan soldiers were disarmed and placed under guard in the guard room. In addition to the soldiers, telegraph employees (twenty men and twelve women) were on duty. They were all searched and held in rooms on the third floor of the building. They offered no resistance. The Soviets turned off the equipment with the help of Afghan experts. The captives were fed, calmed down, and provided with a place to sleep for the night. The next morning, they were all released to return to their own houses. Neither side suffered casualties. After capturing the telegraph building, the Soviets established outside guard posts to control the building entrances.[33]

Taking Down the Police Station and Ministry of Internal Affairs

At 1930, two platoons of paratroopers and fourteen Spetsnaz from Zenith led by Yuri Mel'nik began the assault on the Ministry of Internal Affairs (MVD) building and the *Sarandoy* (National Armed Police) headquarters, which were in the same compound. They worked quickly and decisively. Three open-bed trucks approached the site and stopped at the traffic control post (KPP). They hit the compound with a salvo of seven hand-held RPG-18 antitank grenade launchers, creating confusion among the 350-man security force. This allowed the paratroopers to dash quickly from the KPP to the MVD building. When the attackers were fired on from the building, the assault group conducted a resolute attack and, in a few minutes, had driven the guard from the ground floor and taken possession of it. Then the paratroopers, using continuous fire and throwing grenades, ascended the stairs. It took 15 minutes to seize the remaining floors. The Afghans, not understanding what was happening, were demoralized, and the resistance stopped.

During the gunfight, Captain Anatoliy Muranov of Zenith was shot through both thighs. Major V. Sisin, the MVD adviser, attempted to help him and took him to the embassy medical clinic where Muranov died of trauma and loss of blood. A large number of Afghans were taken captive. The Soviet MVD advisers assisted the paratroopers and Spetsnaz.

Kosogorskiy, the MVD senior adviser, ordered the arrest of Minister of Internal Affairs A. Sh. Payman, but he was not in the MVD building. Payman, still in his underwear, ran to the residence of Soviet MVD advisers where Major N. Nazarov discovered him. On the morning of the following day, Payman was brought to the operations directing staff. General B.S. Ivanov had him write a message to the Afghan people appealing to them to preserve calm and order in the country. At 1400 on 28 December, his message was broadcast on the radio. On 29 December, new Minister of Internal Affairs S.M. Gulyabzoy and the new commander of the *Sarandoy*, Lieutenant Colonel Asgar, arrived at the MVD building and began work. They had been Amin's prisoners in the Pul-e Charki prison.[34]

Taking Down the Central Army Corps Headquarters

The headquarters of the Afghan Central Army Corps (CAC) and its security subunit were situated in the building complex known as the

"House of the People." In all, there were over 1,000 men with artillery, BTRs, and small arms. A company of paratroopers, six Spetsnaz from Zenith, and six Soviet military advisers were allocated for its capture. Their mission included seizing the objective; taking over the CAC staff's command, control, and communications; identifying staff personnel who were sympathetic to the new government to screen out and isolate Amin's supporters; and using the staff to prevent Aghan military actions against the Soviet forces.

The group was split into subgroups. At the start of the operation, the first subgroup's mission was to capture the caserne, the air defense battalion's weapons, the artillery park located at the House of the People, and the signal battalion's caserne. The subgroup commander telephoned the senior Afghan officer, who was a division political officer, and through an interpreter, advised him that Amin was overthrown. He told him that a democratic government had come into power and that Soviet forces were providing assistance in supporting order in Kabul at the new government's request. The Soviet commander gave a clear ultimatum and demanded that all conditions be met without bloodshed. The Afghan officer accepted all the Soviet conditions with alacrity and, together with the battalion chief of staff, carried them out. The military adviser to the signal battalion commander convinced his counterpart not to resist. By 2015, the subgroup completely controlled its assigned sector.

A BTR and small arms fired on the other Soviet subgroup as it entered the corps staff's territory. The paratroopers and Spetsnaz returned fire and quickly suppressed the resistance and destroyed the BTR. The subgroup commander called an Afghan staff officer and, through an interpreter, congratulated him on the victory of the democratic forces of Afghanistan. Then he demanded that the Afghan officer disarm the security company and the corps staff officers.

One of the captured Afghans volunteered that the corps commander, General M. Dust, was in one of the staff rooms with ten soldiers and his bodyguard. When the assault group rushed into the building and demanded that Dust surrender, the defending Afghans answered with gunfire. As the fight was joined, the assault group suppressed the resistance with automatic fire and grenades and captured the corps staff, except for the corps commander and his security guards who escaped across the roof of the military publishing house.

The subgroup commander, taking advantage of the lull, organized a fire-fighting detail to extinguish a fire started during the gunfight. He also directed the rescue of weapons and equipment from the fire. Parts of both details were Afghan officers and soldiers who proclaimed their loyalty to the new regime. By the morning of 28 December, the fire in the building was extinguished, and the signal center was back in working order. All the combat vehicles of the group occupied defensive positions around the objective. At the back of the building, two BMD crews fired machine guns and automatic weapons to suppress centers of Afghan resistance.

As dawn broke, the Soviets began combing the staff building and surrounding area. They detained an Afghan soldier who stated that General Dust was hiding in the military publishing house. The group commander had the soldier convey a surrender demand to Dust after explaining in detail the political situation to the soldier. When Dust was convinced that the Soviet officers were speaking the truth, he surrendered.

The group commander, together with the Soviet military advisers, quickly began to use the corps commander to issue orders to the CAC divisions and regiments. The orders recognized the new government and directed resistance to cease. Dust issued orders to the following units: the 88th Artillery Brigade; the 4th and 15th Tank Brigades; the Pukhantun Military Academy; the 26th Parachute Regiment; the 37th "Commando" Brigade; the 7th and 8th Infantry Divisions; the 190th Artillery Regiment; the CAC reconnaissance battalion; the 9th Mountain Infantry Division; the 41st Infantry Regiment; and separate units and subunits located in Bamian, Wardak, Parwan, Kapisa, Kabul, Logar, and Nangahar provinces.

On the morning of 28 December, the CAC staff intercepted a telegram from the governor of Nangahar province that ordered an infantry division and the 444th "Commando" Regiment to advance on Kabul. The adviser to the CAC knew that Colonel Sabur, the division commander, was the captive CAC signal battalion commander's brother. The Soviets convinced the captive commander to talk by phone with his brother, explain the political situation to him, and convince him to side with the new Afghan government. In this manner, the advance on Kabul was broken up. Later that morning, joint Soviet-Afghan posts provided CAC headquarters security. On the following day, the corps staff returned to the House of the People and to work.[35]

Countering Counterintelligence

Capturing the Afghan Military Counterintelligence Building was rather difficult. Two paratrooper platoons, twelve military advisers, and six Zenith Spetsnaz were detailed to capture this objective. Rafael Shafigulin headed the force that also included three BMDs, two GAZ-66 trucks, and two air defense weapons. The group developed a plan and coordinated it with the advisers. The attack would penetrate the perimeter at three entry points. BMDs would conduct the breakthrough, approaching and then securing the main building. Dismounting personnel would disarm the outside guards, and the "capture group" of twenty-one men would enter the main building, disarm the personnel inside, and detain designated personnel. They decided not to engage the security force but to cut it off from the objective using BMD machine gun and air defense weapon cross-fire. They moved out at 1830.

During the breakthrough, one of the BMDs was damaged and lost mobility. The group commander was in this vehicle, and he decided that his part of the group would assault the closest door. Under the cover of BMD machine gun fire, the group burst into the building and joined up with Chuchukin, the Soviet adviser, who had been there since before the start of the operation. The group then began to carry out its primary mission and suppress the mounting fire. The Spetsnaz and paratroopers of the second group burst through the building's main entrance. The combined group's actions were quick and resolute. Enemy troops inside the building decided not to resist and surrendered their weapons. All the counterintelligence personnel on the Soviet capture list and some members of the government were among the prisoners. The Afghan security personnel who were cut off from the objective heard the noise of battle and left. During the night, separate groups returned and surrendered their weapons. There were about 150 captured soldiers. The Afghan guards at the remaining buildings and soldiers assigned to the site surrendered after hearing Soviet demands on a megaphone.

The other objectives in the Afghan capital were captured without significant problems. On the morning of the 28th, Babrak Karmal was fully in power in Kabul, which was controlled by 103d Airborne Division paratroopers. Soviet ground divisions pushed resolutely southward to gain control of the main lines of communication and airfields in the country. The capture of Kabul was a clear success. The Soviets planned to hold it and other key points while the new DRA president turned his army to fighting the Mujahideen resistance. This was not to be. The DRA army was unable to defeat the Mujahideen, and quickly the Soviet army was dragged into combat in the countryside. The 201st Motorized Rifle Division and other units arrived to reinforce the 40th Army. The Soviet army was now involved in a foreign civil war on some of the toughest terrain on the planet. The brilliance of the capture of Kabul was soon eclipsed by fruitless Soviet operations that accomplished little. The Soviet army was stuck in Afghanistan for nine bloody years.

Analysis

The coup de main is so different from the normal experience of bloody, deliberate urban combat that this account may seem out of place in this volume. However, that is the main point. Any military professional who studies urban combat quickly concludes that it is not the place to fight. But sometimes cities cannot be avoided. If a city has to be taken, it is usually best taken with surprise and audacity.

The Soviet coup de main model was markedly successful in rapidly gaining control of Afghanistan and its main cities. This stands in contrast to the disastrous October-November 1956 operation against Hungary in which the Soviets lost 669 killed in action (KIA), 1,540 wounded in action (WIA), and 51 missing in action. In the August-October 1968 Soviet invasion of Czechoslovakia, the Soviets greatly improved and only lost 11 KIA, 85 killed in accidents, and 87 WIA. The initial December 1979 incursion in Afghanistan resulted in Soviet losses of 24 KIA, 44 killed in accidents, and 74 WIA. In January 1990, the Soviets again used this model in Azerbaijan, where they lost 29 KIA and 98 WIA. When examining other methods and examples of combat in cities, the well-planned coup de main is clearly the best, and least bloody, option. In December 1994, the Russians ignored their own coup de main model in Chechnya with calamitous results.

The main elements of the Soviet coup de main model follow:

- Place advisers and forces on the ground well beforehand.

- Identify key points and personnel that must be quickly taken or neutralized.

- Conduct extensive General Staff reconnaissance.

- Use a cover or deception operation to divert attention away from the main operation.

- Neutralize air defense and communications.

- Have combat air patrol coverage on call.

- Use Spetsnaz, advisers, and paratroopers to seize key points.

- Centralize planning and decentralize simultaneous execution.
- Follow up occupation with ground forces.
- Install a new government.

The invasion of Afghanistan was a military operation the KGB supported, but the capture of Kabul was a KGB operation the military supported. KGB officers were in charge of taking the various objectives. KGB planning predominated. The KGB determined the time to launch the assault. KGB head Yuri Andropov was the first one in Moscow to learn of the mission's success. The KGB tried to disguise Amin's overthrow as an internal Afghan matter with the Soviet Union acting as a good neighbor to calm down the country and help protect the government from internal and external enemies. There were some Afghans who cooperated with the Soviets, but most, including Babrak Karmal, were cooperating for the sake of their own agendas and political advancement. Karmal promised 500 warriors to support the coup; one showed up. Clearly, the KGB called the shots and made the difference.

The KGB plan succeeded, sometimes despite the Soviet penchant for secrecy. Soviet Ambassador to Afghanistan F.A. Tabeev was not briefed on the operation, and as explosions and gunfire rocked Kabul, he called his KGB adviser for an explanation. The KGB adviser told the ambassador that he was busy, but he would give him a complete briefing in the morning. The commander of the 103d Airborne Division, the largest Soviet military force in Kabul, was not briefed and blissfully entered the office of the Afghan chief of staff not realizing that his escort was there to kill the chief of staff. Soviet military doctors who looked out for President Amin and his family's health were not warned that their patients were going to be poisoned. The doctors heroically saved Amin's life and thwarted the initial plan. One of the doctors paid for his dedication with his own life during the assault on the palace. Soviet paratroopers fired on buildings containing Spetsnaz because no one briefed them on what was happening. Secrecy was so compartmented that even the most trusted KGB Spetsnaz were not given the complete plan. This frustrated coordination among the various objectives. Yet, despite the extreme secrecy, there are indications that some of the Afghan personnel had an idea that a hostile enterprise was afoot.

Another potential problem was that the Soviets violated unit integrity throughout the fight and throughout the war. Ad hoc units of

KGB Spetsnaz, GRU Spetsnaz, paratroopers, border guards (part of the KGB), and military advisers were quickly put together and had little opportunity to train and rehearse together before the combat. That it worked is a compliment to the professionalism of the officers involved. Indeed, most of the KGB Spetsnaz were officers.

Fratricide was also a problem. In the assault on the Tadzh-Bek Palace, personnel from the Muslim battalion and the KGB Spetsnaz identified one another by the white armbands on their sleeves, the challenge and password "Misha-Yasha," and Russian cursing. But everyone was dressed in Afghan uniforms and shooting, and grenade throwing took place over a distance. Also, in the dark and confusion, it was difficult to keep track of who had on white armbands and who did not. When the Soviets began to take Afghan prisoners, they found that some Afghans were also wearing white armbands on their sleeves. Many of the Soviets were wounded by 7.62mm rounds. Amin's personal bodyguard was armed with 9mm submachine guns.

Many of the Soviets were armed with 7.62mm weapons, although some had the new 5.45mm AK74 assault rifle. Ricocheting 23mm bullets from supporting ZSU-23-4 fire wounded many Soviets. The ZSU fire was supposed to lift before the assault force dismounted. However, during the assault, a BTR ran off the road into a ditch. The vehicle commander got on the radio and continually asked for assistance, thus blocking the command net. No one else could communicate while he was transmitting, and consequently, the commander could not radio the ZSUs to cease fire. Finally, his messenger physically had to go to the ZSUs to convey the order to cease fire.

The main requirements for a coup de main are planning, audacity, and surprise. The Soviet effort depended on having personnel on the ground well before the event. The assault force commanders had seen the ground—they had physically driven the route, conducted reconnaissance at the objectives, and planned their assaults. The judicious use of ZSU-23-4s and heavy machine guns aided fighting during the approach to the objective. The Soviet soldiers were elite, well-trained forces in prime physical condition. The rapid destruction or capture of key communications curtailed the Afghans' ability to react. The Afghans simply were unable to react because the senior leadership was quickly neutralized. It was a masterfully executed operation.

Notes

1. Webster's Collegiate Dictionary defines a coup de main as a sudden attack in force, whereas a coup d'etat is a violent overthrow of an existing government by a small group. In common use, coups d'etat are by internal forces, whereas coups de main can be by internal or by external forces. Immediately after the 1979 Soviet coup de main in Afghanistan, many articles described the act. Over the years, more facts have emerged that strongly contrast with what was originally published. This chapter incorporates new, original source material in the hope of more accurately describing this pivotal event.

2. *Grif sekretnosti snyat: Poteri Vooruzhennykh Sil SSSR b voynakh, boevykh deystviyakh i voennykh konfliktakh* (*Removing the Secret Seal: Casualty Figures of the Armed Forces of the USSR in War, Combat Action, and Military Conflicts*), G.F. Krivosheev, ed. (Moscow: Voyenizdat, 1993), 397-98.

3. Spetsnaz are "forces of special designation" or special troops. In this chapter, they are highly trained reconnaissance forces trained for ranger and commando-type actions. There were Spetsnaz forces belonging to the KGB and to the Ministry of Defense in this operation. The Ministry of Defense Spetsnaz were part of the General Staff Intelligence Directorate (GRU).

4. Victor Markovskiy, *Zharkoe nebo Afghanistana* (*The Hot Skies of Afghanistan*) (Moscow: Tekhnika-Molodezhi, 2000), 68.

5. Aleksandr A. Lyakhovskiy, *Tragediya i doblest' Afgana* (*The Tragedy and Valor of the Veteran of Afghanistan*) (Moscow: Iskona, 1995), 82, 107, and 131.

6. Ibid., 134.

7. Map 1 is from The Russian General Staff, *The Soviet Afghan War: How a Superpower Fought and Lost*, Lester W. Grau and Michael Gress, eds. (Lawrence, KS: Kansas University Press, 2001), 16.

8. Percy Sykes, *A History of Afghanistan* (London: Macmillan & Co., Ltd., 1940), 64.

9. Louis Dupree, *Afghanistan* (Princeton, NJ: Princeton University Press, 1980), 161.

10. Ibid, 161-65.

11. Aleksandr A. Lyakhovskiy and Lester W. Grau, *Russia's Afghanistan Tragedy*, manuscript undergoing translation and preparation for publication. Most of the material in this chapter is taken from this source, and if the source is not specified, it is from this manuscript.

12. Map 2 created by author based on a map of Kabul produced by the Sahab Geographic & Drafting Institute, Tehran, Iran.

13. "*Spetsoperatsiya v Kabule!!!*" ("Special Operations in Kabul!!!"), *Russkie kommandos* (*Russian Commandos*) (Moscow: International Patriotic Organization "Vimpel," 1999), 54-55, and Lyakhovskiy and Grau.

14. *Boevaya Mashina Pekhota* (BMP), an infantry combat vehicle, is a tracked armored infantry fighting vehicle mounting a 73mm cannon (BMP-1) or 30mm automatic cannon (BMP-2), plus a 7.62mm machine gun and antitank missile launcher. It carries a three-man crew and a squad of eight soldiers. *Bronetransporter* (BTR), an armored personnel carrier, is an eight-wheeled infantry transport that carries eleven personnel and mounts a 14.5mm machine gun and a 7.62 mm machine gun.

15. *Zenitnaya Stanovka Upravlenie* (ZSU) is a self-propelled air defense system. The ZSU-23-4 is an armored tracked system with quadruple-mounted 23mm machine guns. It fires 4,000 rounds per minute.

16. S. Kozlov, "*Kak byl vzyat dvorets Amina*" ("How Amin's Palace was Captured"), *Spetsnaz GRU: Pyat'desyat let istorii, dvadtsat' let voyny* (*GRU Spetsnaz: Fifty Years of History, Twenty Years of War*) (Moscow: Russkaya panorama, 2001), 101. During the takedown, Kozlov was using the code name Kolesnik and is known in many histories only by this code name.

17. Ibid, 105.
18. Lyakhovskiy and Grau.
19. Markovskiy, 68.
20. Lyakhovskiy and Grau.
21. Kozlov, 104.
22. Lyakhovskiy and Grau.
23. Kozlov, 107. Map 3 is from page 109.
24. Lyakhovskiy and Grau.
25. *Boevaya Mashina Desanta* (BMD), an air assault combat vehicle, is an air-droppable, tracked armored infantry fighting vehicle issued to paratroop units. It carries up to nine men (normally a maximum of seven). The BMD-1 has a 73mm cannon while the BMD-2 has a 30mm cannon. Both mount three 7.62mm machine guns. See also Lyakhovskiy and Grau.

26. Ibid.
27. Ibid.
28. Ibid., based on Soviet interrogations of the surviving aide.
29. "*Spetsoperatsiya v Kabule*!!!" 43-44.
30. Ibid.
31. Lyakhovskiy and Grau.
32. Ibid.
33. Ibid.
34. Ibid.
35. Ibid.

Operation JUST CAUSE in Panama City, December 1989

Lawrence A. Yates

Operation JUST CAUSE, the U.S. invasion of Panama in December 1989, brought a quick and decisive end to the dictatorial regime of General Manuel Antonio Noriega, the country's political strongman and commander of the Panamanian Defense Forces (PDF). As official U.S. briefings later proclaimed with only slight exaggeration, approximately 27,000 American troops hit twenty-seven targets in Panama on 20 December, achieving most of the stated combat objectives within hours. Of these targets, many were located in Panama's two principal cities, Colón and Panama City, thereby providing the U.S. military its first significant experience in urban operations (UO) since Vietnam.[1] The following assessment will focus on UO in Panama City, the largest of the two urban areas and the capital of the country (see Map 1).

Operation JUST CAUSE opened the climactic act in a drama that had begun in mid-1987 as an internal crisis for the Noriega regime, but which by early 1988 had escalated into a U.S.-Panamanian confrontation, especially after two federal grand juries in Florida indicted the dictator on drug trafficking charges.[2] As the crisis unfolded, the U.S. Southern Command (SOUTHCOM), established in 1963 to oversee U.S. military activities in Central and South America, carefully monitored daily developments, particularly the PDF's activities. This task was facilitated by the fact that SOUTHCOM headquarters was located in Panama, perched atop Ancon Hill at Quarry Heights, with a clear view of downtown Panama City and several PDF installations in the area.[3]

Before the crisis, SOUTHCOM and the forces assigned to it had worked closely with the PDF. By early 1988, however, the mounting tensions had strained that relationship, a result of the PDF's increasing harassment of American military personnel and incursions onto U.S. military facilities. To enhance security for both people and property, the commander in chief, SOUTHCOM (CINCSO), General Frederick F. Woerner, Jr., augmented his forces by bringing several U.S.-based units—mostly military police (MPs)—into Panama. Woerner also considered it prudent to begin writing contingency plans for the crisis in case the PDF's behavior became more belligerent. The first of these operation orders (OPORDs) appeared in March 1988 and described

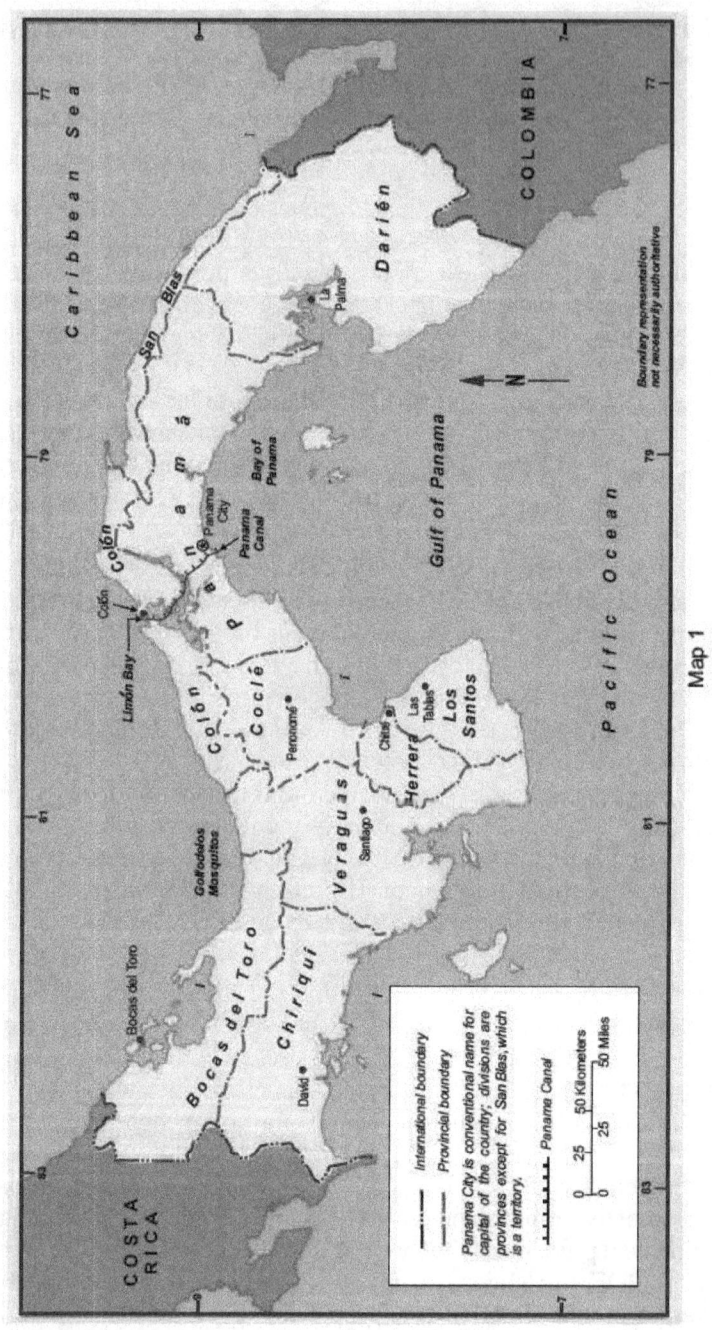

Map 1

defensive, offensive, and civil-military actions U.S. forces could take in the event of hostilities.[4] Nearly two years of continuous planning followed, a process that was still ongoing when General Maxwell R. Thurman took over as CINCSO on 30 September 1989, just days before the PDF brutally crushed an in-house attempt by some disaffected officers to overthrow Noriega. The abortive coup left Thurman and others convinced that U.S. military intervention would be necessary to remove the dictator from power. Accordingly, planners concentrated their efforts on fine-tuning the OPORD, code-named BLUE SPOON, for offensive operations in Panama.

As presented by Thurman to the Joint Chiefs of Staff (JCS), BLUE SPOON called for the United States to employ overwhelming force in a surprise assault on over two dozen targets in Panama. The "trigger event" for this attack would be another coup attempt, the killing of a U.S. citizen, or some other extreme provocation. H-hour was set at 0100 (as it had been throughout the planning process) to help achieve surprise, limit civilian casualties, and take advantage of U.S. night-fighting capabilities. The objectives of the operation would be to protect American lives, property, and interests; capture Noriega and his "accomplices"; neutralize and, if necessary, destroy the PDF; and engage in stability operations aimed at restoring law and order and assisting a new Panamanian government.[5]

Given these objectives, Panama City found itself at the "bull's-eye" of the combat plan.[6] As the seat of government and home to several PDF facilities, half a million Panamanians, and most of the thousands of American civilians living in the country, the city could not be bypassed or besieged if the BLUE SPOON mission was to be accomplished in a timely way. Rather, U.S. forces would have to seize control of the capital from the PDF and maintain order there afterward until a new Panamanian government could begin functioning effectively.

This would be no simple undertaking. Panama City, which traced its origins back to 1519, occupied in 1989 a broad strip of coastal territory along an axis running eastward from the southern (that is, Pacific Ocean) entrance of the Panama Canal (see Map 2).[7] As the country's capital, the city housed key government buildings, foreign embassies, and the Panama Canal Commission. It was also a center of economic activity that emphasized manufacturing, banking, tourism, service industries, and the retail market. Balboa Harbor was a major port area, while Panama's principal commercial airport, Torrijos International, was adjacent to the Tocumen military airfield on the eastern outskirts of the city. Another airport at Paitilla serviced small planes. Also located

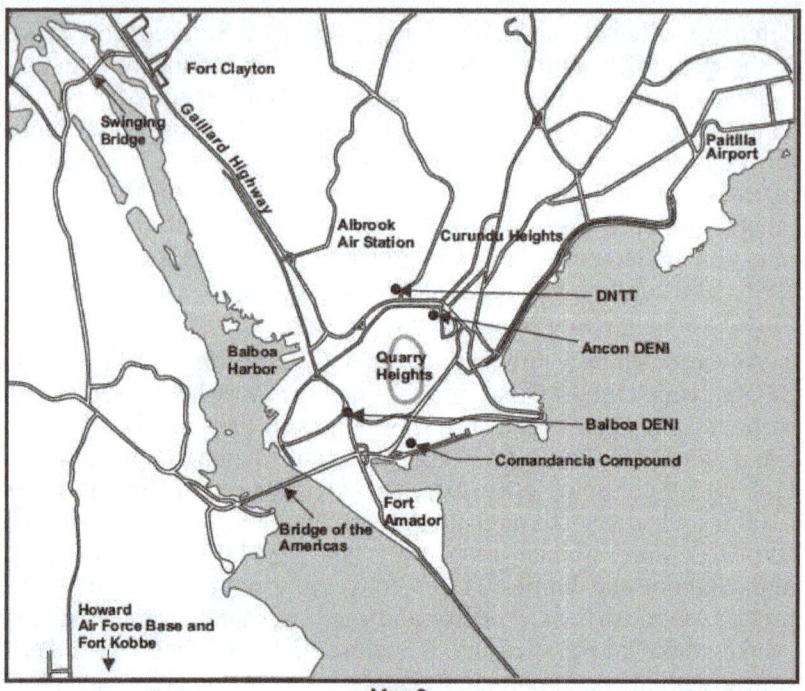

Map 2

throughout the capital were the various water, power, sanitation, medical, communications, and government services critical to the functioning of any major city. As with most urban areas that had evolved over centuries, Panama City was a mixture of old and new, with its varied landscape revealing high-rise apartments and business buildings, more common one- to three-story commercial buildings and private homes, upper- and middle-class residential neighborhoods, working-class areas, slums, and historic sites. Only a few main avenues crisscrossed the city, in contrast to the maze of narrow streets found in the downtown area. Vehicular traffic was moderate to heavy, ensuring some degree of congestion, especially downtown, throughout the day and into the night.

Panama City was also home to a sizable portion of the PDF, the umbrella organization for virtually all the country's uniformed personnel: infantry, special operations forces (SOF), riot control units, highway patrol and police, customs officers, and conservation officials. Of a force totaling 15,000, approximately 3,500 PDF were regarded as combat troops, assigned mainly to infantry companies.[8] In the capital, several of these units and organizations ringed Ancon Hill (see Map 3). From Quarry Heights, SOUTHCOM personnel looked down to the south upon the *comandancia*, the PDF main headquarters. Moving clockwise from there brought into view the Balboa National Department of Investigations, or DENI, station to the west; the Department of Traffic and Transportation, or DNTT, and the PDF engineer complex to the north; and the Ancon DENI station to the east. South from the *comandancia*, within clear sight across the Bay of Panama, was Fort Amador where the PDF 5th Infantry Company had its barracks. From the Amador causeway, one could also see Flamenco Island where elements of Noriega's Antiterrorist Security Special Unit (UESAT) were located. Farther away, between Ancon Hill and the northeasterly outskirts of the city, were a cavalry squadron at Panama Viejo, the 1st Infantry Company at Tinijitas, and the 2d Infantry Company and Panamanian Air Force at the Tocumen military airfield. Well east of the airport, but within striking distance of Panama City, was Battalion 2000 at Fort Cimarron. Besides these PDF units, the capital also accommodated the Dignity Battalions—club-wielding civilians and PDF sans uniforms organized to intimidate Noriega's opponents.

While the PDF had a significant presence within Panama City, the adjacent Canal Area was crammed with U.S. military sites and personnel. A short journey up the canal from its Pacific entrance passed by Fort Kobbe, Howard Air Force Base (AFB), the Arraijan fuel depot, and Rodman Naval Station and Ammunition Supply Point on the left bank; Quarry Heights, Albrook Air Station, and Fort Clayton (headquarters of U.S. Army South, or USARSO) on the right. The troops and sailors located at these and other facilities nearby could easily participate in military operations in and around the capital. Some of the units and headquarters were permanently stationed in Panama, belonging to SOUTHCOM or one of its components. USARSO's 193d Infantry Brigade fell into this category, as did the Special Operations Command, South, with its joint mix of SOF. Also available were elements brought into Panama over the course of the crisis to augment the in-country forces. These included Task Force (TF) Hawk, consisting of aviation assets from the 7th Infantry Division (Light); a battalion from the 5th Infantry Division (Mechanized); two U.S. Marine companies, one with light amphibious vehicles (LAVs); and several MP units (see Figure 1).[9] Since most of SOUTHCOM's forces on the Pacific Ocean side of the isthmus abutted the western edge of Panama City, they would not, in the event of hostilities, have to fight the

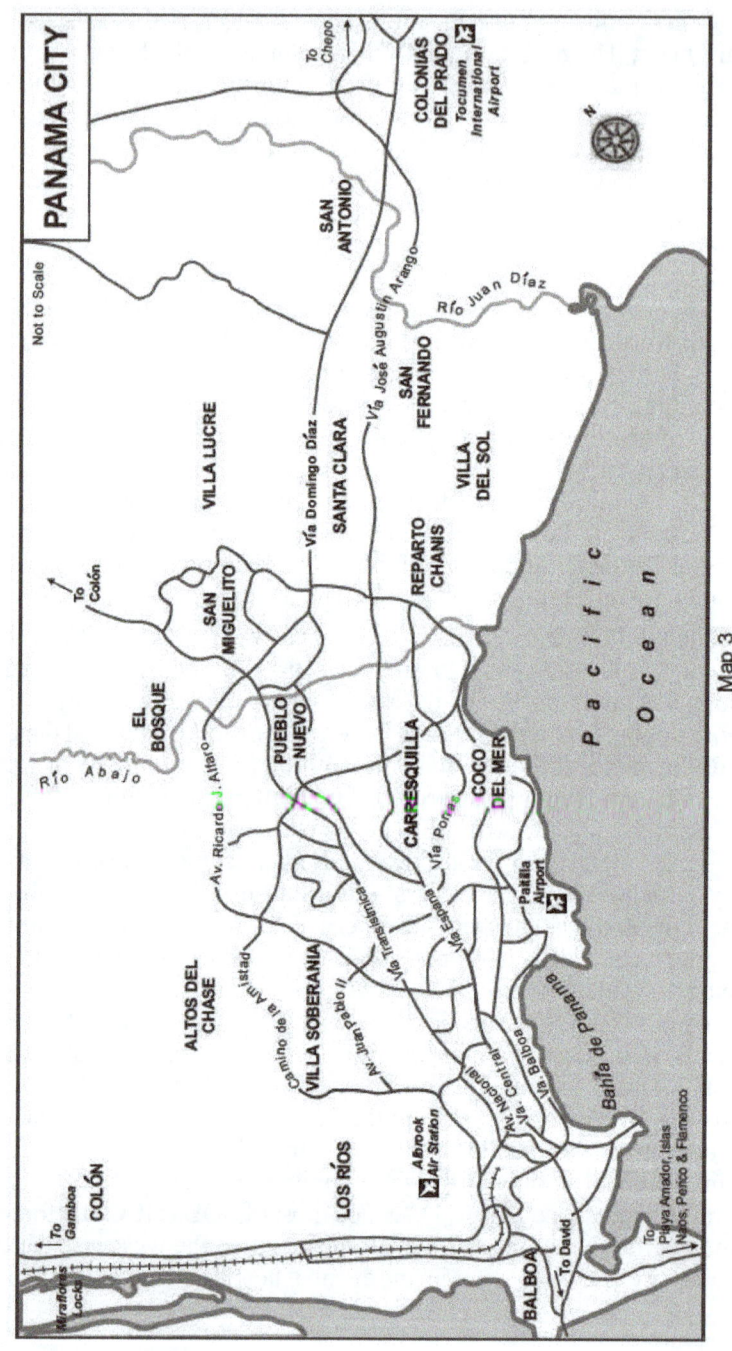
Map 3

U.S. Forces in Panama, December 1989

Stationed in Panama

U.S. Navy South
U.S. Air Force South
U.S. Marines South
U.S. Army South (USARSO)
    193d Infantry Brigade
    92d Military Police (MP) Battalion
    228th Aviation Battalion
Special Operations Command, South

1988 Security Enhancement Augmentation

MP brigade
    MP units
    TF Hawk (7th Infantry Division [Light] aviation assets)
    U.S. Marine company

1989 NIMROD DANCER Buildup

    Brigade Headquarters, 7th Infantry Division (Light)
    Battalion, 7th Infantry Division (Light)
    Mechanized Battalion, 5th Infantry Division (Mechanized)
    U.S. Marine light armored infantry company
    Battalion for Jungle Operations Training Center

1989 ELOQUENT BANQUET Insertions

    AH 64 Apaches
    OH 58 Kiowas
    M551 Sheridans

Army 9,254

Total 13,171

Figure 1

PDF for the approaches to the capital; for all practical purposes, they already controlled them.

A more pressing issue was whether SOUTHCOM had enough forces in Panama to attack the PDF and, simultaneously, to defend the Canal Area. In early 1988, CINCSO thought available forces would be hard-pressed to do both, and the initial BLUE SPOON OPORDs limited the participation of in-country forces to securing U.S. facilities within the Canal Area and isolating the battlefield in Panama City.

Taking down the critical PDF command and control elements in the capital itself would fall to SOF strike forces deploying from the United States.[10] Planners modified this initial concept of operations, however, once the continuing crisis saw additional U.S. troops deployed to Panama. By late 1989, in-country forces had acquired responsibility for several *offensive* missions under BLUE SPOON, many in and around Panama City.

While the city served as the bull's-eye on the BLUE SPOON template covering H-hour targets throughout Panama, the bull's-eye within the capital itself was the *comandancia* compound. If Noriega hoped to mount a coordinated response to an American attack, it would most likely be directed from the PDF's main headquarters. To neutralize the facility and any troops defending it was the mission of TF Gator, led by the mechanized battalion already in Panama. Moving outward from the bull's-eye, the first ring around it included Balboa Harbor, Fort Amador, the Bridge of the Americas, Ancon Hill, and PDF positions around the base of the hill. Within this area, U.S. Navy sea-air-land forces (SEALs) were to disable specific vessels in the harbor while TF Wildcat, led by a battalion from the 193d Infantry Brigade, was to secure Ancon Hill and neutralize the PDF sites around it. The 193d's other battalion, as the principal element of TF Black Devil, was to secure Fort Amador. Marines were to block the Bridge of the Americas against possible reinforcements from PDF barracks at Rio Hato 60 miles to the west. (A U.S. Ranger battalion deploying from the United States was responsible for neutralizing the Rio Hato complex, ideally before any PDF troops there could move on Panama City.)

The outer ring in the target template covering the greater Panama City area included the city's three airports and the PDF units at Panama Viejo, Tinijitas, and Fort Cimarron. The mission of securing Paitilla Airport fell to Navy SEALs, while a second Ranger battalion from the United States was to seize the Torrijos-Tucumen complex and secure the runways for a brigade of the 82d Airborne Division, also deploying from the States. Once the paratroopers were on the ground, they were to mount air assaults on Fort Cimarron, Panama Viejo, and Tinijitas. These operations were designed not just to neutralize the PDF but also to isolate the main battle at the *comandancia* and the anticipated combat around Ancon Hill and at Fort Amador.

The BLUE SPOON concept of joint operations, while simple enough to explain in general, was in its details highly complex and dependent upon efficient interaction between SOF and conventional forces. To ensure unity of command, Thurman had formally named

Lieutenant General Carl Stiner, commander of the XVIII Airborne Corps at Fort Bragg, North Carolina, "my warfighter" (see Figure 2). The corps was geared to contingency operations and, for that reason, had been involved since early 1989 in the BLUE SPOON planning effort. Under Thurman's command and control arrangement, the plan's execution would require Stiner and his staff to deploy to Panama and stand up Joint Task Force (JTF) South. Nearly all units engaged in the operation would be under Stiner's control. That included TF Bayonet, the operational appellation of USARSO's 193d Infantry Brigade, commanded by Colonel Mike Snell, which, in turn, controlled the three conventional battalion TFs operating in the *comandancia*-Ancon Hill-Fort Amador area. In a more unorthodox arrangement, Stiner would also have under him the Joint Special Operations Task Force (JSOTF) that controlled, among other assets, the SOF elements assigned H-hour targets in and around Panama City.[11]

Having achieved unity of command, Thurman and Stiner still had to anticipate the fog and friction of war, although even their worst-case scenarios excluded the possibility of an American defeat. Few if any U.S. officers considered the PDF to be a formidable force. The combat units were certainly well armed with Soviet-bloc weapons—AK-47s, rocket-propelled grenades (RPGs), cadillac-gauge vehicles, and the like—but leadership was poor, the soldiers lacked discipline, and,

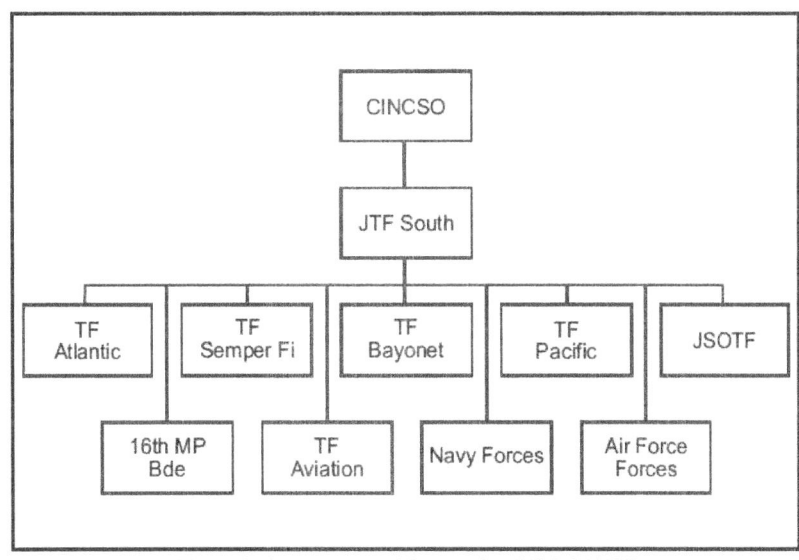

Figure 2. Command and Control for JUST CAUSE

according to intelligence sources, morale in many units was low. Noriega himself was exhibiting increasingly erratic behavior, appearing drunk and belligerent at public and private functions. In SOUTHCOM's best estimate, the U.S. advantage of surprise, darkness, overwhelming force, and effective psychological operations (PSYOP) would result in most of the PDF deserting their posts or surrendering, perhaps after token resistance. Small PDF teams might be able to stage ambushes or launch shoulder-held missiles at U.S. aircraft, but even if successful, such limited measures would not turn Panama City into another Stalingrad. U.S. forces might have to clear several buildings, but they would not have to fight their way through the city block by block. With a U.S. victory preordained, the only question was, "At what price?"

In answering this, planners recognized that their calculations would have to contain more than an estimate of the casualties U.S. forces would suffer. As noted, BLUE SPOON also contained the mission of protecting U.S. citizens in Panama—canal employees, businessmen, retirees, family members, military dependents, and others—an estimated 30,000 to 40,000 of whom lived in the capital. There was a separate plan for evacuating American civilians—a noncombatant evacuation operation (NEO) in military jargon—but by late 1989, as Thurman concentrated on the BLUE SPOON option, doubts persisted about the feasibility of executing both plans in tandem. To do a NEO just before BLUE SPOON would deprive the incoming combat units of the element of surprise, an essential ingredient in the invasion plan. To conduct the two plans simultaneously—extracting thousands of Americans from Panama while bringing in and supporting thousands of troops—would guarantee congestion and confusion, possibly resulting in the kind of prolonged urban combat that the BLUE SPOON concept sought to avoid. Besides, as one XVIII Airborne Corps planner made clear, the tens of thousands of American citizens who had ignored official warnings to leave Panama had to have understood the risks involved in staying.[12] U.S. forces would do what they could to protect housing areas in which American citizens were concentrated, but there was no way to guarantee in the midst of the fighting that some Americans would not fall victim to stray rounds, hostage-taking, or PDF vengeance. In the planners' opinion, the best means for keeping the civilians safe was to defeat the PDF quickly and decisively. Besides determining how best to fight the PDF and safeguard American citizens, BLUE SPOON planners also had to address another aspect of the "end state" sought by the Bush administration: a stable, democratic, and friendly government in Panama that could exercise effective leadership soon after the old regime had been swept away. To help ensure that outcome, U.S. combat operations had to keep physical damage and civilian casualties to a minimum. Planners considered most Panamanians to be friendly or neutral toward the United States; every effort, therefore, had to be made to avoid putting these people or their homes and belongings at risk unnecessarily. Nor could Panama's political, economic, and social infrastructure be destroyed, or even severely damaged, if Washington hoped to achieve its strategic objectives. Yet, SOUTHCOM realized that combat in a congested urban area would inevitably entail casualties among noncombatants, some destruction of private property, and some disruption of law and order and basic services. Shelter, food, and medical facilities had to be available to civilians who suddenly found themselves refugees. Furthermore, any looting, rioting, or demonstrating had to be controlled quickly and without resort to excessive force.

With these considerations in mind, the rules of engagement (ROE) set forth in CINCSO's BLUE SPOON OPORD directed that "To the maximum extent possible, commanders should use the minimum force necessary to accomplish the military objectives." The supporting JTF South OPORD preferred the imperative voice: "Conduct all operations to minimize collateral damage to nonmilitary personnel and facilities, and limit economic hardship to PANAMA."[13]

The need to "minimize collateral damage" led to other restrictions, particularly in the area of fire support. Field artillery was available, but it was not to be used in Panama City if at all possible. A barrage simply risked causing too much damage in a densely populated and, in places, highly combustible urban area. Thus, any tactical unit requesting artillery support in the city had to obtain authorization from a colonel or higher. For similar reasons, BLUE SPOON made no provisions for an air bombardment of the capital. At best, a few U.S. units were slated to receive fire support from AC-130 gunships, each armed with a 105mm howitzer and other destructive but very precise weapons. At the *comandancia*, TF Gator would also have the supporting fires of four LAVs and four M551 Sheridan armored reconnaissance vehicles. A limited number of Cobra and Apache attack helicopters were also available to hit selected targets, but most infantry units would have to rely mainly on rifles, grenades, machine guns, mortars, antitank weapons, and recoilless rifles for firepower.[14]

The assumption at SOUTHCOM was that the "trigger event" for launching BLUE SPOON would occur sometime in January 1990. This estimate meant that the OPORD, even after the JCS had approved it in

November 1989, could not be shelved. In both Panama and the United States, planners continued to amend the plan and to test it using Joint Army Navy Uniform Simulations (JANUS). At the operational level, there was the ongoing need to perfect the communications for a joint undertaking and to ensure that the nighttime airspace over Panama City, which would be crowded with a variety of U.S. military aircraft during BLUE SPOON, was "deconflicted." Beginning soon after the October 1989 coup attempt, Thurman arranged for monthly planning sessions in Panama between his officers, the XVIII Airborne Corps staff, and other supporting headquarters. One of these meetings occurred during the week of Thanksgiving, at which time SOUTHCOM received a warning that a Colombian drug cartel intended to detonate car bombs against U.S. military targets in Panama. With Stiner and his staff already in Panama, Thurman used the threat to stand up JTF South for a trial run. The bomb scare turned out to be a hoax, but it provided the key BLUE SPOON command element the opportunity to gain some practical experience and to identify problems.[15]

As planners tweaked the OPORD almost daily, those tactical commanders—generally at division, brigade, and battalion levels—who had been read into the plan and knew their units had been assigned targets in Panama City had to prepare the troops for UO. In this undertaking, U.S. forces already in Panama enjoyed some advantages. Since May 1989, as a result of an escalation in the crisis, they had been engaged in a variety of exercises and operations designed to assert U.S. treaty rights. That meant, among other things, switching the participating units' mission essential task list from jungle warfare to what was then called military operations in urbanized terrain, or MOUT, the tactical doctrine for which appeared in U.S. Army Field Manual 90-10. It also meant that many of the exercises and operations could be geared to BLUE SPOON missions, with platoon- and squad-size units unwittingly rehearsing the plan by moving to the proximity of what were, unbeknown to them, H-hour targets.[16] The exercises accustomed the PDF to the constant movement of American forces but also allowed in-country U.S. commanders to establish a deceptive signature. For example, when airborne troops conducted air assault exercises onto Fort Amador, they landed the helicopters in front of the PDF 5th Company barracks, even though BLUE SPOON called for a flanking attack.[17] In addition to these troop maneuvers, the American military in Panama familiarized itself with the terrain and the enemy by conducting personal reconnaissance together with more formal staff exercises, map exercises, jeep exercises, and tactical exercises without troops.[18]

BLUE SPOON units based in the United States also enjoyed certain advantages. Hundreds of miles from the PDF, they used existing MOUT training sites or newly erected mockups of their assigned targets to conduct elaborate rehearsals (one of which, by chance, was completed just days before the invasion of Panama). Virtually all affected units, whether located in Panama or not, had ample time to develop battle books containing detailed information and photographic images of the designated targets, conduct sand table exercises, and engage in live-fire exercises, employing terrain that resembled or had been improvised to resemble downtown Panama City. In one case, troops turned their own barracks into a MOUT training area, learning to clear rooms with rolled-up socks serving as grenades.

Since World War II, U.S. forces had been deployed in contingency operations to Lebanon (1958, 1982), the Dominican Republic (1965), and Grenada (1983), generally on short notice and without adequate preparation. In contrast, the troops who would execute BLUE SPOON in Panama were as primed to perform their missions as one could hope. If they lacked anything, it was actual combat experience. Below battalion level, there were few battle-hardened veterans. How the others would take to their baptism of fire was problematic.

The answer came sooner than expected. On Saturday, 16 December, a car carrying four U.S. Marines ran a PDF roadblock near the *comandancia*. The PDF opened fire, killing one occupant, Lieutenant Robert Paz. This proved to be the anticipated "trigger event." On Sunday afternoon, President George Bush received a briefing on the incident and the status of BLUE SPOON. His decision: "Okay, let's go." Soon thereafter, BLUE SPOON received a nobler sounding name, JUST CAUSE. It would begin at 0100 Panama time, Wednesday, 20 December.[19]

Following the president's directive, much had to be done. Fortuitously, Stiner and his staff were scheduled to arrive in Panama on 17-18 December for the monthly planning session. With some changes in personnel, that group now showed up at Fort Clayton with orders to go to war. They continued to modify the plan until the last minute, identifying "war stoppers" and reexamining known problem areas. On Monday night, 18 December, some commanders were formally notified of the president's decision; others received word the next day, in time to give their troops a few hours to prepare for combat. Intelligence reports revealed that some PDF officers knew the United States was on the verge of taking military action, thus diminishing, but not eliminating, the element of surprise at the tactical level. Further complicating matters as H-hour approached, SOUTHCOM learned that an ice storm had hit Pope AFB, adjacent to Fort Bragg, thus calling into question the timely arrival of the brigade from the 82d Airborne Division slated for operations around Panama City. Fortunately, other units concentrating on the capital were ready to move out. To compensate somewhat for the loss of complete surprise, Thurman approved launching the attack on the *comandancia* fifteen minutes early. At 0045, specialized U.S. aircraft jammed Panamanian commercial broadcasting and PDF tactical communications, and AC-130s began pounding the *comandancia*. JUST CAUSE was under way and, with it, the battle for Panama City.

Designating 0045 as H-hour was, in this case, an operational convenience. In fact, well before that time, various U.S. units were en route to their targets while others were already carrying out their assignments. Among these units were several SOF elements working for the JSOTF commander, Major General Wayne Downing. Downing had the H-hour missions of capturing Noriega, rescuing an American citizen from a Panamanian jail, and neutralizing various PDF capabilities, including Paitilla airfield, Balboa Harbor, and the Torrijos-Tocumen Airport complex in the Panama City area. Of these, only the Balboa Harbor mission went off without a hitch.[20] Intended to destroy any vessels that could be used to disrupt U.S. operations or to help Noriega escape, the operation fell to Navy SEALs identified as Task Unit (TU) Whiskey, part of the JSOTF's TF White. Well before H-hour, two SEAL swim teams crossed the canal in combat rubber raider craft launched from Rodman Naval Station. Once at the harbor, they swam to Pier 18, where they attached their demolitions to a docked patrol boat. On schedule, at 0100, the boat blew up and sank. (Much later, during daylight, TU Whiskey helped seize Noriega's yacht, thus depriving the dictator of one avenue of escape.)

In contrast to TU Whiskey's nearly flawless success, the Navy SEAL operation at Paitilla airfield resulted in a deadly firefight with the PDF.[21] Situated on Punta Paitilla, a strip of land jutting out from the coastline a couple of miles east of the *comandancia*, the field's one runway served private planes and some commercial aircraft. One hangar housed Noriega's Learjet. That fact, together with the airfield's potential use by any PDF reinforcements flying into the capital, put the facility squarely on the list of H-hour targets for JUST CAUSE. With the southern end of the runway virtually touching the Bay of Panama, the mission for infiltrating the airstrip fell to SEAL Team 4, also part of TF White. As with many other units involved in JUST CAUSE, the team had rehearsed the operation just a week before receiving the execution order. The plan, in brief, called for forty-eight SEALs in three platoons, supported by an offshore command element and by an Air Force combat control team that would coordinate with the AC-130 assigned to the mission, to run boats from the canal's west bank up the bay to a beach near the southeastern tip of the runway. From there, the SEALs would move onto the airfield, secure the perimeter, destroy Noriega's jet, and obstruct the runway so as to make it unusable to the PDF. Spotty intelligence reinforced by wishful thinking held that the team would encounter only a few security guards.

At 2100 Tuesday, SEAL Team 4 began its more than three-hour voyage to Punta Paitilla. Still planning to begin their assault at 0100, the SEALs learned en route of the fifteen-minute change in H-hour at the *comandancia*. The battle there began right after the team landed, forcing it to hasten its approach to the hangars. As two platoons began moving up the runway, they received some critical information—a helicopter possibly carrying Noriega was heading to Paitilla. It was also possible that a PDF column with V-300 armored vehicles was moving toward them. (Some in the raiding party fell out to set up an ambush position in case the latter report was true.) When the SEALs interpreted another message to mean that they should disable, not destroy, Noriega's jet, confusion was added to their sense of urgency.

After subduing some private security guards at one hangar, elements of the team ran into the PDF at another. A firefight erupted in which two SEALs were killed instantly and two others died as the exchange of gunfire intensified.[22] In time, the PDF defenders were either killed or routed, after which the SEALs secured the airfield, obstructed the runway, and disabled Noriega's jet. They had accomplished their mission but at a price: four killed and eight wounded, a very high number for a small unit. Different assessments of the operation arrived at various conclusions, with the SEALs' misfortune being variously attributed to last-minute changes in command arrangements, the designated H-hour, and the presumed mission, as well as to tactical lapses on the ground, conflicting intelligence, and poor communications between the SEALs and the AC-130 overhead. For some critics, however, the Paitilla losses were the result of a failure to use the right force for the mission. According to this view, Army Rangers, who train specifically for seizing airports, should have been employed, not Navy SEALs.

The Rangers did, in fact, draw an airfield mission, that of seizing and securing the Torrijos-Tocumen complex on the eastern outskirts of the city.[23] TF Red-T was composed of the 1st Battalion, 75th Ranger Regiment; a Ranger company from the regiment's 3d Battalion; PSYOP and civil affairs teams; and an AC-130 gunship and two AH-6 Little Bird attack helicopters. The plan called for the Rangers, following preparatory fires from the AC-130 and Little Birds, to parachute into the airport. Their targets were the Panamanian air force and the PDF 2d Infantry Company at Tocumen, and the International Terminal at Torrijos Airport. Seizing the air complex would prevent its use by the PDF and would provide a base for follow-on operations, beginning with those assigned to the brigade from the 82d Airborne Division scheduled to arrive at the airfield forty-five minutes after the Rangers began their assault. The timely arrival of the brigade was viewed as essential, lest PDF units near the airport mount a counterattack against the Rangers or, potentially even more disruptive, against U.S. units operating around the *comandancia*.

Generally speaking, the Ranger operation mirrored the plan. At 0100, the original H-hour, the gunship and the attack helicopters opened fire on the PDF barracks and other positions at Tocumen. Many of the PDF had already fled, leaving as soon as they heard sounds of fighting at the *comandancia*. Others were killed or wounded in the barrage. Still others took cover. When the Rangers parachuted in at 0103, they met with little resistance from the infantry company, the air force, and the security guards. Consequently, the battalion suffered only one fatality, the result of sniper fire received while clearing PDF positions. In a little over two hours, the TF had secured Tocumen, taken prisoners, and captured almost all of the Panamanian air force intact.

Unexpected difficulties arose, however, when Company C, 3d Ranger Battalion, moved to secure the terminal at the adjacent Torrijos International Airport. One reason BLUE SPOON planners had chosen 0100 as H-hour was that there would be no commercial flights into Torrijos at that time. But in the wee hours of 20 December, a late-arriving Brazilian aircraft unloaded a few hundred civilian passengers into the terminal just before the Ranger assault began. As Company C approached the building, it confronted the risk of harming these civilians or of encountering a hostage situation. The latter, in fact, did occur on the first floor of the terminal, where, as Rangers were evacuating most of the civilians, nine PDF goaded by a Cuban diplomat seized two American girls—one account says a woman and a baby—and used them to hold a Ranger platoon at bay. After a standoff of over two hours, the Ranger company commander arrived and simply threatened to kill the hostage-takers if they did not surrender. Within minutes they did.

While the hostage situation was evolving, another platoon from Company C, employing one squad per floor, was clearing the terminal's second and third levels. From a restroom on the second floor, a couple of PDF soldiers opened fire on the Rangers, wounding two. The Rangers threw in grenades, but the stalls absorbed the fragments. That left little choice but to enter the facility. In the fight that followed, both defenders were killed.

As buildings at Torrijos-Tocumen were being cleared, the first planeload of paratroopers from the 82d Airborne Division began dropping in, a process that would drag on until 0430 because of delays caused by the stateside ice storm. The brigade from Fort Bragg experienced further problems when various elements and equipment landed well off target, often in swamp or tall grass. Given the cumulative effect of these delays, operations against Fort Cimarron, Tinijitas, and Panama Viejo could not be mounted until after dawn. Fortunately, most PDF units in those outlying areas had not intervened in the battle for Panama City. The one unit that had tried was Battalion 2000 from Fort Cimarron. U.S. Special Forces and two AC-130s, however, stopped its advance on the city.[24]

Along with the harbor and airports, Downing's JSOTF had another mission in Panama City, a highly sensitive one. Timed to coincide with the attack on the *comandancia*, the operation involved elite assault forces freeing an American citizen incarcerated in the *carcel modelo*, a prison compound across the street from the PDF headquarters. As executed, most of the rescue mission went according to plan: the assault force "neutralized" the PDF guards and, after extracting the American from his cell, placed him aboard an MH-6 helicopter on the roof of the jail. As the chopper lifted off, it was hit by PDF fire and crashed into the street below, injuring all aboard except the civilian. Quickly, three M113 armored personnel carriers (APCs) arrived on the scene to scoop up the men and rush them to safety.[25]

The M113s had been waiting nearby in case they were needed. They belonged to TF Gator, the conventional force conducting the main H-hour assault on the *comandancia*. The PDF headquarters, three stories high and made of concrete and reinforced steel, was the largest of ten buildings within a walled compound and had always been viewed by BLUE SPOON planners as Noriega's most critical command, control, and communications node. One problem with mounting an attack on the compound was that it was located in *el chorrillo*, a poor and crowded barrio with narrow and erratic streets; buildings of various sorts and sizes, including a sixteen-story high-rise right behind the *comandancia*; and significant vehicular traffic even late at night.

A subordinate element of TF Bayonet, TF Gator was led by Lieutenant Colonel James Reed, commander of the 4th Battalion, 6th Infantry Regiment (Mechanized).[26] It was no accident that the battalion, which had rotated into Panama as part of the ongoing show of force President Bush had initiated earlier in the year, belonged to the 5th Infantry Division (Mechanized), a unit still equipped with the M113 APC. In the narrow streets and constricted terrain of downtown Panama City, U.S. planners believed, the M113's size held an advantage over that of its replacement in the Army's inventory, the larger Bradley fighting vehicle.

Reed's companies B and D formed the core of TF Gator. The plan called for them to set up a series of squad- and platoon-size blocking positions around the *carcel modelo* and *comandancia* compounds, designated A and B, respectively, on Map 4. Meanwhile, Company C, 1st Battalion, 508th Regiment (Airborne), a unit attached to TF Gator from USARSO's 193d Brigade, was to secure and clear the buildings behind the PDF headquarters in the vicinity of the high-rise. From intelligence reports, Reed knew that the ratio of American to PDF troops at the *comandancia* would be at best 1:1 (350 U.S. to 390 PDF). Conventional wisdom, however, holds that to guarantee a successful assault, the attacker-to-defender ratio should be at least 3:1 and preferably higher, 4:1 or 5:1, in UO. To compensate for the manpower shortfall, Reed had operational control of four LAVs and four Sheridans for fire support. He could also count on two AC-130s overhead and AH-6 attack helicopters. Rounding out the TF were two MP platoons (for placing roadblocks around the combat zone), an engineer platoon broken down into two- to three-man demolition teams, and a PSYOP team. With this force, Reed planned to isolate and pound the PDF headquarters, after which U.S. troops could enter the compound to clear the buildings. Because of the SOF-led rescue mission at the *carcel modelo* across from the *comandancia*, TF Gator would begin its attack under Downing's operational control but with Reed directing the battle for the PDF headquarters. The transfer of control from TF Bayonet to the JSOTF took place on Monday, well before the operation.[27]

As a result of repositioning his units on the Saturday night Lieutenant Paz was killed, Reed had both of his mechanized companies on the canal's east bank, the same side on which the *comandancia* was located. Company D was at Fort Clayton, with Company B a few miles to the south at Corozal. Shortly before the attack, Reed brought the LAVs and Sheridans—labeled Team Armor—over to the east bank as well. Last-minute preparations included hydrating the troops for combat in a tropical clime, getting intelligence updates (which

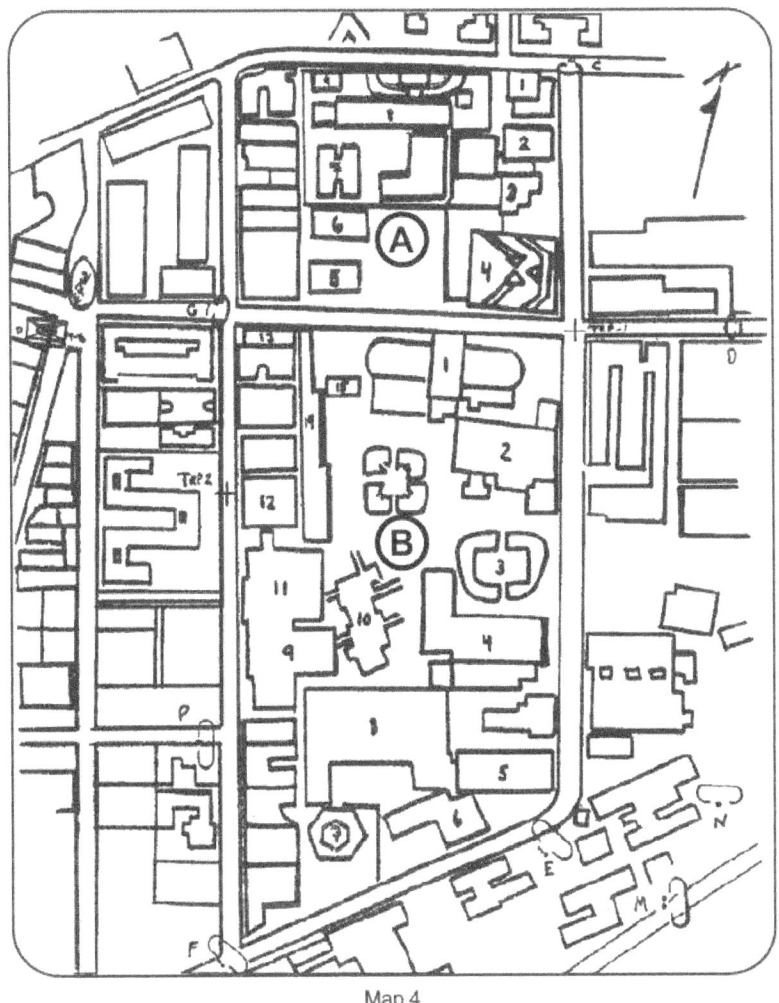

Map 4

indicated the PDF knew the attack was coming), applying glint tape to uniforms and equipment, and disseminating passwords. These latter measures were designed to reduce the risk of friendly fire, an overriding concern U.S. commanders shared throughout the theater of operations but especially in the congested area of the *comandancia*.

The decision to move H-hour ahead by fifteen minutes caused some adjustments but little disruption to TF Gator's schedule as it set out toward the target. When Team Armor reached Ancon Hill, it moved out of formation and took up firing positions on the hillside overlooking the compound. Company B settled in briefly next to Quarry Heights and waited for Company D to move into position around Balboa Avenue. Once that was done, both companies advanced in M113s toward their blocking positions. Meanwhile, Company C, 1/508, moved dismounted into the builtup area adjacent to the compound. The entire TF was now committed to the attack, a fact that concerned Reed deeply. TF Gator had no combat reserve. If additional forces were needed, they would have to come from the reserve Colonel Snell controlled at brigade—that is, TF Bayonet—level.

As companies B and D set out, they immediately saw that the PDF had put its advance knowledge of the invasion to good use. Well before the two units reached their positions, they encountered roadblocks covered by intense small-arms and RPG fire, especially from the builtup area and high-rise apartment building. Reconnaissance by U.S. Special Forces had discovered a couple of the roadblocks, but another had gone undetected. The worst roadblock was one that stacked heavy dump trucks two deep. In trying to negotiate the obstacles, both columns stalled, with Company B suffering one fatality, a corporal who was killed while providing suppressive fire against the PDF. Innocent bystanders also paid a price, as M113s climbing over vehicles in their way could not always distinguish between empty cars and those with civilians inside.

As the columns approached the *comandancia*, the battle became more heated. The AC-130s and AH-6s pounded the compound, and to those watching, the 105mm howitzers of the Spectre gunships seemed to pulverize the main headquarters building. In reality, the damage inflicted, while extensive, was restricted largely to the top floor, as the howitzer rounds failed to penetrate the second and first floors before detonating.[28] From Ancon Hill, Team Armor also opened fire, although some of the vehicles found their line of sight to the *comandancia* obscured either by trees on the hill or by the smoke, fire, and debris that soon engulfed the target. Consequently, the team's impact on the early part of the battle was marginal. Once Reed realized this, he moved some of the M551s off Ancon Hill and gave one each to the two companies assaulting the PDF complex.[29] From their new positions, the Sheridans were much more effective against the compound's walls and defenses.

All of the U.S. assault force initially encountered heavy firing from the compound and the builtup area around it, especially from the 16-story high-rise. Restricted somewhat by ROE designed to limit civilian casualties, the Americans generally showed remarkable discipline in returning fire, although on occasion they unleashed indiscriminate suppressive fires on the apartment building, assuming that, after a certain point, the civilians within had taken appropriate cover.

It took an hour for Company B in the north to secure its positions and an hour or so longer for Company D in the south. At one point in the fighting, the PDF shot down an AH-6, which ended up landing inside the *comandancia* compound. The pilot and copilot managed to get out of the craft, hide out, make their way to a segment of the wall, climb over, and scurry to the American lines, shouting something en route that sounded more like profanity than the password. They both made it to safety, narrowly escaping a tailor-made opportunity to become friendly fire victims. One mechanized platoon, however, was not as fortunate. As its APCs approached the compound, one of the AC-130s tracking PDF V-300s changed the target acquisition system on the gunship to obtain a better image. When the gunner reacquired the target, it was the wrong one. It was not the V-300s but U.S. M113s. The AC-130 hit all three of the platoon's vehicles and wounded 21 of 26 of their occupants. Reed had a fire support officer located with the JSOTF, and when it became apparent what was happening, communication with the plane ended the firing before it inflicted additional damage. Miraculously, no one in the platoon was killed, but the unit was incapable of further action. The preinvasion fears of a major friendly fire incident in a congested urban area had been realized.[30]

While this was going on, Company C, 1/508, was waiting for word to enter and clear the *comandancia* compound. But Reed never issued the order. In the meantime, heavy sniper fire and grenades rained down on the company, resulting in three soldiers' deaths. After that, the unit pulled back to a safer area.

Shortly before dawn, the shooting had been reduced to sporadic sniper fire. At 0430, TF Bayonet resumed operational control of TF Gator from the JSOTF. Remaining was the task of clearing the buildings. Reed had not issued the order to Company C, 1/508, to start the procedure because, after talking to Snell, he decided to await the arrival of a Ranger company from the Torrijos-Tocumen operation to lead the effort. Reed felt that the Rangers had more expertise and experience in clearing rooms than did his mechanized troops, despite their pre-JUST CAUSE UO training. The company arrived around noon on 20 December. With the support of Apache helicopters Reed had requested and a platoon of TF Gator troops providing covering fire from the roof of a nearby gymnasium, the Rangers began clearing the prison and other facilities in compound A and then moved on to buildings in compound B, which included the *comandancia* itself. Company C, 1/508, joined in. By late afternoon on the 20th, the area was secure. TF Gator had lost four soldiers killed in action (KIA) and had several more wounded. PDF casualties were unknown but were assumed to be substantial. The fact that few of the PDF fighting at the *comandancia* wore uniforms hindered an accurate count.

Leaving a platoon to secure the PDF headquarters and its contents, TF Gator engaged in several follow-on operations that included helping Navy SEALs clear Flamenco Island and securing a Panamanian television station near the Ancon DENI. Potentially most challenging would be securing the San Filipe DENI station without harming one of its occupants, a PDF colonel who was also a U.S. intelligence "asset." Reed wondered how he would extract the colonel if a firefight erupted while the officer was still inside the DENI. His speculation ended, however, when U.S. units arrived at the DENI to find that all PDF except the colonel had fled.

Looking back on the battle at the *comandancia*, Reed reached several conclusions. One confirmed the value of the M113 APC in UO. Planners had wanted the M113 because of its size and, in case civilians needed to be evacuated from certain areas, its interior capacity. To these attributes, Reed added the vehicle's freewheeling .50-caliber machine gun that could be trained on the upper stories of high-rise buildings and used much more readily for suppressive fire than the Bradley's more precise 25mm cannon. He also noted that infantry in the M113 could stand and fire from the troop compartment without obstruction, in contrast with the Bradley, in which they could only do so when the turret on top was pointed to the front.

While Reed praised the M113, he was lukewarm regarding the performance of Team Armor's Sheridans and LAVs from their positions on Ancon Hill. The noise and debris the Sheridans created did have a psychological value at the outset of the fighting, he argued, and once the clearing operations got under way that afternoon, both the Sheridans and LAVs helped to suppress sniper fire. But neither of the vehicles had created much physical damage from Ancon Hill during the night assault, although the Sheridans Reed pulled out of position to assign to companies B and D proved very effective against the compound walls. As for the AC-130s, he conceded that they were highly accurate and could bring devastating supporting fires to bear, thus affording a tremendous asset when they hit the right target. That they did so most of the time at the *comandancia* was offset by the one serious incident of friendly fire.

Other key observations TF Gator put forward dealt with a variety of issues. Reed believed that U.S. snipers had been too constrained by the ROE, thus limiting their effectiveness against the PDF snipers who bedeviled the TF. The fact that few PDF soldiers fought in uniform also created a dilemma for U.S. troops under strict orders to avoid civilian casualties. What a legitimate target was and when to shoot at it were not always clear, although no friendly KIAs could be attributed to any indecision over when to use deadly force. During the battle, Reed also realized that his medical station was too far away from the fighting, so he approved setting up an intermediate one closer to the action. Finally, TF Gator was not prepared to cope either with the large number of refugees that appeared at dawn on 20 December or with the widespread looting that afflicted Panama City soon thereafter.

The battle for the *comandancia* saw some of the fiercest fighting to occur during Operation JUST CAUSE. With a 1:1 force-to-force ratio, TF Gator could not afford to find itself outflanked by PDF reinforcements. As Reed put it, "I had no ability within my own resources to fight the deep battle . . . ." That being the case, the Rangers, the 82d Airborne Brigade, Marines, and Special Forces were to block any enemy forces coming in from distant locations. That left PDF personnel in the immediate vicinity of Ancon Hill to worry about. To make sure that none of these forces interfered in the battle downtown was the responsibility of TF Wildcat, another task-organized unit within TF Bayonet.[31]

Commanded by Lieutenant Colonel William Huff III, TF Wildcat had at its core infantry companies A, B, and C from the 5th Battalion, 87th Infantry Regiment, 193d Brigade, headquartered at Fort Clayton. Rounding out the force was Company A from Reed's mechanized battalion, and a headquarters and headquarters company (HHC) with an antitank (AT) platoon, a scout platoon, and a mortar platoon assigned to it. In what was labeled a supporting attack for the *comandancia*, TF Wildcat received the mission of isolating and fixing PDF targets in the Ancon Hill area. Moving clockwise around the hill from its southwest base in the Balboa section of Panama City, Company B was responsible for all of Balboa, including the DENI station located along TF Gator's route to the *comandancia* and TF Black Devil's route into Fort Amador. Northward, Company C targeted the DNTT building and the Ancon DENI station, the latter situated at a critical intersection where two main avenues merged into Gaillard Highway. Company A picked up the PDF engineer compound mainly because the company commander lived near the target and knew the terrain. The attached mechanized company was to set up five roadblocks at critical intersections to block any PDF reinforcements that might show up from Tinajitas, Panama Viejo, and Fort Cimarron. MPs and an infantry platoon were to secure Gorgas Army Hospital, the Panama Canal Commission, and several power and communications buildings on Ancon Hill. Before all this, the TF's scout and AT platoons were to reconnoiter routes and targets; once the operation began, they were to serve as Huff's reserve.

The scouts pulled out the back gate of Fort Clayton about 0030 and proceeded toward the target area. At that time, there was some shooting between U.S. MPs and the PDF at Pier 18 in Balboa Harbor, an isolated incident that "alerted a number of people that something was going on." Despite hearing the gunfire, Huff's reconnaissance element imparted the appearance of being on a routine exercise. That meant, among other things, stopping for traffic lights. The scouts wore soft caps and kept their weapons out of sight, a modicum of deception that, at one red light, enabled them to avoid a firefight with ten PDF soldiers nearby who, despite training their AK-47s on the U.S. vehicles, seemed confused as to what was transpiring. "Again, it could have gone very bad very quickly," one officer later remarked, but it did not. The scouts went on to fulfill their mission, reporting to headquarters the status of the targets they had reconnoitered.

Soon after the scouts left, the word that H-hour had changed led Snell to authorize TF Wildcat's main elements to depart early. Companies B and C and the one mechanized infantry company at Fort Clayton departed for their objectives around 0045 while most of Company A began moving out from nearby Curundu. Some of the units attracted PDF fire, but only Company B encountered serious resistance before reaching its objective. As the troops traveled down Gaillard Highway toward Balboa, they were ambushed by PDF occupying a bus and two squad cars in the vicinity of Albrook Air Station. In the ensuing firefight, U.S. security police at Albrook joined in, much to the chagrin of Company B's officers who were apprehensive about friendly fire in the confusing nighttime exchange. The shooting temporarily slowed the company, but with only three soldiers wounded, it pushed the bus aside and drove on to its targets. Soon thereafter, higher headquarters learned that the short battle had resulted in the first American civilian fatality: a schoolteacher who, in a car with her husband, had been riding home.[32]

As Company B closed on Balboa, the mechanized company reached 4th of July Avenue and began setting up three of its five roadblocks, in the process suffering the only fatality in the TF. Meanwhile, Company

A, 5/87, infiltrated the area near the engineer compound, and Company C began to fix its targets. Huff set up his jump tactical operations center (TOC) in the vicinity of the Panama Canal Administration Building on Ancon Hill, where with the help of retransmission stations, he enjoyed good communications with each of his companies. He could also move the jump TOC to either side of the hill to influence whatever target required his immediate attention. As it turned out, once TF Wildcat crossed its line of departure, each of its four targets went "hot."

Initially, Huff regarded the engineer compound, given its location and size (estimated at "a couple of football fields") as the TF's main effort. The plan was to fix the compound; block the PDF's escape routes; alternate PSYOP with fire demonstrations to induce the defenders to surrender; and then sweep the fourteen buildings, moving from northwest to south. Once the operation commenced, hardly any PDF gave up in response to broadcasts by the PSYOP loudspeaker team attached to Company A. (The PSYOP results at the compound were so disappointing that the team was sent to Balboa to assist Company B.) Later, captured defenders said they were convinced the Americans would kill them if they surrendered. Furthermore, during the first part of the fight, their own officers were threatening to shoot them if they tried to give up. At some point, Company A realized that it was not fighting engineers but civilian-clad infantry teams and snipers organized by UESAT and officers from other elite units for the purpose of defending most of the PDF facilities in TF Wildcat's area of operations.

With the help of U.S. snipers and 90mm recoilless rifle fire from the support platoon on a hill overlooking the compound, Company A began systematically clearing the buildings around 0400, putting to good use the concealment offered by the terrain around the compound. The company commander, in keeping with the unit's UO training, employed a leapfrog method in which a platoon would clear a building, then rest as another platoon cleared the next building. When the objective was secure shortly after noon, five PDF were dead, about twice that number wounded, and eighty-five were enemy prisoners of war (EPWs), many of whom gave up after their officers had fled. Company A suffered three casualties, two from ricochets and one from broken glass.

As Company A was carrying out its mission at the engineer compound, Company C was moving against its two principal targets, the Ancon DENI and the DNTT. The company commander encountered communications problems between the two sites, primarily because of the obstructions houses and natural terrain posed, but once he moved his jump TOC to another location on Ancon Hill, the problem was resolved. (On a more general level, TF Wildcat discovered that its PRC-126 radios did not work that well inside or between buildings.) From intelligence reports, Company C was hopeful that the defenders, assumed to be policemen, would not fight at either objective. These hopes, however, were quickly dashed. At both the DNTT and DENI station, as at the engineer compound, ad hoc commando units formed around a core of UESAT officers and troops were conducting the defense.

At the DNTT, the hastily mounted defense did not work entirely against the U.S. force, as several barriers placed to keep American troops out of the main building actually kept the PDF from escaping. U.S. troops used bullhorns to encourage the PDF to surrender, but there was some doubt as to whether the defenders could hear the offer. In any case, they opened up on the assault force with small-arms fire, and the battle commenced. At one point in the ensuing fight, an AC-130 became available, and TF Wildcat asked for fire support at the DNTT. The request was canceled, however, when one of two marking rounds from the plane exploded dangerously close to Company C's 3d Platoon. The attackers next called for fire support from the TF's 81mm mortars placed in an athletic field on Albrook Air Station, but when a mortar base plate settled, causing a round to land behind friendly forces, that request, too, was canceled. The next step was to fire the company's 60mm mortars in a direct-fire mode, a decision that produced "good results," as did raking the building with .50-caliber machine gun fire from a newly arrived M113. Once in the DNTT building, elements of Company C engaged in room-clearing operations, with some PDF defenders, especially the snipers, not giving up until U.S. troops were right outside the door or, in one case, until a 90mm round had been fired into their position.

As in the case of the engineer compound, UO training paid off at the DNTT. But training cannot replicate all aspects of combat, especially the psychological impact. After the battles, Huff made reference to the movie, "Aliens," a 1980s' science-fiction thriller, in recounting the sensory experience his troops shared once they entered what one of his officers described as the "catacombs" of the building. The power had been cut and the lights were out. With flashlights, the soldiers could see steam escaping from pipes, and they could hear its hissing, an eerie sound in the near dark. This was punctuated by the noise of materials crashing to the floor in the combat-damaged building. As the soldiers moved from hallway to hallway, their flashlights cast bizarre shadows. The cumulative effect of all this was a dark and surreal ambience, one that elevated the troops' fears and slowed them down. Still, they got the job done, pushing their flashlights into a corner, a hallway, a room to see if the light would draw fire. If it did, they lobbed grenades at the source. Working from the ground up—not the top down, as called for in doctrine—the men cleared the building.

At the company's other objective, the Ancon DENI station, resistance was heavy, more so than at any other TF Wildcat objective, so the company commander ordered the building riddled by a .50-caliber machine gun. Then, with his troops set to enter the structure, he ordered a 90mm round fired through the door. In this case, the proximity of a housing area to the station precluded the use of mortars. As with the DNTT, the station had to be cleared room by room. In that operation, U.S. snipers proved very effective against several PDF soldiers who, having fled into a business area across the street, were firing on the Americans trying to secure the DENI. Of seven PDF the snipers engaged, all were killed.

As elements of TF Wildcat were seizing the DNTT, engineer compound, and Ancon DENI, two platoons from Company B secured Balboa, while a third platoon began neutralizing the DENI station there. Many PDF soldiers escaped into an adjacent residential area, while those who remained in the station ignored appeals to surrender. Subsequently, the U.S. troops who had the building surrounded demonstrated their substantial firepower. That included the platoon's 90mm recoilless rifle, one round from which became lodged under the building's roof and started a fire. The platoon had not intended to burn the station to the ground, yet in the midst of the H-hour battles, their requests for a firetruck went unanswered. Huff later remarked sardonically that the fire was "very unfortunate."

Once its four principal H-hour targets were secure, TF Wildcat still had to deal with snipers, refugees, looters, and prisoners. The TF also began follow-on operations, many of which took it into housing areas around Ancon Hill. The sweeps sought to ferret out PDF troops trying to evade capture, a task that under intense UO conditions could be fraught with danger. Most of the remaining PDF, however, knew that it was futile to resist. As U.S. troops combed the houses, Panamanian males of military age had to prove that they were not in the PDF. If they could not, they were taken to the EPW compound at Albrook Air Station for questioning. The sweeps also uncovered weapon caches and

PDF documents. Going into Friday, 22 December, TF Wildcat had suffered only one KIA.

As with TF Gator, TF Wildcat later submitted a list of lessons learned. One item praised the 90mm recoilless rifle and its impact on the battle. Each platoon had a 90mm, and according to Huff, the weapon was loud, better than AT-4s and light antitank weapons (LAWs) for subjecting the enemy to psychological stress in a confined UO environment governed by restrictive ROE. Like TF Gator, however, TF Wildcat was skeptical of the AC-130's utility over a congested urban target. In another lesson, units at several sites commented that they needed to "eliminate" street lights during the fighting. Also noted were the excessive manpower demands that looking after a significant number of EPWs placed on the TF—a lesson that caused Huff to recommend developing methods for removing prisoners from the battlefield more expeditiously.

Huff's subordinates also pointed out that they did not have the personnel necessary to handle all the PDF documentation they captured or to process information contained therein. "We could have used about 1,000 S-2s right at that moment," Huff said with slight exaggeration, "just to cover our battalion." Another officer observed that each company in TF Wildcat could have used an intelligence team, and that information the battalion sent up the chain often took days to come back as usable intelligence. Also noted were the problems that last-minute changes in communications frequencies caused. Finally, Huff observed that, in urban combat, glass, shards, and fragments made gloves as well as elbow pads and kneepads essential.

In conjunction with TF Wildcat, TF Black Devil, the third TF under Snell's TF Bayonet, also had the mission of neutralizing a PDF target near the *comandancia*, in this case the 5th Infantry Company at Fort Amador.[33] Lieutenant Colonel Billy Ray Fitzgerald commanded TF Black Devil, the core of which consisted of the HHC and airborne infantry Companies A and B, 1st Battalion, 508th Infantry Regiment (Airborne), located at Fort Kobbe. Rounding out the TF were MPs and, from the mechanized battalion, a platoon of scouts with ten vehicles. In preparing for its mission, the 1/508 employed terrain models and UO simulations that converted the barracks at Fort Kobbe into training sites. It also conducted actual air assault exercises onto Amador as part of the program to assert U.S. treaty rights. When the time came to execute its BLUE SPOON mission, the principal complicating factor for TF Black Devil was the presence at Fort Amador of a housing area for U.S. military dependents directly across an athletic field from the 5th Company barracks.

On the night of 19 December, Fitzgerald began infiltrating his HHC, scout and AT platoons, and mortars onto Amador. They were in position by 2200, three hours before H-hour. Around 0015, following television announcements that indicated U.S. military action was imminent, movement within the PDF barracks was detected. Around 0030, at the time the shooting at Pier 18 began, the 5th Company's activity increased. Fitzgerald, who was on the scene, spotted a PDF bus that appeared to be getting ready to leave the fort. Consequently, he asked and received permission right before H-hour to close the front gate at Amador. As the troops sent to do so arrived at the gate, they saw the bus approaching at high speed, with PDF soldiers hanging out the windows firing at them. Having rehearsed just such a scenario, the U.S. troops returned fire, causing the bus to swerve and hit a tree. As the firefight continued, a Toyota Corolla appeared, with its PDF occupants also trying to escape by shooting their way out the gate. In this, they fared no better than their comrades on the bus.

As elements of TF Black Devil started to close the causeway at the other end of the fort, members of the mortar platoon began knocking on the back doors of the American-occupied houses, informing the occupants of pending hostilities and offering to take them out, if they insisted. The better course of action, the occupants were told, was to take cover.[34] Meanwhile, to retain some element of surprise, Fitzgerald requested that the air assault be launched early. JTF South, however, concerned about "deconflicting" the airspace over the southeastern part of the city, denied the request. By that time, the battle at the *comandancia* had started, with what Fitzgerald described as an incredible number of rounds from that nearby fight landing on or near Fort Amador.

At 0100, the first elements of the air assault began to arrive, with Cobra attack helicopters covering the troop-carrying Black Hawks. Once the first lift discharged the soldiers aboard, the second lift came in, just as a PDF soldier hit an OH-58 Kiowa with small-arms fire. The chopper crashed, killing the crew of two, the only KIAs in TF Black Devil. As the assault force assembled, the PSYOP broadcasts began. Fitzgerald allowed them to go on for over an hour because of rumors that the 5th Company was about to surrender. When it became clear that the PDF officers were only stalling, the attack began. At the outset, the troops fired M60 and .50-caliber machine guns, AT-4s, and 90mm recoilless rifle rounds at the PDF mess hall. The firing then extended to other buildings. When the PDF refused to surrender, Fitzgerald waited until dawn and then ordered the barracks cleared. The process was slow and methodical, with no U.S. casualties initially. Just as the troops were becoming comfortable, however, perhaps to the point of letting their guard down, the PDF in one building opened fire with RPGs, machine guns, and sniper rounds. By 1800, the barracks were secured after a battle that was later remembered for the use by U.S. troops of a 105mm howitzer in a direct-fire mode. More important to TF Black Devil was the fact that it had incurred no casualties on the ground and had inflicted no unnecessary damage.

All the H-hour battles in Panama City encountered the fog and friction of combat, yet all turned out pretty much the way the planners and commanders had anticipated. The PDF put up heavier resistance than expected in some locations, but in no single battle, except the shootout at Paitilla airfield, did enemy forces inflict anywhere near an unacceptable toll upon U.S. troops. The live-fire exercises, the training events, the rehearsals, and the other forms of preparation had all paid off, a point made in virtually every after-action report. Casualties for the attacking force are supposed to be high in UO, but U.S. discipline, training, and firepower, in conjunction with an inadequately trained and generally poorly led enemy, negated most of the inherent advantages the defending force should have enjoyed. Ammunition expenditures in UO are also supposed to be high, and in some of the H-hour battles in Panama City this proved to be true. But given the short duration of the fighting, resupply was not a problem. By the evening of 20 December, all the H-hour objectives in Panama City had been taken. The outcome had never really been in doubt.

There were, of course, unexpected developments en route to the victory. For U.S. forces in the southeastern part of the city, one surprise was having to deal with large numbers of civilians during and after the H-hour battles. The planners knew that people concentrated in a major urban area could create a variety of problems during a military operation. Innocent bystanders could become hostages or, worse, casualties. As anticipated, the PDF did take hostages, at Torrijos International Airport and later at the Marriott Hotel in downtown Panama City. There were other isolated cases as well. Yet, the worst fears of several U.S. planners—a wholesale roundup of Americans living in Panama—were not realized. Nor did Noriega's supporters attempt to capture key U.S. military and civilian personnel whose names appeared on a PDF "hit list."

Ironically, the first fatality in an operation designed to protect U.S. citizens in Panama was the American schoolteacher riding with her husband. Another American civilian to die violently during JUST CAUSE was a computer science teacher whom four PDF members kidnapped two hours after the fighting began. He was shot in the back of the head, execution style. A third U.S. citizen, a young college student returning home from a late party, was killed when, possibly intoxicated, he drove through one of TF Wildcat's roadblocks.

Most civilian fatalities were Panamanian, an estimated 200 to 300. Some were killed by the PDF, others inadvertently by U.S. troops. More civilians almost certainly would have been killed or wounded had it not been for the discipline of the American forces and their strict ROE. In the end, the number of Panamanian dead was large enough to stimulate debate over the need for an invasion to remove Noriega but not large enough to generate a sense of outrage in Panama or abroad, or to turn the Panamanian people against the U.S. intervention or the nation-building program that followed it.[35]

Where the planners sorely underestimated a civilian problem was with respect to refugees.[36] People would be displaced by the fighting in Panama City; that was to be expected. But it was also assumed that the number of refugees would be manageable: the pinpoint accuracy of U.S. weapons would minimize "collateral damage," as would the anticipated short duration of the planned attacks. This was not an unreasonable assumption, but it did not foresee an entire neighborhood going up in flames, which is exactly what happened to the barrio of *el chorrillo* located next to the *comandancia.* Whether set off by stray rounds from the fighting or ignited deliberately by the PDF in retaliation for the neighborhood's well-known anti-Noriega sentiment, a fire engulfed the entire area before dawn on 20 December. Soon, both TF Gator and TF Wildcat found thousands of homeless and frightened Panamanians—not the much smaller number that was predicted—crossing into their lines even as combat operations were still in progress. As Huff recalled his reaction, "I could not believe it!" Reed shared this amazement.

To remove the civilians from harm's way and that of the engaged U.S. troops, both commanders had refugees directed to nearby Balboa High School, the site of TF Gator's main medical station and its logistical/administrative center. Consequently, the school had to be converted into a refugee center immediately, an improvised process that overtaxed the few U.S. officers and troops located there. By the end of the day, thousands of Panamanians had situated themselves inside the building or outside on the athletic field. At its peak, the number of refugees at the school was estimated at 10,000.

Quickly, toilets backed up. Food, sanitation, and hygiene became serious concerns. So did the mix of people: families with children, young toughs, criminals, even PDF soldiers all mingled together. Some inside the camp had weapons; some had drugs. Once adequate rations and water arrived to feed the refugees, the biggest need became diapers and baby formula. Fortunately, during this chaotic period, the PDF did not try to disrupt the activities of the refugee center by firing on it or by attempting to subvert its efforts. Either course would have adversely affected U.S. credibility and the well-being of the refugees.

Initially lacking the number of military personnel needed to secure and run the camp, U.S. officers at the school decided to get the occupants themselves involved in those tasks. Committees were set up, each with a function and responsibility. Within days, the makeshift center was running more smoothly. Security had been beefed up, portable toilets brought in, many undesirables had been removed, and some of the refugees had been able to return home or relocate to better accommodations. As combat operations subsided, screening procedures sought to retain in camp only those refugees who had lost their homes. The others were fed, treated medically if necessary, and released to return to their residences. Despite these efforts, however, numerous Panamanians remained homeless after the invasion, the source of a scandal a year later when many of them were still living in a "tin city" set up at Albrook Air Station.

Looting posed another problem that planners had anticipated but not on the scale that actually occurred. The temporary breakdown of law and order triggered by the invasion and the subsequent destruction of the PDF offered temptations in urban areas that many Panamanians, particularly from poorer neighborhoods, could not resist. Not long after JUST CAUSE began, looting in Panama City and in Colón on the Atlantic side had become endemic, and U.S. troops were initially spread too thin to deal with the lawlessness. Once enough troops became available to deal with the problem, they restored order through the use of minimum force: threats, apprehensions, flex-cuffs, and firing into the air. Still, the spectacle of mobs running loose in downtown Panama City had, as with the plight of the refugees, created a public relations nightmare for SOUTHCOM and the Pentagon.

These episodes should not suggest that all encounters between U.S. forces and the population of Panama City during JUST CAUSE were negative or counterproductive. As polls would later show, most Panamanians supported the U.S. intervention. After Noriega sought safety within the papal *nunciature* in Panama City, angry crowds gathered outside to demonstrate. U.S. officers trying to negotiate the deposed dictator's surrender used the demonstrations to increase the pressure on him. If he did not give up, Noriega was told, the crowds might get out of control and storm the premises. His safety—his life—could not be guaranteed. Negotiators invoked the example of Benito Mussolini, the deposed Italian dictator lynched by a mob during World War II. Noriega got the point and soon thereafter turned himself over to U.S. drug enforcement agents.

Demonstrations against Noricga were only one means by which the many Panamanians supporting the invasion sought to assist in putting an end to the dictatorship. Within hours after hostilities began, people accosted American troops and flooded official phone lines, offering a variety of helpful information: the whereabouts of PDF soldiers trying to evade capture, the location of arms caches, the best way to win the war. Much of the information these Panamanians had to offer was valuable, and some of it was put to good use. But much of it was ignored: SOUTHCOM, JTF South, USARSO, and other headquarters did not have the organization, procedures, or personnel at hand to deal with this kind of fortuitous windfall.

Nor were there personnel and procedures in place to implement a "guns for money" program once the fighting subsided. Weapons could be picked up readily in some places of the city, and arms caches were rumored to be numerous. In the transition to a new government and with civilians appearing in the streets once the combat had subsided, removing small arms from the populace assumed a high priority. One way to achieve that goal was to pay Panamanians to turn in their firearms and other weapons. Several U.S. units designated to carry out the transaction, unfortunately, did not learn of the program until after it had started, thus making life precarious for any well-intentioned citizen approaching an American checkpoint with a weapon to sell. Another difficulty early on was that the money was not available to pay out, which led to the issuance of IOUs that unscrupulous elements could easily duplicate. After some glitches, administering the program became much smoother, with PYSOP officers providing leaflets from which the populace could learn the procedures for turning in weapons. But as in most programs of this sort, a very small percentage of the guns in Panama City actually were removed from the streets.

For some soldiers in Panama City, the biggest postcombat adjustment came when they learned that a new organization, essentially a police force, would replace the defunct PDF and that recruiting for that force would begin on Friday, 22 December, just two days into the invasion. To establish the new organization as quickly as possible, its cadre would consist of PDF members who had been vetted to eliminate those with records of flagrant abuses and misdeeds. With combat operations still winding down, this decision, together with a plan to begin U.S.-led patrols with the police force as soon as possible, did not sit well with many American soldiers.

The initial recruitment took place in the parking lot of the DNTT building, and it was here that the last significant armed resistance to U.S. forces in JUST CAUSE took place.[37] By late Friday morning, control of the DNTT was in the hands of a platoon from TF Wildcat's Company C. In the parking lot, about 100 Panamanians, many of whom had just shed their PDF uniforms, had shown up to be screened for the new police force. Shortly after the process began, a group of 20 to 30 PDF "rebels" in a warehouse next to the DNTT opened fire on the crowd with small arms. The U.S. platoon responded with what firepower it had, which was minimal. At almost the same time that the shooting began, a motorcade with one of Panama's new vice presidents came speeding down the road, the target of an ambush attempt along its route. The U.S. troops at the DNTT almost fired on the vice president who, once identified, was whisked to safety inside the building.

An hour into the firefight, rounds from 40mm grenades launched from Ancon Hill landed in the parking lot. By then, wounded Panamanians were being evacuated to nearby Gorgas Hospital, and Company C's commander was maneuvering his other two platoons to deal with the hostile forces. Meanwhile, Lieutenant Colonel Huff got the battalion AT platoon and AT sections from A and B companies to form another assault force. Once in position, these units opened up on the warehouse with LAWs, 90mm recoilless rifles, and the only two TOWs fired during JUST CAUSE. Using high-explosive rounds had the desired effect. A fire started in the warehouse, and the shooting stopped. Several PDF bodies were later found on a slope running down from the warehouse. In assessing the episode, some U.S. analysts suggested that the recalcitrant PDF had used the area's storm drains to enter the warehouse undetected. Whatever the case, the defeat of this "counterattack" on 22 December essentially ended the combat phase of JUST CAUSE. Drive-by shootings and sniping would continue, but as of Friday evening, the war in Panama City, and the country, was over.

Once the screening process at the DNTT produced the desired number of recruits, the newly installed government of Panama quickly stood up the new police force. The need to restore order and to acquaint the population with its new constabulary dictated "joint" patrols in Panama City. That meant that former PDF members, now clad in hastily procured police uniforms and sporting .38-caliber revolvers, took to the streets accompanied by U.S. MPs or soldiers. Some U.S. infantrymen who drew this assignment objected strenuously: they considered the duty to be police work, not soldiering, and the patrols forced them to cooperate with men who just days before could have been trying to kill them. Huff, for one, had sought to prepare his men for this eventuality. The in-country U.S. forces, which included his battalion, were going to have to live in a post-JUST CAUSE Panama for some years to come. That meant, Huff told TF Wildcat shortly before it went into combat, that once the fighting was over, "We're going to have to pat these guys [the PDF] on the back and say, 'All is forgiven.'" Undoubtedly some in his audience did not take this message to heart, but many others understood the reality he addressed. The troops stationed in Panama knew the country, had friends among the Panamanian people, and held out some hope for the country's future. One can only speculate, however, how the requirement for "joint" patrols was received by soldiers who had deployed from the United States, who regarded all PDF members as the enemy, and who, upon redeployment, would evince little concern for what happened in Panama.[38]

Caring for refugees, cracking down on looting, collecting weapons, and establishing the new police force—U.S. planners had raised these and other issues while discussing the stability operations an invasion of Panama would necessitate. That U.S. combat units performing these activities were often not prepared or trained to do so was to some degree the result of what many considered to be the most conspicuous lapse in the planning process: the failure to coordinate adequately the combat operations called for in BLUE SPOON with the civil-military operations (CMO) contained in an OPORD code-named BLIND LOGIC.

In part, the failure to coordinate derived from the division of labor among the planners. XVIII Airborne Corps was solely responsible for drafting the JTF South version of BLUE SPOON, while SOUTHCOM's J5 shop was responsible for BLIND LOGIC. The two staffs had some contact but no meaningful coordination. This, in turn, was partly the result of how the relationship between the two OPORDs had been conceptualized. From the outset of the planning process in 1988, the CMO OPORD had been labeled "postcombat" despite historical evidence that CMO issues are likely to arise while combat operations are still in progress, not just afterward. Consequently, the need to synchronize the two OPORDs never received the priority it deserved. When the issue of coordination was finally placed on the planners' agenda for mid-December, it was too late.

There were also problems with BLIND LOGIC itself. Its basic concept was sound: the United States would have to address CMO issues in three phases. The first stage would focus on immediate, life-threatening conditions concerning public safety, public health and sanitation, and population control. The second stage would concentrate on restoring essential services and transferring responsibility for rebuilding Panama from the U.S. military to the American Embassy's country team and to Panamanian institutions. The last phase would involve the United States working with a Panamanian government to ensure a stable, democratic Panama.

Execution of this concept, however, was based on a number of assumptions, two of which were outdated by December 1989. The first was that a U.S. military government, with CINCSO as the military governor, would run Panama for at least 30 days following BLUE SPOON operations. That assumption fell by the wayside when a slate of candidates opposing Noriega clearly won the May 1989 presidential election in Panama, prompting the dictator to annul the results. By the time of JUST CAUSE, the Bush administration had decided to install these three men—the truly elected president and two vice presidents—as the new government in Panama. Thus, there would be no need for a U.S. military governor. The second outdated assumption was that the U.S. president would call up 200,000 reservists to participate in the CMO follow-up to BLUE SPOON. By December, it was clear that President Bush had no intention of doing this. Early that month, the SOUTHCOM J5 sent BLIND LOGIC to USARSO at Fort Clayton for review, only to be informed that the OPORD needed extensive changes. Last-minute efforts to revise BLIND LOGIC collapsed for want of time. Once JUST CAUSE began, SOUTHCOM forwarded a much-shortened version of the CMO plan to the JCS, who approved execution of what senior Pentagon officials renamed PROMOTE LIBERTY. In conducting CMO under the new OPORD, annexes from BLIND LOGIC proved very helpful.

The belated review and rewriting of BLIND LOGIC, when combined with the lack of coordination with BLUE SPOON, had several ramifications. One has already been addressed: U.S. combat units, principally from outside the country but not entirely so, participated in CMO, humanitarian assistance, and police activities in

Panama City for which, as "warriors," they lacked adequate training. Nor were they psychologically prepared to adjust within hours to the much more restrictive ROE that these activities demanded. Another consequence was the belated deployment of CMO volunteers. By the time the volunteers arrived, they found their participation superfluous or behind schedule. (On the Atlantic side, by the time two civil affairs officers showed up in Colón, a battalion commander from the 7th Infantry Division [Light] had the administration of the city so well in hand that he essentially relegated the two men to clerical work.) The last-minute attention to BLIND LOGIC/PROMOTE LIBERTY also created organizational difficulties. As the U.S. Army's 96th Civil Affairs Battalion and volunteer reservists arrived in Panama, no fewer than five organizations became engaged in CMO. Procedures hastily drawn up to facilitate coordination among the groups were never able to eliminate the duplication of effort, the insufficient sharing of information, and the plague of having some important matters just "fall through the cracks."

The confusion surrounding the initial stages of PROMOTE LIBERTY was most apparent in and around Panama City. That is where the greatest number of the CMO activities took place, where the various CMO-related organizations were headquartered, where the new Panamanian government was seated, and where the U.S. and international news media were concentrated. It was also where General James Lindsay, commander of the U.S. Special Operations Command (USSOCOM), MacDill AFB, Florida, sent a staff officer to find a way to rationalize the stability operations and nation-building efforts. Preoccupied with JUST CAUSE, General Thurman welcomed Lindsay's assistance, which resulted in USSOCOM putting forward two options, both of which involved an umbrella organization that would handle the midterm and long-range CMO. The first option harked back to the Vietnam war and a nation-building organization with the unwieldy title, Civil Operations and Revolutionary Development Support (CORDS). CORDS had employed both civilian and military personnel, with many of each serving in supervisory positions. The second option was based on the Special Action Forces (SAF) of the 1960s, a strictly military organization that had been disbanded after Vietnam. Lindsay, an advocate of reviving the SAF, favored this approach in Panama, and Thurman agreed.[39] In January, USARSO began setting up the military support group (MSG) at Fort Amador. While the new American ambassador to Panama was officially responsible for U.S. nation-building there, the military-staffed MSG provided him the organizational mechanism for implementing the program.

By the time the MSG was actually functioning, most of the JUST CAUSE combat units that had deployed from outside Panama had returned to their home bases. That left Major General Marc Cisneros, commander, JTF Panama, in charge of the MSG. As the midterm and long-term stability operations got under way, Cisneros iterated one overriding assumption: the "honeymoon" period during which the U.S. military could be *visibly* involved in nation-building would be short-lived. After a certain point, Panamanians would begin complaining about the inevitable imperfections of any program; if the United States was still overtly engaged in nation-building, the criticism would fall on Washington and U.S. forces in Panama. The rule of thumb, therefore, was to transfer responsibility on a variety of matters to the new Panamanian government and police force as soon as it was practicable to do so. Following this guidance, Colonel James Steele, who ran the MSG for Cisneros, enjoyed significant success. In January 1991, when PROMOTE LIBERTY came to a formal end, the MSG was disbanded.

The U.S. government hailed Operation JUST CAUSE as an unqualified military victory even before its official termination in January 1990. The United States had ousted a tyrannical dictator, destroyed the military/police organization that supported him, provided security for Americans living in Panama, and offered a new chance for the Panamanian people to live in a democratic society. JUST CAUSE had also demonstrated force projection, the ability to have U.S. forces strike virtually anywhere in the world. It was this theme that the Army would take with it into the post-Cold War 1990s.

Only toward the end of that decade did the Pentagon turn to another theme, also present in JUST CAUSE but except for the after-action reports and a few articles, largely ignored: urban operations. Army doctrine at the time called for bypassing urban areas in any conventional war. But events in the Balkans, the Russian battles in Grozny, America's own experience in Mogadishu and Port-au-Prince, demographic projections, and threat assessments concerning future conflicts all indicated that the U.S. military might find itself operating more and more on urban terrain. This prediction led to a new focus on UO that, in turn, led to a search for relevant case studies. There were several from which to choose, including JUST CAUSE.

On a UO spectrum running from total war to peace and stability operations, JUST CAUSE would fall somewhere in the middle. It featured urban combat, but, when compared with Stalingrad, Grozny, or Manila, it was combat of a limited nature. The worst of the fighting was over in a matter of hours, not days or weeks, and the cities involved (mainly Panama City and Colón) were left well intact with little damage to their infrastructure and basic services. Most of all, the high casualties and use of resources usually associated with all-out urban warfare did not occur. The United States suffered 23 military personnel killed and 324 wounded; estimates of Panamanian casualties are placed around 600 dead, military and civilian, and several hundred wounded.

The reasons for the limited nature of UO in JUST CAUSE include the nearly two years SOUTHCOM and others had to plan the operation, the extensive MOUT training that U.S. units participated in shortly before they executed the plan, and the skillful use of America's advantage in firepower combined with strict control over fire support weapons. Most of all, however, the overwhelming success of JUST CAUSE must be attributed to the fact that the PDF did not put up serious or sustained resistance. Most fled their posts as the invasion got under way, leaving some junior officers or hastily formed commando-type units to fight U.S. troops. In places, the resistance was stiff but still overcome in a matter of hours. Had the PDF been a more formidable force, the outcome of JUST CAUSE would have been the same—an American victory—but the cost of the invasion in both lives and property would have been tremendously higher.

The greatest flaw in planning UO in Panama was the failure to coordinate combat with stability operations, the latter of which would take place primarily in the country's two largest cities, Panama City and Colón. Thurman, once he became CINCSO, gave little thought to the BLIND LOGIC OPORD, while Stiner at Fort Bragg had been directed to work only on BLUE SPOON. Attempts in December 1989 to revise BLIND LOGIC and link it with the planning for BLUE SPOON came too late to accomplish either goal. When PROMOTE LIBERTY began on 20 December, the effort lacked synchronization and focus, in part because key assumptions underpinning the original plan—for example, a reservist callup—were no longer valid. Furthermore, the lack of coordination meant that U.S. combat troops were unprepared for much of the chaos they encountered aside from battle (the variety and magnitude of civilian activities, for example) and the numerous stability operations they were called on to perform during the first days of JUST CAUSE. Several of the "disconnects" during this period, especially as they affected the refugee issue, proved a source of some friction between the U.S. military and the new Panamanian government in the year after JUST CAUSE.

U.S. military operations in Panama City during JUST CAUSE and PROMOTE LIBERTY provide a case study for UO that involves combat and stability operations in an urban environment in which most of the population is regarded as friendly and every effort is made to limit damage to the city and its inhabitants. The fact that the United States already had forces stationed in Panama should not detract from the value of the case study. Something analogous could have developed or could still develop in places where U.S. troops occupy urban areas for any length of time. That being the case, JUST CAUSE stands as an instructive example of UO somewhere in the middle of a spectrum that includes Stalingrad and similar cases at one extreme and Port-au-Prince and similar cases at the other.

Notes

1. One could argue that the first significant UO experience for the U.S. military after Vietnam was that of the Marines in Beirut from 1982-84, but, in fact, the Marine positions were located on the outskirts of the city, near the international airport, not in the city itself.

2. For background and details of the crisis in Panama, see Kevin Buckley, *Panama: The Whole Story* (NY: Simon & Schuster, 1991); and Frederick Kempe, *Divorcing the Dictator: America's Bungled Affair with Noriega* (NY: G.P. Putnam's Sons, 1990).

3. SOUTHCOM headquarters was located in what had been the old Canal Zone and in what was still U.S. territory until 2000. At the beginning of that year, according to treaties signed in the late 1970s, the Panama Canal and U.S. property surrounding it would have been turned over to the government of Panama. By 1989, some U.S. territory had already been transferred to the Panamanian government, and SOUTHCOM was exploring ways to vacate the country before the 2000 deadline.

4. Woerner sought authorization to write the contingency plans from the Chairman, Joint Chiefs of Staff (CJCS), Admiral William Crowe. Crowe granted Woerner's request in late February. Message, CJCS to USCINCSO, 28 February 1989. To date, the best overview of the planning process for the crisis in Panama can be found in Ronald H. Cole, *Operation Just Cause: Panama* (Washington, DC: Joint History Office, Office of the Chairman, Joint Chiefs of Staff, 1995). The most thorough account of the planning for CMO is John T. Fishel, *The Fog of Peace* (Carlisle Barracks, PA: Strategic Studies Institute, 1992).

The initial OPORD the SOUTHCOM J3 staff produced was code-named ELABORATE MAZE and, once fleshed out, contained five phases for operations in Panama. The first three phases entailed defensive operations; the fourth phase, combat; and the fifth phase, CMO. The plan was soon broken down into a separate OPORD for each broad category: defensive, offensive, and CMO. Together with an evacuation plan, the revised OPORDs were collectively code-named the PRAYER BOOK. (The plans, it should be noted, were deliberately drafted as OPORDs, not operation plans, in part because of the possibility they might have to be executed soon after being completed.)

5. USCINCSO OPORD 1-90 (BLUE SPOON), 30 October 1989. A sanitized copy of this OPORD has been declassified. The final version of BLUE SPOON covered the contingency in which hostilities would begin with "no notice" and would require the in-country forces to conduct the battle until deploying units could arrive. It also covered the contingency in which the United States would initiate hostilities and thus have time to prepare. Since the

latter scenario is what actually occurred, it is what will be emphasized in this chapter.

6. The "bull's-eye" metaphor is from Captain Joseph M. Nemmers et al., *United States Army South Staff Ride: Operation JUST CAUSE, 20 December 1989 31 January 1990,* updated reprint (Fort Clayton, Panama: Historical Office, Headquarters, USARSO, 1998), 10.

7. The city was burned to the ground by privateer Henry Morgan in 1671 and rebuilt slightly west of its original site.

8. Nemmers et al., *USARSO Staff Ride*, 9.

9. There were two major buildups of U.S. forces in Panama during the crisis. The first came with the security enhancement augmentation of 1988 and included MP units, TF Hawk, and one Marine company. The second augmentation occurred as a result of the violence surrounding the Panamanian elections in early May 1989, elections that Noriega's opponents clearly won, but which the dictator nullified. This troop buildup, Operation NIMROD DANCER, included the mechanized battalion; a brigade headquarters and a battalion from the 7th Infantry Division (Light); and a second company of Marines, the one with the LAVs.

10. The first CINCSO ELABORATE MAZE OPORD gave virtually all offensive missions to SOF, most of whom would deploy from the United States. These elements would be commanded by a JSOTF, located during the planning phases at Fort Bragg, and answering directly to CINCSO. Woerner also activated another organization, JTF Panama, commanded by his Army component commander and headquartered at Fort Clayton to manage the crisis day to day and to draft supporting plans for conventional operations. Initially, as indicated, most of these operations were defensive.

11. Cole, *Just Cause*, 17, 22-23. For a variety of reasons, the Joint Staff in late 1988 had named the XVIII Airborne Corps as the executive agency for planning BLUE SPOON. The formal handoff of that responsibility, however, JTF Panama did not occur until early 1989.

As for command and control arrangements, the JSOTF under Woerner's concept of BLUE SPOON reported directly to CINCSO, an arrangement that Thurman believed violated the principle of unity of command. His solution of placing the JSOTF under Stiner's operational control risked angering SOF commanders who were always concerned that a conventional commander would misuse their assets. But Stiner's extensive background in special operations mitigated, if not negated, this concern.

12. Oral history interview, XVIII Airborne Corps staff officer, 20 December 1989, Fort Clayton, Panama, interviewed by the author.

13. USCINCSO OPORD 1-90 (BLUE SPOON), 30 October 1989; JTF South OPORD 90-2 (BLUE SPOON), 3 November 1989.

14. The four Sheridans and six Apaches were deployed secretly to Panama in November.

15. According to journalist Bob Woodward, Thurman's activation of JTF South during the bomb scare caused some consternation in Washington, as expressed to the CINC by the president's national security adviser, Gen. Colin Powell. In Powell's view, Thurman did not have the authority to activate JTF South on his own since it involved the XVIII Airborne Corps, a headquarters over which CINCSO had no control *until* BLUE SPOON was executed. Still, once Thurman had set up JTF South, Powell saw no reason to deactivate it until the bomb scare was over. *The Commanders* (NY: Simon & Schuster, 1991), 142-44.

16. Operations security dictated that most of the troops involved in the various U.S. military exercises in Panama not know that they were rehearsing a contingency plan. Those who did know were generally officers who had a "need to know" and the requisite top secret security clearance. For the critical attack on the *comandancia*, TF Gator officers down to platoon leaders were aware of the plan. For most other targets, the inner circle excluded officers below battalion or company commanders and staffs.

17. Oral history interview, Maj. Gen. Marc Cisneros, 1990, Fort Clayton, Panama, interviewed by the author.

18. Preparations for MOUT in what would become Operation JUST CAUSE are discussed in various oral history interviews, including Col. Michael G. Snell, 1 January 1990, Fort Clayton, Panama; Lt. Col. James W. Reed, 6 January 1990, Fort Clayton, Panama, interviewed by Maj. Robert K. Wright; Ibid., 29 January 1990, Fort Clayton, Panama, interviewed by the author; and Lt. Col. William Huff III, 29 January 1990, Fort Clayton, Panama, interviewed by the author. In an e-mail to the author, Huff, commander, 5th Battalion, 87th Regiment, 193d Infantry Brigade, noted: "We took the guys over to the old coast artillery positions on the Atlantic side and used them for the fundamental of room and building clearing from the leaders on down. . . . The detailed mechanics of getting inside a room without killing yourself, but insuring all the enemy was neutralized is pretty standard stuff today, but a few years ago it wasn't as well known outside the CT/SWAT community. Hints like 'make sure the grenade goes off before you enter the room. . .' became important later on." E-mail, Huff to author, 6 February 2002.

19. Woodward, *Commanders*, 167-73.

20. The operation at Balboa Harbor is discussed in U.S. Special Operations Command, *USSOCOM History* (MacDill AFB, FL: USSOCOM History and Research Office, nd), 29; and Thomas Donnelly, Margaret Roth, and Caleb Baker, *Operation Just Cause: The Storming of Panama* (NY: Lexington Books, 1991), 120-21.

21. For the Paitilla airfield operation, see *USSOCOM History*, 28-29; Donnelly et al., *Just Cause*, 113-20; and Malcolm McConnell, *Just Cause* (NY: St. Martin's Paperbacks, 1991), 51-78.

22. Accounts differ as to the beginning of the firefight. Some hold that several PDF guards in the hangar opened up on the SEALs (see McConnell); others state that only one PDF guard fired initially, killing the first two SEALs and wounding six others (see Donnelly).

23. This account of the Rangers at Torrijos-Tocumen is based on *USSOCOM History*, 22-24; and Donnelly et al., *Just Cause*, 188-213.

24. The travails of the brigade from the 82d Airborne Division did not end at the Torrijos-Tocumen complex. Several paratroopers in the unit that air assaulted into Panama Viejo landed in the mud flats there, becoming immobilized as they sank into the mire. Helping to extract them from the mud were Panamanian civilians, no doubt perplexed by the sight that confronted them. The operations of the 82d Airborne units, together with the Special Forces battle against Battalion 2000 at the Pacora River bridge, are covered in Donnelly et al., *Just Cause*, 124-30. One additional aside: the 82d's 1st Brigade that deployed in JUST CAUSE was not the brigade that had rehearsed the mission at the MOUT site at Fort Bragg. The 3d Brigade had conducted the rehearsal but by 20 December had been replaced as the division ready brigade by the 1st Brigade.

25. The rescue of civilian Kurt Muse has been recounted in several books, articles, and television interviews and documentaries. See, for example, Donnelly et al., *Just Cause*, 130-34. The PDF had arrested Muse for his clandestine political activities before Panama's presidential elections in May 1989. The rumor circulated among U.S. forces in Panama that, should the United States invade the country at any time, Muse's guards had orders to kill him. President Bush personally made Muse's rescue a priority mission of Operation JUST CAUSE.

26. Unless otherwise noted, the following account of TF Gator is based on Nemmers et al., *USARSO Staff Ride*, 47-62; Donnelly et al., *Just Cause*, 135-60; Oral history interviews, Col. Michael G. Snell, 1 January 1990, Fort Clayton, Panama; Lt. Col. James W. Reed, 6 January 1990, Fort Clayton, Panama, interviewed by Maj. Robert K. Wright; and Ibid., 29 January 1990, Fort Clayton, Panama, interviewed by the author.

27. From his assets, Reed also created two ad hoc squads. One was to put in roadblocks along Balboa Avenue, the other—made up of mechanics and "some people back there at our base camp"—to "decommission" a radio antenna on Quarry Heights. On the issue of command and control, Reed was not sure at what time on Monday TF Gator would go under the JSOTF. This doubt created some confusion when he received conflicting orders from the USARSO/JTF Panama commander, Maj. Gen. Cisneros, who wanted to

continue routine U.S. exercises in Panama so as not to signal the PDF an invasion was imminent and from the JSOTF that worried that any such exercises might set off the war prematurely. Oral history, Lt. Col. Reed, 29 January 1990.

28. The inability of the AC-130 rounds to penetrate beyond the top floor was a problem the U.S. Air Force remedied after JUST CAUSE.

29. Reed also provided two LAVs, one Sheridan, and six M113s to the JSOTF so that SOF elements would have a small TF to assist in extricating American personnel from the U.S. Embassy. The problem for Reed, however, was that once he relinquished the vehicles, he did not see them again for several days.

30. Donnelly et al., *Just Cause*, 150-52; and Telephone interview, Lt. Doug Rubin, 5-6 April 1990, interviewed by the author. Rubin was platoon leader of the unit the AC-130 fired on.

31. Unless otherwise noted, the following account of TF Wildcat is based on Nemmers, et al., *USARSO Staff Ride*, 22-36; Donnelly et al., *Just Cause*, 153-55; Oral histories, Col. Michael G. Snell, 1 January 1990; Lt. Col. William Huff III, 29 January 1990, Fort Clayton, Panama, interviewed by the author; Ibid., 20 June 1990, Fort Clayton, Panama, interviewed by Capt. John Hollins; and Lt. Col. William Huff III and senior officers of the 5/87th Infantry, 193d Infantry Brigade, 5 January 1990, Fort Clayton, Panama, interviewed by Maj. Bob Wright.

32. That only three U.S. soldiers were wounded in the "kill zone" outside Albrook was attributed by Huff to "flukes." "People just escape with their lives by flukes," he later commented. "Bullets impacting on swivels, impacting on a front sight post, and bullets impacting on the stock of an M-16, and also on a SAW [squad automatic weapon]. Just unbelievable." Oral history, Lt. Col. Huff, 5 January 1990.

33. Unless otherwise noted, the following account of TF Black Devil is based on Nemmers et al., *USARSO Staff Ride*, 37-46; Donnelly et al., *Just Cause*, 162-83; Oral histories, Col. Snell, 1 January 1990; Lt. Col. Billy Ray Fitzgerald, 27 January 1990, Fort Kobbe, Panama, interviewed by the author; and Ibid., 20 June 1990, Fort Clayton, Panama, interviewed by Capt. John Hollins.

34. One critique of USARSO's postcombat planning is that it did not provide for marital counseling. Several families at Amador and in other areas U.S. military dependents inhabited often had combat taking place right outside their homes. Some spouses would later blame the military family member for not revealing that an invasion was pending. The stress created by the feeling that one family member had put the others at risk threatened some marriages and required counseling for some families.

35. Regarding the deaths of the three American civilians, see Donnelly et al., *Just Cause*, 233-34. See Ibid., 390, for Panamanian casualties. A few years after JUST CAUSE, the American news media gave wide play to allegations that U.S. troops had executed thousands of Panamanians and buried them in mass graves. Investigation of the allegations showed them to be groundless. While the exact number of Panamanian casualties could not be determined precisely, the number of dead probably did not exceed 600, to include both military and civilian. As for mass graves, several did exist but were hardly meant to be a carefully guarded secret. The principal one in Panama City was the subject of a third-page story in the *Christian Science Monitor*, 29 December 1989.

36. The problems created by the unexpected number of refugees are discussed in oral histories by Lt. Col. Huff, 5 January 1990, 29 January 1990, and 20 June 1990; Lt. Col. Reed, 6 January 1990 and 29 January 1990; Col. William Connolly, 29 January 1990, Fort Clayton, Panama, interviewed by the author; and Lt. Col. Les Knoblock, January 1990, Fort Clayton, Panama, interviewed by the author.

37. For the creation of a new PDF and the "counterattack" at the DNTT, see Fishel, *Fog of Peace*; Oral histories by Lt. Col. Huff (see previous note).

38. Ibid., and comments from various soldiers who conducted the patrols.

39. Oral history interview with USSOCOM staff officer.

Bibliography

This brief account of Operation JUST CAUSE in Panama City relied heavily on documents that I collected during and after the U.S.-Panamanian crisis and that are in my possession at Fort Leavenworth, Kansas. As the notes make clear, I also relied heavily on oral history interviews that I, and others, conducted with participants in the crisis. Without the candor of the interviewees, this chapter would have read much differently.

Buckley, Kevin. *Panama: The Whole Story*. NY: Simon & Schuster, 1991. An engrossing account of the U.S.-Panamanian relationship focusing on politics and personalities.

Cole, Ronald H. *Operation Just Cause: Panama*. Washington, DC: Joint History Office, Office of the Chairman, Joint Chiefs of Staff, 1995. A declassified version of an official history, Cole's work is a superb overview of JUST CAUSE from the JCS perspective. The first half of this monograph offers a thorough analysis of the planning process.

Donnelly, Thomas, Margaret Roth, and Caleb Baker. *Operation Just Cause: The Storming of Panama.* NY: Lexington Books, 1991. As of this writing, this is still the best comprehensive study of JUST CAUSE available.

Fishel, John T. *The Fog of Peace*. Carlisle Barracks, PA: Strategic Studies Institute, 1992. A detailed overview of the planning and execution of Operation PROMOTE LIBERTY.

Kempe, Frederick. *Divorcing the Dictator: America's Bungled Affair with Noriega.* NY: G.P. Putnam's Sons, 1990. One of the first accounts after JUST CAUSE to detail the diplomacy of the Reagan administration in its efforts to oust Noriega.

McConnell, Malcolm. *Just Cause*. NY: St. Martin's Paperbacks, 1991. A very good overview of JUST CAUSE, based in part on the input of various participants.

Nemmers, Capt. Joseph, et al. *United States Army South Staff Ride: Operation JUST CAUSE, 20 December 1989 31 January 1990*. Updated reprint. Fort Clayton, Panama: Historical Office, Headquarters, USARSO, 1998. An excellent staff ride guide to Operation JUST CAUSE that uses the operations logs and participants' recollections to construct a detailed account of TF Bayonet's role in the operation.

U.S. Special Operations Command. *USSOCOM History.* MacDill AFB, FL: USSOCOM History and Research Office, nd. This unclassified history offers an overview of the role of special operations forces in several operations, including JUST CAUSE.

Woodward, Bob. *The Commanders*. NY: Simon & Schuster, 1991. An excellent and very accurate account of the Panama crisis from the perspectives of the Bush administration, the JCS, and CINCSO.

Todo o Nada
Montoneros Versus the Army: Urban Terrorism in Argentina

Lieutenant Colonel Alan C. Lowe, U.S. Army

Unlike the other chapters in this anthology on urban warfare, this entry highlights the asymmetrical (an overused term currently in vogue with little clarity of meaning) nature of fighting within cities. This chapter addresses the challenges that prolonged guerrilla warfare poses within the context of an urban environment. Conventional force-on-force confrontations that characterized the nature of city fighting in Stalingrad, Manila, and Aachen are absent in this unconventional urban battlefield. This is a battlefield in which, using terror repeatedly, small cells of revolutionaries ambushed a government in the very heart of a nation—its capital city.

In general, this chapter explores how a government responded militarily to an insurgent group that undermined its legitimate political authority and threatened society overall. The specific case under examination focuses on the *Montoneros*, an insurgent group of urban guerrilla fighters who were active in Argentina from 1969 through 1977. The type of urban guerrilla warfare that the *Montoneros* practiced can be considered as being representative of other urban insurgent groups in Latin America that conducted a prolonged campaign of terror in an attempt to bring about political and social change within a nation through violent means.

In the course of examining asymmetrical or unconventional methods of warfare, another unique feature emerges that distinguishes this chapter from the rest in this anthology: the problem of terminology. Unlike conventional force-on-force operations where doctrinal terms and definitions are commonly addressed and understood through repetitive application and familiarity, unconventional warfare terminology, in many cases, lacks the clarity of precise definitions. Terms such as asymmetry, insurgents, and terrorism, to name a few, may be used commonly but often fall short of definitional agreement. Consider the case of the *Montoneros* as an example. Although they used acts of terror routinely to achieve their goals, they would never have considered themselves to be terrorists; rather, they were revolutionaries. Likewise, the Argentine military, when tasked to defeat insurgent groups, resorted to acts of terror even more atrocious than their enemies, yet they did not

consider themselves to be terrorists either. Numerous definitions abound regarding terrorism and what constitutes an act of terror. For this chapter, terrorism is defined as the indiscriminate "use of violence, or the threat of violence, to create a climate of fear in a given population ... through the publicity and fear generated by their violence, they (terrorists) seek to effect political change."[1] This definition can be applied to describe the methods and techniques that both the insurgent guerrillas and the armed forces eventually used during this era in Argentine history.

Another dissimilarity to the other chapters is inherent in the nature of the conflict being examined. Revolutionary war conducted by guerrilla organizations on one side fighting government counterinsurgency operations on the other, both coupled with an element of terror, provides an example of political warfare in the extreme. As such, historians who have written about this dark period in Argentina's history have focused on the political aspects of events. Consequently, specific operational and tactical details on urban engagements between forces have not been written, have been suppressed by government authorities, or were not considered sufficiently pertinent to the historical account as political events unfolded. While detailing selected and somewhat spectacular urban tactical engagements, this chapter really examines the larger issues and consequences to military forces when confronted with a situation that the *Montonero* example provides.

In selecting an appropriate case study on urban terrorism in Latin America to examine, many potential examples exist. The most often-cited cases include the activities of numerous leftist revolutionary groups that operated in Brazil, Uruguay, and Argentina; over recent years, Colombia could probably be added to the list with the emergence of narcoterrorist groups. Because the insurgent war in Colombia is still ongoing, the other potential examples provide the advantage of greater historical perspective.

Brazil, Uruguay, and Argentina possess many commonalities in that all three countries consist of democratically elected governments and most of their populations reside in cities. In the 1960s and 1970s, all three countries experienced, in their major cities, the proliferation of numerous insurgent groups that resorted to kidnappings, assassinations, raids, and bombings, all standard fare for terrorist movements bent on overthrowing the established order. Within this backdrop, the *Montoneros* were just one of many revolutionary groups of the period that used terror as a political weapon.

Using the *Montoneros* as the primary case study for this chapter has some advantages over an examination of either the Brazilian National Liberating Action (ALN) or the better-known *Tupamaros* of Uruguay. Although the ALN in Brazil operated in the large cities of Rio de Janeiro, São Paulo, and Belo Horizonte, the movement lasted only about four years. Throughout that period, the ALN never developed the level of threat the *Tupamaros* or *Montoneros* attained and only marginally influenced Brazilian politics at the time. The *Tupamaros* of Uruguay, on the other hand, were significantly more successful than their revolutionary brethren in Brazil. They were truly the first urban insurgency in Latin America that was able to sustain its revolutionary effort. Early on they were successful in their efforts to draw adherents to their cause, executing some well-coordinated and successful terror-type operations (mostly kidnappings and robberies). They also gained minor victories in rallying popular support and in affecting Uruguayan politics. However, the *Tupamaros* started organizing almost as a conventional force by establishing fixed urban bases, supply depots, and even hospitals, all of which eventually jeopardized their mobility and security—critical tenets of guerrilla warfare. The *Tupamaros* became overly professionalized, appearing more like the military forces they were facing.[2] Additionally, as the *Tupamaros* gained some political clout, they attempted to change the system from within, through the electoral process, while simultaneously maintaining an armed terror campaign that isolated them from the urban masses they claimed to represent. The inconsistency of this policy ultimately contributed to their demise as popular support waned and the government began a program of repressive measures.

Similarly, the *Montoneros* in Buenos Aires built upon the example that the *Tupamaros* started just on the other side of the Rio de la Plata in Montevideo. Although the *Montoneros* were not the only revolutionary group active in Argentina, they lasted as a significant threat to Argentine stability for about ten years. Throughout their life span, the organization at times commanded widespread popular support and, for a while, garnered significant allegiance from trade unions within Argentina.[3] Unlike the *Tupamaros*, *Montonero* operations occurred more frequently, with attacks usually being well-coordinated and planned as well as being a bit more daring in scope and spectacular in execution. The *Montonero* example, better than other examples, illustrates how it affected a nation as it dealt with a long-term struggle in which violence on both sides tended toward escalation. Thus, the *Montoneros* in Argentina provide greater opportunities to gain insights into unconventional urban operations (UO) and into the themes, considerations, and lessons that emerge for military forces engaged in this type of conflict.

This examination of the *Montoneros* will underscore the dissimilarities and challenges that a conventional military force faces in an unconventional (or asymmetric) UO campaign. Simply stated, in traditional force-on-force UO, conventional militaries usually fight in a somewhat linear fashion from building to building, street to street, and ultimately block to block. High casualty rates, increased lethality, and usually the destruction of the urban terrain characterize this type of combat. Conversely, guerrilla or unconventional combat operations are conducted on a smaller scale with minimal physical destruction and are usually infrequent occurrences. In fact, combat is almost absent from the landscape, emerging only as an episodic event over a broader expanse of time. As such, it becomes easy to reduce the problem to one under the purview of specialized forces—law enforcement agencies, special weapons and tactics teams, Special Forces, paramilitary, or national guards. In truth, this type of warfare encompasses the participation of all armed government organizations, including conventional forces, that can and do play a significant role.

Although the focus of this chapter is to address the military challenges to an urban terrorist threat, some general background on the nature of revolutionary guerrilla groups in Latin America is necessary to appreciate and understand *Montonero* motivations, methods, actions, and goals. While this background is essential to understanding insurgent groups of the period, it also will explain why these movements gravitated to the cities and became urban terrorist groups. This chapter will not explain the convoluted and confusing politics that characterize perceptions of Latin America or Argentina, but some political context is essential to help understand *Montonero* successes and failures. Politics and revolutionary ideology cannot be avoided due to the nature of this type of warfare. They are the "tangible" aspects of the unconventional urban landscape, just as brick and mortar are for conventional UO fighting. Insurgent guerrilla groups, by definition, conduct political and ideological warfare more than they pose a significant military threat, a fact that military forces tend to neglect.

When studying the course of political events in Latin American countries, probably the most important shaping influence to recognize is the role that tradition plays in Latin culture. Tradition in Latin culture changes very slowly.[4] At the risk of sounding too stereotypical, "one of the keys to understanding the Latin American mind-set is the awareness that, both in its communities and among individuals, there exists a strong tradition of resorting to violent means in order to settle, suppress, or challenge sociopolitical conflict."[5] Historically, since insurgent and guerrilla activities overthrew Spanish colonial rule in the early nineteenth century, political change in Latin America has often been promoted through violence and subversion rather than through democracy by means of the ballot box. The Mexican Revolution, *La Violencia* in Colombia, and Argentina's *Guerra Sucia* (Dirty War) are three of the numerous chilling examples of the levels of ferocity that can be achieved in Latin America. In this respect, the insurgent guerrilla movements in Latin America of the post-World War II era did not deviate from a long tradition of foisting political change through violence.[6]

Over the last fifty years, many Latin American countries have had insurgencies for a variety of reasons. These factors include extensive political, economic, and social needs of a rapidly expanding but poor population; the government's actual or perceived ineffectiveness in meeting those needs; and the potential for organized opposition to the government and its security forces by dissatisfied segments of the citizenry in response.[7] Add to these factors a cultural proclivity for violence with a strong sense of nationalism or the alluring promises of an ideological component, and the potential for revolutionary action increases significantly.

During the Cold War, most of the insurgent organizations in Latin America shared some common characteristics. First, they were usually driven by a leftist ideology. Generally, the ideological component was Marxist-Leninist based, but rarely was it preached or practiced in its pure form. Latin leftist ideologies could include elements of Trotskyist, Maoist, Guevarist, and Castroist ideas mixed with nationalist, populist, or even fascist underpinnings. Many groups that started out waving a particular ideological banner often ended up subscribing to a different theory. An indiscriminate mixing of leftist concepts usually occurred and could result in ideological confusion and vague political agendas. Second, regardless of the political or ideological differences between insurgent groups, they all shared the common desire to overthrow the established order and replace it with a Marxist-inspired state. Third, they used violence to achieve their sociopolitical goals and were committed to armed struggle. These groups could not conceive of change without armed struggle. Political violence was seen as the way to enlighten the masses to the contradictions in the existing system and spark a popular uprising. The last common characteristic these groups shared was their clandestine nature. They generally remained underground for their entire existence or part of it, an indication of their inability to survive as legitimate open organizations.[8]

As the Cold War progressed into the 1960s and 1970s, Latin insurgent groups started operating more and more in cities for a variety of reasons that will be discussed. For now, however, the point of departure for the transition from rural insurgency to urban begins with the revolution in Cuba in the 1950s. All Latin leftist insurgent groups harked back to the triumph of the Cuban guerrilla fighters in 1959 as their battle standard and inspiration. Fidel Castro's success provided the impetus for a revolutionary fire that spread along the mountains, jungles, countryside, and cities in Mexico, Central America, and South America in the coming years.[9] It would be hard to underestimate the impact the Cuban revolution had on these groups, not only symbolically as a model for a successful Marxist revolution in a Latin country but also in the support the Castro government would come to provide to most groups in their own revolutionary struggle. It was with the Cuban revolution that segments of the Latin American left really began to consider armed struggle as a viable means of achieving political objectives.[10]

Besides Castro, probably the most influential Latin theoretician and practitioner on conducting rural guerrilla war to emerge from the Cuban experience was Ernesto "Che" Guevara. Che, along with his French colleague, Regis Debray, worked on a version of revolutionary war modeled after the Cuban example that could be easily exported. Che and Debray based their theory on three basic assumptions. The first assumption was that popular forces could always defeat a regular army in guerrilla war. Second, the main area of operations for guerrillas would be the countryside (although with the later move to cities, insurgents considered the countryside important but not primarily important for a successful revolution). The last assumption asserted that the preexistence of these conditions was not necessary for making a successful revolution; small cells, or *focos,* of professional revolutionary cadres could either create the right conditions or simply do without them. Che's *foco* theory on revolutionary war became the philosophical touchstone for radical movements conducting insurgencies.[11]

By the mid to late 1960s, adherents of Castro and Che's brand of rural insurgency were active in many countries in the Western Hemisphere. Among the most important places were Guatemala, Colombia, Venezuela, and Peru. Additionally, Che led a direct Cuban effort to export revolution regionally in Latin America through Bolivia.

Castro and Che envisioned making Bolivia the center of another "Vietnam war" in the Americas with the ultimate goal of a continental revolution spreading from Bolivia to neighboring countries.[12]

Beginning in 1967, the Cuban hemispheric efforts received some serious setbacks, starting with Che's death in October, thus ending the grandiose plan for Bolivia. Domestically, Castro was faced with a failing Cuban economy that diverted not only his attention but also his support to external affairs. Finally, the exported rural *focos* began to falter and would fail by the end of the decade. It soon became increasingly obvious to insurgents throughout Latin America that rural Castroism had failed despite some limited short-term successes. Now several groups began to consider an alternative approach to revolutionary armed struggle with a move to urban insurgencies.[13]

Another major reason for this fundamental change in revolutionary strategy besides failures of rural movements was recognizing that most of the people in Latin America no longer resided in the countryside. By 1967, at least half of the population of every South American state, except Peru, lived in cities, with some, such as Uruguay and Argentina, registering an urban population of well over 70 percent. The shift in insurgent emphasis to cities was a logical, if not intuitively obvious, step to foment revolution. Quite simply, a revolutionary movement needing people to gain support and form an army logically should locate to where the people are. The revolutionary strategy of the 1970s would of necessity be urban and would include a relationship with the working class.[14]

Urban guerrilla warfare was hardly a new concept, and Latin revolutionaries had a number of contemporary examples from which to draw. Urban terror methods had appeared to succeed in Cyprus with the National Organization of Cypriot Fighters' (EOKA) campaign against the British in 1955 to 1959 and the *Front de Liberation Nationale* against the French in Algeria from 1954 through 1962. What was new for Latin American movements was the shift in primary emphasis from the country to cities. Urban guerrilla warfare had been employed for years as an ancillary to rural insurgency. This was primarily due to the hard-line Castroist influence in which cities played an almost insignificant role in a successful insurgency. Both Castro and Guevara firmly believed in rural guerrilla warfare, and the city, as they saw it, was the guerrilla's grave.[15]

Cities, however, would provide advantages for the insurgent that the countryside did not. Faceless dense crowds of mutual strangers populate large cities. Amid the daily rush and routine of city life, guerrillas can pass unnoticed in a way they never could achieve fully in the countryside. Concentrations of large populations reside in areas that usually have a high concentration of buildings as well. The sea of houses that characterizes large cities provides the urban guerrilla with two of his primary concerns for survival—sanctuary and anonymity. As potential battlefields, cities also provide distinct advantages over rural landscapes. Dense concentrations of buildings make ideal areas from which to conduct close ambushes of police or other government forces that can be cut off from each other with relative ease. Intricate and intertwining roads can assist guerrilla actions by facilitating egress and dispersion after an operation. Cities also provide guerrilla fighters with advantages in the area of support. Banks can be robbed to fund insurgent organizations and operations. Food and medical supplies can be obtained with relative ease. Arms can be purchased or stolen. Intelligence can be collected quickly, and networks can be compartmented and established secretly.[16]

The nerves of the modern city provide a heavy concentration of lucrative targets for insurgent movements as well. Telecommunication facilities that are critical to governments for information dissemination and population control are potential guerrilla targets. Government ineffectiveness can be illustrated to the masses through disrupting essential services such as electric power and water plants. Foreign embassies become potential sites for terror bombing. Diplomats and business executives who live and work within the greater metropolitan areas become targets for kidnapping and assassinations. If the city happens to also be the capital, guerrilla attacks can literally threaten the seat of government.[17]

City centers are also where the media conveys information to the rest of the country and the world, providing potential instantaneous public exposure for an insurgent organization to a mass audience. This exposure can work to the guerrilla's advantage by highlighting the perceived impotence of government authorities and bureaucracy in maintaining control and solving social problems. The underlying assumption insurgent leaders made as they shifted their operations to cities was the belief that society and the government could best be paralyzed using guerrilla action in main population and commerce centers.[18]

Despite all the advantages that cities promise for guerrilla forces, there are some disadvantages to operating in cities. The factors of time and space can work against guerrilla organizations. In the countryside, the authorities are more distant and require a greater response time.

Government control of rural areas not only consumes time but also requires more troops covering areas that extend for tens or hundreds of miles. Large urban areas are usually the locus of the national police apparatus as well as the ruling regime's military might. As such, government response times to attacks or intelligence tips can be measured in minutes and are usually limited to just a few miles.[19]

Regardless of the advantages or disadvantages that cities provide to the insurgent fighter, a general analysis of urban guerrilla warfare shows that it is not significantly different in application than rural guerrilla warfare. The same broad requirements for popular support, recruitment, security, intelligence, and materiel hold true for any insurgency, regardless of the physical setting. The methods and techniques of fighting in cities require adjustments to the new urban environment.

As guerrilla organizations shifted their main efforts to metropolitan areas, revolutionary leaders published guidelines internally on how to specialize in urban insurgency. Uruguayan guerrilla leader Abraham Guillén published his *Strategy of the Urban Guerrilla* in 1966. In it, he called for a continental revolution a year before Guevara's more famous message did the same. Probably the most famous and widely used document regarding urban insurgencies was Brazilian guerrilla leader Carlos Marighella's 1969 *Minimanual of the Urban Guerrilla*. This brief communiqué, written specifically for Marighella's Brazilian fighters, became the urban guerrilla's "doctrine," covering a variety of tactics, techniques, and procedures for conducting armed revolutionary warfare within cities.[20]

Although brief in size (a mere 44 pages), the scope of the *Minimanual* is fairly comprehensive, articulating the uniqueness of the city environment in relation to that of the countryside. Because it was universally used by Latin American urban insurgent groups (including the *Montoneros*) as a "how to fight and win" manual, it is helpful to highlight a few areas of note. Marighella covered topics of critical importance for the urban guerrilla's survival and success. He provided instructions on how to organize, lead, train, conduct offensive tactical operations, obtain resources, recruit, gather intelligence, and enforce operations security. Tactics were adjusted to the peculiar nature of fighting in cities, such as the notion of remaining close to the enemy to frustrate him in applying mass or heavy firepower, thus negating his conventional tactics and weapon systems. Marighella stressed how to maintain the advantage of the initiative in cities through the elements of surprise, knowing the terrain, mobility and speed, and information. Another section addressed the qualities necessary for an urban guerrilla:

bravery, decisiveness, imagination, initiative, flexibility, and determination. These qualities compensated for inferior numbers when confronting government forces. Other passages are devoted to individual training and the skills in which all guerrillas need to be conversant as well as a section on how to conduct organized action. Additionally, the *Minimanual* listed fourteen specific offensive missions that urban guerrillas conduct, including assaults, ambushes, executions, kidnappings, raids, and terrorism—all acts of violence. Of all the missions listed in the guerrilla's repertoire, it is interesting to note that terrorism is the only activity "the revolutionary can never relinquish."[21]

It was largely the political ideology, writings, and insurgent examples provided by revolutionaries such as Che, Guillén, and Marighella that the *Montoneros* built upon to pursue their goals in Argentina. However, political theory and ideology have to be applied to be effective in a revolution. Guerrilla leaders in each country still had practical matters to consider in how best to link acts of terror to political and social revolution to the seizure of state power. Although political and social revolutions are inherently intertwined, they both require different approaches and strategies in actual execution. "The seizure of state power is itself the policy objective of political revolution, whereas it is but a means to social transformation in the case of social revolution."[22] Social revolution must rely on and encourage greater mass participation than with the mere replacement of a government administration through political revolution. Since governments and their armies do not simply disappear, they must be destroyed. This is the role of the armed segments of the insurgency—those that execute military operations. The dilemma facing guerrilla leaders was balancing and coordinating the efforts and relationship of the political and the military arms of the organization. How much emphasis should be placed on rallying the public at large for revolt? How much on implementing a military action program to employ violence in the revolutionary process? These were the practical questions insurgent leaders needed to address as they planned operations. The revolutionaries' application of violence had to be measured, clear, precise, and tied to the political aim of undermining the government by provoking repression without alienating the people in the process. Ultimately, by soliciting a repressive response through using violence, the guerrilla walks an indistinct line between garnering public sympathy and causing public opposition. The guerrilla command structure becomes a crucial factor in blending the political and social facets of insurgent warfare together to maximize both efforts while not allowing violence to become counterproductive to the cause.[23]

Overall organization and command of urban insurgent groups generally follow the pattern of small cellular networks, not unlike those that partisans and resistance fighters have used throughout history. The cell structure assists the overall guerilla organization in maintaining secrecy and operational security. This is achieved through "compartmentalization," which is essentially a matter of information as each cell acts without knowing very much about other cells' activities. Operational capabilities are distributed throughout the organization so that each cell can execute a wide range of missions and limit the amount of damage caused by losing any one cell. Likewise, individual cell members know only what is required to conduct their activities. Only a select few members know the details of any particular action, while only the central executive leadership knows the specifics of strategic planning. This practice of tactical autonomy and strategic centralism ensured that base units operated on their own initiative but within the guidelines established at the top and with special regard for the central command's priority decisions. This type of arrangement can only work effectively if all members understand the movement's politics, overall organization, and strategy.[24]

Argentina was ripe for exploitation by radical movements in the 1960s. It was during this decade that Latin America experienced a period of rapid economic modernization. Regionally, most South American countries experienced a surge in growth, expansion of capital cities, and the gradual emergence of a modern socioeconomic middle class that contributed to a sense of rising expectations by all segments of society. For most countries in South America, this process of development was uneven, causing new social, political, and economic demands on governments. A climate of friction emerged that pitted old systems against new, creating intense ideological competition. Argentina was no exception to this phenomenon as the political system's disillusionment and dissatisfaction affected a whole generation of young Argentines, with the largest concentration of the disenfranchised residing in the slums and shantytowns of Buenos Aires.[25]

Buenos Aires is not only the capital of Argentina but also the largest city and chief port. In addition to being the seat of government, the city represents approximately 70 percent of the nation's wealth. It is the hub of Argentine commerce, transportation, energy, and industry and comprises the greater part of the nation's economy. Of Argentina's 23 million inhabitants, about three-quarters are urbanites, with almost half of the population concentrated in the city and province of Buenos Aires.[26]

Radical movements of the period took advantage of the urban nature of Argentine demography not only as sources of popular support but also as an area that was ripe for exploitation. High inflation, unemployment, and a large concentration of a naturally rebellious, poor youthful population characterized conditions in Argentina. The *Montoneros* arrived on the political scene during some of the stormiest years of social conflict their country ever experienced. Within this overall context of Buenos Aires, both as an actual and symbolic source of power and potential discontent, it is not surprising that urban guerrilla warfare prospered in Argentina.[27]

The *Montoneros* were just one of many unrelated guerrilla groups that appeared in Argentina at this time. The groups that surfaced represented a wide range of political philosophies, including Nazi, Communist, and unique to Argentina, Peronist views.[28] Two of the more active and resilient movements that the *Montoneros* would periodically join forces with in operations were the People's Revolutionary Army (ERP), a Communist guerrilla organization, and the Revolutionary Armed Forces, a Marxist-Leninist-Peronist movement.[29]

The *Montoneros* were a leftist Peronist faction. Peronism, named after former President Juan Domingo Perón, was a national popular movement professing anti-imperialistic and antioligarchic tenets under a banner of *socialismo nacional.* Peronism, as a matter of political reality, was often vague, contradictory, and variously defined by Perón and his supporters who found the message of ultranationalism highly emotive and generically unifying. At the time of the emergence of the *Montoneros* in the late 1960s, Perón was in the closing years of his exile in Spain, maneuvering to return to Argentina. The *Montoneros* saw in Perón a socialist leader in their own mold. The exiled Perón accepted their support and endorsed the movement's actions through published statements advocating resistance and revolutionary war. Committed to the goal of a socialist homeland, the *Montoneros* interpreted Perón's messages as providing carte blanche support to justify violent measures. The *Montoneros* set out to fuse urban guerrilla warfare with the popular struggles of the Peronist movement.[30]

Taking their name from the early nineteenth-century "wild horsemen" who supported Argentina's independence heroes in liberating Spain's colonial hold on their country, the *Montoneros* viewed themselves as the modern version of the free Argentine *gaucho,* or cowboy, liberating the country from oppressive rule. Their very motto evoked a fierce resolution of purpose—"*Todo o Nada*" (All or Nothing). Steeped in romantic symbolism, the movement's founding members, Fernando Abal Medina, Carlos Gustavo Ramus, and Mario Eduardo Finnenich, began to prepare a program to wage armed struggle.[31]

The *Montonero* leaders thrust themselves and their organization on the Argentine political landscape in spectacular fashion by assassinating a former president. On the morning of 29 May 1970, two young men wearing army officers' uniforms presented themselves as bodyguards to Argentina's ex-president, retired Lieutenant General Pedro Aramburu. After some polite conversation accompanied by coffee, one of the guards flashed a submachine gun from under his military raincoat and announced to Aramburu, "General, come with us." The two men escorted Aramburu to a waiting vehicle, thus initiating Operation *PINDAPOY*, or the *Aramburazo* as it was more publicly called. They drove through the city on a circuitous route designed to avoid known areas of congested traffic and police checkpoints, and along the way they made several stops to change vehicles as an added security precaution.

Early in the evening hours, the kidnappers and hostage arrived at a ranch house in the country. It was at this ranch house that Aramburu was told that he had been "arrested" by a Peronist revolutionary organization and that he would be placed on trial. The trial was relatively brief with a foregone conclusion—Aramburu was found guilty of 271 crimes against Perón and the people stemming from actions he authorized as president in the mid-1950s. At dawn on 1 June, Aramburu was informed of the guilty verdict and told that he would be executed in half an hour. With a handkerchief placed over his mouth, Aramburu was positioned near a wall in the basement of the house, and the leader of the group unceremoniously fired several 9-millimeter pistol rounds into the politician's heart.[32]

Unpopular as Aramburu was for the severe government repression of the immediate post-Perón years, the abduction and execution of so prominent a leader served several political purposes. The kidnapping and sentence demonstrated the organization's use of military action to make a political and ideological statement. Aramburu's maneuvering toward a return to power, a fact that was widely known but ineffectively opposed, was destroyed with his death. The Aramburu incident also was a significant act in escalating labor unrest and revolutionary violence against the sitting administration of President Juan Carlos Ongania and contributed to that regime's downfall less than a month later.[33]

At the time that Aramburu was assassinated, the *Montoneros* numbered only twelve members, of which ten actively participated in the operation. The careful planning and daring of the act, followed immediately by other impressive operations conducted in the aftermath of Aramburu's assassination, provided the *Montoneros* a notoriety that was out of proportion to their numbers. With this dramatic beginning, the *Montoneros* launched a program of terrorist actions that would last about ten years. During the movement's height in 1973-74, it would expand to about 7,000 revolutionaries, with up to hundreds of thousands of Argentine supporters rallying behind their banners.[34]

Regardless of how large the cadre of active revolutionaries became, the movement adhered to the urban guerrilla organizational practice of a cellular and compartmented structure for security reasons. The basic fighting unit was the military command, the *commandos,* usually named after individuals memorialized by the movement or in honor of significant events. Cross-cutting this structure were the functional subdivisions of the organization: the maintenance department, responsible for acquiring vehicles and providing logistics support to operations; a documents department, specializing in counterfeit military and police papers; a war department that planned operations; and a psychological action department that was in charge of public declarations and announcements. This structure was remarkably grandiose for a movement that numbered slightly more than twenty members by the end of 1970.[35]

Likewise, *Montonero* operational tactics were typical of the type most urban guerrilla groups conducted. As small elite bands of revolutionaries, the commandos would conduct operations consisting of—

> . . . scattered surprise attacks by quick and mobile units superior in arms and numbers at designated points but avoiding barricades in order not to attract the enemy's attention at one place. The units will then attack with the greatest part of their strength the enemy's least fortified or weakest links in the city. The struggle would be 'prolonged,' consisting of many small victories which together will render the final victory.[36]

However, victory would not be exclusively a military affair because these armed tactics were designed to work in concert with and assist in the popular political mobilization the movement hoped to instigate.

The *Montoneros* struck quickly and dispersed immediately following the *Aramburazo,* but they did not disappear. While 22,000 men were mobilized to search for Aramburu's body and the kidnappers, the *Montoneros* launched a second dramatic blow to demonstrate that they were capable of a sustained challenge to the regime. For two hours on 1

July 1970, four *Montonero* units "occupied" La Calera, a town of about 5,000 located ten miles from the capital. In a coordinated effort, about twenty-five guerrillas knocked out the town's communications equipment and simultaneously took over the local bank, police station, and town hall. During the course of the operation, about $26,000 was "liberated" from the bank, while guns and the dispatch radio were obtained from the police station. During the humiliating ordeal, the policemen were jailed and forced to sing the "Peronist March" at gunpoint.[37]

La Calera was chosen for this operation because it was near the military base that was the home of an airmobile infantry regiment. The assault was designed to illustrate that the *Montoneros* could strike with impunity and to demonstrate the government's inability to react rapidly to the takeover and protect its citizenry. Through classic guerrilla tactics of surprise and mobility, a force of twenty-five could occupy a city and make the government appear weak and incompetent in the eyes of the public, foreign investors, and international banking. To this end, the operation was a huge success, but the withdrawal went wrong. Until the raiders convoyed out of La Calera, led by an imitation police car with its siren screaming, the operation had gone without a hitch.

Trouble began for the guerrillas when a car broke down outside the city. The police caught up with the broken-down car and captured two *Montoneros*. Information almost immediately extracted from the two guerrillas, presumably through methods of torture, resulted in a dozen arrests of *Montonero* suspects and the killing of the leader of the La Calera operation, Emilio Maza, in a gun battle. *Montonero* losses were significant; apart from the death of *Comandante* Maza, the organization lost weaponry, safe houses, a contact list of 167 sympathizers, and organizational security. The police now had a better idea of the organization's molecular structure. The movement was almost wiped out as a result of further police manhunts and arrests. The few key remaining *Montoneros* went underground for several months in safe houses another Peronist guerrilla organization lent them.[38]

Meanwhile, on the national political scene, a military coup deposed President Ongania just one week after the Aramburu execution. General Roberto Marcello Levingston became the new head of state in the aftermath of the coup. When the *Montoneros* reemerged from hiding in September, acts of violence and terror escalated alarmingly. Kidnappings, assassinations, bombings, bank robberies, and raids on military posts for equipment and weapons became commonplace. The government's inability to handle the situation effectively resulted in increased popular sympathy and support for the *Montoneros*, along with sounding the death knell for the Levingston administration after only nine and one-half months in office.[39]

In March 1971, a three-man junta led by General Alejandro Agustin Lanusse deposed Levingston in another military coup, and Lanusse replaced him. During the Lanusse regime, the *Montoneros* tempered their application of violence, not as a sign of support for Lanusse but, rather, to garner and build popular support. The *Montoneros* began to wage an effective propaganda campaign against the government. Sympathetic responses to *Montonero* activities were carefully cultivated by using extreme discrimination in selecting targets not only for their political effect but also for their symbolism, a unifying aspect to which all Peronist supporters could relate. For example, over 100 bombs went off on the twentieth anniversary of the death of Eva "Evita Montonera" Perón, destroying many foreign businesses. The public could not help but grasp the political significance of these explosions. Likewise, other targets were selected because they were symbols of the ruling class elites such as the numerous jockey clubs and luxurious country clubs throughout Buenos Aires. These bombings were executed with a sense of "revolutionary style" that also contributed to the romantic aura of the *Montoneros* as Robin Hood-type protectors of the less privileged, an image that the organization cultivated. While the clubs of the wealthy were being bombed, approach roads were closed off with signs reading "Danger! Dynamited Zone."[40]

Economic problems, which had in part contributed to the end of Levingston's term, subsequently grew worse. The Argentine peso continued to be devalued while inflation spiraled up to 70 percent in 1972. Government credit was almost nonexistent, and Argentina faced one of the most serious economic crises of the century. By helping to create a climate of insecurity and social disorder during this period of economic emergency, *Montonero* guerrilla activity was a behind-the-scenes factor in other semi-insurrectional challenges that shook the government such as strikes, demonstrations, and antigovernment rallies. After nearly seven years of control, many military leaders were tired of trying to solve Argentina's political and economic mess. They were willing to turn the country's problems back to civilians. The time was right for Juan Perón's return to Argentina. While awaiting Perón's arrival, the *Montoneros* did not completely abandon their armed struggle. Violent guerrilla actions continued but with less frequency, mostly to indicate to the generals what they could expect if the scheduled 1973 elections were canceled. For the most part, however, the *Montoneros* redirected their energies toward mass political activity surrounding the Perón return and then in winning the general election campaign. Ultimately, the *Montoneros* became a modest legitimate political force in their own right by winning a few elected seats in the Perón-dominated parliament.⁴¹

However, briefly stated, the time that Perón was in power was just as tumultuous for Argentina as the preceding years had been. It did not see an end to guerrilla activity or acts of terror. The honeymoon period between Perón and the Peronist left was a brief one, shattered as an ideological gulf appeared between the *Montoneros* and *el Líder*. As a politician, Perón looked more to compromise as the means to deal with all political factions in an attempt to get Argentina back to solvency and stability. Whereas Perón emphasized class alliance, the *Montoneros* still advocated class struggle as the answer to the problems that beset society. In poor health, less aggressive, and content with his vindication by the Argentine electorate, Perón was not inclined to promote any dramatic social changes. Faced with mounting labor unrest; commodity shortages, including food staples; and economic strife, Perón antagonized the left with his conciliatory approaches. The *Montoneros* became more and more critical of the government and lost their naiveté concerning Perón, especially after he denounced the more violent aspects of the left. In response, the radical left initiated a new wave of terrorist attacks in Argentina's main urban centers. Collectively, the various movements conducted over 500 kidnappings that netted ransoms in excess of $50 million in 1973. Assassinations began anew as well but focused principally on the split between right-wing and left-wing Peronists.⁴²

With Perón's death in July 1974, the situation in Argentina grew worse. Perón had named his second wife, Isabel, as his running mate in the 1973 election, and she inherited the presidency with Perón's passing. A former nightclub actress with only six years of formal schooling, Isabel's background and education poorly equipped her to be vice president, much less president. Within two weeks of Isabel taking office, the cities were swept again with a surge in violence. Assassinations reportedly averaged one every nineteen hours. In partial response to the rampant lawlessness, the unofficial, yet government-sanctioned, infamous "Triple A" (Argentine Anticommunist Alliance) death squads started cracking down on leftist movements.⁴³

By September 1974, the *Montoneros* were underground and declared a "total popular war" on a government deemed "neither popular nor Peronist." In November, Isabel formally declared Argentina to be in a state of siege, and the government imposed a "temporary" suspension of constitutional rights that remained in place for six years. In December, she petitioned congress for broad powers to call up the military to combat subversion and assist in maintaining security. For the first time since the military withdrew from power, the army was authorized to join the police to fight against the guerrillas. They launched an all-out offensive against the ERP in mid-February 1975. Meanwhile, in retribution, guerrillas staged some devastating attacks in or on the outlying areas of Argentina's largest cities, targeting army and navy installations, airports, and federal prisons. All told, by the end of 1975, over 1,700 people from all walks of life were reported to have been killed as a result of political violence during the eighteen months Isabel was president.[44]

The *Montoneros*' return to clandestine activity was intended as a defensive measure in response to an enemy offensive involving the Triple A, police forces, and the military. Once the *Montoneros* could successfully survive mounting offensive pressure, they looked to regroup and conduct a counteroffensive. The primary objective of the counteroffensive would be to "exhaust," not "annihilate," the enemy forces because they could never hope to match the combined strength of the government security forces. During the rebuilding phase, the *Montoneros* relied on the biggest advantage the cities afforded to the movement—the urban population. Thousands of activists and supporters joined the *Montonero* ranks in reaction to the government's repressive actions.

With this groundswell of support, the leadership attempted to build a *Montonero* army. A new organizational structure, along with a division of functions, took place. Unlike the previous years, in which units were trained in both political and military action, specialization became the order of the day, with political and military functions segregated. Additionally, combat platoons (*pelotones de combate*) replaced the old commandos as the basic operational cell. The new "platoons" were subordinate divisions of a far more elaborate military "column" structure. Military ranks were assigned to the members of the organization as well. Accompanying this reorganization was a vast expansion of the movement's infrastructure. Logistics bases, "safe houses," assembly areas, printing equipment, "people's prisons," training facilities, and munitions workshops were all formally established and organized. By 1974, these new changes enabled the *Montoneros* to mobilize 1,500 people nationally and conduct about 100 *operaciones* such as Molotov cocktail attacks on targets of repressive affiliation, distributing leaflets, raids, occupations, and mass demonstrations in any city they desired.

During their peak year of 1975, the *Montoneros* were able to organize the support of up to 5,000 revolutionaries for various actions, if needed.[45]

Building a genuine guerrilla army required an abundant supply of weapons and equipment. The *Montoneros* focused their efforts on obtaining the necessary funds to equip and train their army. Kidnapping for ransom seemed like the best way for the *Montonero* leaders to acquire funds quickly on the scale required to underwrite their expansion and future operations. Chief executives of the international corporation of *Bunge y Born* were selected as targets. Juan and Jorge Born were the director and general manager, respectively, of this business empire. As the Born brothers rode in their chauffeured limousine from their home in the plush Buenos Aires suburb of Beccar on 19 September 1974, *Montonero* operatives followed them. At one point, the limousine was directed to detour from the main road by "policemen." Once off the main road, about twenty to thirty "telephone repairmen" ambushed the occupants of the car. With the chauffeur dead, the Born brothers were whisked away to stand "trial" for acts against the workers, the people, and national interests. Subsequently convicted of their crimes, the brothers were sentenced to one year's imprisonment in a "people's prison." The *Montoneros*, in a communiqué, announced that they would release the "criminals" if their demands were met. The demand, a ransom of $60 million, was a world-record sum. Described as "bail," it was for the release of Juan and Jorge.[46]

Negotiations with *Bunge y Born* representatives became prolonged as the company balked at paying such a large sum. To expedite payment, the guerrillas applied additional pressure to the business conglomerate by kidnapping another executive, later ransomed for half a million dollars, and through intimidating other high-ranking partners with numerous death threats. The pressure worked, and the company finally gave in to the guerrillas' demands nine months after the kidnapping.[47]

The successful *Bunge y Born* operation not only provided the *Montoneros* with a sizable financial base that exceeded one-third of the national defense budget but also demonstrated the viability and strength of their organization. Several months later, the *Montoneros* followed the success of the Born brothers' operation with the kidnapping of a Mercedes Benz executive that added another $5 million ransom to the insurgency's coffers. With the payoffs from these kidnappings and other operations totaling more than $70 million, the *Montoneros* were guaranteed financial independence to purchase anything the organization required. All this occurred at a time when the Argentine economy faced its worst financial crisis since the 1930s. Inflation hit an annual rate of 200 percent, and unemployment reached unprecedented levels. A former economic minister characterized the condition as "the total destruction of its (national) economic order."[48]

Financially secure, better armed, and more numerous, the *Montoneros* became ever more ambitious in operations against the government and its armed forces. Vengeance killings now became a staple of *Montonero* justice. On top of the list was Federal Police Chief Alberto Villar who had ties to the dreaded Triple A. Villar and his wife were killed as they launched their small yacht from the Tigre boat dock, a recreational harbor up river from Buenos Aires. A powerful bomb had been placed underneath the yacht's floorboards near the engine. As the craft began to maneuver from its mooring, the heat from the engine triggered the explosives and blew the boat apart. Three other former federal police chiefs were killed shortly thereafter, along with other government officials who either collaborated with or were part of the Triple A "death squads." Violence for the sake of violence became the order of the day as *Montonero*-conducted assassinations continued almost indiscriminately.[49]

This move to indiscriminate killing motivated by hate, revenge, and a desire for blood ironically proved to contribute to the demise of the *Montoneros* just at the time when they were the strongest militarily. This surge in killing public officials, for the most part, was not met with public outrage because many of the targets themselves were unpopular, but there were just as many other killings whose significance was lost on the general public. Public support and legitimacy as a "people's movement," critical components for a revolutionary army's survival, began to wane as violence became divorced from political ends that the public could understand. Everyone who worked for the government or wore a police uniform became the enemy.[50]

The killing could partly be attributed to the increasing tendency toward regular military warfare and a more conventional military approach to achieving objectives through killing the enemy. The *Montoneros* fell into the same trap of overprofessionalization that hurt the *Tupamaros* in Uruguay. In one sense, the *Montoneros* became more "symmetrical" in relation to the forces they faced. This move toward greater militarism drew the movement into what they called the dialectic of confrontation—"a reactive spiral of violence which tempted *Montoneros* to increasingly respond to enemy moves rather than seize and retain the initiative."[51]

Besides the campaign against the state security apparatus previously mentioned and the propaganda efforts, the guerrillas launched two other tactical military offensive campaigns in the period 1974-1976. The first saw the initiation of genuine military and paramilitary activity with major attacks primarily directed against the armed forces. The last campaign, set in motion in 1976 on the eve of yet another coup, was principally aimed against the police forces. In both campaigns, the guerrillas selected targets in and around major urban areas to illustrate to the public the government's impotence in securing its own installations. The campaign against the military is the more noteworthy because it saw occasions where the *Montoneros* rampaged at will through Argentina's major cities and dealt significant blows to all three traditional military services: the army, navy, and air force.[52]

This campaign started in July 1975 and at first involved blocking roads, temporarily occupying the city of Córdoba (twice) through superbly synchronized raids, and attacking police stations. In addition to the two attacks on Córdoba and a similar attack in Buenos Aires, nine police stations, twenty stores, two press offices, three town halls, and an artillery headquarters were bombed. What the *Montoneros* achieved by these actions was to show that the police alone could not maintain order despite introducing sand-bagged machine gun nests and strictly controlling traffic around police stations and other likely targets. Police casualties began mounting at least as rapidly as *Montonero* losses, thereby prompting the army to demand the lead in the national counterinsurgency effort.[53]

The army no longer limited its intervention against urban insurgent groups to the times when the police seemed overwhelmed. The shift to a military lead in this war signaled that matters of stability and order were no longer primarily police matters. From the moment the army took control of the counterinsurgency effort, the *Montoneros* considered every uniformed man a representative of repressive institutions and thus a potential terrorist target. The *Montoneros* next lashed out against the military with great ferocity.[54]

Well-coordinated guerrilla operations illustrating a high degree of technical planning and proficiency characterized the latter months of 1975. During this time, the *Montoneros* launched some of the largest guerrilla operations ever undertaken in Argentina. The campaign began when 100 *Montonero* bombs exploded throughout Argentine cities on key revolutionary anniversary dates in August and September, almost as the herald of a new phase in an armed struggle. After this opening salvo of terror bombing, the campaign against the armed forces commenced with attacks on all three armed forces. These guerrilla operations were designed to administer serious psychological blows to the military's public image, if not a clear military defeat for government counterinsurgency efforts.[55]

First, the navy was hit in a well-orchestrated attack. The *Montoneros* blew up the navy's prize possession, a newly acquired, and their first, modern missile-carrying frigate, the 3,500-ton *Santisima Trinidad*. A *Montonero* unit that studied underwater attacks from World War II meticulously planned this operation. Approaching at night in a collapsible camouflaged boat, *Montonero* frogmen attached underwater demolition charges to the ship's hull as it was lying in a naval shipyard protected by guards. Although the resulting explosion did not sink the ship, it did knock out all the electronics aboard, setting operational deployment back by at least a year.[56]

The *Montoneros* then attacked the air force. This attack occurred at an airport in the city of San Miguel de Tucuman. This operation, like the one on the navy, also occurred in a guarded military zone, but the *Montoneros* took advantage of slack security practices. A *Montonero* platoon found an abandoned tunnel that ran under the runway at the airport and packed explosives in a drainage pipe that ran perpendicular from the tunnel and up to the runway. As a C-130 military transport plane rolled down the runway for takeoff, the explosives were detonated by remote control as the aircraft rolled over the drain's location. The explosion damaged the runway and destroyed the C-130. The plane exploded with a military antiguerrilla unit on board. Five people were killed and forty injured in this well-timed and planned operation.[57]

The operation that had the honor of being the most elaborately planned and audacious in scope was reserved for the army. It was early October 1975 when the *Montoneros* attacked the garrison of the 29th Regiment, Mounted Infantry (R29) in the Argentine city of Formosa, located 930 kilometers north of Buenos Aires and close to the Paraguayan border. This northern provincial capital was not a *Montonero* stronghold, so consequently, combatants and equipment had to be transported from a *Montonero* base in Rosario about 800 kilometers away. A total of sixty members composed the whole force, made up of thirty-nine fighters in the assault element and twenty-one support personnel pre-positioned in Buenos Aires, Santa Fe, and Formosa. Success depended on the synchronization of three separate actions, the first being hijacking an *Aerolineas Argentinas* Boeing 739 en route from Buenos Aires to Corrientas. This task was entrusted to four guerrillas, including some doctors among the hijackers, who were to force the pilot to land at the Formosa airport instead of its planned destination. Next, nine guerrillas would take over the airport as the plane was circling overhead. The third action, a convoy of six vehicles consisting of twenty-six people (some in army uniforms), attempted to head undetected to the R29 garrison to conduct the attack and demand the post's surrender.

The assault element achieved some initial success in approaching the garrison undetected. This success can be attributed to the fact that the military was not expecting an attack so far from Buenos Aires. Additionally, the approaching convoy appeared routine to the camp's guards, and the guerrillas dressed in army uniforms were quite literally "hiding in plain sight." The garrison personnel only began to react once the guerrillas approached near the compound gate and fired their weapons. Once firing began, the assault element started taking heavy machine gun fire from various guard towers. The guerrilla force was only able to penetrate the R29 garrison as far as the camp armory where they took some weapons, including a machine gun, that was put to immediate use. The battle that ensued was brief but furious. The *Montoneros* took high casualties, and five of the six vehicles were immobilized. As army reinforcements began to arrive from nearby residential quarters, eleven surviving guerrillas piled into the only remaining vehicle, an F-350 truck. There was just enough room in the truck for the attackers with their weapons to make a getaway. Another four guerrillas ultimately reached the airport independently. Once at the airport, the surviving fighters took off in the Boeing and a four-seater Cessna 182. The wounded were provided with blood transfusions while in flight. The hijackers forced the pilot of the Boeing to land in a field outside Santa Fe where other guerrillas with ten vehicles awaited their arrival. The guerrillas then vanished, preventing police pursuit by simply scattering nails on the roads behind them.[58]

It is interesting to note that the attack on the infantry regiment in Formosa was probably the *Montoneros*' most important "military" operation, but it was also their last.[59] It was these spectacular operations against the armed forces that, in part, contributed to the military reasserting control over the Argentine government. After the attack on the R29 base, the army demanded a larger role in dealing with subversive threats to the military, society, and the nation overall. The army pressured the government to approve its proposal for a National Council of Internal Security and a National Defense Council. The internal security council served essentially as a rubber-stamp organization for all antisubversive actions deemed appropriate by the military; the defense council would enforce the internal security council's policies. Military repression was now given official sanction and would be carried out against all organizations in which subversion was believed to exist. These included known rural and urban guerrilla organizations, combative trade unions, "factory guerrillas," and university student groups. To assist the military in this effort, the two councils gave the armed forces the power to coordinate and centralize all of the nation's agencies, including control over the federal police who could assist in repressing anyone deemed subversive.[60]

Also, by late 1975 and into 1976, economic reverses continued; the rate of inflation reached 350 percent, and the prolonged internal warfare brought Argentina to virtual anarchy. President Isabel Perón was ineffective in bringing any economic or political stability to the national situation. Furthermore, when she was accused of mismanagement and corrupt practices, she was forced to relinquish her position as head of state. The military, its position already strengthened politically by its increased role under the charter of martial law as the central agency controlling antisubversive policies, reasserted itself into the government leadership role. General Jorge Rafael Videla took charge in the aftermath of a military coup following Isabel's removal from office and established a military dictatorship. The army took the lead in running the government, but the navy and air force each shared a third of all governmental responsibilities in an awkward division of power.[61]

Meanwhile, the *Montoneros* continued fighting through 1976 against the police and the military, but none of their subsequent actions ever achieved the level of sophistication, scale, or drama as the ones conducted in the latter part of 1975. As the military began an extreme but effective program of eradicating insurgent groups in 1976, *Montonero* operational capacity became limited to random acts of terrorism. The press, now suppressed by the dictatorship, robbed the *Montoneros* of their last true political weapon—media publicity. Popular support to the movement all but evaporated as the public grew weary from all the civil strife, and the government's reign of terror, the "Dirty War," began. Instead of flocking to their ranks in the face of unbearable repressive conditions as the *Montoneros* hoped, many potential recruits came to regard guerrilla groups as being solely responsible for the repression that occurred nationwide, mostly in the cities but in the countryside as well. By 1977, the *Montoneros* were virtually decimated as a fighting force due to the military's antisubversive measures. Armed resistance came to a complete halt in 1979 when an exiled group of guerrillas returned to conduct a counteroffensive and was almost annihilated. Although the *Montoneros* continued as a movement into 1980, it was estimated that no more than 350 members remained. Although the *Montoneros* never acknowledged defeat, by 1980, nonviolent methods became the rule. The *Montonero* watchword became "to resist is to win," a far cry from the inspirational *todo o nada*.[62]

The military dictatorship after 1976 was no better equipped than its predecessors to deal with the vexing social and economic questions that had beset Argentina for so long. In true military fashion, the dictatorship focused on a problem it could solve—the issue of subversion and security. Officially known as the "final resolution" but more popularly known as the "Dirty War," it included Nazi techniques of mass arrests, imprisonment, unprecedented levels of torture, murder, and burial in mass graves of anyone deemed politically undesirable. No one in Argentina was safe from the parallel clandestine state the military erected in its zeal to "save" the nation. Between 1976 and 1983, upwards of 30,000 Argentines disappeared through the practices of political genocide. Ostensibly occupied with combating terrorism, the government's cure for subversion resulted in the intimidation of the entire population, with no segment of society considered safe or totally secure.[63]

In one sense, the military became what it was fighting—terrorists. What started as urban warfare between two asymmetrical forces—one revolutionary and guerrilla, the other a professional conventional military—during the course of prolonged and frustrating conflict moved toward an unanticipated stage of symmetry. The insurgents became more militarized as the professionals became more clandestine and criminal.

One of the underlying assumptions of this chapter is the notion that a study of past insurgencies or radical revolutionary movements can provide insight into similar situations faced today or in the future. At the tactical level, this brief examination of the *Montoneros* illustrates that, modern refinements notwithstanding, almost everything radical movements practice today has been used in the past. The specific methods may differ, say crashing an airplane into a skyscraper, but the tactical principles are the same. The efficacy of small mobile assault groups operating "behind the lines" to harass the enemy, attacking his symbols of national strength, and terrorizing the citizenry have not fundamentally changed over time. In this type of warfare, though, military tactics are employed and political objectives are sought.[64] Military forces need to understand this and prepare to deal with the challenges that the asymmetrical type of warfare poses. The fact that radical movements have been inseparably linked to ideological forces hostile to the United States presents this issue in a more urgent light.

As a practical matter, militaries that operate in an unconventional urban environment need to understand that technology and weapons alone will not provide the solution to countering asymmetrical threats. Unfortunately, state-of-the-art technology also increases the power of radical movements since ideologically motivated insurgents or terrorists can either construct or secure devices or weapon systems that, for a short time, put them on a roughly equal footing with a country's constituted authority. This technological parity can be a disadvantage to a conventional force, even if its equipment or troops are numerically superior. The threat can "mass" at the critical point and time of its choosing, knowing full well that even with superior numbers the military cannot possibly be everywhere. This point becomes clearer as one considers that the *Montoneros*, although labeled as urban guerrillas, operated throughout the country in other cities, occasionally in the countryside, and as far away as a remote border garrison near the northeastern city of Formosa. They were "urban" in the sense that cities provided a base for operations, safety, funding, logistics support, and intelligence networks, but they could and did strike with impunity anywhere they chose.

Probably the greatest challenge for conventional military forces that engage in an unconventional operating environment is to understand the different nature of the "combat" situation and adjust their traditional battlefield frameworks accordingly. A template type of response to an insurgent threat over a prolonged period of time often fails. Key terrain in these types of operations becomes the symbolic and real centers of government power. One only has to look to the recent examples of the World Trade Center and Pentagon attacks to validate this point. The battleground to be won is not city sectors or districts; it is a fight for minds. This is especially true in a classic revolutionary struggle where both sides are attempting to gain the population's support. Conventional force reliance on massed firepower and maneuver is not only politically inappropriate but also, as a practical matter, very difficult to execute against guerrillas operating in congested, complex city terrain.

Military leaders and planners need to keep in mind that generally these operations involve counterinsurgency and are not necessarily combat operations. At the national level, effective government counterinsurgency programs should include both rewards and punishments. Political and economic development programs must be integrated with military operations designed to eliminate hostile opposition to maintain a legitimate governing authority. It is also necessary to reduce the number of people seen as "the enemy" so we do not alienate public opinion or stifle legitimate dissent.[65]

Another lesson for military professionals to consider when examining the legacy of urban guerrilla warfare is that effective counterinsurgency doctrine is for both specialized forces and conventional forces. Conventional forces need to understand and train to perform counterinsurgency tasks. The potential always exists for U.S. forces assigned to a peacekeeping mission to be tasked to provide support directly to a host nation or in conjunction with a coalition to a region undergoing an insurgency. The U.S. Army found itself in this type of situation as it supported the UNISOM II mission in Somalia in the early 1990s. Understanding the role that conventional forces play in these kinds of operations can assist in maintaining peace. Conventional forces can collect essential intelligence; sweep, clear, and hold areas; and provide a rapid-reaction capability. According to scholars Georges Fauriol and Andrew Hoehn, "in the end, both insurgent and counterinsurgent activities seek one objective; the maintenance and control of political power."[66] In that regard, a military force engaged in these endeavors needs to be prepared to exercise the full range of operations: offense, defense, stability, and support.

The Argentine military response to threats to its society demonstrates an extreme example of how to provide domestic security. A larger lesson that emerges from this case study is that no exclusively military solution for urban violence exists. Urban terrorism is not peculiar to any specific form of society, and under certain conditions, terrorists can succeed in breaking down the fabric of the most resilient democratic society. The measures and level of power the Argentine military exercised may be a remote possibility in a society that has a strong democratic tradition such as in the United States. The challenge to our society, if faced with similar conditions, is to find another way to resolve threats to stability and security without resorting to the Argentine model. This makes it important to consider the problems of national response in these situations. The first requirement is that the government under attack, whether the attack is from an internal insurgent or external terrorist, must show both the resolution and the capacity to respond with necessary force. Just as important as the first requirement is the ability to show restraint in applying force when appropriate. Last, effective UO of any kind require good, timely intelligence coordinated in conjunction with all components in the fight.[67]

One other issue emerges for consideration as a result of this case study on an asymmetrical threat—a cautionary note. To evaluate the phenomenon of the *Montoneros* in Argentina merely from the standpoint of winners and losers overlooks more fundamental issues of concern for modern military professionals. It is true that the *Montoneros* lost in their goal of initiating a popular uprising and replacing the existing regime. In most instances, however, they made a deep impression well out of proportion to their numbers or the strength of their financial and logistics resources. They caused a significant amount of the nation's resources and energy to be applied to the threat they posed. Even when they were able to mount an effective operational challenge in 1975, they were still ultimately defeated by efficient, though brutal, counterinsurgency operations.[68] The tragedy in all this is that the professional military, the defender of freedom and liberty, eventually turned its energies inward, repressing the society it was supposed to protect. In that sense, the *Montoneros* affected millions of lives as democracy was destroyed in the process. From a Clausewitzian perspective, this case study illustrates how a country is thrust into descent when the factors of emotion and passion dominate rationality and control. Unfortunately, the real losers in this situation were Argentina and its people. Perhaps the greatest lesson the *Montonero* example provides is one of caution for governments and societies that may face somewhat similar situations. When a society gives up its core principles and values of governance in the name of greater state security, the society loses.

Notes

1. Microsoft Bookshelf '98 Reference Library.
2. Richard Gillespie, *Soldiers of Peron: Argentina's Montoneros* (Oxford, UK: Clarendon Press, 1982), 81-82.
3. For brief but excellent summaries about ALN activities in Brazil, the *Tupamaros* in Uruguay, and the *Montoneros* in Argentina, see Liza Gross, *Handbook of Leftist Guerrilla Groups in Latin America and the Caribbean* (Boulder, CO: Westview Press, 1995), 16-21, 29-32, 145-49.
4. William Columbus Davis, *Warnings From the Far South: Democracy versus Dictatorship in Uruguay, Argentina, and Chile* (Westport, CT: Praeger, 1995), 2-3.
5. Gross, 4.
6. Ibid.; *Latin American Insurgencies*, Georges Fauriol, ed. (Washington, DC: National Defense University Press, 1985), 9. Fauriol also provides a brief historical overview that concisely traces the development of insurgent groups in Latin America after World War II. See 11-17.
7. Ibid., 163.
8. Gross, 3-4.
9. Ibid., 1.
10. Richard Gillespie, "The Urban Guerrilla in Latin America," *Terrorism, Ideology & Revolution*, Noel O'Sullivan, ed. (Boulder, CO: Westview Press, 1986), 151.
11. Richard Gillespie, *Soldiers of Peron: Argentina's Montoneros* (Oxford, UK: Oxford University Press, February 1986), 48. A footnote on page 48 briefly explains *foco* theory. For readers who may be unfamiliar with *focoism*, the note is reproduced here: "The theory of the *foco*, or *foquismo* (subscribed to by *foquistas*), though originally elaborated with rural warfare in mind, contends that revolutionaries should begin to wage armed struggle even if some of the 'conditions' for a successful revolution are not yet present in their country; that guerrilla activities help to create such conditions; and that, by exploiting the classical guerrilla advantages of mobility, flexibility, and surprise, small armed nuclei can develop into popular revolutionary armies, capable of defeating regular armies." See also Regis Debray, *Revolution in the Revolution* (Harmondsworth, UK: Penguin, 1969); Ernesto Guevara, *Guerrilla Warfare: Che Guevara* (Harmondsworth, UK: Penguin Books, 1969); and Brian Train, "The Terror War" at <www.islandnet.com/~citizenx/Twbody.html>, 2-3.
12. Fauriol, 168-70; in Martin Edwin Andersen, *Dossier Secreto* (Boulder, CO: Westview Press, 1993), Guevara saw as his mission to make "one, two . . . many Vietnams" in the Americas, 57; Robert Moss, *The War for the Cities* (NY: Coward, McCann & Geoghegan, 1972), 148.
13. Fauriol, 170-71; Moss, 148.

14. *Armed Forces & Modern Counter Insurgency*, Ian F.W. Beckett and John Pimlott, eds. (NY: St. Martin's Press, 1985), 116; James Kohl and John Litt, *Urban Guerrilla Warfare in Latin America* (Cambridge, MA: The MIT Press, 1974), 324; and Davis, 28-29.

15. Walter Laqueur, *The Guerrilla Reader: A Historical Anthology* (Philadelphia, PA: Temple University Press, 1977), 187, and *Armed Forces & Modern Counter Insurgency*, 116.

16. John D. Eliot, "Transitions of Contemporary Terrorism," *Military Review* (May 1977), 9; Train, 4-5; and Kohl and Litt, 18.

17. Eliot, 9.

18. *Armed Forces & Modern Counter Insurgency*, 117, and Kohl and Litt, 19.

19. Ibid., 18.

20. Fauriol, 172.

21. Carlos Marighella, *Minimanual of the Urban Guerrilla*, 1969. No publication data available. Copy in possession of the author.

22. Kohl and Litt, 15-16.

23. Ibid., 15-19, and *Armed Forces & Modern Counter Insurgency*, 123.

24. Kohl and Litt, 20-23.

25. Fauriol, 4, and Gillespie, *Soldiers of Peron*, 60-63.

26. Davis, 74; Gillespie, *Soldiers of Peron*, 76; Laqueur, 231.

27. *Armed Forces & Modern Counter Insurgency*, 116, and Gillespie, *Soldiers of Peron*, 47.

28. Simply stated, "Peronist views" were based on three unifying principles: political sovereignty, economic independence, and social justice. Gillespie, *Soldiers of Peron*, 8.

29. Davis, 107, and Gross, 7, 14. In addition to the *Montoneros*, the ERP, and the Revolutionary Armed Forces, Gross lists four other "leftist" guerrilla movements prevalent during the 1960s and 1970s: the Guerrilla Army of the People, a Marxist-Leninist-Guevarist group; the Armed Forces of Liberation, a Marxist-Leninist movement with Maoist overtones; the Peronist Armed Forces, a leftist-Peronist group; and the *Uturuncos* "Tiger-Men," a Peronist-Castroist movement, 7-22.

30. Gillespie, *Soldiers of Peron*, 17, 25, 40, 48; Gross, 17; and Davis, 89, 96.

31. Gillespie, *Soldiers of Peron*, 1, 57-60, and Gross, 17.

32. For detailed accounts on the Aramburu assassination, see Gillespie, *Soldiers of Peron*, 89; Gross, 16; Kohl and Litt, 343; Andersen, 65; and *Terrorism in Argentina*, 1979, no publication data available, 35-38. This book is a compilation of news articles and communiqués published by the military dictatorship that took over Argentina in the late 1970s and conducted the Dirty War. Through brief introductory narratives followed by sensational

newspaper accounts depicting the horrors of guerrilla actions, the book is an attempt to justify the ruling regime's draconian measures to keep order and security. Regarding the Aramburu assassination, pages 35-38 are interviews with some of the *Montonero* members who conducted Operation *PINDAPOY*. Of particular note are the extensive planning, preparations, and methods the guerrillas used in gathering intelligence on Aramburu's movements and details of his apartment along with the ways they obtained military-type uniforms, vehicles, and other support.

33. Kohl and Litt, 324-25, and Davis, 106-107.

34. Gillespie, *Soldiers of Peron*, 87, 90; Gross, 16-17; and *Latin American Insurgencies*, 26-27.

35. Gillespie, *Soldiers of Peron*, 84-85. *Commandos* had the following names: Eva Peron, a name that all units eagerly competed for; *Comandante Uturunco*, *nom de guerre* of Argentina's first modern rural guerrilla leader; General Jose de San Martin, after the Independence hero; Felipe Vallese, the first Peronist youth martyr; and 29 May, date of the *Cordobazo*. Later on, *Montonero* units were christened predominately with the names of slain combatants.

36. Ibid., 79.

37. Gillespie, *Soldiers of Peron*, 95-96, and Davis, 107.

38. Gillespie, *Soldiers of Peron*, 95-97. Although Gillespie does not specifically state that torture was used to extract information from the two *Montoneros* captured in the La Calera operation, the amount of intelligence gained and the speed with which the police reacted suggests that this was the case. Gillespie does state that after the Maza funeral, public sympathy for the "Montoneros being tortured in prison" became evident.

39. Davis, 107. For a detailed chronology of all the significant guerrilla and government events during Levingston's short term in office, see Kohl and Litt, 343-52.

40. Gillespie, *Soldiers of Peron*, 111.

41. Davis, 109-11, and Gillespie, *Soldiers of Peron*, 119.

42. Davis, 112-14, and Gillespie, *Soldiers of Peron*, 146-47, 150-51.

43. Davis, 114-16, and Gillespie, *Soldiers of Peron*, 163.

44. Davis, 115-16, and Gillespie, *Soldiers of Peron*, 163, 184.

45. Ibid., 174-79.

46. Ibid., 180-81. See also Lester A. Sobel, *Argentina and Peron, 1970 1975,* for additional information on the Born brothers' kidnapping. The specific charges the Born brothers had been "tried" on consisted of exploitation of Argentine workers by Bunge and Born, and the corporation's support to the 1955 military coup that deposed President Peron. "In addition to the $60 million (a figure Bunge & Born neither confirmed nor denied), the

company also distributed $1.2 million worth of food and clothing in poor neighborhoods around the country," 146.

47. Gillespie, *Soldiers of Peron*, 181.
48. Ibid., 181-82, and Davis, 116-17.
49. Gillespie, *Soldiers of Peron*, 183-84, 188, and Andersen, 120-21.
50. Gillespie, *Soldiers of Peron*, 186-92.
51. Ibid., 192.
52. Ibid., 193.
53. Ibid., 193-94.
54. Ibid., 201.
55. Ibid., 196.
56. Ibid., 196-97.
57. Ibid., 197.
58. Ibid., 197-200.
59. Anderson, 232.
60. Donald C. Hodges, *Argentina, 1943 1976, The National Revolution and Resistance* (Albuquerque, NM: University of New Mexico Press, 1976), 178.
61. Hodges, 168-70, and Davis, 117-19.
62. Gillespie, *Soldiers of Peron*, 204-205; Gross, 20-21; Andersen, 12-13.
63. Donald C. Hodges, *Argentina's "Dirty War," An Intellectual Biography* (Austin, TX: University of Texas Press, 1991), 19, 177; Patricia and William Marchak, *God's Assassins: State Terrorism in Argentina in the 1970s* (Montreal: McGill-Queen's University Press, 1999), preface.
64. Fauriol, 1, 167-68, 191-92.
65. Moss, 240-41.
66. Fauriol, 191.
67. Moss, 240; *Terrorism, Legitimacy, and Power, The Consequences of Political Violence*, Martha Crenshaw, ed. (Middletown, CT: Wesleyan University Press, 1983), 6, 31-35.
68. Gross, 1-2, 5.

Humanitarian Operations in an Urban Environment: Hurricane Andrew, August-October 1992

Jerold E. Brown

In the early morning hours of 18 August 1992, a WC-130 of the U.S. Air Force Reserve's 815th Weather Flight, the "Storm Trackers," took off from Keesler Air Force Base (AFB), Mississippi, to gather data on an as yet unnamed tropical storm in the mid-Atlantic 1,000 miles east of the U.S. mainland. The National Hurricane Center (NHC) at Coral Gables, Florida, requested the mission to learn more about a growing storm then moving westward across longitude 55 degrees west.[1] The center named the storm, the first hurricane of the 1992 season, "Andrew." Hurricane Andrew became the most destructive and costly natural phenomenon in U.S. history. The U.S. military response to Andrew was the most extensive humanitarian and relief operation in a long history of providing comfort and assistance to the American people in times of need.

The Storm Trackers' mission on that August morning was only the first of more than two dozen missions into the eye of the storm. The trackers flew continuous missions, twenty-four hours a day, watching the storm grow in intensity and tracking Andrew's progress from the Lesser Antilles, across the southern tip of Florida, over the Gulf of Mexico, until it finally made landfall on the Louisiana coast, not far from Keesler AFB where the first mission originated. Each mission lasted ten to thirteen hours. The 815th first established a forward operating base on Antigua in the West Indies to be closer to the storm, then moved to Charleston, South Carolina. Personnel from the 403d Maintenance Squadron at Keesler struggled to keep the 815th aircraft in the air, working twelve-hour shifts without a break while their families in Biloxi prepared for the storm bearing down on their community.[2]

The timely and accurate information the trackers provided allowed authorities to make critical early decisions that undoubtedly saved many lives. A full twenty-four hours before Andrew made landfall in Dade County, just south of Miami, Florida's governor declared an emergency, initiated the first steps of an evacuation of the area in the storm's path, and called up the first contingent of Florida National Guardsmen. Some of these 600 guardsmen would remain on duty for weeks, dealing with the aftermath of Andrew's rage.[3] The Guard performed yeoman duty assisting civil authorities in a variety of tasks, but most important, it performed a law enforcement role. The guardsmen patrolled neighborhoods ravaged by Andrew's 160-mile-per-hour (mph) winds, detained looters and other suspected criminals, directed traffic, and guided follow-on military units to critical locations. The Florida National Guard's training and knowledge were critical in dealing with the chaos Andrew created in more than half a dozen communities of south Dade County. The arriving Florida National Guard units, however, were merely the first act of a massive U.S. military response to the devastation Andrew left behind as it moved across south Florida.

Hurricane Andrew was the most destructive natural disaster ever to strike the United States. Cutler Ridge, Perrine, Kendall, Old Cutler, Country Walk, Homestead, and Florida City were in the 100-square-mile area in south Dade County that Andrew completely leveled. Another 200 square miles, including the cities of Miami and Miami Beach, suffered significant damage. Two dozen south Floridians lost their lives, and property damage rose to an estimated $1 billion, although the total cost can never be accurately determined. Lost wages and earnings, business income, tax collections, tourist trade, and personal assets are incalculable. Perhaps more important, the psychological and spiritual damage to the residents of the stricken area who lived through the terrifying hours of the storm and its aftermath will require years, if not decades, to heal. Into this area of destruction where all public services had ceased to exist, U.S. military forces deployed hundreds, then thousands, of troops and vast quantities of equipment to deal with the crisis. The U.S. military response in south Florida in the days and weeks after Hurricane Andrew became the most extensive urban rescue and humanitarian operations in American history.

The primary responsibility for dealing with local crises and disasters in the United States, whether natural or man-made, historically fell on local authorities.[4] In all too many instances, however, local governments were unequipped to deal with other than minor situations. Local authorities were either too poorly organized, lacked adequate resources, or were simply overwhelmed by the magnitude of the disaster. Thus, state and local governments frequently turned to the militia and, later, the National Guard as the organizations most capable of handling large-scale emergencies. On some occasions, however, disasters were even beyond the National Guard's resources and abilities to deal with the loss of life and disrupted public services. On those occasions when crises overwhelmed state Guard units, governors called upon the president to provide federal resources and manpower to assist local authorities or assume full responsibility for managing the crisis. Throughout the nation's history, the Regular U.S. Army troops responded to these calls for assistance and contributed both directly and indirectly to operations involving rescue, relief, security, and restoration of public services.

On numerous occasions in the nineteenth and twentieth centuries, the Regular Army answered the summons to assist or take control of humanitarian and disaster relief operations. For a number of reasons, military forces are better suited to deal with natural disasters and their consequences than are other government agencies. Among these reasons are leadership, experience, organization, equipment, a trained and disciplined force, and resources that are generally not available even to government agencies specifically created to deal with both natural and man-made disasters.

The Chicago Fire

Perhaps the best-known natural disasters in the last 150 years of American history are the great Chicago fire of 1871, the Johnstown flood of 1889, and the San Francisco earthquake of 1906. In each of these cases, the government responded differently, depending on the presence of military units in the area and local commanders' leadership initiatives. A brief look at each of the disasters will demonstrate the absence of planning and preparations to deal with civil catastrophes.

By the middle of the nineteenth century, Chicago, with a population of 300,000, was a major business, communications, meatpacking, and manufacturing center. Ten railroads converged in Chicago, making it one of the nation's leading transportation hubs. Like most nineteenth-century American cities, Chicago's dwellings and many public buildings were wooden-frame, clapboard, shingle-roof construction. The city's fire department was barely adequate and struggled to keep up with the growth of an expanding metropolitan area. The fire that broke out on Sunday evening, 8 October 1871, in a cow shed behind a residence on Chicago's DeKoven Street spread quickly in the tinder-dry neighborhood of wood-frame buildings.[5] Within hours, the flames engulfed a vast area near the city's center. Lieutenant General Philip Sheridan, commander of the Division of the Missouri, whose headquarters, located across the street from Chicago's courthouse, was destroyed early in the conflagration, responded quickly. He ordered troops at the local garrison to begin demolishing buildings in the fire's path to create a firebreak, keeping the fire to the north and saving the area south of Harrison and Wabash streets. The Army's work, however, had just begun.

By Tuesday, the fire had destroyed three and a half square miles of Chicago, killed several hundred residents, and left more than 100,000 people homeless and destitute. Thousands of hapless Chicagoans roamed the devastated city looking for food, shelter, and anything of value. Widespread looting and the near outbreak of riots prompted Chicago's mayor, Roswell B. Mason, to proclaim martial law on Wednesday and ask Sheridan to take charge of reestablishing civil order. Sheridan readily accepted the responsibility. He mustered a force of Regulars and local militia, subsequently called "Sheridan Guards," to bring order to the city and begin providing relief for the thousands of dispossessed. He ordered six infantry companies from Nebraska and Kansas to Chicago to patrol the city and set up relief centers. When this number proved inadequate, he ordered six more companies to the city, some coming from as far away as Kentucky. Sherman also provided hundreds of thousands of Army rations and thousands of tents and blankets to those in need of food and shelter.

Sheridan not only ordered his troops to arrest and detain looters and cutthroats but also cracked down on profiteers and others attempting to take advantage of the displaced population. Although martial law ended in Chicago on 23 October, fifteen days after the fire started, the Army continued to provide relief services for a considerable period thereafter. Despite the fact that Sheridan had initially acted on his own authority, his superiors, Commanding General of the Army William T. Sherman and President Ulysses S. Grant, fully supported his actions and authorized whatever military resources necessary to provide relief for the inhabitants of the burned-out areas.

The Johnstown Flood

The story of the Johnstown flood offers a different perspective on the military's role in local disaster relief. On Thursday evening, 30 May 1889, a massive storm front moved eastward over the Allegheny Mountains and began to dump huge quantities of rain on an area from those mountains to New York City to the mouth of the Potomac in the east to the southern boundary of Virginia. By Friday, an average of 6 to 8 inches of rain had fallen on this vast area. Not a single community or acre of ground was spared. Central and western Pennsylvania received the heaviest downpours. In some areas, the rain had fallen steadily at the rate of an inch an hour. One source estimated that 4.32 billion tons of water fell on 1,200 square miles of western Pennsylvania in less than thirty-six hours. With such a quantity of water, local flooding was predictable. As events were to prove, however, the consequence of so much water was the most disastrous and devastating flood in U.S. history.[6]

By Friday evening, many towns and villages along the Susquehanna River's tributaries, the West Branch, the Juniata, and the North Branch, were already inundated. Clearfield, Renovo, Lock Haven, Williamsport, and Montgomery, to name just a few of the towns along the Susquehanna system, measured high water above any previous flood levels. By Saturday morning, 1 June, most towns along the upper Susquehanna experienced flooding or effects of the rising water. Generally speaking, these towns and cities coped with the situation on their own. Few outsiders came to help them.

To the west of the Allegheny divide, a number of small tributaries converge to form the Allegheny River. The Allegheny flows westward to meet the Monongahela at Pittsburgh where the two rivers form the Ohio. Along the Allegheny's upper tributaries, scores of small cities and towns lie in the valleys and hug the steep riverbanks. The largest, and perhaps the most important, of the urban centers on the Conemaugh, one of three primary Allegheny tributaries, is the city of Johnstown. Located at the mouth of Stony Creek, Johnstown is the financial and cultural center of the area. At least a dozen other boroughs and incorporated communities along the Conemaugh and Stony Creek, including Cambria, Geistown, Millville, Prospect, Woodvale, Moxham, and Morrellville, are generally identified as part of Johnstown. In the 1880s, small factories, logging operations, mills, iron works, and rail yards sustained the region's population.

A half-century earlier the state of Pennsylvania had built a large earthen dam 16 miles upstream from Johnstown on the South Fork, another tributary of the Conemaugh, to supply water for the series of canals then used to move natural resources and finished goods between Pittsburgh and Philadelphia. The South Fork dam was 931 feet long, 272 feet wide at its base, 72 feet high in the center, and 20 feet across at the top. The dam compounded a reservoir of over 400 acres. In 1854, the first train crossed the Alleghenies on the newly opened Pennsylvania Railroad system between Philadelphia and Pittsburgh. Thereafter, the canal system declined, and the state increasingly neglected to maintain the dam. The Pennsylvania Railroad purchased the dam in 1857 but performed little maintenance on it. The dam broke for the first time in 1862 but caused little damage downstream because the reservoir was only half full at the time. The dam was repaired, and the lake it formed served as a recreational area for summer visitors to the area. Twenty-seven years later the tale would have a very different end.

By noon on Friday, 31 May, several towns on the rail line along the Conemaugh and South Fork were flooded, and water was in some cellars and streets of Johnstown proper. The rain that was swamping towns and communities east of the mountains was also soaking the ridges and valleys to the west. The drainage into the South Fork reservoir was quickly overwhelming the dam's spillway, 9 feet below the crest of the dam. In spite of the fact that 6,000 cubic feet of water was going over the spillway every *second*, the water behind the dam rose at a rate of *10 inches per hour*. The pressure was too much. Just before 1500, the center of the dam gave way, and 20 million tons of water poured through a 430-foot-wide gap in the dam.

The distance from the South Fork dam to the Johnstown bridge is 16 miles, and the elevation drop over this distance is 400 feet. Down the narrow valley of the South Fork into the Conemaugh, a massive wall of water, estimated at 40 feet high, gathered speed and rushed headlong, breaking up and carrying away every man-made and natural obstacle that stood in its path. Trees, buildings, bridges, animals, locomotives, and human beings were swept along in the unimaginable torrent. Entire towns and villages disappeared. By the time the wall of water reached Johnstown, it had been reduced to perhaps 20 feet high. Nevertheless, the wave still contained enough energy that, as it washed through the city, it carried nearly everything in its path with it. It left only death and destruction behind.

Most of the 12,000 residents of Johnstown, completely disoriented and in shock, spent Saturday and Sunday searching the debris for the living and the dead, and trying to come to grips with the enormity of the disaster. Not until Sunday evening, 2 June, did the local sheriff appeal to the governor of Pennsylvania for troops. The next day, 3 June, the 14th Regiment, Pennsylvania National Guard, was ordered to Johnstown. Five hundred fifty guardsmen of the 14th eventually arrived in the Johnstown area. They provided security details to protect property; set up tent villages for survivors; fed up to 30,000 people per day (including thousands of civilian laborers who came into the area); and supervised the clearing of streets, repair of public buildings, and reopening of the railroads. The 14th Regiment remained in Johnstown until 13 July when all but one company departed the area. The remaining company stayed in Johnstown throughout the summer.

Unlike Chicago, no Regular U.S. military units were stationed near Johnstown. Response to and relief of Johnstown arose largely from local and state committees and agencies. Businesses and industries, especially the railroads, that operated in the devastated area provided most of the resources for clearing roads, streets, and the remaining bridges and brought in food, clothing, and other necessary relief supplies at their own expense. The federal government provided little other than its good offices and offers of moral support to the relief effort.

The San Francisco Earthquake

A third example of the U.S. Army's response to an urban crisis was the San Francisco earthquake and fire of 1906. The Army's role in the San Francisco disaster left a legacy of controversy.[7] To some, Brigadier General Frederick Funston was a hero for his quick and timely reaction to the geological upheaval that engulfed San Francisco a little after 0500 on Wednesday, 18 April 1906. During the following days, Funston created a reputation among many Americans for decisive decisions and inexhaustible leadership under pressure that established him as one of America's leading soldiers. To others, Funston far exceeded his position or authority and unleashed on the citizens of San Francisco bands of undisciplined, untrained, poorly led troops who harassed and murdered innocent people going about their legitimate tasks. The truth may, perhaps, lie somewhere between these two positions, but the alternative to Funston's action was inaction and chaos.

The city of San Francisco occupies one of the most beautiful pieces of terrain in North America. Situated on the west littoral of San Francisco Bay, San Francisco was the largest U.S. city west of the Mississippi River in 1900. The San Andreas fault (actually not a single fault line but a zone of faults) extends from the north-central California coast about 200 miles north of San Francisco, through the San Francisco peninsula, southeast to the Gulf of California. Frequent activity (at least in geological time) along the San Andreas line has shaped and reshaped the California coastline for millions of years. In the early morning hours of 18 April 1906, movement of the great plates hundreds of feet below the surface of the earth sent a tremor of enormous magnitude racing along the fault line from north to south at more than 7,000 mph. In the few seconds the shock wave passed through San Francisco, scores of buildings collapsed or were shaken from their foundations, and water and gas mains under the city streets were wrenched apart, twisted, and broken. Ten seconds later a second shock wave of nearly equal force shook the foundations of the city again.

The unsuspecting city lay devastated. Thousands of terrified and stunned citizens fled their homes for the safety of the streets. An unknown number of men, women, and children died in their beds or while trying to escape disintegrating structures. The city's fire chief was among the first casualties of the disaster. He was perhaps the only man in San Francisco who had an idea how to fight a major fire in the city. His loss was a catastrophe in itself. His knowledge and experience were irreplaceable in the coming battle to save San Francisco.

The disruption of city utilities had two almost simultaneous consequences. First, vast quantities of gas escaping from ruptured gas mains turned a number of small fires into roaring conflagrations. Second, the disruption of the water system left firefighters responding to the emergency without their primary means of dealing with the rapidly expanding sea of flames. Thus, as the fire grew in intensity by the minute, the means to slow or stop the fire was quickly vanishing.

Surveying the extent of the damage and the spreading fires from his residence on Nob Hill overlooking the city below, Funston quickly determined that immediate action was necessary if the city was to be saved. Funston, a war hero and Medal of Honor winner, was acting commander of the Presidio garrison and several other military units in the area. Within an hour of the first tremor and without informing his superiors or receiving higher authorization, Funston ordered the troops at Fort Mason and the Presidio to move. In less than two hours after the shock wave left much of San Francisco in disarray, U.S. Army troops were marching into the city. They would play a key, but controversial, role in the battle to stop the fires and secure both public and private property in the ravaged city over the next seventy-two hours.

Around 0800, with troops already in the city, Funston sent a hasty telegram to Secretary of War William Howard Taft. The message briefly outlined the situation in San Francisco and requested authorization for Funston to take whatever actions necessary to deal with the disaster. Of course, Funston had already initiated steps without authority, and he would soon be issuing additional orders without waiting for a response to his telegram to Taft. After a short meeting with San Francisco's mayor, Eugene Schmitz, and police chief, Jeremiah Dinan, at which Funston agreed that the troops would work under Dinan's "guidance," Funston ordered units from Fort Baker, Alcatraz Island, the Presidio at Monterey, and Vancouver Barracks (Portland, Oregon, more than 500 miles to the north) to San Francisco. These units would arrive over the next several days. The governor sent California National Guard units, and Mayor Schmitz requested U.S. Marines and Navy vessels from Mare Island Naval Station. San Francisco was soon under de facto martial law.

The troops now entering San Francisco were detailed to a number of tasks. Patrols controlled access to the main thoroughfares into the fire area and provided security against looters and rioters; medical units set up hospitals to treat the injured and sick; support units set up tents and shelters for the city's refugees; and demolition squads with dynamite proceeded to blow up buildings in an attempt to stop the fire's spread by depriving it of fuel. Funston lacked any legal basis for some of these activities; other measures, such as the humanitarian activities, were well intentioned, and higher authority would certainly approve them eventually.

None of the officers or men detailed to the disaster areas had been trained to deal with civil upheaval, and there was little opportunity for adequate briefing for the assigned missions between the time Funston alerted the units and their deployment. Reports circulated widely that patrols shot suspected looters without appropriate warnings and, in at least a few cases, held drumhead courts-martial and executed miscreants summarily. (A proclamation Mayor Schmitz issued authorizing such actions was ill-advised and certainly unconstitutional.) Other soldiers were accused of looting or stealing private property, some were seen to be drunk on duty (from pilfered liquor), and yet others abused citizens who were doing nothing more than trying to protect or enter their own property.

The demolition squads proceeded with little or no knowledge of or experience with explosives. They destroyed numerous buildings that were not in danger of combusting; they demolished some buildings that, rather than denying fuel to the great fire, added to that fuel; and they wasted valuable explosives by failing to bring down a number of structures. No doubt the temporary housing, mess facilities, and medical treatment provided for thousands of homeless and desperate San Francisco citizens proved invaluable in the crisis, but whatever good the military did during and after the earthquake and fire cannot condone or excuse the indiscipline, poor leadership, lack of oversight, and misuse of soldiers in jobs they were not qualified to perform. Although his actions during the crisis added measurably to Funston's reputation, the U.S. Army could hardly be proud of its overall performance.[8]

At the beginning of the twentieth century, the U.S. Army was clearly unprepared to step into civil relief-humanitarian operations, although it had done so frequently during the nineteenth century. Whenever a civil or natural disaster occurred, the Army's response was always ad hoc. The type of response and amount of assistance provided depended on location, proximity of military units, resources readily available, and local military commanders' willingness to commit their troops and resources. The Army had no standard procedures, no special training, and no predetermined lines of authority to deal with natural or man-made disasters. And, perhaps most important, the Army had no institutional mechanism to document and capture the lessons learned in these incidents. The Army was better prepared to respond to civil disturbances such as riots and labor disputes, but the training and procedures for those events hardly met the needs for assistance during and after disasters.

Hurricanes

Hurricanes are the most awesome and destructive natural phenomena on earth.[9] Only wars kill more people and destroy more property than hurricanes. Some types of storms—tornadoes and microbursts, for example—may release more energy in a given time period than a hurricane, but they are of very short duration compared with hurricanes. Although hurricanes originate in the tropical and subtropical waters of the world's oceans where they present a serious threat to shipping, most hurricane damage occurs over land. Once hurricanes arrive over inhabited areas, they may persist, often for several days, and cover hundreds, sometimes thousands, of miles. Hurricanes may move as far as 800 miles inland before their energy dissipates.

Hurricanes occur in all oceans, although they may be known by different names. The storms we call hurricanes in the United States originate in the mid-Atlantic and generally visit most of their destructive power on the islands of the Caribbean and the south Atlantic and Gulf coasts of the United States. Hurricanes are seasonal. As a rule, Atlantic hurricanes occur in the late summer or early fall. In the Pacific, west of the international date line, hurricane-type storms are known as typhoons. Typhoons can occur anytime but most frequently develop in the summer. In the Indian Ocean, these types of storms are called tropical cyclones. Tropical cyclones generally occur during the monsoon season. In the Southern Hemisphere, similar storms occur during the opposite seasons from those in the Northern Hemisphere. Nevertheless, all of these great storms are related, and all of them result in considerable loss of human life and cause tremendous damage to property.

All hurricanes require certain specific conditions to form in mid-ocean. These conditions include surface water temperature, atmospheric pressure, wind shear, and the air's moisture content. Atlantic hurricanes normally develop in the area north of 5°N—they rarely form on the equator. When conditions are favorable, vast quantities of warm surface water (usually above 80 degrees Fahrenheit) evaporate and rise quickly in the warm tropical air. The rising moist air creates a low-pressure area at the surface that picks up even more surface evaporation. The more moist air that rises, the greater the low-pressure area formed beneath the developing storm. When there is little wind shear (different wind speeds and directions at various altitudes), the surrounding air is also drawn into the low-pressure area and begins to move around it in a circular fashion. The more uniform the winds around the core, the stronger the storm will become. The storm's core will become its "eye" (the area of lowest barometric pressure) and continue to suck up ever greater quantities of warm surface water. At first classified as a tropical depression, when the winds around the eye—the "eyewall"—reach 74 mph, it is reclassified as a hurricane.

Hurricanes are tracked by the movement of their eyes. Most Atlantic hurricanes move west, then north, or northwest, until they reach landfall. The hurricane itself may have a diameter of as much as 250 miles, and the eye may have a diameter of 20 to 30 miles. Once it begins to move, the hurricane's rate of progress will be between 5 and 20 mph; 15 mph is normal. It may cover as much as 4,000 miles over a period of two weeks or more before it dies out, and the path is unpredictable. Some hurricanes proceed into the Gulf of Mexico where they may actually pick up additional strength from the warm Gulf waters; others move north along the U.S. Atlantic coast, causing destruction as far north as Newfoundland. Predicting the movement of hurricanes is a daunting task.

The NHC in Dade County, Florida, identifies and tracks hurricanes that originate in the mid-Atlantic. Atlantic storms are named alphabetically, beginning anew each hurricane season. The first storm, for example, will begin with the letter A, the second with the letter B, and so on. At one time, storms were assigned only female names, but bowing to protests of gender bias, the NHC began using male names as well. Names may be used many times, but names associated with particularly disastrous hurricanes, such as Hurricane Camille in 1969 or Hurricane Fifi in 1974, will be retired and not used again.

Hurricane damage is caused by the effects of high winds, especially the wind close to the eyewall; by heavy rain the hurricane drops, often measured in feet, not inches; and by strong tidal floods along coastal areas that inundate land normally above the highest high tides. Inland, flooding often causes more damage and takes more lives than the devastation the high winds cause. Hurricanes frequently spawn tornadoes that add more destruction to already severely damaged communities. Hurricanes are classified according to the Saffir-Simpson scale of hurricane intensity.[10] The scale is based on wind speed and storm surge or the height of the sea level above normal high tide resulting from the storm's force (see the table). The first hurricane of the 1992 season, designated Hurricane Andrew, was a category 5 storm.

Hurricane Andrew

In the early morning hours of 24 August, Hurricane Andrew came ashore along the south Florida coast. Over the next eight hours, the storm tore a swath of destruction across south Florida. By early evening, the storm had moved across the Florida peninsula and into the Gulf of Mexico. As the storm moved on, it left behind an area of Dade County south of Miami that looked more like a vast salvage yard than a thriving urban area with a vigorous population. Dade's 1,945 square miles (one-third of which is water) supports nearly 2 million people in ninety cities and towns, many unincorporated or attached to larger urban communities.[11] To the north lies Broward County, another heavily populated county, with the cities of Hollywood and Fort Lauderdale. With the Atlantic Ocean on the east and the sparsely populated Everglades National Park to the west and south, Dade County is itself virtually a peninsula on the Florida peninsula.

Dade County has a racially mixed population—white, 75 percent; black, 20 percent; and Asian and Indian, 5 percent—with 45 percent of it being foreign-born. More than 57 percent of Dade's population speaks a first language other than English, primarily Spanish, and 49 percent claim Hispanic ethnic heritage. Miami is the principal city in Dade County, with one-quarter of the county's population. Another quarter of the population lives in communities in the southern third of the county: Homestead, Florida City, Cutler Ridge, Perrine, and a host

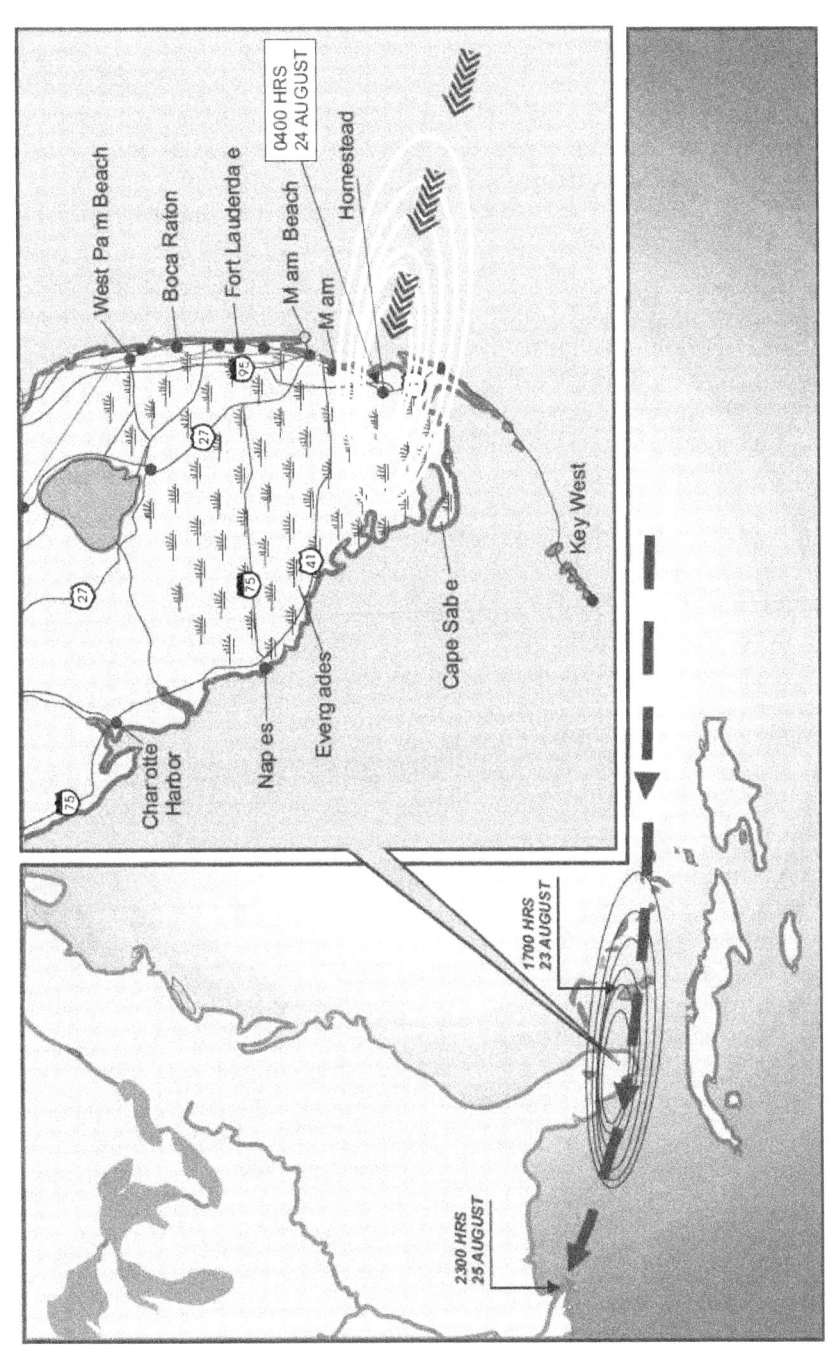

of smaller towns that share common boundaries. This is the area Andrew hit hardest. The populations of these towns range from 27,000 for Homestead to a few hundred for the smallest named communities. Generally speaking, the people of this area are middle- and lower middle-class wage earners, with a higher percentage of whites than north Dade County's towns and cities. Unemployment in 1990 was 7.7 percent.

At the time Andrew struck, the homes and buildings of south Dade County were typical of most suburban communities in the United States. A large percentage of the population lived in single-family dwellings, 51 percent of which were owner occupied. Low-rise office buildings and apartment houses were common, but there were few of the high-rise structures seen farther north in Miami or Miami Beach. Most of the single-family homes were frame construction, although masonry, concrete, reinforced concrete, and concrete block were the preferred construction materials for newer buildings. Like most American cities, power, telephone, and cable lines were overhead, not underground. These were the precise urban conditions most vulnerable to a catastrophic storm.

Those who emerged from their shelters and destroyed houses just before noon on 24 August could barely recognize what they beheld. Many looked around in disbelief at the panorama of destruction, wondering if they were really in some kind of bad dream.[12] There was little that anyone could do that first afternoon. Shock and bewilderment prevailed.

Although many tens of thousands of south Floridians and tourists who had been in the area moved north upon receiving the governor's general evacuation order, thousands of others either chose to stay in the area or had no way to leave. For those who stayed, the night brought fear, anxiety, and sheer terror. Each one has a story to tell, and each story is different. One theme that runs through all of the stories, however, is the increasing uncertainty that they would live through that night. Some of them did not.

As Andrew grew in intensity, everything around the people in Andrew's path seemed to be coming apart. Even the best hurricane preventive measures failed to provide protection against Andrew's fury. In 2000, Dade County building codes required residential construction capable of withstanding 109- to 120-mph winds.[13] Of course, like all building codes, these standards applied only to new construction. Older buildings were often of substantially poorer quality construction and could not be brought up to code because of original

Saffir-Simpson Scale of Hurricane Intensity

Hurricane Level	Wind Speed	Storm Surge	Effects
Level 1 (weak)	74 95 mph	4 5 feet	Minimal damage
Level 2 (moderate)	96 110 mph	6 8 feet	Damage to trees and roofs
Level 3 (strong)	111 130 mph	9 12 feet	Trees down; mobile homes destroyed; buildings damaged
Level 4 (very strong)	131 155 mph	13 18 feet	Extensive damage to buildings; flooding
Level 5 (devastating)	156 ≥ mph	19 feet	Severe structural damage to buildings; heavy flooding

designs or could only be upgraded incrementally. And few owners of older properties had either the resources or the inclination to conform to more recent codes.

Some property owners and residents of south Florida, however, prepared for even more severe hurricane conditions than building codes required. They constructed their dwellings and commercial buildings with heavy beam trusses, concrete and cinder block walls, layered sheathing under glued and nailed shingle or tile roofs, steel bolts, and "hurricane strap" reinforcements of joints and corners. They installed heavy steel doors, emergency lighting systems, and sump pumps. They brought in emergency stores of food, water, fuel, and batteries and had gasoline-powered generators on hand to provide electric power until public service was restored. Nevertheless, all of these heroic measures proved fruitless in the face of Andrew's winds that exceeded 165 mph. (The actual force at the eyewall may have been even stronger, but the official wind gauge broke at 165 mph. At least one source estimated top wind speed at 200 mph.)[14] In a matter of hours, Andrew dismantled homes whose owners had devoted years of preparation to resist just such a storm.[15]

Some coastal residents who initially stayed in the area eventually sought safety farther inland. Even a few miles inland and a few feet higher above sea level seemed to offer some greater degree of security as the winds increased and the surf crashed over the sea walls and around buildings and houses along the shore. This trek inland, however, in addition to being somewhat dangerous, proved to be of little value. The wind did not discriminate as it moved across the Florida peninsula. Buildings along the shore and those inland met identical fates as roofs tore away and walls collapsed. The storm surge was sufficiently high that as far as 5 miles inland buildings flooded or were washed off their foundations. Thus, the seeming safety inland, like the hurricane-proof construction techniques that offered a pseudo peace of mind to some homeowners, turned out to be an illusion.

Perhaps no place in the path of Andrew was hit harder or was the story of survival more dramatic than at Homestead AFB.[16] Homestead had been through hurricanes before, and each time had picked itself up, rebuilt its facilities, and continued operating. But the base had never sustained so much damage that its future would be in doubt. Andrew would change all of that.

During the forty-eight hours before Andrew struck, most of the personnel, dependents, and aircraft of the 31st Fighter Wing at Homestead were evacuated to Air Force facilities to the north. Colonel Stephen B. Plummer, commander of the 31st, selected seventeen officers and airmen to remain with him at Homestead to look after base facilities and two F-16s that could not be flown to safety. Plummer elected to ride out the storm in the base's "hurricane-proof" alert facility, a hardened building that included crew quarters and bays for aircraft. The designation "hurricane-proof" turned out to be a misnomer.

The early morning hours of 24 August were as frightening and terrifying as any the men in Plummer's group, some of them combat veterans from DESERT STORM, had ever experienced. By 0400, the building was coming apart. The wind forced the great hangar doors off their tracks, entered the bays, and picked up the F-16s, twisted them around and smashed them into walls, and then began to disassemble the interior of the alert facility. The airmen scrambled to secure loose items of equipment and tie interior doors shut with bed sheets when a steel hatch came open on the roof, creating a vacuum that threatened to collapse the entire building. One of the airmen, Staff Sergeant Steve Wilensky, volunteered to climb a ladder to close the hatch, thus saving the building and the men inside. The only worry then was whether the roof would remain on the building as it began to dip and sway under the weight of the storm. Andrew did pass, however, and when the eighteen men emerged from the battered alert facility in the morning light, they saw that few other structures remained standing on the once active and thriving base.

For the other military personnel in the storm area, mostly National Guardsmen who had come to evacuate civilians earlier, the hours of darkness were just as trying as for Colonel Plummer's group. The guardsmen sought shelter in a variety of locations. They not only had to cope with the storm raging around them but also were worried about their own homes and families in surrounding communities.[17] For a time after the storm passed, these men shouldered the burden of rescuing trapped and injured victims, recovering the dead, providing assistance to survivors, identifying and opening roads and communications, and supplementing local law enforcement agencies to secure property and deal with looters. The arrival of fresh units with critically needed supplies and equipment brought respite to these tired and weary men.

That Andrew was coming was not a surprise—the Air Force had been tracking the storm for a week, and the Army Operations Center in the Pentagon had already set up a special task force to coordinate anticipated requests for relief supplies. What was a surprise was just how strong Andrew was and how much damage it caused. The aftermath of Andrew's rampage across southern Florida was unlike anything anyone in the United States had seen before. Hardly a single above-ground structure had escaped damage. More than 135,000 homes were destroyed or significantly damaged, most beyond repair. The contents of these buildings and homes were spread over 100 square miles. Hundreds of private boats had washed or been blown ashore from the numerous marinas that dotted the coast, and scores of small aircraft were strewn about the landscape from airports in the area. Public services, including electric power, sewers, telephone communications, water, cable television, and police and fire protection, had generally ceased to exist. An unknown number of dead lay among the wreckage. Most of the deaths resulted from collapsed buildings or flooded areas where victims had sought shelter.[18] Little or no potable water or edible food was available. Medical supplies were in critically short supply. The extent of the disaster was clearly beyond the ability of local and state emergency facilities and resources. Nothing less than the resources of the entire nation would be necessary to respond to a disaster of Andrew's magnitude.

The agency responsible for coordinating the activities of all federal agencies, including the Department of Defense (DOD), during a declared disaster is the Federal Emergency Management Administration (FEMA), which President Jimmy Carter's administration established in 1979. FEMA's purpose is to consolidate federal services during disasters, plan for national emergencies, train civil emergency workers, and pay the federal share of relief operations. Upon declaration of a disaster, FEMA is to implement the Federal Response Plan and determine how federal resources will be used to meet requirements each state identifies. FEMA, like many federal agencies, works adequately in normal operations and even in most emergencies, but it is rarely put to the extreme test. In the extreme test, however, all of the small faults and imperfections in bureaucratic structures have a tendency to appear.

In the first hours after Andrew passed over south Florida and moved into the Gulf of Mexico, FEMA's response was rather lethargic. FEMA's slow action prompted some harsh criticisms. One source claimed that FEMA was "brain dead," and Senator Ernest Hollings of South Carolina said that FEMA was "the sorriest bunch of bureaucratic jackasses I've ever seen."[19] Aspersions aside, some valid reasons may explain FEMA's inability to step in more quickly and launch earlier relief operations. For example, for the first 24 to 48 hours after Andrew, there was general confusion about the true situation in the area. Even the office of Florida's governor, Lawton Chiles, could not provide accurate information about the extent of physical damage or the number of casualties in southern Dade County. Most of the early estimates significantly *understated* the damage to private property and the disruption to public services in the disaster area. Furthermore, the Federal Response Plan, the blueprint for the federal government to mobilize resources and conduct activities to support state and local governments in major disasters, turned out to be almost totally inadequate. While FEMA experienced some difficulties, just before Andrew struck, it succeeded in activating its emergency operations center and notified twenty-six other federal agencies and the American Red Cross of the pending disaster. Although an analysis and critique of FEMA is beyond the scope of this study, it is important to remember that any DOD forces committed to disaster relief operations must work under and coordinate with FEMA.

President George Bush arrived in Miami at 1800 on Monday evening. After touring the area with Governor Chiles, Bush promised that Homestead AFB would be rebuilt, and he ordered the commitment of U.S. military forces to relief operations in south Florida. Bush's first promise was perhaps premature. Congress would eventually decide the future of Homestead. His second promise, however, was quickly translated into one of the largest humanitarian relief efforts in U.S. history.

DOD passed the mission to the Department of the Army (DA), which quickly charged the U.S. Army Forces Command (FORSCOM) to coordinate the deployment and employment of military forces and resources in the disaster area. FORSCOM subsequently directed Lieutenant General Samuel E. Ebbesen, commanding general of the Second Continental Army, to establish Joint Task Force Andrew

(JTFA) to exercise operational control over all military forces involved in relief operations in south Florida. JTFA, officially established on 28 August 1992, was a joint, multinational effort. Its mission was "to provide humanitarian support by establishing field feeding sites, storage/distribution warehousing, cargo transfer operations, local/line haul transportation operations, and other logistical support to the local population." Expanding on this mission statement, the JTFA commander provided his intent and additional guidance:

> Immediately begin to operate feeding and water facilities; priority to the cities of Homestead and Florida City, and the Cutler Ridge area. After a more detailed assessment, expand operations throughout the affected area. Provide assistance to other Federal agencies, state and local governments, and organizations in receipt, storage, and distribution of supplies and equipment. DO NOT engage in law enforcement actions or operations without approval of CG, JTFA. End state is to get life support systems in place and relieve initial hardships until non DOD, State and local agencies can reestablish normal operations throughout the AO.[20]

DOD committed more than 22,000 military personnel to JTFA. Most were Army troops, including a brigade from the 82d Airborne Division from Fort Bragg, North Carolina; a headquarters staff element from the XVIII Airborne Corps; units from the 10th Mountain Division from Fort Drum, New York; and elements of the 1st Corps Support Command. U.S. Air Force, Navy, Coast Guard, and Marine units and Canadian Forces engineer units also participated in the Hurricane Andrew relief effort in the coming weeks. Florida National Guardsmen already in the area and additional Florida Guard units alerted to deploy to the area remained under state control.[21]

There was, however, no headlong rush of military units into the disaster area. The deployment of military units to south Florida and assignment of specific missions required an estimate of needs and a clearer picture of the general situation in the disaster area and close coordination with FEMA and other relief agencies. By statute, a defense coordinating officer (DCO) serves as liaison between the DOD (JTF) and FEMA. Second U.S. Army had earlier appointed a DCO and, on 23 August, the DCO and his team were in Tallahassee assessing the situation and working with his FEMA counterpart, the federal coordinating officer (FCO). Thus, when JTFA officially came into being, much of the structure was already in place, and the designated personnel were working closely together.

The spirit of cooperation established early between the DCO and FCO set the general tone for cooperation down the chain of command. To some extent, the degree and ease of cooperation depended on personalities, local circumstances, and the types of units. Medical units, for instance, seem to have had more difficulty establishing good working relationships than other types of units. One of the most significant problems that plagued the interface between civilian and military organizations was the mutual lack of familiarity and knowledge of respective capabilities, procedures, and equipment. The result was some loss of time and friction. Nevertheless, for the most part, military units under JTFA worked exceptionally well with FEMA representatives and other civilian organizations operating in the disaster area.[22]

Some units, of course, were already operating in south Florida before JTFA stood up. In the immediate aftermath of Andrew, one of the most important tasks was to search for living victims trapped in collapsed buildings or under the rubble. Although large numbers of residents and tourists complied with the governor's evacuation order and moved north, thus reducing the number of potential victims, an unknown number of people remained in the area. The National Guardsmen already in the disaster area were conducting some search and rescue missions, but the task was clearly beyond their limited capabilities. Help arrived. The 301st Rescue Squadron, an HH-60 helicopter reserve unit located at Homestead AFB (and now without a home), established a temporary operations center at Kendall-Tamiami Airport. Joined by the 939th Rescue Wing, Portland, Oregon, the reservists set up a field hospital to treat the injured and flew in pararescue teams with dogs to search collapsed buildings for victims. Coast Guardsmen from the U.S. Coast Guard Air Station at Miami also joined the search and rescue effort. While it is impossible to count the precise number, the early efforts of the Florida National Guard units in the area and the timely arrival of trained and experienced search and rescue units certainly saved numerous lives.[23]

Units alerted for deployment to the disaster area conducted their planning and preparations with the same high level of efficiency normally associated with deployments for other domestic and foreign operations. Training, established procedures, and experience served these units well. Staffs clarified specific unit missions, briefed senior and subordinate commanders, and prepared orders. Reconnaissance teams preceded the main elements to the disaster area to gather firsthand information about local conditions, to identify access routes, and to make initial arrangements for locating troop units. Military units deploying to south Florida moved by air, road, and water. The lead battalion of the 82d Airborne Division left Fort Bragg on Air Force transports less than nine hours after being alerted. Within forty-eight hours, the first elements of a Marine Corps task force departed Cherry Point, North Carolina, by air, and a leadership group from the 10th Mountain Division, Fort Drum, New York, left Griffiss AFB for south Florida. Other units from the 82d Airborne Division moved southward by road. Navy repair and supply vessels sailed from several Atlantic coast ports for south Florida destinations with valuable relief supplies and Seabee personnel.[24]

The tasks assigned to Regular Army units arriving in the first two weeks (phase I) focused on the immediate needs of Andrew's survivors as the JTFA commander's guidance designated (previously noted): to provide food, water, and shelter; to distribute relief supplies such as clothing, personal hygiene items, and health-related items; and to provide security. Once these services were established, Army units expanded their role (phase II) to assist in restoring public services (power, sewage, and so forth), clearing and opening streets and roads, and cleaning up and removing obstructing and dangerous debris. Until their withdrawal (phase III), Army units continued to provide basic services, assist in reestablishing public utilities, and strive to turn over to non-DOD agencies—federal, state, and local governments—responsibility for reconstitution and reconstruction in the disaster area.

As units arrived in the disaster area, they immediately set up operational bases and began to deal with the priority tasks. Other than the search for victims, the most important need was to feed a population that had no means of providing for itself. The Army had already anticipated this need and began to move mobile kitchen trailers into the disaster area during the first few hours after Andrew passed. Within seven days, the Army was operating thirty mobile kitchen trailers at twenty-four sites, serving more than 21,000 meals each day. Over the succeeding two weeks, feeding operations expanded. Mess units prepared meals around the clock and served 35,000 meals per day at the height of the relief effort. The Army served more than one-half million meals in the first thirty days and nearly 900,000 meals before the operation ended.[25] No other military activity directly affected more people than the kitchens did.

Many of the displaced families found temporary shelter in "life support centers," or tent cities, the Army set up.[26] The American Red Cross administered the centers, provided operational guidance, screened victims, and assigned housing space to families. The Army maintained the tents and provided the meals. The centers became more than just living quarters; they became communities, points for distributing all sorts of public and privately donated items, comfort stations where one could get a hot shower and fresh drinking water, day care centers for children, and administrative centers where people could meet with assistance agencies and relief officials. The life support centers were never intended as a permanent solution to the displaced population's problems; the objective was to move people into more substantial quarters and to restore normal community activities, such as schools, as quickly as possible.

Equally as important as providing for the population's physical needs was the need to provide security for both people and property in the disaster area. A common problem in the wake of any urban disaster is looting and pillaging. In the days after Hurricane Andrew, the problem of dealing with looters was compounded by the activities of Miami street gangs. The gangs roamed the devastated areas, taking anything of value they could carry off and threatening residents, relief workers, and military personnel. Many local residents took it upon themselves to defend their property. Armed homeowners confronted looters and forced them to leave the area empty-handed or made citizens' arrests until police could be summoned.

Some units reported incidents involving looters, gang members, and other criminal elements, but such cases did not seriously affect the troops' ability to carry out their missions. Except for military police (MP), regular U.S. Army troops were not issued live ammunition for their weapons. MPs responded to some calls for assistance, and they detained a number of suspects until they could be turned over to the appropriate authorities. As a rule, however, the National Guard assumed the law enforcement role and assisted local police agencies in establishing security, patrolling the area, and dealing with looters and other criminal elements while regular units concentrated on relief and recovery missions. This division of responsibility is based in law and organization. In the first place, the Posse Comitatus Act prohibits regular military forces from participating in law enforcement activities.[27] Governors can endow their National Guard units with law enforcement authority. And National Guard units receive considerably more training in civil control than do regular units. Thus, by not federalizing the Florida National Guard during the crisis, each force was able to concentrate on separate but mutually supporting roles in the Hurricane Andrew humanitarian operation.

Throughout the period of relief operations in south Florida, all military personnel performed their duties to the highest professional standards. Discipline problems were negligible, and complaints about the long hours, the lack of personal comforts, and the extended separation from families were rare. Perhaps this was because here was a case of Americans helping Americans. Every serviceman could see for himself how much the people of the area had lost and how much work was necessary to put things back together. Nowhere, however, was the dedication and professionalism of the military forces more evident than at Homestead AFB. The men and women of Homestead contributed significantly to the relief effort; they had to deal with their own losses as well.

When Colonel Plummer and the seventeen officers and men who had spent the harrowing night in the "hurricane-proof" alert facility at Homestead emerged late on the morning of 24 August, they beheld a scene of utter devastation.[28] Almost nothing was standing as far as they could see. Andrew hit the work areas and the living quarters at Homestead equally hard. Fortunately, other than the small group with Plummer, Homestead's military personnel and dependents had been evacuated earlier. Most of its civilian work force had also moved out of the area along with the general evacuation to the north. Although the Air Force at first announced that Homestead would reopen, the decision on Homestead's future would come later. Nevertheless, the landing facilities at Homestead would play a critical role in the Andrew relief operations, and it was imperative that the runways be made usable.

Even before Andrew came ashore, Air Force planners were preparing for the crisis. The Air Combat Command, Langley AFB, Virginia, directed the Air Force's "total force effort" to deal with Andrew's aftermath. The Air Force focused on two primary missions. The first priority was to make Homestead's runways serviceable so that airlifters could bring men, emergency equipment, and relief supplies into the disaster area. Homestead was soon receiving aircraft. Within the first nine days of the emergency, the Air Mobility Command, Scott AFB, Illinois, flew 529 airlift missions into south Florida, delivering more than 7,000 military and civilian passengers and nearly 11,500 tons of equipment and supplies. This was the largest domestic operation in the Air Mobility Command's history and rivaled the first ten days of tonnage moved to the Persian Gulf in Operation DESERT SHIELD.

Moving large quantities of cargo into Homestead was relatively easy, but Homestead was not designed as a logistics center. Offloading the cargo with the few available forklifts, breaking it down into movable loads by hand, and distributing the supplies to surrounding communities in borrowed deuce-and-a-halfs was exhausting work. Members of the 23d Air Support Group, Fort Bragg, arrived to assist the airmen working around the clock. Teams of specialists in recovery and salvage, and medical units from as far away as Grand Forks AFB, North Dakota, and Mountain Home AFB, Idaho, deployed to Homestead. The base itself, although severely damaged, was transformed into a major logistics center for conducting the relief effort in the surrounding communities.[29]

The second, but not secondary, mission for Homestead was to take care of the thousands of officers, airmen, and their families who called the base home, many of whom had already evacuated the area and had lost virtually everything they owned. Although some of the airmen with critical specialties stationed at Homestead were brought back to assist in the relief effort, more than 2,300 officers and enlisted personnel were reassigned to other AFBs. Special teams went to Homestead to collect medical and financial records and to assess and compile damage reports so that families could be compensated for their personal property loss. A representative of the 1st Mission Support Squadron from Langley arrived at Homestead with Air Force Aid Society funds to provide money for both married and single airmen to purchase the necessary health and hygiene items they lost in the storm. Within one month, the Air Force Aid Society provided $860,000 in loans and grants to Homestead's airmen and their families. Family support centers at AFBs around the United States collected nonperishable food, supplies, clothing, and personal use items for displaced Homestead families.[30] The Air Force's response to the needs of its people at Homestead is an outstanding example for other services to follow if similar disasters occur in the future.

The military presence in the disaster area contributed substantially to establishing a stable, safe environment and meeting the basic needs of most of the residents remaining in or returning to the area. By the middle of September, three weeks after Hurricane Andrew struck south Florida, more than 22,000 soldiers, airmen, marines, and sailors were working for JTFA. The Air Force had brought in thousands of tons of relief supplies, personnel, and equipment while soldiers and marines were feeding and housing thousands of families. Florida National Guardsmen had established a safe and reasonably secure environment so residents could return to their home sites to recover what personal possessions could be salvaged. Army engineers, joined by Navy Seabees and a Canadian Forces engineer battalion, had moved in with everything from chain saws to bulldozers to clear streets and roads, repair and reopen public buildings, and begin the monumental task of restoring power and communications. Army chaplains were performing church services. Army medical teams were providing emergency and routine medical care for anyone in need. Army psychologists were working with civilian mental health teams to help Andrew's victims cope with the post-traumatic stress resulting from the disaster. Army technicians set up and were operating a multilingual radio station to keep residents informed and had distributed 15,000 battery-operated radios throughout the area. Perhaps the single most important indicator of JTFA's success was that, on 14 September, all but 4 percent of the 278 primary, middle, and high schools in the affected area reopened for classes.[31]

Two months after Hurricane Andrew swept through south Florida, JTFA's mission was nearly complete. By 25 October, most of the military units assigned to JTFA had returned home, and the few remaining units were packing up and loading their equipment for the return home. FEMA, which had experienced some initial difficulties during the first days of the disaster, was now fully functioning. FEMA was bringing temporary modular housing units into the area and moving families out of the tents. Public, private, and church-related humanitarian organizations were busy providing every sort of assistance to individuals and families still in need. The Army Corps of Engineers was working with local and state government agencies to rebuild infrastructure. A host of contractors, builders, and tradesmen had swarmed into the area and were at work repairing or rebuilding public buildings and private residences. The people of the area were slowly resuming their lives. Nevertheless, years of hard work lay ahead before the towns and communities south of Miami could return to their normal existence.

Hurricane Andrew struck south Florida in the early morning hours of 24 August 1992 with unprecedented fury. Andrew left behind an unbelievable scene of destruction. When disasters of such magnitude occur—whether the damage is the result of natural or man-made phenomena—local and state resources will inevitably be overwhelmed. This has been the case throughout the nation's history. Even the federal agencies and departments recently created to manage large-scale catastrophes do not possess the manpower, equipment, material, knowledge, and experience to respond adequately in such crises. When overwhelming events befall communities and overwhelm local and state resources, only the military can quickly bring together the human and material resources necessary to save lives, relieve suffering, and protect public and private property until civil authorities are prepared to resume their normal functions.

In many ways, the Army's response to Hurricane Andrew was one more instance of the Army answering the call for assistance from fellow countrymen in need. Just as it responded quickly and unhesitatingly during the Chicago fire and the San Francisco earthquake, the Army moved quickly and deliberately to assist the people of south Florida after Andrew passed. As in previous disaster-relief operations, the Army stayed until the immediate crisis was over and the local situation was stable and under control. In the eighteenth and nineteenth centuries, however, commanders at or near the scene reacted, often without first consulting their superiors, to the crisis; took whatever steps they perceived necessary; and employed locally available resources to save lives, protect property, and restore public order. These commanders then sought authority, approval, or confirmation for their actions as communications and circumstances allowed.

Since World War II, the U.S. Army has participated in numerous humanitarian relief operations. The Army's response to Andrew, however, was more than just a reprise of earlier humanitarian relief operations. The Army's involvement in recent relief operations, and Andrew particularly, has clearly demonstrated that a modern, well-trained, adequately equipped, disciplined military force not only can respond quickly and appropriately to any type of crisis, foreign or domestic, in war or peace, but also is the best-suited force for such missions.

The response to Hurricane Andrew was a Total Army effort to which Regular, Reserve, and National Guard units contributed. The qualities that have led to U.S. Army successes in a variety of war and peace operations around the world—excellent leadership at every level, a wide range of highly developed skills, a positive attitude, dedication to duty, and professionalism—are the very qualities that officers and soldiers demonstrated during their service in the Andrew relief operation. Even those Americans who are critical of or know little about military values and ethics must admit that the men and women who embrace those values and ethics served the nation admirably in the Andrew relief effort. JTFA was also a joint and multinational military effort that worked closely with a number of government and civilian relief organizations. All of the units that made up JTFA were focused on a common objective. Interservice differences and rivalries that plagued many joint operations throughout much of our history played no part in JTFA.

This is not to conclude that the response to Hurricane Andrew was flawless. A number of problems plagued the relief effort. Perhaps the most obvious problem was the unnecessary delay in moving equipment, supplies, and personnel into the most heavily damaged area in the first seventy-two hours of the emergency. This failure was the result of poor damage assessments and lack of an adequate Federal Response Plan. Most participants in the relief effort, military and civilian, were unfamiliar with other agencies' equipment, procedures, and capabilities and with the Federal Response Plan. The Army lacked appropriate doctrine for humanitarian relief operations and, except for Second Army, commanders had relegated training for humanitarian operations to the lowest priority. Mutual training and cooperative planning among the various federal and state agencies responsible for disaster relief, including the U.S. Army, had been almost nonexistent.[32] To avoid these problems and be better prepared for future disasters will require extensive cooperation among all of the agencies involved.

Much of JTFA's success can be attributed to the Army's experience in conducting humanitarian relief operations and the process of learning from those experiences. In the eighteenth and nineteenth centuries, field commanders wrote reports on military actions, and higher-level commanders submitted official annual reports to the War Department on their department and division activities. Most of these reports were narratives whose purpose was to explain or justify a commander's actions. The reports were often self-serving and were rarely critically reviewed for factual accuracy, tone, or content. Furthermore, the Army had no established method to sift through, distill, and disseminate lessons that might be contained in reports. Such reports, therefore, had limited value as instructional material for the Army as it planned and trained for future operations. Thus, the Army learned little from the Great Chicago Fire of 1871, the Johnstown flood of 1889, or the San Francisco earthquake of 1906 that was useful to leaders other than those who were directly involved.[33]

Over the past century, the Army has worked diligently to learn from its experiences to improve leadership, doctrine, command and control, equipment, and training procedures for future operations. With the creation of a General Staff and the establishment of the U.S. Army War College in 1903, the Army carefully began to document and study its own operations. This process has now matured. The current Joint Universal Lessons Learned System (JULLS) provides commanders, planners, trainers, and doctrine writers with a solid pair of shoulders to stand on when looking into the future. Perhaps the U.S. Army's single most important accomplishment of the twentieth century was developing an institutionalized system of critical self-analysis—the after-action review.

JTFA has produced a wealth of studies, reports, and after-action reviews.[34] Each of the units and headquarters that participated in JTFA, including FORSCOM and the Second U.S. Army, conducted internal reviews and completed reports. JTFA staff members then reviewed these reports and included pertinent details and lessons from each in the JTF after-action review. The reports and summaries of JTFA, available from the Center for Army Lessons Learned, Fort Leavenworth, Kansas, are a rich source of insights, ideas, recommendations, and guidance for doctrine preparation, planning, training, and implementation of future humanitarian operations in urban environments. JTFA stands as an example of how well JTFs can operate when the objectives are clear and people and resources are focused.

The U.S. Army's participation in Joint Task Force Andrew marks one of the most successful chapters in the Army's long history of urban humanitarian operations. All of the military personnel returning home from service in south Florida can be proud to have served their fellow Americans in this critical time of need.

Notes

1. Josie Fernandez, "Looking Andrew in the 'Eye,'" *Citizen Airman* (October 1992), 21, and Chris King, "Eye to Eye: Viewing a Monster First-hand," *Citizen Airman* (October 1992), 25-26.

2. Robert Van Elsberg, "The Force Responds," *Citizen Airman* (October 1992), 21-22.

3. W.D. McGlasson, "To the Rescue," *National Guard* (July 1993), 32-34.

4. According to current federal law, local authorities are still primarily responsible for disaster relief. Only after local and state authorities have declared the nature of the disaster and requested federal assistance can federal agencies move into a disaster area. See Robert T. Stafford Disaster Relief and Emergency Assistance Act (Disaster Relief Act of 1974): 88 Stat. 143 [Pub. 93-288, 22 May 1974], as amended in 1977, 1980, 1990, 1992, 1993, 1994, 1995, and 2001.

5. On the Chicago fire of 1871, see Herman Kogan and Robert Cromie, *The Great Fire: Chicago 1871* (NY: G.P. Putnam's Sons, 1971); Paul Andrew Hutton, *Phil Sheridan and His Army* (Lincoln, NE: University of Nebraska Press, 1985), 209-12; and Roy Morris, Jr., *Sheridan: The Life and Wars of General Phil Sheridan* (NY: Crown Publishers, 1922), 334-39.

6. On the Johnstown flood, see Federal Writers' Project, *The Floods of Johnstown* (Johnstown, PA: Mayor's Committee, 1939), and John Bach McMaster, "The Johnstown Flood," *The Pennsylvania Magazine of History and Biography* (1933), 209-43, 316-54.

7. On the San Francisco earthquake, see Gordon Thomas and Max Morgan Witts, *The San Francisco Earthquake* (NY: Stein and Day, 1971).

8. Funston's biographers agree that his reputation was greatly enhanced by his actions during the San Francisco earthquake, but they do not address the controversial nature of some of Funston's decisions during the emergency. See Thomas W. Crouch, *A Yankee Guerrillero: Frederick Funston and the Cuban Insurrection* (Memphis, TN: Memphis State University Press, 1975), 4; John B.B. Trussell, Jr., "The Man Destiny Just Missed," *Military Review* (June 1973), 67-68.

9. On hurricanes, see David E. Fisher, *The Scariest Place on Earth: Eye to Eye With Hurricanes* (NY: Random House, 1994), and Robert H. Simpson and Herbert Riehl, *The Hurricane and Its Impact* (Baton Rouge, LA: Louisiana State University Press, 1981).

10. Gary Barnes, "Hurricane," *The World Book Encyclopedia*, Vol. 9 (Chicago: World Book, 1999), 456.

11. For record-keeping purposes, the U.S. Bureau of the Census designates Dade County as the Hialeah Metropolitan Statistical Area. See U.S.

Bureau of the Census, *County and City Data Book: 1994* (Washington, DC: U.S. Government Printing Office [GPO], 1994), and *The Sourcebook of Zip Code Demographics: Census Edition*, Vol. 1 (Washington, DC: CACI, 1991).

12. Pictures describe the devastation Andrew left better than words. Two excellent photo essays are *The Big One: Hurricane Andrew: Photographs by the Staff of the Miami Herald and el Nuevo Herald*, Roman Lyskowski and Steve Rice, eds. (Kansas City, MO: Andrews McMeel Publishing, November 1992), and Rick Gore, "Andrew Aftermath," *National Geographic* (April 1993), 2-37.

13. See South Florida Building Code (Dade County Edition), Office of Building Code Compliance, Dade County, Florida. In March 2002, Florida promulgated a statewide building code that superseded all local codes. Among the provisions in the new code were revised standards to calculate wind pressure on masonry and wood supporting walls, engineering specifications for roof trusses, requirements for pressure-resistant windows, and prohibition of gambrel roofs. When one considers that Andrew damaged or destroyed even the best constructed buildings in its path, the question arises whether any building codes that are not cost prohibitive can be effective.

14. Gore, 15.

15. Bob Lamm, a resident of Redland, Florida, observed that it took Andrew two hours to tear apart the house he spent five years constructing to withstand a major hurricane. James LeMoyne, "In the Storm," *The New Yorker* (5 October 1992), 85.

16. See Michael J. Haggert, "Andrew's Wrath . . . Wake of the Storm," *Airman* (November 1992), 2-7, and Doug Gillert, "Homestead Sagas," *Air Force Times* (14 September 1992), 12-15.

17. After the storm, about 100 Florida National Guardsmen were released from duty to return home and take care of their families. W.D. McGlasson, "To the Rescue," *National Guard* (July 1993), 33. For an account of a guardsman who moved into the area with his unit to find his home destroyed, see John Daigle, Jr., Bob Hart, Maria LoVasco Jonkers, and Kristi Moon, "Andrew's Wrath Mobilizes the National Guard," *National Guard* (October 1992), 20-23.

18. The death toll was fifteen, relatively low considering the extensive property damage. The dead included a 12-year-old child and a 78-year-old man and ages in between. For accounts of victims as well as survivors' stories, see Gore, 23.

19. Tom Mathews et al., "What Went Wrong," *Newsweek* (7 September 1992), 24.

20. Joint Task Force Andrew After-Action Review (AAR), Overview Executive Summary, U.S. Army Center for Army Lessons Learned (CALL), hereafter JTFA AAR, Fort Leavenworth, Kansas.

21. Ibid., and Gordon R. Sullivan, "Hurricane Andrew: An After-Action Report," *Army* (January 1993), 16-22.

22. FEMA and Hurricane Andrew Disaster Relief: JULLS, CALL Unclassified Restricted Database/Operations Other Than War—Domestic fileroom: Fileroom Folder: HURRICANES, TORNADOS, TYPHOONS/ HURRICANE ANDREW, Fort Leavenworth, Kansas, and JTFA AAR.

23. "Reserve on Top of Storm," *The Officer* (October 1992), 18-20.

24. Peter Madsen and Wayne Whiteman, "Responding to Hurricane Andrew: 10th Mountain Deploys to Florida," *Engineer* (February 1993), 2-4; James T. Palmer and Charles R. Rash, "Operation Hurricane Andrew Relief: Humanitarian Assistance, Redleg Style," *Field Artillery* (October 1993), 31-35. The 1/7 Field Artillery (FA) and 2/7 FA deployed from a field training exercise at Fort Drum to disaster relief in south Florida.

25. JTFA AAR and Sullivan.

26. FEMA and Hurricane Andrew Disaster Relief: JULLS.

27. 18 *United States Code* 1385.

28. Doug Gillert, "Hurricane: Homestead AFB is Just History Now," *Air Force Times* (7 September 1992), and Vickie M. Graham, "Two Years After a Hurricane Demolished Homestead AFB, Airmen are Still Picking Up After Andrew," *Airman* (August 1994), 2-9.

29. "Reserve on Top of Storm," *The Officer* (October 1992), 18-20, and Haggert, 4-6.

30. Ibid., 6-7; Randy Newcomb, Janet Young, and Dan Cappabianca, "Hurricane Andrew—Ridin' the Storm Out," *The Air Force Comptroller* (January 1993), 17-19; and Doug Gillert, "Homestead Evacuees Got Early Support, Help," *Air Force Times* (12 October 1992), 30.

31. JTFA AAR; FEMA and Hurricane Andrew Disaster Relief: JULLS; Sullivan; Keith Butler, "SOF Support for Hurricane Andrew Recovery," *Special Warfare* (July 1993), 12-17; and James Mauro, "Hurricane Andrew's Other Legacy," *Psychology Today* (November/December 1992), 45.

32. JTFA AAR.

33. Neither General Sheridan nor Funston mentioned the disasters that occurred in their respective departments in their annual reports. See Report of Lieutenant General Sheridan in *Report of the General of the Army, Report of the Secretary of War*, Vol. I (Washington, DC: GPO, 1871), 23-24; and Report of the Department of California, Reports of Division and Department Commanders, *Annual Reports of the War Department for the Fiscal Year Ending June 30, 1906*, Vol. II (Washington, DC: GPO, 1906), 179-91.

34. A CALL search produced more than 450 AARs, JULLS, concept plans, SMARTbooks, and other documents generated by units from battalion to JTFA involved in JTFA. See CALL Database Fileroom: Operations Other Than War—Domestic: Hurricanes, Tornados, Typhoons (filecabinet):

Hurricane Andrew: Joint Task Force—August 1992 (filedrawer), CALL, Fort Leavenworth, Kansas.

Urban Warfare: Its History and Its Future

Roger J. Spiller

Why should a modern army invest its professional energies in understanding urban warfare? Armies are optimized when they are used in the open. Armies are not built to work best in cities. If one would wreck an army, tradition argues, send it into a city. The functions armies serve, their fundamental organizing principles, their modes of command and control, their operational and tactical doctrines, and even the standards by which they judge their success—all are tuned to the wide, open spaces of the field of battle. In such spaces, armies have succeeded more often and more decisively. So goes the argument.

But the origin of these prejudices is rather modern. Frequently, the ancient classic *Art of War* by Sun Tzu is held up as the ultimate argument against taking war into a city. But Sun Tzu's often-quoted strictures against cities should be interpreted as being in the nature of a protest. Scholars tell us that in the ancient China of his day, the arts of fortification and siegecraft were well developed precisely because cities were important in war. Sun Tzu seems most interested in rectifying what he sees as unimaginative tactics in attacking cities. Although he regards attacking cities as the least preferable course of action, his conception of war conduces perfectly with the quickest and least costly way to capture a city—by *chi'i*; that is, by indirect means of feints, espionage, disinformation, subversion, and betrayal. Nor did Sun Tzu think that cities could be ignored. The general who left too many towns and cities behind him as he advanced into the enemy's territory, Sun Tzu wrote, was courting danger.[1]

Once, and for the longest time, cities were integral to the conduct of war. Heavily fortified, snug behind their bastioned walls, cities embodied the strength of the state. Cities could be worth taking: a successful siege—that is, one that was not ruinous to defender and attacker alike—quite often concluded a war decisively. Field engagements, however, did not hold out a promise of decisive victory; one might conduct indecisive operations in disputed zones between one strongpoint and another for years. Decisive field operations were always more difficult than sieges to stage and always posed a sterner test for the armies. Whole wars might pass without seeing a field operation that produced any significant result for those engaged.

Campaigns might simply burn themselves out with no meaningful conclusion at all.[2]

Fortresses and the style of war they represented began declining well before the age of gunpowder hurried them along to obsolescence. Fortresses usually were built at command by those who had the resources to give them life. But cities were a collective enterprise, one of the results of constantly redistributing humans and their labors, usually over a course of centuries. From the Middle Ages onward, and especially in Europe, populations were busily rearranging themselves into towns and cities. Between the years 1100 and 1500, the number of towns in Europe doubled.[3] Most faced their enemies without permanent protection. Even when they were not in the lee of a mighty castle, they managed to survive by putting up fierce and prolonged resistance from behind the crudest defenses. Proper sieges of well-prepared fortresses rarely lasted more than a few months, and certain cities held out just as long. One of the longest sieges recorded in that age was against the city of Acre, which defended itself against Frankish Crusaders for almost three years.[4] While the age of the fortress declined, the modern age of urban warfare was beginning. As Phillipe Contamine has observed, a conqueror might now easily avoid a castle, but "it was absolutely vital to control such centres of economic, administrative, and human resources as were represented by towns."[5]

Cities that were not protected by fortifications posed their own kinds of problems for would-be attackers. An unfortified city, if it was to be defended at all, might be more inclined to defend itself in depth, or along a single avenue of approach, forcing an invader to spend itself from building to building, each of which could be made into a redoubt, until the attacker had dissipated its combat power—or its enthusiasm for the fight. Nor were unfortified cities difficult simply because they could be successfully defended. The very human composition of the city could pose yet another set of difficulties. A city full of terrified civilians or a city swollen with equally terrified refugees could produce a corps' worth of friction without ever firing a shot.

The redistribution of the European population was unprecedented but not unique. The rest of the world matched Europe's new patterns of growth, million for million. In 150 AD, the world's population stood at about 300 million. Sixteen centuries of growth were required to double this number.[6] In 1750, the world's population of 600 million began to rise at a rate never before seen. Only fifty-four more years were to pass before the world's population nearly doubled again. By 1804, the world's population had reached 1 billion.[7] The magnitude of this demographic surge is so powerful that neither plagues nor wars nor natural calamities have affected its velocity. During the two centuries since reaching the first billion of population, the world has added 5 billion more.[8] The rate of growth has not subsided, but it has changed shape.

In 1804, London was unique among the world's cities because it had attained a population of 1 million, possibly the first city to do so since ancient Rome. Only 100 years later, cities all over the world contained more than a million inhabitants. Now, one estimate holds that the world contains some 30,000 "urban centers," not megalopolises so much as very large cities. Some of these, such as El Alto, Bolivia, now over 500,000 people, are located close to much larger, better-known cities.[9] By the year 2000, the world contained 387 cities with populations of a million or more—sometimes, much more. The most populous urban agglomeration in the world today is Tokyo, with a population of 26.5 million.[10] Not including the city's several contiguous suburbs, the prefecture of Tokyo proper now covers more than 2,000 square kilometers.[11]

According to a recent UN report, within the next five years, global population will be equally divided between urban and rural inhabitants, but virtually all population growth for the next generation is expected to occur in urban areas. Most of these urban areas are in less-developed regions of the world. During the past five years, urban growth in these regions was six times greater than growth in the urban areas of developed nations. In the more developed nations, 75 percent of the population is already urban areas, a figure that, by current estimates, will increase to 84 percent within the next generation. However, in the world's largest urban agglomerations, for reasons not explained, populations tend to decline. Yet, Dhaka, Bangladesh, and Delhi, India, both defied this trend during the past quarter-century, with populations growing at a rate of 7 percent a year.[12] No evidence suggests that there is any fixed point of maximum urban expansion, a point beyond which a city may no longer serve its purposes.[13] Nor, as noted, is it inevitable that a megacity, once embarked on dramatic expansion, will continue to grow. Mexico City's recent history demonstrates that population surges can indeed abate or even reverse themselves for reasons that have nothing to do with urban dysfunction. In this case, a reorientation of national production and consumption was the proximate cause for revising the city's growth estimates downward.[14]

The world's many cities are as varied as the societies that built them. The standard, common, or normal city does not exist. Cities can be broadly distinguished from one another, however. Geography can impose its own kind of tyranny over how a city grows. Cities that are sited on coastal plains like Tokyo, or those such as Lagos that occupy coastal or estuarial islands, have only so much land available to them. Cities dominated by a particular industry or activity often incorporate it into their design. Capital cities usually fix their national institutions near a ceremonial center where monuments are more numerous than people. This seems to hold true whether the city was originally built for that purpose or later adapted. Washington, DC, St. Petersburg, and Brasilia are modern examples of the former. London, Paris, Berlin, and Tokyo did not begin as capitals but eventually assumed the role. It is possible, too, to distinguish between cities by how they respond to certain social or technical developments. Los Angeles and the automobile culture virtually grew up together, with the result that few cities in the world are so highly integrated with this form of transportation as is L.A. By contrast, modern Athens was required like so many other ancient cities to transplant modern transport patterns onto an urban structure that had not greatly changed in centuries. Comparing cities by one feature or another can be interesting, but it is perhaps not the most effective way to understand the uniqueness of a given city. In this respect, a city is more like a book, to be read and understood on its own terms.

Even so, the modern urbanographer and the modern military professional are unlikely to see a city in the same way. Rio de Janeiro's 764 *favelas*—poverty-ridden urban zones distinguished more by the boundaries of the criminal gangs who operate in them than by any division of orthodox government—may seem to the urban planner to be a collection of political, economic, and, above all, social challenges. The military planner may wonder how—if there is no choice—to move large bodies of soldiers through this zone or whether it is even possible for an army to wrest control from the "federation of gangs" that dominates it.[15] While population and urban experts can contend, theoretically, with China's "floating population" of 100 million homeless agricultural workers displaced by rural modernization and collecting in the nation's cities (1 million in Beijing alone), what theories can a commander and military planner draw upon to contend with his mission in densely populated urban areas?[16]

The art of war clearly has not kept pace with the progressively more complex global urban environment. As a consequence, the military profession is ill equipped to meet the unique demands of modern urban warfare. Unable to avoid operating in urban environments, traditional armed forces tend to regress, their tactics devolving to the lowest common denominator, surrendering the initiative to better-prepared adversaries. Forced to resort to expediencies and improvisations, trial and error, and experiments in the face of the enemy, orthodox military forces face the danger of escalation past the point their strategy can sustain and costs they can endure.

But history has never waited for military theory to catch up, so it has been to history that soldiers have turned to prepare themselves for the battlefields of the future. Each of the twelve cases presented in this volume has been the subject of earlier full-length studies. These larger studies focus on the dramatic and unique characteristics of the events they address. The value of studying these cases in a collective set, however, is that they can be held up in the light of each other. By doing so, one may begin to build a professionally useful body of knowledge about this unique class of military operations.

Just how far urban operations diverge from orthodox military operations can be seen in how differently they are planned and conducted, the constraints under which they labor, how their progress is judged, as well as the results they produce. Sometimes, urban operations are so different from orthodoxy that they seem to belong to another war altogether—as if what happened inside the city had little reference to what happened beyond it. No one involved in the battle of Aachen, on either the Allied or the German side, would have seen the city as being important to a larger fabric of operations. The Germans did not intend to hold the city, and the Allies only wanted to get around it. As Christopher Gabel points out in his case study of the battle, the road network would have accommodated the Allies' original strategy quite nicely. Half of the city had already been destroyed by Allied bombing, although exactly why is unclear because it was not a vital industrial center to begin with. In keeping with the lack of importance both sides assigned to the city, neither side was prepared to fight inside the city. But neither was Adolf Hitler's direct intervention expected, an intervention that had nothing to do with military necessity and everything to do with misplaced sentimentalism. So the German army did not after all withdraw from the city, the Allies could not leave them there, and thus a city battle was fought for reasons of nostalgia as much as any other. Furthermore, while the combat inside the city took on its own character, the rest of the war moved on as before.

Among the cases collected here, the most extreme example of politics and sentiment investing a city with importance is that of Stalingrad. Although Stalingrad is now seen as the archetypical urban battle during World War II, it resembled Aachen in that neither side saw the city as critical to its strategic or operational plans. Neither the German General Staff nor the Soviet *Stavka* assigned much importance to the place. The German army would very likely have passed through Stalingrad on the way to greater prizes in the east had not Joseph Stalin made an issue of the place. That done, Hitler complied enthusiastically. Thus the stage was set for one of the most vicious battles of the twentieth century. While the city might have been of negligible military importance at first, the opposing national leaders ensured that it would grow to strategic proportions.[17]

While neither of the battles for Aachen or Stalingrad could be said to have been intentional and neither was the result of deliberate military planning, the battle for Hue was a critical element in a much larger strategic conception. As Vietnam's old Imperial city, Hue was a cultural icon as well as being politically important. Partly because of its significance, all sides had treated Hue as something of an "open" city, immune to the war that had engulfed the rest of the country. For two years, North Vietnamese strategists planned the campaign known to history as the Tet Offensive. Operational and tactical preparation for the assault on the city itself began six months before the attack. The North Vietnamese Army (NVA) worked to create complete surprise, and its work paid off. For a time, Hue was under control of the NVA.[18] South Vietnamese and American reinforcements to shore up defenses and retake overrun districts were all deployed in the manner of a military emergency—in other words, a think-as-you-go crisis response, always the least acceptable, most expensive course of action.

For all the initial advantages the NVA enjoyed, they were insufficient to guarantee success. The North Vietnamese intended the battle for Hue to conclude promptly and decisively. When their plans were disappointed, they were forced into a series of tactical compromises, including an attempt to reinforce their battle from beyond the city itself. Eventually, the South Vietnamese and the Americans took the initiative away from the NVA. What began as a coup de main ended as a kind of siege in reverse, from the inside out.

Coups de main are not always failures. Nor are coups de main cheap operations, although the importance of subversion, preparation, and speed sometimes may create false expectations of decisive action. Also, unless these sorts of operations are supported properly, they all too often reverse the attackers' fortunes. The NVA's preparations for taking Hue followed the common practice of infiltrating the city well before what the attackers expected would be their decisive blow. The same was true in two other cases here, the Soviet Union's seizure of Kabul and the American seizure of Panama City. In both cases, the attackers enjoyed virtually overwhelming advantages, and both were so planned.

The Soviets came very close to underestimating the regular forces that would be required to consummate the seizure of Kabul. The Americans, on the other hand, were in the peculiar position of invading themselves, so long and well established was their presence throughout Panama. In both cases, the lure of quick, decisive action was too great for the planners to resist. The Americans' concept for invading Panama had a considerably larger scope than the Soviets' concept for Kabul. The Americans planned their invasion to attack many decisive targets as nearly simultaneously as they could to interdict any possible response, but what they wanted in the end was a decision in Panama City. Panama City was the only place, in fact, where decision could be found. The same was true of Kabul, but there the decision had a much shorter life than the one in Panama. The attack on Kabul merely initiated a decade of unrewarding counterinsurgency warfare from which the Soviets had trouble extricating themselves.

Coups de main have never been quite as easy or quite as decisive as they have seemed. But coups de main may be verging on a new popularity if military thinkers can find ways to win a quick decision with new combinations of specialized forces, precision weapons, and cybernetic attack. Conceived in this manner, the coup de main seems a very modern kind of operation, one that aims at only those elements and functions of enemy power that contribute to his resistance. What is more certain is that the very notion of attacking even moderately large cities such as Grozny in the old-fashioned way—first isolating, then dividing the whole into ever smaller areas, reducing the defenders to their final redoubts—is absurd. Any attacking force that takes on an urban population hoping for a soft, compliant target is risking the dissipation of its combat power well before it meets its primary objective.

The presence of civilians, sometimes in the midst of battle, is one characteristic that makes urban warfare unique among all other forms of war. People trapped in cities by war have persisted in the most inhospitable conditions imaginable. A modern urban population may react stoically to the presence of foreign soldiers, but even noncombatant populations must continue to function, no matter what. For an invading army, even the most welcoming population constitutes a kind of resistant medium in which that army must continue to execute its mission. If the fight for a city is part of a larger campaign—such as in the battle for Aachen—fighting elsewhere might drive a new population of refugees into the city, replacing those who had evacuated earlier and arriving just when city services had been wrecked.

All too often, combatant forces have found ways to use civilians to their advantage. In Manila, Hue, Grozny, Beirut, and certainly Sarajevo, civilian noncombatants became critical and, at times, decisive elements of the engagement. Most commonly, the influence of noncombatants will work to the advantage of one side or another; they are rarely a "neutral" force. In the battle for Hue, for instance, South Vietnamese and American rules of engagement would not allow the employment of certain weapons, but the NVA was bound by no such tactical restrictions. Concern for noncombatant casualties in Beirut was said to have prevented the Israelis from penetrating the city's defenses in 1983. In this instance, the Israeli Defense Forces had to contend with the Palestinian refugee camps that worked as a human buffer for the Palestine Liberation Organization defenders behind them in the city proper. By contrast, the siege of Sarajevo was quite explicitly a siege against the noncombatants of the city, inaugurated, as Curt King's essay makes clear, when orthodox military operations failed to deliver the desired result. Sarajevans were, in effect, made hostage to military operations elsewhere, far from the eyes of the international public.

The urban environment, considered in military terms, is a unique environment, both in terms of its essential character and its behavior. Faced with the complexities of this environment, military analysts have resorted to explaining cities as a "system of systems," as if cities were only the product of architectural designs and engineers' drawings. Those would not be cities but monuments. The first, most elementary, feature of any urban environment is that it is a place where people have collected more or less permanently. It is therefore to the human qualities of the urban environment the military planner must first look if he hopes to understand how armies can function in such a place.

When a military force acts in an urban environment, its essential humanness guarantees that the environment acts in return; that is, the relationship between a force and a city is *dynamic*. The dynamic interaction between cities and the military forces operating in them redefines and reshapes those forces over time. Because of its dynamic quality, the urban environment works as an important "third force," uniquely influencing the behavior of all sides engaged. This fundamental interaction cannot be ignored by the armies engaged, regardless of how long or how intensive their operations.

Nor may we assume that the peculiarities of the urban environment will redound to the benefit of one side or another. As Al Lowe has observed in his essay on the long battle for Rio de Janeiro, early in the *Montoneros*' career as urban insurgents, they were happy to adopt the style of the *guerrillero*, fighting a war of poverty against orthodox Argentine forces. But as the war dragged on, both sides gravitated toward each other's methods. Unorthodox methods were increasingly adopted by the state, which conducted its own version of guerrilla operations against the *Montoneros*, including using extralegal death squads. Meanwhile, the methods of the *guerrilleros* slowly became more orthodox until, paradoxically, the movement's appeal to its power base among the urban poor gradually disappeared. Doubtless, neither side expected the environment itself to exercise this kind of power over its behavior.

The commander who enters a modern city unprepared will soon be forced to acknowledge critical differences in how he must operate if he is to accomplish his mission. The cost of everything will go up. He will need more forces and perhaps different forces; more transport, not for his troops but to evacuate noncombatants; or civil affairs specialists to deal with a variety of political and social issues. The presence of refugees and local noncombatants will mean that medical support will be tugged in two directions, toward the rear as well as the front. And in the fighting zones, casualties will begin to mount. Indeed, the historical record consistently shows a rapid increase in the consumption rates of all classes of military supply when a force engages in city combat. These differences are so great that the commander might think he had passed from one theater of operations to another. In a way, he has.

Perhaps the first difference the commander would notice is that his mission had to assume a different shape and his force had to adopt different methods. Time-honored combat formations designed for open fighting would reorganize themselves into ever-smaller groups, perhaps even without his intervention. Command and control would not work as it had. The fluidity with which his force had originally maneuvered would be impeded by the medium in which it now attempted to move. Inconsiderable distances would become deliberate advances under full protection. An attack across a boulevard would take on the character of a river crossing. While the mission tempo would subside, the tactical tempo would intensify. Smaller acts would mean more. Tactical forces would combat smaller targets more fiercely. Buildings would become campaigns, stairs would become avenues of approach, and rooms would become fortresses. In just this way, the worst urban battles of the twentieth century assumed their own shapes and purposes. The battles for the tractor factory in Stalingrad, for the Zoo Flak Tower in Berlin, for the fortress at Manila, and for the Citadel at Hue all exploded the best laid plans of commanders on the spot, forcing them to submit to the tactical demands of the moment.

Modern armies would be mistaken to assume that battles such as these are impossible in the future. The first battle for Grozny that Timothy Thomas describes here, as well as succeeding battles for the city, serves as a warning for those armies that underestimate the challenges of modern urban warfare. Ill-prepared, poorly led, poorly supported, and thrown recklessly against a determined defender whose military assets were modest, a ramshackled Russian army ignored its own history, using firepower as a substitute for thought. Almost a decade after the adversaries began fighting, neither side seems to recognize that fighting is only a means, not an end, certainly not a way of life. So Grozny takes its place alongside those urban battles that have devolved from purpose to habit, where exhaustion rather than the military art offers the only way out. No policy maker or professional soldier should be willing to accept such a verdict.

Modern urban warfare is neither a completely new or completely old military phenomenon; as usual, it is some of both. It is not a phenomenon beyond the reach of professional understanding, and in the past several years, a reawakening of professional interest has occurred around the military world. The professional soldier now has within reach a substantial historical and contemporary literature from which the foundation of new military doctrines and practices can be built. This casebook has been written to contribute to that foundation.

Notes

1. By Sun Tzu's reckoning, the general placed his army in "critical terrain." Sun Tzu, *The Art of War*, Samuel B. Griffith, trans. and ed., foreword by B.H. Liddell Hart (London: Oxford University Press, 1963), 38-39, 78-79. See also *Sun Tzu The Art of Warfare*, Roger Ames, trans. (NY: Ballantine Books, 1993), 111-12, 439.

2. Phillipe Contamine, *The Art of War in the Middle Ages*, Michael Jones, trans. (London: Basil Blackwell, 1983), 219.

3. Spiro Kostof, *The City Shaped: Urban Patterns and Meaning Through History* (London: Thames and Hudson, 1991; paperback, 1999), 108-110.

4. Contamine, 101.

5. Ibid.

6. Kostof, 108-110.

7. The Population Council, "Population," in *The Microsoft Encarta Encyclopedia 99*, 4 (CD-ROM).

8. United Nations (UN), "The World at Six Billion" (NY: UN Population Division of the Department of Economic and Social Affairs, 1999), b-2, b-3 at <http://www.un.org/popin>, accessed 1999.

9. Eugene Linden, "The Exploding Cities of the Developing World," *Foreign Affairs* (January/February 1996), 54-55.

10. This figure includes all inhabitants within Tokyo's urban agglomeration as calculated by the UN Population Division. The UN employs the term "agglomeration" to designate only those urban areas that exceed a population of 10 million. The UN employs the term "small cities" for urban areas of 500,000 and less. See UN Population Division, "World Urbanization Prospects: The 2001 Revision; Data Tables and Highlights" (NY: UN Population Division of the Department of Economic and Social Affairs, 21 March 2002), 1-3, 172. Accessible at <http://www.un.org/popin>, accessed November 2002, hereafter cited as "World Urbanization Prospects."

11. Tokyo.gov, "The Official Tokyo Metro Website" at <http://www.chijihonbu.metro.tokyo.jp>, accessed November 2002.

12. "World Urbanization Prospects," 1-3.

13. This is not to say that once urban growth begins it cannot level off or even reverse itself. Demographic estimates are not predictions of the future. In 1973, estimates of Mexico City's population at century's end ran higher than 30 million, but global and national markets changed radically in the meantime and influenced how economic activity in Mexico was distributed. See Linden, 54.

14. Ibid.

15. David E. Kaplan, "The Law of the Jungle," *U.S. News and World Report* (14 October 2002), 35.

16. Linden, 54.

17. I have discussed the operational value of Stalingrad more extensively in *Sharp Corners: Urban Operations at Century's End* (Fort Leavenworth, KS: U.S. Army Command and General Staff College Press, 2001), 59-60.

18. See Ronnie E. Ford, *TET 1968: Understanding the Surprise* (London: Frank Cass, 1995), especially 66-86.

About the Contributors

Jerold E. Brown is an Associate Professor of History and Fellow of the Combat Studies Institute (CSI), U.S. Army Command and General Staff College (USACGSC), Fort Leavenworth, Kansas. He received a B.A. and M.A. from Purdue University and a Ph.D. from Duke University. He has written and edited several books on military planning and published frequently in military and historical journals, including *The Historical Dictionary of the United States Army*.

Louis DiMarco, Lieutenant Colonel, U.S. Army, is an Associate Professor of Military History at CSI, USACGSC. He received a B.S. from the U.S. Military Academy (USMA), an M.M.A.S. from the USACGSC, and an M.A. from Salve Regina University and is pursuing a doctorate at Kansas State University. He was the lead author of the U.S. Army's urban operations doctrine manual, Field Manual 3-06.

Christopher R. Gabel has served since 1983 on the faculty of USACGSC, where he teaches courses on general military history, military innovation, the Civil War, and World War II. He received a Ph.D. from The Ohio State University. His publications include studies on the U.S. Army during the World War II period, railroad logistics in the Civil War, and a staff ride handbook for the Vicksburg campaign.

George W. Gawrych is currently serving as a visiting professor at the USMA, West Point, New York. He has been a faculty member with CSI, USACGSC, since 1984. He received a Ph.D. from the University of Michigan.

Lester W. Grau, Lieutenant Colonel, U.S. Army, Retired, is a military analyst with the Foreign Military Studies Office, Fort Leavenworth, Kansas. He has published more than ninety articles and studies on Soviet and Russian tactical, operational, and geopolitical subjects. He is the author of *The Bear Went Over the Mountain: Soviet Combat Tactics in Afghanistan* and *The Soviet-Afghan War: How a Superpower Fought and Lost*.

Thomas M. Huber is a veteran faculty member of CSI, USACGSC, where he specializes in Napoleonic warfare and military thought. He received a master's degree from the University of Michigan, Ann Arbor, and a Ph.D. from the University of Chicago. His forthcoming publication is *Density of War: The Interplay of Siege,*

Maneuver, and Guerrilla Warfare From Lexington and Concord to "Olympic" and "Coronet."

Curtis S. King is an associate professor on the Staff Ride Team at CSI, USACGSC. He received a B.S. from the USMA and an M.A. and Ph.D. from the University of Pennsylvania. He spent a six-month tour in Sarajevo, Bosnia, as a NATO historian.

S.J. Lewis was born in Northern California in 1948 and received his B.A. and M.A. degrees from San Jose State University. He received his Ph.D. from the University of California, Santa Barbara, in 1973. He has written extensively on modern European history.

Alan C. Lowe, Lieutenant Colonel, U.S. Army, is currently a military history instructor with CSI, USACGSC. He received an M.M.A.S. from the USACGSC and is currently a Ph.D. candidate in U.S. history at the University of Kansas. He has held staff positions at various command levels both as an infantry officer and in his functional area of psychological operations.

William G. Robertson is the Combined Arms Center Historian and the senior historian and chief of the U.S. Army Training and Doctrine Command side of CSI, USACGSC. He received a Ph.D. in history from the University of Virginia and is the author of *Back Door to Richmond: The Bermuda Hundred Campaign*, *The Petersburg Campaign: The Battle of Old Men and Young Boys*, the Bull Run chapter in *America's First Battles*, and *Counterattack on the Naktong, 1950*.

Roger J. Spiller is the George C. Marshall Professor of History at the USACGSC. His most recent work is *Sharp Corners: Urban Operations at Century's End* (Fort Leavenworth, KS: USACGSC Press, 2001).

Timothy L. Thomas, Lieutenant Colonel, U.S. Army, Retired, is an analyst at the Foreign Military Studies Office, Fort Leavenworth, Kansas. He received a B.S. from the USMA and an M.A. from the University of Southern California. He is the assistant editor of the journal *European Security*, an adjunct professor at the Eurasian Institute, and an adjunct lecturer at the U.S. Air Force Special Operations School.

James H. Willbanks, Lieutenant Colonel, U.S. Army, Retired, is professor of joint and multinational operations at the USACGSC. He is a graduate of Texas A&M University and holds a Ph.D. in U.S. military and diplomatic history from the University of Kansas. He is the author of *Thiet Giap! The Battle of An Loc* and numerous articles on the Vietnam war.

Lawrence A. Yates is an instructor and researcher on the Research and Publication Team, CSI, USACGSC. He received a B.A. and an M.A. from the University of Missouri, Kansas City, and a Ph.D. in history from the University of Kansas. He is the author of several articles on U.S. contingency operations since World War II, has written a monograph on the U.S. intervention in the Dominican Republic in 1965, and is completing book-length studies of U.S. military operations in the Panama crisis, 1987-90 and Somalia, 1992-94.

The editors and authors would like to thank the following persons for their invaluable contributions in preparing this volume: Alice King, Combined Arms Research Library, for her expert assistance in the area of copyrights; Edward J. Carr, Training Support Center, for his superb work in providing standardized graphics and for laying out this book; and Ann Barbuto and Patricia Whitten for applying their editorial skills.

Appendix A. The Future
Our Soldiers, Their Cities

Ralph Peters

© 1996 Ralph Peters

Reprinted by permission from *Parameters*, Spring 1996.

The future of warfare lies in the streets, sewers, high-rise buildings, industrial parks, and the sprawl of houses, shacks, and shelters that form the broken cities of our world. We will fight elsewhere, but not so often, rarely as reluctantly, and never so brutally. Our recent military history is punctuated with city names—Tuzla, Mogadishu, Los Angeles, Beirut, Panama City, Hue, Saigon, Santo Domingo—but these encounters have been but a prologue, with the real drama still to come.

We declare that only fools fight in cities and shut our eyes against the future. But in the next century, in an uncontrollably urbanizing world, we will not be able to avoid urban deployments short of war and even full-scale city combat. Cities always have been centers of gravity, but they are now more magnetic than ever before. Once the gatherers of wealth, then the processors of wealth, cities and their satellite communities have become the ultimate creators of wealth. They concentrate people and power, communications and control, knowledge and capability, rendering all else peripheral. They are also the post-modern equivalent of jungles and mountains—citadels of the dispossessed and irreconcilable. A military unprepared for urban operations across a broad spectrum is unprepared for tomorrow.

The US military, otherwise magnificently capable, is an extremely inefficient tool for combat in urban environments. We are not doctrinally, organizationally, or psychologically prepared, nor are we properly trained or equipped, for a serious urban battle, and we must task organize radically even to conduct peacekeeping operations in cities. Romantic and spiritually reactionary, we long for gallant struggles in green fields, while the likeliest "battlefields" are cityscapes where human waste goes undisposed, the air is appalling, and mankind is rotting.

Poor state or rich, disintegrating society or robust culture, a global commonality is that more of the population, in absolute numbers and in percentage, lives in cities. Control of cities always has been vital to military success, practically and symbolically, but in our post-modern environment, in which the wealth of poor regions as well as the defining capabilities of rich states are concentrated in capitals and clusters of production-center cities, the relevance of non-urban terrain is diminising in strategic,operational, and even tactical importance—except where the countryside harbors critical natural resources. But even when warfare is about resource control, as in America's Gulf War, simply controlling the oil fields satisfies neither side.

The relevant urban centers draw armies for a stew of reasons, from providing legitimacy and infrastructural capabilities, to a magnetic attraction that is more instinctive than rational (perhaps even genetically absorbed at this point in the history of mankind), and on to the fundamental need to control indigenous populations—which cannot be done without mastering their urban centers. We may be entering a new age of siege warfare, but one in which the military techniques would be largely unrecognizable to Mehmet the Conqueror or Vauban, or even to our own greatest soldiers and conquerors of cities, Ulysses S. Grant and Winfield Scott.

Consider just a few of the potential trouble spots where US military intervention or assistance could prove necessary in the next century: Mexico, Egypt, the sub-continent with an expansionist India, the Arabian Peninsula, Brazil, or the urbanizing Pacific Rim. Even though each of these states or regions contains tremendous rural, desert, or jungle expanses, the key to each is control of an archipelago of cities. The largest of these cities have populations in excess of 20 million today—more specific figures are generally unavailable as beleaguered governments lose control of their own backyards. Confronted with an armed and hostile population in such an environment, the US Army as presently structured would find it difficult to muster the dismount strength necessary to control a single center as simultaneously dense and sprawling as Mexico City.

Step down from the level of strategic rhetoric about the future, where anyone with self-confidence can make a convincing case for his or her agenda. Survey instead the blunt, practical ways in which urban combat in today's major cities would differ from a sanitary anomaly such as Desert Storm or the never-to-be-fought Third European Civil War in the German countryside (where we pretended urban combat could be avoided) for which so much of the equipment presently in our inventory was designed.

At the broadest level, there is a profound spatial difference. "Conventional" warfare has been horizontal, with an increasing vertical dimension. In fully urbanized terrain, however, warfare becomes profoundly vertical, reaching up into towers of steel and cement, and downward into sewers, subway lines, road tunnels, communications tunnels, and the like. Even with the "emptying" of the modern battlefield, organizational behavior in the field strives for lateral contiguity and organizational integrity. But the broken spatial qualities of urban terrain fragments units and compartmentalizes encounters, engagements, and even battles. The leader's span of control can easily collapse, and it is very, very hard to gain and maintain an accurate picture of the multidimensional "battlefield."

Noncombatants, without the least hostile intent, can overwhelm the force, and there are multiple players beyond the purely military, from criminal gangs to the media, vigilante and paramilitary factions within militaries, and factions within those factions. The enemy knows the terrain better than the visiting army, and it can be debilitatingly difficult to tell friend from foe from the disinterested. Local combat situations can change with bewildering speed. Atrocity is close-up and commonplace, whether intentional or incidental. The stresses on the soldier are incalculable. The urban combat environment is, above all, disintegrative.

The modern and post-modern trend in Western militaries has been to increase the proportion of tasks executed by machines while reducing the number of soldiers in our establishments. We seek to build machines that enable us to win while protecting or distancing the human operator from the effects of combat. At present, however, urban combat remains extremely manpower intensive—and it is a casualty producer. Although a redirection of research and development efforts toward addressing the requirements of urban combat could eventually raise our efficiency and reduce casualties, machines probably will not dominate urban combat in our lifetimes and the soldier will remain the supreme weapon. In any case, urban warfare will not require substantial numbers of glamorous big-ticket systems but great multiples of small durables and disposables whose production would offer less fungible profit margins and whose relatively simple construction would open acquisition to genuinely competitive bidding.

Casualties can soar in urban environments. Beyond those inflicted by enemy action, urban operations result in broken bones, concussions, traumatic-impact deaths and, with the appalling sanitation in many urban environments, in a broad range of septic threats. Given the untempered immune systems of many of our soldiers, even patrol operations in sewer systems that did not encounter an enemy could produce debilitating, even fatal, illnesses. One of many potential items of soldier equipment for urban warfare might be antiseptic bio-sheathing that coats the soldier's body and closes over cuts and abrasions, as well as wounds. Any means of boosting the soldier's immune system could prove a critical "weapon of war."

Urban warfare differs even in how "minor" items such as medical kits and litters should be structured. Soldiers need new forms of "armor"; equipment as simple as layered-compound knee and elbow pads could dramatically reduce the sort of injuries that, while not life-threatening, can remove soldiers from combat for hours, days, weeks, or even months. Eye protection is essential, given the splintering effects of firefights in masonry and wood environments, and protective headgear should focus as much on accidental blows from falls or collapsing structures as on enemy fire, on preserving the body's structural integrity as much as on ballistic threats.

Communications requirements differ, too. Soldiers need more comms distributed to lower levels—down to the individual soldier in some cases. Further, because of loss rates in the give and take of urban combat, low-level comms gear should not be part of the encrypted command and control network. Radios or other means of communication do not need extended range, but they must deal with terrible reception anomalies. Even a "digitized" soldier, whose every movement can be monitored, will require different display structures in the observing command center. This is the classic three-dimensional chessboard at the tactical level.

On the subject of command and control, the individual soldier must be even better-trained than at present. He will face human and material distractions everywhere—it will be hard to maintain concentration on the core mission. Soldiers will die simply because they were looking the wrong way, and even disciplined and morally sound soldiers disinclined to rape can lose focus in the presence of female or other civilians whom they feel obliged to protect or who merely add to the human "noise level." The leader-to-led ratio must increase in favor of rigorously prepared low-level leaders. While higher-level command structures may flatten, tactical units must become webs of pyramidal cells capable of extended autonomous behavior in a combat environment where multiple engagements can occur simultaneously and in relative isolation in the same building. Nonsensical arguments about the Wehrmacht making do without so many NCOs and officers on the battlefield must be buried forever; not only is the German military of the last European civil war ancient history, but it lost decisively. Our challenge is to shape the US Army of the 21st century.

Personal weapons must be compact and robust, with a high rate of fire and very lightweight ammunition, but there is also a place for shotgun-like weapons at the squad level. Overall, soldier loads must be reduced dramatically at the edge of combat, since fighting in tall buildings requires agility that a soldier unbalanced by a heavy pack cannot attain; further, vertical fighting is utterly exhausting and requires specialized mobility tools. Soldiers will need more upper body strength and will generally need to be more fit—and this includes support soldiers, as well.

Ideally, each infantry soldier would have a thermal or post-thermal imaging capability—since systems that require ambient light are not much good 30 meters below the surface of the earth. Also, an enhanced ability to detect and define sounds could benefit the soldier—although he would have to be very well-trained to be able to transcend the distracting quality of such systems. Eventually, we may have individual-soldier tactical equipment that can differentiate between male and female body heat distributions and that will even be able to register hostility and intent from smells and sweat. But such devices will not be available for the next several interventions, and we shall have to make do for a long time to come with soldiers who are smart, tough, and disciplined.

The roles of traditional arms will shift. Field artillery, so valuable elsewhere, will be of reduced utility—unless the US military were to degenerate to the level of atrocity in which the Russians indulged themselves in Grozniy. Until artillery further enhances accuracy, innovates warheads, and overcomes the laws of ballistic trajectories, it will not have a significant role in urban combat divisions. Because of attack angles and the capabilities of precision munitions, air power will prove much more valuable and will function as flying artillery. Mortars, however, may often be of great use, given their steep trajectories. More accurate and versatile next-generation mortars could be a very powerful urban warfare tool.

The bulk of tactical firepower will need to come from large-caliber, protected, direct-fire weapons. This means tanks, or future systems descended from the tank. While today's tanks are death traps in urban combat—as the Russians were recently reminded—the need for protected, pinpoint firepower is critical. Instead of concentrating entirely on obsolescent rural warfare, armor officers should be asking themselves how the tank should evolve to fight in tomorrow's premier military environment, the city. First, the "tank" will need more protection, and that protection will need to be differently distributed—perhaps evolving to tuned electronic armor that flows over the vehicle to the threatened spot. Main guns will need to be large caliber, yet, ideally, would be able to fire reduced-caliber ammunition, as well, through a "caliber-tailoring" system. Crew visibility will need to be greater. The tank will not need to sustain high speeds, but will need a sprint capability. Further, the tank will need to be better integrated into local intelligence awareness.

While the need for plentiful dismounted infantry will endure, those soldiers will intermittently need means for rapid, protected movement. But this does not necessarily mean mechanized infantry—rather, it may demand armored transport centralized at the division level on which the infantry trains, but which does not rob the infantry of manpower in peacetime or in combat.

Engineers will be absolutely critical to urban combat, but they, too, will need evolved tools and skills. The vertical dimension is only part of the challenge. Engineers will need to develop expanded skills, from enabling movement in developed downtown areas to firefighting. Demolition skills will be essential, but will be a long way from blowing road craters. Tomorrow's combat engineers may have to drop 20-story buildings on minimal notice under fire while minimizing collateral damage.

Aviation is vital to mobility, intelligence, and the delivery of focused firepower in urban environments, but, as Mogadishu warned us, present systems and tactics leave us highly vulnerable. Rotary-wing aviation for urban combat does not need great range or speed, but demands a richer defensive suite, great agility, and increased stealthiness.

Military intelligence must be profoundly reordered to cope with the demands of urban combat. From mapping to target acquisition, from collection to analysis, and from battle damage assessment to the prediction of the enemy's future intent, intelligence requirements in urban environments are far tougher to meet than they are on traditional battlefields. The utility of the systems that paid off so richly in Desert Storm collapses in urban warfare, and the importance of human intelligence (HUMINT) and regional expertise soars. From language skills to a knowledge of urban planning (or the lack thereof), many of the abilities essential to combat in cities are given low, if any, priority in today's intelligence architecture. While leaders are aware of these shortfalls, military intelligence is perhaps more a prisoner of inherited Cold War structures than is any other branch—although field artillery and armor are competitive in their unpreparedness for the future.

Military intelligence is at a crossroads today and must decide whether to continue doing the often-irrelevant things it does so well or to embrace a realistic future which will demand a better balance between systems and soldiers in a branch particularly susceptible to the lure of dazzling machines. Try templating a semi-regular enemy unit in urban combat in the center of Lagos after 24 hours of contact. This does not mean that high-tech gear and analytical methodologies are useless in urban environments. On the contrary, innovative technologies and organizational principles could make a profound difference in how military intelligence supports urban combat operations. But we would need to shift focus and explore radical departures from the systems we currently embrace.

Military police and civil affairs troops will continue to play the important roles they played in urban interventions during the 20th century, but psychological operations (PSYOPS) units, long a step-child, will surge in importance, and may ultimately merge fully with military intelligence to enhance synergy and efficiency. Especially given the potential for electronic population control systems in the next century, PSYOPS may function as a combat arm, even if not credited as such.

Even supply is different. While deliveries do not need to be made over great distances, soft vehicles are extremely vulnerable in an environment where it is hard to define a front line and where the enemy can repeatedly emerge in the rear. All soldiers will be fighters, and force and resource protection will be physically and psychologically draining. Urban environments can upset traditional balances between classes of supply. There may be less of a requirement for bulk fuel, but an intervention force may find itself required to feed an urban population, or to supply epidemic-control efforts. Artillery and ATGM expenditures might be minimal, while main gun and infantry systems ammunition consumption could be heated. Urban combat breaks individual and crew-served weapons and gear, from rifles to radios, and masonry buildings are even harder on uniforms than on human bones. Soldiers will need replacement uniforms far more often than during more traditional operations. Unfortunately, we also will need more replacement soldiers, and all combat support and combat service support troops are more apt to find themselves shooting back during an urban battle than in any other combat environment.

Where do we begin to prepare for this immediate and growing challenge? There are two powerful steps we ought to take. First, the US Army should designate two active and at least one of our National Guard divisions as urban combat divisions and should begin variable restructurings to get the right component mix. Rule one should be that the active divisions are not "experimental" in the sense of nondeployable, but remain subject to short-notice deployment to threatened urban environments. This would put an incredible stress on the unit and, especially, on the chain of command. But today's US Army cannot afford to have any divisions "on ice," and, further, this pressure would drive competence. Two such divisions is the irreducible initial number, since one urban combat division would be rapidly exhausted by the pace of deployments.

Most of the divisional artillery would be shifted to corps-level, while engineers at all levels would be increased and restructured—including the addition of organic sapper platoons to infantry battalions. Composite armor and mechanized elements would be added to light forces at a ratio of one battalion (brigade) to four, with a longer-term goal of developing more appropriate and readily deployable means of delivering direct firepower and protecting the forward movement of troops. Innovative protection of general transport would be another goal. Military intelligence units would have to restructure radically, and would need to develop habitual relationships with reserve component linguists and area specialists. Aviation would work closely with other arms to develop more survivable tactics, while each division would gain an active-duty PSYOPS company. Signalers would need to experiment with low-cost, off-the-shelf tools for communicating in dense urban environments, and an overarching effort would need to be made to create interdisciplinary maps, both paper and electronic, that could better portray the complexity of urban warfare. The divisions' experience would determine future acquisition requirements.

But none of the sample measures cited above is as important as revolutionizing training for urban combat. The present approach, though worthwhile on its own terms, trains soldiers to fight in villages or small towns, not in cities. Building realistic "cities" in which to train would be prohibitively expensive. The answer is innovation. Why build that which already exists? In many of our own blighted cities, massive housing projects have become uninhabitable and industrial plants unusable. Yet they would be nearly ideal for combat-in-cities training. While we could not engage in live-fire training (even if the locals do), we could experiment and train in virtually every other regard. Development costs would be a fraction of the price of building a "city" from scratch, and city and state governments would likely compete to gain a US Army (and Marine) presence, since it would bring money, jobs, and development—as well as a measure of social discipline. A mutually beneficial relationship could help at least one of our worst-off cities, while offering the military a realistic training environment. The training center could be at least partially administered by the local National Guard to bind it to the community. We genuinely need a National Training Center for Urban Combat, and it cannot be another half-measure. Such a facility would address the most glaring and dangerous gap in our otherwise superb military training program. We need to develop it soon.

In summary, an urbanizing world means combat in cities, whether we like it or not. Any officer who states categorically that the US Army will never let itself be drawn into urban warfare is indulging in wishful thinking. Urban combat is conceptually and practically different from other modes of warfare. Although mankind has engaged in urban combat from the sack of Troy down to the siege of Sarajevo, Western militaries currently resist the practical, emotional, moral, and ethical challenges of city fighting. Additional contemporary players, such as the media, and international and nongovernmental organizations, further complicate contemporary urban combat. We do not want to touch this problem. But we have no choice. The problem is already touching us, with skeletal, infected fingers. The US military must stop preparing for its dream war and get down to the reality of the fractured and ugly world in which we live—a world that lives in cities. We must begin judicious restructuring for urban combat in order to gain both efficiency and maximum effectiveness—as well as to preserve the lives of our soldiers. We must equip, train, and fight innovatively. We must seize the future before the future seizes us.

Major Ralph Peters is assigned to the Office of the Deputy Chief of Staff for Intelligence, where he is responsible for evaluating emerging threats. Prior to becoming a Foreign Area Officer for Eurasia, he served exclusively at the tactical level. He is a graduate of the US Army Command and General Staff College and holds a master's degree in international relations. Over the past several years, his professional and personal research travels have taken Major Peters to Russia, Ukraine, Georgia, Ossetia, Abkhazia, Armenia, Azerbaijan, Uzbekistan, Kazakhstan, Latvia, Lithuania, Estonia, Croatia, Serbia, Bulgaria, Romania, Poland, Hungary, the Czech Republic, Pakistan, and Turkey, as well as the countries of the Andean Ridge. He has published five books and dozens of articles and essays on military and international concerns. This is his sixth article for *Parameters*.

www.ingramcontent.com/pod-product-compliance
Lightning Source LLC
Chambersburg PA
CBHW060228240426
43671CB00016B/2882